POLITICAL AND SOCIAL TRANSFORMATIONS IN NORTH INDIA AND NEPAL

The Japanese Association for South Asian Studies
Established in 1988

- **Office Bearers as of 1 November 2006**

  President
  Hiroshi Ishii, Professor Emeritus, Tokyo University of Foreign Studies

  General Secretary
  Shingo Einoo, University of Tokyo

  Members of the Board of Executive Directors
  Norio Kondo, Institute of Developing Economies
  Yoshifumi Mizuno, Tokyo University of Foreign Studies
  Tsukasa Mizushima, University of Tokyo
  Fumiko Oshikawa, Kyoto University
  Masahiro Shimoda, University of Tokyo
  Akio Tanabe, Kyoto University
  Shinkichi Taniguchi, Hitotsubashi University
  Kohei Wakimura, Osaka City University

- **Head Office** (until September 2008)
  c/o Institute of Oriental Culture, University of Tokyo
  7-3-1 Hongo, Bunkyo-ku, Tokyo, 113-0033, Japan
  Fax. +81-3-5841-5898
  Email. jasas@ioc.u-tokyo.ac.jp
  http://wwwsoc.nii.ac.jp/jasas/index-e.html

- **Publications in English**
  1 *JJASAS (Journal of the Japanese Association for South Asian Studies)*, (annual publication in Japanese and English, the current issue: No. 18)
  2 Japanese Studies on South Asia Series
    - No. 1 H. Kotani ed., *Caste System, Untouchability and the Depressed*, Manohar, New Delhi, 1997.
    - No. 2 N. Karashima ed., *Kingship in Indian History*, Manohar, New Delhi, 1999.
    - No. 3 S. Maeda ed., *The Way to Liberation*, Manohar, New Delhi, 2000.
    - No. 4 S. Einoo and J. Takashima eds., *From Material to Deity*, Manohar, New Delhi, 2005.
    - No. 5 H. Okahasi ed., *Emerging New Industrial Spaces and Regional Developments in India*, Manohar, New Delhi, 2007.
    - No. 6 H. Ishii, D.N. Gellner, and K. Nawa eds., *Social Dynamics in Northern South Asia*, Vol. 1: *Nepalis Inside and Outside Nepal*, Manohar, New Delhi, 2007.
    - No. 7 H. Ishii, D.N. Gellner, and K. Nawa eds., *Social Dynamics in Northern South Asia*, Vol. 2: *Political and Social Transformations in North India and Nepal*, Manohar, New Delhi, 2007.

Japanese Studies on South Asia No. 7

Social Dynamics in Northern South Asia

Volume 2

Political and Social Transformations in North India and Nepal

Edited by

HIROSHI ISHII
DAVID N. GELLNER
KATSUO NAWA

MANOHAR
2020

First published 2007
First paperback edition 2020

ISBN 978-93-90035-24-3

Published by
Ajay Kumar Jain *for*
Manohar Publishers & Distributors
4753/23 Ansari Road, Daryaganj
New Delhi 110 002

Printed at
Replika Press Pvt. Ltd.

Contents

Tables and Figures

Preface

In 1997 the Japanese Association for South Asian Studies initiated an academic series entitled 'Japanese Studies on South Asia' under an agreement with Manohar Publishers & Distributors. The initial purpose of the series was (and remains) to introduce the work of Japanese scholars of South Asia to the international academic community. So far, five volumes have been published in this series and the contributors are Japanese authors (previous volumes in the series are listed on the fly leaf). Unlike these previous volumes, the present set, consisting of two volumes, contains articles by scholars from various countries and Japanese scholars make up just half of the authors.

The present volumes (i.e. *Social Dynamics in Northern South Asia*, Vol. 1: *Nepalis Inside and Outside Nepal* and Vol. 2: *Political and Social Transformations in North India and Nepal*) are the outcome of two international workshops held in February and June 2004 at the Research Institute for Languages and Cultures of Asia and Africa (ILCAA or AA-ken), Tokyo University of Foreign Studies, Tokyo. The workshops were entitled 'The Dynamics of Social and Political Change in Nepal' and 'Social Dynamics in Northern South Asia' and included ten and twenty-one papers respectively.

This collaborative study began with two institutional research projects, each with around twenty members (all Japanese except for one Nepali scholar based in Japan). In its preparatory stage, seminars were held as part of a regular research project of the Institute of Oriental Culture, the University of Tokyo 'Reconsidering Anthropological Studies in the Northern Part of South Asia' organized by Katsuo Nawa in 2002. In 2003, an ILCAA research project entitled 'Comparative Study of Sociocultural Changes: On Changes in Northern South Asia' was organized by Hiroshi Ishii. David Gellner joined ILCAA as a visiting research scholar in September 2003. The idea of the international workshops emerged during occasional discussions between them. The main aim of the projects was to achieve a better understanding of the societies and cultures of northern South Asia focusing on various aspects of change in the region.

Revised versions of all but two of the papers from the two conferences have been incorporated in the present volumes. However, in order to group the papers thematically, and in view of the preponderance of papers on Nepal, we considered it appropriate in producing two edited volumes to reorganize the order in which the papers had been originally presented. Thus in the first volume (*Nepalis Inside and Outside Nepal*) we have the following four parts:

1. Urbanization, Ethnicity, and Occupation
2. Marriage, Kinship, and Transformation of Intimacy
3. Transnational Links Inside and Outside Nepal
4. Nepal as Viewed from the Indian Himalayas

In the second volume (*Political and Social Transformations in North India and Nepal*) the subdivisions are as follows:

1. Local Political and Social Change
2. Transformations of Religious Identities and Practices
3. Forms of 'Secular' Activism: Resistance, Negotiation, and Violence and 'Afterword'.

Although the first volume contains chapters on Nepal only (except for the last one), it is impossible, as the book's title implies, to treat modern Nepal in isolation. It is very much a part of the wider region – northern South Asia – indicated by the umbrella title of the set. And at the same time, Nepalis, as described in several chapters in the volume, have forged substantial transnational links with many countries further afield, not least Japan. The final chapter in *Nepalis Inside and Outside Nepal,* by Gerald Berreman, puts forward explicit comparisons with the Indian Himalayas to the west of Nepal in a form which deserves to stimulate debate and further research from Nepal and Himalayan specialists.

It is necessary here to mention what we mean by 'northern South Asia' and why we find it meaningful to see it as one area. We use the term to include north and central India (i.e. India excluding the Dravidian-speaking areas), Pakistan, Bangladesh, Nepal, and Bhutan. As can immediately be seen, it is an area of great cultural diversity. For example, as regards religion, it is characterized by Hinduism, Islam, and Buddhism (all incorporating, of course, numerous forms of local belief and practice). There is conflict between these various traditions, certainly, but also considerable evidence of deep-rooted patterns of coexistence as well. Despite this diversity, there are important cultural and linguistic continuities right across the region, for all that fifty years of nation-building processes have driven neighbours apart from each other and set them on different trajectories.

Northern South Asia is a very rich field for comparison. Take, for example, Nepal and (north and central) India. We can immediately notice many cultural and historical links and similarities in the fields of religious relationships, ideologies of kingship and government, caste system(s), popular culture, clothes and food, and these days even practices of violence and revolution. But at the same time, we can easily point out that similar institutions have different manifestations. Though Islam is not absent in Nepal, communal struggle is much less harsh there than in India. Contemporary castes in Nepal have much less of a history of caste associations, reservations (as affirmative action is known in South Asia) have only just begun to be introduced there, and the way in which the Nepalese state has incorporated subordinate groups differs considerably from similar processes in India. As general historical background, the difference in the experiences of colonialism (direct in India and indirect in Nepal) should be kept in mind.

Comparison between Nepal and Bhutan, though not included in the present volumes, would also produce interesting results. Despite the first obvious similarities of location and mountainous environment, the two countries are contrastive in many aspects: Hinduism *vs.* Tibetan Buddhism, rapid *vs.* slow population increase, and their respective policies towards cultural diversity and nature conservation, are but a few examples of the ways in which the two countries would appear to have taken diametrically opposed paths.

It was one of our initial aims to encourage the comparative study of social change. It is true that only a few of the papers in these volumes take up the challenge to compare explicitly. It is also true that, geographically, the areas dealt with are limited to Nepal and India. Nonetheless, we are glad that some authors are keen on comparison and that the other papers in combination convey detailed and analytical pictures of the many diverse but comparable ways in which local societies of the area are changing. We hope that the present collections will encourage further and deeper comparative studies of the region in future.

Hiroshi ISHII
David N. GELLNER
Katsuo NAWA

Contributors

Biswaroop DAS is Professor at the Centre for Social Studies, Surat in India. He has written extensively on issues related to regional and urban planning, city slums, urban poverty, NGOs and rehabilitation of displaced people. He is the author of *Socio-Economic Study of Slums in Surat City* (CSS, Surat, 1992), *Role and Impact of Micro Finance on Poor* (FWWB-India, 2001), and co-author of *Unknown Leaders of Micro Finance* (FWWB-India, 1999) and *Poor in Urban India: Life in the Slums of a Western Indian City* (Rawat, 2001).

Abhijit DASGUPTA is Reader in Sociology at the Department of Sociology, Delhi School of Economics, University of Delhi. He is the author of *Growth with Equity: The New Technology and Agrarian Change in Bengal* (Manohar, 1998), and has edited several books including *State, Society and Displaced People in South Asia* (University Press Ltd., 2005).

Tatsuro FUJIKURA is Associate Professor at the Graduate School of Asian and African Area Studies, Kyoto University, and an editor of *Studies in Nepali History and Society.* He was a researcher at the Centre for, Social Research and Development (CSRD), Kathmandu from 2004 to 2005. His publications include 'Discourses of Awareness: Notes for a Criticism of Development in Nepal', *Studies in Nepali History and Society* 6 (2): 271-313 (2001), 'The Role of Collective Imagination in the Maoist Conflict in Nepal', *Himalaya* 22 (1): 21-30 (2003), and 'Vasectomies and Other Experiments with Modernity: A Reflection on the Discourses and Practices of Family Planning in Nepal', *Journal of the Japanese Association for South Asian Studies* 16: 40-71 (2004).

David N. GELLNER is Professor of Social Anthropology and a Fellow of All Souls College in the University of Oxford. From 2003 to 2004 he was a Visiting Professor at the Research Institute for Cultures and Languages of Asia and Africa, Tokyo University of Foreign Studies. He is the author or editor of many books on Nepal and Northern South Asia, including *Borderland Lives in Northern South Asia* (Duke, 2013),

Religion, Secularism, and Ethnicity in Contemporary Nepal (OUP, 2016), *Global Nepalis: Religion, Culture, and Community in a New and Old Diaspora* (OUP, 2018), *Vernacular Religion: Cultural Politics, Community Belonging, and Personal Practice in the UK's Nepali Diaspora* (Vajra, 2019), and a special issue of *Contributions to Nepalese Studies 46.1: Nepali Dalits in Transition* (CNAS, TU, 2019)

Krishna HACHHETHU is Reader in Political Science and associated with the Centre for Nepal and Asian Studies (CNAS) Tribhuvan University. He is the author of *Party Building in Nepal: Organization, Leadership and People* (Mandala, 2002) and *State of Democracy in Nepal* (SDSA/N and International IDEA, 2004), and the co-author of *Leadership in Nepal* (Adroit, 2001), *Women and Governance: Re-imagining the State from Gender Perspective* (Nepal Chapter) (S2, 2002), and *Nepal: Local Leadership and Governance* (Adroit, 2004). He has contributed articles to several academic books and journals published in Nepal and abroad.

Hiroshi ISHII is Professor Emeritus at the Research Institute for Languages and Cultures of Asia and Africa (ILCAA), Tokyo University of Foreign Studies. He has conducted anthropological research among the Newars, the Parbate Hindus, and the Maithils in Nepal since 1970. He has published *Nepal: A Himalayan Kingdom in Transition* (UNU Press, 1996, with P.P. Karan et al.), as well as other books and articles in both Japanese and English.

Surinder S. JODHKA is Professor at the Centre for the Study of Social Systems, Jawaharlal Nehru University, New Delhi. Previously he taught at the University of Hyderabad and at Panjab University, Chandigarh. He has been working in the fields of agrarian change and social identity and has published extensively, including *Community and Identities: Contemporary Discourses on Culture and Politics in India* (ed., Sage, 2001).

Mrigendra KARKI is Lecturer in Sociology in Tribhuvan University, Kathmandu, and a member of the Centre for Nepal and Asian Studies.

Lancy LOBO is the Director, Centre for Culture and Development, Vadodara. Earlier, he also served as Director, Centre for Social Studies, Surat. He has conducted extensive studies on Dalits, tribals, OBCs, and minorities in rural and urban Gujarat. He has authored five books and many articles in professional journals. He was an international fellow of the Woodstock Theological Centre, Georgetown University, Washington DC in 1999-2000.

Keshav L. MAHARJAN is Professor in the Graduate School for International Development and Cooperation, Hiroshima University. He conducts research and lectures on Rural Economics and South Asian

Studies. He is the author of *Peasantry in Nepal: A Study on Subsistence Farmers and Their Activities Pertaining to Food Security* (Research Center for Regional Geography, Hiroshima University, 2003) and *Impacts of Irrigation and Drainage Schemes on Rural Economic Activities in Bangladesh* (Research Center for Regional Geography, Hiroshima University, 1997). He is also one of the main contributors to H. Ishii (ed.), *Ryudo-suru Nepal (Social Dynamism in Contemporary Nepal)* (UTP, 2005), and has several book chapters and journal articles to his credit in Japanese and English.

Minoru MIO is Associate Professor of the National Museum of Ethnology, Osaka, Japan. He has written several articles in Japanese and in English, including 'National Discourse and Local Conflict: How Modernity Intervened in a Conflict over the Administration of a Sufi Saint Mausoleum in Mewar, Rajasthan', in H. Kotani et al. (eds.) *Fussing Modernity: Appropriation of History and Political Mobilization in South Asia* (National Museum of Ethnology, 2000) and 'Looking for Love and Miracles: Multivocal Composition and Conflicts among Believers in a Sufi Mausoleum Festival of Rajasthan, India', *Bulletin of the National Museum of Ethnology* 29 (1).

Tetsuya NAKATANI is Associate Professor in the Department of Regional Promotion at Nara Prefectural University. His writings include 'Refugees', in Veena Das (ed.), *The Oxford India Companion to Sociology and Social Anthropology* (New Delhi: OUP, 2003) and 'Away from Home: the Movement and Settlement of Refugees from East Pakistan to West Bengal, India', in Imtiaz Ahmed, Abhijit Dasgupta, and Kathinka Sinha-Kerkhoff (eds.), *State, Society and Displaced People in South Asia* (Dhaka: UPL, 2004).

Katsuo NAWA is Associate Professor of Cultural Anthropology, Institute of Oriental Culture, the University of Tokyo. He is the author of *Nepal, Byans oyobi Shuhen Chiiki ni okeru Girei to Shakaihanchu ni kansuru Minzokushiteki Kenkyu: Mo Hitotsu no 'Kindai' no Fuchi (An Ethnographic Study on Rituals and Social Categories of Byans, Nepal, and Adjacent Regions: Another Constellation of 'Modernity')* (Sangensha, 2002), which was awarded the 30th Shibusawa Prize. His publications in English include 'Ethnic Categories and their Usages in Byans, Far Western Nepal' *European Bulletin of Himalayan Research* 18, 2000.

Kiyoko OGURA is a freelance journalist based in Kathmandu. She is the author of the highly acclaimed *Okoku wo Yurugashita 60 Nichi (60 Days that Shook the Kingdom)* (Aki Shobo), which appeared in Japanese in 1999, in English under the title *Kathmandu Spring: The People's Movement of 1990* (Himal Books) in 2001, and in Nepali as *Janata Jageko Bela (When People Awoke)* (Himal Kitab) in 2004. She has published articles on the Maoist insurgency in several Japanese journals.

Jonathan PARRY is Professor of Anthropology at the London School of Economics and Political Science. He has done field research in various parts of north and central India on various different topics. His publications include *Caste and Kinship in Kangra* (Routledge, 1979), *Death in Banaras* (Cambridge University Press, 1994), *Death and the Regeneration of Life* (ed. with M. Bloch, Cambridge University Press, 1982), *Money and the Morality of Exchange* (ed. with M. Bloch, Cambridge University Press, 1989), *The Worlds of Indian Industrial Labour* (ed. with J. Breman and K. Kapadia, Sage Publications, 1999) and *Institutions and Inequalities* (ed. with R. Guha, Oxford University Press, 1999).

Joanna PFAFF-CZARNECKA is Professor for Social Anthropology at Bielefeld University. From October 1999 to September 2001 she was Senior Research Fellow at the Center for Development Research, University of Bonn, in charge of establishing and managing the Research Programme 'Human Rights and Development'. In 1999 she was Visiting Professor at the University of Tokyo. Her books include: *Ethnic Futures: State and Identity in Four Asian Countries* (ed. with A. Nandy, D. Rajasingham, and T. Gomez, Sage, New Delhi, 1999); *Rituale Heute: Theorien, Kontroversen, Entwürfe* (Rituals Today: Theories, Controversies, Drafts), (ed. with C. Caduff, Reimer, Berlin, 1999; 2001: 2nd edition); *Nationalism and Ethnicity in Contemporary Nepal: The Cultural Politics in a Hindu Kingdom* (ed. with D.N. Gellner & J. Whelpton, Harwood Academic Publishers, 1997). Her articles include: 'Death, Ri(gh)tes, and Institutions in Immigrant Switzerland' in M. Scheinin and R. Toivannen (ed.) *Rethinking Non-discrimination and Minority Rights,* pp. 201-17 (Helsinki: Abo Academy of Human Rights, 2004); 'Demokratisierung und Nation-Building in Geteilten Gesellschaften', in J. Hippler (ed.), *Nation-Building: Ein Schlüsselkonzept für Friedliche Konfliktbearbeitung?,* pp. 49-69 (Eine Welt-Band, Bonn: Stiftung Entwicklung und Frieden, 2004); 'High Expectations, Deep Disappointment: Politics, State and Society in Nepal after 1990', in M. Hutt (ed.) *People's War in a Hindu Kingdom: Maoism in Nepal,* pp. 166-91 (London: Hurst, 2004).

Akio TANABE is Associate Professor at Institute for Research in Humanities, Kyoto University. He is a co-editor of *Gender and Modernity: Perspectives from Asia and the Pacific* (Kyoto University Press and Trans Pacific Press, 2003), *Dislocating Nation-States: Globalization in Asia and Africa* (Kyoto University Press and Trans Pacific Press, 2005), and *The State in India: Past and Present* (OUP, forthcoming).

PART 1

LOCAL POLITICAL AND SOCIAL CHANGE

1

Local Politics and Alternatives in Development in North Bengal

ABHIJIT DASGUPTA

INTRODUCTION

In many parts of rural India, activities pertaining to the formulation and implementation of public goals, and to the distribution and use of political power have been changing in recent years largely due to the decentralization of power to local political bodies known as panchayats.[1] It was believed that the new local power structure under *panchayati raj* would usher in an era of growth and social justice. This paper examines some aspects of relations between local power structures and new development programmes in the state of West Bengal. It also examines the complex relations between local politics and broader goals of equity and development.

Although promises to empower panchayats were made after independence, and two high-powered committees were constituted, very little was achieved in terms of the devolution of power to local bodies.[2] However, in 1992, with the enactment of the 73rd Amendment to the Indian Constitution, a new era began in the history of local administration. This new Amendment made elections to panchayats mandatory in the states, and reserved one third of the seats for women in the three-tier panchayati system. In West Bengal, however, the search for an alternative and efficient local self-government began way back in the early 1970s when a Congress

---

[1] I am grateful to David Gellner, Hiroshi Ishii, André Béteille, B.S. Baviskar, and Masahiko Togawa for comments on an earlier draft.

[2] In 1957 the Balwant Mehta Committee and in 1977 the Ashok Mehta Committee were formed to recommend measures to revamp *panchayati raj*.

government was in power.[3] A new Act to restructure the panchayati system was introduced in 1973. The new Act recommended: (a) the introduction of a new three-tier panchayati system with *gram panchayats* (village councils), *anchal panchayats* (block councils), and *zilla parishads* (district councils); (b) the holding of mandatory elections every fifth year to elect representatives in these bodies; and (c) the use of party symbols and political party support in contesting elections.[4] The rights and duties of panchayat members were spelt out, and the rules for holding elections and carrying out day-to-day business were mentioned. The new Panchayat Act aimed at building political institutions at the grassroots level for the implementation of development projects of the central and state governments.

During the last twenty-five years the Left Front Government (LFG) has carried out several development programmes with the help of panchayats. In 1977, after winning elections at the state assembly, the LFG decided to hold panchayat elections in accordance with the provisions in the 1973 Act. The objectives behind holding panchayat elections in 1978 were twofold: first, to make panchayats vibrant political institutions and, second, to use these local political institutions for the implementation of development projects of the central and state governments. By opting for new panchayats the Left parties presumably decided to play with a double-edged sword. On the one hand, they tried to build a power base at the grassroots level with the help of the panchayats and, on the other, to fulfil the aspirations of the people for overall development. After a gap of two and a half decades, it is abundantly clear that the LFG did show its unique skill in playing with this double-edged sword: it has helped them, both to retain power in the three-tier panchayati system and to implement alternative development projects in the state. Against this backdrop this chapter looks into some aspects of the complex relations between local politics and development projects in a village in the Jalpaiguri district in North Bengal.

The changing politics and development issues in this village were first studied in 1978.[5] A revisit to this village in 2003 offered me an opportunity to compare local politics in the context of development projects initiated by the LFG. I discuss the panchayati electoral politics in 1978 and 2003 and critique development programmes that revolve around panchayats. I point out the inherent contradictions in the functioning of panchayats and

---

[3] After prolonged deliberations the Congress government introduced the new Act in the legislative assembly in 1973 and The West Bengal Panchayat Act, 1973, was adopted subsequently.

[4] West Bengal became the first state in the country to try out party political affiliation in panchayat elections. This is why these panchayats are also known as 'political' panchayats. Political leaders such as Gandhi and Jayaprakash Narayan were against such a move.

[5] See Dasgupta 1981.

development policies of the LFG.[6] Several studies on the *panchayati raj* in West Bengal have highlighted its achievements during the last twenty-five years.[7] This chapter takes up issues that are contentious and the subject of considerable debate. The first part of this deals with the contours of panchayati politics and development strategies in a village called Kamarpur in the Jalpaiguri district of north Bengal. In the next section, I compare local politics and development in 1978 and 2003, and argue that in certain respects local politics in West Bengal has had an adverse effect on the broader objectives of growth and social justice.

During the pre-1978 phase panchayats in West Bengal remained dormant and they had very little to do with political and economic functions.[8] This is clearly evident if we take a look at observations made by anthropologists who studied local-level politics in West Bengal in the 1960s and 1970s. Ranajit Chaudhuri, for example, summed up the situation in the following way:

> The Panchayat is functioning today as a mere adjunct to the administrative machinery of the state government. It rather enables the state to spread its tentacles to the heart of the village and thus bring the entire society within the ambit of its formalized power structure. The politics and programme are decided at state level and the Panchayat is required to merely execute the limited task assigned to it by the state government. As a result the principles of decentralization are receding into the background. The decentralization here comes to mean only the delegation of power to a locally constituted body. (Chaudhuri 1964: 1530)

Marvin Davis, who studied politics in a village in Midnapur district, observed:

> In many ways the activities of the Torkotala village assembly and council do not conform to the provisions of Panchayati Raj legislation. Panchayat members were not chosen in a contested election. Nor was the Upadhyaksha. The assembly and council do not meet regularly. And new council members, or even the leadership, are not chosen every four years. (Davis 1983: 188)

Anthropologist Ralph Nicholas (1965) who examined the dynamics of local politics in two villages in Midnapur district hardly referred to panchayats as the main political institution. He was of the view that village

---

[6]See Mukarji and Bandyopadhyay (1993) for a critical review of the functioning of panchayats in West Bengal.

[7]See, for example, Lieten (1992), Kohli (1987), and Nossiter (1988).

[8]A detailed account of panchayats in West Bengal in the pre-1978 period can be found in Webster (1992).

politics was all about 'faction politics' or in vernacular, what was known as *daladali*. One can cite more such examples to highlight the state of affairs in the functioning of panchayats in West Bengal before the new Act came into existence.

The West Bengal Panchayat Act (WBPA) of 1973 replaced two earlier Acts of 1957 and 1963. Since its enactment the WBPA had been amended as many as sixteen times.[9] Through these amendments, various loopholes in the WBPA were plugged and detailed rules regarding election procedures, counting of votes, declaration of results were incorporated. A legislative measure began to change the dynamics of local politics in West Bengal.

THE RISE OF 'LITTLE RED FORTS' IN NORTH BENGAL[10]

Seven districts in the northern part of West Bengal (Murshidabad, Malda, North and South Dinajpur, Darjeeling, Jalpaiguri, and Cooch Behar) constitute what is popularly known as 'North Bengal' or *Uttar Banga*. As an administrative unit Jalpaiguri district came into existence on 1 January 1869. Previously it was a subdivision of the Rangpur district (now in Bangladesh). The eastern part of the district, which was known as Western Duars, was brought under the jurisdiction of Jalpaiguri in 1869.[11] Since its inception two towns developed in two parts of the district, Jalpaiguri in the central part and Alipurduar in the eastern part. Jalpaiguri, in the course of time, became the chief town and administrative headquarters of the district.[12]

Heroic peasant struggles that took place in Jalpaiguri from time to time are quite popular among many Bengalis. In the late eighteenth century, the *sanyasi* (Hindu hermit) revolt took place in this area, and is regarded as one of India's first nationalist struggles against colonial rule. In the late 1940s, the *tebhaga* peasant movement swept through many parts of the district. This movement was organized in support of the sharecroppers' demand for a two-third share of the crop, and it was led by a peasant organization called the Bengal Provincial Krishak Sabha (BPKS). Again, in the late 1960s, Jalpaiguri drew public attention for the Naxalbari peasant uprisings

[9]For a list of these amendments and changes that were made from time to time, see GWB (1973) and also Webster (1992).

[10]The term 'little red forts' is used here in a metaphorical sense to refer to the panchayats under the control of the Left Front.

[11]Ranajit Dasgupta (1992) discusses in greater detail the early history and various aspects of economy, politics, and social life of the district.

[12]However, Siliguri has now emerged as the chief metropolitan town of north Bengal. Located 15 kilometres away from the village, Siliguri is the gateway to Nepal, Sikkim, Bhutan, and also a transit point for travel to the north-eastern states of India.

that initially sparked off in the neighbouring Darjeeling district but spread to the whole of north Bengal within a short span of time. In recent years, the district has become the epicentre of the Kamtapuri liberation movement of the indigenous ethnic groups, a movement spearheaded by the Rajbangshis, Koches, and Meches for a separate state in north Bengal. Thus for many years the district has been the centre of peasant movements and resistance.

The village Kamarpur is located in the Rajganj subdivision of the Jalpaiguri district. It has five hamlets or residential units (in Bengali *para*) of which three have existed since the time of the Permanent Settlement of 1793 and the two came up only after independence in order to accommodate Hindu refugees and migrants from East Pakistan/Bangladesh. I call the former '*jotedari* residential area' and the latter 'new residential area'. These residential areas may be listed in the following way:

1. Central Jotedari
2. East Jotedari
3. South Jotedari
4. New Residence (North), located on the north-western part of the village
5. New Residence (South), located on the southern part of the village, near the South Jotedari (see Map 1.1)

The term '*jotedari*' refers to a special kind of land-tenure arrangement in rural Bengal. The word is derived from the term '*jotedar*', or big landowner. The *jotedar* used to be the central figure in this type of residential area. The *adhiars* or sharecroppers used to live close to the residence of the *jotedar*. The average size of the '*jote*' was a little under 150 acres. They were the original reclaimer of the soil and held the land at an easy rent. In this respect they were more like *raiyat*s than zamindars.

Although the village population and the number of households increased between 1978 and 2003, the location of the five residential areas remained as before. In 1978, Kamarpur had 480 households (2,676 persons) out of which 217 households were entirely dependent on land for their livelihood. These 217 households may be classified into three main agrarian classes: landowners (84), sharecroppers (26), labourers (61), and as many as 46 households had mixed agricultural occupations, for example landowner-sharecropper, landowner-labourer, and sharecropper-labourers. The two numerically dominant castes in Kamarpur were the Namasudras (45 per cent) and the Rajbangshis (23 per cent), two well-known scheduled castes of Bengal. In terms of numerical strength, the Kayasthas (12 per cent) and the Brahmans (3 per cent) came next. A very high percentage of scheduled caste population (68 per cent) does raise the question whether this is a typical village in West Bengal. It needs to be emphasized that such

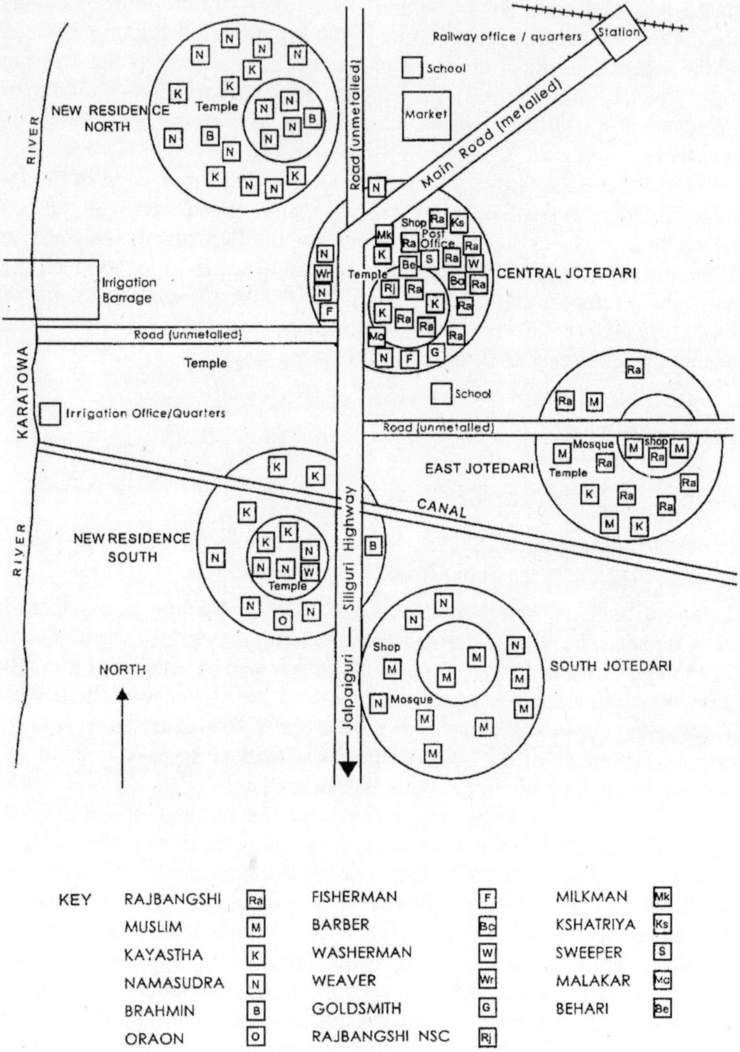

Map 1.1 : Kamarpur Village Settlement Pattern.

a high percentage of scheduled caste population is commonly found in the North Bengal districts of Jalpaiguri, Cooch Behar, the traditional dwelling place of the Rajbangshis. The influx of the Namasudras from East Bengal after Partition only increased the percentage of the Scheduled Caste population. Thus, this kind of demographic composition is typical of villages in these two districts. The Muslims (12 per cent) too had a sizeable population. The Hindu Namasudra castes arrived in Kamarpur from the erstwhile East Bengal, some as refugees or as voluntary migrants. The influx of population from the other side of the border continued for nearly five decades. As mentioned earlier, the immigrants lived in the two new residential areas in the village.

Panchayat elections in Kamarpur were held in June 1978, in accordance with the provision in the new Act. They coincided with my fieldwork in the village. The elections offered me an opportunity to study the impact of universal adult franchise, secret ballot, and party political affiliations on local-level politics. For the first time the residents of the village had the chance to elect their representatives by means of a secret ballot. The new Act allowed the political parties to enter in a big way into the arena of village politics. In 1978, Kamarpur had 1,775 voters. It was a part of a *gram panchayat* called Bina. The voters were to elect only three candidates for the Bina panchayat, which formed a single constituency.[13] For the three coveted seats, nine candidates with different political party affiliations were in the fray (Table 1.1).

The CPI (M) put forward three candidates for the contest, all of whom were Namasudras, whereas the Congress (I) fielded one each from the Rajbangshis, the Namasudras, and the Muslims. There were two candidates, one Rajbangshi and the other a Kayastha, who represented the Congress (N), and a Muslim businessman contested as an independent candidate.[14] All of the candidates were over thirty years old and, with two exceptions, all owned two to five acres of land. It was clear that small farmers were going to dominate the new panchayat. In terms of educational background all except two had completed primary schooling. The left political parties claimed that the main objective behind holding elections with party political affiliation was to get rid of the vested interests that dominated local politics. Indeed, with these elections political power shifted from the hands of the rich peasants to a group of leaders who belonged to the middle peasant strata (Table 1.1). However, neither the CPI (M) nor the Congress (I) was successful in nominating sharecroppers and agricultural labourers as panchayat election candidates.

---

[13]Bina panchayat included several villages in the central part of the Rajganj Block. Please note, all the names of places and persons are pseudonyms.

[14]In 1978, Congress (I) was led by Indira Gandhi, and Congress (N) had Nijalingappa as its leader. Therefore, (I) stands for Indira and (N) for Nijalingappa.

Table 1.1: Socio-Economic Background of Panchayat Election Candidates of Kamarpur, 1978

Name	Age	Caste	Religion	Residence	Occupation	Literacy	Party	Vote Secured
Ganesh Sarkar (Won)	50	Namasudra	Hindu	New Residence (North)	Landowner (3 acres)	up to Class VI	CPI (M)	**268**
Hari Das (Won)	47	Namasudra	Hindu	New Residence (South)	Landowner +Business (1 acre)	up to Class VIII	CPI (M)	**257**
Banik Biswas (Won)	34	Namasudra	Hindu	New Residence (South)	Landowner +School Teacher (4.34 acres)	School Final	CPI (M)	**279**
Paresh Roy	45	Rajbangshi	Hindu	Central Jotedari	Landowner +School Teacher (22.13 acres)	up to Class X	Cong (I)	149

Amir Ali	32	-	Muslim	East Jotedari	Landowner (5 acres)	up to Class II	Cong (I)	137
Sham Mondal	35	Namasudra	Hindu	New Residence (North)	Business	up to Class V	Cong (I)	173
Aminur Rahman	42	-	Muslim	South Jotedari	Landowner +Business (2 acres)	up to Class II	Inde-pendent	8
Amal Dey	40	Kayastha	Hindu	Central Jotedari	Landowner (3 acres)	up to Class X	Cong (N)	15
Naren Roy	51	Rajbangshi	Hindu	East Jotedari	Landowner (4 acres)	up to Class VII	Cong (N)	5

Note: Column 6 presents total landholding of the candidate's household. Where none is shown the household owns no agricultural land.

At the time of the panchayat elections, the village was polarized on caste and party lines. The Namasudras sided with the CPI (M) whereas the Rajbangshis and the Muslims offered support to the Congress (I) candidates. The CPI (M) polled the maximum number of votes in the two new residential areas, the Congress (I), on the other hand, obtained votes mostly from the *jotedari* residential areas. The numerical strength of the Namasudras put the CPI (M) in a commanding position in the 1978 electoral battle. Castes became crucial in determining the political fate of the CPI (M) and Congress (I) candidates. The Rajbangshis and the Muslims showed their traditional loyalties to the Congress (I). The Namasudras, most of whom were immigrants, found the CPI (M) sympathetic towards them since the Party stood against the high-handedness of the Congress leaders in solving the problems of the refugees.[15] The political issues that dominated electoral politics may be classified into general and specific. The general issues were those that cut across the boundaries of the village and brought national- and state-level politics into the arena of village politics. Specific issues, on the other hand, refer to those that have immediate relevance to the village. Several general issues had been raised by the Congress (I), for example, that panchayat elections with party symbols and party affiliations were introduced by the CPI (M) to create divisions among the villagers, and that the LFG failed to stop the rise in prices of essential commodities. The candidates raised several specific village-level political issues, for example, that a Congress (I) candidate organized a folk dance to raise some funds for the village school but the CPI (M) leader refused to buy a ticket. The opponents alleged that this clearly showed lack of concern for the schoolchildren in the village. The CPI (M) selected only Namasudras as candidates for the elections, which proved beyond doubt – it was claimed – that they were sectarian. The CPI (M), on the other hand, raised several general issues: that the Congress rule had made panchayats in the state defunct, that they were responsible for the emergency rule in the country which was throttling individual freedom. They were still more vocal with village-level specific issues such as that the Congress (I) called in ruffians to terrorize their candidates, that they ignored interests of the Namasudras, that only the camp followers of the Congress (I) benefited from the developmental work in the village. It was a unique combination of these two different kinds of political issues that made the panchayat elections of 1978 very special.

Election activities required a large number of active supporters for work such as preparing posters, leaflets, walling (writing slogans on the walls of the brick-built houses), arranging open meetings (by hiring microphones, chairs, tables for the speakers), passing messages to the

[15] I have discussed this at length in another paper (A. Dasgupta 2002).

block- or district-level political leaders, assisting candidates in their door-to-door campaigns, and so on. Both the Congress (I) and the CPI (M) employed a large number of village youths to carry out these functions. Numerically, the CPI (M) had more such youths than the Congress (I). The village youths emerged as important political actors in the wake of the panchayat elections. Political aspirations developed especially among those youths who came from economically poorer strata. The CPI (M) youth cadres from the poor and middle peasant families became active in village politics. The growing importance of the village youths in politics was another feature of the elections in 1978.

For many decades, political parties have tried to enter into the arena of village politics through various bodies, for example organizations for peasants, agricultural labourers, youths, women, castes, and so on. These organizations tried to address the grievances of the groups that they represented and helped in raising political consciousness. In this context, the role of the Krishak Sabha in raising political awareness among the peasants deserves special mention. The Krishak Sabha, the CPI (M)-led peasant organization, was most active in the village. The Congress (I) and other political parties too had their organizations but they never functioned as systematically as the Krishak Sabha did.[16] The activities of the Krishak Sabha became popular in Kamarpur after the emergence of the United Front Government in 1969. The CPI (M), the main partner of the Front, used the Krishak Sabha to mobilize poor peasants against 'vested interests', and to occupy forcibly illegally owned land of the *jotedar*s. In 1977-8, the Krishak Sabha re-emerged in the village scene with new demands, such as payment of Rs.10, the minimum wage to agricultural labourers, recognition of rights to homestead land of the poor, disbursement of interest-free loans to small farmers and liquidation of usufructuary debts, and introduction of 'food for work' for rural employment. The district- and block-level Krishak Sabha leaders maintained links between the village-level organization and the provincial organizations. These leaders were especially active during the time of the panchayat elections in establishing rapport with the villagers, and in helping the contesting candidates in their campaigns. Some of them spoke in open meetings in support of the three CPI (M) candidates.

Thus, with the introduction of party politics, universal adult franchise, and the secret ballot in three-tier panchayati elections the insular character of local politics underwent a radical change, and power shifted from the hands of the *jotedar*s to a group of small farmers. A group of new leaders emerged on the village political scene, whose socio-economic background was different from the traditional panchayat leaders. Two numerically significant castes in the village were politically polarized, the Namasudras

[16]For a detailed discussion on the Krishak Sabha in Bengal, see Béteille (1974: 171-87).

supported the CPI (M), the Rajbangshis and the Muslims sided with the Congress (I). An unintended consequence of the new panchayat elections was that it gave caste a new lease of life in local politics. Caste 'vote banks' turned out to be significant in the panchayati elections. Both general and village-level issues dominated elections. The main rival parties made a judicious mixture of the two in carrying out their political campaigns. With these elections the contours of local politics began to change, and the little red forts found roots in rural Bengal.

PANCHAYATS AND THE NEW DEVELOPMENT AGENDA

To improve conditions in the agrarian sector several steps were undertaken by the LFG in 1977-8. Land ceiling provisions were implemented, measures were taken to confiscate surplus land and to redistribute it among the poor, tenurial rights of the *bargadars* and *adhiars* were protected with the help of Operation Barga (henceforth OB), and minimum daily wages were fixed for agricultural labourers.[17] This was an experiment that P.C. Joshi (1975) described as "land reforms from below". Local-level political organizations like the Krishak Samiti and panchayats were involved in the planning and implementation process (Dasgupta 1998: 114-16). In Kamarpur, by the end of 1978, a total of 79.82 acres of land had been distributed to the poor, out of a total of 200 acres of surplus land that had been confiscated from the *jotedars*. A list of beneficiaries from among the Scheduled Castes and Scheduled Tribes was also prepared and they received most of the surplus land that was distributed.

To protect the interests of the sharecroppers an amendment to the Land Reforms Act was passed in 1977. The objective was to stop evictions of sharecroppers. A landowner was allowed to take a 50 per cent share of the crop when he supplied all the necessary agricultural inputs: in all other cases a landowner was entitled to one third of the crops (Dasgupta 1998: 100-3). OB marked a breakthrough in tenancy reform as it was a unique method to register the names of the sharecroppers to confer them with tenurial rights. The registration of names was carried out with the help of government officials, panchayat members, and Krishak Sabha activists. After identifying priority areas with a high concentration of sharecroppers, teams were formed to visit these areas. The teams conducted meetings with the sharecroppers and their landowners and distributed official certificates to the sharecroppers acknowledging their rights. OB helped in recording names of 700,000 *bargadars* in the state in the late 1980s. To encourage

---

[17] Sharecroppers in North Bengal are called *adhiars* whereas in other parts of the state they are known as *bargadars*.

productivity in leased land, loans were offered at a low rate of interest. The OB ushered in a new era in agrarian reforms (Dasgupta 1998: 157-8).

Several steps were taken to ameliorate conditions of the agricultural labourers, for example, fixing wages for a standard eight-hour working day. The food-for-work programme was stepped up to create more man-days. By the end of 1981 the target of nearly 141 million man-days had been achieved, and land distribution had benefited 1.4 million families dependent on agricultural labour in the state (GWB 1979). Land redistribution was undertaken on a war footing in the backward districts of North Bengal. The decision to recognize rights over homestead land was yet another step that benefited poor and landless labourers.

Besides these new strategies, in order to increase productivity, agricultural inputs, for example, seeds, fertilizers, and pesticides, were made available to poor peasants and sharecroppers. In the 1980s the gross cropped area irrigated in the districts increased from 24.3 per cent to 45.5 per cent. The productivity of the three main crops, i.e. *aman* (winter rice, the most popular crop in Bengal), *boro* (summer rice), and wheat, showed a significant rise (Boyce 1987: 62-7). Subsequently several new development projects of the central and state governments like National Rural Employment Programme (NREP), the Jawahar Rozgar Yojana (JRY or Rural Employment Programme), the Indira Awas Yojana (IAY or Rural Housing Programme), etc., began to change the rural landscape. These were indeed the golden days of agrarian reforms. The local bureaucracy, Krishak Sabhas, and panchayats were the main institutions which carried them out.

CHANGING LOCAL POLITICS: 'LITTLE RED FORTS' IN 2003

Between 1978 and 2003, panchayat elections took place on six occasions (1978, 1983, 1988, 1993, 1998, and 2003), at intervals of five years.[18] The sixth panchayat elections were scheduled to take place on 11 May 2003. A carnival-like atmosphere struck me when I arrived in Kamarpur. Political banners, posters, leaflets, and pamphlets made it clear that a special event was in the offing: the once-in-five-years elections, when Kamarpur's residents exercise their franchise, show their preferences for a party and a person that they think ideal for running the panchayat. In this great battle the new political parties in the state, such as the Trinamul Congress (TMC), the BJP, and the BSP, all tried their luck. Local politics had changed a great deal. However, the Left parties, especially the CPI (M), are still skilfully playing the old game of the two-edged sword, winning election after

[18]For detailed studies of electoral politics and panchayats in West Bengal, see Togawa (1997) and Kumar and Ghosh (2002: 2-35).

election, helping local-level democratic institutions to flourish, and at the same time carrying out their development agenda with the help of the panchayats. Political ups and downs have taken place almost all over the country, but the LFG has managed to hold on to its forts with great skill.

Between 1978 and 2003 Kamarpur's population and households almost doubled (Table 1.2). The percentage of the population dependent on land cultivation decreased, and more and more residents of the village are now pursuing non-agricultural occupations. The percentage of the SC population has gone up because of a higher birth rate and an influx of migrants from bordering districts in Bangladesh. Owing to demographic changes, the number of seats for the panchayats had been raised from three to four; the village population, which had been 2,676 in 1978, was 4,308 in 2003. The residents of the village now elect four candidates from four different constituencies which have been demarcated according to the residential units; each *para* has one seat, except the South Jotedari and New Residence (South). These two residential units have been merged to form one constituency.

As in 1978, the two principal political parties that were contesting the elections were the CPI (M) and the Congress (I). New political parties have made inroads in the village, the most important of which are the BJP and the Trinamul Congress (TMC). The BJP candidates won one of the seats in the 1998 elections, and in 2003 they fielded two candidates from the New Residence (North) and East Jotedari residential area. The TMC contested

Table 1.2: Economic and Demographic Changes in Kamarpur between 1978 and 2003

	1978	**2003**
Population	2,676	4,308
Number of Households	480	887
Operational Land (in Acres)	586	362
Landowners (Persons)	168	221
Sharecroppers (Persons)	60	12
Agricultural Labourers (Persons)	89	117
Mixed Agricultural Operations (Persons)	92	122
Number of Households Belonging to SC	344	647
Number of Households Belonging to ST	4	9
Number of Muslim Households	52	115
Agricultural Wage (Daily)	Rs.8	Rs.50
Total Panchayat Seats	**3**	**4**
Total Number of Voters	**1,775**	**2,637**

seats on earlier occasions. The entry of new political parties is giving local politics a new look; bipolar politics is now moving towards multi-polarity. The elected panchayat members enjoy more power and legitimacy, the right to rule, and to use resources for village development. They are the spokespersons of the village and liaise with government officials.

The socio-economic background of the candidates reveals several points: all were Hindus, two thirds were in their thirties and forties (though one was over 60), and they were more educated than the candidates who contested the 1978 elections (Tables 1.1 and 1.3). The Namasudras and the Rajbangshis are not politically polarized into two rival camps any more; the emergence of other political groups has created new political alignments. The New Residence (North) witnessed a straight contest between the CPI (M) and the BJP. In the East Jotedari constituency, a multi-cornered contest took place. The occupational background of the candidates has diversified. The non-landowning group has emerged to become as important as the small landowners. Except for one, all candidates were contesting in their respective residential areas. In 1978, like the Rajbangshis, the Muslims supported the Congress, and this is why the Congress party fielded one Muslim candidate in that year. In recent years, Muslim candidates have been nominated only in areas where they are numerically strong. However, a Muslim candidate with clout and political skill can make a difference. The electoral success of the CPI (M) in the Muslim-dominated area in 2003 points to a shift in the latter's political allegiance.

The election results showed that the New Residence (North) is no longer a happy hunting ground of the CPI (M). Similarly, the Congress (I) lost its political control among the Rajbangshis of the East Jotedari area. The Central Jotedari area has now emerged as the citadel of the Congress (I).[19] A neck-and-neck battle took place in New Residence (South) and South Jotedari where the Congress candidate lost by a margin of only two votes (Table 1.4).[20]

No clear correspondence between caste and politics could be established from the outcome of the 2003 elections. For instance, in New Residence (North), where 95 per cent of the residents were Namasudra, a traditional 'vote bank' of the CPI (M), the BJP secured nearly 43 per cent of the votes. In the East Jotedari area the Rajbangshis returned a CPI (M) candidate. The relationship between caste and politics in Kamarpur is turning out to be more fluid than it was in 1978. The loss of support of the two main political parties among the Namasudras and the Rajbangshis provided space to other political parties to manoeuvre. In 2003, the BJP succeeded in making use of this space in one constituency. On earlier

---

[19]The Congress (I) won this seat in 1988, 1993, and 1998.

[20]The BJP won this seat in 1998.

Table 1.3: Socio-Economic Background of Panchayat Election Candidates of Kamarpur, 2003

Name	Age	Caste	Religion	Residence	Occupation	Literacy	Party	Votes Secured
1. Naresh Mondal (Won) constituency I	45	Namasudra	Hindu	New Residence (North)	Businessman & Landowner (2 acres)	10 Class Pass	CPI (M)	**270**
2. Ram Mondal constituency I	44	Namasudra	Hindu	New Residence (North)	Timber Merchant	up to Class VIII	BJP	208
3. Anjana Das constituency II (Reserved for women)	32	Kayastha	Hindu	Central Jotedari	Housewife	up to Class VII	CPI (M)	277
4. Shilpi Mohanta (Won) constituency II (Reserved for women)	32	Rajbangshi	Hindu	Central Jotedari	Housewife	up to Class X	Cong (I)	**300**

5. Naresh Sarkar constituency III	52	Namasudra	Hindu	New Res.(S) & South Jotedari	Landowner (4 acres) & Business	Cleared Class X	Cong (I)	250
6. Dasu Mondal (Won) constituency III	56	Namasudra	Hindu	New Res.(S) South Jotedari	Business	up to Class VIII	CPI (M)	**252**
7. Nitu Roy constituency IV	63	Rajbangshi	Hindu	Outsider	Landowner (3 acres)	up to B.A. First Year	Cong (I)	241
8. Subal Das (Won) constituency IV	33	Namasudra	Hindu	East Jotedari	Landowner (3 acres)*	up to Class X	CPI (M)	**371**
9. Sibu Roy constituency IV	34	Rajbangshi	Hindu	East Jotedari	Office Work	up to Class XII	BJP	175

Note: Figures in column 6 indicate landholding per household. Where none is shown the household owns no agricultural land.

Table 1.4: Votes Secured by Different Parties in Four Constituencies, 2003

Parties	New Residence (North) (Voters 548) Constituency I	Central Jotedari (Voters 653) Constituency II	New Residence (South) &South Jotedari (Voters 563) Constituency III	East Jotedari (Voters 873) Constituency IV
CPI (M)	270	277	252	371
Congress (I)	-	300	250	241
BJP	208	-	-	175
Invalid Votes	7	9	13	1
Total Votes	485	586	515	788

occasions, other parties like the Trinamul Congress and the Bahujan Samaj Party contested for this space.[21]

'*JOTER RAJNITI*': HIDDEN ALLIANCES

Joter rajniti or the politics of alliance is now an integral part of the democratic political system in contemporary India. Alliances or coalitions are indispensable at the national, state, and panchayat levels. Political alliances of like-minded political groups are in conformity with democratic politics and they are certainly desirable in certain circumstances. However, in panchayat elections, local factors force different political groups to forge alliances, and in many such cases political ideologies take a back seat. Parties that enter into such alliances do not admit it in public. The consent of the party leader is required before forming such alliances, but neither the public nor the media is supposed to know the details of the alliance.

Such alliances are rampant in many parts of the state. In South Dinajpur, for instance, in a Block called Tapan, the RSP (Revolutionary Socialist Party) won ten out of eleven *gram panchayat*s in the 1998 elections; only one remained under the control of the CPI (M). To put an end to the RSP hegemony in this area, the CPI (M) went for an alliance with the TMC and the BJP. In this Block, in as many as fifty *gram panchayat* seats, the CPI (M) fielded candidates against the RSP, despite being in alliance with it at the state level.[22] In Purulia, where the Forward Block (FB) was strong, the

[21] Other parties which tried their luck in the electoral battle in the village are the Socialist Unity Centre, and the Uttara Khanda Dal (a political front for the Kamtapuri Liberation Front or KLO).

[22] *The Statesman*, 10 May 2003, p. 2.

BJP, the Congress, the TMC, and even the CPI (M) formed alliances to defeat the FB candidates. In Arsha, where the CPI (M) was strong, the BJP, Congress, and FB joined together to defeat the CPI (M) candidates. In this district the incumbent MLA of Arsha constituency belonged to the FB. The two police stations that come under this constituency were Bagmundi and Arsha. In the former the two LFG partners, the CPI (M) and FB, were at loggerheads. Here, to defeat the FB candidates, the CPI (M) tied up with the BJP, the Congress, and the TMC. In Bagmundi, in as many as sixty-nine *gram panchayat* seats, the CPI (M) fielded candidates against the FB. In Arsha, where the CPI (M) had a strong base, the FB candidate joined with the Congress, the TMC, and the BJP in order to try and defeat their own partner of the Front.[23]

There are also electoral alliances on a larger scale. At the time of the 1998 panchayat elections, the BJP allied with the TMC with the tacit support of the Congress, which fielded candidates for 47 per cent of the seats leaving the rest to the BJP-TMC coalition. When alliances on a large scale like this take place, they are described as *mahajot* (grand alliance). Grand alliances are not hidden. Both grand alliances and the other. more local form of alliances are of short duration. They cease to function as soon as the elections are over.

In Kamarpur, *joter rajniti* is now an integral part of electoral politics. In 2003 two such alliances were formed. In New Residence (North), the Congress (I) made an alliance with the BJP to defeat the CPI (M) candidate. In order to avoid the anti-CPI (M) vote being split, the Congress (I) withdrew its candidates. In East Jotedari the Kamtapuri People's Party (KPP) had a number of followers. But the KPP formed an alliance with the CPI (M) because one of their leaders was released from jail before the election on the condition that he should ask the KPP supporters to extend their support to the CPI (M).[24]

Joter rajniti is justified by political leaders on the grounds that it is carried out in order to put an end to the *adhipotto* (dominance) of one political party. The CPI (M)'s *adhipotto* among the Left Front partners is extremely well known. Right from its inception the CPI (M) enjoyed overwhelming dominance in the LF. The very first election results in 1977 gave them dominance since they won as many as 177 (61 per cent) seats out of a total of 293 in the state assembly. At that time the CPI (M) could have formed the state government on its own, but the party opted for LF unity and projected the Front as an alternative to the Congress and other opposition parties. Since then the LF partners have remained together and contested elections for the assembly and parliament after arriving at a

---

[23]*The Statesman,* 10 May 2003, p. 2.

[24]In 1993 a candidate from Uttara Khand contested from this constituency.

consensus on the question of sharing seats. Cracks began to surface in the unity of the Front members after a decade when the CPI (M) began to act as the dominant partner of the Front. The CPI (M)'s numerical strength in the state assemblies (in West Bengal and Kerala) and in parliament, their growing influence with organizational networks in the districts and blocks, a steady increase in the number of members of party cadres, and the emergence of some of the members as important political figures in national politics are some of the factors that helped the CPI (M) to enjoy dominance in the Front. Panchayat elections offered an opportunity for weaker partners to come out in the open with their differences and to show their strength in rural Bengal against one-party dominance. This dissent was not confined to allegations and counter-allegations made at Front meetings; the weaker partners openly defied the directive of seat adjustment in panchayat elections and fielded candidates against the dominant partner. Kamarpur's residents informed me that the beneficiaries of development projects are those who do not question the *adhipotto* of their benefactors.

The political hegemony of a few has led to another development that questions the efficacy of participatory democratic politics. From the early 1980s, in many parts of Bengal, candidates in the three-tier panchayats were declared as elected 'unopposed', which means winning the elections uncontested. For instance, in 1988, as many as 4,200 (7.99 per cent) of *gram panchayat* seats were uncontested. The number of uncontested seats in 1993 was 1,716 (2.81 per cent), and in 1998, in 668 (1.3 per cent) seats no contest was held. The percentage of seats that returned candidates unopposed has consistently decreased ever since the 1988 elections, but the problem of non-representation still persists. This is hardly desirable in a democratic political system.

WOMEN IN PANCHAYATS

The laudable objective behind the reservation of seats for women in the three-tier panchayati system is the empowerment of those who have been kept out of local power structures for far too long. In accordance with the Amendment to the 1973 Act, 33 per cent of the seats in the three-tier panchayats have now been reserved for women on a rotational basis.[25] This 33 per cent reservation should apply in the case of reserved constituencies for the SCs and STs too. In Kamarpur, one seat had been declared as

[25]The rotation takes place in the following way. A *gram panchayat* with 10 seats will have reservations for women in the following order: 1, 4, 7, 10. This order will change in the next election to 2, 5, 8, 1 and it will be 3, 6, 9 and 2 in the following election. It will go back to the first order in the subsequent election.

reserved for women at the time of the 2003 panchayat elections. Two women candidates from Central Jotedari, one from the CPI (M) and the other from the Congress (I) contested the seat (see Table 1.3). Both candidates were housewives whose husbands were active in politics. The Congress (I) candidate, who won, was the spouse of the panchayat member between 1998 and 2003. Nitu Roy, the Congress (I) candidate in East Jotedari, was looking for a berth in Kamarpur because the seat that he had won in 1998 from another village was reserved for a woman candidate in 2003. He asked his daughter to contest from that seat. He was, therefore, an outsider in Kamarpur's panchayat elections.

How effective is this step in empowering women? Are there enough well-trained women to take up the task of carrying out day-to-day administration? To what extent are women from the weaker sections in the rural areas making use of the reservation benefits? Answers to these questions are obviously linked to the status of women in West Bengal. Some recent studies have highlighted pervasive gender discriminations in rural Bengal. Gupta (2002), for instance, reported from her survey in villages in Medinipur and North 24 Parganas districts that most women in her samples are doubly disadvantaged, within the household and at the workplace. The heavy burden of dowry has forced many to cut down on what they spend on their education and many of them drop out at an early age. Those who work in the fields encounter discrimination as their male counterparts always receive higher wages than they do. Gupta cites several such examples to point out how the voices of women are throttled and how social justice is denied them. This raises doubts about the role of women in the political arena.

The lack of representation of women from the weaker sections has led many to believe that the new reservation policy has replaced one form of inequality with another. The successful women candidates in 1993 and 1998 were from upper-caste and middle-class backgrounds. In Kamarpur, for instance, both the women candidates who contested for the Central Jotedari seat were from economically well-off small farmers' households. The spouse of one of the women candidates pointed out that it is difficult to combine *gharer kaj* (housework) with *gramer kaj* (village work); only women from the better-off strata can take the risk of combining the two. This is why a 1997 survey of Jalpaiguri district showed that in *gram panchayats* very few representatives come from the families of agricultural labourers or sharecroppers. Only ninety-seven seats (4.86 per cent) were held by people from agricultural labouring families, and only fifty-one seats (2.55 per cent) were won by those from sharecropping families.[26]

[26]Government of West Bengal (1997). It may be noted that no reservation benefit is offered to the Other Backward Classes (OBCs).

The system has also led to what may be described as 'proxy membership' since a reserved seat returned a woman whose husband had represented the same seat earlier. This is the 'rotation method' now popular in many parts of Bengal. The reserved seat would rotate between spouses, and in some cases when the wife is incapable of contesting for some reason, the seat goes to another member of the family, to her sister or to the daughter of the incumbent. After a gap of five years, when the seat becomes unreserved, the husband contests again. Almost all the political parties have been following this rotation method in panchayat elections. This is why women candidates are turning out to be dummy candidates.[27] Girish Kumar noted that in a *gram panchayat* a woman from one family was nominated by three parties for lack of suitable candidates. He observes, " ... such a situation arises because reservation is enforced without ascertaining the ground realities ... " (2002: 43). As mentioned above, the policy of reserving one third of the seats for women in Kamarpur too suffers from this general malaise.[28]

CIVIL SOCIETY ORGANIZATIONS

In West Bengal, as mentioned earlier, civil society organizations dominated the public sphere for a long time. Some of the popular movements were led by them. In the vernacular they are often referred to as *nagarik sangathan* (citizens' associations). These associations functioned for women, youths, students, workers, peasants, and so on, and maintained close links with the political parties. In recent years, however, panchayats have marginalized many organizations that had been involved in mass movements for decades. For instance, WBPKS, a vibrant political organization which took up many issues for poor peasants, sharecroppers, and agricultural labourers is now almost defunct in Kamarpur and in many parts of North Bengal. When the first United Front assumed office in 1967, the WBPKS launched a land-grab agitation to occupy illegally held (*benami*) land and to redistribute it among the poor. During the first few years of the Left Front rule, the WBPKS was so popular in the state that its membership increased phenomenally (Dasgupta 1998: 163-4). The Left Front made full use of this newly resurgent organization in dealing with the agrarian reforms, especially in implementing the Operation Barga programme, till the end of 1980s. However, with the completion of the first panchayat elections,

---

[27] Several such cases were reported in the media at the time of the panchayat elections.

[28] In order to solve the problem the state government has undertaken several programmes to train women candidates in cities and towns, but many women were conspicuous by their absence. Those who have never been out of the house without either husband or children found it too inconvenient to attend such training camps.

interest in WBPKS began to fade away since panchayats became the epicentre of political and economic power. As panchayats began to take a firm grip over almost all social, economic, and political matters, the WBPKS and other organizations became defunct. As a result, in the rural areas, there are hardly any organized protests against landowners for higher agricultural wages or against eviction of sharecroppers. The poor peasants and agricultural workers have lost a weapon with which they had won many battles over many years.

The WBPKS is not the only casualty. Other organizations that had been active in rural Bengal have lost their significance too; for example, women's associations, youth and students' organizations, and the like. By contrast, in Andhra Pradesh, instead of marginalizing community organizations a large number of self-help groups have been encouraged to function side by side with the panchayats. In a study it has been pointed out that in Andhra Pradesh there are as many as 37,885 youth employment groups, 6,616 joint forest management groups, 10,292 water users' associations, 36,436 mother committees, 99,618 school education committees, 5,499 watershed committees (Powis 2003). The number of these groups is high also in states like Rajasthan, Madhya Pradesh, Maharashtra, Gujarat, and Kerala where a Left Front government was in power for a long time. In West Bengal, however, vibrant civil society organizations have lost their relevance in the wake of panchayat-centric politics. As stated before, peasant organizations, women's groups, students' and youth organizations are hardly functioning in the village.

ALTERNATIVES IN DEVELOPMENT

A shift of emphasis can be noticed in West Bengal as far as the development agenda is concerned. The state government with the help of panchayats is implementing several state and central government projects for rural employment, housing, agricultural credit, health, and education. New roads, electrification, new houses built for the poor, assistance to those below the poverty line, and a public distribution system have brought about perceptible changes in the countryside. But these projects have received more attention than the agrarian reforms programme of the Left Front with which they began their rule way back in 1978. The shift in emphasis has affected two groups the most, the sharecroppers and the agricultural labourers. Thus a recent report states, "the proportion of landless rural households in West Bengal increased from 39.6 per cent in 1987-8, to 41.6 per cent in 1993-4, to as much as 49.8 per cent in 1999-2000" (GWB 2004: 39). This means that by the end of the decade, nearly half the rural households in West Bengal were landless. And while commenting on the condition of sharecroppers, and referring back to Operation Barga, the same report notes, "the pace of the programme tapered off in the mid-1980s and since then the rate of the additional registration has been negligible" (GWB 2004: 39).

In 1978, as many as 226 out of 480 households in Kamarpur were either fully or partially dependent on agriculture. The tenurial rights of the sharecroppers were recognized at the time of Operation Barga. In the 2001 census operations, only thirty-seven persons registered their names as sharecroppers in the village. However, in 2003 the number of sharecroppers went down to twelve. Lack of protection from the state, pressure from the landowners to vacate the land, and the heavy burden of production expenses are forcing sharecroppers in the village to quit an occupation which they have followed for many generations. Som (2004) examined the conditions of recorded sharecroppers in Jalpaiguri and Cooch Behar in 2002-3. Out of a sample of 122 sharecroppers spread over 12 villages, 61 per cent of the total sample have surrendered their *barga* land to their landowners either partially (21 per cent) or totally (40 per cent). Som observed that the incidence of surrender is high where the landowner and sharecropper belong to different castes and when landowners and sharecroppers reside in different villages. He argues that one of the fallouts of OB is that landowners do not lease out land to sharecroppers any more.

The chances of finding an agricultural labourer's job in Kamarpur are now slim. Although government projects have succeeded in creating employment opportunities for the erstwhile agricultural labourers, such jobs are too few and available only for a short duration. To supplement household income many labourers visit the nearby town of Siliguri in search of odd jobs. The beneficiaries of *patta* (surplus land earlier distributed among the poor) are now selling off the land for lack of resources to use for cultivation. This has only accelerated the process of rural proletarianization in the village. In a recent study Bardhan and Mookherjee noted:

> An increase in the Left share of GP seats from 68 per cent to 75 per cent was associated with a statistically significant drop in land areas covered by either land distribution (*patta*) or sharecropper registration (*barga*) programmes, and in the proportion of households receiving *pattas*. (Bardhan & Mookherjee 2004: 967)

Besides pointing out the inverse relations between the popularity of the village panchayat and performance in land redistribution and registration, Bardhan and Mookherjee considered five broad areas for evaluation: the delivery of farm inputs and anti-poverty programmes, IRDP credit programmes, distribution of agricultural minikits, employment generation programmes, and fiscal performance. They observed:

> Local democracy may not function well in some contexts, e.g. where the distribution of assets, literacy and social status is highly

> unequal, a tradition of widespread political participation does not exist and political competition is lacking. (ibid.: 965)

Panchayat interventions have not made much impact on the development of other sectors like education and health. Data on literacy among *adivasis* as a proportion of the total population shows that the all-India averages are better than West Bengal's. In the 1991 census, in West Bengal, 32.3 per cent of male *adivasis* were recorded as literate as compared to the all-India figure of 32.5. In the case of *adivasi* women it was 12 per cent as against 14.5 per cent (Ramachandran et al. 2003). The fifth quinquennial survey on employment and unemployment conducted by the NSS (50th round, July 1993-June 1994) presents data on the principal activity by age group. One such activity is 'attending educational institutions'. Commenting on the NSS Report, Ramachandran et al. (2003: 15) noted:

> If the proportion of persons ... in the age group 5-14 years is taken as an approximation of children in that age-group who attended school regularly, West Bengal's performance in respect of school attendance was poor in 1993-4, particularly in rural areas ... In rural West Bengal only two-third of children in the age-group 5-14 attended school.

By contrast, Kerala, where a Left Democratic Front (LDF) ruled for many years, has excelled in education. In 1991 Kerala recorded a literacy rate of 94 per cent among males and 87 per cent among females. The literacy rate among SC women was particularly high by all-India standards: 74 per cent of SC females were reported to be literate. Efforts by missionaries and various civil society organizations have made Kerala advanced in the field of education.

In the health sector too, state-level data does not show perceptible changes in the rural areas of West Bengal. It is lagging behind many states if one takes into account vital indicators like per capita income, infant mortality rates, life expectancy at birth, fertility control, and the control of diseases and epidemics. In some states, bold steps have been taken to involve the panchayati system in propagating the principle of having a small family. Under the two-child norm policy, Haryana, Madhya Pradesh, Andhra Pradesh, and Tamil Nadu have banned a person with more than two children from contesting for the post of *sarpanch* (head). West Bengal has not yet done so.

CONCLUSION

This paper has critiqued some aspects of panchayats, politics, and the development agenda of the LFG in West Bengal. Twenty-five years ago I studied panchayat elections in a village in Jalpaiguri district in North

Bengal. I went back to that village in May 2003 to observe panchayat elections once again. This chapter highlights my observations on panchayat elections and politics in 1978 and 2003. In 1978, panchayat elections were held for the first time under a new Act. The introduction of party ideologies brought about change in the faction-ridden village politics. In spite of democratization, the Namasudras and the Rajbangshis, the two dominant castes, remained polarized, as the 'vote banks' of the CPI (M) and the Congress (I) respectively. Local, village-level issues dominated electoral politics. The newly elected panchayats became the crucial political institutions in carrying out the LFG's development policies. In the 2003 panchayat elections, castes were not as polarized as in 1978. The emergence of new parties and the politics of alliance have altered the nature of local politics. The rise of panchayats as monolithic local political institutions and panchyat-centric political and development programmes have had an adverse effect on other civil society organizations which had been vibrant and active for many years. The declining role of the Krishak Sabha is a case in point. Political achievements are, however, far more significant than performance in some economic sectors. The double-edged sword of the Left Front is not as sharp as it was in 1978; one side of it has lost much of its shine and sharpness.

REFERENCES

Bardhan, P. and D. Mookherjee. 2004. 'Poverty Alleviation Efforts of Panchayats in West Bengal'. *Economic and Political Weekly* 39 (9): 965-74.

Béteille, A. 1974. *Studies in Agrarian Social Structure*. Delhi: Oxford University Press.

Boyce, J. 1987. Agrarian Impasse in Bengal: Institutional Constraints to Technological Change, Oxford: Oxford University Press.

Chaudhuri, R. 1964. 'Panchayats and Interest Groups: Study of a Bengal Village'. *The Economic Weekly*, 19 September: 1527-30.

Dasgupta, A. 1981. 'Land and Politics in West Bengal: A Sociological Study of a Multi-caste Village'. Unpublished D.Phil. thesis, University of Sussex.

——. 1998. *Growth with Equity: The New Technology and Agrarian Change in West Bengal*. Delhi: Manohar.

——. 2002. 'Refugees as Political Actors: The Displaced Bengalis in West Bengal', in C.J. Thomas (ed.), *Dimensions of Displaced People in North-East India*, pp. 316-46. Delhi: Regency Publications.

Dasgupta, R. 1992. *Economy, Society and Politics in Bengal; Jalpaiguri 1869-1947*. Delhi: Oxford University Press.

Davis, M. 1983. *Rank and Rivalry: the Politics of Inequality in Rural West Bengal.* Cambridge: Cambridge University Press.

Gupta, J. 2002. 'Women Second in the Land Agenda'. *Economic and Political Weekly* 36 (18): 1746-54.

GWB (Government of West Bengal). 1973. *Paschim Banga Panchayat Rules*. Calcutta: Department of Panchayat and Rural Development.

——. 1979. *Tebhaga Theke Operation Barga*. Calcutta: Government Press (in Bengali).

——. 1997. 'Socio-economic Profile of Panchayat Members (Jalpaiguri)'. Calcutta: Government Press.

——. 2004. Development and Planning Department. 'West Bengal Human Development Report'. Calcutta: Government Press.

Joshi, P.C. 1975. *Land Reforms in India*. Bombay: Allied Publishers Ltd.

Kohli, A. 1987. *The State and Poverty in India: The Politics of Reform*. Cambridge: Cambridge University Press.

Kumar, G. 2002. *Constitutionalizing Panchayats: The Response of State Legislatures* (Occasional Paper). Delhi: French Research Institute in India.

Kumar, G. and B. Ghosh. 2002. *West Bengal Panchayat Elections 1993: A Study in Participation*. Delhi: Institute of Social Sciences.

Lieten, G.K. 1992. *Continuity and Change in Rural West Bengal*. Delhi: Sage.

Mukarji, N. and D. Bandyopadhyay. 1993. *New Horizons for West Bengal's Panchayat*. Calcutta: Government of West Bengal.

Nicholas, R. 1965. 'Factions: A Comparative Analysis', in M. Banton (ed.), *Political Systems and the Distribution* (ASA Monograph 2). London: Tavistock.

Nossiter, T.J. 1988. *Marxist State Government in India: Politics, Economics and Society*. London: Pinter.

Powis, B. 2003. 'Grass Roots Politics and "Second Wave of Decentralization" in Andhra Pradesh'. *Economic and Political Weekly* 38 (26): 2617-27.

Ramachandran, V.K., M. Swaminathan, and V. Rawal 2003. *Barriers to Expansion of Mass Literacy and Primary Schooling in West Bengal: A Study Based on Primary Data from Selected Villages* (Working Paper 345). Trivandrum: Centre for Development Studies.

Som, B.B. 2004. 'Operation Barga and its Aftermath: A Case Study of Two Districts in North Bengal'. Paper presented at the national seminar on *Panchayat Experience in West Bengal*, held at North Bengal University, January 2004.

Togawa, M. 1997. 'Untouchable or Scheduled Castes? A Gram Panchayat Election in West Bengal in 1993', in H. Kotani (ed.), *Caste System, Untouchability and the Depressed*, pp. 275-99. Delhi: Manohar.

Webster, N. 1992. *Panchayati Raj and the Decentralization of Development Planning in West Bengal*. Calcutta: K.P. Bagchi & Co.

2

Beyond 'Culture' and 'Agriculture': Agrarian Change and Caste-Conflict in Rural Punjab

SURINDER SINGH JODHKA

INTRODUCTION

Social science research in India witnessed several shifts during the decades of the 1980s and 1990s.[1] Until then a large majority of scholars working on India were preoccupied with issues emanating from the process of development and economic change initiated by the independent Indian state after the colonial rulers left in 1947 (Das 1990). Subjects such as social and economic inequalities, poverty, rural development, agrarian change, and industrial and urban development were among the priority areas. However, it all began to change during the 1980s. The axis of the new paradigm rested on categories like culture, identity, and citizenship. With this 'paradigm shift', the focus of research moved to issues such as nationalism, ethnicity, environment, human rights, and gender (Jodhka 2001).

What brought about this shift? Though some of this was inspired by the new fashions in Western academy and the ascendance of a variety of 'post-modernist' perspectives, there were also many factors that were local in character. The decade of 1980s was a critical phase in Indian history. It saw the rise of a variety of 'new social movements'. Some of these movements, such as the environmentalist mobilization against big dams or

---

[1]This paper is part of my ongoing work on the subject and draws from some earlier papers (Jodhka 2000, 2002, 2004). The fieldwork was carried out with the help of Volunteers for Social Justice, an NGO active in Punjab, and it was funded by ActionAid India. I am grateful to David Gellner, Hiroshi Ishii, Akio Tanabe, Minoru Mio, Jonathan Parry, and other participants for their valuable comments. The usual disclaimers apply.

farmers' movements for remunerative prices were directly in response to changes that had come about with the process of development. Development produced new interest groups and new disparities. Some communities and groups felt marginalized or threatened by the process of change. Living in the new nation-state and its political culture also posed its own challenges to different communities and categories of population.

The question of caste also came back to the centre stage of Indian academy during this period. Various 'backward' and Dalit caste communities began to mobilize themselves for a greater share in jobs and higher representations in public institutions. This assertion of caste during the 1980s was not merely a new avatar of the 'ancient' institution.[2] This was a reflection of the changing realities on the ground. Repeated experience of participating in the democratic system initiated a process of competitive politics. The older structures of power and hierarchy also began to lose their hold over the 'village community'. The emergence of a new class of educated and articulate elite within these categories began to see caste as a resource, which could be mobilized into regional and pan-Indian identities to demand better deals for their respective communities from the new democratic system. The question of caste this time was being raised from below.

How did this substantialization of caste (Dumont 1971; Fuller 1997) become possible? Was it purely an outcome of the changes in the political sphere, the politicization of caste, as Rajni Kothari had put it long ago (Kothari 1973)? Or was it also facilitated by the changes taking place in the social and economic structures in rural India? How did the rise of this new identity politics in turn influence the older structures of dependencies and power relations on the ground?

While a good amount of literature is now available on the rise of backward-caste and Dalit politics in India, most of it deals with castes at the macro level, in terms of their participation in electoral politics, or the mobilization of caste identities at the regional and national levels. As against these macro-political perspectives, I shall try to look at the changing contours of caste and emerging caste conflict in the micro setting. On the basis of my fieldwork in rural Punjab, carried out during 2001 and 2003, I shall discuss the changing nature of everyday caste relations: how they have been conditioned by the agrarian transformation experienced in the region over the last four or five decades; and, how the new caste identities in turn impact upon agrarian social relations in rural Punjab.

Further, in much of the scholarship on India, caste has been seen in unitary terms, a pan-Indian reality, and without any significant variations in its structure or ideology across different regions or subregions of India/

---

[2]An expression used by Srinivas in the title of his book (Srinivas 1996).

South Asia. Popular discourses, as also 'mainstream' sociological writings, have tended to emphasize the underlying cultural/ideological consensus across castes on its governing normative order (Dumont 1971; Moffatt 1979). Despite many criticisms of these theories and the available empirical evidence from the field that contradicted such claims, theories such as Dumont's continue to dominate academic discussions of caste (Gupta 2000: 3).

Such views on caste tend to look at it almost purely in cultural terms, a system of values and ideas which is peculiarly Indian. Its association with Hinduism, where it supposedly had sanction from scriptural sources, further reinforces such a stance. The fact that caste differences exist among non-Hindu Indians is invariably seen only as an evidence of their Hindu ancestry.

Though caste, in a sense, is a pan-Indian reality, its actual frames of reference are regional in character, which ought to be looked at historically. As is widely known, there are different sets of caste groups in different regions. Even "the preoccupation with purity and pollution was not equally marked in every part of the country" (Béteille 2000a: 172). The specific historical trajectory, the patterns of politico-economic changes experienced during the colonial and post-independence period, and the composition of different ethnic communities determine the actual working of caste relations in a given region.[3] Overlooking these obvious facts about caste also makes it appear like an unchanging reality.

Interestingly, it is not only the literature on caste or identity politics that has tended to ignore the link they have with the regional political economy; those working on development and economic change have also rarely looked at how a given set of caste relations could influence the process of economic change, and in turn the implications such changes could have for the caste order. Similarly, even when it is recognized that modern democratic politics has transformed the operative principles of caste quite fundamentally, its essential features are still viewed as being 'traditional' or 'pre-modern'.

CASTE AND COMMUNITIES IN PUNJAB: HISTORICAL BACKGROUND

Despite being rather small in size, occupying a little less than two per cent of the total geographical space and having a little more than two per cent of India's total population, the contemporary Indian Punjab enjoys a rather important place in the cultural and political life of India. Bengal and Punjab

---

[3] Some recent scholarship has begun to recognize this more explicitly in relation to the colonial period. For example, see Rogers (2004), Caton (2004).

were the only two provinces that were partitioned in 1947, at the time of independence from colonial rule. Apart from its active involvement in the freedom movement, Punjab has also witnessed some of the most powerful identity movements during the last century.

Sociologically, the significance of Punjab also lies in the fact that it is on the 'periphery' of India and is one of the few states where Hindus, who constitute more than 80 per cent of India's population, are a minority. Despite being non-Hindus, the 'low caste' Sikhs of the state have the distinction of being included in the list of the Scheduled Castes, a status that was not granted to their counterparts in the other minority communities, i.e. Muslims and Christians. Even the Buddhists and Jains were not considered for such a status. It was only from the 1991 census that the neo-Buddhist converts began to be registered as Scheduled Castes. According to the 1961 census, of the entire Scheduled Caste population of India, 98.56 per cent were returned as Hindus and the remaining 1.44 per cent as Sikhs (as reported in K.S. Singh 1995: 10). Among the Sikhs, the Scheduled Castes constituted 29.2 per cent (Purandare 1995: 45).

Despite the popular image of Punjab being a Sikh state, it was only in 1966, after its reorganization in response to a strong movement for a Punjabi-speaking province, that the Sikhs became a majority in the state. The pre-partition Punjab was a much bigger province where, in religious terms, the Muslims outnumbered the Hindus as well as the Sikhs. According to the 1911 census, the proportion of the Muslim population to the total population of the united Punjab was 51 per cent and that of the Hindus 36 per cent. Only around 12 per cent had reported their religion to be Sikhism. Another approximately 1 per cent were Christians (as in S.K. Sharma 1985: 178).

The population exchange that accompanied the partition of the subcontinent in 1947 changed the demographic profile of Punjab very significantly. Almost the entire Sikh and Hindu population of the western Punjab crossed over to the Indian side and the Muslims living on the Indian side left for Pakistan. Thus, in the post-partition Indian Punjab the Hindus came to constitute a majority. However, the Sikhs too gained in demographic terms. Apart from their proportion going up to around 35 per cent, they came to be concentrated in some specific districts of the Indian Punjab. When the linguistic surveys were carried out to reorganize the provincial boundaries, Punjab was declared a bilingual state with the Sikh-dominated districts being reported as Punjabi-speaking areas and the Hindu-dominated districts as Hindi speaking areas (Brass 1974).

The Sikh leadership (mostly upper caste) saw in the new demographic scenario the possibility of a Sikh majority province. After a long-drawn struggle, Punjab was reorganized in 1966 by taking out the Hindi-speaking areas from it (the southern districts were put together into the new state of

Haryana and the Hindu majority/Hindi-speaking hill districts were merged with Himachal Pradesh). In the post 1966 reorganized Indian Punjab the Sikhs became the majority religious community. As per the 1991 census, Hindus constituted only around 35 per cent of the total population of Punjab. The Sikhs were around 63 per cent and the rest were Muslims and Christians. Another important aspect of the demographic composition of religious communities in Punjab is their uneven rural-urban distribution. Despite being a minority at the state level, the Hindus overwhelmingly dominate urban Punjab while the Sikhs are concentrated more in rural areas, where in some districts they make up to nearly 90 per cent of the total rural population.

In its ideological self-image, Sikhism is a religion without caste. Not only were the Sikh gurus "beyond all doubt, vigorous and practical denouncers of caste" (McLeod 1996: 87), the Sikh reformers in the late nineteenth century also used its anti-caste message to establish Sikhism's distinctiveness from Hinduism. Contemporary Sikh scholars also underline this point very sharply. The following passage provides a good summary of the Sikh claims on caste:

> Guru Nanak championed the cause of an egalitarian society as against the hierarchical structure of the Hindu community. He severally denounced the caste oppression ... Identifying himself with the 'lowliest of the lowly', he addressed to the oppressed strata of the society ... To make an actual beginning in this direction he initiated the egalitarian practices of Sangat (religious congregation), Langar (free community kitchen) and Pangat (unstratified arrangement of sitting). (Singh 1986: 49)

Their claim is certainly not a superfluous one. The Sikh gurus indeed advocated equality of human beings, at the social plane as well as in relation to God. For Guru Nanak the aim of salvation was union with God, which transcended the cycle of birth and death. Since the divine presence was everywhere, it was available to everyone. He denounced ritualism, ascetic practices, idol worship, and renunciation. An important aspect of Guru Nanak's philosophy was his emphasis on the values of everyday life, a 'thisworldliness'.

The second guru standardized the Gurmukhi script, which eventually became a vehicle for the Punjabi language and identity. Earlier, Guru Nanak had consciously rejected Sanskrit in preference of the indigenous spoken language. When the fifth guru, Guru Arjun, compiled the first canon of the faith, the *Adi Granth*, he included the writings of some of the Sufi poets and popular saints from the shudra and 'Untouchable' castes (such as Ravidas, a cobbler; Sadhan, a butcher; and Sain, a barber). Bhai Budha who was appointed the first reader and custodian (*granthi*) was a Jat by caste. Of the 'five beloved' who were the first to be baptized as Khalsas on the day of Baisakhi in 1699 by the tenth guru, four reportedly came from castes belonging to the 'middle' or 'lower' categories in the ritual hierarchy.

However, the Sikh movement's opposition to the prevailing Brahmanical world view was primarily ideological. The material base of the caste system, the prevailing structures of agrarian relations in a rural society where caste divisions had become important functional prerequisites for the working of the agrarian economy, remained relatively unaltered, though the influences of Islam and Sikhism would have indeed made the workings of caste look very different in Punjab.

When they established their rule in the province some of the British colonial rulers appear to have been surprised at the absence of a rigid caste hierarchy in the region. Some of the Western observers went to the extent of saying that Punjab was a "notable exception" to the caste system in India (O'Malley, cited in Nayar 1966: 20). Commenting on the status of 'low castes' in the province, a colonial government report, for example, observed in the 1920s:

> It would be misleading to attach too great importance to the existence of caste in the Punjab. ... Not only is it the case that the Brahman has no practical pre-eminence among Hindus, but as between 'caste' and 'non-caste' Hindus the distinction is not so strongly marked as to create the political problem found elsewhere in India.[4]

Social differentiation in Punjab, some of them felt, had more in common with Europe than with the mainland India. As another observer wrote: "Nowhere else in Hindu India does caste sit so lightly or approach so nearly to the social classes of Europe." (Anderson, cited in Nayar 1966: 20)

Perhaps the most striking aspect of the practice of caste in the region was that it functioned without the presence of what is considered as the most important actor in the system, viz., the Brahmans. Though Brahmans as a caste community did exist in Punjab and continue to be there even today, they were ritually important only for the upper-caste Hindus who numerically constituted a small proportion of the total population of the state. Even among the Hindus of Punjab, Brahmans did not enjoy a superior status. Questioning the popular fourfold classification, Denzil Ibbetson in his census report in *Punjab Castes* argued that the varna model of hierarchy did not operate in Punjab at all and there were instances where Brahmans were "looked upon as outcasts by those who under the fourfold classification would be classed as Sudras" (Ibbetson 1916: 2).

[4]Great Britain Indian Statutory Commission, Memorandum Submitted by the Government of Punjab (1930), cited in Nayar (1966: 20).

Similarly, writing on the social life in colonial Punjab, Prakash Tandon, an upper-caste Khatri Hindu, comments in his celebrated autobiographical *Punjabi Century* that the Brahmans of Punjab lived a 'frugal life', and it was rare to find 'an affluent Brahmin' in the region (Tandon 1961: 77). Most Brahmans in his native village were treated as members of a menial caste. Like other menials, they too were mostly dependent upon the food they collected from their *jajmans*. Giving a vivid description of their social status, he writes:

> With us brahmins were an underprivileged class and exercised little or no influence on the community. Perhaps Muslims had so discouraged temples and external worship that the brahmins had no place left from where to exercise their authority.
>
> Our brahmins did not as a rule even have the role of teachers, because until the British opened regular schools, teaching was done by Muslim mullahs in the mosques or by Sikh granthis ... in the Gurdwaras. Our brahmins were rarely erudite; in fact many of them were barely literate, possessing only a perfunctory knowledge of rituals and knowing just the necessary mantras by heart.
>
> (Tandon 1961: 76)

Similarly, Saberwal, an anthropologist who studied a small town of Punjab during the late 1960s, writes:

> ... even if the Brahmins were able to carve a ceremonial place at Ranjit Singh's court for themselves, there is no evidence that they acquired much land or that they were able to enforce the social circumstances that they would have required for maintaining high levels of ritual purity; and therefore the lowest castes in Punjab had to carry only a light burden of ritual impurities, much lighter, physically and socially, than the burden elsewhere in India.
>
> (Saberwal 1976: 7)

Joyce Pettigrew, another anthropologist, argued that the rural society of Punjab differed radically from Hindu India because of the absence of caste among the Sikhs (Pettigrew 1975: 4). However, not everyone who has studied Punjab agrees with such a position. Paul Hershman, who did his fieldwork in a village near Jalandhar, completely disagrees with Pettigrew's thesis that the ideas of purity and impurity did not exist in Punjab at all (Hershman 1981: 21).

Hershman's claim is certainly closer to reality. Even Pettigrew had recognized the presence of division between upper castes and Dalits. While "Jat, Khatri, Aroras, all ate with one another and there were also an increasing number of cases of intermarriage between them", Jats in the villages "did not visit the houses of Mazhabis, take food from them, eat with them or intermarry with them" (Pettigrew 1975: 44).

Further, it is important to underline here that caste is not merely a religious or ideological reality. In rural Punjab, social relations in the village community and the political economy of agriculture were closely structured around caste. While the ideological stranglehold of Brahmanism and rigidities of caste hierarchy were certainly much weaker here, different groups of servicing castes were tied to the landowning cultivators within the framework of the *jajmani* system, also known locally as the *sepidari* system (see H.C. Sharma 1996; Kesinger 1974).

I.P. Singh (1975, 1977), who did his fieldwork in a village near Amritsar during the late 1950s, provides a fairly good idea of the nature of caste relations in a Sikh village. The Sikhs living in the village were divided into two groups, the Sardars (the upper castes) and the Mazhabis (the lower-caste scavengers). The first group included the Jats, Kambohs, Tarkhans, Kumhars, Sunars, and Nais. Though the agriculturist Jats considered themselves higher than the other groups in this category, Singh found no feeling of caste-based avoidance or prejudice among them. They visited each other's homes, inter-dined, attended marriage functions, and celebrated most of the festivals together. In terms of the village settlement also, no demarcation existed in the houses of these groups.

However, the Mazhabis, who constituted nearly half of the village population, were treated differently. They lived on one side of the village. They had a separate well while all the other castes used a common well. At village feasts, where everyone was invited, the Mazhabis sat separately. Since many of them worked as labourers in the fields of the Jat landowners, the latter visited the houses of the Mazhabis but they did so as a patronizing gesture.

There were also occasions, Singh found, where untouchability was either not practised or its extent had been declining. Many Jats in the village let the Mazhabis enter their houses and did not consider their touch polluting. One of them had also employed a Mazhabi to clean utensils in his house. The practice of untouchability was minimal during drinking sessions. Mazhabis and Sardars drank liquor together but mostly outside their home, during fairs, and occasionally in the fields. When tumblers were scarce, they even drank from the same glass (Singh 1977: 76).

The practice of untouchability was also minimal in religious affairs. There was only one Gurdwara in the village, where everyone was allowed entry. The priest, who himself belonged to a low caste (Cheemba, Washerman), served all the castes without any discrimination. He performed all the marriages in the villages irrespective of any caste distinction. This was in complete contrast to the way a Brahman priest had functioned earlier. Before a *granthi* was appointed in the Gurdwara in the 1920s, the Brahman used to perform rituals for both Sikhs and Hindus, but he served only the upper castes among them.

REFORMS AND MOBILIZATIONS AGAINST CASTE

Apart from the historical specificities of the nature of caste relations in Punjab, the region also witnessed many social movements which had a lasting impact on the social structure of Punjabi and Sikh society.

The establishment of British colonial rule also opened Punjab to the activities of Christian missionaries who came with the intention of spreading the message of the Church. The appeal of the Church attracted members of untouchable castes the most. The first conversion took place in 1873, when a man named Ditt from the Chuhra caste was baptized in Sialkot. "To the surprise of the missionaries, Ditt was followed by hundreds of thousands of others from lower castes, and Punjab Christianity became a de facto movement" (Juergensmeyer 1988: 181). In the given power structure, "conversion would have been a risky act of rebellion" for these 'untouchables' (Webster 1999: 96-7).

According to Juergensmeyer, the Christian missionaries had not really intentionally targeted the low castes for conversions. Apparently "it was the untouchables who came out seeking conversions to Christianity" (1988: 184). They would have obviously seen a potential for social mobility in conversions:

> Originally, the missionaries of the Punjab had only attempted to convert the upper castes, since they regarded others as beyond the reach of the methods they preferred – intellectual argument and moral suasion. The enthusiasm of the first convert, Ditt, and the subsequent lower caste requests for conversion not only baffled the missionaries but embarrassed them: they saw no sensible or moral reason for keeping the lower castes out, yet feared that allowing them in would sully the church's reputation (Juergensmeyer 1988: 184).

The fears of the missionaries were not unfounded. When a newspaper article in *The Tribune* of 19 October 1892 reported that the rate of conversions would soon turn Punjab into a Christian region, "a tremor of fear ran through the upper caste Hindu and Sikh elite" (Juergensmeyer 1988: 181). There was a virtual competition among the religious communities, the Christians, the Hindus, and the Sikhs, to win the Untouchables over to their side. It was around this time that the militant Hindu reformist organization, the Arya Samaj, made its entry into Punjab.

The colonial administrative structure had also begun to deploy new categories of social aggregation and classification. They thought of populace in terms of religious communities and looked at them accordingly in the process of governance (Cohn 1996). They "encouraged members of each community to present their case in communitarian terms" (Grewal

1989: 195). As elsewhere these administrative discourses of British rulers had far-reaching influences on the process of identity formation in the region (Fox 1985). The introduction of the census thus made the 'religious communities' sensitive about the numbers. "Numbers were generally equated with strength, particularly for employment under the government" (Grewal 1994: 131).

While the Muslim population of Punjab remained stable at around 51 per cent between 1881 and 1911 and the proportions of Sikh and the Christian populations went up marginally, the Hindus declined from about 41 per cent in 1881 to around 36 per cent in 1911 (Jones 1976: 324). The upper-caste Punjabi Hindus, who were already feeling marginalized by the Bengali clerks whom the British had brought with them from Calcutta for administrative work, would have obviously viewed the decline in the Hindu population with much concern. The passing of the Land Alienation Act in 1901, which stopped the transfer of agricultural land from the agricultural castes, mostly Sikhs and Muslims, to the non-agricultural castes, mostly Hindus, had also been seen by the Hindu elite as an act of discrimination against them.

The militant reformism of the Arya Samaj appeared to provide an answer to the crisis of the upper-caste Hindu elite of the region. It offered 'a progressive ideology based on traditional values' (Juergensmeyer 1988: 38). Swami Dayanand had launched the Arya Samaj in Bombay in 1875 and visited Lahore in 1877. He stayed on in Punjab for nearly eighteen months during his first visit and set up branches of the Samaj in almost all the big towns of the province (S.K. Sharma 1985: 40).

Unlike the other Hindu reform movements, the Arya Samaj not only attacked 'foreign' religions who had been converting locals into their fold but also severely criticized many of the existing practices of the Hindus including the practice of untouchability. The Swami advocated going back to the ancient Vedic religion wherein Untouchables were presumed to have been a part of the Hindu religion. He attacked Brahmanical hegemony in religious affairs and emphasized the need to spread modern education among the Hindus. Along with bringing back those who had converted to Christianity, he also advocated the need to bring the lower castes into the Hindu fold through a process of religious purification or *shuddhi*. Since untouchability was presumed to emanate from ritual impurity, it could be removed through a religious ritual to render untouchables touchable, which would automatically raise their status (Pimpley & Sharma 1985).

However, despite their criticisms of the Brahmanical orthodoxy within Hinduism, the strategy of the Arya Samaj for elevating the status of the untouchables was worked out within the framework of purity and impurity. The very notion of *shuddhi* involved affirmation to the idea of ritual purity as being the criterion for status enhancement. Neither did they reject the framework of varna. Though some ex-Untouchables from the caste of Odes were solemnized using *shuddhi*, its long-term impact was limited, both because not many took the ritual and because the upper castes went on treating those who did just as before. All the same, the movement helped the Hindu Punjabi elite to consolidate their position in the region and they were able to retain a large section of Dalits within the Hindu fold.

The militant assertion of Hindu identity by the Arya Samaj had already sparked off a debate on the question of Sikh identity. Sikhs began to assert that theirs was a separate religion and that they should not be classed with the Hindus (Oberoi 1994). The practice of untouchability or discrimination against the low castes among the Sikhs was attributed to the continued influence of Hinduism on the community. Thus the struggle against caste and untouchability, which were seen as the core Hindu values, came to be implicated in the movement for a separate Sikh identity.

In other words, the Singh Sabha movement for the liberation of Sikh Gurdwaras from the Hindu Mahants launched during the 1920s also became a movement for the de-Hinduization of the Sikh religion. One of the main demands of the movement was "unquestioned entrance to Sikh places of worship" for all (Juergensmeyer 1988: 28). Some members of the Sikh Khalsa Diwan tried to create their own 'depressed class movements' to encourage Scheduled Caste support. The movement was not confined to the liberation of historic Sikh Gurdwaras.

Its impact went very far. I.P. Singh in his study of a village in Amritsar district reported that the decline of the Brahmans in the village began around the time these reform movements were launched, i.e. 1922-6. It was after these movements that a low-caste Sikh was appointed priest in the local Gurdwara and he began to give equal treatment to members of all castes in the village (Singh 1977: 81-2). The insistence of Sikh reformers that the 'community' should distance itself from the Hindus and the legal recognition granted to weddings performed according to Sikh rituals (namely, the Anand Karaj) made the village Brahman priest redundant. Unlike the Brahman, the Sikh priest could be from any caste and, as mentioned above, the priest in the village that I.P. Singh studied was actually from a lower caste. He had been trained to be a priest at the Sikh Missionary College, Amritsar. Priesthood among the Sikhs had thus become an achieved rather than an ascribed status.

While the Sikh reformers attacked caste, the Sikh leadership, having become aware of the significance of numbers, did not deny the existence of caste among the Sikhs or that the low castes among the Sikhs faced disabilities due to their birth. The Sikh leadership, in fact, had to lobby a great deal with the national leadership that, along with the Hindus, certain Sikh castes should also be included in the list of the Scheduled Castes for the provision of special benefits and reservations. They were obviously worried that if the reservation benefits were not extended to Sikhs, the low castes among them might declare their religion as Hinduism.

Apart from the competition among the Christians, the Arya Samaj Hindus, and the Sikhs, during the colonial period Punjab also witnessed autonomous mobilizations by the local Dalits. The most important of these was the Ad Dharm movement. New opportunities opened up by the growing demand for leather goods such as boots and shoes for the British army had brought some prosperity to some of the enterprising members of the Chamar caste. This mobility was particularly evident in the Doaba subregion of Punjab from where some Chamars had even gone to the United States and England where they had been a part of left-wing organizations. The introduction of secular education along with the social mobility that some individual untouchables experienced prepared the social ground for such autonomous mobilizations.

The Ad Dharm movement took off with the arrival of Mangoo Ram on the scene. Mangoo Ram was the son of a rich Chamar but his family had had to bear the stigma of untouchability. He spent much of his early life in the United States where he got involved with the Gadar movement. By 1925 he had come back to Punjab. On his return home, he set up a school for lower-caste children with the help of the Arya Samaj, but very soon he distanced himself from the Samaj and took over the Ad Dharm movement.

The Ad Dharm movement saw itself as a new religious movement. Its proponents advocated that the 'untouchables' were a separate *qaum*, a distinct religious community similar to those of Muslims, Hindus, and Sikhs, and that the *qaum* had existed from time immemorial (Juergensmeyer 1988: 45). When the 1931 census approached, the Ad Dharmis insisted that they be listed as a separate religious community and not be clubbed with the Hindus. In the very first conference of the organization, they declared:

> We are not Hindus. We strongly request the government not to list us as such in the census. Our faith is not Hindu but Ad Dharm. We are not a part of Hinduism, and Hindus are not a part of us. (cited in Juergensmeyer 1988: 74)

Despite stiff opposition from the local Hindu leadership, their demand was accepted. A total of 418,789 persons reported themselves as Ad Dharmis in the 1931 Punjab census, almost equal to the Christian population of the province. They accounted for about 1.5 per cent of the total population and around a tenth of the total low-caste population of Punjab. Nearly 80 per cent of the low castes of Jalandhar and Hoshiarpur districts reported themselves as Ad Dharmis (ibid: 77).

After independence, the Ad Dharmis were listed as one of the Scheduled Castes of Punjab and were classified with the Hindus once again.

Though attempts have been made to revive the Ad Dharm movement during the post-independence period, there has not been much response. However, the Scheduled Castes of Punjab have been attracted by some new religious reform movements, such as the Radha Swamis. They have also formed their own organizations, both at the level of individual caste communities as well as across the Dalit castes.

AGRARIAN CHANGE AND CASTE IN CONTEMPORARY RURAL PUNJAB

As mentioned above, contemporary Indian Punjab is a much smaller province than the pre-1947 Punjab. A good proportion of the agricultural lands that were developed by the British during the late nineteenth century, viz., the canal colonies, went to Pakistan. The post-partition Indian Punjab also had to deal with a huge influx of population of Hindus and Sikhs which came over to the Indian side of Punjab after the new international border was drawn, as a result of which riots broke out. However, Punjab recovered very quickly. Its performance in the agricultural sector was particularly spectacular.

The quality of the land, state investments in the development of infrastructure, and the experience of its population in developing agriculture in the canal colonies all worked together to provide a conducive environment for the success of the Green Revolution technology when it was introduced in the region in the early 1960s. So spectacular was the success of Punjab that even though the new technological package was also introduced simultaneously in other parts of the country, it came to be identified primarily with Punjab. The success of the Green Revolution in north-west India nearly solved the perennial problem of shortage of food grains in the whole of India.

The available statistics on various indicators of agricultural growth speak for themselves. Of all the states of India, agriculturally Punjab's growth rate was the highest from the 1960s to the middle of the 1980s. The annual rate of increase in the production of food grains between 1961-2 and 1985-6 was 6.4 per cent. The corresponding figure for the country as a whole was only 2.6 per cent. The percentage of high yielding varieties (HYV) of seed in the total area under food grains in Punjab was as high as 73 per cent in 1974-5 (all India 31 per cent) and 95 per cent in 1984-5 (all India 54 per cent). While Punjab had 17,459 tractors per hundred thousand holdings, the all-India figure was only 714. More or less the same is true of other such indicators (Kohli & Singh 1997).

As a consequence, Punjab came to be known as the food basket of India. Though it occupies only 1.5 per cent of the total geographical area of

India, "Punjab produces 22 per cent of the country's wheat (12.7 million tons), 9 per cent of its rice (6.8 million tons) and 24 per cent of its cotton (0.3 million tons). It contributes 60 to 70 per cent of wheat and 40 to 50 per cent of rice to the central pool."[5]

> Economists who looked at the Punjab experience closely also found that the size of holding did not deter the adoption of new technology. A well-known study showed not only that smaller Punjabi landowners were just as eager to adopt the new technology but that the per-acre income from their land was slightly higher than that of the bigger farmers. (Bhalla & Chadha 1983: 78)

The adoption of new technology and growing surplus production began to transform village social structure and its relationship with the market. However, as mentioned earlier, the scholarship on agrarian change in India has largely operated within the framework of class analysis. Working mostly within the Leninist framework of capitalist development, or simply with an acreage classification, economists have mostly looked at the agrarian social structure and the changes through general categories, such as landlords, farmers, peasants, tenants, and labourers (see, for example, Rudra 1990; Patnaik 1990; Bhalla 1976). This has been the case even with some of the anthropological writings on agrarian social structure and change in India (for a critical discussion on the subject see Thorner 1982; cf. Jodhka 2003). Caste largely remained a preoccupation with functionalist social anthropologists who carried out 'village studies' during the 1950s and 1960s without paying much attention to the agrarian economy of the village (for a critical survey of village studies see Jodhka 1998).

CASTE IN CONTEMPORARY PUNJAB

As discussed earlier, notwithstanding the significant influences of Islam, Sikhism, and various other reform movements in the region, caste has not disappeared from Punjab. Perhaps the most significant fact about caste in Punjab today is that it continues to be an important indicator of social inequality. Caste in rural Punjab has a close correlation with land ownership. Virtually all agricultural land in Punjab is under the direct control of the traditionally cultivating castes, particularly the Jats. Though Punjab has the highest proportion of Scheduled Castes of any Indian state, the agricultural land owned by them is virtually negligible. They constituted 28.3 per cent of the total population of Punjab in 1991 (much higher than the all-India average of around 16 per cent) and only 4.8 per cent of them were reported to be working as cultivators. The all-India average of cultivators

---

[5] As in the official website of the Punjab Government 2004 <punjabgovt.nic.in>.

among the Scheduled Castes as a whole was above 25 per cent. In the neighbouring Himachal Pradesh as many as 67.7 per cent of them were cultivators. Even in Uttar Pradesh 42.6 per cent of Dalits were cultivators.[6] One of the possible reasons for such a low percentage of Dalit cultivators in Punjab could be colonial policies towards different caste communities of the province. Under the Land Alienation Act of 1901, for example, Dalits and artisan castes were classified along with the moneylending and urban trading castes and were barred from purchasing land from the 'agricultural castes'.

It is against this background that I now provide a brief summary of the findings of an extensive fieldwork carried out in 2001 covering fifty-one villages selected from three subregions of Punjab, viz., Majha, Malwa, and Doaba (for a more detailed account see Jodhka 2002). The main questions that I tried to probe in this survey were (i) to explore the manner in which caste and caste-related differences work in everyday life in rural Punjab; (ii) to see how the agrarian changes accompanying the Green Revolution had impacted upon these relations; (iii) through this to see if one could explain/understand the emerging caste conflict in rural Punjab and the rise of the new Dalit identity at the regional level; and (iv) to understand how Dalits appropriate available political resources in their everyday struggles with the locally dominant castes.

The Framework

One common feature of caste, particularly in the rural setting, has been its emphasis on social exclusion/segregation and ritual purity/pollution. Segregation of individual castes or groups of castes in the village was the most obvious mark of civic privileges and disabilities. There were also restrictions on the kind of work an individual could do. Each caste was expected to consider a particular occupation as its legitimate calling.

Perhaps the two most important things that have happened over the last century are (a) a legal derecognition of the practice and (b) a near complete change in the consciousness of those at the receiving end of the hierarchical system. Dalits have almost everywhere become much more assertive about their human and political rights (Mendelsohn & Vicziany 1998: 1). Whatever might have been the case in the past, there would be very few among the ex-Untouchables today who would regard themselves as impure or justify their low status on the grounds of misconduct in some previous life, a "fact of nature" (Charsley & Karanth 1998). Today they "all aspire to more comfortable material circumstances; all demand more dignity" (Deliège 1999: 199). This, however, has not necessarily resulted in the

---

[6] *Journal of Indian School of Political Economy* (special issue on Scheduled Castes edited by André Béteille), vol. 12 (3 & 4), 2000b, statistical supplement, p. 615.

alleviation of their social conditions. Some scholars have argued that while ideologically caste has considerably weakened and the older forms of untouchability are receding, atrocities committed on Dalits by the local dominant castes have in fact increased (Mendelsohn & Vicziany 1998; Bèteille 2000b; Shah 2001).

Extending the framework used by I.P. Desai (1976) and Ghanshyam Shah (2000) in their surveys of caste relations in rural Gujarat, I have classified rural social space of contemporary Punjab into three categories. The first is, what could loosely be described as the 'private sphere' and sphere of those relations that were traditionally governed by the framework of the *jajmani* system; The second category is those relations of everyday social and economic life that were not necessarily governed by caste but were influenced by the overall values of the system. The third relates to modern institutions, which have traditionally not been part of the rural life and are, at least in principle, 'caste-free'.

THE PRIVATE SPHERE

Jajmani *Ties and 'Unclean' Occupations*

The *jajmani* system provided a framework of organizing economic life in the village. Different caste groups were typically required to pursue certain occupations deemed to be the calling of their caste. Though not everyone would have ever been employed in the 'callings' of their castes, every caste group was identified with a specific occupation.

It was in this kind of a framework that the involvement of Dalits with 'unclean occupations' was viewed as the primary reason for their 'pollution'. Dealing with dead cattle, scavenging and other occupations that were considered polluting in the Hindu culture were left to the Dalits. Many radical changes have taken place with regard to the involvement of Dalits with such occupations.

First of all, large numbers of Dalits have consciously *dissociated* themselves from their traditional occupations. Only a small number of them (from less than 5 to a maximum of 10 per cent) are still involved in such occupations. There are also variations by caste. The Chamars (including Ad Dharmis and Ramdasis) have almost completely moved away from their traditional occupation of handling dead cattle. They have even begun to *distance* themselves from agriculture and seek employment that will not involve any relationship with the locally dominant caste.

Who then is doing the work that was traditionally done by the Dalits, viz., scavenging or picking up the dead cattle? And what implications do these changes have for the village economy and the traditional structure of *jajmani* relations?

Interestingly, some of these occupations are no longer identified with any specific caste group in rural Punjab. For example, removing dead cattle has become a completely commercialized enterprise. The village panchayat generally gives the work on contract to an individual contractor, who may be from another villages or a nearby town. The contractor typically employs a few workers (not necessarily local Dalits) who work on the dead cattle in the village. Birds and dogs eat much of the meat. There is a lucrative market for the skins and bones. Most of those involved in this business are quite well off and are often regarded with envy even by the upper castes.

There has also been some degree of commercialization of other Dalit or *jajmani* occupations. Barbers, carpenters, blacksmiths, all now have shops. Thus, along with commercialization, a process of *dissociation of caste and occupation* is underway. There are many among the Dalits who still work as barbers. They, however, do not work in the way barbers used to do in the traditional structure of *jajmani* relations. Most of them have set up small outlets, often near the village bus stop. Some Dalits have also taken up carpentry, particularly in villages where the traditional carpenters have left for the towns.

The only 'unclean' occupation where a degree of continuity exists is that of scavenging. Though a large majority of those involved with scavenging work continue to be Balmikis and Mazhabis, the castes with which it was traditionally identified, only a few families from these castes actually work as scavengers. Even in scavenging, the traditional structure of *jajmani* relations has almost completely changed. The cleaning of drains and toilets or sweeping of the houses is mostly done on commercial basis. In most villages a scavenger is employed for an individual street. Each household in the street pays a fixed sum to the scavenger on a monthly basis (the going rate at the time of this study was Rs.10 per household). Interestingly, in some cases, the scavengers preferred to work in the neighbouring village rather than in their own, obviously to avoid any element of familiarity and patronage of the traditional variety being invoked by the households they serve.

The traditional idea of pollution was practised most vigorously in the sphere of personal relations and food. Restricting Dalits' entry into upper-caste houses has been one of the most strictly observed practices in most parts of rural India. A large majority of respondents across caste groups reported that such restrictions are not practised any longer.

Apart from some other factors or processes, this has happened because of the significant changes experienced in the lifestyles of the rich farmers of Punjab during the last three decades. The Green Revolution brought prosperity and provided them with extra income. Though most of the rich farmers of Punjab continue to live in villages, they have all the modern amenities of urban living available in their homes. Their children go to school in the towns and their women desire the luxuries of urban living. Many of these households have begun to employ Dalit women to help with domestic chores. Our surveys found that at least ten to twelve Dalit women were regularly employed for domestic help in almost every village where they performed various kinds of domestic chores such as sweeping and mopping, washing clothes, and, in some cases, even washing kitchen utensils. As is the case with such employment in towns, the Dalit women worked in a couple of houses and were typically paid a fixed sum by each household, ranging from Rs.100 to Rs.300 per month, along with some occasional 'gifts'. Though the upper-caste farmers or their women did not mind Dalit women entering their houses or even the kitchen, only some Dalit women were considered fit for such jobs. For example, those who worked in the cattle shed were rarely considered 'suitable' for domestic chores. Only those who kept themselves 'clean' were employed for domestic work. Similarly, in some households, while they were asked to sweep and mop the house and clean the toilets, their upper-caste employers did not let them enter the kitchen. There were also a few cases where the utensils from which the Dalits ate food were kept apart from the utensils used by the upper-caste family.

A large majority of Dalits in Punjab have traditionally been employed in agriculture, mostly as labourers. Some of them also worked on a long-term basis with the landowning Jats. The traditional variety of attached labour, called variously *sajhi* or *siri*, has given way to a more formal, market-type relation, based on a written contract and specified annual wages, but even a modernized form of a long-term relationship of this form still leads to dependency and unfreedom for the worker. It was clear that Dalits do not like getting into such arrangements. In the Doaba region, where Dalit mobility has been more pronounced than elsewhere in the state, very few of them worked as attached labourers. Of the thirteen villages studied in Doaba, in as many as eight, none of the Dalits worked as attached labourers. However, Malwa still had many who were doing so. Of the twenty-six villages studied, twenty-one had Dalits working as attached labourers (ranging from five to fifty per village).

However, on the whole, the process of occupational diversification is quite pronounced everywhere. Wherever they can afford to do so, Dalits have stopped working regularly on the land. In the villages of Doaba, for example, we were frequently told that much of the labour work is done by migrants and that the local Dalits do not want to work on the land. They only perform seasonal labour and for the rest of the year prefer working in towns or bringing work home. The most popular work that the Dalits of Doaba did while living in the village was rope making. These ropes were woven for urban markets and were sold through a middleman who also supplied them with the raw material.

The local markets in rural Punjab have become nearly free of caste prejudice. Dalits freely enter the village shops run by the upper castes and buy things from them without any experience of untouchability whatsoever. In fact, some Dalits have also opened shops in the villages. Though most of their shops are located either in Dalit localities or on the main road, near the village bus shelter, they are also patronized by the upper castes, albeit, less frequently.

Some of the Dalit shopkeepers reported that, given the choice, some members of the upper castes in the village avoid visiting their shops. One of the Malwa villages, for example, had a single flour mill being run by a Dalit. Though the majority of the villagers of all castes got their wheat ground at this *chakki*, there were some upper castes who went to the neighbouring village to have it done. The obvious reason for this was their caste prejudice.

There was no evidence of untouchability with regard to the labour market. Most of the manual labour in Punjab villages is done by Dalits. They are employed by all categories of villagers for jobs on farms or in house construction.

SOCIAL LIFE

Social Ecology of the Village and Segregation

According to the traditional norms governing rural life, Dalit settlements were supposed to be located outside the main village, preferably on the western side where the sun sets (*lahindey passe*, as it is called in Punjabi). This norm has perhaps never been followed strictly in Punjab. There were several villages in our survey where Dalit houses have traditionally not been located to the west. However, in a majority of the villages, Dalit houses were indeed constructed on the outskirts of the main village settlement.

More important are perhaps the changes experienced in the housing patterns over the last two or three decades. The growing population and a continual expansion of residential areas have, to some extent, diluted the old settlement structure of the village. As the newly prosperous upper castes make newer and bigger houses on the peripheries of the village, Dalit settlements are no longer as isolated as they once were. In fact, all categories of villagers have constructed new houses on the peripheries.

There were also some interesting cases where upwardly mobile Dalits had purchased houses in upper-caste localities from those who had left the village for towns or had migrated to the West. This has happened particularly in the Doaba region. Of the fifty-one villages studied as many as four villages had some manner of 'mixed housing' (three in Doaba and one in

Malwa). Interestingly, there was little resistance from the neighbouring upper-caste residents to Dalits buying houses in their localities.

Providing housing to the Scheduled Castes has been an important component of official developmental schemes for their uplift. A good number of villages in Punjab have such schemes working. These schemes are obviously welcomed by the Dalits for the simple reason that many of them find it very difficult to build houses on their own. However, most of these housing schemes are located at a distance from the village. Since the houses under this scheme are allotted exclusively to Dalits, it reinforces their segregation from the main village. Being located at a distance from the village, these settlements also lack certain amenities that are accessible to those living within the village. Some do not even have working electricity connections. Or, in some cases where such amenities have been provided, the back-up services are of poor quality.

Housing structures have a direct influence on daily life. Segregated settlements impose restrictions on social interaction. For example, in such villages Dalit and upper-caste children play separately. However, it is not so everywhere. Such restrictions are imposed 'strictly' only in fifteen of the fifty-one sample villages. In another eight, such restrictions are followed to 'a lesser degree'. In the remaining villages Dalit and upper-caste children often play together without much restriction.

Unlike some other parts of India, there are virtually no cases of overt discrimination/untouchability or any kind of restrictions on Dalits' access to the common public spaces in the village. No one reported any kind of restrictions on Dalits passing through the streets of the village. They could also take out their own processions through the village streets and are allowed to make a fanfare at the time of marriages or other festive occasions.

Perhaps the most pronounced practice of discrimination against Dalits happens during festivals and village feasts. This discrimination takes various forms. We observed that Dalits, for example, could not participate on equal terms in celebrations of local festivals unless they organized them on their own in their Gurdwaras or *dharamshala*s (community centres). Perhaps the most obvious occasion when Dalits are discriminated against in village festivities is when food is served. They would often be asked to wait until everyone else had eaten and left. Though not so pronounced, there were also reports of separate utensils being used for the Dalits during festivals or village feasts. A Dalit from a village of the Verka block of Amritsar told us that, though they are invited by the upper-caste Jats for weddings in their families, they are served food and snacks at separate tables.

Even on less formal occasions, Dalits and upper castes rarely eat together. Though the prohibition on Dalits entering the houses of upper castes has been considerably relaxed, restrictions on eating together continues. Thus, we found that Dalits and upper castes did not interact so closely that they would visit each other's houses for lunch or dinner on a regular basis.

The most visible division between the upper castes and Dalits is with regard to the cremation grounds. Though there were some villages that had only one cremation ground where everyone cremates their dead, the upper castes generally do not like Dalits using the village (upper-caste) cremation ground. Interestingly, Dalits themselves prefer to have their own separate cremation grounds. There were several cases where Dalits complained that they have to use the common cremation ground because the dominant land-owners had encroached upon the land where they had their own cremation ground and had turned it into fields.

The source of drinking water is another area about which the upper castes used to be very touchy. Traditionally Dalits and upper castes had different sources of drinking water even in rural Punjab. While all the upper castes (including the backward castes) could take water from the village wells, Dalits could never do so. They had to depend exclusively on their own wells.

Much has changed with regard to the access to drinking water. Wells are no longer the primary source of drinking water anywhere in rural Punjab. While in some villages taps have been installed under government-funded programmes, at others handpumps have replaced wells. This change seems to have completely transformed the attitude of the rural population towards drinking water as a potential arena of caste prejudice. Though the sources of drinking water were as such separate for Dalits and the upper castes, it was found that there were many fewer restrictions on the access of Dalits to the taps and handpumps used or owned by upper castes. However, it may be useful to add here that though Dalits could and did access water from the upper-caste sources quite regularly, the frequency of upper castes taking water from the sources used by Dalits was much less, though not completely absent.

Dalits and Religious Places

In his classic study of the practice of untouchability in rural Gujarat, I.P. Desai pointed out that Dalit conversions to Islam or Christianity did not make any difference to their status at the local level because the dominant upper-caste Hindus continued to treat them as before (Desai 1976). In the case of Punjab, however, not only do a section of Dalits follow Sikhism but a large majority of the dominant groups in the village are also Sikhs for whom the practice of caste has no religious justification.

Followers of Sikhism constitute nearly 80 to 90 per cent of the rural population of Punjab. Even among those who are registered as Hindus, such as the Ad Dharmis, in the census enumeration, many practise Sikh rituals and visit Sikh Gurdwaras. Apart from worshipping *Guru Granth*, they have also begun to follow the Sikh rituals, such as getting married through the Anand Karaj ritual. Though formally there are no restrictions on Dalits entering Gurdwaras, there were several cases where Dalits felt that they were not really welcomed by the locally dominant castes who control these Gurdwaras in the village.

During a group discussion with Dalits in a village of Firozepur district we were told that through subtle and not so subtle messages, they are told to stay away. Their children are told to come for the *langar* (the food served in Gurdwaras) after everyone else has finished eating. In another village in Mukatsar district, Dalits reported that they are often asked to sit in separate lines for the *langar*. While the Gurdwara management formally invites all the others, Dalits are not even informed about the special programmes and festivities. A frequent complaint was that they are not allowed to participate in the cooking and serving of the *langar*.

In another village of the same district, the Mazhabis and Meghs (the local Dalit castes) reported that they were often told to sit outside the main door of the Gurdwara and were served *langar* only after the upper-caste Jats had finished eating. The Dalits in the village have for that reason stopped going to the local Gurdwara. Even on special occasions, such as religious festivals, they preferred to stay at home and have their own private celebrations.

Dalits have worked out their own ways and strategies of resisting this kind of discrimination. The most popular strategy of resistance has been to construct separate places of worship for themselves. Of the fifty-one villages studied, Dalits had separate Gurdwaras in as many as forty-one villages. In fact there were some villages where they had more than one Gurdwara. In most cases separate Gurdwaras are built in order to assert *autonomy* and to avoid the humiliation encountered in the dominant caste Gurdwaras. A Dalit of a village near Phagwara in Kapurthala district told us:

> There used to be only one Gurdwara in the village. The local Jats always thought that it was their Gurdwara because they were the ones who had financed its building. We used to visit the Gurdwara but they never liked it. They would not let us cook *langar*. So when we could mobilize some resources, we decided to build our own Gurdwara in our own basti.

The construction of separate Gurdwaras by Dalits has, however, rarely been met with resistance either from the dominant castes in the village or from the religious establishment of the Sikh community. However, though the upper castes do not mind Dalits constructing their own Gurdwaras, some Dalits reported that the Jats and other upper-caste Sikhs do not have the same reverence for Dalit Gurdwaras that they have for their own. Even when the Dalit Gurdwara is closer, Jats prefer visiting their own. If an upper-caste family in the village needs to bring the *Guru Granth* home, rarely do they take it from the Dalit Gurdwara, even when it is convenient to do so. However, there were some villages where upper-caste individuals had started visiting Dalit Gurdwaras, particularly on special occasions.

Though there are very few Hindu temples in Punjab villages, the practice of untouchability is much greater there. We asked a Dalit woman in a village near Patiala if she also visited the Shivji Temple located in the village. "They do not like even our going anywhere near the compound wall of their temple. Why would we be going there?" she responded. Apparently a couple of years back a few Dalit children were chased out of the temple complex during a festival and this had offended the local Dalits.

In another village of the same district, a Hindu saint called Moni Baba performs *yajna* every year in the month of December. This *yajna* is supposed to be for the general welfare of the village. The Baba also organizes *bhandara* (a kind of *langar* where food is served free to the devotees) for a couple of days during the *yajna*. He obviously get donations from the villagers. However, he does not accept donations from Dalits. Chanan Ram, a Mazhabi, told us that when he went to donate ten litres of milk on the occasion of a festival in December 1999, it was not accepted and he was asked to take it back. Caste distinctions are also observed quite openly during the *bhandara*. The building where the food is served is divided into two parts by a wall, one side for the upper castes and the other for the Dalits.

CASTE IN 'CASTE-FREE' SPACES

Apart from the continued practice of untouchability in the private sphere and the everyday social and economic life, the system of caste hierarchy and its ideology of purity and impurity also percolates into the new 'caste free' institutions. For example, unlike the traditional Hindu system of education, the modern institutions of learning are not supposed to discriminate on the basis of caste or gender. In fact, secular education has been a vehicle of Dalit mobility. However, given the nature of the institution of caste, these too cannot always escape being influenced by past values. Schools, public distribution system (PDS) outlets, post-offices, milk cooperatives, panchayats, and modern hospitals, all discriminate against Dalits.

Caste in Schools

From a Dalit perspective, the introduction of the modern secular education was one of the most important changes introduced by the British colonial rulers. Modern secular education – schools, colleges, and universities – is, in principle, open to everyone. However, it is mostly the upper castes and the rich who have accessed modern education and who continue to dominate these institutions. Thanks to the growing awareness about the uses of education among them and the official policy of keeping some posts reserved for the members of the Scheduled Castes, some Dalits too have been able to acquire education. Some of them have also become schoolteachers.

What was the experience of Dalits in the schools of rural Punjab? By and large, the practice of untouchability was not very visible in the village schools. Rarely were Dalit children made to sit separately. In most cases the upper-caste and Dalit children interacted with each other without any problem and drank water from the same source. But there were some cases where distinctions were observed, overtly or subtly. Dalit teachers in the schools also felt that they were not completely accepted by their upper-caste colleagues. They tended to interact more with other Dalit teachers.

More than untouchability, perhaps, the problem was with the quality of education being imparted in the government-run village schools. The number of teachers employed was normally less than required. Even those employed did not take their work very seriously. Rarely do the rural schools have enough infrastructure in terms of rooms, labs, and furniture required for the proper functioning of the school. As a consequence, more ambitious and well-to-do parents have started sending their children to urban schools. In some villages the mushrooming of private schools, mostly at the nursery and primary level, is plainly visible. The main attraction of these schools is that they claim to instruct in the 'English medium'. However, they charge fees while the government schools are virtually free. Only the landed upper-caste and better-off families can afford to send their children to these schools.

This withdrawal of upper castes from the government-run schools has had a further negative impact on the quality of education in these schools. In some of the villages, the government schools have begun to be called Dalit or Harijan schools. Since the influential upper castes do not send their children to the government schools, there is little interest among them to demand improvements in standards of teaching in the local schools.

In a village of Amritsar district, a Dalit student of class 8 told us that out of 37 children in his class, only four were Jats. The rest were all Dalits or from other 'backward castes'. In the neighbouring district of Gurdaspur, the headmistress of the village primary school had a similar story to tell. Of the 108 students in her school, only around 14 or 15 come from families of the landowning Jats. The rest are mostly Dalits. The village also has an *anganwadi* (a crèche) with around seventy young children. They all come from Dalit or 'backward caste' families.

Caste and Panchayats

The introduction of local-level political institutions based on the principle of universal adult franchise and representative democracy has had far-reaching implications for the rural power structure. Like other institutions of Indian political democracy, panchayats too have seats reserved for the Scheduled Castes, both for ordinary membership and for *sarpanch*es (the presidents). Given their population in the Punjab countryside, some Dalits have been able to get elected as *sarpanch*es even in 'open' seats. In our sample villages, as many as seventeen had a Dalit *sarpanch* and another six had had them in the past. Of the seventeen Dalit *sarpanch*es in office, nearly half were women. They could become *sarpanch* primarily because the seats were reserved for Dalit women. In the remaining twenty-eight villages, no Dalit had ever become a *sarpanch*. The number of Dalit *panch*es (ordinary members) varied from one to five, depending on the size of the village and the panchayats.

This democratization of the local political institutions has made a lot of difference to the Dalits. It has given them a sense of dignity and the power to bargain for improvements. Universal adult franchise has forced the upper/dominant castes to recognize the value of Dalit votes. Their being able to be elected as *sarpanch* has also forced the members of the upper castes to renegotiate their relationship with them. Dalits have become an important ally for everyone in the factional politics of the village.

However, despite these radical changes in the rural power structure, caste-related structures of domination have not completely disappeared from everyday life. Nor have the Dalits become empowered everywhere. For example, some Dalits still feel compelled to stand up in the presence of an elderly upper-caste person. They are not treated equally in the panchayat buildings. These buildings are seen as upper-caste community centres. Similarly, though they have been able to get elected as *panch*es and *sarpanch*es, power in the village still lies with the dominant castes. In most cases Dalits could contest and win elections to the village panchayats because they had the support and patronage of some members of the dominant castes. Even where the post was reserved, the dominant castes invariably had a say in deciding who amongst the Dalits should contest it.

As with Gurdwaras, rural Dalits of Punjab have also been building separate community centres of their own, sometimes with a grant from the Department of Social Welfare, sometimes with their own money. Having their own Gurdwaras and community centres has given them a sense of *autonomy* and reduced their dependence on the locally dominant castes.

CASTE AND CASTE CONFLICT IN RURAL PUNJAB: CONCLUDING REMARKS

For a large majority of Dalits living in rural Punjab, caste has only been a disabling structure. Thanks to the various social movements and the processes of economic development, they no longer have to encounter overt untouchability in their everyday life. They have also been investing in the accumulation of the symbolic resources that would help them to lead a life of self-respect and dignity.

With a near complete decline of *jajmani* relations, the traditional association of castes with certain specific occupations does not seem to hold good for rural Punjab any longer. As discussed above, some of the traditional 'unclean' occupations, like picking up the dead cattle, have become commercialized. Though most of the villages in Punjab still have carcasses, the work of picking up the dead cattle is mostly done on a contractual basis. Even where some of Dalits are still engaged in their traditional occupations, they no longer work in the framework of *jajmani* ties. However, despite this process of *dissociation* being so visible it would still be virtually impossible to find any of the upper-caste Punjabis employed in traditional Dalit occupations.

Perhaps more than the idea of pollution, the subordination of Dalits in rural Punjab was institutionalized through the prevailing structures of agrarian relations. Being landless, they are almost completely dependent on the landowning castes for employment and other economic needs. While working on the land continues to be the most important source of employment for a large majority of them, they have also, and quite consciously, begun to move away from agricultural labour. Their attempts at *distancing themselves* from agricultural labour have perhaps more to do with their acute dislike of the dependency relationship with the farmer than the nature of the work itself.

However, such a distancing is possible only where alternative sources of employment become available. The opening of the village economy and its growing linkage to towns has made it physically possible for them to look for other sources of employment, and many of them have been doing precisely that. But this is not an option easily available to all.

As Lynch observed, under conditions of change caste does not necessarily disintegrate into some other type of social group (Lynch 1969: 203). Dalits in rural Punjab do not necessarily want to forget their caste identities. However, they do want to be treated with dignity and respect. To live a life of dignity, they need their own autonomous cultural resources. The traditional Hindu social order prohibited them from acquiring such resources. They were not allowed entry into temples and centres of learning. The Sikh religion does not advocate discrimination against any caste or creed. But, in practice, Sikhs belonging to the landowning dominant castes have not shed all their prejudices against the Dalits, particularly at the village level. While Dalits are allowed entry into the village Gurdwaras, they are not permitted to cook or serve *langar*. Wherever they could mobilize resources, the Dalits of Punjab have tried to construct their own Gurdwaras and other local level institutions in order to attain a certain degree of cultural autonomy from the dominant castes.

At another level, these processes of dissociation, distancing, and autonomy have also disintegrated the traditional ties of the village community, a direct implication of which is the growing tensions and conflict on caste lines.

Though caste has always been a fact of life in Punjab, it never led to any major incidents of violence or 'caste-wars' as have often been reported from some other parts of India. Caste has also not been an idiom of political discourse in the state. It was perhaps for the first time in the recent history of the region that a case of caste-related conflict was reported from the state of Punjab and was prominently highlighted. In the first week of June 2003, in a village called Talhan located at a distance of around ten kilometres from the town of Jalandhar, an ongoing conflict between the landowning Jats and the Dalit Ad Dharmis reached a flashpoint. The tension was so sharp that the local administration had to intervene and had to seal off the village for a couple of days.

Relations between the two communities in the village had been quite strained for some time over the issue of the Dalits' demand for participation in the management of a local shrine. As mentioned above, different caste communities generally have their separate Gurdwaras. In Talhan Dalits also have a Gurdwara of their own. The disputed shrine did not really belong to any particular caste. It was built in memory of a Sikh artisan who died while fixing wheel in a newly dug well. Since he died while working for the village, he was declared a martyr (*shahid*) and the villagers erected a small structure (*smadh*) in his memory, at the place where he was cremated. Over the years, the *smadh* began to attract devotees. With devotees came money. It was gradually turned into a proper religious shrine and the Sikh holy book was also placed close to the *smadh*. The locally dominant Jats who controlled the village panchayat appointed a committee to look after the shrine. Though this committee had members from different caste groups, no Dalit was ever made a member even though they account for nearly two thirds of the total population of the village. Given their numbers no one can be elected *sarpanch* of the village without their support. However, when they demanded representation in the management of the shrine, the Jats refused. The Ad Dharmis approached the local administration and even the court of law. It was during one of the demonstrations by them in the town of Jalandhar that violence broke out, the police opened fire and one Dalit was killed.

The agitation continued for nearly six months and eventually the Ad Dharmis were accommodated on the managing committee. Though it did not significantly alter the power equation, either at the local level or in the region, Dalits elsewhere in Punjab were inspired by the story of Talhan. During 2003-4 there were more than half a dozen cases where local-level tensions came out into the open and were reported in the local newspapers. The issues of contention vary from village to village. They range from demanding a share in the agricultural lands owned and leased out by the village panchayat, drainage rights, or simply contesting elections for panchayat positions against the Jats.

However, notwithstanding the divergent nature of issues, all these stories have a common theme. Everywhere Dalits are making new claims. They are asking for equal rights and a legitimate share in the resources that belong commonly to the village but which had so far been in the exclusive control of the locally dominant caste. Perhaps the most interesting feature of these conflicts is that though the issues are all local in nature, the language and politics they deploy in their struggle are 'imported' from outside the village. These are not simply instances of 'caste-oppression' or violence against Dalits but should, in fact, be viewed as cases of 'Dalit assertion', coming from below, and making a positive claim.

It is for this reason that one has to look at such instances of assertion and conflict in the overall frame of village social structure. Such assertions become possible only when the old structures of dependency and power begin to weaken. Given the specific nature of their dependencies and the relation that caste had with agrarian structure, Dalits have negotiated a space for themselves through the strategies of dissociation, distancing, and autonomy. How do we then talk about the village? This is certainly a question worth asking.

REFERENCES

Béteille, A. 2000a. *Chronicles of Our Time*. Delhi: Penguin Books.

——. 2000b. 'The Scheduled Castes: An Inter-regional Perspective'. *Journal of Indian School of Political Economy* 12 (3-4): 367-80.

Bhalla, G.S. and G.K. Chadha. 1983. *Green Revolution and Small Peasants: A Study of Income Distribution among Punjab Cultivators*. Delhi: Concept Publishing House.

Bhalla, S. 1976. 'New Relations of Production in Haryana Agriculture'. *Economic and Political Weekly* 11 (13): A23-30.

Brass, P. 1974. *Language, Religion and Politics in North India*. Cambridge: Cambridge University Press.

Caton, B.P. 2004. 'Social Categories and Colonisation in Punjab, 1849-1920'. *The Indian Economic and Social History Review* 41 (1): 33-50.

Charsley, S.R. and G.K. Karanth (eds.). 1998. *Challenging Untouchability: Dalit Initiative and Experience from Karnataka*. Delhi: Sage Publications.

Cohn, B. 1996. *Colonialism and Its Forms of Knowledge: The British in India*. Princeton: Princeton University Press.

Das, V. 1990. 'Introduction', in V. Das (ed.). *Mirrors of Violence: Communities, Riots and Survivors in South Asia*. Delhi: Oxford University Press.

Deliège, R. 1999. *The Untouchables of India*. New York: Berg.

Desai, I.P. 1976. *Untouchability in Rural Gujarat*. Bombay: Popular Prakashan.

Dumont, L. 1971. *Homo Hierarchicus*. Delhi: Vikas Publishers.

Fox, R. 1985. *The Lions of Punjab: Culture in the Making*. Berkeley: University of California Press.

Fuller, C.J. (ed.). 1997. *Caste Today*. Delhi: Oxford University Press (paperback edition).

Grewal, J.S. 1989. 'Changing Sikh Self-Image before Independence', in P.C. Chatterjee (ed.), *Self-Images, Identity and Nationalism*. Shimla: Indian Institution of Advanced Studies.

——. 1994. *The Sikhs of Punjab*. Cambridge: Cambridge University Press (Indian edition by Fountain Books, Delhi).

Gupta, D. 2000. *Interrogating Caste: Understanding Hierarchy and Difference in Indian Society*. Delhi: Penguin Books.

Hershman, P. 1981. *Punjabi Kinship and Marriage*. Delhi: Hindustan Publishing Corporation.

Ibbetson, D. 1916. *Punjab Castes*. Delhi: Low Price Publications (2002 reprint).

Jodhka, S.S. 1998. 'From "Book-View" to "Field-View": Social Anthropological Constructions of the Indian Village'. *Oxford Development Studies* 26 (3): 311-31.

——. 2000. 'Prejudice without Pollution?: Scheduled Castes in Contemporary Punjab'. *Journal of Indian School of Political Economy* (special issue on Scheduled Castes edited by André Béteille) 12 (3-4): 381-402.

——. (ed.) 2001. *Community and Identities: Contemporary Discourses on Culture and Politics in India*. Delhi: Sage Publications.

——. 2002. 'Caste and Untouchability in Rural Punjab'. *Economic and Political Weekly* 37 (19) (May 11): 1813-23.

——. 2003. 'Agrarian Structures and Their Transformations', in V. Das (ed.), *Oxford India Companion to Sociology and Social Anthropology*. Delhi: Oxford University Press.

——. 2004. 'Sikhism and the Caste Question: Dalits and Their Politics in Contemporary Punjab', *Contributions to Indian Sociology* 38 (1-2): 165-92.

Jones, K.W. 1976. *Arya Dharma: Hindu Consciousness in 19th Century Punjab*. Berkeley: University of California Press.

Juergensmeyer, M. 1988. *Religious Rebels in the Punjab: The Social Vision of Untouchables*. Delhi: Ajanta Publications.

Kesinger, T.G. 1974. *Vilayatpur (1848-1968): Social and Economic Change in a North Indian Village*. Berkeley: University of California Press.

Kohli, D.S. and N. Singh 1997. 'The Green Revolution in Punjab, India: The Economics of Technological Change', Conference paper.

Kothari, R. 1973. *Caste in Indian Politics*. Delhi: Orient Longman.

Lynch, O. 1969. *The Politics of Untouchability: Social Mobility and Change in a City of India*. New York: Columbia University Press.

McLeod, W.H. 1996. *The Evolution of the Sikh Community: Five Essays*. Delhi: Oxford University Press.

Mendelsohn, O. and M. Vicziany. 1998. *The Untouchables: Subordination, Poverty and the State in Modern India*. Cambridge: Cambridge University Press.

Moffatt, M. 1979. *An Untouchable Community in South India*. Princeton: Princeton University Press.

Nayar, B.R. 1966. *Minority Politics in the Punjab*. Princeton: Princeton University Press.

Oberoi, H. 1994. *The Construction of Religious Boundaries: Culture, Identity and Diversity in the Sikh Tradition*. Delhi: Oxford University Press.

Patnaik, U. (ed.). 1990. *Agrarian Relations and Accumulation: The 'Mode of Production Debate in India'*. Delhi: Oxford University Press.

Pettigrew, J. 1975. *Robber Nobleman: A Study of the Political System of the Sikh Jats*. London: Routledge and Kegan Paul.

Pimpley, P.N. and S.K. Sharma. 1985. '"De-Sanskritization" of Untouchables: Arya Samaj Movement in Punjab', in P. N. Pimpley and S. K. Sharma (eds.), *Struggle for Status*, pp. 86-101. Delhi: B.R. Publishing Corporation.

Purandare, C.K. 1995. 'People of India: Some Prima Facie Inferences with Reference to S.C.s and S.T.s', in P.C. Jogdand (ed.), *Dalit Women in India: Issues and Perspectives*. Delhi: Gyan Publishing House.

Rogers, J.D. 2004. 'Introduction: Caste, Power and Region in Colonial South Asia'. *The Indian Economic and Social History Review* 41 (1): 1-6.

Rudra, A. 1990. 'Class Relations in Indian Agriculture', in U. Patnaik (ed.), *Agrarian Relations and Accumulation: The 'Mode of Production Debate in India'*, pp. 251-67. Delhi: Oxford University Press.

Saberwal, S. 1976. *Mobile Men: Limits to Social Change in Urban India*. Delhi: Vikas Publishing House.

Shah, G. 2000. 'Hope and Despair: A Study of Untouchability and Atrocities in Gujarat'. *Journal of Indian School of Political Economy* 12 (3-4): 459-72.

Shah, G. (ed.). 2001. *Dalit Identity and Politics*. Delhi: Sage Publications.

Sharma, H.C. 1996. *Artisans of the Punjab: A Study of Social Change in Historical Perspective*. Delhi: Manohar.

Sharma, S.K. 1985. *Social Movements and Social Change: A Study of Arya Smaj and Untouchables in Punjab*. Delhi: B.R. Publishing Corporation.

Singh, G. 1986. *Religion and Politics in the Punjab*. Delhi: Deep and Deep Publications.

Singh, I.P. 1975. 'A Sikh Village', in M. Singer (ed.), *Traditional India: Structure and Change*. Jaipur: Rawat (Indian reprint).

——. 1977. 'Caste in a Sikh Village', in H. Singh (ed.), *Caste among Non-Hindus in India*. Delhi: National Publishing House.

Singh, K.S. 1995. *The Scheduled Castes* (People of India, National Series Volume II). Delhi: Oxford University Press.

Srinivas, M.N. (ed.). 1996. *Caste: Its Twentieth Century Avatar*. Delhi: Penguin Books.

Tandon, P. 1961. *Punjabi Century 1857-1947*. New York: Harcourt, Brace and World.

Thorner, A. 1982. 'Semi-Feudalism or Capitalism? Contemporary Debate on Classes and Modes of Production in India'. *Economic and Political Weekly* 17 (49, 51): 993-9; 2061-86.

Webster, J.C.B. 1999. 'Leadership in Rural Dalit Conversion Movement', in J.T. O'Connell (ed.), *Organizational and Institutional Aspects of Indian Religious Movements*. Shimla: Indian Institution of Advanced Studies.

3

Social Change and Leadership: A Case Study of Bhaktapur City

KRISHNA HACHHETHU

INTRODUCTION

This paper sets out to examine social and economic changes in Bhaktapur city, Nepal, during the second half of the twentieth century and to analyse their impact on the emergence of new political leadership at the local level.[1] It begins with an introduction to Bhaktapur city and a review of the scholarly literature on it. This is a critical review in that I disagree with the basic premise shared by these previous studies, namely, that Bhaktapur is a timeless or unchanging city. Change in Bhaktapur is presented here in two parts. The second section of the paper is about my own observations of change in a particular locality of Bhaktapur, Lakolache, where I was born. The last section covers changes in the social, economic, and political spheres of the city at large.

Robert I. Levy's *Mesocosm* (1990) is an intensive and extensive study of Bhaktapur city. It is indeed a comprehensive text introducing the city and the colourful life of its population in several aspects. Located 14 km east of Kathmandu (the capital of the country), ringed by fertile agriculture land, and circled by temples of the *asta matrika* (eight mother goddesses) and the *nava durga* (nine female goddesses), Bhaktapur is a small city of 6.88 square kilometres and its latest population is 72,543 (CBS 2003). It is an agrarian city with an overwhelmingly Newar population. Robert Levy's main interest was to explore the culture of the city, shaped predominantly

---

[1]I would like to acknowledge David Gellner for his valuable inputs and editing of this paper. Professor Lok Raj Baral, Dilli Ram Dahal, and Dhruba Kumar also helped with comments on a preliminary draft.

by religion, tradition, and history. Bhaktapur, like its two neighbouring cities (Lalitpur and Kathmandu) of the Kathmandu Valley, enjoyed the status of independent principality before the unification of Nepal in 1769. Based on an extensive survey, carried out between 1973 and 1976, of its symbols (Hinduism), ideology (caste), and rituals (based on caste and religion), Levy interprets Bhaktapur in terms of several key concepts:

- as an archaic city, meaning that it is supposedly typical of cities before the 'Axial Age' (i.e. before the rise of the world religions);
- as typical of 'the continent in the great divide' (i.e. as typical of agrarian cities before the industrial revolution);
- as exemplifying a 'civic ballet' (i.e. with a rich repertoire of carefully choreographed public festivals);
- as possessing a rich fund of 'marked symbolism' (i.e. gods that stand out and seize the attention);
- as a 'Hindu climax city' (i.e. as the place where the culture of rural Hinduism reaches its apogee).[2]

In Levy's understanding, Bhaktapur city, though divided vertically (i.e. by division into localities), forms an integrated, homogeneous, and territorially defined community marked by a strong value consensus.

Steven M. Parish's *Hierarchy and its Discontents* (1993) demonstrates a continuity of scholarly interest in the complex social system and culture of Bhaktapur. Based on fieldwork between 1984 and 1986, he found Bhaktapur the same as it was a decade earlier when Levy worked there: "Newar Bhaktapur, even today, is a city of caste ... caste life as central to the lives of people ... caste has central role in organizing life" (1993: 5, 29). But Parish's perceptions, both theoretical and empirical study of inter-caste relations among the Newars, are in contrast to Levy's projection of this community as a homogeneous and culturally integrated group. On the debate over the unity of culture, one reviewer states that Levy and Parish are on opposite sides (Gellner 2001a: 308). Parish's contribution is in exploring differences, divisions, clashes of opinion between the unequal people of Bhaktapur city at two levels, one between the upper castes and the Jyapus and the other between pure castes and untouchables.

Though caste is central to people's lives in the city, Bhaktapur is much more than caste. Niels Gutschow and Bernhard Kölver's *Ordered Space* (1975) and Ane Haaland's *Bhaktapur: A Town Changing* (1982) both project Bhaktapur as a city of 'cultural heritage' and as a 'living museum'. Bhaktapur's inclusion in the World Heritage list shows the preservation of medieval characteristics such as cultural events, festivals, *bhajans* (hymns),

---

[2]See Gellner (2001a: 297-300) for a discussion of Levy on these points.

daphas (prayer recitation groups), dramas, folk dances, and *guthis* (a formal social association). The retention of medieval characteristics of Bhaktapur city in its culture, art, architecture, and historical monuments (temples, palace, and shrines) is also covered in larger studies, such as Bernier's *The Temples of Nepal* (1970), Anderson's *The Festivals of Nepal* (1971), and Slusser's *Nepal Mandala* (1982). Works on Bhaktapur by native academics are different from foreign scholars both in methodology and in content. Acharya and Ansari's report (1980) focuses on the question of economic development related to the basic needs of Bhaktapur town. Class content in the caste conflict between the upper-caste landlords and the Jyapu tenants is briefly touched on in Pandey's empirical study of land reform in rural and urban areas of Bhaktapur district (1985). Pushpa Raj Chalise's *Nepalko Prajatantrik Andolanma Bhaktapurko Bhumika* (*Role of Bhaktapur in the Democratic Movement in Nepal*, 1994) is a chronological account of oppositional politics in Bhaktapur district over a period of five decades from 1940 to 1990.

Which aspects of Bhaktapur are attractive to researchers, and to foreign scholars in particular? What are their specific interest areas? What image of the city are they seeking to convey? These questions should be taken into account when we try to understand why some aspects of Bhaktapur are explored and re-explored and other features are ignored. The literature on Bhaktapur, particularly that written by foreigners, tends to highlight a particular image of Bhaktapur city with its three distinct characteristics: its unique position, its cultural heritage, and its specific Newar ethnography.

Unique Position

Bhaktapur is portrayed as "a repository of much of the cultural and social history of South Asia ... untouched by Western influence" (Levy 1990: 2, 4); "a city imagined, dreamed up, and conjured into existence" (Parish 1993: 21); and "conditioned by pre-industrial forms of production" (Gutschow & Kölver 1975: 13). Haaland is highly impressed and excited by the beauty of Bhaktapur: "Hardly anywhere else in Asia – or in the world – does one find an almost undisturbed culture, where people still live in buildings that might all have been precious museum pieces in the West, surrounded by exquisite temples and shrines from an unbelievably rich artistic and cultural period of the country" (1982: 57).

Bhaktapur is, in one respect, rather unusual in Nepal. Nepal is home to over a hundred caste/ethnic groups, ninety languages and/or dialects, and nine different religions (CBS 2002). This is a country of minorities, and the largest group, the Chetri, constitutes only 15.8 per cent of the total population. But whereas nationally Nepal is a plural and diversified society, Bhaktapur is a homogeneous city dominated by one particular ethnic group (Newar), one minority language (Nepal Bhasha), and one religion (Hindu

Table 3.1: Caste, Language, and Religion of the Population of Bhaktapur Municipality (in percentage)

Contents	Year	1971	1981	2001
	Total population	40,112	48, 472	72,543
Caste/ethnicity	Newar	na	na	88.2
	Non-Newar	na	na	11.8
Mother tongue	Nepal Bhasha	na	83.4	87.6
	Nepali	na	14.0	6.3
	Other	na	2.6	6.1
Religion	Hindu	90.4	94.8	88.7
	Buddhist	7.5	2.5	10.7
	Others	2.1	2.7	0.6

Sources: CBS 1975, 1984, 2003.

ism), as shown in Table 3.1. However, as will be seen below, there is plenty of diversity within the Newar ethnic group.

Bhaktapur is a city without some stereotypically urban characteristics. Agriculture remains the primary occupation of the majority population. It is neither an industrialized city nor a big business centre. Bhaktapur is much less and more slowly exposed to the outside world than the other two cities of the Kathmandu Valley, namely, Patan (Lalitpur) and Kathmandu, which is both a cause and a consequence of its social demography. In the early 1950s, the Newars constituted 68.4, 78.4, and 97.4 per cent of the urban population of Kathmandu, Lalitpur, and Bhaktapur respectively (Nepali 1965: 24). Now the proportion of Newars in the populations of the three cities is reduced to 31.7, 50.1, and 88.2 respectively (CBS 2003). The decrease in the proportion of the Newar population in the last five decades in Bhaktapur is 9.2 per cent, which is insignificant in comparison to the decline of 36.7 per cent in Kathmandu and 28.3 per cent in Lalitpur. These figures correspond with the data of migration and its impact on population growth. The annual population growth in Bhaktapur recorded was 0.67 (1952-61), 1.7 (1961-71), 1.91 (1971-81), and 2.37 (1981-99) per cent and the figure of population growth in the corresponding period is 1.78, 2.15, 3.07, and 3.72 per cent in Lalitpur, and 1.83, 2.2, 4.57, and 5.83 per cent in Kathmandu (Sharma 1989; KC 1998). If migration is taken as an indicator of exposure to the outside world and as an instrument of change, Bhaktapur stands in a disadvantageous position in comparison to its two neighbouring cities. Table 3.2 shows that the number of outsiders – whether immigrants (foreign born) or migrants (native born) – residing in Bhaktapur is much lower than the equivalent figures for Lalitpur or Kathmandu.

Bhaktapur's economy is dominated by agriculture and its general pre-industrial position. As Table 3.2 shows, there is insignificant migration from outside the city. Bhaktapur certainly lags behind Kathmandu and Lalitpur in the modernization process. Does this mean that Bhaktapur is an

Table 3.2: Internal and International Migration to Urban Areas of the Kathmandu Valley

	1981			1991			2001		
Cities	Total Population	Foreign born	Native born	Total Population	Foreign born	Native born	Total Population	Foreign born	Native born
Bhaktapur	48,472	6	1,610	61,405	155	1,389	72,543	339	8,841
Lalitpur	79,875	398	6,397	115,865	2,879	14,628	162,991	4,326	50,694
Kathmandu	235,160	2,862	29,127	421,258	13,100	82,526	671,846	24,964	271,228

Sources: CBS 1984, 1993, 2003.

underdeveloped and a static society as portrayed by so many foreign scholars, except Gregory Grieve. It is not surprising that they see Bhaktapur as an isolated and changeless city since their studies focused primarily (a) on immobile symbols and cultural artefacts, i.e. temples, palace, shrine, deities, and festivals, and (b) on relatively less dynamic social institutions, i.e. caste, marriage, *guthi*, *bhajan*, *dapha*, etc.

Cultural Heritage

Books written about the Bhaktapur Development Project (BDP) have contributed significantly in popularizing Bhaktapur as a cultural city. The BDP, a German-aided project locally known as 'the German project', ran for twelve years, from 1974 to 1986, working primarily on the renovation of historical monuments, though its manifest objective was "improving the living conditions of the inhabitants". Gutschow and Kölver's small book (1975) is about the medieval town planning of Bhaktapur with an analysis of its historic temples, shrine, streets, lanes, squares, and festivals. Haaland's book (1982) is mainly an account of the achievements of the BDP in the renovation of historical and religious monuments and infrastructure building, i.e. paving roads, providing sewerage and sanitation, private and public toilets, facilitating water supply, and repairing courtyards, and so on. It was the BDP that began the process of highlighting Bhaktapur's reputation as a traditional city, a historic city, a Hindu Mediaeval city, and a culture capital. It is, in the opinion of one critic, a "romantic historicist 'myth'" to justify conservation work on the monuments of the city (Grieve 2002: 286). The 55-windowed palace, the Nyatapola temple, the Dattatreya *math* (priest's house), Taumadhi square, the Siddha *pokhari* (pond), the Banshagopal *satal* (public inn) are just a few of the more famous of the 150 historic temples and monuments, 172 *patis* (arcades), 27 *satals* (meeting houses), 19 *maths*, 34 ponds, 152 wells, and 77 sunken water spouts (BM 2001: 9), which together go to make up this ensemble of medieval art, culture, and architecture.

The conservation and preservation of heritage has been continued by the local government of Bhaktapur municipality (BM). Using the slogan "Creation of our predecessors – our art and culture", the BM is aiming to achieve official recognition of Bhaktapur as a cultural city. The main motivational factor behind this agenda is to convert the city into a tourist destination and thereby generate a new source of income. Grieve rightly remarks, "In the present global economy, tradition is a valuable commodity that can be used not only to gain distinction, but also monetary capital. The traditional city is constructed by translating local practices into romantic Orientalism" (2002: 304). The BM introduced a US $1 tourist entry fee in 1993. The rate increased to $5 in 1996 and to $10 in 2001. Earnings from the tourist entry fee have contributed considerably more than 50 per cent of the BM's annual income in the past few years (Hachhethu 2003: 59). Projecting Bhaktapur as a cultural city has become an easy and lucrative source of income; consequently, the BM has been aggressively campaigning to promote the reputation of Bhaktapur as a cultural city. A brochure published by the BM gives prominent place to A.E. Powell's quotation: "Were there nothing else in Nepal save the Darbar Square of Bhaktapur, it would still be amply worth making a journey halfway round the globe to see" (BM 2001).

Ethnography of the Newars

The Newars, the indigenous group of the Kathmandu Valley, are a distinct community following the system of caste hierarchy. The division of the Newars to several social rankings dates back at least to the medieval period when King Jayasthiti Malla is said to have divided his *praja* (subjects) into sixty-four castes on the basis of their occupation. G.S. Nepali's book (1965) and Colin Rosser's article (1966), give detailed accounts of caste among both the Hindu and the Buddhist Newars of the Kathmandu Valley. The former covers a wide content of rituals (birth, marriage, death), social institutions (caste, family, kinship, festivals) and the material/economic life of the Newars. Rosser concentrates on the upward mobility of individuals among the Hindu Newars and status downward of a group belonging to Buddhist Newars. *Contested Hierarchies* (Gellner & Quigley eds. 1995) covers all the major caste groups within the Newars, but nearly all the book's detailed discussion focuses on Kathmandu or Lalitpur, or villages in the west of the Kathmandu Valley. Levy, Parish, Gutschow and Kölver, and Haaland concentrate principally on the social and cultural lives of the Newars of Bhaktapur city. Levy's (1990) account of ethnography of the Hindu Newars of Bhaktapur is as intensive as Gellner's observation of the rituals of the Buddhist Newars of Lalitpur (Gellner 1992).

Levy found 350 *thar*s (clan names) and arranged them in twenty district levels (ranked from Brahman to untouchable) in Bhaktapur's urban macrostatus system. For the sake of the present analysis, the Hindu Newars of Bhaktapur can be regrouped into four basic categories in hierarchical order: upper caste (Brahman, Chathari, and Shrestha) at the top, Jyapu in the middle, low-caste groups in the lower middle, and untouchable at the lowest position. The caste system dominates the life of Bhaktapur. An anthropologist observes, "Newar Bhaktapur, even today, is a city of castes, of culturally valued inequalities, the social and symbolic life of the city is organized in terms of these inequalities" (Parish 1993: 5). The system of hierarchy and inequalities can be observed in the social practices, settlement patterns, class differences, occupations, and cultural symbols of Bhaktapur city (Table 3.3).

The two dominant groups among the Newars of Bhaktapur are the upper castes and the Jyapu, a majority community comprising around 60 per cent of Bhaktapur city's population. They are distinct groups in many respects. "The stereotype of the Shrestha is that of the well-to-do merchant, clean, well-dressed, highly literate, well-mannered and well-educated, fastidious, cultured, essentially urban in outlook and orientation: the stereotype of the Jyapu is that of a mud-bespattered fieldworker, poor, rough in manner and speech, illiterate, essentially a peasant and worker" (Rosser 1966: 92). The upper-caste Newars have a collective identity – *svasya* (superior), *sahu* (merchant), *madhyam barga* (middle class) – that distinguishes them from other groups. It refers to their caste status, class position, and occupation. They include the descendants of the Malla kings of the medieval period and families of their advisers and administrators. They are traditionally landlords and merchants. They are also involved in trade, business, bureaucracy, teaching, and other learned professions. The term 'Jyapu', a Newari word, means peasant. Peasant refers to the occupation of farming across the caste hierarchy. Peasant as an occupational group includes Brahmans as well as untouchables. However, the meaning of Jyapu in Bhaktapur is not confined only to the agricultural occupational group. If a person is called a Jyapu this refers to his/her social and economic position in the society. The Jyapu's social status is lower than that of upper-caste Newars and the term also implies that the person so referred to is likely to be poor.

Lower caste groups – 'impure but not untouchable' – consist of several clans, i.e. Gatha, Bhan, Kata, Chalan, Khusa, Nau, Kau, Pun, Sami, and Chipa. They are all associated with different traditional craft or ritual occupations. Their social status is lower than the Jyapus and their economic condition in general is worse than that of the Jyapus since their traditional occupation is neither agriculture nor business. Below this group are the untouchables. The three major castes among them are Nay, Jugi, and Pwah. Nays are hereditary butchers who sell buffalo meat, Jugis are tailors, and Pwahs are Sweepers. In Bhaktapur all three still follow their traditional occupations.

Table 3.3: Conventional Distinctions between the Newars of Bhaktapur City

	Upper castes	Jyapus	Low castes	Untouchables
Social status	Higher	Middle	Lower	Lowest
Social practice	Don't accept boiled rice and certain food from the person of lower status	Take all food items from a person of high caste but not from lower castes	Take all food items from a person of high caste but not from lower castes	Prohibited to enter the houses of touchable castes
Settlement	Centre of town and bazaar area	Lanes	Corner of city	Outside city boundary
Rituals	Take front seat in chariots and festivals	Sit behind the upper castes	Outside chariots	Prohibited to enter temples and chariots
Occupation	Business and landlords	Tenants and farming	Specific job ascribed by tradition	Meat selling, tailoring, and cleaning
Class	Rich and middle	Poor and lower middle	Poorer and lower middle	Poorest

Note: Newar Untouchables are not included in the official government lists of Dalit castes, for reasons which have to do with the politics of ethnicity and the concern of Newar ethnic leaders not to split the 'Newar community'. So they are referred to as Untouchables here, in line with their traditional designation.

What aspects were left out in previous studies of Bhaktapur city? Levy admits, "We have for the most part neglected economy, social dynamics, ecological relations, material culture, and so on" (1990: 8). Parish explores the discontent of the lower-status Newars against the system of hierarchy and inequality but he does not explore how such resistance has brought about changes in inter-caste relations. Haaland describes the contribution of the BDP in bringing change to the physical appearance of the city. However, she does not really do justice to the subtitle of her book – *A Town Changing* – as she fails to describe a significant aspect of change, namely, the consequences of such innovations and renovations on the social and economic dynamics of city life. Acharya and Ansari (1980) provide some statistical data on indicators of basic needs, i.e. housing, food, sanitation, drinking water, education, etc., but they ignore the social and political dynamics of economic development and underdevelopment. Chalise (1994) gives an account of political development without linking it with the social and economic changes of the people of Bhaktapur district. In short, the harsh judgement that Mikesell passes on Levy's book is equally applicable to other studies of Bhaktapur as well:

> His major mistake is that he wants to make an understanding of the city as a whole while limiting himself to the religious realm and religiously framed normative one without integrating it into the historically arisen material one – production, reproduction, consumption, distribution, exchange, classes, non-religious forms of representation and orientation, and so forth. (Mikesell 1993: 232)

This paper focuses on the social, economic, and political changes in Bhaktapur that have been ignored by previous studies. It also poses a question about the validity of a generalization – made by many authors about Bhaktapur – that the city is underdeveloped, undynamic, static, and unchanging. Change in Bhaktapur city is presented at two levels, the micro and the macro, by two different methods. For description at the micro level, I will give a personal account of change in the neighbourhood – Lakolache – where I was born in 1960 and grew up. Changing Lakolache can be taken as typical of what was going on in many parts of the city. The subsequent section deals with macro-level change within Bhaktapur city, focusing on education, income, occupations, and new associational life. All of these are aspects of social life in the city which I consider to be both *instruments of change* and simultaneously *outcomes of change*.

CHANGING LAKOLACHE

I begin with a brief introduction to Lakolache *tol* (locality) (see Levy 1990: 184). It covers an area either side of a narrow path 200 metres long; it is subdivided into three small *tol*s: Gahiti, Chapal, and Twale. There are one public inn, two wells, three public taps, four shelters (*phalcha*), and two Ganesh temples. This lane, like many other parts of the city, is inhabited predominantly by Jyapus. There are a few upper-caste families, both Chathari (Joshi, Timila, Dhaubadel, and Hora) and Shrestha (Hachhethu and Sikhwal), among the total 120 households of Lakolache. My observations of the changes in Lakolache are presented here in three different time periods. The first period covers the time of my childhood and school years up to 1975; the second period is about my youth (1976-90); and the last phase is an account of new developments which I, as a frequent visitor to Bhaktapur, have observed since 1991, the year when I migrated to greater Kathmandu. Though living outside Bhaktapur, I have visited the town of my birth almost once a week (usually on Saturdays), in addition to staying with my parents at festivals and other major rituals.

At the age of five, I was admitted to a primary school (Baradayani School) near by my house. All the schoolchildren were Newars and half of my classmates up to grade five belonged to the Jyapu families of the surrounding areas. In the morning before school, I usually played with neighbouring boys (both Jyapus and other castes) of my age at gambling – not for cash but in kind, i.e. *chakki* (cigarette box), *champati* (the seed of a kind of sour fruit), and *gucha* (marble). In the evening, we (both boys and girls) generally played different non-gambling games, such as *telkasa* and *aspas* (both forms of hide and seek). Circumstances were rather different when I joined Vidyarthi Niketan High School. It was one of six high schools in Bhaktapur district at that time, four of which were located around the Darbar square area and the remaining two were in Thimi and Sanothimi (4-5 km west of Bhaktapur city). There were a considerable number of students from the hill Bahun/Chetri castes of the rural areas of Bhaktapur district in my school. However, the overwhelming majority were still Newars, mostly belonging either to the upper or to the lower (i.e. lower than Jyapu) castes. Children from Jyapu families constituted nearly 20 per cent of the students up to grade eight but declined to 5 per cent by grade ten. The Jyapu boys of my neighbourhood, both those who dropped out of school and others who had never been sent to school, were found in different spots at different times, some singing *bhajan*s or playing *dapha* music in wayside *phalcha*s before sunrise and after sunset, and others playing cards at noon. But it would be difficult to find them in the city in the daylight hours during the farming season.

Up to the age of ten, I, like my playmates, used the sides of the lane and garbage pits as toilets. Even the elder members of my family and neighbours used these places late at night. To urinate in the daytime, they entered a house nearby and used a space on the ground floor under the stairs. This space is a personal garbage pit which was set in the ground floor of almost all the Jyapu households, and used for making compost fertilizer. For defecation they used open places – specified separately for men and women outside the city and called *khele* and *malain* respectively. No one saw any need for a private toilet. When visiting the *khele* I often saw the male members of some Jyapu families working with dust, waste, and dry stool to make compost. Other noticeable things at the riverside and ponds were people bathing and women washing clothes. Most people of my locality used well water for cooking and drinking. Whenever I got sick my parents took me to a *vaidya* (traditional medical practitioner) for *jharphuk* (exorcism by brushing with a broom) and visited temples to pray for my recovery. All our neighbours did the same. People went only very rarely to a hospital and only when a person fell seriously ill.

My uncles were in business. They collected vegetables from the Jyapu houses and sold them in Kathmandu. Every morning they went to Kathmandu with a full truckload of vegetables, returning only in the evening. Most male Jyapus of my neighbourhood of all age groups hung around in wayside shelters doing nothing or playing cards during the agricultural off-season. The women Jyapus were, however, usually found to be working, e.g. *thajya yayegu* (spinning thread), making beaten rice with wooden foot-operated pestles, drying agricultural products in the sunlight, etc.

In those days the Jyapus were distinct from us in many respects. They used predominantly indigenous kin terms, such as *bajya* (grandfather), *aji* (grandmother), *abwa* (father), *ama* (mother), *aka* (uncle), *mama* (aunty), *taju* (elder sister-in-law), *ata* (elder sister). Upper-caste Newars used different terms, borrowed from the Nepali language, for those same relatives, namely, *baje*, *bajya*, *ba*, *ma*, *kaka*, *kaki*, *bhauju*, and *didi* respectively. The menfolk of some Shrestha households organized *bhajan*s (devotional hymns) to the god Ganesh of Gahiti *tol* once a week, on a Tuesday. The songs they sang were modern in style and composed separately in both Nepali and Newari languages. They used modern musical instruments, i.e. the harmonium (*harben*) and the tabla drums (*tamal*). Their songs and musical instruments were and are different from those of classical Newari songs and musical instruments used in *bhajan* and *dapha*. Almost all Jyapu families had members who participated in *bhajan* and/or *dapha*. The Jyapus, even the men, wore homemade (handloom) clothes, whereas we wore shop-bought finished products. For Jyapu women it was a matter of pride to appear in their home-made thick black saris with a red border. The radio was a luxury item available only in my house and the houses of other upper-caste families of my locality. Only a few Jyapu households had electricity. Some other distinct features of the Jyapus were walking barefoot, using straw for cooking, carrying loads on their shoulders, wearing dirty clothes, and marrying young.[3]

During my childhood I sometimes accompanied my grandfather and mother to feasts at our Jyapu neighbours' houses. We, along with other invitees of the same caste, were seated separately in the *chwata* (second floor) and we were not served some items, like *takha la* (cooked and frozen jellied buffalo meat, served in winter). Upper-caste Newars did/do not take cooked rice and some other food items such as *takha la* from the lower castes. Sometimes my family invited the Jyapu neighbours for feasts, for example, for the ceremony of *kayta puja* (caste initiation for boys), marriage, and *sraddha* (ceremony commemorating deceased ancestors). Our Jyapu neighbours were placed in the *matan* (first floor) and served all food items (i.e. they could accept everything from us, but not vice versa). When they had finished eating, they collected and threw away the *chipa lapte* (polluted leaf plate) themselves. After I and four of my cousins had jointly gone through the ritual of *kayta puja*, our grandfather and other family

---

[3]Most male Jyapus of my neighbourhood married between the ages of 12 and 16. Many of my Jyapu classmates in Bhaktapur Campus were already married before they entered higher education.

members of the older generation told us that we could no longer take boiled rice, *takha la*, and some other food items from the hands of Jyapus. Jyapu neighbours, even though they were not our tenants, would voluntarily serve my family by carrying out what were defined in the traditional culture as low-status tasks, e.g. carrying the *batacha* (a metal pot containing water used to wash the hands of someone offering rice balls to the ancestors) during the *sraddha* ceremonies, and carrying the *musyami* (a kind of lamp) in the funeral processions. Shresthas would never have dreamt of reciprocating by performing such low-status work for Jyapus.

As I grew older, changes in the lifestyle of Lakolache appeared slowly but steadily. I was the only one from my locality to be admitted to Bhaktapur Campus in 1977 for higher education. I studied to the certificate and diploma level from 1977 to 1983 in Bhaktapur Campus and completed my MA in 1986 from Kirtipur Multiple Campus, Tribhuvan University. There were six other educated persons in my neighbourhood, older than me, and all from the upper castes. Of the total of twenty persons who went in for higher education after me during the nine years of my campus life (1977-86), five, including one female, were from the Jyapu families and the other fifteen, including three females, were my cousins and neighbours from the upper castes. In each succeeding year there was a gradual increase in the number of Jyapu children attending school.

The face of my locality began to change rapidly in the early 1980s. My house is in a lane attached to a public garbage pit surrounded by nine houses. I was able to convince my immediate Jyapu neighbours to accept the financial and material support offered by the municipality to turn the garbage pit into a brick-paved courtyard. A community of adjoining neighbours, observing what we had done, did the same with their garbage pit. We also received a fund of Rs.1,500 for each household from the office of Water Supply and Sewerage under the BDP planning to build a private toilet. The grant was more than sufficient to construct a normal toilet. Moreover, the availability of chemical fertilizer in the market helped to break the traditional link between the garbage pit and farming. The newly constructed private toilets replaced the personal garbage pits under the stairs in the ground floors of the Jyapus' houses. A new drainage system was constructed, followed by stone paving of the lane. We – the Hachhethus, who had expanded to eight households by that time – installed private pipes and taps (at our own expense) together with the construction of private toilets (paid for by the grant), but our Jyapu neighbours waited for another grant before they installed private taps. The people in the north-eastern part of the city received the facilities of private taps and toilets, brick-paved courtyards, sewerage, brick-paved roads/lanes earlier, as the BDP started its work from the upper half of the city. My local lane – so full of faeces during my childhood – became a clean place.

In the 1980s, my uncles began to face problems in their business as middlemen between the Jyapus producing vegetables and the consumers. They ultimately shifted to the transport business as a consequence of the integration of the Jyapus into the cash market. The Jyapus of my neighbourhood and other parts of the city began to deal with the market directly by going to Kathmandu with their own vegetables. As demand grew in Kathmandu they were seen selling in Bhaktapur less and less. The farming of green vegetables largely replaced wheat as the second major crop – rice remained the first major crop – which required more time on their farms. The wages for agricultural labour increased considerably. One phrase I heard very often from my uncles when expressing their dissatisfaction with the Jyapus was: *teis pathi ko phurti* (literally 'twenty-three *pathi* cockiness'). It referred to Jyapu pride and assertiveness, which was the result of the reduction in land rents, and the specification of the Land Reform Act 1964 that tenants need pay rent of no more than 23 *pathi*s of paddy per *ropani* of land. This phrase was generally used by my uncles in two circumstances, either when a well-dressed Jyapu appeared in the lane or when a Jyapu neighbour refused to obey their orders. The improved income flow of my Jyapu neighbours was manifested in many ways. Hardly any house in my locality was left without electricity. Two-in-one radios were the most popular luxury item among the local Jyapus. There was an explosion of *bhatti*s (liquor plus cooked food shops), predominantly run by Manandhars and Chitrakar, both relatively low-caste groups. The Jyapus were and remain both the owners and the principal customers of all the newly opened *bhatti*s in Lakolache.

I was married in April 1986 and to celebrate the wedding, my father organized a feast over two days. The guests on the first day were relatives, kin, and Jyapu neighbours. It was a *bhway* (traditional feast) in line with the traditional caste hierarchy as regards seating arrangements, the serving of food items, and observing other rituals. On the following day we held a buffet dinner (popularly known as a 'party') and the guests were friends of mine, and of my family father and sister), belonging to different caste/ ethnic groups, including hill Bahun/Chetri, Janajati, Madhesias, and the Newars of different caste hierarchies (i.e. both from Bhaktapur and from elsewhere) – upper caste, Jyapu, and lower caste. The wedding 'party' was consciously arranged as a response to the emergence of new forms of associational life and the adoption of a new culture beyond the traditional caste system. At that time, I was chairman of the Gahiti Youth Club (1981-90), teacher at Arniko Secondary School (1981-7), a member of the Pragati Library, and a fresh ex-student of MA in political science. From all these associations I had an extensive circle of friends which included people of many different caste and ethnic backgrounds. They assembled for my wedding party on the basis of equality. The 'party'-style feast symbolized those new values that transcended or ignored the caste hierarchy.

Since I moved to Kathmandu in 1991, I have observed an acceleration in the changes in Lakolache *tol*. I hardly ever see children (whether of the upper castes or of the Jyapus) in the street, in the wayside shelters, or in the *chok* (a wide courtyard) before and after school times, except sometimes when they are playing chase and cricket during the school holidays. Most of them are busy at home playing with toys, watching television, or doing their school homework. *Chakki, champati, gucha, telkasa*, and *aspas* – the popular games of my childhood – are unknown to them. Almost all the schoolchildren of my locality appear from their houses dressed in the uniforms of their respective schools at around 9 a.m. and return in the afternoon around 4 p.m. There are campus boys and girls in many households, including the Jyapus, of Lakolache. As youths and youngsters need to give much time to their education, the younger generation is not to be found in the *bhajan* and *dapha* music groups. Only middle- and old-aged Jyapus do this, and they restrict their musical activities to a few days around major festivals (Bisket, Dasain, etc.). In order to see once again the everyday sights of my childhood – Jyapu women husking rice (*kuti yayegu*), pounding beaten rice (*baji luyegu*), spinning thread (*thajya yayegu*) – I had to attend a special cultural festival organized by the Bhaktapur municipality in 1997.

Making compost fertilizer from a mixture of garbage, waste, and dry stool – which I observed every day at the *khele* during my childhood and youth – has almost totally disappeared. The municipality refuse collectors come twice a day with a small vehicle to clean the lane and remove garbage from the containers. Nowadays people use pharmacies, clinics, and hospitals, instead of *jharphuk vaidya*s, as places for treating diseases. An outsider can no longer easily distinguish the caste status of the younger generation simply by observing the way they are dressed. Even old Jyapus, whether men or women, do not leave their houses without shoes.

Recently I have noticed a change in the organization of feasts. Due to the separation of families and subdivision of houses, hardly anyone in Lakolache *tol*, whether they belong to the upper castes or the Jyapus, has enough space in their own house to hold big feasts, which are organized generally on the occasions of weddings and *kayta puja*. So the public meeting house attached to the big courtyard is used for grand feasts, both *bhway*s and parties. The system of separate sittings or separate days and different food items for one's friendship circle on the one hand, and for relatives and neighbours on the other, is no longer practised. Today everyone eats the same food at buffet parties, and at feasts everyone sits together in rows and is served the same feast as everyone else. A person sitting with you at a feast may be of an upper or a lower caste than you. Restrictions on taking particular food items from the hands of low castes are no longer observed at feasts.

CHANGING BHAKTAPUR CITY

The literacy rate of Bhaktapur city has more than doubled every twenty years – 27 per cent in 1971, 33 per cent in 1981, 62 per cent in 1991, and 74 per cent in 2001 (CBS) – suggesting mass educational awareness. Until recently, education was the privilege of upper-caste and upper-class Newars. The Jyapus lagged behind but their consciousness of the value of education has increased continuously. The Vidyarthi Niketan Secondary School records show that among the students who completed school leaving certificate (SLC) from this school in the 1950s, there were only 2 belonging to the Jyapu families, but their numbers increased to 10 in the 1960s, 82 in the 1970s, and 250 in the 1980s (Vidyarthi Niketan Secondary School 1998). The trend was clear to Haaland in the early 1980s: "Bhaktapurians today feel that education is the ticket to a better life for the new generation" (Haaland 1982: 39).

To be educated means to have exposure to the outside world. For the educated Jyapus of Bhaktapur, the lifestyle of the upper-caste Newars is the model for their upward mobility. In appearance, educated Jyapus are distinct from the uneducated members of their own community and close to that of upper-caste Newars. My Jyapu friends at college gave up wearing handwoven clothes and wore only shirts and trousers made from finished cloth; in their houses they covered the ceilings with thick, cheap white cloth to prevent the dust falling; they arranged wooden chairs, tables, and beds in order to make the rooms attractive; they requested the female members of the house to clean the passages and rooms; and they motivated their brothers and sisters to go to school. In this way educated Jyapus were the catalyst in bringing about changes within the family that moved it away from the traditional inherited ways of doing things.

To get exposure to modernization through educational attainment or other means is an expensive process. For parents, it is not only a question of meeting the cost of tuition fees but also of having to bear the expense of other associated activities. How the Jyapus of Bhaktapur have managed to afford the extra costs of a modern lifestyle is a matter of considerable interest.

The Land Reform Act 1964, was a benchmark in bringing a substantial improvement in the economic conditions of Bhaktapurians, the Jyapus in particular. The Act was the culmination of a series of progressive land reform measures begun in 1951. The system of compulsory unpaid service known as *bethbegar* and *jhara* had been abolished before 1951. The Land Reform Act 1964 guaranteed legal registration of tenancy rights and fixed the land rent at 23 *pathi*s of *dhan* (paddy) per *ropani* (approximately one-eighth of the total production in two crops). Before the enactment of this Act, tenants had no legal rights to the land they cultivated, and the land rent was fixed by an unwritten compromise made between landowners and tenants, which was generally more in the interest of landowners than of the tenants. Usually the tenant had to pay at least half of the crop to the landlord, as well as provide all kinds of other services as well. The significance of this Act in changing the economic condition of the majority population of the city, the Jyapus, can be seen in the figures on land-peasant relations in Bhaktapur city. A study published in 1980 found that only 2.3 per cent farming households owned all the land they cultivated; 58 per cent owned some of the land they worked and supplemented it with additional rented lands; and the remainder were non-landowning tenant farmers (Wachi quoted in Levy 1990: 63). Since more than 95 per cent of the farming households were tenants, the impact of the Land Reform Act in improving the conditions of the masses of Bhaktapur city is quite obvious. The changing position of the Jyapus from the impact of the series of land reform measures was summed up by Narayan Man Bijukche, Chairman of the Nepal Workers and Peasants Party (NWPP): "The position of the Jyapus of Bhaktapur city changed from being slaves before the 1951 [reforms began] to being serfs following the abolition of *bethbegar* and *jhara* systems, and finally to becoming peasants after the 1964 land reform" (interview, 26 December 2001).

After security of tenancy rights was granted, along with fixed low rents and the right to a share if the land was sold, agricultural production increased suddenly. It was also an outcome of a change in farming style, i.e. the use of *bikashi* (improved) seeds, chemical fertilizer, and machine tools. The result has been a big boost to the agricultural economy of Bhaktapur. More recently the Jyapus have taken up large-scale vegetable farming as major cash crops, to meet the ever-increasing demand for vegetables from Kathmandu. The growth of Jyapu income is visible in several ways, for example, the construction of several hundreds of new houses outside the city, increased market activities against the tradition of the barter system, and the rapid increase of the number of students from peasant families. (Compare Maharjan, this volume, for similar processes in the nearby settlement of Nakadesh.)

The BDP has had a major impact on Bhaktapur in two ways: one is the physical appearance of the city and the other is in the diversification of sources of income. In the past Bhaktapur was infamous as a backward, underdeveloped, uncivilized, dirty, and stubborn city. The streets were full of garbage and faeces. The BDP changed its face by renovating historical monuments and providing physical infrastructure, such as brick-paved roads, sewerage, construction of private and public toilets and taps, etc. The city cleaning campaign initiated by the BDP has been continued by the BM. City cleaning is one of the three core ingredients – the other two being heritage conservation and tourism promotion – of its agenda to make

Bhaktapur a cultural city. Seventy per cent of its development budget is allocated for the conservation and cleanliness of the city (BM 2001: 3). Restrictions on pollution-creating industries and the relocation of previously established industries from the core of the city area, a ban on heavy vehicles entering the city, and a prohibition on all kinds of vehicles in the Darbar square area are some other noteworthy accessories in making Bhaktapur a pollution-free city. Credit should be given to the BDP for its programme which changed the reputation of Bhaktapur from that of being the dirtiest to the cleanest city of Nepal.

The BDP helped to improve the living conditions of Bhaktapur city dwellers, particularly the Jyapus. Its contribution was not limited to providing temporary jobs for a large number of people; it also helped to produce trained manpower for construction. The upper-caste Newars failed to take advantage of the jobs and skills training opportunities provided by the BDP because their status-consciousness barred them from getting involved in what they perceived as inferior manual work, for example, art, crafts, and construction. The Jyapus on the other hand, were ready to provide a labour force to the BDP. Most upper-caste Newars were landowners and most Jyapus were their tenants. Having been poor tenants for several decades, the Jyapus have a tradition of hard work. Caste status and its relation to work is also well reflected in the figures for persons 'not in the labour force': among the Jyapus such people make up only 4.8 per cent, whereas among upper-caste Newars 39.1 per cent fall into this category (Acharya & Ansari 1980: 111). Thus the BDP could be considered a pro-Jyapu project, because it created consciousness and enhanced confidence among the Jyapus, while providing them with alternative sources of employment. As a consequence, a large number of Bhaktapur Jyapus are now involved in providing skilled and unskilled labour for the booming construction industries in the neighbouring cities of Kathmandu and Lalitpur.

This trend of diversifying employment among the Jyapus is clear in the statistics. At one time agriculture as an occupation in Bhaktapur actually increased from 65 per cent in 1971 to 77 per cent in 1981 but thereafter it decreased considerably: to 59 per cent in 1991 and 47 per cent in 2001 (CBS 2003). Three factors have significantly encouraged this trend. One is the separation of families and the consequent fragmentation of landholdings that compels those without enough land to search for other livelihoods. The second factor is that increasingly agricultural land is being sold off for the construction of residences, as is happening throughout the Kathmandu Valley. Last but not the least, the number of educated people in Jyapu families has been increasing and they are attracted more to other occupations. Data on the educational backgrounds of 2,924 educated persons involved in farming – 1,296 non-school, 1,368 below SLC, 137 SLC, 70 IA,

28 BA, and 16 MA (CBS 1984) – shows clearly that the higher the level of education, the less likely is the person to pursue agriculture as an occupation. In the next ten years Bhaktapur will start to be dependant upon migrant labour to carry out its farming. Whatever the reasons for occupational change, the continual reduction of farmers in a city dominated by Jyapus suggests a rather radical social change. Traditionally the Jyapus are supposed to be farmers, but considerable numbers of them are now found in other occupations such as owning factories (mostly brick factories), in business (mostly as shopkeepers selling vegetables), in professions (as doctors, engineers, lawyers, teachers), in services, and in construction.

The transformations in education and sanitation, the growth of income, and the changes of occupation of Bhaktapurians, the Jyapus in particular, all of this has an impact on other areas of the city's life. Only 7 per cent of the households had a private toilet in the late 1970s (Acharya & Ansari 1980: 115) but now this facility is available in 90 per cent of the houses (CBS 2003). Today 98 per cent of the houses have electricity (CBS 2003); only 35 per cent had it in the early 1980s (Haaland 1982: 34). In the past well water was used for drinking and cooking; now 90 per cent of the population uses tap water (CBS 2003). Once wood and straw were the main sources of fuel for cooking; now only 18 per cent rely on it (CBS 2003). Seven thousand telephone lines have already been installed in a city of 12,133 households.

The rapid modernization of Bhaktapur over a long period, as described above, has affected significantly the core of the traditional social structure – the caste system – and has tipped the political equation of the city in favour of the Jyapus. In the past, distinctions between upper-caste Newars and Jyapus were multifarious, impossible to avoid, and hard to overcome: social status and class position were reflected in settlement areas, marriage, kinship, and patterns of association. But the new dynamics of change in the social, economic, and political aspects have meant that the gap between these two groups has been radically reduced.

The most remarkable change was the land reform programme which went wholly against the grain of the traditional system of hierarchical interdependence between the Newars of Bhaktapur city. Most upper-caste Newars were landowners and most Jyapus were their tenants. In the conflict between these two groups on the question of Land Reform, the socially inferior Jyapus came out as winners against the traditionally superior high-caste Newars. Land Reform did not only improve the economic conditions of the Jyapus; it was instrumental in introducing a new and non-deferential culture in the relations of Jyapus with upper-caste Newars. Increased assertion by the Jyapus against the traditional domination of upper-caste Newars, following the change in the political economy, has also been reported from Satungal, west of Kathmandu (Ishii 1987). The availability of other sources of cash income meant that Jyapu dependency on upper-caste Newars was reduced. Over time, the caste-based economic disparities between these two groups have ceased to exist. Differences between the upper castes and the Jyapus are also much reduced so far as occupation is concerned. The economic prosperity of the Jyapu community has meant that the caste hierarchy in the social life of Bhaktapur city is much less rigid than before.

Another force resisting the traditional setting of the superior-subordinate position in inter-caste relations among the Newars is the increasing number of educated people in the Jyapu families. Exposure to education has helped in widening the Jyapus' horizon and in bringing about a change in their thinking and behaviour vis-à-vis upper-caste Newars. They are ambivalent in the sense that the lifestyle of the upper-caste Newars remains a model for their upward mobility, but they are, at the same time, discontented with their hereditary subordinate status. Their aspirations and exposure to secular values, such as equality, are being increasingly expressed through new forms of associational life. As Gellner (2001b: 287) remarks in a similar survey, "new economic conditions produce very different cultural demands [from the past]." Friendships, clubs, schools, campuses, picnics, libraries, offices, NGOs, civil society, and political parties are new social institutions – different from the traditional *guthi*, *bhajan*, or *dapha* – in which caste values have no place in interpersonal relations between members of the association. The emergence of new associational forms of life has brought a new culture different from the traditional caste system. Moreover, the emerging trend of inter-caste love marriages between educated youngsters has posed a challenge to the marriage system as the key determinant and perpetuator of caste status.

THE EMERGENCE OF NEW LEADERSHIP

The modernization in the social and economic spheres of Bhaktapur has had a cumulative effect in bringing change to politics in the city. The 1982 local election, held under the partyless Panchayat regime, was a benchmark for the transfer of power and leadership within the BM from the upper castes to the Jyapu community.

In the past, when social stratification and economic disparity between the upper-caste Newars and the Jyapus were high, the upper-caste Newars monopolized political power. The Jyapus were not politically aware in those days. Upper-caste Newars were at the forefront from the beginning of popular politics in the form of opposition against the oligarchic Rana regime in the 1940s. Those who introduced communist politics to Bhaktapur were upper-caste Newars. Some from the groups whose social status was lower than the Jyapus had been active since the time of the anti-Rana movement. The same trends continued in the post-Rana period and during the three decades of the Partyless Panchayat system (1960-90): those who were active in carrying out politics of different ideologies and blocs, i.e. as democrats or progressives or panchas, were either upper caste or lower caste. For this entire long period the Jyapus in general seemed to be a non-political entity, with a few individual exceptions such as Bikulal Bhaila and Mangaldas Chaguthi who were co-opted by the central leaders during the Panchayat period, and few were elected. Out of five persons who held the post of National Panchayat (legislative) member from Bhaktapur district in different periods (1960-80), two were Chetris and three were upper-caste Newars. Of the five persons holding the post of Pradhan Pancha of Bhaktapur Municipality (at that time called the Nagar Panchayat) in the same period, three were upper-caste Newars and two were from the Jyapu community. The two Jyapu Pradhan Panchas (Bishnu Prasad Nepali and Babu Kaji Basukala) and another Pradhan Pancha from the upper castes (Lakhan Das Banepali) had communist backgrounds but only Basukala has retained his association with the NWPP, the communist party which has dominated Bhaktapur's politics since 1980. This shows that the local communists of Bhaktapur city had long since penetrated the local panchayat structure. They managed to reach the top posts of the city's local government not by their own strength but by playing off two factions of the local panchas against each other, one led by Madan Krishna Hada and the other by Ganesh Bahadur Khatri.

The NWPP in those days was a cadre-based underground party and its influence was mainly confined to some places of the city, i.e. Byashi *tol*. The dominant figures in the city politics were Ishwari Lal Joshi (a long-time member of the National Panchayat), Upendra Daibagya (District Chairman of *Gaun Pharka* or Back to the Village National Campaign which filled up the posts in the local government by nomination between 1975 and 1980), and Madan Krishna Hada (former member of the National Panchayat and former Pradhan Panch). All belonged to the upper-caste Newar bloc. Before the 1980 referendum, Panchayat leaders were largely co-opted by the centre and the beneficiaries in the case of Bhaktapur were the upper-caste Newars who enjoyed a status similar to that of the hill high-caste Brahmans and Chetris in the national context. The political history of Bhaktapur shows that the upper-caste Newars had long been in proximity to power in the Shah and Rana courts, in the political parties' local leaderships between 1950 and 1960, and in the Panchayat system's local leadership after 1960.

The domination of upper-caste Newars in the local politics of Bhaktapur ended suddenly after the 1980 referendum. The introduction of direct elections for the selection of leadership was a breakthrough for the emergence of a new leadership representing the majority community of Bhaktapur city. The prevalence of the Jyapu community in the local politics of Bhaktapur was further ensured after the restoration of democracy in 1990. For the last twenty years the leadership of the BM has been mostly constituted by activists of the NWPP coming from the Jyapu community (Table 3.4).

Underlying the political transformation of Bhaktapur are the changes in the social, economic, and political spheres that went against the interests of the upper-caste Newars. The Land Reform Act of 1964 and the role of the communist activists of Bhaktapur (who later, in 1975, turned into a splinter group with a new name, NWPP) in the implementation of the Act in the interest of the Jyapus was the key factor in the present social division of Bhaktapur along party political lines. The local communists of Bhaktapur backed the Jyapus at the critical hour of their conflict with the upper-caste Newars in disputes over tenancy rights and land rents. The beneficiaries were the Jyapus and the losers were the upper-caste Newars.

A leading peasant/communist activist said that the communist party (the CPN-Bhaktapur, the political ancestor of today's NWPP) launched three different peasant movements within Bhaktapur. The *Napi* (survey) movement was launched immediately after Land Reform in 1964: the implementation of the Land Reform Act started with *Napi*, the measurement of the land and registration of the names of both landowner and tenant. The activists of the CPN-Bhaktapur took an assertive role to make sure that the names of tenants were correctly recorded. A second movement called *bali katne* (forcible capture of crops) was launched in 1960-70 in order to organize peasants against landowners who evicted tenants

Table 3.4: Caste Composition of Bhaktapur Municipality Leaders

Castes	1982	1987	1992	1999	% in Total Population
Upper Castes	3 (15.78%)	3 (15.78%)	3 (15.78%)	3 (15.78%)	27.2
Jyapu	13 (68.42%)	13 (68.42%)	14 (73.68%)	15 (78.94%)	59.3
Low Castes	2 (10.52%)	2 (10.52%)	1 (5.26%)	-	7.7
Untouchable	-	-	-	-	3.2
Buddhist Newar	1 (5.26%)	1 (5.26%)	1 (5.26%)	1 (5.26%)	2.2
Non-Newar	-	-	-	-	0.4
Total	19 (100%)	19 (100%)	19 (100%)	19 (100%)	

Sources: Local election results, Bhaktapur Development Project estimates of population.

through manipulation in *Napi*. Dozens of peasants were involved in capturing crops forcibly in favour of tenants who had been illegally deprived of their tenancy rights by landowners. Third, there was the *bharpai* (receipt) movement in the 1960s: this campaign was a movement to make sure that written receipts for land rent were given to tenants by landowners. Some landowners had started to refuse to give written receipts and then used this absence of receipts as an excuse to deprive the tenants of their tenancy (interview with Jyan Bahadur Nyanchain, 27 December 2001).

Because of the party's contribution to the protection of tenancy rights at critical times the NWPP has been considered as the Jyapu party. In fact, the NWPP intensified the social cleavage between the upper castes and the Jyapus of Bhaktapur by redefining the relationship in terms of class struggle. Those who were less affected or unaffected by the Land Reform programme were principally those with occupations other than agriculture: the Buddhists, the low-caste Newars (other than Jyapus), and the Untouchables. Socio-economic cleavages have thus had a deep impact: caste and class have combined within the political equation of Bhaktapur city such that the majority community, the Jyapus, is with the NWPP and the other caste groups favour other parties. Upper-caste Newars vote for the NC (Nepali Congress, a liberal democratic and centrist party), and low castes, Untouchables, and Buddhist Newars are with the UML (Communist Party of Nepal, Unified Marxist-Leninist Party, the largest left party of Nepal). The RPP (Rashtriya Prajatantra Party, a conservative party formed by the former panchas) has some influence in all the above-mentioned caste groups.

The correlation between caste cleavages and political polarization can be illustrated by the plight of the Pwahs (Sweepers), an untouchable caste traditionally involved in raising pigs and fishing. They live in a cluster outside the city and the open spaces near their settlement are used by the Jyapus to dry paddy in October-November. The Pwahs' pigs eat the paddy during the night and the Jyapus sometimes retaliate by killing the pigs; thus there are tensions between the Pwahs and Jyapus every year during paddy drying season. Conflicts between these two groups are manifest in other forms as well. After the NWPP swept virtually all the elected posts of BM in the local election of 1982, the traditional Pwah Sweepers of the BM went on strike. The BM sacked many of them and the vacant positions were filled by people from other castes. Consequently other castes now outnumber the Pwahs in these municipal jobs: of the 196 employees working in garbage collection, only 64 are Pwahs and the other 132 are Jyapus (Dhakal & Pokharel 2005). This is one incident which helps to explain why non-Jyapu Newars prefer parties other than the NWPP.

There are some exceptions to these generalizations, which can be related to class divisions within the Jyapus dating back to the pre-land reform period. For instance, the Kumahs of Talako *tol* (an area adjoining Lakolache) are divided into two groups, the *nayo kumah*s and other *kumah*s. 'Kumah' means potter and they take the honorific surname of 'Prajapati'. Literally, *nayo kumah*s means *kumah* elders. This title refers to their position as rich landlords who had given up their traditional occupation of making clay pots. Other *kumah*s were their tenants and continued to produce clay pots. Most *nayo kumah*s have long been associated with the NC whereas other *kumah*s vote for the NWPP.

At the macro level, however, caste-based political divisions persist. The polarization of such caste-based politics of Bhaktapur city can be illustrated by the example of voting in ward number 11 of the BM in the 1997 local election. In this ward all the other parties made an alliance against the NWPP. There are sizable numbers of upper-caste Newars, Buddhist Newars, and Pwahs, in this ward. The candidate of the RPP, Dhruba Libi, was elected as the Ward Chairman by combining the support of the upper-caste voters, Buddhist Newars, and Untouchables.

Political processes have thus led to a kind of revival of caste, different in shape from the old form of social and economic stratification. This is parallel to several cases in India where caste matters less in modern social life but it is the basis of political organization (Jodhka, this volume, forthcoming). The revival of caste has led to the perpetuation of the typical psychology of Bhaktapur Newars. Each caste group of Newars sees themselves as "We" and treats other caste groups as "They"; at the same time, all Newars consider non-Newars as "Outsiders". The social psychology of 'We, They, and Outsiders' has its own impact on the politics of Bhaktapur city and in keeping the Jyapus in an advantageous position in local politics. The upper-caste Newars are divided into three hierarchical groups: Brahman, Chathariya, and Shresthas. The Untouchables have also three main castes: Jugi, Nay, and Pwah. Those whom I have referred to as low-caste Newars are the most heterogeneous, with a large number of small groups. By contrast, the Jyapus form a more homogeneous and much larger group bound by intra-caste marriage and by *guthi, bhajan*, and *dapha* organizations that provide platforms for their collective activities in cultural affairs. The Jyapus are both a coherent community and a majority group in the total population of the city. Their caste consciousness, and their assertion for political power, lie behind their domination of urban politics in Bhaktapur city. The first-past-the post electoral system provides the mechanism for transforming social strength into political power.

The gains of the Jyapus are the losses of the upper castes. As a consequence of the land reform programme, the position of many upper-caste Newar households deteriorated into the position of *kalcha sin wa manacha jaki* ('one bunch of firewood and one *mana* of rice'). This phrase is used for the upper-caste Newars who, after the implementation of the Land

Reform Act, turned into a poor class to the extent that they were unable to stock groceries for the next few days. The traditional power and position of the upper-caste Newars was also weakened by some other factors. Their primary occupation is trade and business, and this was adversely affected by the closure of the Tibetan border in 1959 and the construction of the Arniko highway linking Kathmandu with the Chinese border. Bhaktapur lost its vitality as a trade centre between the north and south and between Kathmandu and the eastern hills. Since the changes taking place in Bhaktapur do not favour the upper-caste Newars, many of them have migrated in search of better economic opportunities and career development. Following the long tradition of high-caste migration, many upper-caste Newars of Bhaktapur have moved to Kathmandu. This trend has also helped to change the political balance in Bhaktapur in favour of the Jyapus.

The Jyapus' assertion of political power is supported by both social and economic changes. They are now no longer poor and uneducated. The presence of educated Jyapus in considerable numbers means that they have leaders from their own community capable of handling posts of public responsibility. Education is considered an asset and essential factor for a person aspiring to public office. Resistance against the caste-based tradition of hierarchy and inequality, strengthening of their economic position, and a highly developed consciousness of themselves as the majority group of the city helped to place the Jyapus in a dominant position in local politics in Bhaktapur.

The NWPP, a Bhaktapur-based communist party of Nepal, is both an instrument and a beneficiary of the changes taking place in Bhaktapur. Ideologically, it professes Marxism, Leninism, and Mao Tse-Tung thought, and functionally this party is close to North Korea. Irrespective of ideology, the NWPP has built its strong base primarily through the politicization of caste and by addressing the social and economic aspirations of the Jyapus, the majority community of Bhaktapur city. It has popularized the use of the word *kisan* (the Nepali word for peasant) in place of Jyapu. The word 'Jyapu' is used continuously, but in lesser degree, by the upper-caste Newars and also by Jyapus themselves in conversation among themselves. But in inter-caste conversations or in formal contexts, a Jyapu feels hurt if a person of another caste uses this terminology. Their preference for the word *kisan*, and their rejection of *Jyapu* as a formal appellation, is an expression of their resistance to their traditionally ascribed inferior position vis-à-vis the upper-caste Newars. The NWPP, far more than any other party, has strongly cultivated the Jyapus' desire to be treated as equal citizens of the country. The NWPP has an outstanding record of making substantial contributions to the Jyapus' cause at the most important time of tenant-landowner conflicts in the 1960s. This shows that there has been a long concerted effort to organize the Jyapus politically by the local communists who later formed the NWPP. The most important contribution made by the NWPP is to build confidence among the Jyapus, hitherto a suppressed community, by providing them with opportunities to play the lead role in the political, social, and cultural affairs of the city.

CONCLUSION

In many respects Bhaktapur city today is different from the city that Levy, Parish, and others had studied. But many of the changes that I have described here were well underway when they carried out their fieldwork and could have been addressed by them. The caste system continues to function but its scope has been increasingly narrowed so that it is now limited to the practice of arranged marriages and the observance of rituals following death. Inter-caste love marriages are on the rise, posing a fundamental challenge to the existence of castes as endogamous groups determining the status of a person in society. Despite its politicization, discussed earlier, caste is, therefore, no longer the core of city life. A new form of associational life which transcends traditional caste values and custom is thriving as far-reaching changes in the social and economic spheres are translated into interpersonal relations. The pace of change is so fast that preservation and conservation have become the topmost priority of the local government of the BM. Changes in Bhaktapur city stand out in two particular aspects: (a) the change in its reputation, from that of being one of the dirtiest places in Nepal to being a model clean city; and (b) the transfer of political leadership from the traditional elite (upper-caste Newars) to the masses (Jyapus).

REFERENCES

Acharya, R. and H. Ansari. 1980. *Basic Needs and Government Services: An Area Study of Bhaktapur Town Panchayat, Nepal*. Kathmandu: Centre for Development and Administration, Tribhuvan University.

Anderson, M.M. 1998 (1971). *The Festivals of Nepal*. Delhi: Rupa and Co.

Bernier, R.M. 1970. *The Temples of Nepal*. Delhi: S. Chand and Company Ltd.

BM 2001. *Bhaktapur: A Cultural City*. Kathmandu: Bhaktapur Municipality (BM).

CBS. 1975. *Population Census 1971 (Urban Characteristics)*. Kathmandu: HMG, NPC Secretariat.

——. 1984. *Population Census 1981 (Urban Characteristics)*. Kathmandu: HMG, NPC Secretariat.

——. 1993. *Population Census 1991 (Urban Tables)*. Kathmandu: HMG, NPC Secretariat.

——. 2002. *Population Census 2001: National Report*. Kathmandu: HMG, NPC Secretariat, CBS in Collaboration with UNFPA Nepal.

——. 2003. *Population Census 2001 (Selected Urban Tables)*. Kathmandu: HMG, NPC Secretariat.

Chalise, P. 1994 (2051 V.S.). *Nepalko Prajatantrik Andolanma Bhaktapurko Bhumika (Role of Bhaktapur on Democratic Movement in Nepal)*. Kathmandu: K.L. Udaya.

Dhakal, S. and S. Pokharel. 2005. 'Local Movements, Political Processes, and the Transformation of Bhaktapur: A Case Study of Bhaktapur Municipality', ms.

Gellner, D.N. 1992. *Monk, Householder, and Tantric Priest: Newar Buddhism and Its Hierarchy of Ritual*. Cambridge: Cambridge University Press.

——. 2001a. 'Does symbolism "Construct an Urban Mesocosm"? Robert Levy's Mesocosm and the Question of Value Consensus in Bhaktapur', in D.N. Gellner, *The Anthropology of Buddhism and Hinduism: Weberian Themes*, pp. 293-315. Delhi: Oxford University Press.

——. 2001b. 'From Mandalic Sacred Centres to Communist Strongholds? On the Cities of the Kathmandu Valley', in D.N. Gellner, *The Anthropology of Buddhism and Hinduism: Weberian Themes*, pp. 276-92. Delhi: Oxford University Press.

Gellner, D.N. and D. Quigley (eds.). 1995. *Contested Hierarchies: A Collaborative Ethnography of Caste among the Newars of the Kathmandu Valley, Nepal*. Oxford: Clarendon.

Grieve, G. 2002. 'Signs of Tradition: Compiling a History of Development, Politics, and Tourism in Bhaktapur, Nepal'. *Studies in Nepali History and Society* 7 (2): 281-307.

Gutschow, N. and B. Kölver. 1975. *Ordered Space: Concepts and Functions in a Town of Nepal*. Wiesbaden: Kommissionsverlag Franz Steiner GMBH.

Haaland, A. 1982. *Bhaktapur: A Town Changing*. Kathmandu: Bhaktapur Development Project.

Hachhethu, K. 2003. 'Municipality Leadership and Governance: A Case Study of Bhaktapur', in L.R. Baral et al. *Nepal: Local Leadership and Governance*, pp. 33-72. Delhi: Adroit.

Ishii, H. 1987. 'Social Change in a Newar Village', in N. Gutschow and A. Michaels (eds.), *Heritage of the Kathmandu Valley*, pp. 336-54. Germany: VGH Wissenschaftsverlag.

Jodhka, S.S. forthcoming. 'Changing Caste and Local Democracy: Assertion and Identity among the Dalits of Rural Punjab', in D.N. Gellner and K. Hachhethu (eds.), *Local Democracy in Nepal and South Asia*.

KC, B.K. 1998. *Trends, Pattern and Implications of Rural-to-Urban Migration in Nepal*. Kathmandu: Central Department of Population Studies, Tribhuvan University.

Levy, R.I. 1990. *Mesocosm: Hinduism and the Organization of a Traditional Newar City*. Delhi: Motilal Banarsidass.

Mikesell, S.L. 1993. 'A Critique of Levy's Theory of the Urban Mesocosm'. *Contributions to Nepalese Studies* 20 (2): 231-54.

Nepali, G.S. 1988 (1965). *The Newars*. Kathmandu: Himalayan Book Sellers.

Pandey, S.R. 1985. *The Political Economy of Nepalese Land Reform*. Kathmandu: Himalayan Pioneers for Public Service and Research.

Parish, S.M. 1997 (1993). *Hierarchy and Its Discontents: Culture and Politics of Consciousness in Caste Society*. Delhi: Oxford University Press.

Rosser, C. 1966. 'Social Mobility in the Newar Caste System', in C. von Fürer-Haimendorf (ed.), *Caste and Kin in Nepal, India and Ceylon*, pp. 68-139. Bombay: Asia Publishing House.

Sharma, P. 1989. *Urbanization of Nepal*. Honolulu: East-West Centre.

Slusser, M.S. 1998 (1982). *Nepal Mandala: A Cultural Study of Kathmandu Valley*. Kathmandu: Mandala Book Point.

Vidyarthi Niketan Secondary School. 1998. *Golden Jubilee Souvenir 1998*. Bhaktapur: VNSS.

4

The Transformation of Caste Relationships in Nepal: Rethinking 'Substantialization'

HIROSHI ISHII

INTRODUCTION

This paper attempts to describe and analyse the transformation of caste relationships in the latter half of the twentieth century in Nepal.[1] The empirical data is mainly drawn from a Newar village in the Kathmandu Valley, situated to the west of Kathmandu city.[2] I will also refer briefly to a village in Dhading district inhabited by Parbatiyas.[3]

Conceptualizing Caste Relationships

Before proceeding to particular cases, it is important to try and clarify what I have in mind when I speak of a 'caste', 'caste relationships', and 'the caste system'. The caste system, in my interpretation, consists of the following three aspects:

1. A caste is a hierarchized and named social category which is "exclusive (no one belongs to more than one group)" (Bailey 1963: 121), "exhaustive (everyone belongs to some group)" (ibid.), and hereditary. (This

---

[1]I thank David Gellner for his constructive comments as well as English editing, and Katsuo Nawa for his careful editing.

[2]The Newars have traditionally made the Kathmandu Valley their homeland. Their mother tongue is Newari, one of the Tibeto-Burman languages. My main research trips were in 1970-2, 1978-9, 1984, and 1996. I made brief visits in other years also (1989, 1997, 1998, 2002, 2003, etc.).

[3]The Parbatiyas are the Hindus in the hill areas of Nepal whose mother tongue is Nepali, which is Indo-European. I carried out fieldwork in this village in 1977-8 and 1996 (see Ishii 1982, 1999).

does not mean that the boundary of each caste is clearly defined. See Mayer 1960 on this point.)

2. Following Bouglé and Dumont, I consider hierarchy, separation/repulsion, and the division of labour (based on hereditary specialization) as the main characteristics of caste relationships (Bouglé 1971: 9; Dumont 1980: 21).
3. However, I disagree with Dumont's claim that these three principles rest solely on the opposition of the pure and the impure. The pure-impure opposition is very important but it should not be considered as "a single true principle" (Dumont 1980: 43). Rather, it is one of two factors – the other being state-level political power – which integrate hierarchy, separation, and the division of labour into a system.

Thus I do not subscribe to Dumont's core notion of the disjunction of status and power nor to that of the encompassment of the politico-economic domain by religion. There is more than one dimension to caste relationships and they may be in conflict with each other. There is also more to caste relationships than religion alone.

Even in the ritual sphere, caste relationships may be contested. We will see below that Shresthas (not Brahmans) appear as the central figures in the most important festival of the Newar village I studied. This aspect, which I characterize as 'ritual-organizational', should be distinguished from the ritual hierarchy based on commensality in which the Brahman occupies the topmost position (see also Ishii 1995b: 111-14). Thus the ritual-organizational sphere and ritual hierarchy appear side by side and cannot be reduced to a single principle.

It is not easy to integrate political and economic elements into the consideration of caste relationships. But, as was clearly exemplified by the Rana regime in Nepal in the nineteenth century, the government sometimes plays a crucial role in controlling relationships between castes. At the local level, we will see that the political empowerment of one of the middle-status castes can lead to a (partial) restructuring of the commensal hierarchy. Much has been written about the correlation between economic status and hierarchy. At one end stands Dumont who admits no correlation between them and at the other are such authors as Barth (1960) and Bailey (1963) who assert and advocate the existence of "summation" .

> The simultaneous comprehensiveness and clear definition of units which characterizes caste systems results from the summation of many part-statuses into standardized clusters, or social persons, each identified with a specific caste position. Thus, in a Hindu caste system, there is a diversity of economic statuses and ritual statuses, but these are interconnected ... (Barth 1960: 113)

> Barth re stated [*sic*] ... the positive correlation between ritual status

> and politico-economic status found in the middle-ranges of the caste system. ... The summation of roles has a clear empirical connection with the co-operative element, for, ... castes have become competing political groups only in so far as political and economic roles are not [*sic*] longer clustered and the system is no longer involute. (Bailey 1963: 119)

When Srinivas writes, "It was possible for strategically located groups to move up in the local hierarchy through the capture of political power, the acquisition of land, through trade ... " (Srinivas 1996: x), he is no doubt siding with the latter authors. (Deliège 1999 may be added to them though he does not use the word 'summation'.) I also side with them but with the reservation that summation prevails in a vague way and in many cases does not extend to Brahmans (Bailey 1963: 120).

I regard the concept of the dominant caste (Srinivas 1959) as very important when analysing caste relationships. The same could be said of kingship which has been made the focal point more recently (Das 1977: 1-56; Dirks 1987; Quigley 1993: 114-69; Burghart 1996: 35-58). However, due to the limitations of my materials I will not deal either with kingship *per se* or with ascetics in this chapter. The notion of the *jajmani* relationship (Wiser 1988) is, as we will see, relevant to some extent in the Newar context, though it by no means covers the whole inter-caste division of labour (I abstain from calling it the *jajmani system*: see Fuller 1989). On the other hand, the relevance of auspiciousness (Raheja 1988) is rather low in the societies I studied; there seem to be significant cultural/regional differences within South Asia as regards this point.

Changes in vs. *Changes of the Caste System*

Anthropologists and sociologists have been dealing with changes of the caste system for more than fifty years. As early as the 1960s, Bailey pointed out the increase of competition between castes and asserted that the caste system in a true sense (i.e. in terms of his elaborate definition) had ceased to exist (Bailey 1963: 107-24). At about the same time Srinivas paid attention to "the freeing of caste from its traditional, local, and vertical matrix" and maintained that "[t]he coming into existence of new opportunities, educational, economic, and political, brought about an increase in horizontal solidarity" (Srinivas 1966: 114).

Barnett (1977: 393-416), though ethnosociologically oriented, made use of Dumont's notion of "substantialization" and wrote of a shift from a holistic hierarchical ideology to a non-holistic substantial ideology. He also understood "substantialization" as the transition from caste to "ethniclike" [*sic*] regional caste blocs. Though he stressed other interesting points, such as the need to distinguish changes among touchable and untouchable castes, his use of the term "substantialization" was rather uncritical (as we shall see below) and did not sit well with his ethnosociological preoccupations (see also David 1977 'Introduction': 42-52).

In 1996 there appeared two anthologies on caste (Fuller 1996; Srinivas 1996). The very fact of publication itself implies that the editors and authors think that it is still relevant to talk about caste. Needless to say, the changes that have occurred in the half century since caste began to be studied in the modern way have been considerable. It is noticeable, however, that contemporary authors face problems similar to those faced by authors in the mid twentieth century (or even before).

Some prominent scholars of caste, such as Srinivas, Béteille, and Mayer, have been observing changes over several decades; the former two as insiders (in terms of nationality) and the latter from outside.[4] Adrian Mayer who had studied Ramkheri in central India in 1954-6 studied it again in 1983 and 1992. Paying attention to commensality, occupation, relationship of caste, wealth, and power and the internal dimension of caste, he traces and analyses the change and continuity and points out that:

> The dominant morphology of caste is no longer primarily that of ranking, rather it is of separation; and the normative basis is less that of purity than it is of difference within which lies familial solidarity. (Mayer 1996: 62)

This is quite similar to the earlier quote from Srinivas. We will see changes parallel to it in rural changes in Nepal; being a village study what Mayer presents is highly comparable to the material I put forth in this chapter. It is necessary to add here that in his or others' studies political factors, including such elements as elections and reservations, occupy a very important place in considering caste.

Fuller, discussing Mayer's contribution to his edited volume *Caste Today*, states that "the pattern of change is consistent with Dumont's substantialization thesis that, at the ideological level, structure yields to substance and each caste becomes like a collective individual with its own distinctive culture and 'way of life'" (Fuller 1996: 12). Two pages later he refers to substantialization as "a breakdown in hierarchical interdependence between the two castes" (ibid. 14). Recently Toffin, commenting on Gellner's paper (2003) on Newar ethnicity and the rise of caste organizations among them, and referring to the rejection of old obligations by Jyapus (Maharjans), states that "[s]uch a process, called 'substantialization of caste' by Louis Dumont, is a clear indication of the progressive disintegration of the old order ... " (Toffin 2003: 135). The term substantialization thus looks highly relevant to the present issue, but a critical assessment of it is necessary before proceeding further.

---

[4] Another notable study is by Wadley (1994).

On Substantialization

In the 'Introduction' to *Contested Hierarchies: A Collaborative Ethnography of Caste among the Newars of the Kathmandu Valley*, Gellner, referring to my article, makes the following remark:

> Whichever perspective is adopted for understanding it, the traditional Newar caste order is, all agree, in a rapid process of change. Ishii (1978: 527) has noted that "intercaste cooperation and interdependence are in a process of collapse. ... [A]t the same time intracaste cohesion seems to be increasing." This is the process Dumont (1980: 227 [*sic*: the page number should be 222]) called "substantialization", the replacement of an interdependent, continually segmented hierarchy by competing internally egalitarian blocs. (Gellner 1995a: 34)

I was not unaware of Dumont's "substantialization" when I wrote the article cited but thought (and still think) that it has limited applicability, because it is heavily loaded with Dumont's own notions of structure, the caste system, and change (or rather changelessness).

In introducing the subject, Dumont goes back to Ghurye's account of changes in relation to the caste organization:

> Ghurye points out that hierarchy is attacked by the non-Brahman movement ... , notions concerning impurity being much weakened ... and the rules concerning food and drink considerably relaxed, especially in the towns. The freedom of the new professions means that the caste no longer prescribes occupation. As a counterpart, endogamy continues to hold sway with undiminished force save for certain differences of nuance ... Emphasis must be placed on the caste associations or sabha. ... The community-aspect of caste has thus been made more comprehensive, extensive and permanent. (Dumont 1980: 221)

It is noted here that recent changes in Nepal show many aspects parallel to the above points in general, though there are differences also. (I will return to this point later.) Dumont puts forward the term "substantialization" shortly after this as follows:

> In short Ghurye ... has put his finger on an essential phenomenon, which may be called the substantialization of caste. In fact a number of the features quoted together indicate the transition from a fluid, structural universe in which the emphasis is on interdependence and in which there is no privileged level, no firm units, to a universe of impenetrable blocks, self-sufficient, essentially identical and in competition with one another, a universe in which the

> caste appears as a collective *individual* (in the sense we have given to this word), as a substance. (ibid. 222; original emphasis)
>
> All this suggests, finally, that what used to be a caste *system* with a religious basis is tending to become a collection of closed groupings corresponding to modern ideas of social stratification. (ibid.: 413-14 [Note 112e]; original emphasis)

This would seem to indicate that substantialization, which can literally be paraphrased as a change "from the world of structure to the world of substance" (ibid. 40), refers to a process which can take place over a certain period of time. (This can be called "a view of substantialization as a process".) However, we encounter statements which lead us to the opposite extreme if we are to follow Dumont in a rigorous way. Having in mind changes occurring *within* Indian society from 1780 to the present day, he states:

> One thing is certain: the society as an overall framework has not changed. The castes are still present, and untouchability still effective ... [T]here has been change *in* the society and not change *of* the society. ... To say that there has been no change *of* the society is roughly to say that there has been no revolution or overall reform: a form of organization does not change, it is replaced by another; a structure is present or absent, *it does not change.* (ibid. 218-19; original emphasis)

The above statement leaves no room for substantialization to be taken as a progressive process, because a structure, according to Dumont, is only replaced by another and the transition (roughly) takes place as a revolution. Substantialization is defined, therefore, as a change crossing a categorical threshold. Thus he criticizes the theories of change of other scholars such as Srinivas and Bailey:

> But ... this alleged modification ... remains incomplete. It bears on the politico-economic domain of social life ... the politico-economic domain is encompassed in an overall religious setting. ... Everything happens as if the system tolerated change only within one of its secondary spheres. ... we would conclude that the facts they adduce display neither reinforcement [i.e. Srinivas' view: HI] nor any essential transformation [Bailey's view: HI] of the system, but only a change involving its minor areas. (Dumont 1980: 228)

Summarizing the discussion so far, Dumont's main points on the present theme can be listed as follows:

1. Substantialization is the transition from one structure to another.
2. A structure is either present or absent, it does not change (except when a revolution occurs).

3. All changes (so far observed) bear on the politico-economic domain and are therefore secondary.
4. The structure of the caste system has not changed.

If we are to follow Dumont, therefore, we have to conclude that substantialization has not actually taken place yet. Here Dumont's core notions or axioms, when combined, lead inexorably to the clear-cut conclusion that we can only talk about substantialization at a time of revolutionary social change, which could be dubbed 'the view of substantialization as a revolution'. This makes it difficult for us to use the concept as an analytical tool for dealing with social change, because it limits the possibility of substantialization being observed to very special occasions. Thus Dumont's concept is necessarily limited in its applicability. His theory is "too consistent" (Quigley 1993: 39-53) and "extreme" (Inden 1990: 203) to be analytically practical. But this is what makes Dumont's theory uniquely his.

In order to adopt the view of 'substantialization as a process', we have to either think that Dumont himself was not attentive to his axioms (namely, points 2 and 3 above) when he was talking about substantialization (which does not seem very probable), or that his axioms are unnecessary or in need of modification. In fact, point 2 above does indeed look too rigid. Dumont himself seems to have had doubts, at least to the extent of suspecting that changes might have been taking place, though in a hidden way, which could bring about such a revolution any day:

> If we are entitled to state that so far the changes that have occurred have not visibly altered what we have taken to be the heart, ... who can say but that these changes have not built up their corrosive action in the dark, and that the caste order will not one day collapse like a piece of furniture gnawed from within by termites?
> (Dumont 1980: 218-19)

Dumont is unwilling to accept genuine changes to be taking place quite overtly even when he sees changes and suspects that they may be leading to an overall reform. One wonders at this point why he could not resort to the analogy of a building having windows through which the observer can spot the changes and decay inside, instead of just imagining the activities of termites in a black-box-like piece of furniture. It would have been more productive to base judgements on visible phenomena. I would maintain, following Lévi-Strauss, that it is necessary to pay attention to "the diachronic changes of the structure" (Lévi-Strauss 1963: 309).

The above point is fundamentally related to Dumont's axioms of the disjunction of status and power and the encompassment of the politico-economic domain by religion, by resorting to which he discards every change in the politico-economic domain as irrelevant (to the main problem at least). Dumont's theory based on these concepts has been criticized by many scholars on the basis that it is too Brahman-oriented, too Orientalist, or otherwise overstated (for example: Berreman 1979: 155-63: Inden 1990: 152, 203; Quigley 1993: 37-53). I too think that Dumont has carried his perspective too far. His assertion that all changes are confined to the secondary sphere is a typical example. It is as if he has forgotten his own summary of Ghurye, including the attack on hierarchy and weakened notions concerning impurity. True, it is important and inescapable to start from the understanding of the subordination of power to status, but we should also pay attention to the aspect of their conjunction (Quigley 1993: 48) and the phase in which the politico-economic domain attains primary importance.

Now substantialization can only be understood as a process by modifying points 2 and 3 above. But, in doing so, we have to depart from Dumont's own formulations to a considerable extent. It is by downplaying his core themes that we can save the applicability of the term 'substantialization'. (Or we are returning to its more literal and wider meaning.) This could be one alternative. For example, Fitzgerald, defending Dumont and suggesting that Ambedkar's approach has something in common with Dumont's theory, gives a different interpretation to this notion. He points to "Dumont's notion of a partial shift from structure to substance at the level of caste" (1996: 286), but, as we have seen above, Dumont's theory of structure leaves no room for the notion of a 'partial shift'. Thus when Fitzgerald says "[c]astes become substantialized as political associations ... " (1996: 287), I would say he is unconsciously taking a wider and freer view of the term.

In short, if we are to use the term 'substantialization', we have to be attentive to its applicability, its connotations, and its relation to other interpretative notions.

SATUNGAL

In this section I try to give a summary picture of how caste relationships have changed in Satungal, a Newar village about 7 km to the west of Kathmandu. I have written on related themes in relation to this village in several places.[5] I will add new materials of the changes from the mid 1980s and a new analysis, though some overlap in the data presented is inevitable.

This village used to depend mainly on paddy, wheat, and other crops

[5]See Ishii (1978, 1980, 1986, 1987, 1993, 1995a, 1995b, 1999). I will not list my publications in Japanese here. My other publications on this village in English, plus one Japanese article, are listed in Ishii (2001).

but has changed its occupational structure considerably in recent years. There have been big improvements in amenities. For example, electricity reached the village in 1971 and I found from my survey that more than half of the households had TV sets in 1996. In the same year about two thirds of the households had toilets though there were none in 1970. New factories, schools, and many shops have been built within the village area which draw many people from outside.

Table 4.1 shows the main castes of the village, their household numbers and population and the figures for 'temporary residents' in 1970, 1978, 1984, and 1996. The increase in temporary residents in recent years is quite noticeable. It also shows that the population increase of the more populous castes has been considerable unlike the castes with smaller populations (for example, compare the Shresthas and the Maharjans to the Khadgis). This

Table 4.1: Number of Households and Population

	1970			1978		
	Number of households	Population	Average household members	Number of households	Population	Average household members
Brahman	1	4	4.0	1	4	4.0
Shrestha	63	389	6.2	68	466	6.9
Maharjan	100	568	5.7	116	705	6.1
Putuwar	10	41	4.1	8	49	6.1
Nakarmi	1	9	9.0	1	10	10.0
Manandhar	1	8	8.0	1	10	10.0
Khadgi	17	100	5.9	17	109	6.4
Kapali	1	2	2.0	1	1	1.0
Others						
Temporary residents	0	0	0.0	4	17	4.3
Total	194	1121	5.8	217	1371	6.3

	1984			1996		
	Number of households	Population	Average household members	Number of households	Population	Average household members
Brahman	1	6	6.0	1	3	3.0
Shrestha	90	551	6.1	122	714	5.9
Maharjan	133	782	5.9	180	986	5.5
Putuwar	9	52	5.8	13	64	4.9
Nakarmi	1	10	10.0	2	13	6.5
Manandhar	1	9	9.0	1	10	10.0
Khadgi	18	115	6.4	20	138	6.9
Kapali	1	1	1.0	1	5	5.0
Others	1	8	8.0	3	22	7.3
Temporary residents	6	17	2.8	137	275	2.0
Total	261	1551	5.9	480	2230	4.6

Source: Author's own fieldwork.

may be related to the difference in their socio-economic conditions, though it is hard to be definitive on this point.

Shrestha Dominance and How It Has Changed

The Shresthas have been the dominant caste in this village since at least the latter part of the Rana period (1846-1951), though their position has been wavering in these decades as we shall see later.[6] Two (maximal) Shrestha lineages are said to be the descendants of the founder of the village who, they say, was given land here by the king of Patan (Lalitpur, a town south of Kathmandu; Satungal was once included in Lalitpur *ilaka* [district].) and later invited Maharjans (Jyapus) to work for them.[7] The practice of inviting service castes to settle has continued even until recent years; the latest is the case of a Napit (Barber) family who came to Satungal around 1989. A Nakarmi (Blacksmith) family and a Brahman family came in the 1950s. The Brahmans came from Patan and the Nakarmis and Napits from Kirtipur (a town two kilometers to the east of Satungal). These three castes already had service relations with Satungal villagers before they moved in and were provided with rooms or houses on their arrival. A Manandhar family came also from Kirtipur in the 1940s. But unlike others, they have had no caste-specific relation with the villagers (see below).

Shrestha elders preside over the important festivals of the village including the Vishnudevi[8] and Mohani (Dasain) festivals. The responsibility for holding these festivals falls to these elders together with the relevant *guthi*s (organizations with a hereditary membership whose main purpose is carrying out ritual matters).[9] Appointed because of their seniority within

---

[6]There are two Licchavi inscriptions in this village including Amsuvarman's which attest to the antiquity of the settlement (Vajracharya 2030 v.s. (1973): 196-7, 263-5) but it is not possible to relate the present residents to anything written there.

[7]For 'maximal lineage', see Ishii 1995b: 137-40.

[8]'Vishnudevi' is a local name for Vaishnavi, one of the seven or eight mother goddesses. For the organization of the festival, see Ishii 1978.

[9]The *guthi*s in this village are divided into two kinds, namely, the funeral *guthi*s or *sana-guthi*s, on the one hand, and those relating to festivals and some important rituals on the other (for the former, see Ishii 1996). The names of the *guthi*s in the latter category are: Silan *guthi*, Mahadip *guthi*, Mari *guthi*, Arati *guthi*, Gahsi *guthi*, Mohani *guthi*, Marthi Amai *guthi*, Yenya Punhi *guthi*, Salhu *guthi*, Bhindyah *guthi*, Krishna *guthi*, Buddha Punhi *guthi*, and Sora Shraddha *guthi*. Each *guthi*, except the Buddha Punhi *guthi* (which is comparatively new), is an mono-caste organization and the members of the *guthi*s in this category excepting the cases mentioned below are Shresthas. The first five of the above are the *guthi*s related to the Vishnudevi festival, among which the Gahsi *guthi* consists of Maharjans only. Plural *guthi*s of the same name are found within the village in the cases of Salhu *guthi* and Sora Sraddha *guthi*; there are Salhu *guthi*s among the Shresthas, Maharjans, and Khadgis, and Sora Shraddha *guthi*s among the Shresthas and Maharjans. They are all intra-caste *guthi*s. Activities in most of the Salhu *guthi*s (to go to worship the Red Matsyendranath monthly) have declined in recent years.

the (maximal) lineages that happen to be the original settlers of the village, these elders enjoy very prestigious positions. They are said to 'become god (*dyah*)'[10] during the sacrificial rituals of the Vishnudevi festival and Mohani. Even though a village Brahman participates, it is not considered that he 'becomes god'. He only plays an instrumental role in executing necessary rituals. The central figures in the festivals are the Shrestha elders.

In the Rana period, there was a village functionary called *dware*, which roughly corresponded to the village head. Though there were exceptions, *dware*s used to be appointed by the government from among the Shresthas. *Thari*s were elders whose role was to support the *dware*. It is said that originally they were appointed by the government, but from a certain point their position became hereditary and to this day the senior-most elder of each of the five prestigious (maximal) lineages of the Shresthas has assumed the *thari* role (which is limited to ritual).

This structure of Shrestha dominance has changed to a considerable extent due to the modernization of Nepal after 1951, especially by the introduction of elections to the village in the 1960s. Broadly speaking, this gave power to numerically larger groups, though other factors such as education, economic condition, and human relations were also important. In short, the Maharjans, who in this village were the most numerous, grew confident and began to reject their subordinate status to the Shresthas by withdrawing from some of their caste-specific roles, sometimes acting in cooperation with other castes. This led to changes in various ritual organizations as well as in day-to-day relations which caused the villagers to complain that village harmony had been destroyed (*ga milay ma jula*).

In the Panchayat era (1962-90) the village head (Pradhan Panch) was elected by either direct or indirect election (see Ishii 1986, 1987). This village constituted one administrative village (except for a short period after the late 1970s) together with a neighbouring village B, the majority of whose population are Maharjans. It was quite common for kin and caste mates to act collectively at the time of elections, though fission and antagonisms leading to intra-caste factions or group coalitions across caste boundaries were not rare. Against this background, the leading factions of the Shresthas and the Maharjans in this village confronted each other, at the same time trying to get support from people in the neighbouring village, sometimes physically confronting and hurting their opponents. Largely speaking, the confrontation was the severest in the 1960s and 1970s (see Ishii 1986, 1987). But the intensity of the conflict has cooled mainly due to the Maharjan leader's (and his family's) loss of prestige (because of the arrest of his son for theft) and the coalition of the Shrestha mainstream and the anti-mainstream groups of Maharjans. The emergence of active figures

---

[10] It is not specified what kind of god they become.

of a new generation was also a factor that accelerated this trend. Thus, in the elections for village head in the 1980s, the Shrestha mainstream elder (the topmost elder in terms of lineage prestige, generation, and age) and a young Maharjan leader who was on good terms with the mainstream Shresthas were elected in succession. After that, the Shrestha elder retired from political activity (while continuing to fulfil his ritual roles and to act voluntarily in socio-religious activities). Meanwhile the old Maharjan leader's household split, which decreased its centripetal potential. Younger leaders no longer confronted each other as their predecessors had and, as we shall see, the two castes have come closer to each other in some respects.

This situation was made more fluid by the democratization of 1990, which made political parties legal and changed the Village Panchayat into the Gau Vikas Samiti or Village Development Committee. Political parties rather than castes and kin became the focus of attention in people's political alignments. When I asked about the situation of socio-political opposition between castes in 1996, people referred to the Shrestha-Maharjan quarrel as a matter of the past. What was talked about instead was who supported which party. The picture of political alignments was no longer so clear-cut. People of different castes appeared among supporters of each national party. Some close relatives were found to support different parties and even former opponents were named as supporters of the same party. It was not unusual for people to change party affiliations.

The constitutional reforms of 1990 permitted the freedom of association and numerous voluntary associations sprang up all over the country. In this village the formation of 'youth clubs' has been particularly noticeable. So far three clubs have been formed and registered. Having around fifty to eighty members who pay membership fees, they claim to (and to some extent actually do) carry out various social activities such as the construction and repair of public buildings, public health service, adult education, enforcement of public discipline (control of gambling, drinking, etc.), and in some cases the promotion of sports. Some try to raise money by resorting to nearby companies, NGOs, and individuals including politicians, but a shortage of money is one of their chronic problems. Most of their members are from the Shrestha and Maharjan castes of this village though a few members from other castes can also be found. Each club has a chairman, other officials, and a steering committee but no caste monopoly can be observed concerning the positions. On the other hand, it is not rare to hear that the three clubs are related to three main political parties; the Nepali Congress, the Communist Party of Nepal (UML), and the National Democratic Party (RPP). This perception depends mainly upon the party affiliation of those who occupy the leading positions. These affiliations are by no means fixed. Due to the unstable political situation, individual profit motives, sometimes induced from outside, and changes in personal relationships, people shift their affiliation rather freely. There seems to be more scope for individual choices than before, though traditional social constraints have by no means disappeared. Overall the former Shrestha dominance (in the political sphere) has metamorphosed into a loose Shrestha-Maharjan combination divided into party alliances. Other small (especially low) castes are left in a situation where they face a larger (but less solid) dominant layer (i.e. the Shresthas and Maharjans).

Occupational Change

After 1951, Nepal took the path of economic development and modernization. Agricultural development, including land reform, proceeded in the Kathmandu Valley. This village was no exception. Old forms of land tenure such as *birta*[11] and *rakam*[12] were abolished resulting in the alleviation of farmers' burdens. In the mid 1960s the village saw an increase in the production of rice and wheat due to the introduction of high-yield varieties and chemical fertilizers. At the same time the number of villagers employed in the city increased and this accelerated the development of a cash economy. Accordingly, traditional systems of agricultural labour exchange declined and were replaced by hired labourers. The development of communication and education, symbolized by the introduction of radio (1951) and TV (1985) broadcasting, and the penetration of school education, has affected people's ways of thinking and behaviour.[13]

Tables 4.2 and 4.3 show the primary occupations of males above the age of fifteen in 1970 and 1996 respectively. Table 4.4 contains the graphs of the proportion of the male population in the main occupational categories, and Table 4.5 shows the change of the proportion of the number of households combining agriculture with other work at four points between 1970 and 1996. This data shows that even in 1970 more than half of the adult males in Satungal had jobs other than agriculture as their primary occupation, and that about two thirds of the households combined agriculture with other work. The main categories of non-agricultural occupations are construction work, commerce, and employment in various sectors.

Up to 1984, there was a small and gradual increase in construction work, and the overall change was also gradual. The proportion of the non-agricultural households in 1970, 1978, and 1984 stayed at the level of

---

[11] Land grants made by the state to individuals, usually on an inheritable and tax-exempt basis; abolished in 1959 (Regmi 1976: 233).

[12] Unpaid and compulsory labour services due to the government from peasants cultivating *raikar* (including *jagir*), *kipat*, and *raj guthi* lands; abolished in 1963 (Regmi 1976: 235).

[13] See Ishii 1980 and 1993 for the economic change in this village between 1970 and 1978, and the change of agricultural labour recruitment.

Table 4.2: Primary Occupations of Males above 15 (Satungal 1970)

Occupational categories		*Br	Shr	Mhj	Ptw	Nkm	Mdr	Kdg	Total
Construction work	Contractors (Thekdar)		1	1					2
	Carpenters (Sikarmi)		13	1					14
	Brickmasons (Dakarmi)		4	23	1				28
	NCCN⁺ (Brickmasons etc.)		1	5					6
	Labourers†		6	18	2			1	27
	Total		25	48	3			1	77
	Percentage		24.3%	29.3%	27.3%			3.2%	24.5%
Commerce	Shopkeepers/-tenders#		8			1	1	(1)	10
	Grain merchants		6	4					10
	Milk sellers		2	1					3
	Firewood sellers			2	3			8	13
	Yoghurt sellers		3	8	2				13
	Total		19	15	5	1	1	8	49
	Percentage		18.4%	9.1%	45.5%	50%	50%	25.8%	15.6%
Employees in government offices and others	Government and municipal offices		8	3					11
	Teachers		1	1					2
	Gardeners			3					3
	Army		1						1
	Ropeway (to carry loads)		4	7				8	19
	Migrant workers			1					1
	Technical trainees (paid)			2					2
	Total		14	17				8	39
	Percentage		13.6%	10.4%				25.8%	12.4%
Others	Caste-specific occupations (including priests)$^{\Delta}$	1				(1)		5	6
	Domestic helpers		2	1					3
	Music teachers			1					1
	Owners of water mills							2	2
	Total	1	2	2				7	12
	Percentage	100%	1.9%	1.2%				22.6%	3.8%
Agriculture, students, no outside job			43	82	3	1	1	7	137
	Total		43	82	3	1	1	7	137
	Percentage		41.7%	50.0%	27.3%	50.0%	50.0%	22.6%	43.6%
Grand total		1	103	164	11	2	2	31	314

Source: Author's own fieldwork.

Notes: *Abbreviations of caste names: Br = Brahman, Shr = Shrestha, Mhj = Maharjan, Ptw = Putuwar, Nkm = Nakarmi, Mdr = Manandhar, Npt = Napit, Kdg = Khadgi, Kp = Kapali

⁺National Construction Company of Nepal

† Including those who work as agricultural labourers in farming seasons. Labourers who only engage in agriculture are classified in 'Agriculture'.

A Khadgi owns a meat shop in the village, which is shown in brackets. He is included in the number of 'Others - Caste specific occupations'. Two tailors (Damais) who commute from outside are not included in this table.

$^{\Delta}$ A Nakarmi (Blacksmith) works in his smithy. In this table, he is counted among the 'Shopkeepers/-tenders'.

Table 4.3: Primary Occupations of Males above 15 (Satungal 1996)

Occupational categories		Br	Shr	Mhj	Ptw	Nkm	Mdr	Npt	Kdg	Kp	Total
Construction work	Contractors (Thekdar)		1	10	1						12
	Carpenters (Sikarmi)		8	11	2				1		22
	Brickmasons (Dakarmi)		8	36	1				2		47
	Labourers *		9	11	4				2		26
	Total	0	26	68	8	0	0	0	5	0	107
	Percentage	0%	10.8%	20.9%	42.1%	0%	0%	0%	13%	0%	16.7%
Commerce	Shopkeepers/-tenders+		47	31		1	2		(20)		81
	Grain merchants		0	2							2
	Milk Sellers			0							0
	Firewood sellers								1		1
	Land Merchants		2	5							7
	Factory owners, etc.†		7	2							9
	Total	0	56	40	0	1	2	0	1	0	100
	Percentage	0%	23.2%	12.3%	0%	25%	40.0%	0%	2.6%	0%	15.6%
Employees in government offices and others	Government and municipal offices		13	7	2						22
	Teachers		4	3							7
	Army			2							2
	Gardeners		1								1
	Salt trading company			4					3		7
	Private enterprises, shops, or factories		30	28	5					1	64
	Total	0	48	44	7	0	0		3	1	103
	Percentage	0%	19.9%	13.5%	36.8%	0%	0%	0%	7.7%	100%	16.1%
Others	Caste-specific occupations					2		4	21		27
	Drivers, conductors, driving assistants		16	21					2		39
	Hand-cultivator driver			1							1
	Moneylenders			1							1
	Tax collectors			1							1
	Tailoring (New)		3	3							6
	Weaving		2	3		1					6
	Poultry farming			3							3
	Landlords (= House owners)		16	16							32
	Politicians, village chief		3								3
	Total	0	40	49	0	3	0	4	23	0	119
	Percentage	0%	16.6%	15.0%	0%	75%	0%	100%	59.0%	0%	18.6%
Agriculture	Agriculture only		25	75					3		103
	Agricultural labourers or Attached labourers		1	2	1						4
	Total	0	26	77	1	0	0	0	3	0	107
	Percentage	0%	10.8%	23.6%	5.3%	0%	0%	0%	7.7%	0%	16.7%
Students	High school, college	1	39	46	1		3		3		93
	Total	1	39	46	1	0	3	0	3	0	93
	Percentage	100%	16.2%	14.1%	5.3%	0%	60.0%	0%	7.7%	0%	14.5%
No outside job			6	2	0				1		9
	Total	0	6	2	0	0	0	0	1	0	9
	Percentage	0%	2.5%	0.6%	0%	0%	0%	0%	3%	0%	1.4%
Unknown					2						
	Total	0	0	0	2	0	0	0	0	0	2
	Percentage	0%	0%	0%	10.5%	0%	0%	0%	0%	0%	0.3%
Grand total		1	241	326	19	4	5	4	39	1	640

Source: Author's own fieldwork.

Notes:* Including those who work as agricultural labourers in farming seasons. Labourers who only engage in agriculture are classified under 'Agriculture'.

+ They work in grocery shops, tea shops, cloth shops, vegetable shops, meat shops, etc. Twenty Khadgis (Kdg) are shopkeepers/-tenders of meat shops: they are counted in 'Others - Caste Specific Occupations'. Eleven among them work in the village and nine outside.

† Furniture factories, brick, rice/flour mills, owners of vehicles.

Table 4.4: Changing Occupations of Males above 15 in Satungal

	1970	1978	1984	1996
A. Construction work	24.5%	22.0%	26.3%	16.7%
B. Commerce	17.2%	18.2%	10.9%	15.6%
C. Employees in government offices and others	12.4%	10.6%	17.1%	16.1%
D. Others	2.2%	6.0%	11.6%	18.6%
E. Agriculture		33.7%	23.8%	16.7%
F. Students	43.6% (E+F+G)	6.8%	6.5%	14.5%
G. No outside job		2.7%	3.8%	1.4%
H. Unknown	-	-	-	0.3%

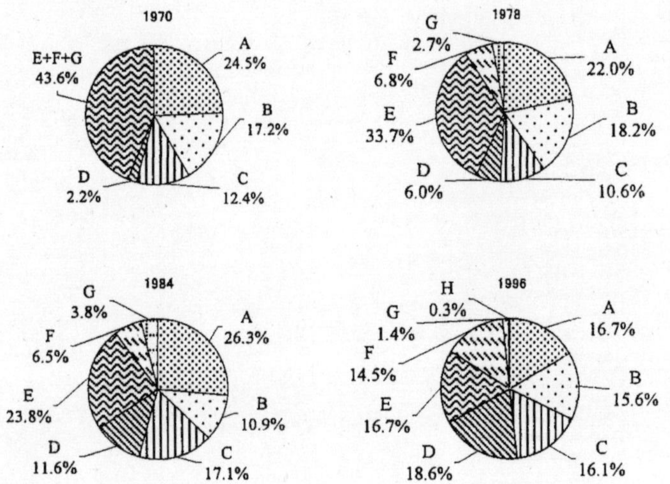

Source: Author's own fieldwork.

Graphs for Table 4.4

a little more than 6 per cent; more than 93 per cent of all households engaged in agriculture to some extent. In those years, though there were many non-agricultural jobs, agriculture still occupied the main place in the villagers' livelihood. This situation changed greatly in the mid 1980s. The single most important factor was the establishment of factories in the village. Table 4.6 lists the factories together with the information about the owners, number of employees, and the year of establishment. It shows that many of them were introduced within a rather short period, that the larger factories were owned by outside entrepreneurs, and that only small factories belonged to the locals. The main factors that facilitated the establishment of factories in Satungal were the government's policy of economic deregulation, the geographical conditions of this area (the existence of plain land, closeness to the capital with a convenient road access), and comparatively lower land prices and taxes. The entrepreneurs bought many acres of land in the village. Villagers who sold their lands sought other ways to earn their living; some bought cars or trucks, some built houses, and others opened shops or tried to acquire other jobs.

Dependence on agriculture declined and the number of people working in other sectors increased. It was noticeable that comparatively few villagers went to work in the factories; fewer than seven per cent of all the employees of the factories (24 out of 400) were from this village (of these eleven were female, mostly young). Villagers might or might not work within the village, but many tended to avoid the big factories which were mostly run by Marwaris whom they regarded as foreigners (despite the fact that they may well have had Nepali citizenship). The aspiration for higher salaries and more freedom in work were reasons cited for working elsewhere. Taking up new occupations, including opening shops, was commonplace.

Employees in the factories included people from nearby villages, Nepalis from distant areas, and some Indians. Most of them lived in or near the village and rented rooms from the locals. Thus many villagers (90 in 1996) became landlords, often constructing new houses or reconstructing their houses for the purpose. Most of them have other jobs and only for one third of them does the rental constitute their primary income.

In 1996, the proportion of adult males in each of the six occupational categories (including 'students') was almost equal; those with agriculture as their primary occupation were thus only one sixth of the adult male

Table 4.5: Changes in the Proportion of Agricultural and Non-Agricultural Households in Satungal

	Number of agricultural households				Number of households combining agriculture and other jobs				Number of non-agricultural households			
	1970	1978	1984	1996	1970	1978	1984	1996	1970	1978	1984	1996
Brahman	0	0	0	0	0	0	0	0	1	1	1	1
Shrestha	15	15	13	8	44	49	71	87	4	4	6	26
Maharjan	35	27	22	27	63	86	106	127	2	3	5	26
Putuwar	2	2	0	0	7	6	9	6	1	0	0	7
Nakarmi	0	0	0	0	0	0	0	0	1	1	1	2
Manandhar	0	0	0	0	1	1	1	1	0	0	0	0
Napit	0	0	0	0	0	0	0	0	0	0	0	2
Khadgi	0	1	0	0	13	15	16	10	4	1	2	9
Kapali	1	1	1	0	0	0	0	0	0	0	0	1
Others	0	0	0	0	0	1	0	0	0	3	1	1
Total	53	46	36	35	128	158	203	231	13	13	16	75
Percentage	27.3%	21.2%	13.8%	10.3%	66.0%	72.8%	77.8%	67.7%	6.7%	6.0%	6.1%	22.0%

Source: Author's own fieldwork.

Table 4.6: Registered Factories in Satungal Development Committee

Types of industries	Establishment Year	Number of employees (Satungal villagers in parentheses)	Owners*
Vegetable oil processing	1984	50 (5)	M
Plastic sheets manufacture	1985	7 (0)	M
Corrugated iron	1986	83 (6)	M
Textile (polyester)	1988	16 (3 - including 1 woman)	M
Match factory	1989	40+ (6 - including 4 women)	N
Textile (polyester)	1989	27 (0)	N
Juice factory	1989	35 (0)	M
Tile production	1990	31 (0)	N
Peanuts processing	1991	28 (6 - all women)	M
Wool importer (warehouse)	1991	15 (0)	P
Plastic pipe	1991	9 (0)	N
Iron galvanizing	1993	16 (0)	N
Electric wire	1995	35 (0)	M+N
Electric bulb†	1995	–	M
Magnesite warehouse	(Only purchased land)		

Source: Author's own fieldwork.

Notes: M: Marwari (with Nepalese citizenship), P: Parbatiya, N: Newar

* All from outside.

+ An approximate.

† Soon closed down by the government order.

population. It should be noted that there are many households which continue to have agriculture as their secondary or tertiary occupation. The number of non-agricultural households had increased greatly by 1996 but it was still 22 per cent (Table 4.5). Furthermore, the numbers in Tables 4.2–4.5 do not include the temporary residents shown in Table 4.1. If we take them into account, the proportion of those reliant on non-agricultural work in the population will be much higher.

Almost all the temporary residents in 1996 were non-agricultural workers (though we have to note that in the busy agricultural seasons agricultural labourers came from outside and stayed in the village). Temporary residents generally do not stay for long. Less than one third of the temporary residents had been in Satungal for more than three years. Some of them had been in Satungal for several years (none had stayed more than eight years). As for their places of origin, just about a half of them were from the hill areas ranging from Bajhang in the far west to Dharan (Sunsari district) in the east. The other half were again divided into two groups (of approximately the same size), namely, from the Kathmandu Valley and Tarai-India. Most of the people in the last category are from the Nepalese Tarai east of Bhairahawa. It is noteworthy that there were seventeen people from Jhapa district (in the south-east corner of Nepal) and fifteen from India (Bihar, etc.).

Among the temporary residents, all the adult males, a little less than half of the adult females, and a few of the children were working for money. The rest of the adult females were housewives. About a half of those working were hired by factories, companies, or schools (as teachers) nearby or in Kathmandu. Some people commuted to Kathmandu by bus every day. Twenty per cent of those working were engaged in commerce either running shops, as hired workers in others' shops, or as middlemen. There were some construction workers (6.3 per cent), motor (taxi, minibus, and truck) drivers (3.4 per cent), a few menial workers, and one owner of a motorcycle workshop.

There was a clear disproportion in the age and gender breakdowns in 1996. Only thirty per cent of the temporary residents were women and the number of children, (e.g. under fifteen) was less than 20 per cent. Most of the males were in their twenties and thirties and there were about thirty males over forty and just a few over fifty. As might be deduced from the gender disproportion, many were living with their kin and/or friends, though there were also married couples with children.

It should be noted that 14 per cent of the working temporary residents were engaged in their caste-specific occupations as gold- and silversmiths, blacksmiths, tailors, or barbers. The largest group among them (70 per cent of these caste-specific temporary migrants) were the gold- and silversmiths. There was a big group of twelve people consisting of one couple (in their early thirties) with two children and their kin, neighbours, and friends who were all males between the ages of fourteen and twenty-seven. They came from Dolakha district in 1995 and rented rooms from a Khadgi in the village. They used them as workshop to make gold and silver ornaments to order and had not opened a shop. Among the rest there were three tailors, two barbers, and one blacksmith. The barbers were from Siraha district in the Tarai.

There was another big group of nine males who were said to be friends. Coming from Dharan in 1995, the group consisted of seven Rai males between fourteen and eighteen, a Shrestha aged seventeen, and a Brahman who was thirty-one years old. They rented rooms from a Putuwar and worked in a carpet factory. Their education level was rather low. Many of them quit school after the third or fifth grade and none of them had passed SLC. Big groups like these, however, are rather the exception. Most of the temporary residents live in groups of two to several people or alone.

Villagers including the landlords are mostly indifferent to their 'neighbour' temporary residents. In some cases they don't even know the surnames of the people to whom they rent their rooms.[14] This contrasts

---

[14]These days landlords can no longer be ignorant of the names of the house/room renters as, according to David Gellner, a police regulation was issued in 2003 that all landlords had to record this information (so that they could check up on Maoists moving into the Valley).

clearly with their traditional intra-village relationships, which are dense, intimate, and sometimes complicated.

In the winter, when some of the agricultural lands are turned into brick factories financed by outside entrepreneurs, many seasonal labourers flow in to work. Most of them live in small temporary huts built near the kilns only during the dry season when bricks are made. These people (numbering about two hundred), along with others who visit or pass through the village are customers of the shops run by residents here or people from outside.

In 1996, I counted 140 shops, selling miscellaneous goods, tea, cloth, vegetables, meat, iron goods, etc.; by way of contrast, in 1970 there were thirteen shops including six grocery shops (two of which also dealt with cloth and timber), three tea shops, a meat shop, a smithy, and two (traditional) tailor shops run by outside Damais commuting to the village.

Since 'students' form one of the 'employment' categories used above, let us take a brief look at education. In order to construct Tables 4.7 and 4.8 I have used the term 'school-literacy rate', which is defined as the proportion of the people who either are attending school, or have attended it, or who can read and write without having been to school. Table 4.7 shows that this rate increased from 24 per cent in 1970 to 68 per cent in 1996. Gender differences remained substantial: in 1996 the rate for the females was 52 per cent whereas that for males was 83 per cent. Both caste and gender differences are evident in Table 4.8. Excluding the category 'Others' (where the number is too small for the tendency to be apparent), there is a high correlation between school-literacy rates and the caste hierarchy: the line for Shresthas is found at the top followed by the lines for Maharjans, Khadgis, and Putuwars. One should note also that these lines do not cross each other, which shows that there have been general improvements across the board which have left the correlation of caste and literacy undisturbed. The lines for females also go up towards the right but most of the female lines are below those of males (including those of the lower castes). Caste difference still prevails, but gender difference is even greater.

Table 4.7: School-literacy Rate above 6 (Satungal)

	1970		1978		1984		1996	
Male	201	45.3%	327	55.9%	476	68.5%	724	83.2%
Female	61	14.4%	86	16.4%	164	25.7%	451	52.2%
Total	262	23.6%	413	37.2%	640	48.0%	1175	67.8%

Source: Author's own fieldwork.

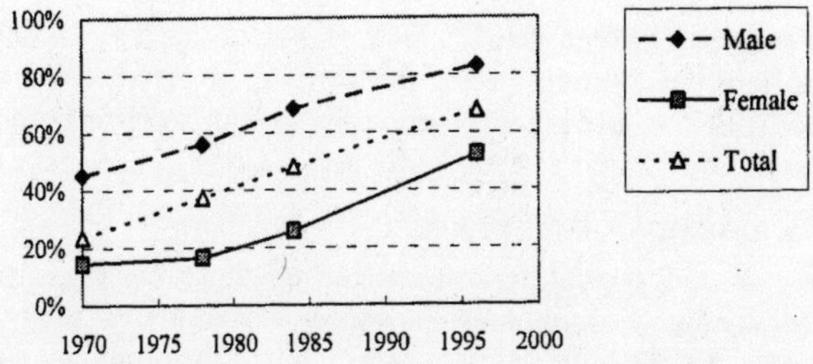

Source: Author's own fieldwork.

Graph for Table 4.7.

Table 4.8: School-literacy Rate above 6 by Caste

	1970	1978	1984	1996
Shr M	49.4%	71.9%	76.5%	91.6%
Shr F	16.8%	30.2%	39.7%	62.6%
Mhj M	47.1%	54.4%	68.0%	79.4%
Mhj F	12.6%	6.3%	16.8%	46.0%
Kdg M	23.3%	37.5%	50.0%	73.7%
Kdg F	0.0%	2.2%	17.9%	37.5%
Ptw M	6.7%	26.3%	42.3%	66.7%
Ptw F	29.4%	5.3%	15.8%	63.0%
Others M	71.4%	75.0%	66.7%	80.0%
Others F	41.7%	75.0%	45.0%	47.8%

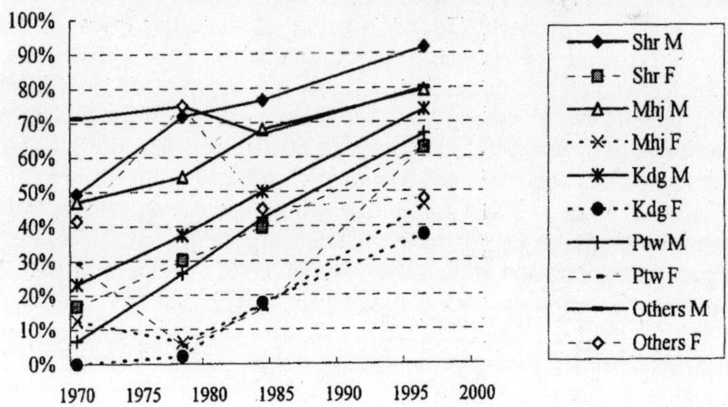

Source: Author's own fieldwork.

Graph for Table 4.8.

Actual Occupations and Caste-Specific Occupations: Correlations

The relationships between actual jobs and stereotypical caste occupations are not uniform; with some castes the correlation between them is high, with others it is low, and in yet other cases it is not so clear because of the ambiguous nature of their caste-specific occupations.

SHRESTHA, MAHARJAN, PUTUWAR

The Shresthas are typical representatives of those castes whose caste-specific occupation is ambiguous. As we have seen above, they were (and still are, especially in formal ritual organizations) the dominant caste in the village. In other words "their traditional function is to patronize other groups" (Quigley 1995: 80). As for their caste-specific occupations, people may list, for the sake of convenience, landowners, bureaucrats, shopkeepers, etc. In rural areas it is taken for granted that landownership is the most basic factor for patronage to prevail. The fact that the Shresthas still pass on the legend about their ancestor being given land by the king of Lalitpur suggests the importance of landownership with regard to their position (at least in their own self-image).

The present landownership and occupational structure does not indicate Shrestha dominance in any straightforward way. In almost all these spheres, the Shresthas face competition from other castes, especially the Maharjans. In landownership (Table 4.9), the two castes are not very different though the proportion of those who own no or only a little land is slightly higher among the latter. Most of the landowners are farmers and many of them combine agriculture with other jobs (seasonally, throughout the year, or by having some household members work outside). Partly because of this, it has become a common practice to hire agricultural labourers (mostly from outside) when there is high demand for it. In the past, labour exchange prevailed to a larger extent (Ishii 1993). The Maharjans are known in Newar society as the farmer caste and many of them do indeed practise agriculture but, as Table 4.9 shows, they do not have a monopoly. However, when we look at the occupations of the Shresthas and the Maharjans, we notice that there is a certain tendency which differentiates them. Both Shresthas and Maharjans are found in the same categories of work in Tables 4.2 and 4.3, but in terms of percentage, nearly twice as many Shresthas are employed in government offices, companies, etc., and engage in commerce. On the other hand, more Maharjans are found in the category of construction work and agriculture. The tendency and difference of this kind did not decline between 1970 and 1996. Rather, in some cases such as construction work, the difference has become larger. Thus, even though it is only as a general tendency, stereotypical caste occupations and functions continue to have some relevance in the actual choice of jobs. It can be added that the Putuwars are comparable to the Maharjans of the lower economic stratum as far as the present point is concerned.

Table 4.9: Landholding by Caste

(*unit: household*)

1970

Area (ropani)	Br	Shr	Mhj	Ptw	Nkm	Mdr	Kdg	Kp
0	1	6	11	3	1	0	10	0
0-5	0	14	35	3	0	1	7	1
5.0-10.0	0	24	29	3	0	0	0	0
10.0-20.0	0	12	19	1	0	0	0	0
20.0-30.0	0	4	4	0	0	0	0	0
30.0-	0	3	2	0	0	0	0	0
Total	1	63	100	10	1	1	17	1

1978

Area (ropani)	Br	Shr	Mhj	Ptw	Nkm	Mdr	Kdg	Kp
0	1	3	10	4	1	0	10	0
0-5	0	27	48	1	0	0	7	1
5.0-10.0	0	17	34	2	0	1	0	0
10.0-20.0	0	15	19	1	0	0	0	0
20.0-30.0	0	4	4	0	0	0	0	0
30.0-	0	2	1	0	0	0	0	0
Total	1	68	116	8	1	1	17	1

1984

Area (ropani)	Br	Shr	Mhj	Ptw	Nkm	Mdr	Kdg	Kp
0	0	11	8	2	1	0	7	1
0-5	0	38	53	5	0	0	8	0
5.0-10.0	0	23	45	1	0	1	3	0
10.0-20.0	0	16	22	1	0	0	0	0
20.0-30.0	0	1	4	0	0	0	0	0
30.0-	0	1	1	0	0	0	0	0
Total	0	90	133	9	1	1	18	1

1996

Area (ropani)	Br	Shr	Mhj	Ptw	Nkm	Mdr	Npt	Kdg
0	1	29	31	5	2	0	2	9
0-5	0	66	88	7	0	0	0	8
5.0-10.0	0	23	45	1	0	1	0	2
10.0-20.0	0	7	14	0	0	0	0	0
20.0-30.0	0	1	0	0	0	0	0	0
30.0-	0	0	1	0	0	0	0	0
Total	1	126	179	13	2	1	2	19

Source: Author's own fieldwork.

SERVICE CASTES

Most of the service castes (whose population is small) show a high correlation of stereotyped and actual occupations. Some of them retain *jajmani*-type relations but some have turned to cash payments.

The Brahman gives religious and ritual services, mainly to the Shrestha households, in several important festivals carried out by the relevant *guthi*s or ritual organizations, and on some occasions to the village in general (for example reciting religious stories during the monsoon season in the village square), though on some occasions they serve the Maharjans also. For his role relating to the *guthi*s, he receives a stipulated amount of grain for each function, but in addition receives unstipulated amounts of grain, other food, cloth, cash, etc. as religious gifts.[15] When necessary other Brahmans are invited from outside to perform rituals. But it can cause problems if it is done in a way that implies a slight to the village Brahman.

The Nakarmi (Blacksmith) and the Napit (Barber) are typical service castes but they differ from each other considerably in the ways they are remunerated. The work of the Nakarmi was until recently mainly the repair of agricultural tools, but it has expanded to include other kinds of work because of the increasing demand for other iron goods such as railings for houses and some machines. They have absorbed welding as one of their techniques. As early as 1970 about two-thirds of village households were paying for the Nakarmi's services in cash. The remaining one-third were giving grain twice a year. The amount was fixed loosely and the households giving it judged it according to the work they had received during the year (no calculation proportionate to the number of household members was made). If Nakarmis (or Napits) visited the threshing floors of their customers at the time of rice harvest, they could get some additional grain on the spot (called *khal bhag*). Those who made this kind of payment were found, both in 1970 and in 1996, only among the Shresthas, Maharjans, and Putuwars. The proportion of such households had declined still further by 1996 when more than 80 per cent of all households (not including temporary residents here) were paying in cash. In this way, the *jajmani*-type relation between the Nakarmis and other castes has declined, even though the Nakarmis have continued to follow their caste occupation.

The Napit's work is of two distinct kinds: that done in daily life and that done on the occasion of life-cycle rituals or post-mortuary rites. For the ordinary services, Napits circulate around villages and cut hair and nails and shave anyone on request. For the latter he/she is specifically invited to the patron's house (or place where a ritual is being held) and provides the appropriate services (of shaving or nail-cutting, which are for purification)

---

[15] In Table 4.3 for 1996, the Brahman is recorded only as a student. He was practising as a priest even at that time. After that he became a full-time ritual specialist.

at the proper time and place. It is customary at important rituals, such as boys' and girls' initiations, that the household's Napit is invited to the feast and given some food and money. Twice a year the Napit receives regular prestations of grain.

There are several Napits who have fixed relations with Satungal villagers and it is only at the time of rituals that a villager has to invite the Napit to whom he is related and offer regular payment; for ordinary haircutting and shaving, he can be served by any Napit visiting the village for work. It should be noted that the Napits do not serve the Khadgis and Kapalis at their life-cycle rituals. The situation is more complex in the case of the Nakarmis, Putuwars, and Manandhars: they do not have Napits cut their nails at their life-cycle rituals but have Khadgi women do it instead (see Gellner 1995a: 17, 1995c: 270-1 also). Unlike the Nakarmis, most Napits are paid in grain even today; in 1996 I found nearly 80 per cent of the households paying Napits in grain. The amount is more fixed than in the case of the Nakarmis. The endurance of the *jajmani*-type relationship in the case of the Napits compared to the Nakarmis can certainly be related to the fact that the services of the former are indispensable at important rituals. The Nakarmi's work is not related to rituals at all and has been much less resistant to the influence of monetization.

The Khadgis are known as butchers though they have various ritual and other roles (see also the next section). As 'Butchers' Khadgis here act as meat-sellers and traders of buffaloes.[16] Their role is required in important festivals (carrying out buffalo sacrifice to goddesses and for feasts), in life-cycle and other rituals (for feasts), and for the consumption of buffalo meat on secular occasions. They are given meat and feasted for ritual roles but otherwise demand money and a portion of the meat. However, some Maharjans and Putuwars began to slaughter buffaloes themselves from the mid 1990s for their own (secular) consumption. Their reason was to economize expenses but it was also said that the Khadgis claimed to be too busy to do it. Whatever the reasons, this is a considerable change in people's notions about something that used to be seen as caste-specific work.

When we turn to Tables 4.2 and 4.3 and look into their actual occupations, we notice that the number and proportion of Khadgi males engaging in their caste-specific work increased to a considerable extent from 1970 to 1996. Whereas only 5 men out of 31 (namely 16 per cent) engaged in meat- and buffalo-selling in 1970, 21 men out of 39 (54 per cent) were doing so in 1996. Among the latter, there were some who had meat shops outside the village (mostly nearby and in Kathmandu in a few cases). The increasing

---

[16]Khadgis in this village have not been making the selling of milk their main occupation as they do not keep buffaloes except for a short period before selling or slaughtering them (for a different situation, see Gellner 1995c: 265, 270).

size of the local population, including the in-migrants, many of whom are meat consumers, accounts for such a change. The Khadgis were so busy in their meat/buffalo business that they sometimes were reluctant to work as butchers for the villagers. In 1970 many of the Khadgis were working as coolies in the ropeway terminal at Teku in Kathmandu, and as fire-wood-sellers.[17] The demand for such jobs declined because of the development of road transportation, the spread of the use of kerosene and propane gas, and the forest conservation policy. What many Khadgis had chosen instead by the middle of the 1990s was their own caste occupation. They must have judged it more profitable to do so under the prevailing conditions of population movement and increase but it can also be said to some extent that they evaded competition with other castes by choosing as they did.

There is only one household each of the Manandhar and the Kapali castes. The former runs a grocer shop and combines it with agriculture and (later on) government service. The correlation of their actual jobs with their caste-specific occupation (oilpresser) is not so high though oil is included among the commodities they sell.

No Kapalis here are tailors but their ritual roles are still indispensable on various occasions. In this village a Kapali woman receives food offerings 'in the name of the deceased' at post-mortuary rites such as Lohcha (sixth day) and Nhaynhuma (seventh day). People begin big feasts and some calendrical rituals (e.g. Gu Punhi and Hamo Salhu) after giving food to a Kapali. In the Gatha Muga ritual (to drive away evil), the Kapali is the first to burn wheat straw with bugs and throw it at a *mabhi chwasa* (an inauspicious ritual disposing place).

Socio-Ritual Structure: Vishnudevi Festival, De-bhway, *and Inter-Caste Relationships*

VISHNUDEVI FESTIVAL

In this village the organization of the Vishnudevi festival offers a paradigm of the traditional village order. As I have analysed the Vishnudevi festival organization before (Ishii 1978), I only summarize the main caste roles in the festival.

Shrestha: To oversee the whole festival, to supervise the god's land, to carry out the functions of the four *guthi*s of the festival, to conduct main acts of worship;

Brahman: To perform puja (worship with offerings to deities) in a few important sacrificial and other rituals;

[17] They had been agricultural labourers before that.

Maharjan: To prepare for the festival (washing and decorating the images of deities), to support Shrestha elders and ordinary villagers in acts of worships, to carry ritual goods, to take apart and keep the parts of the palanquin of the goddess, to carry out the functions of one of the *guthi*s of the festival (Maharjan elders are caretakers of the Vishnudevi temple also.), to play long wind instruments or *ka* [discontinued, resumed, and became optional – see the text];

Putuwar: To carry rice-beer pots (regarded as Bhairava) and ritual goods;

Khadgi: To announce the arrival of the festival as village messengers, to usher processions with music (of drums), to kill buffaloes in sacrificial rites;

Kapali: to usher processions with music of a wind instrument (*mwahli*, a kind of oboe), to carry auspicious red powder to the sacred place where a buffalo sacrifice is done;

(The two castes below are from other villages.)

Pahari (Pai in colloquial Newari): to support Maharjan elders, to guard the image of the goddess, to accompany sacrificial animals, to accompany processions with an old sword;

Dyahla (Poh, Pode): To dispose of and make use of offerings.

The above are regarded as the formal participants in the festival. It is noteworthy that the Nakarmis, Manandhars, and Napits are not included; they are newcomers and have no rights or duties in the festival. The same applies to newcomer lineages from those castes that do have roles. The Brahman is an exception in this respect.

The above festival organization clearly demonstrates the centrality of the Shresthas; they are the overseers, conductors, and main performers of the festival, as well as being the recipients of the services of the other castes including the Brahman. The festival organization also demonstrates the hierarchy of roles to some extent: Maharjan elders are the supporters of Shrestha elders, a Pahari supports Maharjan elders, Dyahlas dispose of offerings, and others participate in auxiliary roles.

It is notable that this festival has been celebrated every year without a break as far as locals can remember (i.e. for more than sixty or seventy years at the very least). The basic organization has not changed much, though there were times when villagers thought it was in danger. The political dispute discussed earlier resulted in the withdrawal of the *ka* horns by the Maharjans, which in turn caused severe conflicts between the two castes. The *ka* withdrawal was regarded as very serious. For the Shresthas it was a blemish on sacred tradition. They have been negotiating with the Maharjans for many years to resume the playing of the *ka* but with only partial success. Up till now (2003) *ka* horns have been blown in some years and not in others. The Maharjans have come to understand that they have the option of playing or not and people would say that the role has changed from being an obligation to being an optional addition to the festival.

In retrospect, despite all the passion and uproar it generated, this event changed the festival only very marginally. Maharjans did not claim to replace the Shrestha elders themselves and the latter's centrality persists even to this day. But we have to be careful to specify that it is in the Vishnudevi festival organization and the Mohani (Dasain) *guthi* that we can assert this. Maharjans claim equality in more outright ways in other ritual matters, not to mention the political sphere.

The Vishnudevi festival and Mohani (Dasain) are the two biggest festivals in this village. The former is the most revered despite its local character. The latter is highly prestigious, being the biggest national festival, pan-Indian, and deeply related to family, kin, and village bonds. Villagers are quite pious, especially as regards the deities related to these festivals, though no doubt there are gender, generational, and individual differences. Many think it imperative to carry them out in the proper way lest the village face the absence of divine protection. Local people's piety is encountered in other contexts too. For example, it is not rare to hear people say that the Buddha image in the centre of the village square really sweats when the state faces some danger such as war.

It is in the two main festivals that Shrestha elders are said to become 'gods' (*dyah juyegu – dyah* in these cases referring to goddesses). Some elders may become possessed by 'gods' when they walk holding swords in the ritual of *paya* (sword procession) on the last day of the main period of Mohani. But people say that the most important rituals in which they 'become gods' are those of slaying a demon (symbolized by a gourd) inside the gods' house at Mohani, and the main sacrificial rituals (in which a buffalo is sacrificed) in the Vishnudevi festival, both of which are hidden from the eyes of ordinary villagers. People believe in the divine character of these core rituals and no one has questioned the right of Shrestha elders to play the central roles in them.

De-bhway

Usually held once a year, *de-bhway* is a village feast, in which, ideally, one member from every household (regardless of the precedence of settlement) participates. The goddess Vishnudevi is worshipped in order to rid the village of illness and sin, with the sacrifice of a buffalo and/or sheep, whose meat is consumed at the feast as a gift from the goddess. Its organization is not so tradition-bound as the Vishnudevi festival and has experienced fissions and fusions. In 1967, it split into two, namely, the Shrestha *de-bhway* and the Maharjan *de-bhway*, each attracting some members from the other as well as from different castes. The main reason was said to be the Maharjan elders' (unsuccessful) demand for equal treatment in the climax ritual of the feast, or the *si biyegu* (or *si ka bhu*) in which *si* or eight parts of the face of the animal sacrificed are given to the eight elders. The election for Pradhan Panch, which gave more self-confidence to the numerically strong Maharjans, was certainly relevant. In the meantime Khadgis began to hold their own *de-bhway*. In 1979 Shrestha leaders set out to reintegrate the feasts and were successful (see Ishii 1987 for more detail up to this time). The resumed *de-bhway* continued for some years but became less regular in the late 1980s. In 1992 it was held under the leadership of traditional Shrestha leaders and new Maharjan leaders, but no more in the next year. The reason most openly given was that there were too many participants to have seats in the precinct of the Vishnudevi temple. Some added that there was Maharjan discontent about being assigned seats lower than the Shresthas. Another reason may be that the *si ka bhu* was no longer held. It is presumed that its absence had the effect of making the Shresthas less interested in the *de-bhway*. In 1995 the Maharjans and the Nays held their *de-bhway*s separately, but none has been held since then. *De-bhway*(s) disappeared along with the disappearance of the ritual that differentiated the members and expressed hierarchy between them.

Other Ritual Organizations, Roles and Their Changes

If we conceptualize ritual organizations along a spectrum from rigidity to frailty, various *guthi*s are situated in between the above two. Generally speaking, newer *guthi*s are more prone to changes such as splits, membership change, and disappearance. As such, the Buddha Punhi *guthi*, organized with Shrestha and Maharjan members in 1966, disintegrated after the 1982 election, and the Bhindyah *guthi* and Krishna *guthi* organized in the 1940s and 1950s, respectively, have experienced internal quarrels, fission, and change of membership. These are also related to the movements of funeral organizations (*sana-guthi*s) but we cannot go into this aspect here (see Ishii 1996).

The Bhindyah and Krishna *guthi*s are among those of the Shresthas. In order to carry out their function, including the observation of festivals of the deities concerned, *guthi*s need the services of other castes. A Brahman is needed for various kinds of worship and sacrifice. For some *guthi*s, Maharjans serve as messengers and caretakers, and a Kapali ushers palanquin processions with music. It was obligatory for Shresthas, Maharjans, and Khadgis to play music by turn, at the palanquin processions. But these days, people say they show up of their own accord in order to make festivals lively.

In the past, various castes had more roles to play at ritual occasions either directly serving the Shresthas or in other ways subordinate to them. Representative of this was the playing of *ka* horns by Maharjans; it was necessary not only during the Vishnudevi festival but also at the funerals of

Shresthas. But the latter service was withdrawn in the late 1960s, about the same time when there was a quarrel about the playing of *ka* at the Vishnudevi festival.

Maharjans used to serve as cremation caretakers (*gwan*) at Shrestha funerals. For that role, two old Maharjan lineages used to provide several males in turn. But after a small quarrel in the early 1960s, they ceased to serve the Shresthas in this role forcing the latter to carry out cremations themselves. It was also thought to be obligatory for Maharjans to provide Western-style band music at Shrestha weddings. But they stopped doing it in the late 1960s, though they continued to play at their own weddings. However, from the 1980s Damai bands, whose music and costumes are more fashionable, have been replacing the Maharjan bands even at the latter's weddings.

Another Maharjan service which is dwindling is their role as messengers. Just as some *guthi*s have their messengers, most of the Shrestha households had hereditary relationships with Maharjans or Putuwars who were to carry invitations or messages on the occasion of life-cycle rituals, death, etc. In many cases the Maharjan or Putuwar servants are or were tenants of or agricultural labourers related to the patron households. Their numbers have been decreasing along with the withdrawal of other services and, at the same time, due to the development of alternative means of communication and transportation such as telephones and cars. However, even today there are still a few Shrestha households that have messengers they can call on. A few Maharjan or Putuwar women used to be midwives, and they also provided some auxiliary services in the purification rituals after the childbirth. Their services have been declining as more and more people are resorting to hospitals for childbirth.

A similar point applies to the services of Khadgi women who used to cut the umbilical cord of the higher castes and to the role of Khadgi males to dispose of the soil of the floor of the death bed of the higher castes. Khadgi drums (*naykhi*) were also necessary for funeral processions. These services are also declining as more people are dying in hospitals than at home, but it is also said that the Khadgis totally stopped accepting this role in the late 1990s. The Khadgis' roles were also necessary at the time of Shrestha weddings; they used to carry the bride in a hammock-like carrier (*du*) bound to a carrying pole and provided music for the procession; both services have become obsolete as decorated cars and Damai music have become popular these days.

Seating Order at a Wedding Feast and Some Changes in Customs Relating to Cooking and Food

It is not only the *de-bhway* (village feast) that has changed. Many *guthi* feasts (including those of death *guthi*s) have shrunk both in terms of frequency and size. On the other hand, feasts accompanying life-cycle rituals seem to fluctuate depending on the economic condition of the household(s) concerned, government regulations, etc. Large-scale feasts are not rare even these days. And in these kinds of feasts we can observe the relationship between castes and its change in a visible way (in contrast to buffet-style parties, an urban fashion which villagers have begun to adopt to a limited extent). As examples, I cite here a *de-bhway* held in 1971, and a wedding feast (on the bridegroom's side) of a Satungal Maharjan held in 1997. The latter was a traditional feast in which people sat on the seats spread in one corner of the village square and were served beaten rice (*baji*), meat, vegetable dishes, liquor, etc. Curtains were put up on two sides of the place where there was no house, and long straw mats were placed as seating in six rows. It was said that there were more than seven hundred guests who were fed in six sittings. People from other villages were usually fed in earlier sittings, participants of the wedding procession later, and those who worked as waiters in the last sitting. The way people sat at this feast showed a different order from that of the past feasts such as the *de-bhway* (Chart 4.1) in which people of different castes sat in separate rows or if in the same row, separately.

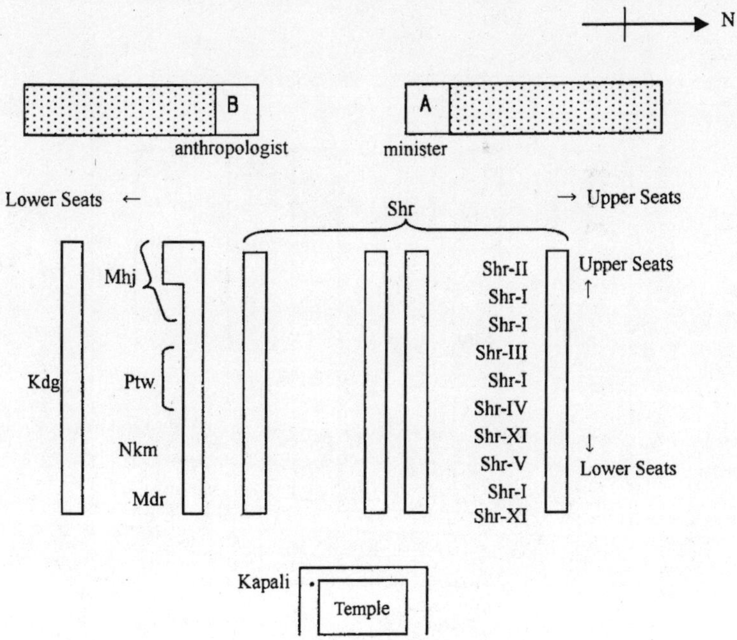

Chart 4.1: *De-bhway*

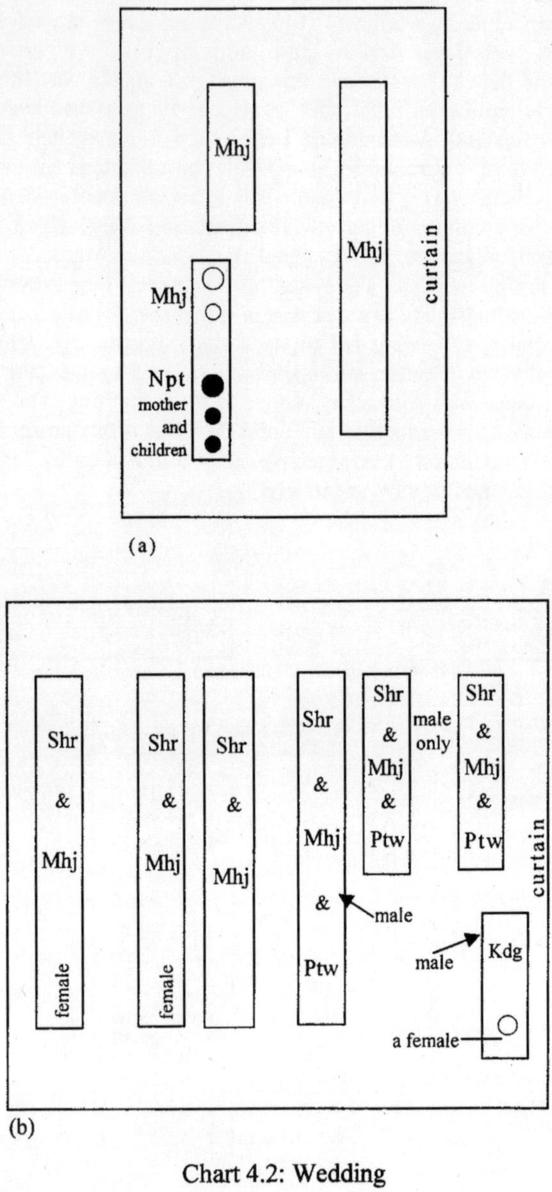

Chart 4.2: Wedding

The main features of the 1997 wedding feast are as follows (I show the seating orders in the third and the fourth sittings in Chart 4.2a, b).

1. Shresthas, Maharjans, and Putuwars did not sit separately but were mixed. Those who were on good terms sat with their shoulders touching regardless of caste.
2. The Khadgis and the Napits who came in these turns sat in the same row as the above people. There was a gap (equivalent to about two persons' width) without any straw mat between the Khadgis and others. The Napits sat on the same long straw mat as the Shrestha-Maharjan-Putuwar group, but there was a similar space between the two groups.
3. There was a tendency for males and females to sit in separate rows, though it was not systematically observed.

In this feast, some changes were observed regarding a particular food and those who cooked it. *Tahkah* (Np. *thalthale*) is a popular winter dish of (usually buffalo) meat cooked in water which turns to jelly in the low temperature, and is not regarded as in the same category as the ordinary feast food, but is categorized with boiled rice (e.g. rice cooked in water). As such, *tahkah* (just like the cooked rice) should not be accepted from the hand of someone of a lower caste than oneself. However, it has been customary for this food to be served at feasts with participants of various castes. For example, it was served at Maharjan weddings where Shresthas were invited. But in such cases, Shresthas used to work as cooks (of at least of the *tahkah*) and also as waiters. However, this complex adaptation was not observed in the above wedding feast; among the cooks there were both Maharjans and Shresthas but there was no distinction as to who should cook *tahkah*. People would say that these days Shresthas do not usually mind taking such food (as *tahkah*) from the hands of Maharjans though there are some old people who still refrain. In this way the commensal barrier between these two castes has been lowered.

CONCLUSION

There have been challenges to the traditionally dominant caste. Along with this has been the withdrawal of some caste-specific services by the middle and lower castes. Severe conflicts prevailed for some time but in recent years a partial merging of the higher and middle castes can be observed in the socio-political as well as the commensal spheres.

The lower (water-unacceptable) castes have remained more separate. Among them, the Khadgis have been resuming their caste-specific occupation to a considerable extent. Gellner's comment on the Newar low castes that "for the moment the barrier between the 'unclean castes' and the rest remains high" (Gellner 1995b: 290) is (more than) applicable here. Furthermore, they are in a situation in which they have to resort to their traditional occupation in order to pursue their economic ends.

A continuity of caste roles is clearly seen among the Kapalis and the Brahmans who stand at the two extremes (of the hierarchy in terms of commensality). In other places (presumably in urban areas), however, "Kapalis are abandoning their specialism" (ibid. 278) and "(w)ith the rise in the economic status of stigmatised castes, discarding caste-bound duties will continue" (Shrestha 2002: 413). A parallelism to the so-called "rigidity of the poles" (Quigley 1993: 159; Bailey 1957: 266) seems to obtain as far as the data on this village is concerned but we cannot go too far into this line.[18]

The contrast between the Napits and the Nakarmis is noteworthy; the *jajmani*-type relationship is retained by the former whereas the latter have largely turned to monetary payments. But it should be noted that the latter have not abandoned their traditional occupation, though they have transformed the contents of their work to a considerable extent. The Khadgi case above is similar in that they pursue their caste occupation within the cash economy.

We find a comparable situation among the Kamis (Blacksmiths among the Parbatiyas) in a village I studied in Dhading district, where the number of Kamis working in metal has increased. Young Kamis there have learned how to make and repair copperware, returned to their village and engaged in the work on cash basis. This has improved their economic position and made it unnecessary for them to depend on Brahman landowners who had previously hired them as agricultural labourers. In this case also, they use the niche of their caste occupation for economic ends in spite of its stigmatizing connotations. (Though not dealt with in this chapter, the cases of sweepers employed by municipal governments in Nepal and India can be viewed in the same light: see, for example, Gellner 1995c: 286-8.)

We have seen that the division of caste roles in the principal festivals is largely preserved. As for the contrast between the Napits and the Nakarmis, dealt with earlier, we can attribute the persistence of the *jajmani*-type relationships of the Napits to their essential role in rituals. On the other hand, certain ritual services have been withdrawn, many feasts economized, and some ritual organizations abolished. Factors such as prestige, economic considerations, ritual needs, and human relations seem to have been at work in the selection processes. It should be noted here that not many people now are making a living from caste-specific ritual roles, though a

---

[18] Quigley (1993: 160) argues that "Brahmans and Untouchables are often not seen as belonging to opposite ends of the spectrum, 'poles apart'. On the contrary, they are often assimilated." Though this does not apply to the present material, it is certainly the case in Mithila where there are many Mahapatra Brahmans.

good number still have such roles and carry them out at festivals and in rituals.

Actual occupations are diverse. But it is mainly the higher- and middle-ranking castes who can take the greatest advantage of them. As the Khadgi case shows, there is no condition of equal competition. The data on education shows caste (and gender) differences clearly and we can see this reflected in the distribution of various occupations.

Looked at this way, we realize that we are not far from the situation described in Dumont's summary of Ghurye cited in the introduction of this chapter, including the continuance of endogamy, though we have to replace the "non-Brahman movement" by "non-dominant castes" and add some points of continuity and resumption. As for the comparison with Ghurye's emphasis on caste associations, we can see from Gellner's recent studies that caste-based organizations with their centres in urban areas have been emerging in post-1990 Nepal in spite of the fissiparous tendency of larger Newar castes (Gellner 1995b, 2003: 106-28). The village under study is within the area of the activities of one of them (i.e. the Jyapu Mahaguthi). But it still remains to be seen whether such organizations will develop on lines comparable to caste associations in India.

Now, is it possible to talk about substantialization as regards the present materials?

1. Strictly speaking, only the view of substantialization as a revolution should be called Dumont's. If we take this view, we have to say that substantialization in Dumont's sense has not taken place in the society described.
2. Talk of substantialization as a process is possible if we ignore Dumont's core themes. In that case we have to be sure of what we mean by 'substantialization'. If we follow Dumont's terminology but leaving aside his notions of the changelessness of structure and the disjunction of status and power, substantialization refers to the transition from the world of interdependence to the world of substance (consisting of collective individuals). This is a holistic definition; what is at stake is the change of a whole society, not changes of its parts.
3. However, what we observe is usually partial; we encounter phenomena such as the weakening of relationships between certain castes. When we apply the term 'substantialization' (as a process) to them, we are supposing that the whole society is proceeding towards the world of substance. This, however, is an assumption which needs to be empirically verified.
4. The most notable recent changes in the village studied are the partial merging of the upper and middle castes and the resumption of the traditional occupation by a lower caste. The former came about some time

after the long period of conflict accompanied by the weakening of inter-caste relationships between the castes concerned. In this stage, each caste concerned looked 'substantialized', but what followed in the course of time was not the strengthening of separation and collective individuality but the (partial) merging mentioned above. It is rather questionable whether we can grasp this recent phenomenon by use of the same analytical tool. The resumption of the occupation of a lower caste has been taking place as part of the cash economy. Nonetheless, the occupational relationships involved are not freed from the relational basis of caste. It is not improbable that this will persist for some time even under present politico-economic conditions. What prevails here is not the traditional inter-caste dependence but a division of labour based on caste mediated by the cash economy. In some important ritual matters, we can still observe a division of roles between castes. Things are clearly relational in this sphere. On the other hand, many kinds of roles, including the playing of music by various castes, have evolved from obligatory duties to voluntary services. On the level of observation, we may encounter similar actions (such as a person playing the musical instrument unique to his caste) to those of several decades ago, but in such cases the nature of the relationship has changed enormously. The relationship has not been 'substantialized', even in a broader sense, but has surely undergone an important change.

5. Thus what we are actually dealing with are multidimensional transformations under conditions of economic, political, and social change. Caste relationships have indeed metamorphosed, but the direction is by no means unilinear. It is not that every caste is transforming itself into an equal individual entity. We will be misled if we assume that the collapse of inter-caste relations in a certain part of the society automatically implies the appearance of Dumont's world of substance.

REFERENCES

Bailey, F.G. 1957. *Caste and the Economic Frontier*. Manchester: Manchester University Press.

——. 1963. 'Closed Social Stratification in India'. *Archives Européennes de Sociologie*, IV-1: 107-24.

Barnett, S. 1977. 'Identity Choice and Caste Ideology in Contemporary South India', in K. David (ed.), *The New Wind*, pp. 393-414.

Barth, F. 1960. 'The System of Social Stratification in Swat, North Pakistan', in E.R. Leach (ed.), *Aspects of Caste in South India, Ceylon and North-West Pakistan*, pp. 113-46. London: Cambridge University Press.

Berreman, G. 1979. *Caste and Other Inequalities*. Meerut: Folklore Institute.

Bouglé, C. 1971. *Essays on the Caste System by Célestin Bouglé*, tr. D.F. Pocock. Cambridge: Cambridge University Press.

Burghart, R. 1996. *The Conditions of Listening*. Delhi: Oxford University Press (ed. by C.J. Fuller and J. Spencer).

Das, V. 1977. *Structure and Cognition: Aspects of Hindu Caste and Ritual*. Delhi: Oxford University Press.

David, K. (ed.). 1977. *The New Wind: Changing Identities in South Asia*. The Hague and Paris: Mouton.

David, K. 1977. 'Introduction', in K. David (ed.), *The New Wind*, pp. 1-58.

Deliège, R. 1999 (1995). *The Untouchables of India*, tr. N. Scott. Oxford: Berg.

Dirks, N.B. 1987. *The Hollow Crown: Ethnohistory of an Indian Kingdom*. Cambridge: Cambridge University Press.

Dumont, L. 1980. *Homo Hierarchicus: The Caste System and Its Implications* (complete Revised English Edition). Chicago and London: The University of Chicago Press.

Fitzgerald, T. 1996. 'From Structure to Substance: Ambedkar, Dumont and Orientalism'. *Contributions to Indian Sociology* (n.s.) 30 (2): 273-88.

Fuller, C.J. 1989. 'Misconceiving the Grain Heap: A Critique of the Concept of the Indian Jajmani System', in J. Parry and M. Bloch (eds.), *Money and the Morality of Exchange*, pp. 33-63. Cambridge: Cambridge University Press.

Fuller, C.J. (ed.). 1996. *Caste Today*. Oxford: Oxford University Press.

Fuller, C.J. 1996. 'Introduction: Caste Today', in C.J. Fuller (ed.), *Caste Today*, pp. 1-31.

Gellner, D.N. 1995a. 'Introduction', in D.N. Gellner and D. Quigley (eds.), *Contested Hierarchies*, pp. 1-37.

——. 1995b. 'Sakyas and Vajracaryas: From Holy Order to Quasi-Ethnic Group', in D.N. Gellner and D. Quigley (eds.), *Contested Hierarchies*, pp. 209-39.

——. 1995c. 'Low Castes in Lalitpur', in D.N. Gellner and D. Quigley (eds.), *Contested Hierarchies*, pp. 264-97.

——. 2003. 'From Cultural Hierarchies to a Hierarchy of Multiculturalisms: The Case of the Newars of the Kathmandu Valley, Nepal', in M. Lecomte-Tilouine and P. Dollfus (eds.), *Ethnic Revival and Religious Turmoil*, pp. 73-131. Delhi: Oxford University Press.

Gellner, D.N. and D. Quigley (eds.). 1995. *Contested Hierarchies: A Collaborative Ethnography of Caste among the Newars of the Kathmandu Valley, Nepal*. Oxford: Clarendon Press.

Inden, R. 1990. *Imagining India*. Oxford: Blackwell Publishers.

Ishii, H. 1978. 'Structure and Change of a Newari Festival Organization', in J.F. Fisher (ed.), *Himalayan Anthropology: The Indo-Tibetan Interface*, pp. 505-27. The Hague & Paris: Mouton.

——. 1980. 'Recent Economic Changes in a Newar Village'. *Contributions to Nepalese Studies* 8 (1): 157-79.

——. 1982. 'Agricultural Labour Recruitment in a Parbate Village in Nepal', in D.B. Bista et al., *Anthropological and Linguistic Studies of the Gandaki Area in Nepal*. Monumenta Serindica 10, pp. 40-80. Tokyo: ILCAA.

——. 1986. 'Institutional Change and Local Response in a Newar Village', in H. Ishii et al., *Anthropological and Linguistic Studies of the Gandaki Area and Kathmandu Valley in Nepal*. Monumenta Serindica 15, pp. 1-39. Tokyo: ILCAA.

——. 1987. 'Social Change in a Newar Village', in N. Gutschow and A. Michaels (eds.), *Heritage of the Kathmandu Valley*. Nepalica 4, pp. 333-54. Sankt Augustin: VGH Wissenschaftsverlag.

——. 1993. 'Agricultural Labour Recruitment among the Newars and Other Groups in the Sub-Himalayan Areas', in C. Ramble and M. Brauen (eds.), *Anthropology of Tibet and the Himalaya*. Zurich: Ethnological Museum of the University of Zurich.

——. 1995a. 'Affinal Prestations in a Newar Village'. *Journal of Asian and African Studies*, 48-49: 419-42.

——. 1995b. 'Caste and Kinship in a Newar Village', in D. Gellner and D. Quigley (eds.), *Contested Hierarchies*, pp. 109-57.

——. 1996. 'Sana-guthis (Funeral Organizations) in a Newar Village: Characteristics and Change', in S. Lienhard (ed.), *Change and Continuity: Studies in the Nepalese Culture of the Kathmandu Valley*, pp. 39-54. Turin: CESMEO.

——. 1999. 'A Comparative Study of Life-Cycle Rituals of the Newars, Parbate Hindus and the Maithils', in R.B. Chhetri and O.P. Gurung (eds.), *Anthropology and Sociology of Nepal: Cultures, Societies, Ecology and Development*, pp. 27-47. Kathmandu: Sociological and Anthropological Society of Nepal.

——. 2001. 'Japanese Studies on the Himalayas and Nepal'. *European Bulletin of Himalayan Research*. 20 (1): 165-208.

Karan, P.P. and H. Ishii. 1996. *Nepal: A Himalayan Kingdom in Transition*. Tokyo: United Nations University Press.

Lecomte-Tilouine, M. and P. Dollfus (eds.). 2003. *Ethnic Revival and Religious Turmoil: Identities and Representations in the Himalayas*. Delhi: Oxford University Press.

Lévi-Strauss, C. 1963. *Structural Anthropology*, tr. C. Jacobson and B.G. Schoepf. New York and London: Basic Books.

Mayer, A. 1960. *Caste and Kinship in Central India: A Village and Its Region*. London: Routledge and Kegan Paul.

——. 1996. 'Caste in an Indian Village: Change and Continuity 1954-1992', in C.J. Fuller (ed.), pp. 32-64.

Parry, J. 1979. *Caste and Kinship in Kangra*. London: Routledge and Kegan Paul.

Quigley, D. 1993. *The Interpretation of Caste*. Oxford: Clarendon Press.

——. 1995. 'Sresthas: Heterogeneity among Hindu Patron Lineages', in D. Gellner and D. Quigley (eds.), *Contested Hierarchies*, pp. 80-108.

Raheja, G.G. 1988. *The Poison in the Gift*. Chicago: The University of Chicago Press.

Regmi, M.C. 1976. *Landownership in Nepal*. Berkeley & Los Angeles: University of California Press.

Shrestha, B.G. 2002. *The Ritual Composition of Sankhu: The Socio-Religious Anthropology of a Newar Town in Nepal*. Den Haag: CIP Data Koninklijke Bibliotheek.

Srinivas, M.N. 1959. 'The Dominant Caste in Rampura'. *American Anthropologist* 61: 1-16.

——. 1966. *Social Change in Modern India*. Berkeley & Los Angeles: University of California Press.

Srinivas, M.N. (ed.). 1996. *Caste: Its Twentieth Century Avatar*. Delhi: Penguin Books India.

Toffin, G. 2003. 'Comments (to D. Gellner)', in M. Lecomte-Tilouine and P. Dollfus (eds.), pp. 132-6.

Vajracharya, D. 2030 v.s. (1973). *Licchavikalka Abhilekha (Inscriptions of the Licchavi Period)*. Kirtipur: INAS, Tribhuvan University (in Nepali).

Wadley, S.S. 1994. *Struggling with Destiny in Karimpur, 1925-1984*. Berkeley & Los Angeles: University of California Press.

Wiser, W.H. 1988 (1936). *The Hindu Jajmani System: A Socio-Economic System Interrelating Members of a Hindu Village Community in Services*. Delhi: Munshiram Manoharlal.

5

Understanding the Ethical Basis of Local Democracy: Towards Post-Postcolonial Transformation in Rural Orissa

AKIO TANABE

INTRODUCTION

This paper is an attempt to describe, analyse, and understand how people in contemporary rural Orissa, India, are trying to reconstruct socio-political relationships which will mediate their embodied cultural ethical values with ideas and institutions of democracy.[1] I will draw my examples mainly from Garh Manitri, Khurda district, Orissa where I conducted intensive fieldwork for twenty-one months during 1991-3, and which I visited quite often in the period 1995-7 while living in Puri as well as on several occasions since then.

There are several important social changes that have taken place since independence in Indian society. One significant aspect is that there is an increasing participation by the 'lower'[2] caste population – along with other oppressed groups – in democratic politics.[3] While this democratization process has been noted at the level of national electoral politics (Yadav 2000), the increasing political participation of the 'lower' castes has also

---

[1]I would like to thank Jonathan Parry, who acted as discussant, and all other participants at the conference for incisive criticisms and comments. I am also grateful to the editors of this volume for helpful suggestions and English editing.

[2]I am conscious that to describe some caste groups as 'lower' is to adopt a hegemonic discursive framework. I use the word for want of a better expression and will keep it in quotation marks throughout.

[3]In the field of election analysis, the increasing participation of the subalterns or 'mahajans' in the 1990s has been termed the 'second democratic upsurge' by Yogendra Yadav (2000).

brought about important transformations of socio-political relationships at the local level. In this paper, I would like to show how the increasing political participation of the 'lower' castes is connected with the reconfiguration of inter-caste relationships in local society, and how this overall socio-political change has been concomitant with the reformulation of indigenous cultural values.

In particular, I intend to pay attention to the creative agency of the people in providing the ethical basis of what I would like to call 'post-postcolonial transformation' in rural Orissa, which became visible in the 1990s. This period marked an important social change which brought about the democratization of local politics and made the structure of hierarchy and dominance less relevant for the public life of the community. It may indicate the beginning of the end of the post-colonial form of hierarchy and dominance which centred around the landholding structure and the ritual authority of the Brahmans. It is notable, however, that this democratization process has not brought about equality of individuals in rural Orissa, where social differences in terms of caste and gender remain a salient feature. What it did bring about is more equal representation of different caste groups and women in the decision-making process in local politics. This is in part explained by the effect of caste and gender reservation measures in the panchayat reformation in 1990 taken by the state government of Orissa.[4] But that cannot explain everything. In my reckoning, there has been social transformation from below from the 1970s and 1980s which has been combined with the political institutional change in the 1990s. New kinds of socio-political relationships are emerging in which the aspects of hierarchy and dominance are downplayed and the aspects of equality of different caste groups in terms of their participation in and contribution to the community are more emphasized. Notably the 'lower' castes – as 'subalterns' – draw on the sacrificial idioms of 'service' and 'duty' to legitimize and insist on their equal participation in the public sphere.

For present purposes, the 'subalterns' can be defined as those who can only be given subordinate positions in the hegemonic or 'superalternate' discourse of values (Gregory 1997). They are the people who are given no voice in hegemonic discourse and must employ 'subalternate' discourse for resistance.[5] In the Indian context, the discourse of hierarchy and dominance belongs to the superalternate, whereas that of ontological equality

[4]In Orissa, some of the new reservation measures for 'lower' castes and women in panchayat elections were decided in 1990 and applied in 1992 prior to the 73rd Amendment to the Constitution of India.

[5]On the concept of 'superalternate' and 'subalternate', see Gregory (1997). Gregory draws largely on Guha (1985). On the question of whether the subalterns can speak, see Spivak (1988).

belongs to the subalternate. Here I would like to suggest that although the subalterns' voice is oppressed in hegemonic discourse, they can speak in *another voice* (cf. Spivak 1988), and that this voice is – at least at first glance – winning for itself a broader space for enunciation in the post-postcolonial sphere. This process entails a potentiality of creating new ethics but is also subject to the working of power which attempts to ignore and marginalize subaltern voices in a new way. In the end, what we see is a mixed result for the subalterns.

By focusing on the creative agency of ordinary people, I propose to contribute to the debate over the ethical basis of modern India not through conceptual arguments but by paying attention to the possibilities inherent in people's practices as moral and reflexive agents. There is much lamentation and concern in contemporary India over the 'great divide' among Indian intellectuals over whether priority should be given to the rights of modern individuals ensured by the state or to the virtues of 'traditional' community maintained by society (Bardhan 1998; Bose & Jalal 1998; Nandy forthcoming). In this paper, I suggest that we start by paying attention to the actual situation in society, that we see how these two different values and discourses coexist, and how they are employed by people as cultural resources in order to formulate new patterns of practices – albeit with incoherency and dilemmas. It is my contention that people do indeed possess significant agency that enables them to bridge over and mediate the dichotomies of the post-colonial predicament – variously seen in terms of 'individual' *versus* 'community', 'right' *versus* 'virtue', 'outer' *versus* 'inner', 'modern' *versus* 'traditional', 'rational' *versus* 'religious'.[6]

This paper aims to shed light on the human agency that works through dilemmas and inconsistencies in the life-world, mediating contradictions in practice in situ in contemporary rural India (Demmer in press). It argues that there are significant attempts by subaltern people to reconstruct social relations and discursive frameworks which can and do help them deal with post-colonial dilemmas and to fulfil both their politico-economic interests and their cultural-moral identities. I believe that by describing this kind of politico-moral negotiation in contemporary rural India today anthropology based on ethnographic fieldwork can contribute to contemporary issues and problems.

This paper is also a critical response to previous anthropological works on Indian society which have mainly concentrated on the issues of 'status'

---

[6] I agree with Corbridge and Harriss's observation that "People live more comfortably on the borders between rural and urban worlds, 'western' and 'eastern' worlds, modern and pre-modern worlds, than some prophets or critics of high modernity allow" (2000: 32). However, it is also true that these colonial dichotomies also have turned into tools of oppression and resistance in colonial and post-colonial histories of India (Chatterjee 1993, 2004).

and/or 'power' to discern the essence of the Indian order of things. In such studies, scholars have attempted to describe Indian 'society' and 'culture' as a system with a consistent order in which people's status in hierarchy could be explained and the role of power in defining socio-political relationships could be clarified.[7] In this kind of scheme, 'caste' was often proposed as the key to understanding Indian society and much effort was spent on solving the enigma of caste, namely, whether caste was about status or power. This debate has been played out in many avatars,[8] the most recent one being between Dumont (1980) and the neo-Hocartians (Dirks 1987; Quigley 1993; Raheja 1988b). To put it simply, while Dumont argued that caste was about hierarchical status with the Brahman at its apex, the neo-Hocartians opposed him and proposed that caste is mainly about power centring on the king or the dominant caste.

I have more to say later about this debate, but I would like to mention here that my aim is not to adjudicate between the opposing sides in this argument, but rather to point out shared methodological presuppositions. Both sides of the debate are intent on locating a single Indian 'social order' in which persons are placed, in a prescriptive manner, in particular positions with specific ranks, capacities, and duties. What is lacking in this kind of methodological standpoint is the aspect of situated agency, the acknowledgement that people have the power to reconstitute ethics and aesthetics as regards interpersonal relationships. The norm-centred view does not account for the fact that people are not just embedded within a social order to obey the prescriptive and the coercive but have reflexive and creative capacities by which they gauge themselves in social interaction and relationships. Although people do not usually have the capacity to change the social hierarchy or the power structure themselves, except in extraordinary cases, as agents they do have the capacity to be creative in the formation of ethical and aesthetic practices vis-à-vis others in everyday life.[9] As the socio-political context changes over time, people manifest their capacity to reformulate their practical-moral relationships to fit the new circumstances, as can be seen in the case of rural Orissa in the 1990s.

---

[7]See Overing & Passes (2000), Overing (2003), and Demmer (in press) for criticisms of anthropological views of 'society' and its prescriptive 'rules'. See also Asad (1983) for criticism of Geertz's 'cultural system'.

[8]The previous avatar of this discussion was that between structural-functional analyses, which put stress on 'positions' and 'roles' (status in the social structure) (e.g. Mayer 1960 and Srinivas 1952), and Marxist analyses, which argued that caste was basically about class (power relationships) which was disguised as culture and religion (e.g. Mencher 1974).

[9]Overing has rightly pointed out as regards previous academic focus on reason, that "The power of actors' *thinking as social and moral beings* is neglected and thereby denigrated absolutely" (1985: 5, emphasis added).

SOCIAL PRACTICE AND CULTURAL RESOURCES

How, then, can this aspect of people's agency be described? In order to deal with this question, following Shotter (1993) and Demmer (in press),[10] I shall focus on two aspects of cultural-political agency: social 'practice' and cultural 'resources'. The first aspect is related to the social practice of people who are embedded in certain relationships but have the capacity to reflect and dialogically act upon self and others.[11] This agency of the self is based on 'the autonomous I' which 'is ever implicated within and joined with an intersubjectivity' (Overing & Passes 2000: 2). Here, 'identity' of the 'autonomous I' can only be constructed in relation to 'others' in one's responsive practices and their intersubjective ethical evaluations. Such ethical intersubjectivity is realized by the 'reflexive and embodied agency' of the people.[12]

It should be noted that reflexivity and embodiedness point to the basic human condition. Reflexivity is a capacity of human beings to cast a reflective gaze upon the self and the world and to assign various levels of significance to them (Mohapatra 1990: 27; Taylor 1985), which has to do with the characteristic of a human being as "self-interpreting animals" (Taylor 1985: 45-76). Human agency requires such reflective capacity to ponder on the meaning and effects of one's action on self, others, and the world. Moreover, this reflexive self is always situated and embedded in particular circumstances since human beings are embodied beings. Embodiedness places the human agent in a particular space and time and in a specific nexus of social relationships.

It is the reflexive and embodied character that makes the human agent an ethical being in embedded relations in the sense of seeking to act in a good and meaningful manner in everyday practice. However, in order for human agency to work, it requires cultural resources of meanings and values which can be employed to reflect upon and assign significance to the world. The second aspect of cultural-political agency involves the cultural resources that people draw upon during negotiative practices in order to secure moral legitimacy (Demmer in press; Pardo 2000).

An essential point here is that these resources of meanings and values

---

[10] Demmer mentions two aspects of a rhetoric culture as being "the social practices of people" and "the resources of symbols and meanings" (in press).

[11] Social practice is based on what Bourdieu calls 'habitus', that is, "systems of durable, transposable dispositions, structured structures predisposed to function as structuring structures, that is, as principles which generate and organize practices and representations" (1990: 53). Actors can be reflectively conscious of what they are doing without a "conscious aiming at ends". I believe that this reflective consciousness is one of important factors in bringing about 'transposability' of patterns of behaviour. See also Yanai (1993).

[12] See Tanabe and Tokita-Tanabe (2003) for discussion on 'agents as reflexive bodies'. For further analysis of body and agency, see Tokita-Tanabe (2003).

are not reducible to a system or a set of rules which prescriptively bind people. Neither do they constitute an unchanging and timeless tradition. Rather, 'living tradition' (Billig 1987; MacIntyre 1981; Shotter 1993) as historically extended and socially shared contestation over appropriate discourses and practices can function as a rich arena for negotiation precisely because it contains cultural resources which present people with dilemmas and inconsistencies. In particular, the existence of superalternate and subalternate frameworks brings about the space for negotiation and contestation. People take advantage of the 'two-sided' and 'dilemmatic' nature of living traditions to negotiate and accommodate their changing situations (Shotter 1993). In this way, these cultural resources are reproduced through usage in people's discourses and practices, enriched with new flows of influences from outside, including modern ones, and undergo changes as the discourses and practices are negotiated and transformed (Demmer in press; Shotter 1993).

It is indeed ordinary people's everyday ethical practice, and the cultural resources employed therein which work to create new patterns of behaviour and new discursive frameworks. The importance and potentiality of social practice and cultural resources for the construction of ethics has been more or less neglected in South Asian anthropology. I shall try to articulate the kinds of practices and resources in Indian culture that make ethically responsive, reflective practice possible.

It is my contention that the post-postcolonial transformation of the 1990s is a culmination of the efforts by subaltern agency since the 1960s to go beyond the colonially 'traditionalized' structure of hierarchy and dominance and to mediate their embodied sense of ethics with modern ideas and institutions of democracy. We must also note, however, that there are attempts by both urban and rural elites to deny, suppress, and/or dislocate such subaltern agency. It is precisely this cultural politics of ethics involving plural 'practical-moral' agencies in the process of domination and resistance in India that I aim to describe.

POST-COLONIAL AGENDA AND POST-POSTCOLONIAL TRANSFORMATION

It is necessary to explain what is meant by the post-postcolonial transformation of the post-colonial history of India. Indian independence in 1947 did not mean that the country became totally free of its colonial legacy. It is true that the colonial rule of difference between the 'colonial state' and 'native society' ended after independence, and that a democratic 'nation-state' was born which was supposed to integrate the people with the state. However, the transfer of power was characterized by a 'passive revolution' in which the independent state as the successor of the colonial state continued to depend on the pre-existing dominant classes for effective rule (Chatterjee 1986: 30; Corbridge & Harriss 2000: 38; Kaviraj 1997). The 'traditionalized' form of hierarchy and dominance in society formulated under colonialism persisted after independence and, in such a context, the important 'post-colonial agenda' came to be how to bring about practical mediation between the democratic institutions designed with the new 'idea of India' (Khilnani 1999) and the embodied values of the people in an unequal society.

At the village level, the continuing characteristics of local society 'traditionalized' by colonialism included the hierarchical aspect of caste with Brahman at its apex and the centrality of the dominant caste based on unequal landholding and the *jajmani* system (Tanabe 1998; Bayly 1999; Dirks 2001). The practice of 'untouchability' was constitutionally condemned, reservation measures for Scheduled Castes and Scheduled Tribes were introduced, and there were several attempts to dissolve socio-economic inequality through land reforms. However, the government's commitment to empower the underprivileged remained at best half-hearted since its political rule was dependent on the support by the old dominant classes of the aftermath of the passive revolution. In the case of coastal Orissa, the old dominant classes consisted of Brahmans, Karanas (Scribes, equivalent to Kayasthas in other areas), and Khandayats. Brahmans and Karanas were mostly the local elites who possessed fairly large estates and often held government jobs, while the more numerous Khandayats constituted the dominant landholding caste.

The commitment of the Indian people and the government to the institution of electoral democracy, however, did have gradual effects on the nature of political practices in the long run. A new wind began to blow in the 1960s with an expansion of the participatory basis of Indian democracy. There was an increase in overall voter turnout as the 'lower' caste population started to enter the political world and political competition became serious with the emergence of real alternatives to the one-party dominance of the Congress (Yadav 2000). Democratization in India meant a downward expansion of the participatory basis of democratic politics in which the underprivileged in terms of caste, class, and gender increasingly took an active part.

Indira Gandhi responded to the wave of democratization with populist measures. In order to capture the votes of the masses, she resorted to pork-barrel politics of distributing state resources in return for electoral support. The 'subsidy raj' (Bardhan 1984) was used not only for state control of the economy but also to ensure the continuing political support of the people.

In this situation, in rural coastal Orissa, factional politics became more intense from the 1960s and 1970s as village people attempted to influence the flow of governmental resources (Tanabe 2004).[13] Since these state resources were of considerable importance in the local cash economy, decision-making regarding their distribution was an important political issue in the village. The factional groups were led by dominant caste leaders who governed matters of resource distribution at the village level through the factions they led. Although state resources came mainly in the name of community development and the alleviation of poverty, resources were distributed and consumed among the main factional members who belonged to the dominant caste. The practice of factional politics was closely related to corruption in government.[14] Administrative staff and politicians received a certain 'percentage' as they influenced the flow of the state resources and overlooked its embezzlement by the local factional members (Tanabe 2002; Visvanathan & Sethi 1998; Wade 1982, 1985).

The importance of state resources for the local economy was acute since Oriya villagers experienced hardly any increase in agricultural productivity or any cash income outside agriculture. The green revolution, which started in Punjab in the 1960s and covered West Bengal by the 1980s, never reached most areas of Orissa.[15] Furthermore, opportunities for cash income outside agriculture were very limited since there was strong state control of the market economy under the 'licence raj'. The only significant means of cash income for Orissan villagers was the production of cash crops like betel leaves and oilseeds such as cashew nuts and peanuts. The land for planting such cash crops, however, was limited and mostly in the hands of local elites and the dominant caste. The rule of the old dominant classes thus persisted through the 1970s and 1980s in rural Orissa with the unequal landholding structure and the political control of the flow of state resources by the local elite and the dominant caste. This can be seen as an aspect of persistence of the post-colonial condition of rural India.

This was the situation when important policy changes came in the 1990s. The effect of economic liberalization policies undertaken by the central government in 1991 became visible even in rural Orissa by the mid 1990s. Cash income became more accessible in the private sectors as well as in small-scale businesses. People also saw future prospects in getting themselves and their children educated to obtain salaried jobs. As people

---

[13] See Lewis (1958), Nicholas (1963: 114) and Bailey (1963, 1969) for studies of factions in Indian villages. See Brass (1965) and Washbrook (1976) for studies of factions at intermediate levels. See also Hardiman (1982) for a critique of these works.

[14] On corruption in India, see Wade (1982, 1985), Gupta (1995), Mohapatra (1997), Visvanathan & Sethi (1998), Fuller & Bénéï (2000), and Parry (2000). It is often pointed out that corruption has become deeply entrenched in the post-colonial Indian administration. Béteille points to the "criminalisation of our [India's] economic and political life" (1994: 565).

[15] Major irrigation plans are underway in Orissa today and their effects are yet to be seen.

found it economically more rewarding to participate in the market than factional politics, the number of people interested in factional politics decreased.

In this context, the *gram panchayat* came to have a more significant role in decision-making processes from the mid 1990s. With the decline of dominant-centred factional politics, the *gram panchayat* came to acquire agency and began to do what it is supposed to do: discuss ways of improving the common welfare. The democratic nature of the *gram panchayat* was strengthened in Orissa also with the reform of the 'panchayati raj' (local government) by the state government of Orissa in 1992. This was in anticipation of the 73rd Amendment to the Constitution in 1993, which prescribed reservation measures not only for the lower-caste population but also women in one third of municipal and panchayat seats (Bates 2004). The full reforms, in accordance with the Amendment, were implemented in Orissa in 1997. This reform in the panchayat system together with the diminishing popularity of factional politics led to further democratization in the representation and functioning of the *gram panchayat* meetings. An encouraging example of this, though it is a result of the reservation measure, can also be seen in the fact that a woman is currently (from 2002) the head of the *gram panchayat* (*sarpanch*) of Garh Manitri. The effect of the panchayat reforms is as still too early to evaluate, but the very presence of 'lower' castes and women in the panchayat meetings would certainly make a gradual difference. As their presence is normalized, their voice will hopefully begin to count in the public sphere.

What can be already observed is the change in the place of local decision-making. Whereas previously, actual decisions on distribution of resources were made in meetings of the main factional members and *gram panchayat* meetings had only nominal importance, today the *gram panchayat*'s discussions over matters regarding the improvement of local welfare are taken into consideration and attempts are made to put their decisions into effect.

Of course not everything is so bright. Corruption still continues and seriously inhibits the effectiveness of development schemes. Also, factional politics persists with more castes participating though with less involvement of the dominant caste. However, at least there is no longer unofficial control of local politics by members of the dominant caste. It is the *gram panchayat* with more democratic representation in terms of caste and gender that has started discussing and suggesting ways for improving the local life. The democratization process seems to have reached the local level in this respect. This shift from the domination of local politics by the old dominant classes to the active participation of the previously underprivileged in the *gram panchayat* can be said to represent an aspect of post-postcolonial transformation in rural Orissa.

THE ETHICAL BASIS OF POST-POSTCOLONIAL TRANSFORMATION: WHERE DOES IT LIE?

What I would like to call post-postcolonial transformation of rural Orissa does not end here. The democratic functioning of the *gram panchayat* represents only the political aspect. What is the cultural change that accompanied this transformation? To put the question more specifically, where does the ethical basis of this transformation lie?

It has been often assumed that with the advent of modernity, tradition will gradually be replaced. Here modernity is considered to be some kind of a force from outside which makes people reflect critically upon their traditional norms and frees them from those norms (Beck et al. 1994; Giddens 1990, 1991). It is assumed that, in the process, people will gradually internalize modern values. In this kind of modernization theory, the ethics of modern India are often seen to come from outside influence. For example, Fuller and Harris (2000: 14), along with Parry (2000: 29), interpret the existence of criticism of corruption by the people as a sign of internalization of "the impersonal norms and values of the modern state". I do not deny that modern values have been very influential in people's practice and thought, or that the state has played an important role therein. The democratization process would not have been possible without the intervention of the state. It was the political institutional change that allowed subaltern voices space in the public sphere. However, it is also important to pay attention to the agency of the people, not only that of the modern state, in the post-colonial history of ethical development. The role of indigenous politico-moral resources and their utilization by the people should be taken seriously as well. The ethical values mobilized at the local level after the reforms of the early 1990s are not restricted to 'modern impersonal norms' but also include an embodied sense of subalternate morality which has a longer history in Indian society.

What modernity does is not to gradually replace or marginalize the indigenous ideas and values, but to increase existing cultural resources by adding new ideas and values to the sociocultural reservoir, and to influence the way the ethical practices are formed out of these hybrid semantic resources.[16] It should be noted that we cannot assume an exclusive opposition between traditional structure and modern values in which either the existing structure persists or the external forces take over.[17] Rather, the

---

[16] I borrow the idea of 'reservoir' in this sense from Demmer (in press).

[17] As Bose says, in place of the dichotomy of tradition and modernity, the "problem of reconfiguring the relationship between nationalism, democracy, and development needs to be relocated in the very different context of the dialectic between domination and resistance, privilege and deprivation at the global, national, and local levels" (1997: 59).

process of transformation involves the usage of resources that derive from both old "internal dispositions" and "external forces" (Bourdieu 1990: 55).

In my opinion, we must recognize the coevality of the traditional and the modern,[18] and, moreover, go beyond the supposed identification of tradition only with the structure of status and power – represented respectively by caste hierarchy and the *jajmani* system – in the case of India. From the point of view of modernity, which stipulates the freedom of individuals, tradition associated with status and power will have to be denied in the logic of axiomatic contradiction. However, I would like to point out, first, that the ideas and institutions of old and new elements coexist in a hybrid manner in everyday practice. There is a logic of commonplace contradiction where inconsistencies and dilemmas provide a space not only for antagonism but also for negotiation and mediation.[19] Second, and more importantly, status and power are not the only historically accumulated living cultural resources in India. There is an alternative resource, which allows human agents to reflect ethically and aesthetically upon the appropriateness of conventional patterns of social behaviour. It is this third kind of cultural tradition as an ethical resource which I want to emphasize in this paper.

The kind of cultural tradition I am referring to here has been preserved in the socio-religious tradition of caste cooperation, sacrifice, and devotionalism (*bhakti*). It is here that we can find the ethical resources of ontological equality. These resources are now employed by the subalterns to mediate their embodied sense of morality with modern ideas of equal political participation and cooperation for public welfare.

What I am suggesting here is that there has been a particular form of democratization in rural Orissa because there was a mediation of an indigenous value of ontological equality with democratic ideas. Such mediation was possible because the space for subaltern agency has expanded and there have been sociocultural negotiation and transformation over patterns and meanings of practice. How can we understand this transformation? Since the value of ontological equality, which, I suggest, forms the ethical basis for the post-postcolonial democracy in rural Orissa, can be observed in the social practice of caste, sacrifice, and devotionalism, let us now turn to this topic.

---

[18]Fabian (1983) described how anthropology created an 'othered object' by denying coevality. See also Gregory (1997).

[19]On "commonplace contradictions" and "axiomatic contradictions" and their implication for anthropological studies, see Gregory (1997).

CASTE AND SACRIFICIAL ETHICS IN INDIA: BEYOND STATUS AND POWER

As regards the cultural resources for social cooperation in India, I focus on the ethical aspect of caste organization that worked as a subalternate basis for organic cooperation in local society in conjunction and in tension with relationships defined in terms of a superalternate structure of hierarchy and domination.

The hierarchical view of caste represented by Dumont (1980) has recently received much criticism. It has been noted that the kind of view of India which put caste hierarchy as its foundation stems from Orientalist discourses based on Brahmanical representations of Indian society (Burghart 1990; Das 1994; Raheja 1988b). Recent scholars have repeatedly pointed out that caste hierarchy came to prominence thanks to forces unleashed by colonialism and in idioms provided by Orientalist discourses (Dirks 1987; Inden 1986, 1990; Raheja 1988a; Van der Veer 1988: 52-8). However, it seems to me that enough has now been said about the Western hand in creating a distorted image of India and about the need to 'deconstruct' Orientalist knowledge.[20] What we must do now, while being sensitive to the working of colonial/Orientalist power, is to change our perspective from paying attention on the colonizers'/Orientalists' views and how they influenced Indian society to analysing the practices and views of the multitudes of Indian people in the politico-social situation they are placed.

The recognition that there are plural and possibly conflicting values and points of view in India opened the way for a new area of investigations.[21] The most fruitful of them so far have been those concerning kingship and dominance. Recently, there has been an impressive amount of work focusing on the socio-cosmological significance of kingship and dominance in Indian society (Dirks 1987; Madan 1985, 1987; Marglin 1985; Raheja 1988b; Shulman 1985). Recognition of the cosmological importance of the institution of kingship has led a number of scholars to return to and adopt Hocart's scheme for understanding Indian society, in which the centrality of the king rather than the purity of the Brahman is given importance as the pivot of Hindu social organization (Hocart 1950, 1970). It seems that the definition of caste as a 'sacrificial organization' following Hocart holds sway in much of the recent literature (Dirks 1987; Inden 1990; Quigley 1993, 1994). It is also my contention that caste practices in the local community should be understood as having sacrificial significance.

---

[20]Richardson succinctly says 'Enough Said' (2000). Quigley says that Orientalist criticism would leave us in 'a kind of intellectual limbo' (1993: 14).

[21]This path of investigation was pioneered by Marriot (1955: 13; 1976).

However, because these neo-Hocartian arguments have been mainly developed as attempts to understand the cultural and cosmological importance of kingship and dominance in Indian society, there has also been a tendency to reduce the meaning of sacrifice to its political or power-related aspect. As a consequence, when caste was defined as a sacrificial organization, the meaning of caste was often reduced to its significance as part of the structure of kingship and dominance (e.g. Dirks 1987; Quigley 1993; Raheja 1988b).[22] Against these views I would like to point out that the meaning of sacrifice in Indian history and its influence on Indian society are richer and wider than can be reduced to a mere political structure of kingship and dominance.

The neo-Hocartians have not only failed to take into account the aspect of hierarchy, which indeed is an undeniable feature of caste, but also, and more importantly, have not been able to see the ethical aspect of sacrifice as a cultural resource for subaltern reformulations of social relations. It is indeed constructive to interpret the meaning of kingship and dominance in terms of sacrifice; but this does not mean the reverse. That is to say, sacrifice cannot just be interpreted in terms of and thereby reduced to matters of kingship and dominance.

Sacrifice can be said to be a mechanism by which a sacrificer gains contact with the realm of the sacred so as to allow its energy of life to flow into the process of reproduction.[23] As I will argue by analysing a community ritual, the sacrificial process actually includes both 'hierarchy' of purity and 'centrality' of royalty, but it cannot be reduced to either of them. Moreover, there is a third and most critical aspect of sacrifice, that is, ontological 'equality' which manifests in the phase of devotional submission to the divine. These three values and principles – hierarchy, centrality, and equality[24] – interact and work together in the community sacrificial process to bring about the reproduction of society.[25]

---

[22]Quigley even goes so far as to say that 'Caste is a form of kingship' (2000: 250).

[23]I feel that the most inspiring part of Hocart's theory is his suggestion that a polity-society may be seen as being organized to perform sacrifice in order to contact the sacred "in quest of life" (Schnepel 1988).

[24]Raheja's notion of 'shifting positionality', where positionality and interrelationships shift between the principles of centrality, hierarchy, and mutuality according to context and viewpoints, is useful in doing away with the scheme of presenting an overarching principle as in the Dumontian (hierarchy) or neo-Hocartian (centrality) positions (1988b). However, her notion tends to fall into postmodernist relativism where everything is reduced to context and viewpoints, and lacks sensitivity to the actual politico-social structure in history in which these principles were placed in the interrelationships of domination and resistance. Also, for understanding the sacrificial process, the principle of 'ontological equality' is more important than 'mutuality', by which Raheja seems to mean equal exchange relationships.

[25]Admittedly, there are other qualities that human beings get from contact with the sacred. The most important among these, other than the generative power for reproduction in the Indian context, are perhaps transcendental knowledge (*jnana*), divine sweetness or ecstasy

REVOLVING VALUES IN SACRIFICE: SUPERALTERNATE AND SUBALTERNATE

Let me illustrate my point with the example of a community ritual I have observed in Garh Manitri. In this ritual, there is a transformation of the goddess's power in three phases: (a) the arrival of the goddess's power of fertility received with devotional submission, at which point ontological 'equality' is manifest; (b) the union of the goddess with royalty mediated by the Brahman who represents the order of 'hierarchy'; (c) consumption of the product of the union in the form of remnants of sacrifice and exercise of the power so gained in accordance with the structure of royal 'centrality'. It is a very complicated ritual with many interesting details, but I can only give a brief outline of it here.[26]

At the beginning of the festival, on the night of *mahasaptami*, a Khond ('tribal') priest performs *puja* (ritual of worship) on the hill where the goddess resides and a Saora ('tribal') medium becomes possessed. A procession led by the medium, who is now considered to be the goddess, descends the hill and enters the village. The procession proceeds to the temple dedicated to the goddess where the chief awaits with the 'king's sword' laid down on the ground. This is a challenge by the chief to test the divine power of the medium/goddess. The medium must lift up the sword to demonstrate his divine power, in which he succeeds. The chief and the people become convinced of the power of the goddess within the body of the medium and offer *pranam* (reverential bowing) to her. This scene represents the phase of the 'equality' of beings in front of the divine. Then the medium is invited to enter the king's palace, and offerings are made to the goddess in the name of the king. After that, the medium/goddess proceeds towards the main fort area where the houses of warriors, including that of the chief, are located. On the way the goddess accepts offerings from the chief and other villagers who wash the medium's feet and worship him as the goddess. The procession finally reaches the 'sword hut' (*khanda ghara*) constructed near the chief's residence. A Brahman priest throws rice and flowers on the medium/goddess, chanting a mantra. Then the medium places the sword in the hut. The sacrifice of a goat, called the 'royal sacrifice' (*sarakari bali*), takes place. The sacrificial goat is first sanctified by the Brahman priest chanting a mantra in its ear. Just after the goat is sacrificed the medium drinks its blood which results in the goddess leaving his body. Here the Brahman intervenes to pacify and control the power of

---

(*rasa*, *bhava*), and ultimately liberation (*moksha*), which are significant in renunciatory and devotional traditions. My contention is that the principle of sacrifice permeates these traditions also. But it would be out of place to discuss these matters here.

[26] See Tanabe (1999) for the details of this ritual and its interpretation from a different point of view.

the goddess, a manifestation of 'hierarchy'. From then on, the goddess is said to reside in the sword, which is worshipped in the sword hut by the Brahman acting as priest and by the chief as the worshipper. The meat remaining from the royal sacrifice, that is, the fruit of the union of the goddess and the king, is distributed and consumed by the families of the various castes making up the local community. The meat is distributed in equal proportions, except that the head goes to the king (*kachari*) and the penis and testicles go to the chief. This represents the structure of centrality where the ontologically equal but functionally different parts are integrated with royalty at the centre (head). The sword, which represents both the power of the goddess and the authority of the king, is taken by the chief on *Dashahara* night two days later when he leads a pseudo-military procession with other warrior-caste men through the village. This is an exercise of power by the reconstructed community centring around the chief whose authority is sanctioned by the goddess and the king.

The basic mechanism for the transformation of the goddess's power (*shakti*) through three stages is sacrifice. Sacrifice, in a word, is a process of self-transformation through symbolic death. By destroying the offering identified with the sacrificer, the sacrificer and the community represented by him go through a process of death and regeneration. In this process, the self without borders acquires immanence with the sacred that lies beyond the self and then re-structures the new self recharged with sacred power.[27] The manifestation of the ontological 'equality' in the phase of the devotional submission corresponds to the process of death and deconstruction that is the first part of the sacrifice. Then the second part, namely, the process of rebirth or reconstruction of the new self and social order, is achieved through the principles of 'hierarchy' and 'centrality'. I say the phase of devotional submission is the most critical aspect of sacrifice because it is this devotion and submission, that is offering of the self or self-destruction, which makes contact with the sacred possible.[28] It is also the stage in which the aspects of 'status' and 'power' are denied and the ontological equality and oneness of beings are represented. As I see it, it is the ontological equality and oneness of beings represented in the devotional phase that provide the politico-moral resources for mutual respect and recognition, and these are the key to interpersonal 'ethics'. I deem it to be a crucial aspect of the sacrificial process which is utilized to reflect upon and transform everyday practices from a subaltern perspective.

---

[27] For theories of sacrifice, see Hubert & Mauss (1964, esp. pp. 9-18), Bataille (1976), Hocart (1970), Inden (1978: 36), and Tanaka (1991).

[28] This is the phase referred to as liminality in the anthropological tradition starting from van Gennep (1960) and developed by Turner (1969). As Das correctly says, "[t]he paradigm of liminality par excellence is death" (1982: 120). This is an aspect of the existential condition of human beings that grounds their ontological equality: we all die.

The contrast drawn here between the devotional phase of sacrifice which represents ontological equality and the hierarchy and centrality phases which represent status and power is reminiscent of Victor Turner's formulation of 'structure' and 'communitas' or 'anti-structure' (Turner 1969). I draw inspiration from Turner's two distinct modes of social togetherness, and, following Bauman, I connect it to the argument of ethical potentiality of 'subalternate' values (Bauman 1993: 116-19). I would like to note, however, that Turner's formulation suffers from the priority given to the functional reproduction of the structure. The phase of communitas is said to be 'anti-'structure and only defined as the opposite of structure, serving functionally to reproduce the social structure in the end. The 'equality' phase does indeed negate status and power, but I would argue that its meanings cannot be reduced to its 'anti-' character. It has a rich semantics and needs to be analysed on its own terms. It would be more fruitful to take the two forms of togetherness to be – overtly or, more often than not, covertly – in constant tension and inconsistency, offering alternate forms of social togetherness as cultural potentialities.

The importance of the co-presence of the three phases in the sacrificial process – hierarchy, centrality, and equality – is that they represent alternate formulations and values of socio-political relationships. Like Turner's formulation of two opposing kinds of social formation, the aspects of status and power can be seen as the 'superalternate' structures placed from above as prescriptive norms of hierarchy and centrality for the management of society, while the aspect of equality not only denies structure but also works as a foundation for a 'subalternate' sociality of spontaneous relationships based on the ethics of ontological equality with mutual dignity and recognition (Bauman 1993; Gregory 1997).

The contradiction and contestation between the domination of superalternate values and the resistance of the subalternate value constitute the real dilemmas of human socio-political relationships that are played out in ritual mechanisms and in everyday interactions. It seems to me that the coexistence of these two forms of social togetherness is at the heart of the dilemma of human life (Gregory 1997). The reason why I emphasize the importance of the value of ontological equality represented in sacrifice is that I believe it is the most important ethical resource for constituting the subalternate form of sociality. This subalternate form of sociality, in my opinion, has the potentiality to go beyond the structure of hierarchy and centrality represented by status and power.[29]

[29]Compared to the importance of the process of contestation and dilemma between the superalternate values and subalternate values, the contradiction between the Brahmanical hierarchy and royal centrality or that of individual and the community, though important in today's discussion, actually seem to me to be epiphenomenal superficialities in understanding the potentiality of ethical basis in Indian society.

In other words, the values and social configurations of hierarchy, centrality, and equality are all present and legitimate in Indian society. It should be noted that I am not arguing for caste-distinct or class-distinct values. By the terms 'superalternate' and 'subalternate', I am not suggesting that certain values are for the ruling class and others for the oppressed class. Rather, the superalternate and subalternate values are *alternate* values that have relevance in different situations and contexts for everybody. Whereas the superalternate values have the function of constructing social order through prescriptive norms, the subalternate values have the function of deconstructing such norms and bringing people back to the basis of human ethics, that is, ontological equality. From that basis, people have the chance to reflect and reconstitute new social relationships.

Furthermore, it is important to recognize the existence of plural and conflicting values in Indian society rather than one overarching value that is shared by all and determines the social structure (Dumont 1980; Moffatt 1979). It is indeed true that the value of hierarchy, for example, is accepted and utilized even by those who are considered the most impure, as ably demonstrated by Moffatt (1979).[30] But this does not mean that hierarchy is the only value that has relevance in society. Rather, it is truer to say that the three values of hierarchy, centrality, and equality are all accepted and utilized by everybody depending on the situation and context. These values and viewpoints can be said to constitute the cultural resources for forming different kinds of social relationships. The aspect of equality is a potential indigenous resource for going beyond hierarchy and power and for establishing participatory democracy.

I would like to suggest that the three values constitute 'revolving values' after Malamoud's idea of 'revolving hierarchy' in which the encompassing and encompassed values revolve, depending on which point of view is taken (Malamoud 1981). This means that a particular value may dominate in a certain context, other values being encompassed and subordinated for the time being, but if another point of view is taken, another value can be seen to encompass other values. The superalternate values of hierarchy and centrality hold sway in most situations. However, there are always situations and viewpoints when the subalternate values can be seen to be most relevant. The superalternate and subalternate values are always in tension, even if this is hidden under the shared repetition of social practices that cover up the potentiality of multiple interpretations.

Thus, the superalternate aspect of Brahmanical hierarchy as well as that of kingship and dominance, which have dominated previous interpretations constitute only a part of the larger sacrificial process in India. There is another crucial aspect of ontological equality which represents the

---

[30] See Deliège (1992) and Mosse (1994) for relevant discussions of Moffat's scheme.

subalternate value and which makes the spontaneous commitment of members towards organic cooperation possible. Moreover, it is significant that the degree of importance and the semantic contents of each aspect – hierarchy, centrality, and equality – have changed in history. This is due not only to the workings of power in history that have been emphasized in works of 'ethnohistory' of kingship (Cohn 1987; Dirks 1987), in critiques of colonialism/Orientalism (Ahmad 1991; Inden 1990; Raheja 1988a), or in studies of politico-economic change (Fuller 1996; Fuller & Harris 2000). These authors are correct to point out the inappropriateness of the Dumontian insistence on an ahistorical and changeless hierarchy. However, they fail to address the role played by ordinary people's agency and their ethical and moral concerns. It is this 'third' space – a sphere of ethics and morality not captured by a focus on social status or political power – that I propose to address.[31]

THE RECONFIGURATION OF CASTE RELATIONSHIPS FROM BELOW

How do people utilize the cultural resource of subalternate values to realize ethical relationships?[32] It is undeniable that the superalternate values of status and power dominated socio-political relationships in rural Orissa in the post-colonial era. The subalternate value of ontological equality remained a subdued potentiality. As we have seen, factional politics controlled by the dominant caste held sway in village public life in the 1970s and 1980s. The Brahmanical hierarchy also persisted in the norm-centred representation of the caste order given by village informants. It would be one-sided, however, if we did not look at the aspect of social practice in transformation that resisted the post-colonial structure of hierarchy and dominance and slowly attempted to undermine it. In addition to the downward spread of democratization, from the 1960s there was also a subaltern movement of social transformation from below. Notably, there were workings of subalternate agency that slowly changed the pattern of inter-caste relationships.

The caste-based division of labour in the local community underwent a

---

[31]The term 'third space' was suggested by Demmer in a personal communication. The term 'th[illegible]d' is after Shotter (1993). Shotter contrasts 'practical-moral' knowledge to 'practical-technical' knowledge – knowing 'how' – and to 'theoretical-conceptual knowledge' – decontextualized knowing –, and calls it "knowing of the third kind" (Shotter 1993: xiii, 142). Social status can be related to theoretical-conceptual knowledge of the social system, whereas political power is related to practical-technical knowledge to attain one's interests. The sphere of 'moral society', referred to here as the third space, is related to this third kind of practical-moral knowledge (Tanabe 2002).

[32]In this section and below there are some passages drawn from Tanabe (2002).

transformation which reflected the gradual empowerment of the 'lower' castes as I have argued elsewhere (Tanabe 2004, 2006). For instance, in the case of Garh Manitri, the amount[33] of the annual payment of paddy grains[34] became negotiable in the so-called *jajmani* relationships between 'master' (*saanta*) and 'servant' (*sebaka*) households. Today, at the time of the annual transaction, there is often bargaining between the patrons and the service providers such as Barber (Bhandari), Washerman (Dhoba), Blacksmith (Kamara), and Astrologer (Jyotisha). Carpenters (Badhei) and Potters (Kumbhara) have even changed their forms of payment to daily wage and a piecework system, respectively, thus retaining 'master-servant' relationships only in name. Also, the economic importance of the master-servant relationships seems to have declined in quantitative terms as everyday commodities are more often purchased in the market.

Let us take the example of a young Barber man, Gobinda Barika,[35] who opened a hair "saloon" (the English word for a barber shop) in Garh Manitri in 1990. This was the first time in this village that a Barber offered the service on payment basis outside the so-called *jajmani* relations.[36] I asked him why he wanted to open a haircutting saloon. He said, "Instead of serving masters (*saanta*), I wanted to do my work on my own. Here, it is my shop and I am the owner (*malika*)." Gobinda Barika decided to remove himself from '*jajmani*' relations and become the independent owner of a barber shop. He did not opt to remain in the 'moral economy' where the patron-client relationship would at least give him an assurance of survival and a guarantee of subsistence. He preferred to put himself in the market, which might lack guarantees but would grant him the position of an independent owner and place him on equal terms with his customers.

Another noteworthy phenomenon is that several castes have started to refuse to perform hereditary allotted work which they find degrading. For example, Cowherds refused to carry palanquins for the 'upper' castes for

---

[33]The measure used on this occasion is called *nauti* or *gauni* in Khurda region, Orissa. It is a cylindrical basket about 25 cm in diameter and 25 cm in depth which is usually made of cane or tin. This is what is called a four seer *gauni* and it can hold four seer (= about 3 kg of paddy rice or nearly 5 kg of threshed rice).

[34]In the pre-colonial period, in addition to land given as part of the share, the performer of the service was given one bundle of paddy stalks a year from each service-receiving household, as the name of the gift *bira barttana* (bundle salary) suggests (Tanabe 2005). This practice continued until the 1960s with some of the servants. According to the villagers, the arrangement was that the Barber and the Washerman received one bundle every year per couple in the family, and the Blacksmith per bullock plough.

[35]All personal names in this paper are pseudonyms.

[36]Here I say "so-called" *jajmani* relations because it is problematic to include different kind of relationships (*jajman*-Brahman, master-servant etc.) under the umbrella term '*jajmani* relations'. In Garh Manitri, the word *jajman* is used only for the patrons of a Brahman priest. The word *saanta* (master) is used in relation to so-called service castes.

their marriage ceremonies in the 1970s. The 'upper' castes threatened them and argued that they should perform their traditional duty. The Cowherds responded by saying that their real traditional role was only to carry the palanquins of gods in religious rituals, but subsequently the 'upper' castes had forced them to carry them as well. They argued that this deviation from real tradition should be rectified. When the discussion did not result in agreement, the Cowherds told the 'upper' caste people that if they continued to force them to carry palanquins for them, they would not carry palanquins for deities in the village festival, which was considered the Cowherds' role. As the time of the village festival approached, the 'upper' castes had to give in and gave their word that henceforth they would only ask the Cowherds to carry the palanquins of deities. More disputes followed after the festival, but as the vehicle used for the bridegroom in marriage processions gradually changed from the palanquin to the Ambassador car in the 1980s, the topic was no longer brought up.

Here we can see the reconstruction of tradition taking place through a selective procedure. The Cowherds saw the work of carrying palanquins for the 'upper' castes as degrading according to their sense of dignity. However, instead of denying the traditional role altogether, they decided to redefine what they saw as constituting 'real tradition'. When this was denied by the 'upper' castes, the Cowherd people resisted by refusing to play their ritual role in the village festival. The 'upper' castes had to give in, probably because they did not want to be held responsible for disturbing the proper performance of the community festival. This kind of revision of the existing customs comes about as people begin to reflect upon the prevalent social set-up as being something that can be changed and look for possibilities of alternatives.

In another example, Sweepers (Hadi) are now reluctant to clean the village before community rituals. I was walking with a Khandayat (the dominant peasant-militia caste) leader, Narayana Srichandan, in the village before the Ramachandi festival in 1991, which is the most important community festival in the region. There was a Hadi ('untouchable' Sweeper-Drummer caste) man, Rama Naik, cleaning the street. Narayana Srichandan said to me, "Hadi people clean the whole village before the festival." Then, Rama Naik turned to me and said, "If we do not clean, these people hit us," pointing at Narayana Srichandan.

Narayana Srichandan, one of the Khandayat leaders, seems to have wanted to imply the idiom of organic ethics in order to emphasize the harmonious, cooperative aspect of the community festival in which different caste people have different responsibilities. However, the harmonious model was immediately contradicted by Rama Naik. His statement clearly indicated that he was doing the cleaning job because of violent sanctions threatened by the dominant caste group and not because he accepted the present system. Rama Naik was well aware that there are alternatives to the present social set-up and refused to take the present one for granted. These cases of resistance can be seen as attempts of the 'lower' caste to empower themselves and redefine their 'traditional' duty in order to maintain their dignity and self-respect (Tanabe 2002).

The 'lower' castes attempted to transform the caste-based division of labour and patron-client relationships in the local community in a way that would undermine the unquestioning reproduction of the old superalternate structure of hierarchy and dominance. The 'lower' castes slowly transformed the contents of practices so that they would be in a more respectable position with self-dignity and economic independence.

But we must ask ourselves a question here. Does this mean that caste as a social mechanism as a whole has been deconstructed? The answer seems to be 'No'. The transformation of *jajmani* relationships should not be understood only as the destruction of pre-market, customary exchange relationships by the intrusion of the market principle. Instead of just considering the workings of such anonymous market principles, we should note the conscious workings of 'caste associations' (*jati sabha*) as a unit of subaltern agency which resisted and/or negotiated with the patron dominant-caste households to pursue fairer transactions (Tanabe 2006). In the case of the Potters, who succeeded in transforming the system of exchange from the customary 'master-servant' relationships to a piecework system, they negotiated with the dominant caste in an organized manner through their caste association. The local leader of the Potters' association proudly told me that they had all cooperated together to rectify the unfair system of exchange. Caste as the basis of identity and agency continues in the subalternate attempts to achieve social transformation and improvement of their position.

The persistence of caste, however, is not only related to the phenomena of 'substantialization' where independent caste groups continue as units for endogamy and the reproduction of the caste tradition (Dumont 1980; Fuller 1996). What is important in understanding the phenomenon of caste as a reservoir of community ethics is that the aspect of sacrificial cooperation based on ontological equality seems to have continued and gained importance in inter-caste relationships in today's rural Orissa. Attempts at social transformation can be seen as being based on these subalternate sacrificial ethics rather than on, say, liberal individualism.

It should be noted that although several castes refused to perform roles which they deem degrading, they are more willing to accept what they consider as their proper 'traditional' ritual roles. Let us again take the case of Gobinda Barika. His father is the head barber who undertakes ritual tasks, such as carrying a torch in processions as part of the community festival. When I asked Gobinda Barika whether he wished to take over his father's role in the festival, he said, "When the time comes, I will decide. If I feel that I want to do it, I will do it. I do not want other people to tell me to do so. Previously, I did not feel like doing it, but now I am gradually beginning to think that I should do it. It is honourable work. It is service (*seba*) for the goddess." Gobinda Barika seems to accept that there is some meaning in the community ritual. He says he will do it not because of the pressure from the community, but because he feels it is his 'service' for the goddess. As I understand it, it is this attitude of service or self-sacrifice for a higher principle that is at the basis of the subaltern ethics of cooperation. Similarly, in the case of the Cowherds who refused to carry palanquins for the 'upper' castes, they were ready to accept their role for the deities and they continue their ritual role of carrying deities in the festival till today. They say that carrying the palanquins of gods is their original true 'duty' (*kartabya*) and 'work' (*kama*) whereas carrying palanquins for the 'upper' castes was only later imposed on them by the 'upper' castes. Thus, it is not the paradigm of the sacrificial organization itself that is denied. Rather, it is the contents of specific sacrificial duties that are coming to be redefined from below as subaltern agency expands its space and influence.

In exactly the same way, although the Sweepers are reluctant to clean the village, they take pride in acting as drumbeaters in the community ritual. The same Rama Naik who criticized the dominant caste for forcing him to clean, accepts the drumming role in the community goddess festival rather more willingly. He said to me with a touch of pride, "Unless we beat the drum, the goddess does not come to the village." Many young male Hadi work in the cities nowadays, but some even come back to the village during the festival in order to play the drums for the goddess. This shows that the idea of playing one's role in the organic whole itself is not rejected as long as there is an egalitarian respect for each role. Rama Naik was defying what he saw as hierarchical and oppressive but he accepted the role that allowed him a sense of pride and dignity as well as an indispensable position in the community.

It is notable that when it comes to explaining their 'proper' traditional role, 'lower' castes emphasize the aspect of devotionalism and the sacrificial ethics of duty (the belief that everyone can approach the divine through service). It is based on the idea of ontological equality of beings who are all capable of approaching the divine by offering their work as sacrifice.[37] The equality is at the level of the right to approach the divine through their work and not at the level of the content or choice of service. Therefore I call it *ontological* equality which is different from individual equality, which would involve freedom of choice of work. They deem their caste

---

[37]This philosophy is most eloquently expounded in the *Bhagavad Gita*, a scripture which is often discussed in local society.

identity and role indispensable and honourable in the collective sacrificial endeavour, while denying or at least minimizing the aspects of hierarchy and dominance in inter-caste relationships by redefining their 'traditional' role and position.

The semantic transformation or the shifting of emphasis in the interpretation of caste sacrificial organization seems also to be at work in Garh Manitri in the understanding of the community ritual, the Ramachandi festival. Although there are obvious aspects of Brahmanical hierarchy and royal centrality in the ritual, and the Brahmans and the dominant caste tend to emphasize their authority and privileges, in villager discourse in general it is the aspect of devotional submission, or offering of the self, that is emphasized today as the most important feature of the sacrificial ritual. Even Brahmans and members of the dominant caste admit that devotion is the most important aspect in conducting the ritual. 'Everybody does their own duty as service (to the goddess)' is the set phrase that one hears repeatedly about sacrificial organization. This is consistent with the villagers' insistence on the significance of the values of 'duty' and 'service', as well as with the ontological equality of each caste for the community and local deity.

By contrast, hierarchy and dominance are underplayed today and villagers, especially the 'lower' castes, are in effect shifting the semantics of the caste order to sacrificial cooperation and solidarity, in which each caste performs its role on an equal basis. The negotiations over *jajmani* exchanges and the redefinition of the content of their traditional duties can also be understood as the subalternate efforts towards this end. Thus, there seems to be a development of a form and idea of caste as sacrificial organization in contemporary local society in Orissa which highlights organic cooperation based on ontological equality while underplaying both purity-centred hierarchy and the political structure of dominance.

Nonetheless, since sacrifice in Indian history has long been related to ideas of hierarchy and dominance, it is not possible simply to discard its implications in caste organization. There will continue to be a process of renegotiation of meaning in the field of unequal power relationships. The idiom of 'cooperation' is also employed by the 'upper' castes as an ideological discourse to maintain the structure of hierarchy and dominance. For example, the dominant caste attempts to legitimize the cleaning job of the Sweepers by claiming that it is their traditional duty and that their cooperation is necessary for the proper running of the community. However, this does not mean that we should belittle the creative agency of the local people by simply assuming that the maintenance of caste-based duties necessarily always leads to the reproduction of the power structure. As identity rather than self-interest has become arguably the most important focus in contemporary Indian politics – whether local or national – the matter of values has become a serious politico-cultural concern of the villagers. Values and ethics, which are the basis of identity, are not mere ideology of power but constitute an important politico-cultural concern for villagers (Tanabe 2002). We should pay sufficient attention to subaltern efforts constantly to negotiate and transform the content and meaning of caste duties into democratically acceptable and existentially meaningful ones.

DEMOCRACY AND SACRIFICIAL ETHICS

The attempts at reformulation of social practice seem to have been limited mainly to the social and ritual sphere of community rituals and *jajmani* relationships in the 1970s and 1980s. For the village political economy, the landholding structure and the factional politics that centred around the dominant caste still largely dominated the scene in the 1970s and 1980s. There was thus a disjunction between the reformulation of caste relationships towards equal participation in the socio-ritual sphere and the power of the dominant caste in the politico-economic sphere in this period.

This disjunction represented the paradoxical nature and the fragmented form of life of the post-colonial predicament. The practice of the socio-ritual life of the community gradually accepted subalternate values whereas the sphere of politics, supposedly based on the principle of democracy, in reality remained dominated by the logic of power and number.

There were preliminary attempts to apply the moral sense of sacrificial ethics to transform the practices in the larger socio-political spheres in the 1980s and early 1990s. The questioning and criticizing by the 'lower' castes of the existing power relationships did not remain confined to the sphere of inter-caste exchange but gradually extended to the sphere of politics.[38] They more often than not covertly and sometimes overtly criticized the over-politicization and corruption of the dominant caste. In 1991-3, during my first fieldwork, the 'lower' caste population often angrily condemned the active factional members, in their absence, for

[38]Akhil Gupta describes a similar situation as follows, "Growing economic opportunities that enabled lower castes not to rely as heavily on agricultural labor in the village ... together with the rhetoric of social equality and the dependence of the upper castes on the electoral support of the lower castes, led to a phenomenal transformation in the confidence with which lower-caste people dealt with erstwhile landlords and other socially superior groups. Younger lower-caste men, still primarily wage labourers, publicly criticized upper-caste people, something that their fathers would not have dreamed of doing. Lower-caste people also ... criticized state officials for not implementing government development programs properly" (1998: 17).

'eating up' the subsidy meant for community development and resorting to threats of violence in order to impose their political decisions.

Let us take the example of a young Washerman, Krushna Malik, in local politics. There was a meeting in which committee members for the college in Garh Manitri were to be decided. The factional leaders attempted to include as many of their faction members as possible in the committee. The candidates of the factions were mostly Khandayats. In the course of the meeting, Krushna Malik spoke out and said that there should be a representative from each hamlet in Garh Manitri in the committee. His statement was met by loud shouts from faction members telling him to keep quiet. One faction leader suggested that the committee members should be elected on the basis of merit and recommendation. The discussion went back again to selecting people from the two factions. After the meeting, one Khandayat made a comment about Krushna Malik's statement: "It is all very well to say that there should be one representative from each hamlet. But that would not work. Committee members must possess a certain quality. What quality do they have? Each family has had its role in the village. We have been the leaders of the village in history and this quality cannot be acquired overnight." Krushna Malik later said to me, "The factions are destroying the village. Everybody must cooperate to develop the village. That is why I said there should be a representative from each hamlet. Then there can be real cooperation involving everybody."

The idea of representation has long been a part of the moral sense of justice in the political field. It has acquired legitimacy, along with the idea of democracy, in the discursive space of what constitutes proper administration and government. There seem to be two conflicting ideas of representation here. The logic of 'representation of particulars' demands that each social group should be represented, whereas the logic of 'represen tation of the majority' says that the majority should rule. The latter is supported by the democratic institution of electoral politics where numbers matter. The faction leader employed the logic of 'representation of the majority', which works in favour of the political primacy of the dominant caste, the Khandayats. Krushna Malik, in contrast, employed the logic of 'representation of particulars' when demanding that there should be a representative from each hamlet of the village. Since the composition of each hamlet more or less corresponds to a caste group, this suggestion had in effect advocated caste-wise proportional representation.

In factional politics, state resources have to be distributed in proportion to political influence in order for a maximum number of votes to be secured. In the public meeting described above, this factional logic of political society reigned at the beginning. But when Krushna Malik presented a legitimate argument based on the logic of representation of particulars, the faction leaders had to respond by resorting to another legitimate discourse. So, one Khandayat leader took up the logic of meritocracy and connected this to the logic of majority representation.[39]

In this complex situation, plural and contestatory ideas and discourses regarding rightness and goodness appeared on the scene. These included ideas of 'representation of particulars', 'representation of the majority', and meritocracy. Moreover, it is interesting to note that there were also two forms of sacrificial ethics legitimizing two opposing political positions. When the Khandayat man mentioned the necessity of a certain 'quality' in a committee member, he employed the discourse of sacrificial ethics in the sense that each man should stick to his traditional position in the hierarchy. This 'hierarchical sacrificial ethics' worked along with the logic of 'representation of the majority' to deny representation to the 'lower' castes. Meanwhile, Krushna Malik employed the discourse of sacrificial ethics in the sense that each person should have a properly recognized and respectable role. This discourse of 'egalitarian sacrificial ethics' was combined with the logic of 'representation of particulars' to promote representation from different sections of the community. It is interesting to note that this suggestion by Krushna Malik indicates a mediation between the paradigm of sacrificial organization, the service of each caste for the whole, and democratic representation. Although this suggestion was not taken up seriously by the majority dominant caste, the fact that such a proposition was made in public suggests that there was increasing opportunity for the subalterns to speak up for themselves.

It was in such a situation that the combined effect of liberalization policy and the reformation of the *gram panchayat* brought about the 'democratization' of the local political process in the mid 1990s. When we look at the re-establishment of the function of the panchayat and the demise of the dominant-caste centred factional politics in Orissan villages in this period, it seems to me that the values of democracy and sacrificial ethics have been connected to legitimize and support the kind of representation practised in the new *gram panchayat*. The vocabularies used by the villagers to describe the work in the *gram panchayat* strikingly resemble the semantic resources developed in the socio-ritual sphere. People talk about doing their 'duty' as 'service' for the village community.

The logic of representation in the *gram panchayat* today (in 2003) almost exactly follows the kind espoused by the young Washerman about ten years earlier. He espoused the logic of 'representation of particulars', which demands that each social group should be represented, in contradistinction to the logic of 'representation of majority', which demands that the

---

[39]The opposition between the logic of proportional representation and that of meritocracy is a familiar topic in regard to the problem of reservation in state-level politics as well.

majority should rule. The ward-wise election of the panchayat members, where a ward more or less corresponds to a (few) hamlet(s) dominated by a (few) caste group(s), as well as the reservation measure ensure that there will be representation of different caste groups in the *gram panchayat*. The way the *gram panchayat* is organized, with the representatives of different caste members and the discursive framework employed in it to talk about 'service' and 'duty' for the common welfare demonstrates how the sacrificial ethic, mainly developed in the sphere of inter-caste relations, is now beginning to transform itself beyond the ritual sphere and to provide the basis of morality in the political sphere. What we are witnessing in contemporary Indian society may be a process of creation of an Indian form of local democracy based on the creative mediation by the people between indigenous ethical resources and ideas and institutions of democracy.[40] Here, both cultural values and forms of democracy are being modified to suit each other.

THE POST-POSTCOLONIAL AGENDA: DEMOCRACY AND DEVELOPMENT

Although India seems to be developing its own form of local democracy, at least in its politics of representation at the level of the *gram panchayat*, this does not yet seem to be connected with any process of mutual cooperation for community development. The reason why there came to be less popular participation in factional politics in the 1990s was that there was a decrease in the relative economic importance of the state resources distributed through factional channels. The democratization of the *gram panchayat* in the 1990s took place not because the dominant castes learned to internalize democratic values, but because they saw better opportunities in the market and became less obsessed with controlling local politics, whereas the 'lower' caste groups took the new opportunity of participating in village politics enthusiastically.

Meanwhile, state corruption continues, which results in the misuse of the state resources and the malfunctioning of development schemes. In this situation, although democratization has indeed taken place in terms of the representative constitution and the working of the *gram panchayat*, it has

---

[40]However, I am not arguing that there exists a single form of Indian democracy. Rather, it is necessary to see contestations of different potential forms of democracy in India. This echoes the warning by Sugata Bose and Ayesha Jalal that we should bear in mind "the contestations that animated the creative efforts to fashion a vibrant culture and politics of anti colonial modernity" instead of overemphasizing differences as Partha Chatterjee has done (Bose & Jalal 1998; Chatterjee 1993). See Sen (1998) for similar criticisms of "communitarian understandings".

not resulted in effective functioning for local development. There is now growing dissatisfaction and frustration over the present working of community development programmes. There is also increasing criticism and despair regarding corruption in the state administration, especially from the underprivileged who are apparently empowered in terms of democratic participation but remain poor, if not poorer, in the current situation.

Today, successful participatory democracy – even with its ethics of sacrificial cooperation – is not effective for local community development, since democracy under the present poor governance is not able to translate the increasing political participation of the subalterns into proper distribution and usage of state resources. It is the malfunctioning of the state apparatus – corruption – which is at the root of the problem. Moreover, economic activities in the market are basically individual affairs independent of the community. As more people – especially those with means – are interested in developing their own welfare in the market, there is less incentive for them to spend time and energy on community development. In this situation, there is a growing disjunction between the democracy of representation and economic development under liberalization. Hence there now seems to be a change of agenda. The post-postcolonial agenda seems to be to find a way to make participatory Indian democracy compatible with the global market economy.

CONCLUSION

The post-colonial agenda of independent India was to mediate the newly established democracy with the social values and practices of people in an unequal society. It is my contention that the pivot of the mediation lay in people's agency with their subalternate values of ontological equality which gradually transformed the social scene dominated by hierarchy and dominance. It is this space of mediation, in post-colonial India, between the democratic ideas and institutions and the people under social dominance and hierarchy – and yet with transformative agency and embodied moral sense – that I have tried to describe, using the case of rural Orissa.

For villagers, there has been an uneasy coexistence of imported and indigenous discourses and values. But, at the same time, this coexistence has entailed considerable potential.[41] The hybrid coexistence of fragmented and incoherent cultural resources is not only a source of dilemmas for people, but also a rich politico-cultural reservoir for reconstruction and manoeuvre of practices and discourses. Here, we can go beyond both the

[41]Bishnu Mohpatra remarks: "In fact the language of community and the vocabulary of civil society coexist uneasily (but sometimes with a lot of possibilities) in Talajanga" (2001: 671).

modernist teleology of Benedict Anderson (1991) and Ernest Gellner (1983), and the cultural determinism of 'civic culture' as posited by Robert Putnam et al. (1993). Fragmentary resources "afford" (Gibson 1979) people to construct and negotiate a pattern of social practice that can meet contrary and dilemma-strewn post-colonial circumstances.[42] This, however, does not mean that they are only of an ad hoc nature with no consequences.

There seems to be a larger structural transformation from below which has been successful in establishing socio-political practices that connect the present democratic set-up with the subalternate value of sacrificial ethics. As I have repeatedly contended, the present socio-political process in rural Orissa is witnessing a politico-moral translation of sacrificial ethics of ontological equality into a political demand for equal participatory democracy of different groups. Here, there is a subaltern attempt of mediation between embodied ethical sense and democratic ideas and institutions. This involves the process of reinterpretation and reconstruction of the 'image of community' (Li 1996) – from hierarchy and dominance to sacrificial cooperation based on ontological equality – as well as forms of democracy – participatory equality not of individuals but caste groups – in an attempt to create viable democratic practice in Indian society.

This, however, does not mean a story with a happy ending. There is an ongoing dynamics of domination and resistance between the dominant classes and the subaltern people. This dynamics is related to the *longue durée* contestation between superalternate values of hierarchy and dominance and subalternate value of ontological equality. While the subalterns seem to enjoy their spring in the *gram panchayat*, the battlefield for the dominant classes seems to have shifted since liberalization to the global market economy rather than local politics for control over the state resources. The subalterns seem to have claimed their victory only in a place where the dominant classes have already lost interest and evacuated the field. Now the real challenge for the subalterns seems to be to extend their battlefield to the economic. Meanwhile, there have been attempts by some of the dominant classes to pursue both economic success in the global economy and imposition of the superalternate values on to society in the name of 'Hindutva'. If the purpose of democracy is to ensure not only formal political rights but also capability towards freedom in Amartya Sen's sense (1993, 1999), the post-postcolonial agenda for India must be to mediate the success of participatory politics with the development of

---

[42]The Gibsonian approach to perception has opened the way to see how we are keeping-in-touch with the world that is permitting us to do certain things – to experience the world in a certain way, rather than individuals perceiving the world in their consciousness in a one-directional manner. However, what the Gibsonian framework lacks is the perspective upon how a certain way of perception of the world is granted recognition and legitimacy in society (Shotter 1993: 86). This is where the question of the cultural-politics of ethics enters.

overall well-being. It remains to be seen how, by whom, and what kind of cultural resources will be utilized in order to reformulate new kinds of social practices that would make this mediation possible.

REFERENCES

Ahmad, A. 1991. 'Between Orientalism and Historicism: Anthropological Knowledge of India'. *Studies in History* (n.s.) 7: 135-63.

Anderson, B. 1991. *Imagined Communities: Reflections on the Origin and Spread of Nationalism*. London: Verso.

Asad, T. 1983. 'Anthropological Conceptions of Religion: Reflections on Geertz'. *Man* (n.s.) 18: 237-59.

Bailey, F.G. 1963. *Politics and Social Change: Orissa in 1959*. Berkeley: University of California Press.

——. 1969. *Stratagems and Spoils: A Social Anthropology of Politics*. Oxford: Blackwell.

Bardhan, P. 1984. *The Political Economy of Development in India*. Oxford and New York: Blackwell.

——. 1998. 'The State against Society: The Great Divide in Indian Social Science Discourse', in S. Bose and A. Jalal (eds.), *Nationalism, Democracy, and Development: State and Politics in India*. Delhi: Oxford University Press.

Bataille, G. 1976. *Theorie de la Religion* (Oeuvres Completes 7).

Bates, C. 2004. 'The Development of Panchayati Raj', in S. Basu and C. Bates (eds.), *Rethinking Indian Political Institution*. London: Anthem Press.

Bauman, Z. 1993. *Postmodern Ethics*. Oxford: Blackwell.

Bayly, S. 1999. *Caste, Society and Politics in India from the Eighteenth Century to the Modern Age* (The New Cambridge History of India, IV. 3). Cambridge: Cambridge University Press.

Beck, U., A. Giddens, and S. Lash. 1994. *Reflexive Modernization: Politics, Tradition and Aesthetics in the Modern Social Order*. London: Polity Press.

Béteille, A. 1994. 'Secularism and Intellectuals'. *Economic and Political Weekly* 29: 559-66.

Billig, M. 1987. *Arguing and Thinking: A Rhetorical Approach to Social Psychology*. Cambridge: Cambridge University Press; Paris: Editions de la Maison des sciences de l'homme.

Bose, S. 1997. 'Instruments and Idioms of Colonial and National Development', in F. Cooper and R. Packard (eds.), *International Development and the Social Sciences: Essays on the History and Politics of Knowledge*. Berkeley: University of California Press.

Bose, S. and A. Jalal 1998. *Modern South Asia: History, Culture, Political-Economy*. London and New York: Routledge.

Bourdieu, P. 1990. *The Logic of Practice*, tr. R. Nice. Cambridge: Polity Press.

Brass, P. 1965. *Factional Politics in an Indian State: The Congress Party in Uttar Pradesh.* Berkeley: University of California Press.

Burghart, R. 1990. 'Ethnographers and Their Local Counterparts in India', in his *The Conditions of Listening: Essays on Religion, History and Politics in South Asia*. Delhi: Oxford University Press.

Chatterjee, P. 1986. *Nationalist Thought and the Colonial World.* London: Zed Books.

——. 1993. *The Nation and Its Fragments: Colonial and Postcolonial Histories.* Princeton: Princeton University Press.

——. 2004. *The Politics of the Governed: Reflections on Popular Politics in Most of the World.* New York: Columbia University Press.

Cohn, B.S. 1987. 'Political Systems in Eighteenth Century India: The Benares Region', in his *An Anthropologist among the Historians and Other Essays.* Delhi: Oxford University Press.

Corbridge, S. and J. Harriss. 2000. *Reinventing India: Liberalization, Hindu Nationalism and Popular Democracy*. New Delhi: Oxford University Press.

Das, V. 1982. *Structure and Cognition: Aspects of Hindu Caste and Ritual.* Delhi: Oxford University Press.

——. 1994. 'The Anthropological Discourse on India', in R. Borofsky (ed.), *Assessing Cultural Anthropology*. New York: McGraw-Hill.

Deliège, R. 1992. 'Replication and Consensus: Untouchability, Caste and Ideology in India'. *Man* (n.s.) 27: 155-73.

Demmer, U. in press. 'Jenu Kurumba Culture as a "Tradition of Persuasion"', in S. Tyler and I. Strecker (eds.), *Rhetoric Culture*. London: Berghahn.

Dirks, N.B. 1987. *The Hollow Crown: Ethnohistory of an Indian Little Kingdom.* Cambridge: Cambridge University Press.

——. 2001. *Castes of Mind: Colonialism and the Making of Modern India.* Princeton: Princeton University Press.

Dumont, L. 1980. *Homo Hierarchicus: The Caste System and Its Implications.* Chicago: Chicago University Press.

Fabian, J. 1983. *Time and the Other: How Anthropology Makes Its Object.* New York: Columbia University Press.

Fuller, C. 1996. 'Introduction', in C. Fuller (ed.), *Caste Today*. Delhi: Oxford University Press.

Fuller, C.J. and V. Bénéï (eds.). 2000. *The Everyday State and Society in Modern India.* Delhi: Social Science Press.

Fuller, C.J. and J. Harris. 2000. 'For an Anthropology of the Modern Indian State', in C.J. Fuller and V. Bénéï (eds.).

Gellner, E. 1983. *Nations and Nationalism.* Ithaca: Cornell University Press.

Gibson, J.J. 1979. *The Ecological Approach to Visual Perception*. London: Houghton Mifflin.

Giddens, A. 1990. *The Consequences of Modernity*. Stanford: Stanford University Press.

——. 1991. *Modernity and Self-Identity: Self and Society in the Late Modern Age*. Stanford: Stanford University Press.

Gregory, C.A. 1997. *Savage Money: The Anthropology and Politics of Commodity Exchange*. Amsterdam: Harwood Academic.

Guha, R. 1985. 'The Career of an Anti-God in Heaven and on Earth', in A. Mitra (ed.), *The Truth Unites: Essays in Tribute to Samar Sen*. Calcutta: Subarnarekha.

Gupta, A. 1995. 'Blurred Boundaries: The Discourse of Corruption, the Culture of Politics, and the Imagined State'. *American Ethnologist* 22: 375-402.

——. 1998. *Postcolonial Developments: Agriculture in the Making of Modern India*. Durham, NC: Duke University Press.

Hardiman, D. 1982. 'The Indian "Faction": A Political Theory Examined', in R. Guha (ed.), *Subaltern Studies I: Writings on South Asian History and Society*. Delhi: Oxford University Press.

Hocart, A.M. 1950. *Caste: A Comparative Study*. London: Methuen.

——. 1970. *Kings and Councillors*. Chicago: University of Chicago Press.

Hubert, H. and M. Mauss. 1964. *Sacrifice: Its Nature and Function*, tr. W.D. Halls. Chicago: University of Chicago Press.

Inden, R.B. 1978. 'Ritual, Authority, and Cyclic Time in Hindu Kingship', in J.F. Richards (ed.), *Kingship and Authority in South Asia*. Madison: University of Wisconsin.

——. 1986. Orientalist Construction of India. *Modern Asian Studies* 20, 1-46.

——. 1990. *Imagining India*. Oxford: Blackwell.

Kaviraj, S. 1997. 'A Critique of the Passive Revolution', in P. Chatterjee (ed.), *State and Politics in India*. Delhi: Oxford University Press.

Khilnani, S. 1999. *The Idea of India*. Delhi: Penguin Books.

Lewis, O. 1958. *Village Life in Northern India*. Urbana: University of Illinois Press.

Li, T.M. 1996. 'Images of Community: Discourse and Strategy in Property Relations'. *Development and Change* 27: 501-27.

MacIntyre, A. 1981. *After Virtue*. London: Duckworth.

Madan, T.N. 1985. 'Concerning the Categories Subha and Suddha in Hindu Culture: An Exploratory Essay', in J.J. Carman and F. Marglin (eds.), *Purity and Auspiciousness in Indian Society*. Leiden: E.J. Brill.

——. 1987. *Non-Renunciation: Themes and Interpretations of Hindu Culture*. Delhi: Oxford University Press.

Malamoud, C. 1981. 'On the Rhetoric and Semantics of Purusartha'. *Contributions to Indian Sociology* 15: 33-54.

Marglin, F.A. 1985. *Wives of the God-King: The Rituals of the Devadasis of Puri*. Delhi: Oxford University Press.

Marriott, M. 1955. *Village India*. Chicago: University of Chicago Press.

——. 1976. 'Hindu Transactions: Diversity without Dualism', in B. Kapferer (ed.), *Transaction and Meaning*. Philadelphia: Institute for the Study of Human Issues.

Mayer, A.C. 1960. *Caste and Kinship in Central India: A Village and Its Region*. London: Routledge.

Mencher, J.P. 1974. 'The Caste System Upside Down, or the Not-So-Mysterious East'. *Current Anthropology* 15: 469-78.

Moffatt, M. 1979. *An Untouchable Community in South India: Structure and Consensus*. Princeton: Princeton University Press.

Mohapatra, B. 1990. 'The Politics of Oriya Nationalism, 1903-1936'. Unpublished D.Phil. thesis, Oxford University.

Mohapatra, B.N. 1997. 'The Problem'. *Seminar* 456: 12-16.

——. 2001. 'Social Connectedness and Fragility of Social Capital'. *Economic and Political Weekly* 36: 665-72.

Mosse, D. 1994. 'Idioms of Subordination and Styles of Protest among Christian and Hindu Harijan Castes in Tamil Nadu'. *Contributions to Indian Sociology* (n.s.) 28: 67-106.

Nandy, A. forthcoming. 'Democratic Culture and Images of the State: India's Unending Ambivalence', in M. Kimura and A. Tanabe (eds.), *The State in India: Past and Present*. Delhi: Oxford University Press.

Nicholas, R.W. 1963 (1958). 'Village Factions and Political Parties in Rural West Bengal'. *Journal of Commonwealth Political Studies* 2: 17-32.

Overing, J. 1985. 'Introduction', in J. Overing (ed.), *Reason and Morality*. London and New York: Tavistock Publications.

——. 2003. 'In Praise of the Everyday: Trust and the Art of Social Living in an Amazonian Community'. *Ethnos* 68: 293-316.

Overing, J. and A. Passes. 2000. 'Introduction: Conviviality and the Opening up of Amazonian Anthropology', in J. Overing and A. Passes (eds.), *The Anthropology of Love and Anger: The Aesthetics of Conviviality in Native Amazonia*. London and New York: Routledge.

Pardo, I. 2000. 'Morals of Legitimacy: Interplay between Responsibility, Authority and Trust', in I. Pardo (ed.), *Morals of Legitimacy: Between Agency and System*. New York and Oxford: Berghahn Books.

Parry, J. 2000. 'The "Crisis of Corruption" and "the Idea of India": A Worm's Eye View', in I. Pardo (ed.), *Morals of Legitimacy: Between Agency and System*. Oxford: Berghahn Books.

Putnam, R.D., R. Leonardi, and R.Y. Nanetti. 1993. *Making Democracy Work: Civic Traditions in Modern Italy*. Princeton: Princeton University Press.

Quigley, D. 1993. *The Interpretation of Caste*. Oxford: Clarendon Press.

——. 1994. 'Is a History of Caste Still Possible?', in U. Sharma and M. Searle-Chatterjee (eds.), *Contextualising Caste: Post-Dumontian Approaches*. Oxford: Blackwell.

——. 2000. 'Scapegoats: The Killing of Kings and Ordinary People'. *The Journal of the Royal Anthropological Institute* 6: 237-54.

Raheja, G.G. 1988a. 'India: Caste, Kingship, and Dominance Reconsidered'. *Annual Review of Anthropology* 17: 497-522.

——. 1988b. *The Poison in the Gift: Ritual, Prestation and the Dominant Caste in a North Indian Village*. Chicago: University of Chicago Press.

Richardson, M. 2000. 'Enough Said', in A.L. Macfie (ed.). *Orientalism: A Reader*. Edinburgh: Edinburgh University Press.

Schnepel, B. 1988. 'In Quest of Life: Hocart's Scheme of Evolution from Ritual Organization to Government'. *Archives Européenne de Sociologie* 29: 165-87.

Sen, A. 1993. 'Capability and Well-Being', in M. Nussbaum and A.K. Sen (eds.), *The Quality of Life*. Oxford: Clarendon Press.

——. 1998. 'On Interpreting India's Past', in S. Bose and A. Jalal (eds.), *Nationalism, Democracy and Development: State and Politics in India*. Delhi: Oxford University Press.

——. 1999. *Development as Freedom*. Oxford and Tokyo: Oxford University Press.

Shotter, J. 1993. *Cultural Politics of Everyday Life: Social Constructionism, Rhetoric and Knowing of the Third Kind*. Toronto: University of Toronto Press.

Shulman, D. 1985. 'Kingship and Prestation in South Indian Myth and Epic'. *Asian and African Studies* 19: 93-117.

Spivak, G.C. 1988. 'Can the Subaltern Speak?', in C. Nelson and L. Grossberg (eds.), *Marxism and the Interpretation of Culture*. Urbana: University of Illinois Press.

Srinivas, M.N. 1952. *Religion and Society among the Coorgs of South India*. Oxford: Clarendon Press.

Tanabe, A. 1998. 'Ethnohistory of Land and Identity in Khurda, Orissa: From Pre-colonial Past to Post-colonial Present'. *Journal of Asian and African Studies* 56: 75-112.

——. 1999. 'The Transformation of Sakti: Gender and Sexuality in the Festival of Goddess Ramachandi', in M. Tanaka and M. Tachikawa (eds.), *Living with Sakti: Gender, Sexuality and Religion in South Asia*. Osaka: National Museum of Ethnology.

——. 2002. 'Moral Society, Political Society and Civil Society in Post-Colonial India: A View from Orissan Locality'. *Journal of the Japanese Association for South Asian Studies* 14: 40-67.

——. 2004. 'Democracy and Development in Agrarian India: An Anthropological Reflection on Rural Political Economy'. Paper presented at the workshop on 'South Asia and East Asia: Comparisons and Connections', South Asia Initiative, Asia Center, Harvard University, 2004.

——. 2005 'The System of Entitlements in Eighteenth-Century Khurda, Orissa: Reconsideration of "Caste" and "Community" in Late Pre-Colonial India'. *South Asia* 28 (3): 345-85.

——. 2006. 'Recast(e)ing Identity: Transformation of Inter-Caste Relationships in Post-Colonial Rural Orissa'. *Modern Asian Studies* 40 (3): 761-96.

Tanabe, A. and Y. Tokita-Tanabe 2003. 'Introduction: Gender and Modernity in Asia and the Pacific', in Y. Hayami, A. Tanabe, and Y. Tokita-Tanabe (eds.), *Gender and Modernity: Perspectives from Asia and the Pacific*. Kyoto and Melbourne: Kyoto University Press and Trans Pacific Press.

Tanaka, M. 1991. *Patrons, Devotees, and Goddesses: Ritual and Power among the Tamil Fishermen of Sri Lanka*. Kyoto: Institute for Research in Humanities, Kyoto University.

Taylor, C. 1985. *Human Agency and Language (Philosophical Papers I)*. Cambridge: Cambridge University Press.

Tokita-Tanabe, Y. 2003. 'Aesthetics of the Female Self: Modernity and Cultural Agency of Urban Middle-Class Women in Orissa', in Y. Hayami, A. Tanabe, and Y. Tokita-Tanabe (eds.), *Gender and Modernity: Perspectives from Asia and the Pacific*. Kyoto and Melbourne: Kyoto University Press and Trans Pacific Press.

Turner, V. 1969. *The Ritual Process: Structure and Anti-Structure*. Chicago: Aldine Publishing Company.

van der Veer, P. 1988. *Gods on Earth: The Management of Religious Experience and Identity in a North Indian Pilgrimage Centre*. London: Athlone Press.

van Gennep, A. 1960. *The Rites of Passage*, tr. M.B. Vizedom and G.L. Caffee. London: Routledge & K. Paul.

Visvanathan, S. and H. Sethi (eds.). 1998. *Foul Play: Chronicles of Corruption*. New Delhi: Banyan Books.

Wade, R. 1982. 'The System of Administrative and Political Corruption: Canal Irrigation in South India'. *Journal of Development Studies* 18: 287-328.

——. 1985. 'The Market of Public Office: Why the Indian State is not Better at Development'. *World Development* 13: 467-97.

Washbrook, D. 1976. *The Emergence of Provincial Politics: The Madras Presidency, 1870-1920*. Cambridge: Cambridge University Press.

Yadav, Y. 2000. 'Understanding the Second Democratic Upsurge: Trends of Bahujan Participation in Electoral Politics in the 1990s', in F.R. Frankel, Z. Hasan, R. Bhargava, and B. Arora (eds.), *Transforming India: Social and Political Dynamics of Democracy*. Delhi: Oxford University Press.

Yanai, T. 1993. 'Souki to Hanpuku: Aru Mapuche no Yumegatari no Bunseki (Remembrance and Repetition: Analysis of a Mapuche Dream Narrative)'. Unpublished Ph.D. thesis, Tokyo University (in Japanese).

PART 2

TRANSFORMATIONS OF RELIGIOUS IDENTITIES AND PRACTICES

6

Hindus and Muslims after the 2002 Gujarat Riots: 'Imaging' as Binary Opposites

LANCY LOBO AND BISWAROOP DAS

THE RIOTS

The torching of carriage S-6 of the Ahmedabad-bound train Sabarmati Express at Godhra on 27 February 2002, in which fifty-eight passengers, including twenty-six women and twelve children, were burnt to death, was shocking. But for the burnt corpses of the ill-fated passengers to become the justification for armed squads of the ruling Hindu Nationalist Party with its 'brother' organizations – the RSS, VHP, and Bajrang Dal – to launch a pogrom against the innocent Muslims of Gujarat was hideous.[1]

Around 2,000 Muslims were killed in the post-Godhra riots which continued for months. Eyewitnesses, victims, survivors, and observers put the numbers who terrorized them at less than 2,000; most often, even in remote villages, they were closer to 10,000-15,000-strong mobs armed with deadly agricultural implements. Key men carried guns and rifles. A few in the crowd even carried mobile phones to enable military coordination in the attacks. Dead bodies no longer resembled human beings: they were reduced – whenever they had not been burnt to ashes – to a grotesque and pathetic sight. Rape was used as an instrument for the subjugation and humiliation of a community. Pregnant women's bellies were slit open with swords and foetuses flung in the fire. A chilling and hitherto absent technique was the deliberate destruction of evidence – barring a few cases,

[1]This paper is part of a larger study, 'Geography of Gujarat Riots, 2002: Causatives and Spatial Patterns of Related Factors', Centre for Culture and Development, Vadodara, April 2004. We are thankful to the participants of the seminar in ILCAA where it was presented, and especially to Katsuo Nawa and David Gellner for very useful comments. The usual disclaimers apply.

women who were gang-raped were thereafter hacked and burnt (Genocide 2002).

Contrary to popular belief, the 2002 Gujarat riots were mainly concentrated in the state's central and northern zones, leaving peninsular Saurashtra, Kacch, and the south Gujarat regions largely devoid of direct clashes and riots between the two communities. This becomes evident from the maps showing the spatial distribution of a large number of related variables carefully aggregated, analysed, and plotted under the following heads: (1) triggering events; (2) clashes; (3) rumours; (4) damage; (5) other effects; (6) interventions by agencies towards rescue and relief; (7) state action; and (8) extent and spread of riot.[2] What emerges from these maps is that the cities of Ahmedabad and Vadodara including their outskirts and the *taluka*s of Anand and Chotaudepur in central Gujarat and Kadi in northern Gujarat can be grouped together as *very highly affected* areas. This is followed by the *taluka*s of Borsad, Sojitra, Jetpur, Naswadi, Kawant, Halol, and Nadiad in the central area, Bayad in the north, and parts of Bhavnagar in the Saurashtra region which fall in the *highly affected* category. The *moderately affected* areas were the *taluka*s of Padra, Dabhoi, Khambhat, Petlad, Thasra, Godhra, Limkheda, Mehmedabad, Daskroi, and Viramgam in the central zone; Mehsana, Prantij, Vijapur, Meghraj, Modasa, Himmatnagar, Idar, Vadali, and Vijaynagar in the northern zone; and Jhagadia in the southern zone. Excluding the cities of Ahmedabad and Vadodara and at a much lower scale Surat and Rajkot, riots, clashes, and damage were mainly witnessed in 35 of the 211 *taluka*s or 16 per cent of such blocks in the state. However, of the *taluka*s in the central zone, as many as 31 per cent (19 out of 62 *taluka*s), and of those in the northern zone as many as 24 per cent (10 out of 42 *taluka*s) witnessed a higher intensity of rioting.[3]

THE BACKGROUND

Conflicts and riots among Hindus and Muslims in India are not a new phenomenon. They have, however, been less frequent and not as intense in terms of the scale and nature of violence as in some recent riots. The 2002 Gujarat riots are one among a series that have been exceptionally violent when compared to riots that had occurred previously in the state or when compared to riots that had occurred elsewhere in the country. It may well be said that the 2002 Gujarat riots should properly be called a pogrom because they occurred with the complicity of the state.

---

[2] We collated data from reports in two vernacular newspapers, viz., *Gujarat Today* and *Gujarat Samachar*, for the months of March and April 2002.

[3] For more details and, especially for maps showing the spatial spread of the variables mentioned, see Lobo & Das (2004).

Riots in India during the post Independence period have gradually acquired a character qualitatively different from those that occurred during the British period. These have no more remained assertions to gain economic and political space by subjugating different minority groups at the local and/or regional level. Instead, they now draw their contents from a new form of political discourse that grew first in a latent and subsequently in an explicit form through the sustained introduction of a 'communal' and divisive ideology. Institutionalized through supportive structures, components of it spread wider and, to a large extent, became a pan-Indian phenomenon. Intermediated with the ideology of 'Hindutva' (Hinduness), such a form of communalism has encroached upon spaces that could not be guarded well by forces claiming to oppose such formations. Compelled, as they were, to participate in the framework of a democratic model representing a wide range of caste- and class-based sectarian interests, several political parties responded to changes through accommodations, alliances, and adjustments. To what extent other political parties in the country have been 'secular' within the vote-based political arithmetic of gaining, regaining, retaining, and re-affirming power is difficult to ascertain. It can, however, be said that the contents of political discourse and their articulation in different forms by parties like the Congress has been quite different so far as the degree of inclusion of 'religio-political' discourse is concerned. Evidently, such a discourse formed an explicit part of the appeal of the 'Hindu nationalist' Bharatiya Janata Party (BJP) and its political as well as 'non-political' allies and associates.

The notion of a unified India, propagated through a subtext of 'Hindu nationalism', emerged as an important component of the BJP's project of nation-building. And within this context, the state of Gujarat emerged as one of the foremost states where the BJP witnessed a substantial rise in its political fortunes. This is evident from its having gained a progressively increasing number of seats in successive elections since 1989 except for its recent downfall in the 2004 parliamentary elections. At the state level, however, the party continues to rule after strengthening its position substantially in the 1990 Assembly elections by winning 68 of the 143 seats contested, and subsequently gaining an overwhelming majority in the 2002 Assembly elections.

THE CONTEXT

Forming a large part of western India, Gujarat is one of the most industrially prosperous states of the Indian union. With 82 per cent of its gross state domestic product coming from the secondary and tertiary sectors and a much higher average annual rate of growth compared to other states, it has improved its economic position substantially, especially during the last two decades. In spite of a high rate of growth, growing industrial investments, and an economic environment which facilitated sustained growth of the manufacturing sector the state has been witness to a number of large-scale riots and unrest between Hindus and Muslims.

Available data indicates that the percentage of Hindus to the total population in Gujarat has remained steady at a little below 91 per cent since 1951. In 1991 the Hindu share was 90.83 per cent, followed by 8.73 per cent Muslims and 0.44 per cent Christians. The latter form a significant proportion of the population only in one district of Gujarat, Dangs, where their proportion increased from 1.33 per cent in 1981 to 5.43 per cent in 1991. Surat, adjoining the Dangs, has a Christian presence of 0.94 per cent and Kheda near Ahmedabad 1.48 per cent. In Ahmedabad (including Gandhinagar), Vadodara, and Bharuch their proportion is between 0.5 and 1 per cent. In all other districts of Gujarat, their presence is negligibly small.[4]

Distributed in the entire state, Muslims form nearly 5 per cent or more of the population in all districts, except in the Dangs. Their presence is smaller in the north-eastern districts but rises in the southern Gujarat districts, most of which have a Muslim population of around 10 per cent. Among these, Bharuch has an exceptionally high Muslim presence at 16.60 per cent. In the south-west, within its Saurashtra subregion, the Muslim presence is higher in the western districts of Jamnagar, Junagadh, and Rajkot, and relatively lower in the eastern districts of Surendranagar, Bhavnagar, and Amreli. In Jamnagar, their share is 13 per cent, followed by Junagadh and Rajkot where they form somewhat less than 10 per cent of the population. In Surendranagar, Bhavnagar, and Amreli, their presence is around 6 per cent. The district of Kacch in the north-west has the highest proportion of Muslims in the state. In 1991, they constituted 19.64 per cent of its population. Since 1951, the proportion of Muslims in most districts of Saurashtra and Kacch subregions has remained unchanged, or has declined, while it has shown a slight rise in most districts of the Gujarat subregion, thus keeping the proportion of Muslims in the state as a whole more or less unchanged.

Corresponding to the all-India trends and figures, a larger proportion of Muslims in Gujarat remains located in its urban areas. In 1991, 58 per cent of Muslims as compared to 32 per cent of Hindus were living in cities and towns of the state. The highest proportion of Muslims, at 40 per cent, is in Godhra, Panchmahal district, though their proportion in the district as a whole is only 4.6 per cent. Bhuj in Kacch with a Muslim presence of 24 per

---

[4]For these demographic data, as well as those presented in the following two paragraphs, see Joshi et al. (2003: 66-7).

cent, Patan in Saurashtra with 27 per cent, and Bharuch in south Gujarat with 28 per cent are the other towns with a high Muslim presence. Jamnagar and Junagadh in Saurashtra and Surat in south Gujarat also have relatively high Muslim populations of 20, 18, and 14 per cent respectively. Of the other major cities in the state, the share of the Muslim population is 12.5 per cent in Ahmedabad, 10.28 per cent in Baroda, and 7.55 per cent in Rajkot.

It must be noted that the state has for long been a riot-prone region, though such occurrences became frequent after 1950 reaching a peak during the 1960s with the 1969 riots as the first such major outbreak. Subsequently, the first half of the 1980s witnessed some bouts of intense and widespread rioting, especially in 1985, though the casualties and losses were less than in 1969.

The riots of 1969 had occurred with the 1965 Indo-Pak war in the background and a host of other events and factors which included the then Chief Minister's aircraft being shot down by a Pakistani war plane, the shifting of Muslim votes from the Congress to the Swatantra Party, an RSS rally calling for a Hindu *rashtra* as a reaction to certain demands put forth by some Muslims, the Jan Sangh leader Balraj Madhok's agitation about Muslim protests against an attack on a mosque in the Middle East, protests by sections of Muslims and Hindus on incidents of insult to the *Koran* and the *Ramayana* by a Hindu and a Muslim officer respectively, and the call of Jan Sangh leaders for the formation of the Hindu Dharma Raksha Samiti.[5] As against this, the riots of the 1980s can be placed against a background of latent as well as manifest social unrest, the *Navnirman* agitation of 1974, and the anti-reservation stir against the inclusion of socially and economically backward classes within the realm of benefits from such reservations (Sengupta et al. 2003).

The riots in Gujarat in 2002, which preceded the Assembly elections, not only witnessed unprecedented violence, arson, and looting in terms of their nature as well as intensity, but they also resulted in the definitive exclusion of Muslims in most parts of Gujarat. These riots occurred when the form of political discourse(s) had already witnessed a notable change and the BJP had emerged as the dominant power in the state, whilst also ruling at the Centre. The rise of the BJP during the 1990s was punctuated by the L.K. Advani-led *rath yatra* (chariot tour) starting in Somnath (in Gujarat), the December 1992 demolition of the Babri Masjid (Babri mosque) in Ayodhya, and the communal riots that followed in Gujarat and elsewhere. Thus the intensification of Hindutva was both cause and consequence of the efforts, debates, actions, and reactions to the building of the Ram Mandir (temple for Lord Rama) at Ayodhya, and the general politici-

[5]As quoted in Sengupta et al. (2003) and Shah (1970).

zation of the *Ramjanmabhumi* (birthplace of Lord Rama) issue, after the highly symbolic laying of the foundations of the new Hindu temple, combining bricks contributed from different parts of the country, and the formal inauguration through the ritual of *shilapuja* (thus far no further building has been permitted).

The 1990s gradually witnessed a definite slant in the character of riots, for it was during this period that an otherwise diverse and amorphously based Hinduism began to be projected as a monistic and unified system aimed at giving a new religio-political meaning to Hindutva. This new form of religio-cultural nationalism that defined *we* (the Hindus) vs. *they* (the Muslims, and in some cases the Christians) emerged as a major instrument for the BJP and its associates to harness the support of the 'majority' community at various levels in the social and political arenas.

While a succession of particular events does not necessarily establish any relationship between and amongst them, responses to our in-depth enquiries regarding the underlying causes of these riots put to as many as fifteen scholars and activists associated with a wide range of political, quasi-political, and development organizations revealed that many of these may indeed have been linked with one another. In a nutshell, their conclusions were that:

i. given the ways in which ongoing politico-religious discourses had already shaped public space, the stage was already set for existing animosities to burst into serious conflict;
ii. with the rise of the Patels and changing political equations of the upper and middle castes vis-à-vis other groups, especially after the 'anti-reservation' riots in the state, the space for locating the Hindutva project had widened;[6]
iii. in some regions, especially in central and south Gujarat, the support extended by the non-resident Gujaratis (NRGs) to a number of religious sects was a contributory factor towards the creation and sustenance of an ideology of the 'Hindutva' variety;
iv. a section of unemplcyed youth as well as labourers retrenched from the composite textile mills and associated industries in Ahmedabad may have participated in the riots more vigorously;
v. the loss faced by the BJP in the last panchayat (village-level) elections

[6]Kanbis, an agrarian caste in the nineteenth century, later came to be known as Patidar caste (Clark 1979). Most Patidars use Patel as their surname and hence are known as Patels. However, 'Patel' is a revenue term and is found among other castes and Muslims and Parsis too. The Patidars took part in the Nationalist Movement and then when the 'Land to the Tiller' movement came into being they ceased to be tenants and became landowners (Hardiman 1981). They embraced the Swaminarayan (Vaishnavite) sect and became the dominant caste of the region. They also took to business and trade and, having previously been considered to belong to the Shudra varna, they are now bracketed among the upper castes.

needed a political recovery and the fallout of the riots helped to consolidate specific configurations facilitating its victory in the Assembly elections;

vi. unlike in states such as Bihar and Uttar Pradesh, where the Other Backward Classes (OBCs) and Dalits (ex-Untouchables) wield substantial prominence in the political sphere, political power in Gujarat remains in the hands of stronger caste groups like the Patels who socially as well as politically remain opposed to the Muslims;

vii. a series of activities and programmes linked and associated with *rath yatra*, *shilapuja*, *gaurav yatra* (tours to celebrate the pride of Gujarat), etc., were responsible for sustaining a communally affected social and political environment in the state;

viii. stronger social divisions along caste lines and at the same time potentials of their being invoked on religious lines provided a platform for a call for the 'unification' of Hindu identity at a pan-Gujarat level; and

ix. coupled with the increasing 'ghettoization' of the Muslims, especially after the 1992 demolition of the Babri Masjid, there was a singular absence and lack of any systematic effort on the part of the state as well as 'secular' civic organizations to integrate the Muslims into the larger sphere of the economy and society.

The most striking of many such responses, however, were the reasons cited for the spread of the 2002 riots to a large number of rural areas. Most said that this was a conscious effort by the BJP and its allies to weaken Congress strongholds. A large number of respondents suggested that the dominant group of Patidars (Patels) was especially instrumental in making space for the BJP and also in facilitating the ideology of Hindutva to enter and spread in such areas through a variety of associated institutional structures.

THE STUDY AND ITS METHOD

Notwithstanding the above context and background, the main focus of this paper is to examine how, in the villages of central Gujarat, Hindus and Muslims continued to perceive each other in terms of images and imaging, even one and a half years after the 2002 riots. An understanding of this kind, we believe, is likely to throw light on the sustainability or otherwise of images of one community vis-à-vis the other. In addition, we also gathered views of our Hindu respondents on the meaning of 'Hindutva', for their image of Muslims remains linked with the way they tend to define this concept.

Data was collected from twelve villages in the districts of Kheda and Anand in central Gujarat where the intensity of the riots ranged from high to moderate.[7] The villages selected were Chikhodara, Sarsa, Kasor, Bochasan, Napa, Khanpur, Timba, Pandori, Ghodasar, Umreth, Vadod, and Bhadaraniya. Based on a checklist, relevant information was gathered through focus group discussions (FGDs), several brief interviews with a number of people, and twenty-four in-depth interviews of key respondents representing a variety of Hindu caste groups, and from among the Muslims. The collection of such data was difficult, for many people were apprehensive about responding to such questions and this compelled us to make repeated field visits.[8] It was noticeably more difficult to interview Muslim respondents, as they were still in the grip of fear to speak on issues which had become extremely sensitive after the riots as well as the results of the 2002 state assembly elections. As opposed to this, an aggressive stance among the Hindus participating in the FGDs was frequently evident in their expressions while speaking about Muslims. It should be noted that in case of more than a dozen interviews we were unable to hold a dialogue with our respondents on a one-to-one basis, for these interviews eventually became discussions in which other household members and at times neighbours participated. Projecting sets of images of 'the other' may thus have been influenced by the need to identify with the prevalent image of one's own community. This was, however, beyond our control and we let the interviews proceed without making any efforts to change their character or trajectory. Images appearing here in a rather undifferentiated manner may be largely due to such contingent factors but nevertheless call for a portrayal of forms in which they emerge as encapsulated opposed sets with the potential of being appropriated by vested interests to create and sustain conflicts, contests and complementarities across time and space to the extent possible. It should be noted that the names of respondents appearing in the text are pseudonyms. In the following sections, we narrate the images of Muslims and Hindus vis-à-vis each other and present the meaning of 'Hindutva' as viewed by our Hindu respondents from the villages mentioned above.

HINDU IMAGES OF MUSLIMS

Aggression and its simultaneous legitimization set the tone for the way in which the Hindus in the study tended to identify Muslims. And while doing

---

[7]Kheda was bifurcated into two separate districts of Kheda and Anand by a State Government Resolution dated 15 October 1997, when Shri Shanker Sinh Vaghela was the Chief Minister of the State. Currently Kheda has 615 villages and 10 towns and Anand has 350 villages and 12 towns within its jurisdiction. During 1991, the district of Kheda had a Muslim presence of 10.75 per cent, and in its two urban agglomerations of Nadiad and Anand, respectively 13.54 and 10.20 per cent of the population was Muslim.

[8] Much of the field data was collected from May to August 2003.

so what is projected is a consortium of images which are aggregative rather than differentiated and singular rather than plural. Invariably, such exercises in imaging were negotiated without any defined reference to space and time. Irrespective of variations amongst respondents in terms of income, assets, and caste, riots in general are perceived to have always been triggered by the Muslims. As opposed to that, Hindus see themselves as a group retaliating only in defence. Thus, a dominant image of Muslims is that of 'aggressors' who have internalized and articulate 'aggressive' behaviour.

Muslims as an 'Aggressive Lot'

Within the immediate context of the 2002 Gujarat riots, the attack on Akshardham (the Swaminarayan temple in Gandhinagar, the capital of Gujarat) appears as the major axis around which 'Hindu revenge and retaliation' is legitimized by almost all the respondents. This is further articulated by examples of Muslims having looted the Somnath temple and attacked the twin towers in New York. American 'retaliation' in the form of a war against Afghanistan is legitimized within the same space. Parsottam of Chikhodra, who has studied up to the SSC and owns an auto repair unit, explained the causes of riots in these words:

> Hindus retaliated because their own brothers were attacked in the holy temple of Akshardham. Muslims are also creating terror in America and England and just as America had no choice but to teach them a lesson in Afghanistan, the Hindus in Gujarat had to respond in a similar manner. Two continuous attacks opened our eyes and broke our patience. During the Godhra carnage they kidnapped our girls and raped them. Hindus never indulge in such things ... Muslims live in India but are loyal to Pakistan and celebrate when Pakistani cricket team wins. For long, they have been creating panic and disturbances in cities and have now run away to the villages. But this time the people in the villages too understood their game and taught them a lesson ... Muslims have destroyed more than 300 temples in India during the past. The Somnath temple was attacked and destroyed twice.

Krishna Kant, who is a graduate and a follower of the Swaminarayan sect, echoes similar feelings when he says:

> How long are we going to forgive them? Even if all of them die there would be no repentance on *our* part, for they can never change. If they had kept quiet after Godhra, we would have forgotten it all, but time and again they keep putting bombs and creating disturbances. There is never any remorse or repentance on their part and so we must retaliate in self-defence. (emphasis added)

Nathubhai Patel, educated up to SSC, a farmer and a BJP worker, feels that the aggressive *qaum* (community) of Muslims should be entirely wiped out and says, "When we have money we buy things to decorate and purify our homes but when they get money they buy arms to kill humans and animals." The tone of all our respondents was broadly similar. All of them emphasized the 'anti-national' and 'immoral' aggressive behaviour of Muslims, as opposed to their own nationalistic and naturally patriotic and moral behaviour. So all Muslims get similarly imaged as aggressive and attacking, looters and destroyers, violent sadists, killers and rapists, whereas Hindus are supposedly passive and accommodating, soft and tolerant, respectful and moral, saviours and protectors of truth and non-violence.

That violence and aggression is not only 'natural' to Muslims, but also such a behaviour pattern among them across regions is nurtured, sustained, and reinforced by sets of institutions, was stated by all respondents. To a large number of them, mosques are but fronts for making and storing weapons, and *madrassas* platforms for creating real and potential anti-social elements. Common forms of expressions were the following: 'The Koran also speaks of *ahimsa* [non-violence] and the need for living in peace but the Muslims do not behave in accordance with the Koran. ... Only 5 per cent among the Muslims are good and the rest are given wrong education at the *madrassas* that potentially turns them hostile towards all Hindus. ... From childhood they are taught that Hindus are *kafirs* making the child nurture anger all through his life', 'Of the seventy Muslim families at Kasor only two are in favour of India. ... They particularly incite their community by saying that Islam is in danger and the *kafirs* must be eliminated', 'Vengeful Muslims train their young ones at *madrassas* to work against their own country'. This indicates that there is an overwhelming perception among Hindus that Muslims create and sustain aggression through institutional structures such as *madrassas* and mosques.

Muslims as Anti-Nationals

Across all groups of respondents Muslims are perceived to be loyal to Pakistan and therefore to be anti-Indian and as an extension, anti-Hindu. Nearly all claim that Muslims not only express their joy when Pakistan wins a cricket match but also tend to support terrorist activities in Kashmir. The words of Kanu Rohit are a pointer towards such feelings:

> Ninety per cent of Muslims in India support terrorist activities. This is due to Pakistan's defeat in the 1972 war, following which they no more want to fight a war directly but encourage cross-border terrorism. And because these terrorists are Muslims, the local Muslims support their cause and activities.

In Bharat Trivedi's opinion:

> We shopkeepers hoard grains but they store weapons. If I were Prime Minister, I would hand over Kashmir to Pakistan and chase all the Muslims there and bring in the Kashmiri Hindus to India.

Solanki, who holds a postgraduate degree in social work, echoes the sentiments of others. According to him,

> Muslims pretend to be friends and loyal but betray at the first available opportunity. They are emotionally living in Pakistan and only physically in India. Seventy per cent among them are violent and a nuisance. They behave like 'refugees' in India.

To Kartik of Umreth, in the second year of college, 95 per cent of the Muslims are bad, anti-social, and anti-national, indulging in terrorist activities and occupations like smuggling, bootlegging, and dealing with illegal weapons. Significantly, all responses that tend to label Muslims as anti-nationals simultaneously declare them to be loyal to Pakistan and to be potential traitors not worthy of trust.

Muslims as Violent

Muslims are generally perceived as perpetrators as well as practitioners of violence. A large number of respondents expressed the view that even within a nation where the majority is Hindu, a minority is able to practise its aggression in the public sphere. The essence of many responses was, 'It surely stems from their violent behaviour, supported albeit by vested interests'. Their supposedly violent behaviour is contrasted to other minority groups who are labelled as peaceful, such as the Parsis, 'who have assimilated with the majority community like sugar in milk', and the Christians who have worked to provide health and education for all. That violent Muslims have harassed Hindus for centuries whereas Hindus have retaliated only now and then appears as a dominant trope. Muslims are supposed to have been violent all through history whereas Hindus have been tolerant and accommodative till they had no other choice. Dayabhai, a Rohit by caste and holding a diploma in Mechanical Engineering says:

> Muslims always believe in revenge ... more than 60 per cent of them are anti-Hindu and favour Pakistan. We are good to them but they have always misused our goodness.

According to Dharmishtaben, who has studied up to the SSC and is a housewife:

> Nearly all Muslims carry revolvers and rape Hindu women during any riot.

Prabhu Rohit of Napa at Borsad feels that:

> After the riots the Muslims in my village have now been humbled, though they still continue to possess large numbers of weapons. If they become a majority they would surely turn the whole country into a Muslim country.

In a group discussion at Kapadvanj, some stated clearly that had the Muslims not been so cruel and violent in Godhra, nothing would have happened. According to Jashbhai, who is a graduate and comes from Bhadaraniya:

> The Muslims take part in violence and killings and the killing of an animal and of a human being is the same for them.

In spite of the variations in expressions about the intensity of latent as well as manifest violence among Muslims, it is important to note that not even a single Hindu respondent said that Muslims were no more violent than Hindus or Christians.

Muslims as Always United and Ghettoized

Without exception respondents felt that all Muslims are in continuous support of each other across states as well as the nation. According to many, they tend to live close to each other and are thereby able to insulate themselves, which is necessary for them to carry out illegal activities as well as to gang up against other communities. Some believe that all Muslims are united because Islam is monotheistic and has only one holy book and that this reinforces their togetherness leading to concerted behaviour. Such processes supposedly encourage the growth of a 'closed' mindset which is perpetuated by their *maulavis* at mosques and *ustads* at *madrassas*. That such insulation has been the product of their being staunch followers of Islam was expressed by many. Bharatbhai of Pandori at Petlad believes that:

> Muslims do not want to change and stop their continued misdeeds but we Hindus do not have that unity. ... Even while they are only converted Muslims they are staunch about their religion and continue to hold on to each other for gaining strength.

At a group discussion at Kapadvanj some women said that:

> After Ayodhya the unity among the Hindus has been on the rise ... As opposed to us, Muslims give more importance to their religion. They would prefer to die to save their religion and consider every Muslim as their brother. They do not help others except their own people and more than 50 per cent of the Muslims get excited and agitated in the name of religion and create trouble for their neighbours and the country.

The general feeling across groups throughout our research was that the ghettoized Muslims generally act in concert and that this facilitates the triggering of problems that damage and destroy the otherwise peaceful fabric of the larger society in India.

Muslims as Immoral and Dirty

As perpetrators of violence Muslims are also imagined by many as immoral and dirty. A large section believes that the revengeful and violent Muslim is a rapist, always ready to dishonour Hindu women. Since 'they marry across their own relatives, they do not have any respect for women and neither are able to appreciate the virtues of mothers and sisters'. And it is precisely because of such social behaviour that 'their women are not as virtuous and are often quarrelsome'. For Pravin, studying in the third year of college, "Muslims are a quarrelsome community and continue to harass others". Many Hindus expressed views that Muslim women are quarrelsome and that immorality and revenge are part and parcel of Muslim socialization processes, albeit in different words. A large number emphasized what they identified as anti-normative and deviant behaviour and its perpetuation through specified teachings to children from the very beginning among all Muslims irrespective of their social and economic background. A large number focused on the fact that multiple marriages are allowed to Muslims and on the supposedly higher population growth among them owing to their non-adoption of contraceptives. To some, illiteracy has compounded their immorality and led them to opt for illegal occupations and living in an unclean manner. Across all Hindu groups there was an emphasis on the Muslim consumption of beef. Many said that no moral community can eat cows, which are protected and respected by others as the mother and the goddess. In addition, some pointed out what they labelled as 'opposite' behaviour, for 'why else would the Muslims write from the *wrong* side, wash hands in a *different* way, and produce a lot of children?' Thus the prevalent image of Muslims across all Hindu groups is that they indulge in immoral behaviour and dirty living.

The Hindu Self-Image

Significantly enough, the Hindu self-image is the binary opposite of the image that they have of Muslims. The 'tolerant' Hindus, according to all respondents, have had a raw deal at the hands of Muslim invaders, merchants, violent mobs, and terrorists across regions and over time. Had the Muslims lived in peace and maintained solidarity they would have been safe. To the majority, the riots of 2002 were entirely the Muslims' responsibility. They believe that the Muslims were solely responsible for the Godhra massacre and the attack on the Akshardham temple. So naturally the Hindus retaliated, 'For how long could they have remained soft towards an enemy growing inside?' Nearly all agreed with the tone and opinion of Parsottam Makwan:

> The Hindus have taken a beating for so long and have now retaliated to teach them a lesson. Even the tribals have joined the Hindus to beat them.

Across all groups, respondents individually or collectively were of the opinion that they felt no remorse for what had happened, for they all agreed that, in these riots, the Muslims had not been at the receiving end as much as they should have been. They justified their position by arguments such as 'it was only a natural retaliation against atrocities carried on for so long by the Muslims', 'this time Hindus were compelled to teach them a lesson', 'this was an opportunity to take sustained revenge', 'the Hindus have been suffering at the hands of Muslims since the time of Independence', 'always kind and soft, the Hindus had no option but to fight back this time', etc. What appears important here is the self-image of the Hindus, projected as benevolent, kind, and peaceloving who had to retaliate against the aggression of the Muslims in order to protect their own homes and at the same time weaken the 'united' strength of the Muslims.

That India 'belongs to Hindus' but 'has a secular fabric allowing others to stay' is the essence of the opinion advanced by many. In the same breath there is a celebration of a 'Hindu nation' which is accommodative, tolerating the Parsi and Christian communities who have 'mixed well' and continue to remain partners in the overall project of nation-building, unlike the Muslims who are 'bent upon carrying out anti-national activities'. That the nation is unsafe because of the overwhelming anti-social and anti-national activities carried out by Muslims is an aggregate expression advanced by nearly all respondents. It is significant here that by declaring and emphasizing that the Muslims are anti-nationals, the Hindus automatically emerge as patriotic and 'pro-national' – a point that respondents felt no need to assert or mention explicitly.

The image of immoral and violent Muslims is projected and reinforced by the *moral* act of retaliation in response to attack(s) that have been going on for a long time and tolerated. Thus is 'non-violence' celebrated in a violent way. This is legitimized by the constant portrayal of non-violent and tolerant Hindus reacting only when 'pushed to the wall'. And it is only in a 'no alternative situation' that unabated violence is given legitimacy – ironically as an effort to protect the tenets of non-violence. All Hindus, of whatever occupation, background, or income level, largely shared these views: as far as they were concerned, violence is the domain of the Muslims on which Hindus encroached only temporarily in order to restore order.

The image of Muslims as 'herding together', united, and ghettoized is constantly expressed in pejorative terms, for it is their 'unified' existence, viewed by all respondents as a deliberate strategy, which gives them the edge over Hindus – who are seen as fragmented and divided. Hence the theme of divided *vs.* unified becomes at the same time the reason for Hindus being unable to emerge as a potential countervailing force to the 'united' community of Muslims and the assertion of a need to become a reckoning force, albeit 'for the protection of the Hindu virtues of tolerance, non-violence, and peace'. Thus Hindu violence can be celebrated as a qualitatively different kind of 'moral violence' as against Muslim 'immoral violence'. And since 'their unity' cannot be 'eroded', the need of the hour 'is to become united' and retaliate in a timely fashion.

THE MUSLIM SELF-IMAGE AND THE ROLE OF THE DALITS

From the group discussions and individual interviews held across settlements among the Muslim respondents, there does not emerge any clear Muslim self-image. All that the narratives reflect are the methods adopted by Hindu caste groups in killing members of their families and destroying their assets and property. Across groups, opinions clearly converge that during the riots not only were they unable to protect their belongings but also the lives of their near and dear ones. In a chorus, they speak of planned massacre and attacks at select places by the Hindus, supported often by the police, and that services like firefighters did not arrive in time. A large majority had always believed that riots were a phenomenon which generally remained limited to urban centres and had seldom entered the villages. Overwhelmed by the suddenness of the attack, they were unable to cope with it. Importantly, a clear distinction was made by all Muslim respondents on the aspect of participation by different communities in attacking their *mohalla*s (lanes). All the narratives from villages in Kheda point to the Patels as being in the forefront as well as behind the forces that unleashed the terror, looting, and killing. That in places the Dalits also attacked the Muslims was narrated by many, though a majority of them indicated that most of these Dalits were instigated and in many cases coerced by the Patels to join in attacks on Muslims. Significantly, across Hindu caste groups, the Dalits were found generally to express the view that though Muslims are often aggressive and violent, many among their neighbours were not as bad. Some among the Dalits clearly stated that some Muslims are better than the Patels and it is because the Patels are able to alienate and indulge in Muslim-bashing that the Dalits do not have to face the entire brunt of the Patels' ire and exploitative machinations. A curious mix of macro images of Muslims as violent yet bashful, as both aggressive and anti-social, were expressed by some Dalit respondents, especially within the context of their own settlements.

MUSLIMS AS BINARY OPPOSITES: EXPRESSIONS THROUGH FORMS AND PHRASES

The most important finding of our research is that the imaging of Muslims by Hindus has been reductionist and aggregative in character. As binary opposites, they have been projected as located on the other side of 'positive' norms and/or morals. Such an undifferentiated imaging, among other things, seems to have been determined by constant propaganda and through a systematic articulation of selective patterns of behaviour stripped of their corresponding cultural and temporal contexts. This modality is adapted and celebrated with the singular aim of denigrating a community and it tends to aid the process of their being marginalized and consequently insulated. This process can emerge as an effective instrumentality of gaining as well as appropriating spaces which were hitherto controlled by other agencies.

Evidently such tendencies appear more pronounced with the use of phrases and idioms that were frequently expressed by our Hindu respondents. The Hindus' perceptions about Muslims as anti-normative, anti-national, and a group which always remains engaged in scheming against the majority as well as the nation, were often expressed in phrases such as, 'consumption of dirt always leads to the emergence of dirty thoughts', 'tiger cubs reared with puppies show their true colour only later', 'snakes fed with milk are bound to strike when they get big', etc. Phrases celebrating Hindu revenge, retaliation, and the need for masculine assertion, were often expressed as follows: 'over their black deeds, we will make it red all the way', 'other states strike back harder than we do', 'Hindus are not sitting pretty wearing bangles', 'kicks must be responded to only by kicks', 'it is for the first time in last 54 years that the trigger has popped out to strike', 'wisdom fails when the end nears'; 'with death coming a camel looks up to Marwad and a Muslim towards Mecca', 'a poisonous creeper must be chopped on time', 'a brick thrown must be responded to with a harder stone', and other similar expressions. Phrases like 'a biting dog must be spanked'; 'the dormant fire is ready to burst'; 'an injured lion becomes violent', and 'even a eunuch would rise to the occasion' further substantiate the legitimization of violent retaliation. Placed within their context(s) some of the phrases used frequently by our respondents are listed below.

1. *Dudhma jem sakar male* (*As sugar becomes one with milk*): Used to illustrate how other minority groups such as the Parsis have assimilated and integrated with Indian society whereas Muslims have supposedly not done so.

2. *Temne kalu karyu, ame lal karishun* (*They painted it black, we shall paint it red*): Emphasis on legitimizing the indiscriminate killing of Muslims for deeds that are claimed to have been done to the entire Hindu community across time and space.

3. *Ato matra chamatkar batayvo che, hinduo kai bangdio nathi pahenta (It is only a beginning: Hindus are not sitting pretty wearing bangles)*: Essentially used to legitimize the violence that emerged specifically in the aftermath of the Godhra incident.

4. *Bharela agni* (*Dormant fire ready to burst*): Used to emphasize Hindu tolerance and yet at the same time expressing the idea that it is time to act, for the Muslims had crossed all limits of decency.

5. *Laton no jawab laton thij* (*Tit for tat*): Used to emphasize the need to retaliate against Muslims in the same manner in which they attacked the Hindus. A similar phrase meaning a 'stone for a brick thrown' was also used by many when expressing agitation over what was labelled as the wrongdoing of Muslims at Godhra and Akshardham.

6. *Kadvo velo kapyej par ave* (*A bitter vine must be cut on time*): Generally used in discussions about the characteristics of Muslims where they have been frequently labelled as anti-national, anti-social, unpatriotic, and potential cheats.

7. *Sanpna kanane dudh pivadaviye to moto thai ne fen mande* (*Snakes fed with milk are bound to strike when they get big*): Used to express the popular belief that Muslims have been pampered and have grown because of the concessions granted to them by the state and especially by political parties like the Congress.

8. *Vinash kale viprit buddhi* (*Wisdom fails when the end nears*): Used in the context of post-Godhra and post-Akshardham events that triggered the riots, especially when legitimizing the attacks on the property and lives of Muslims. The point is to explain why the Muslims indulged in such acts of violence, and to say that they would not have done so had they not lost their sanity.

9. *Kachro khaine kachro jeva vicharon ave che* (*If you eat dirt, your thoughts are going to be dirty*): Frequently emphasized to drive home the perceived 'anti-normative' social behaviour of Muslims who consume non-vegetarian food, and are therefore immoral.

10. *Barne bordi na ugadaye ane miyani bhai bandhi na rakhaye* (*Just as a thorny berry should not be grown in one's courtyard, one cannot befriend a Muslim*): Used when claiming that Muslims are untrustworthy, traitors, unpatriotic, etc., across time and space and irrespective of context.

11. *Hindustan murdabad, Pakistan zindabad* (*Hail Pakistan and to hell with India*): Used to describe the alleged attitude Indian Muslims have towards India and Pakistan, be it during a cricket match between India and Pakistan or when Pakistan is allegedly 'stealthily encroaching' in parts of Jammu and Kashmir.

12. *Kutru bachku bhare to lakdi fatkarvu pade* (*A biting dog must be*

spanked): Used frequently to legitimize appropriate punishment towards Muslims who have supposedly been a major irritant harming the larger society for a long time.

The portrayal of Muslims as suggested above and the phrases generally used by respondents while substantiating their narrations, would seem to point to an increasing polarization between Hindus and Muslims. Whether the rise and subsequent emergence of the BJP as the dominant political party in the state, especially since the 1990s, can be directly linked with such increasing polarization between the two communities is difficult to state conclusively, but the responses across all respondent groups in our sample tend to point towards the possibility of such a pattern:

> Hindus were looking for a strong leader who could protect them from Muslim counter attacks and hence they voted for Modi. There will be peace in Gujarat as long as he is in power. BJP is the party which protects the Hindus. (Makwana)
>
> In spite of much corruption in BJP, Hindus were afraid of Muslim backlash in case the Congress won in the Assembly elections. (Kanubhai)
>
> The BJP alone can bring terrorism under control. (Bhavesh Patel)
>
> Hindus feared that if Congress won, it will be Muslim Raj and they will have to face revenge and hence voted in favour of BJP. (Mukesh)
>
> Muslims were harassing us during the Congress rule and so we have brought back the BJP to protect ourselves. Modi is like God to us. He has taken water up to Kathiawad. (Ramjibhai)
>
> The BJP won with the promise of protecting Hindus. (Natubhai Patel)
>
> The Godhra incident enraged all Hindus and they voted in favour of BJP so that the Muslims can be kept under control. (Dhulabhai)

Such responses indicate that a specific kind of portrayal of Muslims placed within as well as outside the immediate context of the post-Godhra riots and the accompanying polarization on the lines of a communal divide aided the process of consolidation of the BJP's power base and its overwhelming victory in the last Assembly elections.

THE CONCEPT OF 'HINDUTVA': HOW THE RESPONDENTS VIEW IT

Since an idea of 'Hindutva' – howsoever fluid or rigid it may be – had been doing the rounds both before and especially after the riots, we were keen to learn how our respondents understood it. We found that people ascribed a wide range of meanings to the term 'Hindutva'. For some, Hindutva means working out strategies by which Hindus can be favoured, while all other minority groups, and especially Muslims, can be treated as subordinate in all walks of social and economic life. To others, Hindutva is a rising force needed to safeguard the interests of all Hindus across the nation. Evidently, for such a group minorities are not only subordinate but also real and/or potential enemies located in opposition to Hindus, if not to the religions tenets of Hinduism. Some expressed the meaning and essence of Hindutva in terms of a national identity where all those born in 'Hindustan' must believe in Hinduism and Hindutva, and those who belong to communities like Parsis, Muslims, Christians, etc., should live in a manner that must work towards being assimilative rather than destructive or disaggregating to the project of nation-building. Significantly, a large number of respondents emphasized that they saw Hindutva as being a way of leading a tolerant and peaceful life in accordance with what they labelled as Hindu rituals, rules, and regulations. They were, however, unable to identify what they meant by such rules and where they had emerged from. Given below are some of the responses:

> One can understand Hindutva by understanding a Hindu individual who is kind, sentimental, and accommodative unlike the rigid and fundamentalist Muslims. (Prabhu Rohit)
>
> Hindutva is a system that is all inclusive, embraces all castes, but excludes the 'minority' religions. (Pravin Mohan)
>
> Hindutva is a strategy worked out by upper castes to keep the lower castes and Muslims perpetually in a subordinate position so that they always remain subservient to their interest. (Bhikhu Vaghela)
>
> Hindutva is the *sanatan dharma* and in its manifest form is continuously working towards assimilating all denominations of the Hindu order. (Ratna Parmar)
>
> Hindutva is a call for Hindu unity so that in India Hindus can always remain in commanding and not in any obeying position. (Natha Solanki)

The broad spectrum of the responses have to be seen as coexisting in a contested arena. However, taken together, they appear to consist of attempts to cleanse, improve, and modify the Hindu self-image from a soft and tolerant position to one that of being able to retaliate and engulf others into the Hindu fold while keeping them at a subservient level. Thus Hindutva would seem to be an overarching modality helping people to achieve a unified platform, a modality which can be easily channelized politically.

In other words, perceptions of Hindutva in our fieldwork area appear to be inherently political, veiled by elements of religious symbolization and pseudo-historical essentialism.

IMAGES HELD BY CITY DWELLERS: EXTRACTS FROM A RECENT STUDY

In this section we make an attempt to juxtapose the images collated from the rural respondents with that of urban respondents from the Gujarati cities of Surat and Vadodara.[9] The general intensity of the riots in urban areas of the state was high, especially along the national highways passing through the north and central regions of the state. However, it needs to be pointed out here that though Surat witnessed very intense riots in 1992 after the demolition of the Babri Masjid, it remained rather calm in 2002. Vadodara by contrast closely followed Ahmedabad in terms of intensity of the violence, arson, and looting.[10]

Desai, while examining the relationship between Hindus and Muslims in Surat after the 2002 riots, comments elaborately on the movement of both communities across select localities within the city, especially after 1992, and labels the phenomenon "the disintegration of a co-existence" (Desai & De 2003). He adds that such movements were more pronounced from within pockets in the old city where previously people of different faiths and sects had lived together for a very long time. Most of the migrants were middle- and upper-caste Hindus and economically better placed Muslims. Importantly, he also points to the movement of Muslims specifically to a few select localities and cites the example of the emergence and growth of more than twenty-five co-operative housing societies of Muslims in a stretch on the Rander Road on the west bank of the Tapi river in the city after 1992. Consciously opting for such collective living

---

[9]This section is based entirely on a study carried out by Desai and De (2003), fieldwork for which was conducted during the first half of 2003. Quantitative data was collected from 100 respondents in each of the cities from among a cross-section of people in pockets with high Hindu presence, high Muslim presence, and mixed localities. Qualitative data was gathered through a large number of informal interviews, select case studies, and focus group discussions. While the narration and analysis presented by Desai for the Surat part of the study are based mainly on qualitative data, the Baroda part worked on by De is essentially based on analysis of the survey data. The report, aimed at understanding relations between Hindus and Muslims, especially in the context of post 2002 Godhra riots, is divided in two parts with the former solely dealing with the city of Surat and the latter the city of Vadodara.

[10]Intensely affected pockets in Ahmedabad included Naroda Patia, Odhav, Amraiwadi, Gomtipur, Meghaninagar, Chamanpura, Paldi, Vatva, Naroda fruit market, and Kabadi market. In Vadodara the most affected areas were Fatehpura, Makarpura, Chipwad, Macchipith, and Hanuman Tekri. For more details on the intensity of these riots across the state, see Genocide (2002).

and moving in with one's 'own people' is manifest also in the efforts of groups belonging to lower- and lower-middle income categories. For example Unn, now a satellite township located at a distance of 10 km from Surat, houses a large number of Muslim migrants from other states working in nearby industries. A substantial share of Unn's population also consists of those Muslims who had suffered during the 1992 riots in Limbayat – a low-income suburb in Surat. Prior to 1992, Unn had a population of little less than 8,000, but it now houses more than 50,000 people.[11]

Emphasizing the practice of Hindus refusing to rent out residential and other premises to Muslims – a phenomenon generally prevalent across most towns and cities in the state – Desai clearly brings out the increased social distance between the two communities and the strengthening of forces that have led to the systematic alienation of Muslims in the spheres of access to select services, jobs, as well as to civil society associations like professionals' collectives, literary groups, unions, Lions and Rotary clubs, etc. Through an analysis of a large number of detailed case studies and focus group discussions, the study concludes that many of the related processes began to intensify after the 1992 riots and became firm and established in the aftermath of the 2002 riots. However, an important point highlighted in the report is that among individuals and groups from both communities having business links and mutual economic dependence, relationships have not eroded altogether with bonds still being alive. In the same study De reports similarly on Vadodara.

Desai and De's study tends to show that schisms between the communities have been largely caused by the anti-Muslim propaganda of the Hindutva forces through a variety of social and political institutions, by boycotts, and by the general marginalization of minorities. The study also shows that, just as in the rural areas, Hindu respondents, by and large, spoke of the Muslims as always united and ghettoized, overzealous about Islam, very staunch and fundamentalist, aggressive, ready to engage in immoral behaviour and to lure Hindu girls, argumentative and quarrelsome, anti-national and anti-social, always pro-Pakistan and pro-Muslim nations. According to the study, Hindus believed that a section among the Muslims were advancing nefarious designs of terror by training their youth at *madrassas* which are nothing but breeding grounds for anti-Hindu and anti-national activities. However, there were also intellectuals and practising lawyers in the urban areas who condemned the politico-religious discourses unleashed by the Hindutva forces.

Desai's analysis also corresponds largely with our data from the rural pockets when he finds the shades of grey and ambivalence of positions

---

[11] For further details on such post-1992 intra-city residential mobility in Surat, aimed at producing collective living amongst one's own group, see Desai & De (2003).

among his Hindu respondents only rarely and in small measure and that too located more among the lower social and economic groups. It appears that, by and large, it is the higher and intermediate Hindu caste groups who hold and propagate the stereotypical images of Muslims both in rural and in urban areas. In this context, the Muslims seem to be in a state of flux and subjugation, often being reconciliatory and accommodative in their responses. We can see this in their failure or refusal to portray any definite image of their own and the fact that they tend rather to narrate their anxieties and woes vis-à-vis the majority community and its 'Hindu-centric' religio-political discourse.

CONCLUSION

It is clear that a mix of civic polity with far from secular discourses was strengthened by the issue of constructing the Ram Temple at Ayodhya, the euphoria around it, and the various *yatra*s (tours, pilgrimages) held by Hindu nationalists to propagate an ideology which could appeal to the larger sections in the society. Though the riots of 2002 in the state may not have been inspired by the contents of the newer modalities of mobilization, for such occurrences are contingent upon a variety of other social and economic factors, yet the riots seem to have facilitated the polarization of Hindus and Muslims as clearly opposed to one another. The undifferentiated and unified response(s) that we get from our data seem to indicate that they have been results of a systematic and an uni-directional projection of one community in its relations with the other. While at a cognitive level, the existence of such a dichotomous and monolithic opposition seems difficult to comprehend, its presence at whatever level of consciousness, even as a temporary phenomenon, across groups and in such a pervasive manner as seen in many of the rural and urban areas in Gujarat, certainly has the potential of being appropriated and exploited by vested interest groups at least in the short run.

REFERENCES

Clark, A.W. 1979. 'Central Gujarat in the Nineteenth Century: The Integration of an Agrarian System'. Ph.D. dissertation, University of Wisconsin, Ann Arbor: University of Microfilms International.

Desai, K. and A. De. 2003. 'Hindu Muslim Relations in Gujarat: Case Studies of Surat and Vadodara'. Unpublished paper, Centre for Social Studies, Surat.

Genocide. 2002. 'Genocide: Gujarat 2002'. *Communalism Combat* (March-April) 8: 77-8. (see also www.sabrang.com)

Hardiman, D. 1981. *Peasant Nationalists of Gujarat: Kheda District, 1917-34.* Delhi: Oxford University Press.

Joshi, A.P., M.D. Srinivas, and J.K. Bajaj. 2003. *Religious Demography of India.* Chennai: Centre for Policy Studies.

Lobo, L. and B. Das. 2004. 'Geography of Gujarat Riots, 2002: Causatives and Spatial Spread Patterns of Related Factors'. Unpublished paper, Centre for Culture and Development, Vadodara.

Sengupta, C., K. Anil, and Y.G. Katy. 2003. 'Communal Riots in Gujarat, 2002: A Study of Contextual Factors'. Unpublished paper, Tata Institute of Social Sciences, Mumbai.

Shah, G. 1970. 'Communal Riots in Gujarat'. *Economic and Political Weekly* 5 (3-5): 187-200.

7

The Spread of Vihar Buddhism among Rural Newars in the Kathmandu Valley

KESHAV LALL MAHARJAN

INTRODUCTION

Modern socio-economic transformations began in earnest in Nepal in the 1950s, i.e. after the end of the Ranas' autocratic rule. The Kathmandu Valley, as the centre of politics, economy, and culture in the country, experienced these transformations in the most dynamic form and its 'native' inhabitants, the Newars, are the single most affected group in the country. These transformations have brought changes in all spheres of their life – political, economic, social, and cultural – and the changes were intertwined with each other.

There is no stark differentiation between Hinduism and Buddhism in traditional Newar society; most Newars are not required to opt for one or the other religion. However, some of the elite Newars who were Vajrayanist Buddhists learnt about Theravada Buddhism during the early 1920s and 1930s, basically in India, and tried to (re)introduce this sect of Buddhism in Nepal (Kathmandu Valley) during the 1930s as a subtle kind of protest against the Rana regime. Initially this sect of Buddhism was supported by the liberal Vajrayanist Buddhists from the upper castes of Newar society who were also rather well-to-do economically. It started to take root in the Kathmandu Valley during the 1950s, amicably accepted by the locals as Vihar Dharma (see next section), which I paraphrase as 'Vihar Buddhism' hereafter. It further spread widely in the Valley among the rural Newars and beyond in the 1980s, which became a firm trend after the democratic change in 1990.

The introduction and the spread of Vihar Buddhism in Nepal, and especially in the Kathmandu Valley, can be understood as both the cause and the effect of the political and socio-economic transformations of contemporary Nepal. Generally, the followers of Vihar Buddhism, especially the monks, the sponsors, and local intellectuals, are regarded as people who have some kind of grudge against society or dissatisfaction with prevailing systems including institutions and networks. Many also resort to Vihar Buddhism in order to protect themselves from the angst of this fast-changing 'world' with which they are unable to keep pace and feel consciously or unconsciously insecure in their livelihood. Declaring oneself as a Vihar Buddhist in the former case may be regarded as a sort of active protest against existing systems, and an attempt to create an alternative avenue for self-realization. By contrast, in the latter the adoption of Vihar Buddhism can be regarded as the passive action of the masses in search of a place/means for self-realization. This is more pronounced since the 1980s when Vihar Buddhism penetrated Newar society deeper and wider in terms of area, community/caste, economic possessions, gender, culture, and network, at times incorporating diaspora Newars and non-Newars, especially after 1990. In general these Vihar Buddhists are more liberal and progressive as well as more concerned, hardworking, and sober-living.

Keeping this in mind, this paper examines the spread of Vihar Buddhism among rural Newars in the Kathmandu Valley by describing the introduction of Vihar Buddhism in a rural setting in the Valley and its spread among villagers on the basis of general surveys, questionnaires, and ethnographic methods.[1] In doing so, first, the socio-economic dynamism of the rural setting is discussed, with a case study, to understand the socio-economic nature of the place, including its people, where Vihar Buddhism has been introduced and is spreading. Then, the actual mechanism/process of the spread of Vihar Buddhism is discussed, taking into consideration its

[1]An earlier version of this paper was drafted in Japanese in 2000 and submitted for publication in 2002, eventually coming out as Maharjan (2005). In the meantime, I had the opportunity to review LeVine & Gellner (2005) and to have a series of interactions with David Gellner. The issues raised in their book have many similarities with those examined here. This gave me a much-needed incentive to rewrite the earlier Japanese version of the paper in English and address a wider audience, to relate the rise of Theravada to general developments in the village, and to update the data. I benefited from discussions in the conference seminar. I also benefited from various informal discussions with Krishna Kumar Prajapati, headmaster of Siddhi Ganesh Madhyamik Vidyalaya (morning), and a social worker of the village. At the initial stage of conducting the village survey, village-resident social workers, Professor Tulsi Man Duwal, campus chief, Sanothimi Campus, and Mr Kailash Bhakta Pradhanang, ex-member of District Panchayat, gave necessary advice. Binod Awale, Santosh Maharjan, and Krishna L. Maharjan aided data collections in the census and sample surveys of the village. The Makita Scholarship Foundation, the Mitsubishi Foundation, and the Inamori Foundation also supported field visits between 1991 and 2004. I would like to take this opportunity to thank all the villagers who welcomed me warmly and patiently participated in all the formal and impromptu interviews.

perception by sponsors, laity, and local people in general. Further, I deal with recent developments after democratization which gave rise to various movements and forms of activism. In the concluding part, I consider reasons for the spread of Vihar Buddhism and its import. But before that, is a brief review of Newar society and religion, especially the relation between Hinduism and Buddhism, the introduction of Vihar Buddhism, and its spread in Nepal, to provide the background information necessary to understand the whole issue.

NEWAR SOCIETY AND RELIGION

In the Newar society of the Kathmandu Valley, Hinduism and Buddhism as practised by the laity exist parallel to each other and are often hard to differentiate. This is especially true for Vajrayana Buddhism and Hindu Tantrism, which became intricately intertwined with each other during the late Malla period. The followers of both religions worship different deities, often with different names but in order to fulfil the same or similar wishes and to obtain the same religious merit. They follow the same annual rituals and the same rites of passage (though minor details may differ). Although *ahimsa* (non-violence) is supposedly essential to the Buddha's teachings, it is relatively less important in Vajrayana Buddhism. Vajrayana Buddhists make animal and plant sacrifices and hold big feasts to gain religious merit and social status. Vajrayana Buddhism is particularly associated with the Bare and Gubhaju castes. They are regarded by other Newars as Buddhist by birth, whereas Dyahbramus (Newar Brahmans), Joshis, and some Sheshyahs (including those who claim to be the descendants of the Malla rulers of mediaeval Nepal and their various courtiers) are regarded as Hindus by birth. But where the vast majority of the population is concerned, whether it is regarded and/or claimed as Buddhist or Hindu, a stark differentiation between the two religions is neither sought nor possible (see also Gellner 1992, and Gellner & Quigley 1995).

However, under the Shah-Rana regime before 1951, Hinduism received preferential treatment, as it was (and is) the religion of the rulers. And these rulers were more authoritarian and had many more Hindu subjects than the Malla kings who preceded them. Buddhism was regarded as an offshoot of Hinduism and secondary if not inferior to it. Buddhist priests were regarded as inferior to Hindu priests regardless of their scholarly and practical ritual achievements. In the caste system supported by the state during the Rana period they were assigned lower status than Hindu priests. Even Newar Hindu priests, the Dyahbramu, were ascribed lower status than the Parbate Hindu priests, the Upadhyaya Bahuns. The rest of the people, including other ethnic groups, were assigned to different levels between the Chetris and the polluting castes, giving due consideration to their contributions to the regime (Höfer 2004). Although the internal Newar caste system, which went back at least to the Malla period, was adapted to this new, state-backed hierarchy, some groups were ascribed higher status than others because of the support they gave to the Ranas. Thus, those Newars who had close relations with the ruling elite became more and more Hinduized (see also Rosser 1966). However, at the local level, Hindus are not always the winners. The fierce Bare - Sheshyah (Buddhist-Hindu) power struggle in the city of Patan has not produced any decisive result yet. Claiming to be non-Hindu is often a sign of protest against the feudalistic and authoritarian regime.

In spite of the strongly Hindu framework, which requires people to commit to Hinduism in their economic and political life, many of them are neutral in their social life. Except for those regarded as Buddhist or Hindu by birth, the laity can claim to be either, although it may be easier to claim to be Hindu. In order to claim to be Buddhist and be regarded as such by others, it would be necessary for them to act publicly with some visible performance. This means that in order to be generally recognized as a Buddhist in the locality it is not enough simply to undertake traditional Vajrayana rituals, but to practise either (Tibetan) Lamaism or Theravada Buddhism. The first thing the laity will have to do in this case is to visit a Lama monastery or Theravadin Vihar regularly, listen to sermons, and participate in regular group worship. The final step would be to become a Lama or Bhikshu, if feasible.

In the case of the Theravada, commitment means first of all a regular visit to a Vihar, a place where there is a statue of the Buddha in a hall where people can be accommodated for worship and meditation. Usually there is also a separate room for the *bhante* (monk, *bhikshu*) to use as living quarters. There are usually also *chibhadyah* (*chaitya*) of various sizes in and around the Vihar, if it has been established in an old, often renovated *baha* or *bahi* (the temple-monastery complexes of traditional Vajrayana Buddhism). The Vihar is also used for teaching Buddhism and for the general education of local children. It may equally be used for local gatherings and other community events. People who visit the Vihar regularly listen to the preaching of the *bhante*, take part in Buddha Puja, and try to practise the teachings of the Buddha in their everyday life, for example, by not offering fowl and animal sacrifices in rituals, by becoming vegetarian, giving up alcohol, and so on. They offer rice, money, and other consumer goods to the *bhante* on the day of Buddha Puja. Later, they start fasting during the Buddha Puja and also take on various practices of *panchashil*, *astashil* (Five Precepts, Eight Precepts), and so on, in order to lead their life according to the Buddha's teachings (Pragya, 1982; Vajracharya & Vajracharya, 1983; Sushobhan 1985; Bajracharya 1986).

They will also participate in the *bhojan* (communal meal) after the Buddha Puja sponsored by the laity. Many people do all this individually, while still participating in the rituals of traditional Buddhism and Hinduism, as members of their family or *guthi*.[2] Annual rituals may be simplified and rites of passage may be modified according to Theravada if the practising person is the family head. Visiting the Vihar and *ahimsa* are the basic symbols of Theravada for the laity and essentially go together. The laity understand it as the Vihar Dharma. For them to go to the Vihar is equivalent to doing *dharma* and they use the expressions *viharay wanegu* (to go to the Vihar) and *dharmay wanegu* (to go [to do] *dharma*) as synonyms. Hence, in order to remain close to informants' own way of describing their religious practice, Theravada as practised in the Valley will be referred to as Vihar Buddhism in this paper, as already mentioned. In addition to visiting the Vihar and observing *ahimsa*, abstention from alcohol and meat, though not essential, are also a symbol of becoming a Vihar Buddhist. Vihar Buddhists are generally regarded as kind and pious people in society who mean no harm to anybody. Although the *bhante*s are opposed to Gubhajus as Vajrayana priests, the laity have no objection to simultaneously worshipping the deities of Vajrayana Buddhism, or, for that matter, to worshipping Hindu deities.

THE INTRODUCTION OF VIHAR BUDDHISM IN NEPAL

Vihar Buddhism was revived[3] in Nepal during the 1930s by people who, dissatisfied with the Rana regime and the religious practices of the time,

---

[2] *Guthis* are characteristic Newar institutions, which bring together a group of Newar household heads for a common, usually social and ritual purpose. Many *guthi*s, though not all, are based on shared kinship (see also Nepali 1988 (1965); Quigley 1985; Regmi 1978a).

[3] It is generally understood in Kathmandu, and confirmed by scholars such as Baikuntha Prasad Lacoul and Labh Ratna Tuladhar writing on Sthaviravada (Theravada) in Nepal and the autobiography of Mahapragya, respectively, that Mahapragya and the contemporary *bhantes* revived Theravada in Nepal. It is also said that in earlier times no clear demarcation was made between the various sects of Mahayana and Hinayana (Sthaviravada or Theravada) in Nepal (Ram 1977; Shrestha 1994; Singh 1990). Accordingly, Theravada Buddhism may have been practised in Nepal in ancient times and it may be right to say that the Theravada was revived in Nepal by Mahapragya in the 1930s. Asha Ram Shakya, commenting on Heinz Bechert's 'Report on a Study of Buddhist Revival in Nepal', even argued that "Theravada Buddhism has introduced nothing new. It has simply laid stress on the need of strictly observing the Vinaya rules of the Buddha's time ... therefore I prefer to call it a 'Revival of Buddhism [and not Buddhist]' (Kölver 1992). The Vihar Buddhism as discussed in this paper could be regarded as the practice since the 1930s, in a way influencing Vajrayana Newar (Nepal) Buddhism and Mahayana Lamaism, but at the same time, its laity, essentially from the pool of the Vajrayanists and the Hindus, keep on practising their religions while going to Vihars. Hence the word 'revived' would also be understood as (re)introduced.

came in contact with it in Kolkata, India, and later in Sri Lanka and Myanmar. The Newar merchant community with trading *kothis* (houses) in Kolkata and influenced by Maha Bodhi Society and its founder Dharmapala, a Sri Lankan *anagarika*, no doubt, played a crucial role in reviving Vihar Buddhism in Nepal. Since people could not protest against the Rana regime openly, they expressed their protests indirectly in the form of undertaking and or encouraging Buddha *dharma*, which was different from Hindu *dharma* as well as being different from Vajrayana Buddhism. Jagat Man Sakya (later Dharmaditya Dharmacharya), Dharma Narayan Tuladhar (Dharma Sahu), and Bhaju Ratna Kansakar are some of the well-known figures who encouraged Buddha *dharma*. Another form of protest that was lurking then was the language movement. Newars were pushing for the recognition of Nepal Bhasha, the Newar language,[4] with a strong sentiment of Newar nationalism. They came together and moved forward jointly by publishing Sanskrit and Pali Buddhist texts in a journal in Nepal Bhasha called *Buddha Dharma* published in 1925 by Dharmacharya. This was the first magazine or newspaper in Nepal Bhasha. Prior to that only Pandit Nisthananda Vajracharya had written books on Buddhism, such as the *Lalitavistara*, depicting the life story of Buddha, in Nepal Bhasha. Later, a monthly journal, *Dharmodaya*, became the platform for such movements. Dharmacharya also organized the Buddha Jayanti on the day of Swanha Punhi (full moon in the month of Baishakh according to the Vikram calendar) in 1926 to celebrate Buddha's birth, enlightenment, and passing away.

The first monks to lead a monastic life with full Theravadin ordination were Mahapragya and Pragyananda in 1932. They were influenced by Chandramani, a Myanmarian monk living in Kushinagar, India, who also ordained Dr Bhimraj Ambedkar in 1956. In fact, they had previously been Tibetan Buddhist monks but changed to Theravada after coming into contact with Chandramani. Chandramani also ordained the Nepali nuns, Dharmapali, Sanghapali, Ratnapali, and Dharmachari, all from the rather affluent families of Uday, the trading community of Newars. But all these monks and nuns received very hostile treatment from the Rana regime and were exiled. In exile they formed the Dharmodaya Sabha, the Buddhist Society of Nepal, in 1944, which still exists in Kathmandu today as an

[4]The language of the Newars is called 'Newah Bhae' in their mother tongue, which when translated in Nepali becomes 'Newar Bhasha' and 'Newar Language' in English. Recently, Newar scholars and activists, in line with the ethnicity movement in the country, prefer this denomination to the earlier one, 'Newari', commonly used in Nepali. Nepal Bhasha is the Sanskritized name of the Newar language used by the language activists and the literary world. Newar language gets that name as the language of the inhabitants of the then Nepal (Mandala); the medieval Newar kingdom of Nepal. Here, Nepal Bhasha and Newar language are used interchangeably according to the context. 'Nw.' will indicate any word in the text specific to Newar language before the word.

umbrella organization for Nepali Buddhists.[5] It was only in the late 1940s that they could return to Kathmandu where they founded Ananda Kuti Vihar in Swayambhu in 1948. It was the official headquarters of the Theravada, headed by Bhikshu Amritananda, and boasted a Buddha relic brought from Sri Lanka. The All-Nepal Bhikkhu Mahasangha was formed in 1950 and Theravadin monks, with a monastic community of about fifty, including *gurumas*, as the nuns were called, started activities openly in an organized manner.[6] Vihars were constructed at many abandoned and often ruined *baha/bahis*, some of which had been used as public toilets or garbage collection centres by the local people. About thirty such Vihars were founded in the Valley by the 1980s. After the end of the Rana regime in 1951, King Tribhuvan made Buddha Jayanti a public holiday in 1952 and sponsored the recitation of Mahaparitran and Buddha Puja in 1953.[7] In 1956, marking the 2,500th year since Buddha's *parinirvana* (death, salvation, and supreme enlightenment), Nepal, under the leadership of Bhikshu Amritananda, hosted the Fourth World Fellowship of Buddhists Conference. This conference was inaugurated by King Mahendra and was participated in by delegates from more than forty countries. Being the first ever interna-

---

[5]Dharmodaya encompasses the Mahayana, Vajrayana, and Theravada sects of Buddhism and all of them are represented in it. The chairmanship and the governing body are rotated among the three sects. All the sub-sects of Lama Buddhism, Ngimapa, Sakyapa, Kagyupa, Gelukpa, Bonbo (Bonpo), come under the Mahayana and are collectively represented in Dharmodaya. In principal, this representation is done on the basis of rotation among the sub-sects, which in turn are again represented by the Lamas of Gumbas according to rotation, and the will and ability of the Lama/Gumba, etc. However, according to Gumba Byabastha Tatha Bikas Samiti (Gumba Development Committee), there are about 4,500 Gumbas in Nepal. Since the Lamas of these sub-sects are scattered throughout the country, including those in the very remote areas, it may not be feasible for all of them to be in constant touch with Dharmodaya. Such exclusion, if any, could be supplemented by the practice of Lamas travelling around different Gumbas for learning and preaching purposes. Currently, only 1,409 Gumbas – Ngimapa 1,125, Sakyapa 27, Kagyupa 156, Gelukpa 6, Bonbo 22, others 17 – are registered with the Gumba Development Committee (Gorkhapatra Sansthan 2005). The committee is vigorously campaigning to register them all and bring them under systematic organization. Newar Buddhism is represented as Vajrayana and the reviving Sthavira Buddhism as Theravada. Hence Dharmodaya is the umbrella organization of Buddhism in Nepal, although some remote institutions of a sect may not necessarily be physically incorporated at a certain stage.

[6]Technically the nuns were not fully ordained nuns (*bhikshuni*) but only *anagarikas* or 'homeless ones', a kind of celibate status between monastic and lay, which, as we have seen above, was adopted by Dharmapala. The status of fully ordained nun had been lost to the Theravada tradition in the eleventh century. It could not be revived because a minimum of five ordained *bhikshunis* had to be present in order to ordain a new one (more recently the Theravada nuns have challenged this conclusion, by taking ordination from Chinese Buddhists: see LeVine & Gellner 2005). Colloquially the nuns are referred to as *guruma* (guru mother), the respectful term used for a Vajracharya priest's wife.

[7]The recitation of *paritran* or 'protection' verses is, other than the worship of the Buddha, one of the main rituals of Theravada Buddhism. A 'Mahaparitran' refers to a collective all-night recitation by a large number of monks.

tional conference held in Nepal, the king and the country got much-needed publicity. This millennial celebration was remembered for a long time by the Newars of Kathmandu.

However, Vihar Buddhism could not develop smoothly thereafter. The introduction of the Panchayat political system after 1960 dealt it a severe blow, as it did to the Newar nationalist movement, including the language movement. Buddhism was regarded as a branch of Hinduism and subordinate to it. To convert a person from one religion to another was forbidden. Hence the Theravadin monks could only reach to Buddhists by birth: basically to the Bare, Gubhaju, and Uday among the Newar community. With few exceptions, *bhante*s and *guruma*s came from these communities. But the mass of the laity came from the Jyapu community. It was not a big problem for them to undertake Vihar Buddhism along with their traditional rituals, Hindu or Vajrayana, and in line with the Panchayat ideology. The practice of Theravada by the monastic community is also much in line with Newar traditional customs. The lay community is involved whenever needed or possible, but there are not too many impositions as far as the issues of gender and impure castes are concerned. The presence of prominent indigenous Newar merchants, Maniharsha, Gyanjyoti, Sanujyoti, and so on, as lay sponsors also may have helped to make it acceptable.

Slowly the monastic communities started to perform rites of passage and to recite sutras to aid in the fulfilment of wishes, to heal ailing family members, to ensure safety when travelling, etc., for their laity, just like the Tibetan Lamas and Vajrayana Gubhajus, or for that matter Hindu Brahman priests. By the 1980s, Vihar Buddhism had spread throughout the Kathmandu Valley and its vicinity, especially among Newars, though much more strongly in some villages and some urban contexts than in others. It had also spread beyond the Valley among the diaspora Newars, at times involving Tamangs, Gurungs, Magars, and even Tharus. After democratization in 1990, it spread faster and much further, involving more of the diaspora Newars and other ethnic groups and even some Parbate Hindus.

Vihar Buddhism also began to be taught in Nepal along with the establishment of Ananda Kuti Vidyapith in 1959 under the management of Ananda Kuti Vihar. This school not only taught *pariyatti* (elementary Buddhism) classes but also general education under the government system of education. In fact this school was one of the leading high schools in Nepal producing the brightest students for some decades thereafter. Some of the present author's college mates and good friends are the able products of this school. They are now leaders in various sectors of the society, some even in foreign countries and international institutions. Later, *pariyatti* classes were started at other Vihars as well. But for higher ordination, one still has to go to India, Sri Lanka, or Myanmar, or, these days, to Thailand. Thus ordination was and is the gateway to foreign connections for many and is one of the reasons the new generation is attracted to Vihar Buddhism, especially in recent years.

It is generally accepted that the people who take to Vihar Buddhism are mostly those who could not adjust to prevailing society for political, social, or personal (familial) reasons. Hence they are regarded as, and in fact many of them are, more liberal and progressive than their contemporaries. This is more often true of *guruma*s and to some extent of female lay people. Vihar Buddhism has flourished with the vigour of such pioneering people (see also Gombrich & Obeyesekere 1988). But whether the movement will remain vigorous is a different question, which will have to be answered by the next generation. This could be crucial for the future path of Vihar Buddhism.

THE SPREAD OF VIHAR BUDDHISM AMONG RURAL NEWARS IN THE KATHMANDU VALLEY

Population growth, urbanization (the massive expansion of city areas in the Kathmandu Valley) (see also Sharma 1993 for the issues of urbanization in Nepal), internationalization (influx of foreigners and foreign investment), new electoral systems, the penetration of governance, spread of education, awareness of public health, etc., have all had their effect on the various aspects of life in the Valley. With farmland in Kathmandu and Patan city areas fast diminishing, the suburban area of the Valley has begun to fill the role of supplier of fresh food – vegetables, milk, poultry, etc., – making rational use of the surplus family labour (see also Acharya 1979, for surplus labour in Nepalese agriculture). Residential and industrial areas have sprawled out to these suburbs. Governance though slow is becoming more systematized and more firm. The need of development was felt everywhere. Leaders with more local interests were starting to being recognized in the electoral politics. More schools were being established and systematized. All these phenomena had their effects on daily life and on people's way of thinking and how they viewed the events around them, sometimes with hope and sometimes with anxiety. People became more aware of their rights and duties, of choices and alternatives in their mode of livelihood, and of a need to create and uphold their identities. Adopting a new religion and/or reviving an old one can be considered as a way to establish social and personal identity in a time of rapid change. The move towards Vihar Buddhism can be understood in the same way.

In fact Vihar Buddhism has spread quite widely, though unevenly, in rural Nepal, especially among rural Newars in the Kathmandu Valley. It experienced slow but steady growth up until the 1980s, as mentioned above. In the 1980s it began to spread faster, especially with the active participation of the second generation of monks and nuns, such as Subodhan, Sudarshan, Gyanpurnik, Buddhaghosh, Ashwaghosh, Dhammawati, and others. In the 1990s, after the democratic movement, the lay community turned to it more and more as an alternative, if not with (high) expectations. Currently, there are ninety Theravadin Vihars in Nepal, of which fifty-seven are in the Kathmandu Valley and its vicinity (Kondanya 2003). One can find a Vihar in almost all the Newar settlements that have existed since the Malla period in the Valley. The nearest ones from central Kathmandu would be Nakadesh (Nw. Nara), Thimi, Sunakothi (Nw. Sunagu), Khokana (Nw. Khona), Bungamati (Nw. Bunga), Sanagaon (Nw. Thashi), Kirtipur (Nw. Kyapuh), Panga, Chobhar, Lubhu, and the farther ones would be Thecho, Harisiddhi (Nw. Jala), Chapagaon (Nw. Wa), Matatirtha, Balambu, Thankot, Banepa (Nw. Bhota), Dhulikhel, Panauti, Khopasi, and Trisuli. Besides, there are more than thirty Buddhist institutions called *sangha*, *samuha*, or centres, which are purely Theravadin and which organize or sponsor Theravadin activities. As for the active monastic community, there are about 200 *bhikshu*s and *sramanera*s and about 120 *anagarika*s (*guru-mas*), some preaching and some still studying (Kondanya 2003). Those who are studying not only learn about Buddhism but also acquire a general education, some even in foreign countries such as Sri Lanka, Myanmar, Thailand, Taiwan, Australia, France, the UK, and the USA.

NAKADESH: A CASE STUDY

Socio-Economic Dynamism of the Rural Setting

The rural setting that will be discussed here is Nakadesh, which is regarded as a part of a bigger settlement,[8] Thimi (see also Lachhi 1989).

[8]Nakadesh, the name as it appears in a plate in a temple in the village, dated 1672 (Nepal Sambat 792) (Malla et al. 2000), is a Newar settlement forming the core part of the Siddhi Ganesh Village Development Committee (VDC: administrative village), the other part being Duncho, a Parbate-Hindu (mainly Chetri but also with some Damai and Sarki) settlement within the village, distinctly separated from Nakadesh by a stretch of farmland. It was incorporated into Madhyapur Thimi Nagarapalika (administrative town) in 1998 along with four other administrative villages. Historically, it is regarded as the expansion (partly a breakaway new settlement) of the core part of Thimi, a medieval city kingdom. The very name Naka (Newar: new) Desh (settlement, country, land) suggests it is a newer settlement (compared to Thimi). Many intra-familial, supra-familial and other social relations of the people in the two settlements amply support this relation. However, some people in the village opine that the village may not be so new, as many settlements in the valley are often rebuilt over the ruins of the settlements from an earlier era, and could even be older than Thimi. Although further studies are needed to establish this, rural elites prefer to use Nagadesh as the name of the village, perhaps to have an identity independent of Thimi, and it is more commonly used in the official documents and formal platforms. According to the villagers, this name (Naga [serpent] + Desh) is derived from Basuki Nag, a Puranic serpent, who takes care of the people, land, and the water in the vicinity. People worship the serpent in the middle

Nakadesh branches out from the centre of Thimi on its eastern side on the less productive uplands of the vast farmland spreading along the bank of the river Manohara. Nakadesh is said to have acquired its character as a Newar settlement during the seventeenth and eighteenth centuries, its identity revolving around a Hindu deity, regarded as the saviour of the settlement (see also Müller 1981 and Levy 1990). This deity is one of seven in the area whose chariots are carried around the region on the occasion of the Biska festival every year, on the first day of the month of Baishakh according to the Vikram calendar. This settlement is dominated by Jyapus, the Newar farmers, but also has a sizeable population of Sheshyah and Nay, with a few houses each of Gubhaju, Kau, Nau, and Jugi (Maharjan 1994). Sheshyahs are regarded as latecomers to the village and claim to be the descendants of the concubine of the last Malla king of Bhaktapur. According to the people,: "they settled here because the deity asked their leading ancestor to do so in a dream when he halted for the night during his flight from the conquering Shah king, Prithvi Narayan, and his men."

The physical order of the settlement is typically Newar. There are three-storeyed houses lining settlement paths, with temples of main gods and other deities, public open spaces, public water spaces (ponds, wells, *hiti*s), and public buildings (*chapah*, *phalcha*). The social order of the society is based on caste and the division of caste roles in performing religious and social functions is all typically Newar, and basically Hindu, understood to have been formed by the end of the Malla period (see also Gutschow & Kölver 1975; Müller 1981; Levy 1990; and Vergati 1995). But at the same time, the *chibhadyah*, the basic element of Buddhism, is to be found in almost all big *nani*s (courtyard-like spaces surrounded by houses, often with a well, *chibhadyah*, and/or some Hindu deities) and *lachhi*s (a wide open space in the Newar settlement with a temple of Ganesh and/or other Hindu deities, *chibhadyah*, used for public gatherings, festival celebrations, public works, drying crops, etc.). Gubhajus, including those from Thimi and Bhaktapur, perform rituals for the Jyapus and act as their domestic priests. Dyahbramus from Thimi are the priests of the Sheshyahs. Some of the Jyapus also use them as domestic priests. Annual festivals,

---

of the terraced land, near a water spring where it is believed to have been rehabilitated after it lost its home, the Valley pond, being drained by Manjushri, and is believed to appear during meaningful occasions (Prajapati et al. 1997). These names in Newar language would be Nakadeh and Nagadeh, respectively. The local people also identify themselves as *Nar(a)mi* (people of Nara [land]) and identify the place as, *Nara(sa)y wanegu* (to go to Nara [land]) or *Naray chwanmha manu* (person living in Nara [land]). Considering the linguistic characteristics of Newar language, it is possible to think that Nakadeh/Nagadeh became colloquially Naradeh and later 'deh' was either dropped or shortened. Hence, Nakadesh and Nagadesh are used interchangeably in this paper according to the context, as explained above.

rites of passage, religious sacrifices and offerings, social values and norms, and understanding of the world, universe, and cosmos are all basically Hindu in nature. All the religiously meritorious deeds, including the hosting of elaborate religious and social feasts, are regarded as ways to secure a proper way to and a proper place in the next world.

Situated on the banks of the river Manohara, the lowland area is good for farming with a good supply of surface water and an underground reservoir from which water can be easily pumped up during the dry season. Land on the riverbank is very fertile in spite of being prone to irregular flooding every year. Hence in modern times the right to ownership of farmland in this area has been controversial and the tenant farmers have always been forced to pay high tenancy rents (also confirmed by M.C. Regmi during personal communications with the present author). Most recently the farmland of this area belonged to the Pashupati Guthi, a *guthi* performing the rituals of Pashupati Nath. The tenant farmers of this land, Jyapus of Nakadesh, were just the tillers and were subjected to a high level of extraction until they acquired secure rights after the Land Reform of the early 1960s. They were very often called on for contributions of *jhar* (free labour) to build and maintain the stucco palaces of the Rana rulers (see also Regmi 1978b). They were deprived of education and had no access to government jobs. Thus, the farmers here were rather poor and could not survive only on farming. They had to strive hard to make ends meet, processing farm products, like pressing mustard oil, preparing beaten rice, preparing yeast ferments used for producing *thon* (rice beer), weaving *suku* (straw mats), making pots and selling them in the cities of the Valley. They were constantly on the move throughout the day, come rain or shine. But their apparent simplicity and habits of hard work were understood in a different way and mocked by the Parbate Hindus, as expressed in the Nepali proverb, *kam kura eka tira, kumlo boki Thimi tira*, meaning 'put aside your work and go to Thimi carrying loads of burden'. This is used to denote people who are unable to perform duties, who put off decision making; the incompetence of such people is supposed to be illustrated by the people of Thimi.

The need to sell goods, basically farm products, away from their own settlement, making door-to-door visits in different villages and cities of the Valley, made these people in due time good salesmen, with a thorough geographical and social knowledge of different settlements and cities. They developed the skills of making good business deals, producing quality goods, and selling with amicable language and salesmanship. They never became angry while making a deal and became experts in developing human relationships. Today they have been able to create their identity as *thimi-narmi banja*, salesmen from Thimi and Nakadesh. They are most well known for Nepali earthen pottery, Hindu deity masks, beaten rice (having represented Nepal internationally as manufacturers of these items), yeast for making alcohol, mustard oil, and *chaku wasah*. This last is a solid cake of molasses cooked along with spices, coconuts, cashew nuts, chestnuts, dry grapes, ghee, and some nutritious ingredients, used as a supplement in the diet of weak persons and the mothers of newborn babies. To all these, the cultivation of flowers and green vegetables has been added recently.

Narmis interact on a daily basis with Parbate Hindu people, principally the Chetris, some Sarkis and Damais, and a few Tamangs who are believed to have settled within the village premises during the period of Jang Bahadur Rana. Some of them also interact with Magars living in the neighbouring settlement. All of these local factors influence in one way or the other the behaviour and thoughts of the Narmis.

CONTEMPORARY DYNAMISM IN FARMING

Although farming is the main occupation of many of the villagers, most of them own very little land. About half of the villagers have less than two *ropanis* (1 *ropani* = 0.05 ha) of farmland and those holding more than four *ropanis* are only about 20 per cent of all the villagers (Maharjan 1998). According to the National Sample Census of Agriculture, the figures for Bhaktapur district are 13 per cent and 63 per cent, respectively (CBS 1993a). Moreover, tenants farm about one-third of the farmland and for more than 60 per cent of the farmers at least some of their land is held as a tenancy.[9] The corresponding figures for Nepal as a whole were 9 per cent and 17 per cent in 1991 (CBS 1993b).[10] These tenant farmers in Nara have to give half of what they produce to the landowners as land rent. Although the Land Reform of 1964 officially set the land rent at *teis pathi* (23 *pathi*s) of paddy per *ropani* of *khet* land, about one-third of the level beforehand, many of the tillers continued to pay half the produce (unofficially) in order to please the landlord, who would otherwise snatch the land away from

[9]Mahesh C. Regmi, in a personal communication, said that Bhaktapur/Thimi farmers are the most exploited in the history of modern Nepal.

[10]According to the latest National Sample Census of Agriculture these figures have become 17 per cent and 14 per cent, respectively (CBS 2004b). This change during the decade can be understood as the partial structural change in the land tenancy market of the country where a relatively smaller proportion of the land is tenanted but there are relatively more tenant farmers than before. However, in the three districts of the Kathmandu Valley, the share of tenant farmers has decreased considerably during the decade but not the share of tenanted land (CBS 2004a). This implies that the trend in the structural change in the land tenancy is different in the Valley and the country as a whole. This point needs to be explored further giving due consideration to the drastic economic and political changes, including the impacts of the insurgency, during the last decade.

them and give it to another tenant. Meanwhile, much of the ownership of *guthi* land was transferred to the *guthi* members (caretakers) and/or the actual tillers. In the process many of the marginal farmers became landless. They had no option but to undertake land tilling from the 'neo landlords' on the basis of sharecropping, without being registered formally as tenants, and they still had to pay half the produce. Thus, one can easily imagine the hard life of the farmers, living on farming alone, especially if they are only producing traditional crops. All the farmers have to be engaged in some petty activities to supplement their subsistence living. As mentioned earlier, they engage in pottery making, mask making, pressing mustard oil, etc. Some of the village *banja*s (vendors) collect these items from other villagers and sell them door-to-door in the city areas of the Valley. These *banja*s link the village with the outer world. They try to supply the needs of the city people by procuring items from the village and also introduce the products of the city to the village people. They thus became the driving force behind change, especially by introducing in the village city-style amenities.

The local farmers were quick to grasp the pressing need of the city dwellers for food. Initially, they sold rice, beaten rice, wheat flour, mustard oil, chillis, etc., as before, and tried to increase the volume of transactions of these products. But they soon realized that the hinterland in which they collected these products was not large enough to meet the growing demand and they began to go further away, as far as Nagarkot and Dhulikhel, to collect them. This was not only time-consuming but it turned out not to be profitable either as they had to compete both with the local traders and with the same products pouring into the Valley from other parts of the country and even from India. In the course of time they realized that their relative advantage lay in supplying vegetables. Thus they started to cultivate the vegetables they saw in the markets, some of them previously unknown to them. They became pioneering farmers and encouraged others in the villages to follow. They also introduced chemical fertilizers, power tillers, irrigation pumps, tractors, and later insecticides. Some of them also became dealer agents for chemical fertilizers.

This was supported by two important infrastructure measures that materialized under the able leadership of the elected Pradhan Pancha during the 1980s (later he was one of the founding members of the Nagadesh Bauddha Samuha). Learning about the plan to construct a ring road which would encompass the core settlements of Bhaktapur and would pass through the middle of the farmland of the village, he worked hard to get higher authorities to sanction the budget so that work could start in his jurisdiction and he persuaded some villagers to part with some of their land and to contribute labour, *shramadan*, to construct a fair-weather road (now part of the road is gravelled with local initiative). Although driving a car is not very smooth on this road, trucks, tractors, and power tillers can easily move around thus enhancing the transportation of farm inputs and farm products in the village.

Another rural project was the construction of an irrigation conduit network which tamed the water from the Manohara river. Here again the Pradhan Pancha managed to get the villagers to contribute *shramadan*, as "the government budget was hardly enough to buy a few sacks of cement to construct the inlet bund at the river side". He also managed to form a beneficiaries group to manage and maintain the conduit system. These two construction works went a long way to stabilize village farming and make the village a vegetable-growing area.

Three crops a year can be grown easily on *awal* and *doyam khet* (first- and second-class rice paddy fields) where irrigation was enabled by the conduit system. Low-lift pumps and dug wells are used to irrigate *sim* and *chahar khet* (third- and fourth-class paddy fields) and *pakha* areas (formerly dry rainfed fields), and intensive farming was carried out here too (see also Maharjan 1998). Spring water is also used to supplement the irrigation for vegetable growing. Deep tube wells are bored in order to irrigate *tar* (plateau) areas. High-yielding varieties of rice, wheat, potato, carrot, radish, cabbage, spinach, eggplant, cauliflower, green onion, tomato, etc., were introduced. New vegetables such as Chinese cabbage, lettuce, broccoli, and asparagus, which were unknown to the villagers before, are also being cultivated. These seeds came from as far away as Bangladesh and Japan. Besides, traditional vegetables with strong demand, such as *pachai* (*Brassica juncea Czen & Cross. Cruciferae*: rape), *tukan* (*Brassica campestris Linn., Cruciferae*: mustard), *chamsur* (*Lepidium sativum L., Cruciferae*: garden cress), *palah* (local spinach), *tusi* (cucumber), *torei* (gourd), *phasi* (pumpkin), *simi* (*Dolichos lablab L., Leguminosae*: horse bean), *bakula* (*Vicia faba*: broad bean) are also cultivated. These vegetables are grown throughout the year in response to the demands of the vegetable markets in the Valley.

The traditional farming patterns on *khet* land of two crops a year (paddy and wheat or potato) changed to three crops a year: paddy–wheat–potato; paddy–potato–potato; paddy–potato–vegetables; paddy–vegetables–vegetables; or vegetables–vegetables–vegetables. Traditional cropping patterns on *pakha* land – maize (intercropped with soybean) followed by mustard or beans; millet–mustard, chilli or summer vegetable followed by mustard or beans – have changed to paddy–fallow or vegetables–vegetables–vegetables–vegetables in places with good water facilities. By contrast, in places with no proper water supplementation, maize intercropped with soybean used to be cultivated in summer and the field was left fallow the rest of the year. Some still cultivate mustard or beans on such land. Barley and millet cultivation has been abandoned and wheat cultivation has decreased considerably. Farming as a whole has become highly intensive and production levels have increased enormously. It can be said that a revolution occurred in the village farming system during the 1980s, which has increased not only land productivity but also labour productivity.

The bulk of family labour goes into cultivation. But every hand in the house is needed to process and market the vegetables. The women of the house can often be seen happily chatting with each other as they sit in the pathways in front of their houses cleaning, bundling, and packing the vegetables to be sent to market early in the morning of the following day. Some of them take the vegetables to the collection centre nearby the same evening. The vegetables thus collected are loaded into a minibus and are sold in the various vegetable markets in the Valley – Asan, Ganabahal, Mahabauddha, Kalimati, Bauddha (Nw. Khasa), Koteshwar, Mangal Bazar, Dhaugal, Lagankhel, Satdobato – often wholesale to the shop owners in these markets. The farmers have bulk buyers, such as hotels and restaurants, and they also supply to jails, army camps, and police headquarters in Singha Durbar, using their old connections. Yet others pack the vegetables on to a bicycle and a male member of the house takes the produce to sell directly to the consumers and thus increase their profit. Their traditional engagement in roaming trade as *banjas* has contributed to their success at vegetable marketing. Recently they have also started to export vegetables to the Middle East on a trial basis. The customers there are none other than Nepali migrant labourers.[11]

Vegetable production in which all members of the family can be engaged has become one of the main activities of the farmers of this village, and they are able to earn a living even from the little land they cultivate. A farmer can easily earn Rs.50,000 per year from a *ropani* of land by cultivating vegetables throughout the year. The yield of paddy has increased 1.6 times and of potatoes 3 times due to the introduction of high-yielding varieties. Thus, a farmer can use his land strategically, by first growing paddy and potatoes for staple food and then to generate cash income by growing vegetables on the rest of the land.

Valley farming as a whole is widely accepted to have gone through a major transformation during the 1980s, and productivity, though varying from place to place, must have gone up in all the rural areas of the Valley.

[11]There are hundreds of thousands of people from all over Nepal working in different countries, hired through job placement agents in Nepal and India. Recently I had an opportunity to talk to dozens of them working at Doha International Airport, Qatar, and was pleasantly taken aback when I was completely unexpectedly asked in Newar language by a ground staff of the Qatar Airways, while checking-in by showing my passport for a flight to Osaka, *'chi yakahcha la, ganan jhayegu?'* (Are you alone, where did you come from?). He was none other than a Dhakhwa (Newar Buddhist) from Nagbahal in Patan, Kathmandu Valley.

This has in general contributed to the much-improved socio-economic status of the Valley's farmers, most of whom, among the Newars, are Jyapus.

OTHER ASPECTS OF SOCIO-ECONOMIC DYNAMISM

The people of the village, including Jyapus, are no longer dependent on farming alone. The transportation of goods and people, the sale of farm products, and the running of corner shops, tea stalls, and restaurants are fast increasing in the village. Butchery, tailoring, iron-smithery, and cobblering are the jobs traditionally undertaken by people of occupational castes (Dalits). Some locals are managing private schools. Government servants, bank clerks, and teachers are also increasingly represented in the village. Some commute from the village to Kathmandu on a daily basis. Some locals manage broiler farms, pig farms, and brick kilns, and there is one carpet factory. There are quite a number of (day) labourers from the Tarai working in brick kilns and from neighbouring mountain districts in the carpet factory. Seasonal farm labourers (Tamangs and Parbate Hindus) come from the neighbouring districts to supplement the scarcity of labour during the peak seasons of planting paddy and harvesting paddy and potato.

In addition to the traditional cottage industries of earthen pottery, mask making, beaten rice production and yeast making, factories producing cold drinks, alcohol, medicine, electrical parts, carpets, and garments have been established nearby, especially from the 1980s. There are also private and government colleges affiliated to Tribhuvan University, an educational materials' centre of the Education Ministry, a national hospital, and other government offices in the area. Suburban residential houses have begun to sprout up here and there. More recently, two systematized residential areas have been developed in the region by the valley town planning development authority. During the early 1990s, land prices in the village swelled to its zenith due to the unexpected urgent demand from Nepalis returning from Hong Kong after it was returned to China by Britain. Some villagers made a fortune selling land at that time. A steady polarization into haves and have-nots is observed to be in progress.

With the diversification of occupations and the contemporary economic dynamism, people's lifestyles have started to change. Often the living patterns of the members of the same family have grown to be different from each other's due to their different occupations. This has tended to undermine the conditions – joint ownership, joint living, joint earning, and joint consuming – that underline joint families and has served to hasten family separation (see also Maharjan 1994). The ideal joint family is becoming hard to find and the members of the younger generation now frequently leave their parents to live by themselves. Even the number of very aged people living alone is increasing. These phenomena affect the daily activities of the Narmi people, as well as their perceptions of the cosmos and of life, both directly and indirectly.

As a whole, the society can be said to be transforming from a stable and low productivity paradigm to a dynamic and high productivity one. In this process of transformation people are coming to feel insecure. The increasing number of aged people living alone most vividly illustrates this. Most of these people tend to submit themselves to some religious practices to gain mental peace and perhaps salvation. One such avenue for them is to join Vihar Buddhism, and it is an option that is becoming widespread in the village.

THE SPREAD OF VIHAR BUDDHISM

Although there were Thimi-Narmi people who used to visit Vihars in Patan and Kathmandu, Vihar Buddhism got its momentum in the region during the 1970s, when the remains of an old *chaitya* were found during the cleaning of a public toilet in Thimi. The laity decided to make a Vihar in the village and started to collect donations from various people. They finally built Thimi Pati Vihar in the early 1980s and a *bhikshu* who was in Dharan before took up residence and started to preach Vihar Buddhism. He had learnt Theravada Buddhism in Darjeeling (India), Sri Lanka, and Myanmar. Now *bhikshus* from other Vihars make visits here and perform joint worship during Buddha Puja and Paritrans. Often *bhikshus* from Sri Lanka, Myanmar, and Thailand also visit. Some of the dedicated laity have become *sramaneras* (monastic novices), as will be seen below, two each of Narmi boys and girls have become novices or nuns and are currently training abroad.

Meanwhile more and more of the Narmis became interested in Vihar Buddhism. Most of them were those who were worried about the dark side of the current social dynamism. They were especially worried about the problem of ageing, the increase in the number of nuclear families with only old couples or a lone old member – far removed from the ideal Newar joint family – the lavish lifestyle and individualistic ways of thinking of the younger generation, and the polarization of local society. They wanted to do something to improve this situation and want to transform society into a more modern, more productive, and more stable one. Hoping to find an answer in Vihar Buddhism, they formed the Nagadesh Bauddha Samuha (Nagadesh Buddhist Group Caucus, a socio-philanthropic voluntary organization) in 1987 with a small but active membership (Nagadesh Bauddha Samuha 1988). Through this organization they began Vihar activities independent of Thimi Pati Vihar. They celebrated the inauguration day by doing *puja* of all the *chibhadyahs* in the village. The Samuha became the donor group for a new Vihar, Nagadesh Buddha Vihar, and they sponsor and/or undertake activities in the Vihar pertaining to a deeper understanding of Vihar Buddhism. The activities are all voluntary. At first there were no external funds and local donations and offerings were rather small. People would gather at different places, mainly in the houses of core members, for their activities. It was difficult even to get a *bhikshu* to spare the time to come there and preach. But their voluntary efforts, including *puja* of *chibhadyahs* in the village on religiously significant days of the month (i.e. *punhi, amai, ekadashi,* and *astami*), kept the spirit alive and they started a campaign to collect donations from beyond the village. They were also successful in getting Bhikshu Pragyalok from Sri Lanka to give religious instruction. The core members also actively participate in various national events of Vihar Buddhism in the Kathmandu Valley, in Lumbini, Pokhara, and so on. They have Bhikshu Dhammashobhan's encouraging guidance for all these activities.

The Nagadesh Bauddha Samuha was given a small piece of abandoned community land on the outskirts of the village by the VDC (the local council). They started to build a hall in the plot, which later would become the main hall of the Vihar. On 1 June 1991, on the 2,535th Buddha Jayanti day, they invited Bhikshu Subodhananda Mahasthavir to inaugurate the statue of the Buddha for the Vihar. Nagadesh Bauddha Vihar symbolically took firm root on this day. In 1994, Bhikshu Thanseth stayed here for the *varsabas* (rains retreat) with the consent of Bhikshu Ashwaghosh Mahasthavir. In the meantime, donations started to come in little by little and went on accumulating. To this a million yen was added in 1995-6 as a donation from a Lions Club in Hiroshima, Japan.[12] Further enthusiastic

---

[12]While conducting the first census and sample surveys on the issues of socio-economic dynamism of the village during 1991-2, I was first approached by the former Pradhan Pancha and a founding member of the Samuha to explore the possibilities of getting aid from Japan for the village. In one of the subsequent visits in 1994-5, when the preliminary findings of the earlier survey study were submitted to the village, many founding members of the Samuha made a strong request for aid. With good timing I found the Hiroshima Rijo Lions Club willing to give a donation for the welfare of the village. All the arrangements for the donation, according to the spirit and principles of the Lions Club, were made with the author as the go-between. Later, a path was paved for relations between the Hiroshima chapter and the Kathmandu chapter of the Lions Club. The money was used to supplement the cost of construction of the Vihar house, the work being monitored by the Embassy of Japan in Kathmandu. Some key members of the Japanese Lions Club visited the village along with the author to make the formal agreement and monitor the building, in March 1996. The Japanese guests were given traditional *pancha kanya* (five virgins) welcome at the airport with flower garlands and the drum troupe (*dhime baja*) of the village, well known as one of the Newar cultural troupe of the valley. Later in the village, they were given an honourable welcome and taken in procession through the village with a cloth banner, *dhime baja*, and accompanied by the lay people. Many villagers showered the procession with rice and flower petals from

donations from the laity followed. With all these donations, offerings from the laity, and *shramadan*, the Vihar building, a community meditation centre, was constructed in 1996 on the slope of the land obtained from the VDC. Statues depicting the life stages of Siddhartha Gautam were established at the side of the entrance of the main hall, near a *chibhadyah* established earlier. Rooms for monks to live in were added later. Gyanjyoti, a pioneer sponsor of Vihar Buddhism also supported the various activities of this Samuha in cash and in kind. Thereafter the Samuha started the preaching of Buddhism by inviting monks from various other Vihars in the Valley. They included Bhikshu Varsambodhi, Bhikshu Kolit, Bhikshu Saddhatissa, Bhikshu Kaludai Mahasthavir, Bhikshu Mahendra Mahasthavir, Bhikshu Aniruddha Mahasthavir, Bhikshu Dhammashobhan, and Anagarikas Dhammawati and Keshavati, besides those already mentioned above. The Samuha had 200 members,[13] including 75 women, in 1996, who participated actively in Vihar Buddhism and in other social activities of the Samuha. They are all active *upasaka*s and *upasika*s. Donations, external assistance, and important information are all clearly recorded, well disseminated among the members, and made public at the general meetings.

The activities of the Samuha include yearly celebrations of Buddha Jayanti, Dharmachakra Prabartan Divas, Ayu Sanskar Divas, mini gatherings once a week, Buddha Puja on every *amai, astami* and *punhi*, daily voluntary prayer and meditation at the community meditation centre, and participation in bigger Buddha Puja events at various Vihars in the Valley. They also organize Buddha Puja processions in the village and worship all the *chibhadyah* in the village on the important full-moon days of the year

---

windows and doors, a Newar way of honouring and showing gratitude. In the Vihar the chief guest's face was covered with the many garlands offered by the laywomen. The building was inaugurated by the president of the Lions Club in March 1997.

[13]Membership of the Samuha is given to the representative of the household regardless of the number of family members participating in Vihar activities. According to the author's census survey of the VDC in 1991-92, there were 641 households, 90 per cent Newars and 10 per cent non-Newars. Among the Newars, 87 per cent were Jyapus, 5 per cent Sheshyahs, 5 per cent Nays, and the rest 3 per cent. Thus it can be said that, with 200 households, 35 per cent of Narmi Newars had at least one Vihar Buddhist in their family. Leaving out the population of the Sheshyahs, especially those who are (or claim to be) descendents of Malla kings, and the Nays, who would be unable to make living if they did not slaughter ruminants and sell the meat as self-conscious Hindus, this figure rises to 40 per cent. Even among the Jyapus there are many such self-conscious Hindus, most of whom have important roles in organizing and supporting Hindu culture, for example in the Biska Jatra festival, or at the 'royal palace' (*layku chen*), a ritual centre of the village, etc. Besides them, there are many who, when asked specifically whether they are Buddhists or Hindus, claim to be either or who make no difference between the two, although some affirm that they are not Vihar Buddhists. There are also some young people who claim to be neither. Thus it can be said that in this village, about one third of the people are Hindu, another one third Buddhists, and the rest one or the other, though some of them could be neither.

(Swanha Punhi, Guru Punhi, Si Punhi, Gunla Punhi). Mini gatherings are accompanied by meditation, reciting Pali sutras, and the exchange of ideas on the Buddha's teachings and their adaptation to daily life. The number of participants in such gatherings varies from twenty to thirty; invariably about half are female. During the Buddha Puja in the Vihar, there will be a *bhante* and sometimes a *guruma* to lead the meditation, recite *paritran sloka*s and give the preachings. He or she will explain about the Buddha's teachings, *panchashil, astashil*, etc., illustrated with various episodes from daily life. At the end of the *puja*, *upasaka*s and *upasika*s give offerings of money, fruits, rice, sweets, incense, etc., to the priest. A ceremonial meal (*bhojan*) of *ja* (cooked rice), *ken* (*dal* soup) and *tarkari* (vegetables), often with *achar* (pickles), a staple diet representative of the Valley, is arranged after the *puja* and members of the laity eat the meal with the priest. Members who remain in the Vihar thereafter discuss various matters for as long as the time allows.

On the occasion of Buddha Puja on Gunla Punhi in July 1996, a *paritran* booklet written by Bhikshu Buddhaghosh Mahasthavir in Nepali and printed in Patan was used. Some of the pamphlets explaining the Buddha's teachings were in Nepal Bhasha (the Newar language). The Puja led by Bhikshu Varsambodhi started around 9:00 a.m. and by 10:30 a.m. there were twenty-six men, thirty-two women, and nine children participating. Thereafter, some people left while others continued to arrive. Finally, there were about fifty people at the time of the *bhojan* after the Puja. The Puja started and ended with meditation, prayer, and the recitation of *sloka*s. The sermon of the *bhante* focused on patience, *ahimsa*, greed, anger, self-help, and so on. Animal sacrifice, big feasts, alcohol consumption, and quarrels between and within families and neighbours were especially discouraged. After the *bhojan*, the *bhante* criticized Vajrayana priests for being hereditary, a practice which restricts people from learning the Buddha's teachings and is not only against the very basic spirit of Buddhism but also acts as a disincentive for the masses to adopt Buddhism. Bhikshu Varsambodhi talked calmly but firmly, making sure that the message was being conveyed. People going in and out of the Vihar would fold their hands and bow, saying, "*bhagawan sharana* ([I take] refuge in the Lord [Buddha])". The Samuha members use this Buddhist greeting instead of the more common *namaste* or more recent (Newar revivalist) *jwajalapa*.

Some of the core members of the Samuha are very learned. One of them was a teacher for eighteen years in the Buddhist high school, Ananda Kuti Vidyapeeth, in Swayambhu, founded by Bhikshu Amritananda Mahasthavir in the 1950s. Many of them are teachers in the local high school. The head teacher and social worker, who is also a core member of the Samuha, is a very diligent and hardworking person with a deep understanding of the Buddha's teachings. He is the key person in the whole movement. He claims to have been influenced by Ambedkar and introduces Ambedkar, Rahul Sankrityayan, and their deeds to the villagers in addition to various Nepali *bhantes* and *gurumas*. He has written about ten books on various aspects of Buddhism in the local context and their understanding on Theravada lines.

Nagadesh Bauddha Samuha is registered at the district office of Bhaktapur as a non-profit (socio-philanthropic voluntary) organization and actively organizes eye camps, in cooperation with Lions Club of Kathmandu and Tilganga Eye Hospital, treating patients from near and far. In 1996 alone about 500 patients were treated on two such occasions. It organized another eye camp in 1998, treating 200 patients. It also organizes literacy classes for adults, women, and children and *pariyatti* classes on Buddhism. Often the Vihar is used by village youths for various purposes. Some members even talk about organizing skill training to help local youths to earn their living. Samuha members also voluntarily contribute to various community works, such as maintenance of roads and drains. They help villagers to cope with complicated official papers regarding bank accounts, asset registration or transactions; they help them to deal with strangers and any issues too complicated for the villagers to handle. Such help ranges from simple facilitation in acquiring citizenship cards to dealing with complicated issues regarding police and civil administration, service delivery programmes of the government and NGOs, elections, transaction of land, and sanction of loans.

As an institution the Samuha also acts as a pressure group along with other similar groups to achieve common goals. In this regard, in 1990, it sent an official letter with seventeen recommendations – including that Nepal should be declared a secular country and that there should be the right to use Nepal Bhasha for official purposes – to the committee drawing up the new constitution. Later it also wrote to protest against the Supreme Court's decision to ban the use of Nepal Bhasha by Kathmandu Municipality and Maithili by Rajbiraj Municipality for official purposes. The Samuha became a member of the Dharmodaya Sabha in 1994, and later, when the Madhyapur Thimi branch of the Dharmodaya Sabha was established in 1999, it started to manage it and now conducts all the activities of the Sabha as a representative body. It registered a letter at the concerned government office condemning the assassination in Lumbini in 1997 of Japanese monk Nabatame Yutaka of Nipponzan Myohoji. It expressed deep sorrow at the Indian President K.R. Narayan's statement that "Buddha was born in India", made when he was the chief guest at a gathering of international Buddhists in Sarnath. It donated Rs.7,450 to the Jyapu Mahaguthi to help it construct the Lotus Pond (Paleswan Pukhu) inside Gautami Vihar in Lumbini. The core members of the Samuha actively take part in various national-level events relating to Buddhism.

The Samuha convenes its general assembly meeting every four years where activities and financial transactions of the period are reported and the secretary proposes a general plan for the next four years. Normally, Buddha Puja and some other meaningful event coincide with it; for example, Swanha Punhi, and people from various walks of life are invited as guests. In June 1995, it held its first general assembly meeting to which Bhikshu Buddhaghosh Mahasthavir was invited as the chief guest. Bhikshu Ashwaghosh Mahasthavir was the chief guest at the second general assembly meeting held in June 1999. The Samuha also sends condolence messages whenever some renowned *bhante* or Buddhist sponsor passes away, and sends felicitation messages whenever some *bhante* or sponsor is publicly honoured or attains some notable achievement. It sponsored a ten-day *paritran* recitation to mourn the death of a local *bhante*, Sramanera Shilratna, who had always supported the Samuha. In fact, forty-six *upasakas* and *upasikas* from the Samuha have died since its formation in 1987, and for each of them the Samuha organized a *paritran* recitation.

LAY PERCEPTIONS OF VIHAR BUDDHISM

This section will analyse Vihar Buddhism as perceived by the people of the village on the basis of a questionnaire survey of fifty-three members of Nagadesh Bauddha Samuha and thirty-five non-members from the other Narmi Newars during 1996-7. The members who were surveyed are active members of the Samuha and the non-members were chosen at random. The questionnaire dealt with the occupation and socio-economic condition of the interviewees, the current problems they were facing, their opinions about Vihar Buddhism, its (probable) role in socio-economic development of the village and in making a difference to their livelihood, the activities of the Samuha members, and the current situation of the village. In addition to this, the members were also asked about the time and reason for joining the Samuha, the ways in which they participate in and contribute to Vihar activities, and the consent of family members in joining Vihar. The non-members were also asked what they expected from the Vihar and whether they would be joining it in the future. They were all asked how much they knew about the Japanese donation.

Perceptions of Samuha Members (n = 53)

Of the fifty-three members surveyed, all owned their own house and eighteen of them, with comparatively large families, had two or more houses. They were all from different families. Twenty-two families were nuclear of which six were made up of only aged people over sixty-five, living either alone or with only their spouse. Two old men living alone had started to live in the Vihar itself. Twenty-one families had a family head above sixty years of age and six of them were females. Forty-one houses had toilets inside the house and twenty-nine had a tap, although the supply of water was not regular. Those who lacked toilets in the house used open public toilets, generally located at some peripheral shady place/slope, often near a waterbody and/or demarcated by walls. Many, including those who had taps, used wells, ponds, public taps, and springs for their water supply. Seven of them were entrepreneurs managing various factories in the village, two were managing buses used for transporting farm goods and people, five had cars for personal use, and another five had motorbikes. Fifty of them owned some piece of farmland but more than half of them had less than five *ropanis*. Some had big and small ruminants, and twenty-two had poultry. Most of them said their main family job was farming. Business, managing factories, running buses, running corner shops, etc., were their secondary jobs. With regard to the family's cash income, one third said they earned more than Rs.50,000 per year, while about 20 per cent said they earned Rs.25,000-50,000, and about 10 per cent earned less than Rs.25,000 per annum. The rest said they either had no cash income or had so little cash, which passed through their hands so quickly, that they could not work out its accumulated value over a year.

As for personal information, one-third of them were in their fifties, slightly more than one third were over sixty, and slightly less than one-third were in their forties. About half of them were literate either with primary education or having graduated from adult literacy programmes. About 20 per cent were illiterate and the rest had education above junior high school; some were even graduates with a Bachelor's or Master's degree. Some 80 per cent of them were farmers, about 10 per cent were teachers, and the rest were salaried job holders and self-employed entrepreneurs. Six of the female members undertook virtually all the housekeeping work in the Vihar.

All fifty-three had been active member of the Samuha for more than five years and 80 per cent of them were founding members who had joined the Samuha at their own initiative. The remainder joined the Samuha after they were asked to do so by their friends and neighbours who were members. All of them had the consent of their family members to become Vihar Buddhists. Some 20 per cent were active in Vihar Buddhism even before the formation of the Samuha. They had previously visited Vihars in Thimi, Patan, and Kathmandu and participated in various Buddha Pujas and gatherings. Some of them also practised traditional Hindu and Vajrayana Buddhist rituals, including *astami brata* and *haribhajan*, but more than half of them had stopped those annual rituals and were proud to be called Vihar Buddhists.

As to the reasons for joining the Samuha, many said they wanted to increase their knowledge of Vihar Buddhism, *thahta thahmhaysinan mhasikegu* (to get to know and understand their own inner self), and to achieve tranquillity. But some 20 per cent also said that they were looking to improve their current life. Although half of them confessed that nothing had changed in their life even after joining the Samuha, the rest felt some changes had occurred. Almost all of them said that their ways of thinking and perceiving things in the society, their relationships with family members, neighbours, and society as a whole had changed. Personal activities and their ways of spending their leisure time had changed, with most of them spending time in the Vihar and focusing on Buddhism, and they were satisfied with the changes. Many of them also had been able to overcome personal greed and other worldly matters. They had been able to control their consumption of alcohol and meat and many had become vegetarians. Women claimed to have lost interest in fancy clothes and jewellery. They were able to perform their household work, farm work, and other work better than before.

They believe that all these changes are due to receiving the teachings of Bhagawan Buddha. They are confident that they have contributed to village society in the best way they can and they are sure that they are perceived well by the villagers. Hence, they want to further contribute to the society in various ways, with actions in unity. And they want to spread Vihar Buddhism further by rightly understanding its teachings and practising it in daily life as far as possible. In order to deepen their understanding of Vihar Buddhism, to lead a life according to it and propagate it, they feel it is important to have a library, to publish more books, to establish a training centre where teachings can be conducted, and to strengthen its publicity. All of them vividly remember the Japanese aid for Vihar in minute detail and are thankful for it. Most of them also hope for more help in the future for the development of the Vihar and the village.

Before these aims can be achieved, they also realize that they need to cooperate among themselves, help each other in economic and health problems, and improve education, literacy, public health, and other social problems. For these purposes, some 80 per cent say they are ready to contribute economically according to their capacity and nearly half of them are also ready to contribute with voluntary labour, some without any limits.

The problems they perceived to be the most serious in the village were garbage (drainage and solid waste) and public health issues, the lack of tap (drinking) water, and the lack of proper means of transportation and communication. Issues related to education, farming, employment, and social discipline followed these. Some were concerned about family issues and personal health issues. Interestingly, none of them cited the economic problem of inflation and general hardships in life, which in society at large are the foremost problems people mention first. Two-thirds of the sample did not feel they had any problems.

Perceptions of Other Villagers (n = 35)

All the interviewees, except one, owned their own house and eight owned two houses. More than half lived in nuclear families. Some 60 per cent of the families were headed by people in their forties, approximately 20 per cent by people in their fifties, and around 10 per cent by people over sixty. The heads of five families were in their twenties and three of them were females. Some 80 per cent had toilets in the house and some 70 per cent had tap water. Those without such facilities used the public facilities. Two were operating minibuses but none were managing factories. Five had cars and four had motorbikes. Very few had domestic livestock. More than 80 per cent had farmland of less than five *ropani*s in extent. The main profession of more than 80 per cent was farming. The remaining 10 per cent included teachers, those in salaried jobs, and businessmen. All had some amount of cash income but 60 per cent did not specify it as the amount was too small; some 10 per cent had an annual family income of more than Rs.50,000, one even having more than Rs.300,000 per year. About half were literate with primary education or from adult literacy programmes, one fourth was illiterate, and the rest were literate with education above junior high school.

The problems they identified in the village and its society did not differ much from those perceived by the Samuha members. They also claimed that the problem of garbage and public hygiene was the biggest faced by the villagers. In second place came the problem of lack of tap water. Some also cited the problems of transportation and communication, education facilities, and social discipline of the people. Regarding personal problems, one third pointed to economic hardship and thought their life would have been better if they earned more cash income. Another one third pointed out problems of health, education, family affairs, and relationships with neighbours. The rest claimed they currently had no problems.

None of them are against Vihar Buddhism and many of them also have visited Nagadesh Buddha Vihar on at least one occasion. On their responses to the religious publicity of Vihar Buddhism, some 80 per cent had a positive opinion, and some 10 per cent said they wanted to be part of it but were either too busy or prevailing circumstances did not allow them to do so. Some 10 per cent also said that every individual should have the freedom of belief and the right to practise whatever religion he or she chooses. About half of them appreciated the behaviour of the Samuha members, some 40 per cent were neutral, while about 10 per cent wanted them to put what they had learnt into practice in daily life.

In general, most expect the Vihar to contribute to the improvement of the morale of the villagers by making them positive and pure-minded, helpful to each other, patient, not overly selfish, accommodative towards different opinions within the family and in the community, and accepting of a "simple life". They want the Samuha members to set an example and help them to lead such a life. They welcome gatherings, Buddha Pujas, preachings on Vihar Buddhism, and other public activities to enhance the participation of the villagers and achieve that objective. They appear to be proud to have a Vihar in their village.

On the voluntary social activities of the Samuha as an NGO, they appreciate its contribution in making the villagers aware of external matters, in germinating cooperation and a progressive attitude, in bringing positive changes to the village, in making the village known to others, and in raising the self-esteem of the villagers. They look to the Samuha members to lead the village in promoting wider participation, irrespective of caste, political affiliation, and economic status. They hope the Samuha people will actively help in solving the problems faced by the village, such as problems of garbage and public hygiene, social discipline, disputes between neighbours, etc.

Thus, it can be said that the villagers expect the Samuha to contribute not only to the religious aspect but also, and perhaps more, to the upliftment of the socio-economic conditions of the people and the village as a whole. They evaluate the Vihar very positively for its contribution in these aspects so far, and they have high expectations of its future activities. Most of them were aware of the Japanese aid for the Vihar and its usage in constructing the meditation house of the Vihar. Some also remember it along with the musical village procession organized to welcome the Japanese guests who came to the village to inaugurate the building.

SUPPORTERS OF VIHAR BUDDHISM

In this section, I will provide a description of some of the people who have been supporting Vihar Buddhism in order to convey how it is understood at the individual level and how Vihar Buddhism has spread within the village. It is based on observation and direct conversations I have had with the people described on various occasions, between 1991 and 1998. It is supplemented by personal discussions with the secretary of the Samuha in 2003 and 2004.

Executive Members of Nagadesh Bauddha Samuha

The chairman is the eldest of three brothers, who lived in a joint family during his young days. Farming was the main job of the family and they tilled 21 *ropanis* of land, most of it *guthi* land, in and around the village.

He collected farm products from around the village, added them to his own family's surplus, and sold them in Mahabauddha bazaar in Kathmandu and to the police in Singha Durbar from 1960, when he was in his teens. He would also roam around the Valley with other villagers to transact goods; not only to sell them, but also to exchange mustard for mustard oil, and earthen pots for paddy, wheat, potato, and chilli. The farm products collected in this way were processed and sold as flour, beaten rice, mustard oil, and chilli powder basically in Mahabauddha. He also collected black soil and manure from various places to enhance the productivity of his land. As he grew older, he also acquired the skill of masonry and became an excellent *dakahmi* in building houses and *chibhadyah*. The family also ran a sawmill in the village selling wooden construction materials: beams, pillars, plywood, and fuelwood for brick kilns, rice mills, and household use. About 10 *ropani*s of land was purchased with these income sources and on this land they constructed four houses for the family in the space of fifteen years. His family led a rather prosperous life in the village and held big feasts from time to time, when they would invite the whole village. The other villagers regarded his family as *jyupin bhipin manuta*, 'respectable people'. He himself was a voracious eater and drinker and was often heavily drunk. He would drink and dance the whole night under the mask of Bhailah Dyah (Bhairava) during Hindu rituals. Even today his physical size is about one and half times that of ordinary villagers.

With the enactment of Land Reform in the 1960s, he had to claim the ownership of the land his family had been tilling in accordance with the new law. He had to engage in hard court battles for more than ten years for this purpose. When his father died in 1985, the issue of inheritance surfaced and suddenly the brothers became engaged in a fierce internal family battle. He lost control of himself and started accusing his younger brothers of numerous faults. In spite of his relatively well-off condition, he could not achieve mental satisfaction in life thereafter. He started to devote more time to singing hymns in the Gyanmala Bhajan Khalah and visiting Vihars in the Kathmandu Valley for mental peace. He began to participate actively in various Vihar gatherings and Buddha Pujas. He learnt about the Buddha's teachings basically by listening. He received considerable personal satisfaction from the fact that he could contribute his voluntary labour to the construction of *chibhadyahs*. He got requests for this from near and far. By the end of 1997 he had helped to construct twenty-eight *chibhadyah*s in the Valley. His human relationships have widened with his volunteering, and with his participation in the Gyanmala Bhajan Khalah and in Vihar Buddhism. Slowly he was able to control his temper, becoming more patient and improving his character. He stopped drinking alcohol, gave up smoking and eating meat, and stopped performing *ban syayegu* (offering animal foodstuffs, e.g. eggs, fowl or animal sacrifices) during *mohani* *nakhah* (Dasain or Vijaya Dasami) in 1987. After controlling his diet and becoming a vegetarian his health improved. Eventually, he gave a large portion of the family property to his brothers and just kept three *ropanis* of vegetable land for himself.

On the day of Buddha Puja in 1985, the year his father died, his uncle, an active member of Thimi Pati Vihar and living separately from his sons, declared his wish at a family gathering to establish a Vihar in Nagadesh, and started to sponsor Buddha Pujas regularly. Soon like-minded people gathered and started to contribute whatever they could to realize the establishment of the Vihar. More and more people came to participate in Buddha Puja and there were more than fifty founding members when Nagadesh Bauddha Samuha was formed in 1987. At that time the current chairman was the founding secretary of the Samuha, his uncle being the founding chairman. In the same year, he acquired a carpet factory in the village with loans from a government bank. Initially the business did not go well but things started to improve once the Vihar was established. He firmly believed that Vihar Buddhism had a positive impact on his new business. He clearly remembered getting a *japamala* (rosary) from Bhikshu Buddhaghosh, which coincided with the turn of his business, and believed it was no coincidence. He left the management of the factory to his son and he himself participated full time in Vihar affairs. He not only donated a handsome amount of money but also played a leading role in raising funds to construct the Vihar building. Further, he was the *dakahmi nayo* (foreman) during the construction of the building and worked day and night until it was completed. Finally he became chairman of the Samuha in 1996 after the death of his uncle and oversees all the Vihar activities. He sponsored Buddha Pujas and *bhojans* and bore much of the cost of maintaining the Vihar. He would recite *paritran slokas*, meditate daily, keep the *panchashil*, and undertake *astashil* as frequently as possible. He consumed a full meal only once a day, in the daytime, and spent most of his time in the Vihar. He would mediate family and community disputes, advising people to be patient, subdue anger, and follow the Buddha's teachings. He took great satisfaction in being able to serve the people. He remained chairman of the Samuha until he passed away of cancer in March 2002.

The vice-chairman is in his forties and is the head of a family of six. He and his wife are both faithful members of the Samuha. He is a teacher in the local high school and also manages a corner shop, which is mostly looked after by his wife and other members of the family. He also owns a *ropani* of *khet* land and a *ropani* of *pakha* land, produces enough paddy and vegetable for self-consumption from these lands and sells the green vegetables regularly. He has a stable source of income and perceives no problems in his daily life. When a young boy he would go to sell grains in

Kathmandu and various settlements in the Valley, including Lubhu, and to fetch manure. He is also a founding member of the Samuha. Before 1987 he was an active member of Gyan Mala Bhajan Khalah in Swayambhu. He always believed in Buddhism and has been practising the teachings of Buddha. Currently he has unresolved issues of property inheritance with his brothers but he would like to tackle the issue with patience, disinterest, and calmness. After becoming a member of the Samuha his knowledge of Vihar Buddhism has deepened; he recently decreased his consumption of alcohol and he finds that he doesn't get angry as quickly as before. Although he is unable to become vegetarian due to various *guthi* obligations, including the *si* (death) *guthi,* he has followed the teaching of *ahimsa* and has stopped offering sacrifices at *mohani nakhah*. He wants to increase the benevolent acts undertaken by the people and contribute to a society in which people help each other. Thus he makes a regular monthly donation of Rs.300-400 to the Vihar. He says any *dharma* should contribute to *samaj kalyan*, the betterment of society, and he is not much interested in differentiating between Vajrayana and Theravada Buddhism or for that matter between Buddhism and Hinduism.

As a teacher he is also an active social mobilizer. He started a small reading room in the village by collecting books from various places, including foreign embassies, and he conducted several adult and female literacy classes when he was a college student. He was also a youth leader in campaigns for village cleaning, maintenance of public toilets, public health, family planning, and tree plantation. He also actively participates as a member of cultural troupes, learning and teaching cultural musical instruments, *bhajan*, and dances. He recently organized the teaching of Bhairava and Mahankal dances (traditional masked dances of the gods), which had been losing popularity ever since the boom of television. He also takes part in the Nepal Bhasha language movement, teaches Nepal Bhasha as an elective language in the high school, and encourages village children, including his own, to learn and speak it. Now he wants to mobilize young people through the various activities in the Vihar for the betterment of society. Thus, he is a Vihar Buddhist who also is a Newar nationalist working for the preservation and spread of its culture and the language.

The accountant, in his fifties, is the head of a family of eleven. All the members of the family are busy in their respective affairs; hence he is the only member in his house undertaking Vihar Buddhism and lives separately from the rest of the family. He runs a fertilizer outlet and a grain shop in the village and supplies vegetables and milk to bulk buyers, such as hotels and *gompas* in Kathmandu. He owns 10 *ropanis* of *khet* land, 3 *ropanis* of *pakha* land, and produces a surplus of food. He is also a rather well-to-do person in the village and a founding member of the Samuha.

He had keen interest in the Gyanmala Bhajan even when he was young and wanted to become a *bhante*. But his mother would not allow him to be one. He had been on pilgrimage to Lumbini and had visited Dhulikhel Vihar several times since 1979 and had sponsored Buddha Puja there twice on the advice of Dharmanand Bhante. He believes Buddha Puja can enlighten people. He has stopped drinking alcohol and eating meat. Recently his family members have begun to show an understanding of his way of life. He feels that after the democratization of the country in 1990 the village has become dynamic and the feeling of unity has grown in the village. He too wanted to do something for the village and therefore undertook this important responsibility. He contributes money regularly to maintain the Vihar's activities.

The director is in his seventies and is the head of a family of eight. He is the only person in the family who follows Vihar Buddhism. His family runs a grain shop and owns 8 *ropanis* of land. They have enough to eat and earn a good income from selling vegetables. The family is economically satisfied. He refers to himself as *jha wane dhunkala* (having crossed the zenith of life) and is leading a retired life. He is also a founding member of the Samuha and also takes part in Vihar activities in Patan and Kirtipur. He was invited to join this Samuha by a neighbour and found the environment good. He harmonizes well with the chairman and felt he could contribute something in spite of his old age. Hence he undertook this responsibility and hopes it will bring merit in his remaining life and stabilize the path to the next life. By daily worship and meditation, he strives to come to know the Buddha but feels it to be very difficult and thinks he may not be successful in this life. He finds tranquillity in undertaking Vihar activities. He has become totally vegetarian and avoids displays of emotions. He also contributes money regularly to maintain Vihar activities. He thinks it is important to undertake activities which would interest the younger generation so that they can also be given some responsibility and made them a part of the movement to spread Vihar Buddhism. He is critical of people who pretend to be pious in the Vihar but act differently in other activities of daily life.

The auditor is in his fifties and the head of a family of ten. He is also the only Samuha member in the family. But his wife is a frequent visitor and he is satisfied with this. At this moment he doesn't want to push his wife too far. He also doesn't feel any lack in his daily life. With 1 *ropani* of *khet* land and 1.5 *ropanis* of *pakha* land he can manage to fulfil the family's needs from the income earned through the sale of vegetables. He was invited to join the Samuha at its foundation. He joined in the hope of improving his health. He likes the calm environment of the Vihar and feels peaceful when he hears people exchanging the greeting, *bhagawan sharana*.

He wants to spread this greeting among ordinary people as well and he hopes they will like it. Earlier he was afraid of being among many people, but this fear has abated after regular visits to the Vihar. He finds he can relax now, he is no longer afraid, and can even speak in front of unknown people. After undertaking Vihar activities he was able to stop smoking and stop performing *ban syayegu*. He thinks his family is living a peaceful happy life due to the blessings of the Buddha and says he would always give first priority to the Vihar's activities. He also contributes money regularly to maintain Vihar activities.

Other Supporters

Gyani (a pseudonym, as are all the names below) is in her twenties, and is a typical Newar lady, with good self-composure, living with her parents in a family of seven. She participates in all the gatherings and *puja*s in the Vihar without fail. Her family manages 4 *ropani*s of vegetable land and has a daily income of about Rs.500 from selling vegetables. The family is content with the current situation. She is also a founding member of the Samuha. Her maternal uncle, a core member of the local Gyanmala Bhajan Khalah, influenced her to undertake Vihar Buddhism. She thinks it is a good way of life and is participating on her own initiative. Her family wholeheartedly supports her decision. She also considers it her duty to support the Vihar by undertaking all the 'ladies' work' in the Vihar. Previously she had observed *brata*, fasting, in the 'Hindu way' to gain religious merit,

> But it was very demanding and harmed my health and prevented me from doing household and farm work the following day. Hindu *brata puja* is also complicated and I didn't understand the meaning. It was just performing things as you are told, like a monkey. I stopped observing such *brata*s once I started visiting the Vihar. In the Vihar also while undertaking *panchashil* and *astashil* one needs to fast but that is only during the morning and is rather easy. As an *upasika* it is convenient to observe such religiously meritorious deeds in the Vihar while also undertaking other works. Since the *puja* is simple I can easily understand it and self-satisfaction is much higher in these Buddha Pujas.

When she first started to visit the Vihar, people in the community were not so nice about it. Whenever she overheard people talking about her and wondering why she had not got married even at her age, she would get very angry. Now she has overcome such feelings of anger. That is because she has learnt to be patient and to subdue anger through the teachings of the Buddha and she and the community have become used to each other, she explained. She has no school education but has become literate by joining literacy programmes in the village. She can read the *sloka* book written in

Nepali, slowly. This brings her peace. She says the teachings of the Buddha are beautiful and are essential for leading a good life. The most important thing for her now is Vihar Buddhism. Hence she doesn't mind undertaking any work for the Vihar. She thinks serving the Vihar enriches her. She is an egg-eating vegetarian and does not want to think of marriage at the moment as that may disturb her self-enrichment. She thinks that in order to realize harmony in the community, it is necessary to create chances for young people to get in touch with Vihar Buddhism and make them realize its beauty in a natural way. In order to do that, in her personal capacity, she often invites, but never presses, her friends to visit the Vihar to observe what goes on there.

Aji is in her seventies and lives alone. Soon after her marriage her husband died. One day, after returning from selling vegetables her husband had an unusually high fever that laid him low for four days. He never recovered. People say her husband had *jha wangu ka* (crossed the zenith of life). After his demise she lived with her in-laws for some time. In 1953 she inherited 2 *ropani*s of land from her in-laws. She says that ever since that time she has made her living by producing vegetables on this land and has lived all alone. She became a member of the Samuha on her own initiative when it was formed. But even before that she used to visit Thimi Pati Vihar and was a pious believer in Vihar Buddhism. She consoles herself by saying that it is her *karma* and the result of doings in her previous life that she can't have a family in this life. She has stopped *ban syayegu* in various rituals and observes traditional festivals very simply. She is living life according to the motto, 'lavishness is the enemy of life'. She has become a vegetarian after joining this Vihar and undertakes *astashil* every week. Thanks to this she has become very patient and her health has improved, she claims. Serving the Vihar by providing labour, participating in all gatherings, *puja*s, and meditations is what she can contribute to enhance Vihar Buddhism in the village and she is willing to spare her whole life for that, so she says.

Ram, in his sixties, is the head of a family of five. After the death of his wife he could not get along with his son and lost his place in the family. He spends most of his day in the Vihar. He became a member of the Samuha on his own initiative, but has been following Vihar Buddhism from even before when he used to visit the Vihar in Thimi. By visiting the Vihar regularly his understanding of Buddhism has deepened and he feels real calm during meditation. Even without special treatment the respiratory disease he sufferred from for eight years has been cured, he says. Before, he used to consume meat and alcohol during festivals, but now he has become a pure vegetarian and has stopped drinking alcohol as well. He also thinks that, in order to spread Vihar Buddhism, it is necessary to involve the younger generation. He owns a *ropani* each of *khet* and *pakha* land and his family makes a living by selling vegetables. He has to depend on the little money his son, who controls everything, is willing to give him.

Bajya is in his eighties and lives with his ailing wife, separate from his children's families. He has long been retired. He rents his land to his son and lives on the proceeds. He fears ageing but expects to benefit from the *punya* he has gained from joining the Samuha at its formation in 1987. He visits the Vihar daily. When he is at home he feels down and lonely, becomes lazy and starts to perceive everything negatively. But in the Vihar he can be free from anxiety, he can meditate, or he can listen to the teachings of the Buddha, thus receiving mental support which promotes positive thinking. He has donated 0.7 *ropani* of land, the *kosah* (bride gift or dowry) of his wife, to the Vihar. He cultivates it and supplies vegetables and grains to the Vihar for the meals that are held there. He is ready to do anything he can to spread Vihar Buddhism and participates in Buddha Puja without fail.

Asa Man is in his fifties and lives with his elder brother's family. One of his eyes doesn't function well. He joined the Vihar on his own initiative. He is a *jharphuke baidya* (a Tantric healer) and used to cure people's illnesses. He used to observe all traditional rituals without questioning their meaning, like other ordinary people. But he has stopped after starting to visit the Vihar regularly. He gets mental peace from listening to the Buddha's teachings and tries to lead a life according to the teachings. However, except for giving up smoking and drinking, he has not been very successful. He believes that the spread of Vihar Buddhism depends on the laity being able to practise the teachings of the Buddha in daily life. He continues to practise *jharphuke yayegu* to make a living.

Kancha is in his fifties and lives alone and has some speech problems. He joined the Vihar on the advice of a friend. He does all the menial work in the Vihar. He owns only 0.25 *ropani* of land and hence cannot make a living. He has been allowed to live in the Vihar. He may not be able to understand the religiosity of the Vihar and cannot follow the sermons, but he shows a very satisfactory expression and is very lively when he is serving the people in the Vihar. He never sits idle and is always doing something. He has stopped smoking and drinking and recently became an egg-eating vegetarian. He says that it is very important for everybody to have good relations with each other and to live in harmony.

In addition to the people described above, there are many women who come to the Vihar every day to carry out all sorts of petty work, such as helping to conduct Buddha Puja, cook and serve *bhojan*, and produce vegetables for the Vihar. They all claim that they have developed patience and are able to suppress anger after undertaking Vihar Buddhism. They say they have stopped gossiping about others and their daily life patterns have changed. They claim that they have decreased their consumption of meat and are more mentally stable than before and can face different aspects of life calmly.

An old lady, a mute from the village, who had been living as a beggar at various places in the Valley, returned to the village in 1995 and started to live in the Vihar. She may not be able to understand Vihar Buddhism but tries to help in the cleaning by copying what others do. People say they can feel her satisfaction from her facial expressions, when her contributions to Vihar activities are recognized by others. People in the Vihar have accepted her as well.

RECENT DEVELOPMENTS

This section summarizes developments between 1998 and 2004. Nagadesh Bauddha Lyayemha Puchah (Nagadesh Buddhist Young People's Group), the brother association of Nagadesh Bauddha Samuha, was formed in July 1999. The Lyayemha Puchah, being the youth organization of the Samuha, has supported all the latter's activities and played an important role in spreading Vihar Buddhism among the younger generation of the village. The Samuha uses the youth power of the Lyayemha Puchah to make the presence of Vihar Buddhism visible whenever possible. For example, it participated in the peace protest procession against the Hindu-Bauddha Conference held in Lumbini in November 1999, along with ten members of the Lyayemha Puchah. The official stand of this conference – protested against by many Buddhist activists – was that "Buddhism is a branch of Hinduism ..." The Lyayemha Puchah and the Samuha members also participated jointly in organizing 'Mikhadan Mahadan' (the gift of an eye is a great gift) conference (March 2001); in the inauguration by Prime Minister Girija Prasad Koirala of the Nipponzan Myohoji Stupa in Lumbini (November 2001); in the commemoration of Disarmament Day (October 2002), in felicitating Bhikshu Gyanpurnik at the Vishwa Shanti Vihar, Manbhawan when he received a degree in Buddhism from Sri Lanka, in the 4th National Gyanmala Conference in Dharan (January 2003), and in the march for world peace organized by Swayambhu Gyan Mala Bhajan Khalah (March 2003). The Samuha also participates regularly in various national and regional Gyanmala Bhajan functions and organizes hymn recitations along with the members of the Nagadesh Gyanmala Bhajan Khalah. Many of the Gyanmala Bhajan Khalah members are also Samuha members. Nagadesh Bauddha Samuha became the Madhyapur Thimi branch of the Dharmodaya Sabha in 1999 and its first general assembly meeting was held in 2001. Some thirty-one Samuha members have taken life membership of the Dharmodaya Sabha. Nine members of the Samuha (including one who was a Jugi by caste, i.e. who would have been considered 'untouchable' in the past), and some members of the Lyayemha Puchah, participated in a temporary Pravrajya (going forth) and Upasampada (ordination) organized by Dharmakirti Adhyayan Gosthi in Lumbini in December 2000. They all became *bhantes* (Buddhist monks) for a week. The Upajjayacharya (presiding learned monk) of this function was Bhadant U Nanissar Sayadaw of Sitagu International Buddhist Academy, Myanmar.

In addition, the Samuha also organizes short and long Buddha Pujas several times a year in the village. Not only has the frequency of such *pujas* increased but the timing of holding the *pujas* has also become thought-provoking for the villagers. For example, in April 2001, it commemorated Rahul Sankrityayan on the very day of Biska Jatra, the most important traditional Hindu festival that goes together with the local identity in the region for many people. It also commemorated the Buddhist King Ashok on the day of *mohani nakhah*, the biggest national Hindu festival, in October 2001, and Disarmament Day in October 2002. According to the secretary of the Samuha, they were just the right days to commemorate such events to make the villagers more aware of the Buddha, the Buddha's teachings, including *ahimsa*, piousness, detachment, and the righteous way of living.

The Samuha felicitated the government for declaring Shankhadhar Sakhwa, who founded the Nepal Sambat in 879, a national hero. It also commemorated the understanding made between Satya Narayan Goenka and Jayendra Saraswati of Kanchikamkoti Pith in Maha Bodhi Society, Sarnath, in November 1999 not to regard Buddhism as a branch of Hinduism and to practise each faith with dignity and with due respect for the other as an independent faith. It campaigned for local people to write 'Bauddha' and 'Newar' in *dharma* and *jati* columns of the 2001 national census survey and sent a letter to the government requesting it to include Pali as an elective language in the courses for students of classes nine and ten. It observed three minutes' silence to protest the Taliban's destruction of the Bamiyan Buddha statues in Afghanistan and sent condolences to the royal family of Nepal after the massacre of June 2001. It accepted a donation from Mrs Krishna Maya Nakarmi, a Kau widow and founder of the Sramanera Shilratna Fund, and honoured her wish that the fund be used to spread Vihar Buddhism.

Eye camps are organized regularly by the Samuha to treat patients. Furthermore, an eye donation campaign to the Nepal Eye Bank was also initiated in the villages and the eyes of the Samuha member who died in July 1999 were donated to two persons from Trisuli and Dhading. It was the first eye donation and so far there have been three successful donations. Earlier, people would think that one would be reborn without eyes if they mistreated their eyes. But with the influence of Vihar Buddhism they have started to realize that *mikhadan* (eye donation) is good as it helps others to see the beautiful world even after one's own death (see also Leve 2002). "Anyway the inner sight is what is most needed for living a pious life and to gain Buddhist wisdom (*gyan/prajna*)", says a donor. There are already 172 men and women, old and young, from both monastic and lay communities, regardless of caste, willing to donate their eyes. Their donation will is filed in a book along with their full profiles and photos and kept safely in the Vihar, as of January 2004. In March 2001, a 'Mikhadan Mahadan' meeting was organized jointly by the Samuha and the Lyayemha Puchah in the Vihar to make people aware of eye donation. On that occasion certificates were given to the eye donors by the Thai ambassador and Bhikshu Ashwaghosh Mahasthavir.

In 1999, an offering of alms to *sramanera*s was held in Nagadesh Buddha Vihar and Bhikshu Varasambodhi stayed for *varsavas* in the Vihar from the month of August that year. Later, in October 1999, two founding members of the Samuha sponsored the offering of the robes ceremony for Varsambodhi at the conclusion of the *varsabas*. Two years later, in July 2000 Bhikshuni Keshavati started *varsavas* in the Vihar. During her *varsavas*, Keshavati Guruma encouraged the village children to study Buddhism and gave *pariyatti* lessons to them. A big Buddha Puja was organized at the end of her *varsabas*. She also inaugurated a small Buddha *stupa* constructed on the roof of the Vihar. In October 2000, twenty-eight children sat for their first year *pariyatti* exams held in Dharmakirti Bihar, under the encouragement of the *guruma*. The results of the exams came out in January 2001, and twenty-six children passed, thirteen in the first division, six in the second division, and seven in the third division. This was a pleasant surprise for the Samuha, and the news travelled rapidly around the village. Soon it was a matter of pride for many villagers. In the *pariyatti* exams of 2003, an *upasika* student of the Vihar topped the all-Nepal Board in the third year lessons, a second pleasant surprise and a matter of great pride for the Samuha. More and more children of Samuha members are taking *pariyatti* exams and are becoming the pool for future *sramanera/anagarika* and perhaps *bhante/guruma* thereafter.

The Sramanera Pravrajya (monastic ordination) of two sons of Lyayemha Puchah members and *upasaka*s and *upasika*s of the Nagadesh Bauddha Vihar was conducted by Bhikshu Ashwaghosh Mahasthavir in Sangharam Vihar, Dhalko, in July 2001. They took the names Nanda Kumar and Rahul Kumar. Similarly, Anagarika Pravrajya (nuns' ordination) of two daughters of the Lyayemha Puchah members and *upasaka*s and *upasika*s of the Vihar was conducted by Dhammawati Guruma in Dharmakirti Vihar, Naghal, in August 2001. They took the names Rupawati and Kshantiwati. All four of them were sent to Sri Lanka for further studies under the guidance of Bhikshu Kolit and Bhikshu Saddhatissa. The *sramaneras* went to Saraswati Poribena and the Anagarikas to the Sanghamitta Education Centre in Horana. In fact Keshavati Guruma is also in Sri Lanka for higher studies at Samanta Lanka Dasashilmatha, Kotare. So the parents of the children feel reassured. Of course, they can also contact them by phone if necessary and they exchange letters regularly. Now the parents of these young monks and nuns want them to study as much as they can, although they were very hesitant at first at the idea of the children leaving home, especially the girls. The Samuha is hopeful that these children – and the core members think at least one of them, if not all – will continue the monastic life after returning from their studies and will become the resident monastics – *bhantes* reared by the Samuha from their own community – of the Vihar.

In fact, Rupawati and Kshantiwati are cousins, daughters of two brothers. Rupawati's father is an *upasaka* and she studied *pariyatti* lessons with Keshavati Guruma when she was just eleven. Keshavati Guruma encouraged her to continue further studies to deepen her understanding of Buddhism. Consequently, Rupawati requested her parents to let her renounce and started to visit the Vihar regularly. She made a point of resisting her parents by telling them that if she got married she would in any case have to leave them. A family meeting, including grandparents as well as maternal and paternal uncles, was called, and after long hours of serious discussion they decided in her favour. At the time it was a hard decision for the family, especially the parents, but everybody is cooperative now. All the family members want her to be successful in her mission. She will be learning Buddhism and general education with other children until she finishes her college education. She will come back once to visit her parents between finishing school and entering college. Though it would be unusual, she can decide to change her mind and not return to Sri Lanka for college. But if she decides to stick to her original plan, she will return to Sri Lanka to continue her studies. She will finally return to Nepal after completing her college-level studies. Thereafter she will have to decide whether to renounce the family for ever or to come back home. There are about fifty *sramaneras* and twenty-five *anagarikas* studying abroad currently. The organizers expect one or two out of every lot of five to ten students that go abroad for studies to become monks.

The current Samuha secretary has published four books on Buddhism recently. *Gautam Buddhaka Samakalin Bhikshuharu*: Bhag Ek (Monks of Gautam Buddha's Time, Part One, Nepali) in June 2001; *Buddhakalin Samajaya Paristhiti wa Thi Thi Halanjwalan* (Social and Material Conditions in the Buddha's Time, Nepal Bhasha) in September 2001; *Nhaykuti Bhagawan: Ek Parichaya* (The Buddha of Nhaykuti: A Study, Nepali) September 2001; and *Triratna Bandana: Paritran ra Bauddha Sanskar Paddhati* (Praising the Three Jewels: the Paritran Rite and Buddhist Life-

Cycle Rituals, Nepali) in July 2002. He has done much to publicize Vihar Buddhism through the written word. His writings have impressed prominent Buddhists such as the late Gyanjyoti and his wife Lakshmi Prabha, Lok Darshan Bajracharya, Bhikshu Kumar Kashyap Mahasthavir, and he has received sponsorship from them to publish his books. He has other manuscripts ready for publication, for instance, Buddhaka Samakalin Bhikshuharu Bhag Dui (Monks of Gautam Buddha's Time, Part Two, Nepali). His earlier short writings also include *Buddha Sharir Hoina Bichar Ho* (Buddha is not a Material Body, He is an Ideology, Nepali) 1989; *Buddha Ek Kushal Chikitsak* (The Buddha as a Skilful Healer, Nepali) 1991; and *Bauddha Jhanda: Ek Garimamayi Pratik* (The Buddhist Flag: A Glorious Symbol, Nepali) 1995.

The third general assembly meeting of the Samuha was held in May 2003 and the chief guest was Bhikshu Kumar Kashyap. The financial and activity reports of the past four years were presented. Twenty-three Samuha members had passed away during this period. They included the past chairman of the Samuha and the wife of the new chairman. During this period, Sramanera Buddhisagar of Chaturbrahma Vihar, Matatirtha, had also passed away. He was the first *sramanera* from the Thimi-Narmi people and one of the pathfinders for the Samuha. His death was observed in the Vihar with Buddha Puja and with a minute's silence.

The life patterns of the laity continue to change. The most visible changes among the laity can be said to be the stopping of *ban syayegu*, a simpler observation of traditional rituals, and the widespread abstention from drinking alcohol and eating meat. Many are performing Buddha Puja on their birthdays. Some are changing the way they observe rites of passage. About ten Samsmarans, or Theravada-style memorial services, were performed during the period 2000-3 instead of *shraddha* carried out under the instruction of a Vajracharya as an annual memorial service for near and far ancestors. During the funeral procession of the Samuha members, all the members, including women, participate while reciting Pali *sutra*. The core members are planning to replace the traditional funeral ceremony itself and put an end to their traditional death *guthi* in the near future. Due to the thought-provoking activities undertaken by the Vihar, people are also changing their earlier cosmological concepts, as in the case of eye donation, the worship of deities, and human relations. Slowly, more and more numbers of the same family are joining the Samuha. However, due also to their age many members pass away every year, which to some extent has reduced the membership. Thus, in spite of gaining publicity, there are only 235 members[14] (representatives of the households) regis-

[14]This is an increase of 18 per cent in about seven years. As for the reference of the total Buddhist population in the region, *National Population Census 2001, Nepal* shows the population of Madhyapur Thimi Nagarapalika, made up of five VDCs (Siddhi Ganesh VDC

tered in the Samuha as of the end of 2003. They have also not been able to get the participation of the Chetri and Tamang communities, although they have influenced the other castes of the Newar community, including the Sheshyah, Nau, Kau, Nay, and Jugi (see also Hartman 1993), who do visit the Vihar and often actively participate in Buddha Puja and other Vihar activities.

CONCLUSION

In the 1980s and 1990s, when rapid socio-economic transformations were taking place in Nepal, particularly in the Kathmandu Valley, many people became dissatisfied with the situation and were unwilling to accept the prevailing traditional systems. Some of them found Vihar Buddhism helpful in solving their problems. However, this may not be the only reason for involvement on the part of the laity. And this paper has shown that many village people have found peace and ways for self-realization by resorting to Vihar Buddhism. In the concluding part, I will consider reasons for the success of Vihar Buddhism in Nara (Nakadesh) and its relation to cultural activism.

In the Thimi-Nara region, Vihar Buddhism started to take root among the laity from the 1980s. Before that, although some individuals participated actively in Vihar Buddhism elsewhere in the Valley, the mass remained basically Hindu in this region (Thimi-Nara-Bode) where Biska Jatra of seven Hindu deities is the centre of the local microcosm. Participation in all the Hindu meritorious deeds (feasts, rites of passage, sacrifices and offerings, etc.) and supporting traditional social values and norms were essential to be identified as *jyupin bhin pin manuta* (respectable people) at that time. Correct Hindu observances were also regarded as the way to secure one's passage to, and a proper place in, the next world.

The accidental excavation of an ancient *chaitya* provided a much-needed alternative for people who were feeling insecure in the rapidly polarizing society. Most of them were aged and have-nots, and many were female; all were, to some extent, the victims of the ongoing paradigm change in society. They came in large numbers to the Vihar to listen to talks by the *bhantes*, to take the precepts of Buddhism, to overcome familial troubles and loneliness, to heal wounds, to gain the will to guard themselves from extreme consumerism and lavish lifestyles, to control their

---

being the smallest and Lokanthali VDC dominated by non-Newars being the largest) to be 47,751, of which, only 11 per cent is Buddhist. It may be significant here to note that Vihar Buddhism has grown not just in numbers but has spread beyond the upper-caste Newar communities, including the Jyapu community even in this Vihar. Of the few Gubhaju (Vajracharya) families in the locality some have also started to participate in Vihar activities.

emotions, to pass their leisure time, and to obtain peace of mind by following a righteous life. Within the region the core following was (and is) larger in number and more regular in Nara, a relatively compact Jyapu-majority settlement where Nagadesh Bauddha Samuha was formed before the foundation of the Vihar and members of the Samuha gathered in the living houses of the members in turn to pray, sing hymns, discuss Buddhism, and listen to the precepts even without a *bhante*. Although most of the then vibrant members of the Samuha were older people, there were also some younger, educated members who were actively taking part in the various social activities in the village, including teaching in the schools, and organizing *shramadan*, adult and female education programmes, health camps, political campaigns, etc. With the active participation of these younger members the Samuha was able to organize Buddha Puja more regularly and could also bring different monks from other Vihars to give instruction. The Samuha became the sponsor and the lay organization of the Vihar. The younger Samuha members helped villagers, including non-members, to cope with the bureaucratic demands of modernization and social transformation.

The donation from a Lions Club based in Hiroshima, which enabled the construction of the meditation house of the Vihar, was very timely. The meditation house provided a definite physical place for Vihar activities. In addition it strengthened bond of solidarity among the Samuha members and encouraged hesitating villagers to become members, making all of them proud of themselves and enhancing their spirit of voluntary cooperation. With this momentum, they also organized several eye camps to treat the patients with eye diseases from near and far, as well as literacy classes for adults, women, and children. The Samuha has also been active as a pressure group along with other similar groups working towards common goals of issues of language (recognition of all languages of the nation, including Nepal Bhasha), religion (freedom of belief and equal treatment for all the religions), and social justice.

Although there is no resident monk in the Vihar yet, the members have been able to invite both renowned and young monks and nuns for *varsabas* in the Vihar, consequently raising the dignity of the Samuha members and at the same time raising the ascetic status of the Vihar among the monastic circle. With the help of these *bhante/guruma,* they have held *pariyatti* classes for children some of whom have set remarkable records, a source of great pride for the Samuha and the village as well. Some of these children, sons and daughters of the Samuha members, have been ordained as *sramanera* and *anagarika* and have gone to Sri Lanka for higher studies. Thus the Samuha, which was sponsor and laity so far, is in the process of becoming monastic by producing *bhante/guruma* from among its own community. In the meantime the Samuha has also been able to involve the

Lyayemha Puchah, the youth organization of the village, in the activities of the Vihar. Together they have participated in various religious and social activities beyond the village, thus making the Samuha more dynamic and compensating for the demise of nearly seventy older members between its formation and 2003.

It may not be easy to single out a reason for the success of Vihar Buddhism and its smooth spread among the people in the region, perhaps different from other rural regions within the Valley. Economic diversification creating both opportunity and angst, nuclearization of the family with frequent break-ups, diminishing social relations, increasing personalization of human relations, changes in food habits, and changes in the political system, all these trends have pushed people to look for an alternative to gain mental peace and self-realization. Vihar Buddhism filled that need and it was made available to the villagers by the Samuha, formed by older members with conventional wisdom, supported by altruistic and capable educated younger members. One of these younger members, currently the secretary of the Samuha, has not only been serving the society, village, and individuals from the Panchayat days when he was just in his twenties, but also has a deep scholarly knowledge of Buddhism and has written many books on this subject in Nepali and Nepal Bhasha. His writings have been widely recognized by monks and wealthier sponsors in the Valley and he has obtained funds to publish new books. This is perhaps a unique feature of this village not easily found elsewhere.

This is not to deny the importance of a vibrant laity, the Nagadesh Bauddha Samuha, whose members, in spite of being aged, were from relatively diverse economic backgrounds and education levels, but mostly from the agricultural profession. They were active in Vihar Buddhism even in earlier decades, all expecting a change in the prevailing socio-economic system, institutions, and network. They expected to get mental peace, which would lead to self-realization, and they readily contributed economically, physically, and mentally to develop Vihar Buddhism. They were supported by non-member villagers, perhaps the future pool of the laity, whose socio-economic state was not much different from the Samuha members, who didn't perceive the problems of the society differently from the members of the Samuha, and who also had an internal wish for the success of the Vihar and felt that the presence of the Vihar in the village raised their dignity. The non-members admire the transparency of the management and want to be a part of its development by contributing in affordable ways when necessary.

The Samuha has been organizing important Vihar activities on traditional festival days traditionally and nationally regarded as very auspicious, such as Biska Jatra and Mohani. Needless to say the Samuha members prefer to join Vihar activities on such occasions, rather than the more traditional ones. Now the penetration of Vihar Buddhism has brought such deep cultural and social changes in the village that the people who earlier believed that they would be reborn without eyes if they mistreated their eyes now readily donate their eyes for the benefit of those who cannot see. Some even say that the *gyan chakshu* (eye of wisdom) is more important than *charma chakshu* (eye of leather [body]) to lead a pious life and to gain Buddhist wisdom (*gyan/prajna*). The life patterns and values of the laity have thus been changing. The most visible changes among the laity can be said to be the stopping of *ban syayegu*, a simpler observation of traditional rituals, and the widespread abstention from alcohol and meat. Many are performing Buddha Puja on their birthdays. Some are changing the way they observe rites of passage. Recently Theravadin-style Samsmarans have been introduced for annual memorial services instead of the Vajrayanist *shraddha*, and *sutra*s are recited during funeral processions. Generally speaking, such laities can be found even in rural settlements where Vihar Buddhism has not taken such deep root as in this village. The ground is already fertile and once they get the guidance of a pious leader, who has the backing of the elders, there is every chance that Vihar Buddhism will take firm root in those settlements as well. Recent developments such as Vihar construction, organization of Buddha Puja, Gyanmala Bhajan Khalah (hymn-singing groups) in the villages of Lubhu, Thashi, Sunagu, Kyapuh (Kirtipur), etc., are worth noticing in this regard.

It will be interesting to see what will happen in the next and following decades. The key question is how this religious reformism will accommodate itself to Newar cultural nationalist activism with its core components of language and culture. The main issues on which the latter movement focuses are the non-observation of elaborate festivals and rites of passage; the nuclearization of the joint family and decay of inter- and supra-familial relations; and the loss of the Newar language (which, though not yet an issue in this village, is a growing problem in the cities and in the diaspora Newar society).

Newar cultural nationalists take pride in the highly sophisticated multi-layered aspects of their culture, and treasure their cosmic values, highly sanskritized at macro- and mesocosms, and also localized at microcosms, regardless of being Hindu or Buddhist. They take part in elaborate observations of festivals and rites of passage, almost always accompanied by big feasts. They also believe in observing and reviving almost all known cultural practices in harmony with the nature. Regarding all such practices as cultural heritage, they are always willing to disseminate them among the Newar diaspora society as well. The recent development of Newar festivals being observed in Sikkim, New York, London, and elsewhere, can be regarded as an example. In accepting and revitalizing these cultural practices, they also accept the embedded caste and gender roles and the inherent caste and gender discrimination therein, although they are generally silent about this issue and/or at least superficially opt for egalitarian recognition of caste and gender.

Some of the Vihar Buddhists may team up with such activists on socio-cultural issues, i.e. structure of society, institutionalization, family types, familial relations, etc., But they may differ vastly in the personal aspects of the culture: worshipping, observation of festivals, rites of passage, food habits, etc. The Vihar Buddhists, as seen in this case study, clearly opt for a simpler observation of festivals and rites of passage, including putting *ahimsa* (non-violence) into action by discontinuing animal sacrifice and cutting down or cutting out feasting and the consumption of alcohol. Thus they lead a simpler life with fewer wants, less envy, less anger, less angst; in short, their life is calmer, more pious, and more tranquil. Needless to say these aspects are not specific to Vihar Buddhists, but their attitude of following sincerely the precepts of Buddhism leads them to a comparatively sober, pious, and hardworking life. Vihar Buddhists are also regarded as more egalitarian as regards age, gender, and caste/ethnicity.

The fact that rural Jyapunis participate more actively in decision-making and undertake more work than their Newar sisters may have to be understood as a caste-specific case and needs further study (see Pradhan 1981 for the details of Newar women's activities and participation in work). In addition to being the followers of the philosophy of Vihar Buddhism, the very people who become Vihar Buddhists are potential activists, either being opposed to current society or feeling insecure in it, and at the same time wanting to bring better changes in the society, as mentioned in the text. As regards other aspects of Newar national activism, they do not differ much, including on the language issue. However, Vihar Buddhists also demand the recognition of Pali, rather than Sanskrit, as a language to be taught in school in addition to promoting the Newar language vis-à-vis other ethnic languages.

Thus, Vihar Buddhists may even play a leading role in Newar national activism, including cultural issues, by means of the work they do towards building an increasingly egalitarian and active society.

REFERENCES

Acharya, M. 1979. 'Surplus Labour in Nepalese Agriculture'. *The Journal of Development and Administrative Studies* 1 (2): 222-43.

Bajracharya, B.R. 1986. *Buddhism of Nepal.* Kathmandu: Ananda Kuti Vihar Trust.

CBS (Central Bureau of Statistics). 1993a. *National Sample Census of Agriculture 1991/2: Bhaktapur.* Kathmandu: HMG (His Majesty's Government of Nepal), NPC (National Planning Commission) Secretariat.

——. 1993b. *National Sample Census of Agriculture1991/2: Nepal.* Kathmandu: HMG, NPC Secretariat.

——. 2002. *Population of Nepal, Village Development Committees/Municipalities: Caste/Ethnicity, Mother Tongue & Religion.* Kathmandu: HMG, NPC Secretariat.

——. 2004a. *National Sample Census of Agriculture, Nepal 2001/2: District Summary.* Kathmandu: HMG, NPC Secretariat.

——. 2004b. *National Sample Census of Agriculture, Nepal 2001/2: Nepal.* Kathmandu: HMG, NPC Secretariat.

Gellner, D.N. 1992. *Monk, Householder, and Tantrik Priest.* Cambridge: Cambridge University Press.

Gellner, D.N. and D. Quigley (eds.). 1995. *Contested Hierarchies: A Collaborative Ethnography of Caste among the Newars of the Kathmandu Valley, Nepal.* Oxford: Clarendon Press.

Gombrich, R. and G. Obeyesekere. 1988. *Buddhism Transformed: Religious Changes in Sri Lanka.* Delhi: Motilal Banarsidass.

Gorkhapatra Sansthan. 2005. 'Nepalka Gumbaharu (Gumbas of Nepal)'. *Gorkhapatra*, August 13, 2005, Saturday Supplement. Kathmandu (in Nepali).

Gutschow, N. and B. Kölver. 1975. *Ordered Space: Concepts and Functions in a Town of Nepal.* Wiesbaden: Franz Steiner.

Hartman, J.-U. 1993. 'Some Remarks on Caste in the Theravada Sangha of Nepal', in G. Toffin (ed.), *Nepal: Past and Present.* Delhi: Sterling Publishers.

Höfer, A. 2004. *The Caste Hierarchy and the State in Nepal.* Lalitpur: Himal Books.

Kölver, B. (ed.). 1992. *Aspects of Nepalese Traditions.* Stuttgart: Franz Steiner Verlag.

Kondanya, V. 2003. 'Theravada Bhiksu, Sramanera, Anagarika tatha Viharharu (2060)'. *Ananda Bhoomi* 31 (1). Kathmandu: Buddha Vihar, Bhrikutimandap (in Nepali).

Lachhi, G. 2046 V.S. (1989). 'Thimiya Laekuchen wa Nagadesh (Thimi Palace and Nagadesh)'. *Nagadesh Gaun Panchayat: Ek Parichaya (Nagadesh Village Panchayat: An Introduction)*, pp. 50-2. Bhaktapur: Nagadesh Village Panchayat (in Nepal Bhasha).

Lacoul, B.P. 1985. *Sthaviravada.* Kathmandu (in Nepal Bhasa).

Leve, L.G. 2002. 'Subjects, Selves, and the Politics of Personhood in Theravada Buddhism in Nepal'. *Journal of Asian Studies* 61 (3): 833-60.

LeVine, S. and D.N. Gellner. 2005. *Rebuilding Buddhism: Theravada Revivalism in Nepal.* Cambridge MA: Harvard University Press.

Levy, R.I. 1990. *Mesocosm: Hinduism and the Organization of Traditional Newar City in Nepal.* California: University of California Press.

Maharjan, K.L. 1994. 'Effects of Modernization on Periurban Families in Kathmandu Valley', in M. Allen (ed.), *Anthropology of Nepal: Peoples, Problems and Processes,* pp. 193-208. Kathmandu: Mandala Book Point.

——. 1998. 'A Study on Farming of Kathmandu Valley in Nepal'. *Journal of International Affairs and Cooperation* 4 (1): 127-51.

——. 2005. 'Kathmandu Toshi Kinko Sonrakuno no Henka to "Vihara Bukkyo" no Tenkai (Dynamism in Periurban Village of Kathmandu and Spread of Vihar Buddhism)', in H. Ishii (ed.), *Ryudo Suru Nepal (Social Dynamism in Contemporary Nepal)*, pp. 203-28. Tokyo: The University of Tokyo Press (in Japanese).

Malla, K.P. et al. (eds.). 2000. *A Dictionary of Classical Newari*. Kathmandu: Nepal Bhasha Dictionary Committee, Chwasa Pasa.

Müller, U. 1981. *Thimi: Social and Economic Studies in a Newar Settlement in the Kathmandu Valley*. Giessen: Selbstverlag des Geographischen Instituts der Justus Liebig-Universität Giessen.

Nagadesh Bauddha Samuha. 2045 V.S. (1988). *Nagadesh Bauddha Samuhako Bidhan 2051*. Bhaktapur: Nagadesh (in Nepali).

Nepali, G.S. 1988 (1965). *The Newars*. Kathmandu: Himalayan Book Sellers.

Pradhan, B. 1981. *Newar Women of Bulu*. Kathmandu: CEDA.

Pragya Rashmi, Bhikshu. (ed.). 1982. *Buddha Dharmaya Ruprekha (An Outline of Buddhism)*. Kathmandu: Gana Mahavihara (in Nepal Bhasha).

Prajapati, K.K. et al. (eds.). 2054 V.S. (1997). *Nagadesh: Ek Parichay (Nagadesh: An Introduction)*. Bhaktapur: Nagadesh Gaun Bikas Samiti (in Nepali).

Quigley, D. 1985. 'The Guthi Organizations of Dhulikhel Shresthas'. *Kailash* 12 (1/2): 5-62.

Ram, R. 1977. *A History of Buddhism in Nepal A.D. 704-1396*. Patna: Janabharati Prakashan.

Regmi, M.C. 1978a. *Land Tenure and Taxation in Nepal*. Kathmandu: Ratna Pustak Bhandar.

Regmi, M.C. 1978b. *Thatched Huts and Stucco Palaces*. Delhi: Vikas Publishing House.

Rosser, C. 1966. 'Social Mobility in the Newar Caste System', in C. von Fürer-Haimendorf (ed.), *Caste and Kin in Nepal, India and Ceylon*. Bombay: Asia Publishing House.

Sharma, P. 1993. 'A Note on Recent Trends in Nepal's Urbanization'. *Nepalese Economic Journal* 1 (1): 33-42.

Shrestha, M.L. 1994. 'Prachin Nepalma Buddha Dharmako Sthiti (The State of Buddhism in Ancient Nepal)'. *The Dharma-Pradipa*, 3 (3): 4-6 (in Nepali).

Singh, H.L. 1990. *Buddhism in Nepal*. Kathmandu: Satish Singh.

Sushobhan, Bhikshu. 1985. *Buddhism at a Glance*. Kathmandu: Ananda Kuti Vihar.

Vajracharya, R.K. and B.R. Vajracharya. 1983. *Nepah Dehya Biharya Tahcha (Key to Viharas in Nepal)*. Kathmandu: Mantrasiddhi Mahavihara (in Nepal Bhasha).

Vergati, A. 1995. *Gods, Men and Territory: Society and Culture in Kathmandu Valley*. Delhi: Manohar.

8

Public Space, Voluntary Associations, and Hindu Nationalism: Changing Urban Festivals in Udaipur, Rajasthan

MINORU MIO

INTRODUCTION

In Udaipur, the central city of Mewar region in Rajasthan, three new urban festivals, namely, Matka For, Ganesh Utsav, and the Garba Dance (a dance associated with the festival of Navaratra and originating in Gujarat), began to be observed about fifteen years ago.[1] And they are quickly expanding both in the number of sites where they are held and in the number of people who gather for the festivals.

As north Indian social history reveals (Freitag 1989), from the nineteenth century onwards religious festivals have served as important occasions to create public arenas in which communities come to be defined symbolically and to form an autonomous sphere against the state. Udaipur has not lacked for such public festivals. For example, the burning of a giant statue of Ravana is staged on a large scale at the central cricket ground of Udaipur city under the auspices of the Sanatan Dharma Society with the cooperation of the municipal committee, with the Maharana of Mewar and other establishment figures of Udaipur city being invited to the event. It is an occasion for the display of social harmony and order under the hegemony of the upper class in the local city. Another festival, Ram Rewari,

---

[1]The data here is based on my field research carried out in 2000 (July to September), 2001 (July to September), and 2003 (September to October). The field research was supported by a grant-in-aid for scientific research from the Japan Society for the Promotion of Science (JSPS). I would like to express my gratitude to all my informants in and around Udaipur city.

which is held on the eleventh of the bright half of the month of Bhadrapad, has also been celebrated on a big scale in Udaipur for a long time. As this festival is planned so that each *jati* or caste performs a parade of its own palanquin (*palki*) through the streets after performing *puja* at their respective Chattrubhujaji temple, it serves as the occasion for the public display of the solidarity of each *jati* community.

The three new festivals in Udaipur are also designed as public performances staged in urban spaces. But their organizers exemplify a clear contrast with the conventional public festivals because the new festivals are organized by voluntary associations of young, urban middle-class males rather than by members of the city elite or by caste elders. Moreover, these festivals are deeply correlated with Indian politico-economic trends in the 1990s and 2000s in three ways:

1. The development of electronic mass media, especially TV, has influenced the creation and the spread of the festivals;
2. The organizers try to cover the costs of the festival by introducing sponsorship and advertisements from local industry;
3. The organizers and participants are very aware of the Hindu religious and political discourses, and when they explain their intentions and activities, they often mention 'the revival of tradition' or 'contributing to the creation and reinforcement of the Hindu nation'. Several organizing voluntary associations are even deeply connected with Hindu nationalist parties and organizations. These festivals can be seen as public occasions through which the developing urban middle class commits itself to Hindu nationalism.

These festivals' names and their features evoke western Indian public festivals. Indeed all of the new festivals in Udaipur originate from Maharashtra or Gujarat. In western India, public festivals organized by local *mandals* (committees) have had a close connection to local politics and the production of a sense of neighbourhood from the 1890s onwards (Hansen 2001: 53). Ganpati Utsav (the Marathi name for Ganesh Utsav) became popular in Maharashtra as it was tied in with the anti-Brahman movement and with emphasis on the great Marathi indigenous tradition. According to Kaur, who analyzed the iconography of Ganpati Utsav *mandap* tableaux historically and ethnographically, for a long period following 1947 they were non-political, but the displays have come to take on a more directly political form in their themes and messages since the 1980s.[2] This

[2]Kaur (2003). *Mandap* tableaux are displays, paintings, and figures specially made for the festival. Ganpati Utsav in Maharashtra is famous for its spectacular mandap tableaux, which often comment on contemporary society or politics.

tendency is closely connected to the rise of the Shiv Sena in Maharashtrian politics. According to Hansen, the Shiv Sena has come to dominate local mandals from the 1980s. It has transformed the style of the festival into a more aggressive celebration of Maharashtrian community. The Shiv Sena even incorporated the Navaratra festival, originating in Gujarat in the 1980s, in an effort to appeal to the wider Hindu community.

There are certainly some similarities between the new urban festivals of Udaipur and the festivals of western India, both in their contents and in the ways in which the organizations that hold the festivals are related to Hindu political parties. At the same time, the new festivals of Udaipur seem to reflect the particular contemporary sociocultural conditions of a specific urban centre and the festival organizers try to secure their own sphere of public activities.

The following discussion is based on field research conducted from 2000 to 2003. The time period for the field research was rather short and data collection is still at an early stage. Thus I consider the present paper as an interim report on the social, cultural, and political implications of the development of new local festivals in an urban environment in the 1990s and 2000s.

THE CREATION OF URBAN FESTIVALS IN UDAIPUR

Overview

Udaipur was constructed by Maharana Udai Singh in the middle of the sixteenth century. His Mewar kingdom resisted the Mughal Empire fiercely and was attacked severely by Emperor Akbar in return. The Maharana built a new capital in a hilly area as a countermeasure to the attacks by the Mughals.

After the seventeenth century, when peace with the Mughal Emperor was established, the Maharanas began constructing artificial lakes, one after another, around Udaipur. The three most famous are Pichola Sagar, Swarup Sagar, and Fateh Sagar, which were constructed to surround the old city. They contain a well-maintained park and the Lake Palace Hotel (which was a Maharana's palace), and attract many tourists, both Indian and foreign.

The Maharana's main palace is situated by Pichola Sagar, and a part of it was also reconstructed as a hotel and a museum; the other part is still used as the ex-royal family's residence. The road connecting the palace and the Jagdish temple was built under the patronage of a Maharana.[3] It has

---

[3]The temple is dedicated to the Jagannath of Puri in Orissa, who appeared to the great-

been the main street of the old city since the Maharanas' time with rows of souvenir shops, small hotels, and offices. It is one of the main places where the new urban festivals are held.

The old and new parts of the town are separated by the rampart. Narrow alleys make the old part a labyrinth, with buildings five or six storeys high with shops on the ground floor lining both sides of the alleys. The town is divided into wards called *mohallas*. A *mohalla* consists of a few hundred households which cooperate with each other as a neighbourhood at residents' life-cycle rituals and on other special occasions. Although a *mohalla* may consist of a single *jati*, usually several *jatis* live side by side in a *mohalla*. The new town developed gradually outside the ramparts after independence, and the residential areas there are comparatively well ordered. New office buildings for commerce or modern business are also situated here. Today Udaipur is the central city for the politics and economy of the Mewar region, with a population of more than 300,000. Tourism and marble production are the main industries.

All three of the new festivals are celebrated on the streets of Udaipur city in both the old and the new city areas. Matka For (pot-breaking) is held on the day after Janamashtami (the eighth day of the dark half of the month of Bhadrapad). The main event of Matka For is the competition to break a clay pot between teams made up of the young men of a *mohalla*. This competition is based on the famous anecdote of Lord Krishna's childhood, which relates how he had his mischievous friends construct a human pyramid in order to steal the clay pot in which his foster mother had hidden his favourite butter.

In Udaipur, Matka For is performed only at the crossroads in front of the Jagdish temple. The event site is the centre of the old town and roads leading to main old town shopping centres converge at this junction. Although the place is very narrow, more than 10,000 people come to watch. Naturally traffic on the roads leading to the junction is disturbed, and the business in shopping centres is also suspended temporarily. In this way, as the crossroads becomes a festival space, the everyday activity of the town is stopped and festive time takes over public space.

Various events are also performed at the main crossroads of each *mohalla* at the time of Ganesh Utsav and the Garba Dance. Ganesh Utsav is celebrated for ten days from Ganesh Chaturthi, the birthday of the Lord Ganesh, to Anant Chaturdashi (from the fourth to the fourteenth of the bright half of the month of Bhadrapad). Although the festival in Pune and

grandson of Maharana Udai Singh, Maharana Jagat Singh, in a dream. Moreover, the image of Krishna to which Mira Bai, the most famous of Krishna's female devotees in Mewar, is said to have directed her worship is also enshrined in this temple. Thus the festivals of Krishna are celebrated on a grand scale here.

Mumbai has been celebrated on a large scale ever since Tilak's innovations at the end of the nineteenth century, in Udaipur only a handful of immigrants from Maharashtra used to celebrate it in their own community hall; other people of the town were indifferent to it. Only in the last ten years has it come to be celebrated more widely.

People set up statues of Lord Ganesh at the corner of a crossroads or in a small open space in a *mohalla* on the day of Ganesh Chaturthi, and participate in quiz shows, dance contests, or other entertainment performances every night for ten days. There are no *mandap*s displaying various scenes as in Pune and Mumbai (Kaur 2003). People in Udaipur simply enjoy participating in or just watching various entertainment events performed in front of the statue of Lord Ganesh.

The Garba Dance takes place from the first to the ninth day of the bright half of the month of Ashvina, at the same time as Navaratra, the festival of the goddess Durga. Actually the dance is a part of Durga worship. Statues of the goddess Durga are placed by the roadside in a *mohalla* in the same way as at Ganesh Utsav, and people enjoy dancing to the Garba songs in front of the statues every night during this nine-day festival.

Ritual processions have become the concluding act of both the Ganesh Utsav (on the day of Anant Chaturdashi) and the Garba Dance (on the day of Vijay Dashami). Each procession is organized by the *mohalla* that hosts the festival, and every procession is led by a *rath* (chariot) which carries a statue of the deity. They head to the *ghat* by Pichola Sagar to immerse the statue in the lake. All of the processions go through the streets and stop at the main crossroads where various martial arts and dances are performed. As the procession route is formed to connect each *mohalla* that observes the festival, the streets are filled with a bustle of *rath*s, participants, and spectators. Everyday activity comes to a halt. Since the event sites are linked by these processions, the whole city is transformed into a festive space.

Transformation of the Festivals

All three festivals have started up in Udaipur within the last ten to fifteen years, and in each case the founder(s) can easily be specified. The Garba Dance was introduced in the late 1980s in a town hall in the new town area by a youth club. This club dissolved soon afterwards, but young people from other *mohalla*s formed their own associations and took up the dance festival. The number of *mohalla*s that perform the Garba Dance has been increasing year by year, and now most *mohalla*s of Udaipur observe it.

Originally the Garba Dance was very popular in Gujarat, and the original style of Navaratra in the Mewar region was totally different from Gujarat's Garba Dance. In Mewar, Navaratra has traditionally been centred on mother goddess temples and shrines. People go to the temples and shrines, dedicate *jo* (barley) plants, and participate in *pujas* to the mother goddesses. *Pujas* take place every day and night during Navaratra and are presided over by Brahman priests or the *bhopas* (mediums of the goddess). Animal sacrifice used to be common in the temples and shrines presided by *bhopas*, and many water buffaloes and goats used to be sacrificed on the ninth or tenth day of Navaratra. There was no dancing in temples, shrines, or streets during Navaratra.

The members of the youth club which first held the Garba Dance in Udaipur happened to visit Gujarat in the late 1980s during the Navaratra season and were fascinated by the beautiful dances being performed there. They introduced the dance event to Udaipur the very next year. Other young people were also attracted to this beautiful and enjoyable dance, and the practice spread rapidly in Udaipur. Now the number of people who come to worship the mother goddesses in temples and shrines is decreasing in Udaipur. Animal sacrifices have also become rare. The traditional way of observing Navaratra in Udaipur has become marginalized.

However, the way the Garba is performed is not a wholesale imitation of the Gujarati original. Whereas in Gujarat no statue of the goddess is brought to the dance arena, in Udaipur people purchase a big statue of Durga to be placed at the dance ground. Neighbours bring barley plants to the goddess's statue instead of to the temple. The final day's procession was also added in Udaipur. The style of the procession was borrowed from the Durga Puja of Bengal. So Udaipur's Garba Dance is a mixture of the traditions of Gujarat, Mewar, and Bengal.

Matka For was started in 1993 by a voluntary association called the Dharmotsav Samiti. The association consists of the young shopkeepers of the Jagdish temple area. The leader is a Brahman in his mid thirties who runs a plumbing supplies shop in front of the Jagdish temple. Before he organized the Dharmotsav Samiti, he had joined another voluntary organization called the Shiv Dal Trust in Rajsamand, a local town of the Mewar region, the aim of which was to revive Hindu tradition. The Shiv Dal Trust started the Matka For in Rajsamand, imitating Bombay's Matka For in the early 1990s. At that time, the shopkeeper participated in this event and had the idea of organizing a similar event in Udaipur.

According to him, he felt a strong sense of impending crisis about "the decline of the Hindu tradition" in those days, and he was especially worried about the Jagdish temple's miserable situation as it "was visited by fewer and fewer people, and regrettably, some people would even drink alcohol in the precincts of the temple" (interview, August 2000). Exactly at this time, the Sangh Pariwar's Ayodhya campaign came to a climax and the Babri Masjid was demolished. "So we came to be proud of our Hinduness in this incident, and I thought that we should also start something in order to make Hindu culture prosperous in our own native town." Then, after discussions with neighbouring young shopkeepers, he and ten others formed the Dharmotsav Samiti. Although their aim has been to support religious events at the Jagdish temple or other Hindu festivals in general, organizing the Matka For is their most important activity. According to him, this event is appropriate for attracting public attention to Hindu culture because it enacts a religious episode and at the same time serves as public entertainment. Although at the beginning it was hard to organize – they had to invite the teams, search for prize sponsors, make the rules, and maintain discipline during the event – it became popular very quickly. Team entries increased year by year and now the audience for the event has reached around 10,000. In order to attract more attention from local people they added an opening performance of a girls' dance show. They also introduced several rules to make the competition, fairer like a sports event. Now the whole event is broadcast by local cable TV networks and has become famous even in the surrounding rural areas.

It was in 1993 that Udaipur's first Ganesh Utsav was held (not counting the private celebrations of the Maharashtrian migrants), when two *mohalla*s started the festival independently. By 1997, ten more *mohalla*s had started to observe it, and the number of *mohalla*s participating has doubled in the last few years. The young people of two *mohalla*s near the Jagdish temple began the festival in 1993. The first group started it because they happened to win the competition of Matka For and had the idea of using the prize money to start a new event. The other group of young people was also motivated to start some event as popular as the Matka For after they were impressed by the excitement generated there. It is interesting that one new urban festival in Udaipur triggered the creation of another, different festival. Both groups chose Ganesh Utsav as the new festival because some of their members had experience of it in Pune or Mumbai when they lived there as migrant workers and because they wanted to start a pleasant entertainment event with plenty of shows and games. The young people of both *mohalla*s also emphasize that they wanted to contribute to the revival of Hindu tradition.

As mentioned earlier, the organizers of Ganesh Utsav in Udaipur have never introduced *mandap* displays which have sometimes been a way for people to make political statements in western India. The organizers in Udaipur seem to be eager to imitate or appropriate performance entertainments only. Thus the Ganesh Utsav of Udaipur can be said to be more focused on pleasure-seeking and entertainment than the western Indian original.

The Organization of the Festivals

These festivals are organized not by temples or by traditional communities such as castes as in the case of conventional religious festivals, but by voluntary organizations of young males. Although these youth organizations tend to recruit their members from the same *mohalla,* and apparently the festivals are held *mohalla*-wide, members join the organization freely and as individuals.

Members of such organizations, which are called *yuvak sangh* or *nav-yuvak mandal* in Hindi, are aged between about fifteen and early thirties, and an organization consists of thirty to a hundred male members. In general, members pay between Rs.5 and 50 as an annual membership fee. When membership fees are insufficient to hold a festival, which is usually the case, members go around the *mohalla* to collect donations from shops and households or to seek sponsors who provide money and goods in exchange for advertisement flags or panels at the event site.[4]

At the time of the festivals, members of the organizations devote themselves to all necessary tasks such as purchasing statues, setting up places for the entertainments, inviting special guests, devising security, planning programmes, etc. They also conduct everyday *puja*s and the final day's rituals by themselves without inviting Brahmans or other religious specialists. Elders of the *mohalla* neither participate actively in nor do they disturb these activities. At most they provide financial support for the younger generation's activities. As long as young people's activities are related to the Hindu religion, elders cannot intervene.

At the moment there is only one organization which holds Matka For. On the other hand, there are many organizations (probably seventy to eighty for each) for the Garba Dance and Ganesh Utsav. This clear contrast in the numbers of organizations between Matka For and the other two festivals is due to the fact that Matka For is much too dangerous and large-scale a festival to start up easily. The organizations for Garba Dance and Ganesh Utsav do not overlap with each other, though some young males belong to both organizations. It is a hard and time-consuming task to engage in activities as a member of a festival organization. Moreover, the timings of these two festivals are contiguous to each other. In some cases there is rivalry between the leaders of the two festival organizations in the same *mohalla*. In such cases one group of youths starts one festival and the other group starts the other, and they compete with each other for popularity in the *mohalla*. Some organizations are planning to hold other seasonal festivals, such as Shivaratri or Diwali.[5]

It is noteworthy that many of these organizations have begun to transform themselves from temporary or seasonal organizations coming together

[4]In some places youths block a crossroads to levy a 'passenger tax' on drivers and passersby to raise funds for the festival.

[5]In Mewar both are traditional festivals. But some youth organizations are planning to hold new events during these festivals.

only for festivals into permanent associations engaged in various, ongoing public activities. One turning point for this change was the Gujarat earthquake in January 2001. Most festival organizations collected relief goods to send to the devastated areas or went there directly to assist in relief work. Thereafter many organizations began engaging in other public activities.

There are also some cases in which festival organizations have direct or indirect relationships with political organizations. The Udaipur branches of both the Bajrang Dal and the Shiv Sena are directly involved in organizing Ganesh Utsav in the *mohalla*s where their branch offices are placed. In one case, the festival organization comprises mainly members of the RSS. Even when the organizations do not have a direct relationship with Hindu nationalist parties, they receive help from the Shiv Sena or the RSS in the provision of security at the festivals or for the reinforcement of staff at the time of the final day's parades. Other aspects of the public and/or political activities of these festival organizations will be discussed later.

Festivals as Entertainments

In these three festivals, ritual activities are marginalized and both organizers and participants concentrate on entertainment. It is true that the festivals are based on religious myths and that statues of the gods or goddesses are always set up at the festival sites, but people pay little attention to those images or to rituals which symbolically connect human beings with the other world. At the time of the parades images of the gods or goddesses are carried through the streets, but this seems only to be the cue for merry-making. In the case of Matka For, participants and spectators enjoy the pot-breaking competition in the manner of a sporting event.

As mentioned earlier, the Dharmotsav Samiti lays down rules for the competition and uses various means to stir up excitement among the participants and the spectators. The teams that compete with each other to break the pot should be comprised of residents of the same *mohalla*. Young people of the *mohalla*s near the Jagdish temple area make a team, and about ten teams take part in the competition. So the game becomes a competition between *mohalla*s. Competitors wear uniforms supplied by sponsors. As also mentioned earlier, to attract larger audiences, the Dharmotsav Samiti has started an opening performance by a music band and added a girls' dance show before the main competition. The Samiti invites entries for the dance show and about twenty local girls perform 'traditional' folk dances in turn. There are several institutions in the city where girls can receive training in 'traditional' folk dances. These dances were performed in the past, but the performers were adult females and usually members of specific low-ranking castes. Moreover, several dances shown in the opening performance of Matka For were supposed to be performed at other rituals.

The opening programme continues for several hours. During intervals between the girls' dances special guests are introduced and make speeches. A puja to Lord Krishna's image is also performed in the tent for the guests during this performance, but participants and spectators pay hardly any attention to it. The latter collect gradually around the space in front of the Jagdish temple, taking their seats on the steps to the temple, on the roofs of the surrounding shops and restaurants, or on the ground outside the fences. The main competition starts around seven in the evening after several hours of the opening performance show, and by this time the Jagdish temple area is closely packed.

Dharmotsav Samiti members measure the height at which the clay pot is suspended (which must be precisely 21 feet above the road surface). The order of turns for each team is decided by lottery. In order to make it difficult to compose a human pyramid firmly many pails of water are thrown by the Dharmotsav Samiti's members in the first round. When every team has tried and failed to break the clay pot in the first round, lots are drawn again for turns. From then on, the height of the pot is lowered by one foot in every round. As only thin mats are laid on the paved road, it is very dangerous when the human pyramid collapses. Several boys are sent to the hospital every year to be treated for concussion as a result of the collapse. When a pyramid is set up successfully and a team comes near to breaking the pot, the audience gets excited. And when the pot is broken at last, the cry, *Krishna Bhagvān ki Jay* (Victory to Lord Krishna), is raised unanimously by the audience. The victorious team parades the trophy through the streets to their *mohalla*, and the festival ends around nine in the evening.

Excitement and entertainment is the main purpose of the Matka For. The audience consumes this event and the background music performed by a band as they enjoy TV shows or action films. Taking pleasure in entertainment is also the main purpose of Ganesh Utsav. At the time of the first puja to the Lord Ganesh, many residents of the *mohalla* come together to worship the god, bringing *laddus*[6] and coconuts as offerings. But, as in other pujas which are carried out regularly over ten days every morning and evening, few people actually attend. Several members of the festival organization play the tapes of *arti* songs for Ganesh and hurry through the ritual.

The attraction for the local people of the *mohalla*s is the various performances held every night in the open spaces in front of the Ganesh statue. They enjoy seeing and participating in amateur entertainment shows in

[6]A *laddu* is a round sweet made of gram flour or thickened milk, with sugar, saffron, and other ingredients. Ganesh is believed to be fond of laddus, so it is the most suitable offering to him.

which both hosts and participants are their *mohalla* neighbours. Above all, they enjoy the dance contest performed to cassettes of fashionable film songs or a quiz show which imitates TV programmes such as *kaun banega crorepati* (the Hindi version of *Who Wants to be a Millionaire?*) (as a local imitation, they entitle their quiz show *kaun banega hazarpati*, 'Who Wants to Win a Thousand?') or *khulja sim-sim.*[7] As there is rivalry among the *mohallas*, when a game show attracts a large audience and many participants on one day, the same show is imitated in other places the next day.

In some places they even entertain themselves with the Garba Dance during Ganesh Utsav. Clearly this performance is out of context. But people do not care much about contextuality as long as it is enjoyable and attractive for residents. The out-of-contextuality of the performance can be seen in the case of the Garba Dance at the time of Navaratra too. As mentioned above, both the dance and the music originated in Gujarat where the language is different from Mewari or Hindi. Usually the organizers purchase Garba Dance music cassettes recorded in Gujarat in the market and play them on the dance platform. Participants enjoy the dance without understanding the meanings of the songs. They form two lines circling around a clay pot in which a votive light is burning. Usually one line consists of males and the other of females, and they dance facing each other. In this way the dance becomes an occasion for young boys and girls to encounter each other. For these participants the meaning of the ritual songs is of no importance. Their prime concerns are fashion and dance styles. In some *mohallas* the organizers even play music cassettes from popular film songs, and this is called the 'disco-type' Garba Dance. As the original meaning is considered of little relevance, they can freely arrange both style and content in accordance with their taste.

Emphasis on the Revival of Tradition

Despite these new features of the three festivals, the organizations' members (and especially the leaders) emphasize that they are not creating new events but trying to revive extinct traditions. The Dharmotsav Samiti and Matka For are good examples. According to one leader, they "did not start a new event, but only revived an old tradition which had been forgotten for a long time." From their point of view, they are undertaking this event in order to re-create Hindu tradition.

Thus the emphasis on tradition or loyalty to the great Hindu land can be discerned throughout the Matka For event and in all the participants'

---

[7]This means 'Open Sesame' and was a simple quiz programme with different prizes hidden in boxes. This and *Kaun banega* ... were the most popular TV quiz shows during my field research.

behaviour. When a human pyramid collapses and the crowds groan with disappointment, the host of the event praises the bravery of the young men who are descendants of the Mewar kingdom that fought against the Mughal emperor's army. When the crowds begin nudging each other and threaten to become disorderly, the host announcer asks them to maintain discipline because they are true patriots of India and heirs of the glorious tradition of Mewar. The songs performed during the event are also patriotic, such as *Vande Mataram* (one of the favourite songs of the Independence movement which is still much loved by Hindu nationalists) or theme songs from patriotic films.

The emphasis on tradition and patriotism can be observed in other contexts also. The opening performance is called a cultural programme. As mentioned earlier, 'culture' (*sanskriti*) here means the dances in which girls dress up in traditional Mewari costumes and perform Mewari folk dances. If the meaning of 'cultural' dance is stretched somewhat, the girls may perform popular film dances, or not only girls but also adult females and males may dance. However, the organizers normally recognize only Mewari folk dances as 'traditional culture' and these are preferred, even if they are being performed out of their traditional context. Other performance genres are neglected. In this way, the opening performance and the main event are consistent as events which perform 'tradition'. The contrast between girls and men, between dance and brave action, is clearly displayed and what are taken to be traditional gender roles are implicitly represented throughout the festival.

The ceremonies inserted at intervals during the opening performance are also interesting. The wonder and glory of 'the continuity of the Hindu tradition' are praised again and again in guests' speeches. Moreover, at an award ceremony in 2001, for those who had contributed to the rise of Hindu culture in the Mewar region, the Mewar military officer who played an active role in the Kargil war of 1999 was invited with his family, and a prize (an imitation sword and shield from the Mewar kingdom era) was awarded to them. Here again the tradition of the Hindus and the Mewaris, identified as brave patriotic spirits, was emphasized.

This case clearly exemplifies typical features of invented traditions, as pointed out by Hobsbawm (1983a). The Matka For of Udaipur was constructed in response to a rapidly changing society, emerged within a brief and dateable period, and is establishing itself with great rapidity (ibid.: 1). Moreover, ancient materials are used to construct a new festival for novel purposes (ibid.: 6). When old materials are adopted, transformed, and enacted for certain purposes, this enactment cannot be a mere unreflexive repetition of convention. There must be a break from the past context, and a performative event is created which is always conscious of spectators and is always taking the effect of ritual into consideration.

The 'tradition' that is emphasized during the opening of Matka For is certainly reflexively constructed, in the sense that the organizers are highly conscious that they are constructing a performance, and that they are doing so for an audience (and the audience and the performers are clearly marked off from each other, more so perhaps than in the context of a traditional village festival). Symbols and actions connected with stereotyped gender roles, the bravery of Mewaris and patriotism are repeatedly conveyed or on show during the festival. The messages of these symbols and actions are communicated to the audience in the midst of the excitement of the games. In the case of Ganesh Utsav and the Garba Dance, some organizers claim that their own festivals are the 'purely traditional' ones and criticize other *mohalla*s for organizing what they see as the 'pleasure-seeking' or 'disco' type. Those organizations that have a direct or strong relation with Hindu nationalist parties are particularly likely to emphasize their festivals' traditional nature.

The festivals themselves, however, are not 'traditional'. And as the festivals are also performative, like Matka For, the emphasized 'tradition' cannot help but appear arbitrary and constructed to the historian of Hinduism (though this does not bother either the organizers, who sincerely believe themselves to be reviving traditional Hinduism, or the audience). The events staged at the 'purely traditional' *mohalla*s' Ganesh Utsav are dances and quiz shows just as in other *mohalla*s. The only difference lies in the content. For example, the dances are not fashionable film dances but traditional folk dances, and the questions asked in the quiz show all relate to Hindu culture. But, as noted above, the folk dances have been removed from their original contexts and reworked to fit the context of a public performance. In the case of the quiz shows, the style and content are a mixture of the modern and the 'traditional': the style is in imitation of TV shows and the content is supposedly Hindu. In my interviews with the leaders they were quite clear: they intend to contribute to the revival of authentic Hindu traditions and they hope to eliminate the pernicious influence of the modern West over Hindu culture by means of these festivals.

In this ambiguity of 'tradition', there may lie the mechanism that allows the public to become involved in the Hindu nationalist movement. In so far as the festival events attempt to re-create or re-establish a link with the past, the nationalists recognize the young people's events as 'tradition' without examining the contents too closely and they support their actions. In Hindu nationalist movements also, 'traditional' rituals have been appropriated and invented, and these 'traditions' have become important means for their political propaganda (Hansen 1999: 159-81). 'Traditional' rituals and festivals have a powerful attraction for Hindu nationalist movements because nationalism evokes nostalgia for a people's glorious past.[8] Although not all of the new festivals in Udaipur were necessarily created or introduced by Hindu nationalists, it is highly probable that the latter regard youth festivals in Udaipur as an important opportunity to broaden their support base among middle-class youth, and our cases seem to illustrate this to some extent, as shown below. For the organizing youths success comes when others recognize their events as traditional. Of course, it is also an important legitimation of their efforts when these festivals are popular among their neighbours, but, in order to secure their domain from intervention by the local establishment or local elders, and in order to expand the events successfully once they have begun, it is also important to obtain recognition from more authoritative organizations. Thus, recognition and support from Hindu nationalists, whose political influence has been getting stronger from 1990 onwards, was of great charm for the youths. Under these circumstances the young men of the Udaipur festival organizations began to get involved in interdependent relationships with Hindu nationalist movements.

Young people may become attached to Hindu nationalist discourse simply through organizing a 'traditional' festival, and thus evolve into supporters of the Hindu nationalist movement. However, such a mechanism cannot tell the entire story. Other youths try to maintain their own realm of activities and to keep their distance from Hindu nationalist politics. In the next section, I focus on the developmental process of the youth organizations and the way their activities extend beyond festivals in order to clarify how these organizations are related to Hindu nationalist parties or, on the other hand, try to avoid them.

THE DEVELOPMENT OF YOUTH ORGANIZATIONS AND HINDU NATIONALISM

We can classify the youth organizations of the new festivals in Udaipur into four categories in terms of the degree of their commitment to the Hindu nationalist movement. Here I take up typical examples from each category in order to examine the nature and process of youth organizations' activities.

Festivals Organized by Branches of Hindu Nationalist Organizations

A typical example of this pattern is an Udaipur branch of the Bajrang Dal, which directly organizes a Ganesh Utsav festival. They set up a statue of

[8] As Hobsbawm (1983b) pointed out, the mass production of traditions in Europe took place precisely in the late nineteenth century when nation-building was at its height.

Lord Ganesh by the roadside in the new town area and organize games and dances every night during the festival in front of the statue. Although there is no apparent difference from other *mohalla*s' Ganesh Utsav, the name of the Bajrang Dal is proudly displayed on the pennant that is hung over the road and the organizing committee consists mostly of members of the Bajrang Dal. A leader of the Bajrang Dal lives there and as he took the initiative to start the Ganesh Utsav here in 2001, this *mohalla*'s Ganesh Utsav came to be organized under the strong influence of the Bajrang Dal.

The Bajrang Dal was established as one of the organizations of the Sangh Pariwar in the late 1980s and has been very active from around 2000 in the Mewar region. One of its main targets is the re-conversion of those in rural and mountain areas who have converted away from Hinduism (most have converted to Christianity). They recruit hundreds of teenagers as members every year and their initiation ceremonies, in which novices are given daggers as a symbol of their being guardians of Hindu virtue, are often given full coverage in local newspapers.

The branch leader is a young Rajput in his early twenties. According to him, he has had an antipathy to Muslims from his junior high school days, and often caused violent confrontations with Muslims. His ancestors were local feudal lords in the past, so he claims that he is only following his family's duty to attack foreign enemies in order to protect his people. He is also angry with establishment leaders, saying that they have not taken any action against the decline of order in Indian civic life and have simply been appeasing the 'enemies' of India, such as Muslim and Christian missionaries.

After graduating from high school, he got a job in a security company. At the same time, he joined the Shiv Sena on the invitation of someone he had known very well in his school days. He was an active member, joining a demonstration against the sale of cows, leading an attack on a movie theatre which showed an 'immoral' film, and organizing a ritual to pray for rain in Udaipur. He was promoted to the head of the Udaipur branch office in just four years. But he was disappointed that the upper posts were rotated among higher-ranking people and there was little hope of gaining further promotion. So he consulted a son of Bal Thackeray directly and moved into the Bajrang Dal. Now he is acting as the leader of the rural areas of Udaipur district and is a director of the Udaipur city branch of the Bajrang Dal.

As the leader of the rural areas, he has formed more than fifty branch committees in villages within two years. He also succeeded in inviting a Hindu saint, Asa Ramji Maharaj, who is highly respected and very famous in western India, and organized a re-conversion ritual of hundreds of converted Christians under the patronage of the saint. Moreover, he eagerly organizes mass demonstrations, such as the gathering on the Akhand

Bharat Diwas (Undivided India Day) on 14 August (the Independence Day of Pakistan) and the commemoration parade on 6 December (the memorial day of the destruction of Babri Masjid) from a city hall to the Jagdish temple.

The celebration of Ganesh Utsav is also a part of the movement for awakening Hindu consciousness. The branch office is situated in a new town area where business families are concentrated and traditional public religious events are rarely celebrated. This leader tries to reconstruct and promote a sense of community in the *mohalla* by organizing the Ganesh Utsav. He invites neighbours to the performance of *arti* to Lord Ganesh every morning and evening during the festival or to the *havan* ritual at night. He also emphasizes that there should only be traditional performances in the night programmes during the festival. So he organizes traditional *bhajan kirtan* instead of dances to film songs. He also stages fancy dress shows, but the participants are only children and the subject is limited to religious themes.

The recruitment of young men to the Bajrang Dal is another main purpose of Ganesh Utsav. Teenagers, especially those who have dropped out of school or failed to find permanent jobs, find it interesting to be part of the staff of the event. The Bajrang Dal accepts them as festival organization members first and gradually directs their interests to other Bajrang Dal activities. In this way many teenagers of the *mohalla* have joined the Bajrang Dal within two years. Aware of Ganesh Utsav's effect for mass propaganda, the branch leader mobilized rural branches to hold their own celebrations of Ganesh Utsav from 2002. The recent penetration of new urban festivals into rural areas of Mewar is certainly a part of the Sangh Pariwar's expansion strategy.

Organizations Involved in Hindu Nationalism

There are also organizations which come to be deeply involved in the Hindu nationalist movement as part of the process of their activity, even if there was no direct relation when they started out. The Dharmotsav Samiti is one such organization.

As mentioned earlier, the Dharmotsav Samiti is an organization formed by young shopkeepers around the Jagdish temple, and its principal raison d'être is to organize the only Matka For festival in Udaipur. The Dharmotsav Samiti was not directly related with the Hindu nationalist movement when it was established. As Matka For grew into a big event which attracted audiences of more than 10,000, its management became beyond the ability of local shopkeepers. They looked to the Hindu nationalist party as the most reliable organization to help with security during the festival and to negotiate with the police and the administrative authorities.

Moreover, when Matka For became an indispensable annual event in Udaipur, the Samiti turned their concerns to other public activities. They collected and sent disaster relief at the time of the Gujarat earthquake. They also started public welfare activities such as blood donation. The RSS and VHP are cooperating actively with the Dharmotsav Samiti in these activities also.

Furthermore, an event took place in 2003 which brought the Dharmotsav Samiti decisively under the strong influence of the Hindu nationalist movements, namely, the trouble that took place at the time of newly started Jagannath Yatra in Udaipur. Although the Jagdish temple is known as a temple to Lord Krishna, the main god enshrined in the high altar of the temple is called Jagannath, the same as the famous god of Orissa. It is said that Maharana Jagat Singh would see Lord Jagannath appeared in his dreams every night and so he became a devout follower of Jagannath. One day Jagannath told the Maharana in a dream that an image of him was buried in a mountain of the Mewar kingdom. When his servants discovered the image in exactly the place described in the dream, the Maharana ordered the construction of the Jagdish temple to enshrine the image. Since Jagannath is identified with Lord Krishna, it was mainly the festivals and rituals of Lord Krishna that came to be performed in this temple in later years.

The Dharmotsav Samiti decided in the late 1990s to start a Jagannath Yatra in Udaipur in order to 'revive' tradition (interview, 2003). The float and the image for the procession were made with the donations of local people and visitors to the Jagdish temple. They collected about one million rupees in four years. The Jagannath Yatra in Udaipur was started in 2003, on the same day as the Jagannath Yatra of Orissa. More than 200 people pulled the float, and a large-scale parade with a music band, horses, camels, and elephants marched through the old town area for several hours.

However, the float was too high to go smoothly through the narrow lanes in the old town as the top touched electric wires in various places. The Samiti members claimed that they had requested the electric company to re-hang the wires higher for the parade, but the request was delivered to the company only a few days before the Yatra. On the day after the Yatra the Samiti members made a protest against the slow service of the electric company, and some of them resorted to violent action, dragging out an employee, undressing him, smearing mud on his face, and hitting him with sticks. The police were called and the assailants were arrested. The leader of Dharmotsav Samiti was also taken into custody temporarily.

The RSS responded to the request of the remaining members of the Dharmotsav Samiti to put pressure on the authorities (a demonstration asking for their release was organized). In various ways it also gave support to the Dharmotsav Samiti during the trial procedure, which was still pending in the autumn of 2003.[9] The Dharmotsav Samiti owed much to the RSS and Sangh Pariwar in these troubles.

As part of the campaign for the Rajasthan assembly election, the RSS and VHP held political conventions frequently in Udaipur in the autumn of 2003. In these conventions, the Dharmotsav Samiti always supplied welcome gates for prominent guest speakers of the VHP and the RSS, and the leader and members of the Samiti showed up to assist in various ways. Until 2003, the Dharmotsav Samiti had restricted its activities relevant to the Jagdish temple only, and they did not participate in political activities openly as the Samiti. But they changed their policy suddenly in autumn 2003. We can discern their debt to the Sangh Pariwar behind this change of policy.

Youth organizations that share a nationalistic outlook and the Hindu nationalist party tend to become mutually interdependent. In this case, the Sangh Pariwar took advantage of the weakness of a youth organization and managed to bring the organization under its strong influence.

Organizations Focusing on Festivals as Entertainment

There are many organizations that seek only to provide entertainment at festivals and are indifferent to political or public activities. A youth organization near the Jagdish temple is a typical example. It is called the Gariya Devra Gangor Ghat Navyuvak Mandal (two *mohalla*s, namely, Gariya Devra and Gangor Ghat, combine here). It was formed to organize the Ganesh Utsav. They also participate in the Matka For as a competitive team, and once their team won the pot-breaking game. They intended to use the prize money in some public way following the model of the Dharmotsav Samiti. But they could not organize a large-scale event. So they decided to start a manageable new Hindu festival and found that Ganesh Utsav was most suitable for their purpose. This organization consists of about eighty men between sixteen and forty years old who pay Rs.80 every year as the membership fee.

According to the leader, who runs a travel agency in the Gariya Devra area, they take care not to form any relationship with a specific religious or political organization as people of various faiths (mostly Hindus and Muslims, but some Sikhs and Jains also) live in this area (interview, 2001). The entertainment presented at the Ganesh Utsav includes magic shows by residents of this area, quiz shows imitating TV programmes, and dance

---

[9]The BJP, the major political party of the Sangh Pariwar, came to power in Rajasthan after the assembly elections of December 2003. Immediately the charges were withdrawn and all the accused in this case were acquitted in 2004.

contests. He claims that these events are in order to have a pleasant time and they do try not to stimulate communal feeling in the entertainments.

Even when funds for the festival are left over, they are saved for the next year and are not used for other public activities. Although the leader wants to contribute to some other public activities, he says that they cannot afford any time or manpower to engage in such activities. The most they have been able to do is to supply relief goods at the time of the Gujarat earthquake and labour power to clean the bottom of the lakes of Udaipur at the time of drought in the Mewar region in response to requests of the Mewar Sena, an active youth organization discussed below.

In the new town area, another organization called the Hindu Ekta Ganpati Utsav Mandal organizes Ganesh Utsav. In their *mohalla*, several collective residences for public service personnel (for workers at the airport, the radio station, etc.) and some buildings reserved for SCs and STs have been constructed recently, so residents do not know each other well. This Mandal aims to cultivate friendship among residents of the *mohalla* by holding the Ganesh Utsav (interview, 2001). Twenty-five members of the Mandal are elected from among residents of the *mohalla*. The funds for the festival are mostly donated by the residents. Since this *mohalla* consists of various religious communities, they do not stage any entertainment which emphasizes Hindu nationalism. The main programme is the dance contest here, but the participants are restricted to children under ten years old. They expect that the dance contest will provide a good opportunity for locals to become acquainted with each other's children and, at the same time, there is little risk of it being used for specifically political purposes. This Mandal does not engage in any other public activities.

In the next *mohalla* of the same area and with a similar composition of residents, however, members of the RSS have joined a youth organization and the influence of Hindu nationalism is clearly observable in the performances of Ganesh Utsav. There does not appear to be any clear correlation between the residential pattern and the strength or influence of Hindu nationalism.

Organizations Engaging in Public Activities Independent of Political Parties

A typical example of organizations independent of political parties is the Mewar Sena which has been organizing the Garba Dance for ten years at Jagdish Chawk, the street between the Jagdish temple and the Maharana's old palace. The leader (I will call him Kapil) is a young Brahman in his late twenties who runs a successful handicrafts shop in this street (interview, 2003). He formed a youth organization called the Jagdish Chawk Navyuvak Mandal ten years ago following the advice of a senior person whom he admired as his own guru. He was still a teenager at that time, and he simply wanted to organize the Garba Dance which was beginning to be fashionable in Udaipur. His guru, however, had political ambitions and dreamed of being a member of the state assembly. It seems that he tried to make the youth organization into one of his support organizations for the election. The guru encouraged Kapil to get involved in public activity and taught him how to mobilize youth organizations for social welfare work, such as cleaning Udaipur's lakes and supporting rural development. The guru died in a traffic accident several years ago without realizing his political ambitions.

Kapil changed the organization's name to 'Mewar Sena' and, while organizing the Garba Dance, he set about organizing other public activities. More than 200 young males of the Jagdish Chawk *mohalla*, ranging from teenagers to forty-year-olds, are members of the Mewar Sena and they each pay Rs.21 as the annual fee. As the organization has expanded throughout the Jagdish Chawk area, the total of members is now over 1,000.

When the Garba Dance season is approaching, in order to raise funds for the festival, they collect donations from residents, invite sponsorship from companies where members are working, and levy a private traffic 'tax' from taxis and rickshaws going through the Jagdish Chawk. They also charge an admission fee of Rs.5 to all those who come to dance. A big Durga statue is set up in front of the Maharana's palace, and they hold a dance function for each of the nine nights of Navratra. Hundreds of young men and women come to dance every night, and more than a thousand people gather in the streets. Prizes are given to the best dancers and most fashionable dressers every night. They sometimes sell lottery tickets also at this festival. In 2002, each ticket cost ten rupees. The first prize was a new Maruti car and the second a new refrigerator, both provided by sponsoring companies. The funds that remain after the festival are used for various public activities.

Cleaning the Udaipur lakes is a typical example of the Mewar Sena's public activities. Usually they clear away waterweeds in winter. When the lakes dried up at the time of the drought in 2000, they cleaned garbage and mud from the bottom of the lakes. They collected funds and equipment from the municipal committee and big industry, and the Mewar Sena and other youth organizations nearby provided voluntary labour. The Mewar Sena also employed farmers from neighbouring villages to help in the cleaning as a measure of drought relief. They were also very active at the time of the Gujarat earthquake.

Now they are expanding their activities into rural areas. They are engaged in a reforestation project in a hill village, a road improvement project in another village, and education aid projects in many villages (donating school uniforms, maps, and blackboards to primary schools; in one case they even constructed a classroom for the school). Furthermore, they award prizes at the time of the Garba Dance to those schoolchildren who have obtained the best results in classwork and sport. They have also organized a pilgrimage bus tour to Amarnath. They place a signboard displaying photographs of all these activities next to the Garba Dance, where everyone can see it.

Kapil has left the organizing of the Garba Dance to other younger members these last few years, and has turned his attention mainly to the expansion of the organization and the management of public activities. Four branches of the Mewar Sena have been set up in Udaipur city itself, and more than ten branches have been formed in the rural areas of the Mewar region. These branches search out necessary public works in their own franchise area and the next projects are decided on the leader's initiative.

Kapil points out that the Garba Dance is a measure to draw young people's attention to the Mewar Sena. The festival is no more than a means for involving youth in public activities. But at the same time, he claims that he is not interested in party politics. He takes care that his organization should have no relationship with any Hindu nationalist organization or other political party, and he is not going to stand as a candidate for any political post. He is critical of the activities of the Bajrang Dal and the Dharmotsav Samiti. He is particularly critical of the latter, whose *mohalla* directly adjoins the base of the Mewar Sena. The members of both organizations have known each other since childhood. Kapil believes that the Dharmotsav Samiti wrongly connects religion with political ambition and has made an error in becoming intimate with the Sangh Pariwar recently.

CONCLUSION

In conclusion, I would like to return to the questions of the motivations of local middle-class youth for engaging in public activities and the future of these voluntary associations in the contemporary Indian social situation.

In his monograph on Tamil society, Mines (1994) started from a contrast of Indian with Western individuality. He pointed out that Indian individuality is contextualized in a concrete social relationship and since its strength differs according to one's role in a certain constituency of social relationships, Indian individuality is conceived to vary from one person to another. He also indicated that those who are going to exercise leadership in Indian society try to form various institutions for public activities and to be the head of them in order to expand their constituency of influence by winning the approval of others. This feature of individuality seems basically applicable to people in Udaipur. And as Hansen (2001) has pointed out, public festivals have provided good opportunities for the acquisition and expansion of such leadership in urban situations in South Asia.

Young males of the emerging middle class in Udaipur have consolidated their local leadership through enthusiastic participation in public activities. At the same time, they have a sense of extreme vulnerability and impending crisis, because of their economic position as shopkeepers or the owners of small companies. The sense of crisis is conceived and expressed as the decline of tradition or the decline of order, as the leader of the Dharmotsav Samiti clearly stated. They are trying to contribute to the public in a certain way and at the same time to acquire new leadership in competition with the conventional leaders, i.e. the upper-class establishment leaders and caste elders who are seen as not coping with public decline satisfactorily.

Founding new festivals, which are therefore not under the control of conventional leaders, is the best means of acquiring leadership. As long as they are religious festivals, new leaders can secure an autonomous sphere of activity which evades administrative intervention as well as criticism by conventional elders. Moreover, since it is easy to include fashionable elements in the new festivals, young leaders can win the approval and support of their young urban neighbours who are familiar with and avid consumers of the entertainments offered by the mass media.

The three new festivals that are very popular in western India must have been part of the cultural repertoire of the new young leaders. They must have known that these festivals would be attractive to urban citizens through having actually seen them or through having heard about them in the mass media. As there is rivalry among leaders, leaders of the same neighbourhood can compete with each other in the introduction of new festivals. So three different festivals, all originating from western India, have come to be staged in Udaipur one after another within a short period of time.

At the same time, the communal tendency has strengthened in these festivals as Hindu nationalist organizations have assumed control of them gradually in their places of origin. So the new festival organizations in Udaipur run the risk of involving themselves in communal politics. As discussed in this chapter, some organizations have indeed become involved in political activities to support Hindu nationalism.

In Udaipur, however, unlike Mumbai where festival organizations have been strongly dominated or influenced by Hindu nationalism, festival organizations are not necessarily deprived of their own initiatives. Some organizations, appropriating entertainment programmes of the original festivals or imitating electronic media content, limit their activities only to the performance of the festivals for amusement or mutual friendship and try to avoid communal politics. Moreover, some organizations like the

Mewar Sena are actively engaged in public activities while keeping their distance from party politics.

The Mewar Sena was originally formed from political ambition. It owes much to the leader's personality, in particular the fact that he has maintained its strategy of independence from politics. However, they can keep engaging in public activities independent of Hindu nationalist organizations mostly because they have been able to secure independent financial resources, and to establish a unique strategy for the recruitment of members (namely, they succeeded in expanding their franchise of recruitment) and for searching out public needs through their own networks. The Mewar Sena deserves our attention because its members are forging a new form of civic society beyond the boundary of communities as conventionally conceived. However, it may be difficult to form an inter-communal organization, which is regarded as ideal for the purposes of preventing communal violence (Varshney 2002), as long as the primary purpose of the Mewar Sena is to carry out a Hindu festival.

At the moment, urban festivals in Udaipur have become a public arena for urban youths' mutually contesting and contradictory projects and perspectives for the public sphere. It cannot be predicted whether this arena will become a resource of grassroots support for Hindu communalism or if it can transform itself into a new civic society based on spontaneous voluntary associations. But it can be safely stated that this new phenomenon is responding to and at the same time influencing the rapid social changes that are occurring in contemporary north-western India.

REFERENCES

Freitag, S.B. 1989. *Collective Action and Community: Public Arenas and the Emergence of Communalism in North India*. Berkeley: University of California Press.

Hansen, T.B. 1999. *The Saffron Wave: Democracy and Hindu Nationalism in Modern India*. Princeton: Princeton University Press.

——. 2001. *Wages of Violence: Naming and Identity in Postcolonial Bombay*. Princeton: Princeton University Press.

Hobsbawm, E. 1983a. 'Introduction', in E. Hobsbawm and T. Ranger (eds.), *The Invention of Tradition*, pp. 1-14. Cambridge: Cambridge University Press.

——. 1983b. 'Mass-Producing Traditions: Europe, 1870-1914', in E. Hobsbawm and T. Ranger (eds.), *The Invention of Tradition*, pp. 263-307. Cambridge: Cambridge University Press.

Kaur, R. 2003. *Performative Politics and the Cultures of Hinduism: Public Uses of Religion in Western India*. Delhi: Permanent Black.

Mines, M. 1994. *Public Faces, Private Voices. Community and Individuality in South India*. Berkeley: University of California Press.

Varshney, A. 2002. *Ethnic Conflict and Civic Life: Hindus and Muslims in India* (2nd edn.). New Haven: Yale University Press.

9

Some Unintended Consequences of Ritual Change: The Case of Funerals in Changru, Byans, Far Western Nepal

KATSUO NAWA

INTRODUCTION

Ritual has often been conceptualized as the prescribed process of religious actions repeated almost automatically by the participants each time.[1] However, there are cases in which the process of a ritual itself is deliberately changed in a drastic manner. The consequences of this kind of change are difficult to predict and are often quite different from what the reformers expected.

This chapter looks at funerals in Changru (Chhangru), a village in Byans, far western Nepal.[2] Why funerals? First, the funeral is the largest

---

[1]An earlier version of this chapter was published as the first half of the 12th chapter of my ethnography (2002: 238-55) and an earlier draft in English was read in Clare Hall ASH Colloquium in Cambridge in June 2003. I thank Dilli Ram Dahal, Takeo Funabiki, David Gellner, Hiroshi Ishii, Alan Macfarlane, Seika Sato, and Akio Tanabe, among others, for their helpful and constructive comments and criticisms on various earlier versions of this paper. I want to express my deepest gratitude to all the people of Byans whom I talked with. Without their patience and kindness I could not have written this paper at all. Any remaining errors and shortcomings are mine.

[2]Fieldwork in Darchula district was carried out for about fourteen months, from 1993 to 1995, while I was an affiliated research scholar of the Centre for Nepal and Asian Studies, Tribhuvan University. The research was financially supported by the Asian Studies Scholarship Program of the Ministry of Education, Science and Culture, Japan. For the research in Byans, I had special research permission in 1993 and 1994 from the Home Ministry, HMG Nepal.

and probably the most important post-mortem ritual in Byans.[3] Second, the funeral in Changru changed drastically within a few decades: The 'traditional' funeral called *Gwon*[4] was replaced by a new one named *Sarat.*[5] Some elders still remembered the days when they had performed Gwon. In this chapter I will discuss how and why this change was introduced, and what consequences it had for the villagers of Changru.

Byans is the geographical region of the uppermost valley of the Mahakali (Kali) River that constitutes the western border between India and Nepal. The area, lying north of the Api Himal, consists of nine villages, only two of which (including Changru) lie within the territory of Nepal, the other seven being in the state of Uttaranchal, India. The main inhabitants have been described as basically 'Mongoloid' people (using the now obsolete term of biological anthropology). They are often called Byansi in Nepal,[6] and rather misleadingly are included in the general category of Bhotiya in India. As I have pointed out elsewhere (Nawa 2000), however, their ethnonym in their mother tongue is Rang, the term usually being paraphrased as the people who live in Byans, Chaudans, and Darma, three adjacent Himalayan regions. Many people in Byans have traditionally conducted trans-Himalayan trade, in addition to agriculture and animal husbandry. In summer, many traders go to Purang (Taklakot) in Tibet from their villages in Byans. In winter, when their villages are cut off from the outside world by snow, they move to Darchula, a hill bazaar on the Mahakali where they have their winter houses, and travel to villages and towns in the southern fringe of the Himalayas in far western Nepal and Uttaranchal for trade. Several scholars have pointed out that they have kept their

---

[3]According to the villagers of Changru, the deceased is cremated on the same day or the next morning on the bank of the river Mahakali. Three days later some bones of the deceased are moved to another place near the village (or their winter residence in Darchula). The family members of the deceased put out a meal for him or her every morning and evening on a stand set in the front yard of their house. The funeral is performed during the next dark half of the lunar month. The bones of the deceased are later brought to Kailash or a sacred place in India. Note that what I call 'funeral' here, following Sherring (1993: 126-32), is not the cremation ritual but the main post-mortem ritual held many days after the cremation.

[4]Byansi is a Tibeto-Burman language with no standardized writing system, and the transcription of Byansi words in this chapter is tentative and incomplete. Accuracy is further compromised because I do not use phonetic symbols and diacritics. Trivedi (1991) and Sharma (2001) give us reliable information on the language based on their research on the Yerjungkhu dialect (villagers of Changru speak the Pangjungkhu dialect), though in some details I disagree with both of them (Nawa 2002: 351-2).

[5]In several villages in Byans and adjacent regions, Gwon was not totally abolished. In these villages, people had to choose either Sarat or a shortened and abbreviated version of Gwon each time. I have analysed the process of a Gwon carried out in 1995 in the village of Shangkan elsewhere (Nawa 2002: 255-63, n.d. b).

[6]The population of Byansi in Nepal is 2,103 according to the 2001 census, though it is not certain whether this number really coincides with the number of the people who think themselves to be Rang.

own culture and traditions, while being influenced by both Tibetan Buddhism and Hinduism.[7]

Professor Dilli Ram Dahal, a prominent Nepali anthropologist, made the following observation on their religion and ritual:

> Animal sacrifice is common in many of their rituals, and they celebrate major Hindu festivals suggesting Hindu beliefs and practices. On the other hand, they also employ Tibetan lamas during funeral, an indication of Buddhist affiliation. (Dahal 1994: 37)

Even though it contains no factual errors on the level of observable ritual practices, this observation is totally inconsistent with the subjective religious affiliation of the people of Changru. As far as I know, no villagers in Changru except Tibetan refugees and some other newcomers admitted that they were Tibetan Buddhists. Many villagers strongly insisted that they were not Buddhists but Hindus, and indeed deeply resented outsiders who regarded them as Tibetan Buddhists (Nawa 2000).

Why, then, did the villagers of Changru, who strongly affirm themselves to be Hindus, call Buddhist monks to some of their funerals? How was it possible for them to deny their Buddhist affiliation? In this paper I will attempt to answer these questions by reconstructing the process of change and transformation of their funerals from the middle of the twentieth century. In so doing, I will try to submit a more elaborate as well as more comprehensive description-cum-analysis of ritual change in the Himalayas than those that rely on the concepts of Sanskritization and modernization. I will do this by focusing on the relationship between ritual practice and several types of utterances that occur during the ritual. In the following I will first describe the process of a Sarat, the new funeral, based on my fieldnotes, and then reconstruct the process of Gwon, the traditional funeral, held in Changru in the first half of the twentieth century, using mainly information obtained by interviews with some elders in the village. Finally I will clarify the discrepancies between the original aims and some unintended consequences of the introduction of the new funeral, and discuss the mechanism through which these unexpected consequences, including the occasional participation of Buddhist monks, were generated.

---

[7] See Dahal (1994), Fürer-Haimendorf (1988 [1975]: 282-4), and Manzardo et al. (1976), all of which are based on information from the Nepali side of the Mahakali River. For more information, see Nawa (2002). Raypa (1974) gives us basic ethnographic information on the Rang in India, while Srivastava (1953, 1966), Raha & Das (1981), Hoon (1996), and Leder (2003) focus on their sociocultural and economic changes and dynamics. For a brief introduction of the people of Nepali Byans, now officially recognized as one of *Adivasi Janajatis* of Nepal under the name of 'Byasi' or 'Vyasi' (HMG 2058 V.S.; cf. Gellner & Karki, this volume), see Ukyab & Adhikari (2000) and the NEFIN webpage (http://www.nefin.org.np/mainsite/content/view/18/40). See also Rana Magar (2057) which is mainly based on data gathered in Darchula and Rapla. Note also that the description in this paragraph is inevitably approximate and oversimplified.

SARAT: THE NEW FUNERAL

Among the villagers of Changru in Nepalese Byans, it was (and certainly still is) the rule that funerals are performed in the way they call 'Sarat'.[8] Putting together my own observations and the explanations given by the villagers, we can safely say that Sarat proceeds in the following order. First, the bones of the deceased are brought into a room of his or her house. Various offerings are presented, and a religious specialist (either a Brahman, a Tibetan Buddhist monk, or a villager) recites a religious text. A meal is served to those who attend the funeral. After the recitation the bones are carried out again, with a typical gesture called *yimo* (see below). The deceased is considered to have metamorphosed into an ancestor, and people carry out a ritual of ancestor worship tossing the offerings into the air, just as they do in other rituals for gods and ancestors (Nawa n.d. a). At night, a ritual called *kirtan* is performed, in which villagers sing songs of praise to major Hindu deities. The next day a ritual of purification is carried out mainly by the clan members of the deceased.

Panel A, reconstructed from my field notes, shows how a Sarat was actually carried out by the villagers of Changru.[9]

Panel A: The Process of a Funeral Held in Darchula in January 1995

The deceased was a woman of Changru in her seventies. The ritual was held in her house, where her daughter, whom I will indicate by her initial G, had lived for some years with her after the death of G's husband. Ritual works for males were managed by P, a son of the co-wife of the husband of the deceased who lived in another house.

Preparation

Many villagers had already gathered in the front yard[10] of the house of the deceased to prepare for the funeral when I arrived there around eight o'clock in the morning. Some of them were pitching a canopy over the front yard, others were cooking meals which would be served in the afternoon. At least one member from each household of the village came intermittently, delivered a fixed amount of rice and liquor, helped with some of the work, and usually returned home after a while.

G, who was barefoot throughout the funeral, walked to the stand set up in the front yard to offer some food and drink to the deceased. The stand

[8] Some villagers told me that the word 'Sarat' was derived from the Hindi and Nepali word *shraddha*.

[9] I owe the use of the 'Panels' as an ethnographic device to Malkki (1995).

[10] A front yard is called *changpang* in Byansi. The dichotomy between *chyukhu* (inside of the house) and *changpang* is crucial in many rituals in Byans.

was a slate placed on a three-pronged branch about one-metre high. She washed away the food that was left on the slate using water drawn from the Mahakali River, then put some homemade bread on it and poured some liquor in a backhand grip.

Within the house preparations were continuing. In a room on the first floor, in which the main ritual would be performed, a small Tibetan-style collapsible table had been set out. Beside it, along the side wall, a box covered with cloth was placed, on which several ritual items such as small metal lamps were laid out. A set of folded and bundled traditional clothes and ornaments used by the deceased had been already placed in front of the box. Several plates of offerings, mainly snack foods and fruits, were carried in. The walls were covered with cloth, on which two posters of Hindu deities were put. Several villagers carried photos and clothes of their family members who had recently passed away and put them near the clothes of the deceased.

Going to Fetch the Bones (chije kan demo)

Later in the morning, P, a young male villager, and I went to a small bush on the outskirts of the town.[11] P carried a knife with him. According to some villagers it was to ward off attack by demons (*sina*). Three days after the cremation some of the deceased's bones had been placed in a metal container and buried in the ground there. P now dug the container up and wrapped it in a white cloth. The young man with us asked P whether or not it was necessary to give a thorny twig (*nache*) to demons,[12] but in the end they did not do so. Then we went back. On the way a male villager asked P, "Isn't it the old custom (*thum*) to carry [the bones] in a *barko*?"[13] P replied, "They said, 'You can also carry them by hand.'" When we reached the house, P first asked some elders who were there, "Shall I put this inside?" and then entered the house. I followed him. The case was placed in front of the clothes of the deceased.

Recitation of Buddhist Text

A Tibetan Buddhist monk[14] was already seated in the main room and had started to read from a Tibetan text. P, a male elder of the sub-clan (hereafter RT), and an elderly man from another sub-clan (hereafter JR), stayed in the room throughout the recitation.

---

[11] According to villagers this programme had to be done by an odd number of people. I was counted as a participant.

[12] A thorny twig is a necessary item for the performance of *changchimo*, the ritual of exorcising demons (*sina*) (Nawa 2002: 168-76, n.d. a).

[13] *Barko* is a thick white cloth used as a sort of women's shawl in their traditional clothes.

[14] This Buddhist monk (*kujo* in Byansi, cf. the Tibetan word *sku shabs* or *sku zogs*, which is a honorific term for lamas) was a Tibetan refugee.

Many plates of offerings, mainly snacks and fruits, were handed first to the deceased (i.e. to the plate on the box), then to the monk, and then to other participants in order of seniority from elder to younger. Several plates of food were also brought in. One of the elders present criticized the process, saying "Everything has been mixed [wrongly]. We have to treat separately things which belong to this house from things which belong to the families whose members' clothes have been carried in".[15] Next, a bottle of liquor from the household of the deceased was brought in and distributed in the same order.

Several more villagers brought sets of clothes, ornaments, and photographs of their own family members who had recently passed away. Each of them then carried a plate of food for his or her own deceased family member and put it in front of the clothes. JR explained to me that the purpose of setting out keepsakes of recently dead villagers and offering them liquor, a meal, and sweets is to invite them to come and take the newly deceased person along with them.

Villagers entered the room one by one, put flowers on the clothes of the deceased, tossed (*thumo*),[16] a small amount of grain (*sherje*) into the air, made a gesture of respect (*dhok*),[17] and offered liquor and/or sweets to the deceased. Some villagers gave her a cigarette. Liquor and sweets were then shared by the participants.

RT tried to hand a plastic bag of puffed rice (*phuru*)[18] to the monk, asking him to throw it to the bones and clothes of the deceased. The monk did not do it, but P took it and threw it to the bones several times. After this, only RT threw the *phuru* several times and a considerable amount remained unused when the monk ended the recitation.

The recitation continued for many hours after the villagers began to salute the deceased. Some of the villagers suggested that I should take a meal with them. I went out to wash my hands and returned to another room on the first floor of the same house. Many villagers had already come and eaten a plate of rice with lentil soup, the common meal for many ritual occasions in Byans. I also ate there. Villagers came to the house intermittently, ate a meal, adult men in the room, the women and children in the front yard, and then returned home.

---

[15]This utterance referred to the fact that they did not distinguish properly the offerings to the deceased from those to the ancestors whose clothes had been brought into the room.

[16]The word *thumo* means to worship, to celebrate, to offer, and to toss up at the same time (Nawa 2002: 164-8, n.d. a).

[17]*Dhok* refers to the gesture of holding out one's hands towards the feet of the person to whom one is expressing respect (and then to join one's hands together before one's own breast).

[18]*Phuru*, called *murmura* in Hindi, is thrown towards the effigy of the dead in Gwon (Nawa n.d. b).

The recitation was still going on when I entered the main room again. In the meantime, the monk took a short rest. He drank a cup of Tibetan tea and started talking with people in Byansi on the difference between Rang and Tibetan traditions.

The monk: We Tibetans (*Pang mang*) say that we must not use meat in funerals.

A villager: According to our tradition (*thum*), meat is indispensable because the deceased has no body.[19]

The monk went out once, came back and continued his recitation until evening, taking several short breaks from time to time. Villagers who sat near him poured Tibetan tea into his cup several times.

During another break, RT, one of the oldest males of the sub-clan, muttered his discontent: "I threw *phuru* several times, but others did not do it at all. Much has still remained." Some minutes later he went on: "In Pangjungkhu people threw away Gwon [the traditional funeral]. In Yerjungkhu[20] they do it even now. We stopped it, saying that it was too expensive. In Yerjungkhu people make an effigy, but here it is enough if there is a *kujo* (Buddhist monk). In the past we played the drums [for funeral], but we gave that up too."

After the Recitation

The monk finished his recitation in the evening. Murmuring some phrases, he wrapped the book with white cloth. He then talked with some villagers about their religion again, asking "Is there no *se yamo*[21] in Changru?" Other villagers talked with each other about the procedures and necessary items of the next part of the ritual.

A bottle of liquor was brought into the room and handed to the monk after a twig was put into it. The monk offered it (*thumo*) to the deceased by pulling the twig out of the bottle and sprinkling drops of the liquor into the air. Other participants tossed (*thumo*) some grains into the air.

P and another man from the sub-clan of the deceased put offerings such as rice, liquor, milk, and holy water into a vessel, after asking advice on what should be included. Several villagers said that the offerings (mainly sweets and grains), already placed separately on a piece of cloth, should be kept separate.

Women came into the room, one after another, put flowers in front of the photograph of the deceased, tossed up the rice grains, made a gesture of

---

[19] This probably referred to the sacrifice in *rhasimo*. See below.

[20] Yerjungkhu and Pangjungkhu are subregions in Byans (Nawa 2000). Changru lies in Pangjungkhu.

[21] A sacred recitation explained in the next section.

respect (*dhok*), and went out again. Some male members of the sub-clan followed them.

The vessel was carried out after a while. According to the villagers, younger female consanguineous relatives (*chame rhingsha mang*)[22] of the deceased have to carry it outside the residential area and throw it away. Several villagers came to take back the clothes and photographs of their recently deceased household members. The monk also went home with his book.

People then discussed where the bones should be carried.

P: Where to place it? In the front yard of the house?

People: To the north.
To the south.

G: I cannot manage to go any places where it should be brought finally. I am busy with my work in the school. But I may have time to go to the south. It is totally impossible to go to Kailash.

People: You should carry them to the north, it would be better to carry them to the north than to the south.

It was concluded that the bones would be carried to the north towards Kailash, after being kept temporarily on the northern fringe of the town. People then started preparing the next part of the funeral, confirming with each other the number of bottles of liquor, the persons required, and so on. The bones were put into another small metallic case and wrapped in white cloth. RT was still complaining, "I threw *phuru* many times. No one else did it. ..."

To Place the Bones

People started making the gesture called *yimo*, turning round one's hand inward horizontally, but they made no sounds while doing so. Normally there is sharp yelling ("hohohohoho ...") at this part of the funeral. I had the impression that the gesture occurred rather sporadically.

P, JR, two other male villagers, and I went out to place the bones outside the town temporarily. Just outside the house we met several women coming back with the now empty vessel. We went northwards again. On the way, P threw the remaining *phuru* on the banks of the Mahakali River. He placed the bones behind a rock near the place where he had dug them out in the morning. Then he covered the spot with several stones and bound a piece of white cloth (*daja*) to a bush nearby. JR told P, "Say [to the deceased] 'I will bring you to the north.'" R tossed grains of rice and

[22] *Chame* literally means a daughter while *rhingsha* means a younger sister. *Mang* is a plural suffix.

splashed some drops of liquor with his finger directly from two small bottles which they had brought with them. The participants then shared the liquor. Then we returned. On the way P threw the two bottles away on the river bank.

Soknu thumo

The room used for the funeral had already been cleaned up when we returned. Some villagers told me that the room should not be cleaned by the younger consanguine females (*chame rhingsha mang*), but by 'married-in' women (*kutisha mang*[23]). Another villager explained to me that now that the deceased had become an ancestor (*simi*), they would worship their ancestors next.

Two bottles of liquor (called *soknu*[24]) were brought into the room. JR offered (*thumo*) the liquor, sprinkling it from the bottle using the twig. Other participants were P, RT, another male villager, and I.

People discussed about the amount of rice to be cooked in the purifying ritual called *rhasimo* the next day, and then checked whether or not all the villagers had visited the house to eat a meal in the afternoon.

G: R, the *lama* (shaman), did not come.

JR: He always eats only in his house [due to the taboos he follows as a shaman]. You can ask him to come [to see the votive lamps].

Seeing the Votive Lamps (kyu)

Before 8 o'clock in the evening, a person from each household that had sent the clothes of its recently deceased member brought one handmade votive lamp made of dough. A two-sided drum and a harmonium were also carried in, not for this occasion but for the programme called *kirtan* to be held at night. M, a village shaman (called *lama* in Byansi), arrived. People discussed the norm that one must not drink liquor or smoke cigarette during *kirtan*.

M: It is possible to smoke in the room over there [i.e. in the next room of the same house], isn't it?

R, another *lama*, arrived. P lit all the votive lamps. M and R sat down and stared at each *kyu* one by one, with great care and almost without moving. Children were sent out of the house and the room became totally quiet.

---

[23]The word literally means married women. In the context of ritual, it often refers to the women married into a village or a clan, and is used in contrast with *chame rhingsha mang*, who will eventually marry out.

[24]See Nawa (2002: 175, n.d. a) for details.

R: All are good. There is something wrong in only one *kyu*.
People: Why is it wrong?
Please see *sherje* (grains used in ritual).

R took out a handful of rice grains (*sherje*) from his pocket, looked through them on his right palm, moved them between his right and left palms, and blew onto them. After doing these things several times, he threw some grains hard to the *kyu*, put several others into it, reshaped and blew into it, and set it out again.

R: Now there is no problem.

R went out of the room a moment later. Before going home, he carried out another divination using *sherje* in the next room at the request of several villagers.

A Meal

A plate of food, identical with the one served in the afternoon, was served firstly to relatives from other villages and then to villagers of Changru. After the meal, some guests stayed in the house until *kirtan*, while others went back home.

Kirtan[25]

At night the villagers and other relatives came to the house in twos and threes. They sat in the house, jam-packed, and sang Hindu religious songs celebrating Ganesha, Narayana, Siva, and other famous Hindu deities. The songs are very popular in Nepal as well as in India, often broadcast and tape-recorded, though the words of some of the songs have been translated into Byansi. A middle-aged male villager who worked at the village health post took the lead as he had extensive knowledge of such songs. I found that many villagers did not always remember the words. Clearly there were considerable differences between the villagers as regards their knowledge of these songs.

Purification (rhasimo)

The next morning I had to leave Darchula to extend my non-tourist visa. Several villagers told me later that they had carried out *rhasimo* on that day. They sacrificed a goat to worship their ancestors and to purify themselves.[26] They said that the meat of the goat was cooked and served to clan members and affines.

This description of a Sarat performed by the villagers of Changru in

---

[25]*Kirtan* is a word of Sanskrit origin used in both Nepali and Hindi.

[26]*Rhasimo* is the infinitive of the verb which means to purify. Some villager referred to the same ritual by the term *chokhyasimo*, a loan word from Nepali (*chokhyaunu*), which also means to purify.

1995 presented in Panel A cannot be said to exemplify a 'typical' Sarat. The details of Sarat were different at several levels each time that it was performed. Some differences were the outcome of carelessness on the part of some participants. That several set of clothes and dishes were brought into the room at the improper time and that the large part of *phuru* remained unused would be examples of this kind of carelessness. In the second place, people often omitted or simplified some parts of a ritual arbitrarily, saying "It will be OK too" or "It will be the same". When P fetched the bones, for instance, he did not use thorny twigs and carried them in his own hands, though other participants had pointed out the more authentic way of doing it. On another level, participants had to choose one alternative or another at several points intentionally. Thus G chose to be barefoot throughout the ritual,[27] and asked a Buddhist monk, rather than other religious specialists, to read a text. Finally, some differences depended on the village. The ritual of *chije kan demo*, for instance, was carried out quite differently in Tinkar, another village of Nepalese Byans. There they used a long white cloth called *am*, and grains of *phuru* were thrown to the umbrella of the man who held the bones on the way. This diversity at many levels, both institutional and accidental, makes it impossible to present a typical way of doing Sarat in detail. At the same time, it is clear that every villager was firmly convinced that they were performing Sarat, despite these considerable differences. In other words, the conviction that they were carrying out Sarat preceded and encompassed the diversity which inevitably occurred in the actual ritual process.

GWON: THE 'TRADITIONAL' FUNERAL

Sarat is not the only form of funeral in Byans. Nor is it the 'traditional' way of performing funerals. Changru villagers knew that they had held their funerals in quite a different way several decades before. Villagers agreed that it took much more time and money to carry out Gwon, the older funeral, than to do Sarat. People were not so sure, however, about the details of Gwon, and the village elders' accounts did not always coincide with each other in every detail. It is not certain to what extent this discrepancy was caused by the actual diversity of Gwon, and to what extent it was generated by their lapses of memory. The following, for instance, is what one male elder in Changru told me. Though his version is not the one and only explanation of Gwon, it roughly coincides with the versions of other elders in the village.

[27] It was a well-known norm that close relatives of the deceased should be barefoot while they were in mourning. However, many villagers pointed out that it was an old custom and that it was one's prerogative to decide whether or not to follow it.

Panel B: A Digest of an Interview in Byansi with a Male Villager of Changru

[Regarded as one of the most knowledgeable people on ritual in Changru, this villager was in his sixties and had worked as the chief organizer and negotiator with other villages in many important inter-village rituals such as marriage ceremonies.]

The first day is called *shin gusimo*. Villagers collect wood (*shin*) for flaming torches and take them to the house of the deceased. Affines (*shisha mang*) of the deceased offer a meal.

The second day is called *ja jyungsimo*. A special type of unleavened bread called *ja*[28] is cooked in the house of the deceased. A *ya*, an animal into which the soul of the deceased will be induced, is fetched. If the deceased is male, it should be a male yak, and if female, a female yak. People take it to the place where the bones of the deceased have been kept, put his or her clothes on its back, and then bring it to his or her house. A special funeral drum called *jendol* is played. *Ja* is offered to the deceased. The household of the deceased offers a meal to participants.

The third day is called *jo yepsimo*. The *ya* is again taken to the place where the bones of the deceased are being kept. The bones are put into a pair of special miniature boots called *simi bapche*, and are put on the back of the *ya* together with the clothes of the deceased. The *ya* is then taken to the front yard of each house in the village. Each household gives it liquor and a meal. In the evening, an effigy is made of wooden sticks and a basket, which is clad with the deceased's traditional clothes. Then *se yamo* is recited throughout the night.

The next day, *pongsimo*[29] is carried out after the *se yamo* is complete. The *ya* is released outside the village and chased away, and the villagers are not concerned about what happens to it thereafter. The sticks and several other items used in the funeral are thrown away. The bones are placed on a high mountain. The 'bad' (*yada*) works are now at an end and people come dancing back to the village. After that, liquor is ritually offered in the house of the deceased.

The fifth day is called *rhasimo*. Each close male relative of the deceased shaves his head and takes a bath. A goat is killed. The household of the deceased invites all the villagers and ritually offers liquor and a special type of small deep-fried bread called *rhe koto*.[30]

It is said that long, long ago, a Gwon took nine days, not five. But we

---

[28]According to him *ja* is a kind of *loni koto*, deep-fried unleavened round bread. Unlike the usual *loni*, it has no projections. Another villager told me that it is a kind of pancake made of bitter buckwheat (*sile koto*).

[29]Raypa (1974: 108) glosses this word as "an act to release *ya*".

[30]According to him, *rhe koto* is a small *loni koto* with two projections.

no longer know what was carried out each day. Then Gwon was shortened to five days, and then to three days.

What this informant did not explain about *se yamo* is that it is an oral recitation with a peculiar tune, carried out by turns by two males called *se yakcha*. It takes nearly a whole day to recite all of it. According to the speaker of Panel B, it consists of six parts. In the first part the process of the particular Gwon that they are carrying out is recounted. The story of the origin of Gwon and three other mythical stories of the ancestors of Rang follow. In the last part, the soul (*rhame*) of the dead is sent by words of *se yakcha*s from south of the Himalayas to the land of ancestors which, according to the recitation, lies in Tibet, further to the north of Mount Kailash. The *se yakcha*s teach the soul of the deceased which paths to follow, how to deal with dangers, how to respect the deities of each place along the way, and so on.

We should be careful not to regard Panel B, one individual's account from memory, as the very programme of Gwon held in Byans many decades ago. Nor can we assume that in the past Gwon was always held exactly in the same way taking the same amount of time. By putting various sources together,[31] however, we can safely say that the funerals in Changru were once carried out in the form of Gwon, that Gwon differed greatly from Sarat, and that the focus of Gwon lay in offering food and liquor to a yak which incarnated the soul of the dead person and in the recitation of the long oral tradition called *se yamo* with the aim of sending the soul to the land of the ancestors. It is also certain that villagers of Changru are well aware of the existence of the two forms of funerals, Gwon and Sarat, and of the fact that Gwon is the 'ancient tradition' of Rang whereas Sarat was introduced in the recent past as a 'new tradition'.

AIMS AND RESULTS OF THE ATTEMPTED CHANGE

The discussion above clarified the fundamental difference between the two types of funeral, Gwon and Sarat. Why has their funeral changed so drastically? Villagers unanimously asserted that they had altered it intentionally. What sort of intention, then, brought about the change?

I would like to begin by quoting words of two male villagers, in their sixties and seventies respectively, who still remembered the occasion when Sarat was performed in Changru for the first time.

---

[31]Sherring recorded the process of Gwon in the early twentieth century (1907, 1993: 120-32). Raypa, an anthropologist from Indian Byans, wrote a detailed account of Gwon (1974: 96-109) from his own Hinduistic point of view. These two accounts basically coincide with each other as well as with Panel B.

Panel C: An Abridged Translation of a Statement Given by a Male Villager of Changru in Byansi

[The speaker, in his sixties, was one of the richest traders in Byans, and a leading village intellectual who graduated from a high school in India.]

About forty-five years have passed since we stopped Gwon. It was people older than we who decided to stop it, so as to follow (or according to) the world.[32] Several young people who had received school education said this first. We decided to do Sarat, as Bahuns[33] used to say various things [about us]. G *kaku*, BS *kaku*[34] and others said this first. Educated people. The elders said "No" and a quarrel arose. But we stopped Gwon, saying "Just do as the Thakur[35] do."

At the outset, it was said that we would offer food in the afternoon, would do *kirtan* at night, and would prohibit liquor and *bidis* (Indian-style leaf cigarettes) at night, so as to purify [our practices]. But it turned out to be wrong. We had supposed that we were doing *kirtan*, but liquor and meat were offered and we smoked *bidis*. A *kirtan* turned out to be a *baira*.

Panel D: An Abridged Translation of a Statement Given by Another Male Villager of Changru in Byansi

[The speaker, in his seventies, was a successful trader who was literate in the Devanagari script.]

These days Sarat has changed a lot. The first one [i.e. the first Sarat] was of JS *kaku*, TS's father. When we decided to adopt Sarat as our custom, the women did not agree. They said, "Let us do Gwon." Then [the men] explained, saying, "To chase a yak away is not good for Nepal." Then the women also slowly came to consent. At that time, everyone had gone to Tibet for trade. So we decided to cut our relations (*ti kilmo*) with anyone who did not come. '*Ti kilmo*' means never to go for any occasion, even for their weddings. Everyone came. Sarat started. We held *kirtan* that night. All came, men and women, and held *kirtan* until dawn. After dawn, we held *kirtan* until evening. When we do *kirtan*, we must not consume liquor, cigarette, or *bidis*. Nowadays, totally collapsed [*sic*]![36] People go outside to have liquor and cigarettes.

---

[32] *Duniya ga anusar*. Both *duniya* and *anusar* are words borrowed from Hindi and Nepali.

[33] 'Brahman' in Nepali.

[34] *Kaku* is a kin term which refers to distant patrilineal consanguineous relatives one generation above the speaker. The word was also used to address them frequently. The speaker thus regarded the reformers G and BS, both already deceased at that time, as people one generation higher than him. G had been a schoolteacher in Changru and BS had once been a very influential politician.

[35] An honorific title in Hindi.

[36] '*Bilkul khatam*'. Both are loan words from Hindi.

The two statements above, together with other evidence, elucidate the following points. First, the change of funeral rituals in Changru from Gwon to Sarat was carried out in the middle of the twentieth century mainly by young educated male villagers, despite the objections of male elders and females. Secondly, they tried to abandon the then existing scheme of funerals totally, replacing it with an entirely different scheme which they believed was authentically Hindu and suitable for the Hindu Kingdom of Nepal. Thirdly, at least two different aims motivated the change: to represent the Rang positively to the outside world according to the standards of high-caste Hindus, and to cut down the time and money expended for the ritual.[37]

The villagers of Changru were exceptional in Nepal for the ease with which they were able to access modern primary education in the first half of the twentieth century. It takes less than one hour to walk from Changru to the school in Garbyang, a village in Indian Byans, and many children in Changru were educated in Hindi there.[38] Some of these students then went on to high schools in the hill stations in Kumaon. Recognizing that they were not Indian but Nepali, and that the socio-political situation of South Asia had changed radically due to Indian independence and the end of the Rana regime in Nepal, they constituted a small but influential reformist group in Changru in the middle of the twentieth century.[39] Their movement, ranging from negotiations with Tibetan officials to abolish their collection of land taxes,[40] to establishing a school in Changru, as well as reforms of their rituals and other customs, can be described as modernist, nationalist, and Hinduist, all at the same time. The change from Gwon to Sarat was the most drastic reform they introduced in the religious sphere.

The two elders, our informants also pointed out that Sarat as performed in the 1990s was significantly different from what was originally planned and carried out in Changru in the mid-twentieth century. Though the exact way in which the first Sarat was performed is not entirely clear, it is almost certain that a meal was offered to villagers and other affines, the Hindu text, *Garud Puran,*[41] was read, probably by a village youth, and *kirtan* was held at night, singing songs in praise of several major Hindu deities. Comparing this basic scheme with the description in Panel A, the difference is quite obvious. In the latter, many distinctly Rang idioms such as liquor and

[37]Raha and Das (1981) treat yak as the sacrificial animal in Gwon. However, I know no one in Byans who would admit to the truth of this statement.

[38]This fact partly explains the extremely high literacy rate of 'Byansis' in Nepal.

[39]Several younger educated youth from Changru went to Kathmandu and became top-level officials in several Nepalese public corporations.

[40]On Tibetan taxes on land in Byans before 1955, see Manzardo et al. (1976: 97).

[41]*Garuda Purana* in Sanskrit. What was actually read might have been a Hindi translation of it.

phuru were used. Gestures of *thumo* and *yimo* were also typically Rang (Nawa 2002: 170-3, n.d. a). There was even a Tibetan lama. True, these educated Changru youths achieved great success on the level of discourse. Every villager of Changru insists that he or she is Hindu, when asked (cf. Nawa 2000). On the level of actual performance, however, their attempt at Hinduization did not accomplish quite as much as they had planned. Actual Sarats in the 1990s were quite eclectic. It would be extremely difficult for an outside observer to deduce from Panel A that Sarat was the relatively new Hinduistic form of funeral introduced just several decades earlier.

How and why has this discrepancy grown up, then? The sentence "*Kirtan* turned out to be *baira*" from Panel C is highly suggestive here. *Baira* are improvised songs sung on the night of marriage ceremonies and other auspicious occasions at which deities, legendary ancestors, and traditions of the Rang are often celebrated. *Kirtan*, on the other hand, are songs with fixed words to praise major deities in the Great Tradition of Hinduism. The sentence above thus seems to suggest that the intentional attempt by young village leaders, which Himalayan anthropologists would call 'Hinduization',[42] had been, as it were, neutralized by the actual practices of ordinary villagers.

The suggestion that the ban on liquor, *bidi*s, and cigarettes was often ignored can be understood in the same way. In many rituals in Byans, liquor was one of the most important and indispensable offerings to their deities. It was strongly recommended for the host of an important ritual to provide *bidi*s and cigarettes to guests as a sign of his hospitality. Furthermore, in a traditional Gwon, liquor was offered on *pongsimo* and according to some villagers several *baira*s were sung that night. There would have been no taboo on liquor or cigarettes on these occasions. It is highly likely that, even within the scheme of the new funeral, villagers acted according to their usual way of carrying out rituals, and thus the attempted 'Hinduization' through *kirtan* turned out to be incomplete.

Why, then, did this infiltration of 'traditional' items and practices occur? One important reason lies perhaps in the fact that the plan for the first Sarat drawn up by the young village leaders was very rough and sketchy from the point of view of actual ritual performance; they could not regulate each action and gesture of the participants. This is absolutely natural. To prescribe every movement and every gesture of each participant of a ritual in detail beforehand is virtually impossible. Furthermore, participants in a ritual cannot carry it out abstractly. If, in the first Sarat, the programme made by the leaders did not prescribe the details of the ritual, the villagers could not but recollect and rely on the knowledge of the funerals with

[42]Here I apply this problematic word only to the movement initiated by several individuals who had the clear intentional aim to change some part of their rituals based on the criteria of Hindus who live to the south of the Himalayas.

which they were familiar. Although, as trans-Himalayan traders they certainly had considerable knowledge of both Hindu and Tibetan Buddhist rituals, the only type of funeral they knew well enough to perform themselves would have been the Gwon ceremony, which they had conducted for years. So they borrowed several small items, gestures, and procedures from Gwon when performing the new funeral ceremony of Sarat. This feedback from the older ritual made the actual performance of the new one markedly eclectic. This process of selective recollection and reiteration of the now abolished old funeral must, inevitably, have been repeated for years, each time Sarat was performed, with a certain amount of deviation. Villagers remembered more or less the way they performed the ritual each time, which in turn could be referred to as precedents in the next funeral. Such tiny memories were accumulated as folk knowledge of how to carry out Sarat, to the extent that many villagers could articulate the way of doing it in some detail. Consequently Sarat was established as 'a new tradition',[43] though quite different from what the initiators had intended. This is my hypothetical reconstruction of the formation process of Sarat in its current eclectic form.

If the discussion above is convincing, the next point to consider is the discrepancy between the two modes of discourse on funerals: the ideological one that objectifies in order to evaluate it in relation to the dominant outside discourse, on the one hand, and the pragmatic mode, on the other, that tries to perform each part of it smoothly and correctly. As Panel A clearly shows, what mattered within the actual process of ritual was the latter, i.e. discussion about concrete details of who should do what, when, where, how, and if any differences of opinion arose, why. They debated with each other quite frequently in order to carry out the funeral properly (cf. Lewis 1980: 19-24). These sorts of exchanges, not necessarily totally consistent with each other, seldom corresponded directly to any abstract and more coherent argument such as "Let's abandon Gwon, otherwise Bahuns will despise us."

It is not that the former village leaders always treated their funeral abstractly as they themselves were undoubtedly compelled to deal with particular dos and don'ts within each real ritual occasion. Nor was it that ordinary villagers remained permanently caged in the non-reflexive world of habitus. Being trans-Himalayan traders, for centuries they had had plenty of opportunity to compare and evaluate their 'tradition' (*thumcharu*) with the Great Traditions both north and south of the Himalayas (Nawa 2002: 131-55). In Panel A, some villagers discussed with the monk the differences between the Rang and Tibetan ways of performing funerals. The people of Changru I met had certainly internalized both abstract and

---

[43] *Nuda thum* in Byansi.

pragmatic modes and used them according to context. It should be noted, however, that considerable differences existed among the villagers as to the degree of internalization of these two modes.

One theoretical corollary of the discussion so far is that people do not always speak about ritual in the same way. Bourdieu's famous dichotomy between doxa and orthodoxy/heterodoxy (1977: 168) is not totally convincing in this regard. First, both can coexist within one ritual. The boundary between them, moreover, is not always clear, as one participant may perform a ritual without any conscious reflection on it while others discuss acrimoniously the authentic way of doing it. Furthermore, it is difficult to locate properly within Bourdieu's schema the kind of short pragmatic utterances occurring within the ritual discussed above. They are different from what he calls doxa, as these utterances are made in full awareness of some difference, real or supposed, intentional or accidental, between what is being done and what should be done. On the other hand, they are much more sporadic and fragmentary than ordinary debates on orthodoxy and heterodoxy, though it is always possible that one of these tiny discrepancies in ritual practice could turn out to be the focus of a major debate over orthodoxy. Finally, it was the accumulation of these small utterances, as well as corresponding practices, that had brought about the transformation of Sarat from the Hinduistic style of funeral once intended to the current more eclectic one with its considerable diversity.

I would like to point out also that the shift from Gwon to Sarat in Changru had had an enormous impact to the villagers' 'cosmology'. For instance, Gwon had provided a clear answer to the question about the place where one would go after death. As mentioned earlier, the last part of *se yamo* was intended to teach the soul of the deceased the correct way of travelling from the southern hills of the Himalayas across Byans to the ancestors' land in Tibet. The soul was supposed to reach the land called *Chunglung Gui Patu* and become an ancestor. Sarat, by contrast, gives no clear vision on the destination of the soul of the dead, at least to ordinary villagers. The following conversation in Panel E clearly shows this.

Panel E: An Excerpt from an Interview Held in a Small Square in Darchula in Byansi

[RP, the interviewee, was a man in his fifties. He was a former Pradhan Panch (governmental village headman before 1990), the son of a powerful *lama* (shaman), and renowned for his extensive knowledge of Byansi oral tradition.]

Nawa: Where does a human being go after death?

RP: I don't know. (Pause) It is said that a person with good *karma* will have a good rebirth, while one with bad *karma* a bad one. I don't know anything except this.

Nawa: Isn't that the Buddhist account?
Youths: Hindus also say the same.
RP: It is not totally suitable to call [our tradition] Hindu, nor is it to call it Buddhist.
Nawa: What happens to the dead according to *se yamo*?
RP: *Se yamo* is just like a recitation of the Bahuns. It shows the way for the peace of the soul.[44]
Nawa: In what language is it done?
RP: In the language of Rang. It is very long. It is recited without looking in any books. It takes a whole day. If a soul listens to what the *se yamo* tells it, it can go adequately. It is better than the recitations of Bahuns. It teaches, "You have to go through this way." We don't know the details any more.

In this interview, RP relied rather vaguely on the South Asian notion of *karma* and reincarnation to explain the destination of the soul of the deceased, instead of the land of the ancestors mentioned in *se yamo.*[45] This explanation may be consistent with the content of Hindu texts recited by Brahmans in some Sarats. It is, however, quite inconsistent with the actual ritual process of Sarat, especially with the gestures of *yimo* and *soknu thumo* for ancestors which indicate that the soul of the dead has turned into an ancestor. In Byansi the soul of the deceased before Sarat or Gwon is called *rhame,* and distinguished from an ancestor called *simi.*[46] And a *se yakcha,* a high school teacher from a village in Indian Byans where Gwon was still carried out answered the question above immediately: "[He or She] will go to *Chunglung Gui Patu.*"

It is undoubtedly wrong to treat this inconsistency only negatively, as a discrepancy or cultural disorder. Indeed, villagers of Changru did not seem to experience any serious problems because of this inconsistency. We should be careful not to introduce false problems of supposed logical contradiction by our presupposition that every native explanation of ritual and cosmology must be totally consistent (cf. Goody 1977: 52-73; Latour 1987: 201; Boyer 1990: 1-23). At the same time, it is obvious that both the composition and the villagers' explanations of Sarat were indeed much less consistent than those of Gwon. The introduction of the new way of performing funerals has made their conception of the posthumous world less

---

[44]He used *atma* for soul and *shanti* for peace. Both words are derived from Sanskrit.

[45]It is wrong, however, to think that Hindus in the southern hills of the Himalayas have a single consistent view on the destination of the soul of the dead. Bennett (1983: 35-40) demonstrates the vagueness as between their conceptions of salvation (*mukti*), reincarnation (*samsara*), heaven (*swarga*), and the abode of the ancestors (*pitrilok*).

[46]This conception resembles the notion of many Hindus that a *pret* is transformed to a *pitr* after several rituals. For the Parbatiya case, see Bennett (1983: 92-120).

coherent, but the villagers of Changru did not seem to find any serious problems with it.

Another related point from Panel E is the way in which the recitation of *se yamo* was discussed and evaluated in relation to foreign religious texts. This juxtaposition, very common among the villagers of Changru, was certainly one example of the point discussed above that they often objectified their own rituals and placed them in relation to other religious traditions that they knew. Indeed, *se yamo* was often explained as the equivalent of the texts recited in Hindu and Buddhist funerals in that, according to them, all of them are supposed to show the right paths for the soul of the deceased to follow.

This equation, moreover, was not merely theoretical. Many villagers of Changru resorted to the equation to justify the replacement of *se yamo* by the Hindu *Garud Puran*. They substituted the former with the latter, because, according to them, they were more or less the same. Nor has the *Garud Puran* been the only substitute for the old *se yamo*. They told me that they hired Brahmans in some Sarat, asked some villagers to read the *Garud Puran* in others, and called a Tibetan Buddhist monk to read their religious texts in still others (as in Panel A).[47] In other words, *se yamo*, *Garud Puran*, and Tibetan Buddhist texts were not only considered to be parallel on the level of discourse but also as alternatives to be chosen in the actual performance of funerals (though in Changru *se yamo* had been banned for decades).

Here could be the key to solve the problem I posed at the beginning of this chapter, i.e. why the people of Changru sometimes hired Buddhist monks to their funerals despite their strong denial of any Buddhist affiliation. In Panel A, the only thing the monk did for villagers as a Buddhist monk was to recite the text. Villagers did not trouble themselves as to the actual content of the text, being simply convinced that it was beneficial for the soul of the deceased. Nor did they care about the other things he did as a Buddhist monk, such as wrapping the book with a white cloth and murmuring some phrases after the recitation. On the other hand, at some points the monk acted not as a Buddhist monk but as an honoured participant of a Rang ritual, notably when he offered a bottle of liquor in the typically Rang manner. In the occasional conversation with some villagers, moreover, he himself admitted that the funeral was based on the tradition of the Rang, quite distinct from that of Tibetans. All these details strongly suggest that the participation of the Buddhist monk is nothing but optional. There can be no direct correspondence between what the monk recited and

---

[47]I have not attended any funeral in Changru in which the *Garud Puran* was recited either by a Brahman or by a villager. On the other hand, the villagers of Tinkar, another village in Nepali Byans, had the option of three types of recitation in their funerals: *se yamo*, *Garud Puran*, and a Tibetan Buddhist text, and I attended each type of funeral there.

what the villagers performed. If the Buddhist monk is substituted by a Brahman or a villager, it would make little difference to the ritual process of Sarat. What was crucial to complete a Sarat was to have someone recite an authentic text for the deceased. As long as this was done, the villagers were wholly convinced that they had carried out a Sarat properly based on their 'new tradition', regardless of the text recited. The fact that the people of Changru sometimes invited a Buddhist monk to their funeral, therefore, does not necessarily mean that they are Buddhists.

To invite a Tibetan Buddhist monk was, I would argue, a rather ironic consequence of the Hinduistic reform movement in the middle of the twentieth century to change radically their style of carrying out funerals. The process may be reconstructed as follows. There had been no place for either Buddhist monks or Brahmans in traditional Gwon. When *se yamo* was substituted with the *Garud Puran*, many villagers understood the change by roughly equating the two ways of recitation to the deceased. This equation was extended in the meantime, enabling the villagers to hire not only Brahman priests but Tibetan Buddhist monks as well. Cost-cutting had been one of the main reasons to introduce Sarat, and in Byans Buddhist monks were not only more accessible but probably less expensive as religious specialists than Brahman priests since around 1960 when several monks started to live there as refugees.

The eclectic and hybrid nature of Sarat in the 1990s was symbolically visible in the arrangement in the room in the Sarat of Panel A. Hanging on the wall to the left of the Buddhist monk were two posters of Hindu deities, under which the bones and traditional Rang clothes of the deceased were placed. Sarat, originally introduced as the Hindu funeral, was in the meantime established as a 'new tradition' of Rang, allowing recitation by both Brahman priests and Buddhist monks.

CONCLUSION

Funerals in Changru changed fundamentally in the twentieth century. As we have seen, it was young educated village leaders who advocated the replacement of Gwon by Sarat in the middle of the twentieth century. They almost certainly executed the plan for two reasons: to curtail the time and money spent on funerals, and to cope with the discourse of high-caste Hindus. Ordinary villagers, while accepting the change of the basic plan of funerals, more or less tacitly reintroduced into Sarat many items, gestures, and procedures of the now abolished Gwon, in order to perform their ritual in actual situations. Thus Sarat revealed its hybrid nature, which was not anticipated by the original planners of the ritual. Furthermore, villagers utilized, perhaps equally tacitly, a relativistic perspective on the recitation for the deceased as well as the claim of cost-cutting of ritual to enable themselves to hire not only Brahman priests but also Buddhist lamas for their new type of funeral.

At first sight it might seem to be that the shift from Gwon to Sarat could well be analysed by such concepts as Sanskritization, Hinduization, and modernization.[48] True, we can say that the village leaders in the middle of the century certainly intended to Hinduize and modernize their funeral, and that they were really successful in doing so on the level of discourse as no villager of Changru today denies that they are Hindus. A brief comparison with the Thakalis of Thaksatsae, also well known as trans-Himalayan traders, would be suggestive at this point.[49] Many scholars have pointed out that, in the first half of the twentieth century, several prominent Thakali leaders brought about sociocultural reforms, from the ban of eating yak meat to the introduction of the new clan names, in order to Hinduize or de-Tibetanize their culture. Both cases can be analysed as an example of intended cultural change by leaders of a Himalayan society who were exposed to the gaze of the Hindu state of Nepal and its elites. The difference lies first in that the reformist leaders of Changru were not dominant and wealthy traders and tax collectors but young, educated, but otherwise ordinary, male villagers. Second, the reform in Changru, unlike the Thakali one initiated several decades earlier, was carried out largely in the context of post-Rana Nepal. Third, the reformers did not intend to change the customs of all Rangs. The Rangs in India had implemented their own reforms, also at the level of the village, in the context of colonial and post-colonial India (Srivastava 1953, 1966; Raha & Das 1981). Moreover, Changru is the only Rang village in Nepal in which Gwon has been totally abolished.

The complex and in part unexpected consequences of the introduction of Sarat, however, makes the straightforward application of such simplistic '-ization' categories wholly impossible. As I have discussed elsewhere (Nawa 2002: 161-3, n.d. a), the concepts of Sanskritization and Hindu-

[48]Raha and Das (1981) analysed the change of funeral of what they called Eastern Bhotias in two phases: Sanskritization and then the revival of their traditional religion due to the changes of the socio-political situation in India.

[49]To summarize adequately the debate on sociocultural change among the Thakalis in the twentieth century, and even to list up the major contributors from Tucci, Kawakita, and Fürer-Haimendorf to many Thakali intellectuals today, is beyond the scope of this chapter. For the three distinct ways of representing Thakalis from the outsiders' point of view, see Iijima's ethnography (1982) in which the history of Thak Khola is sympathetically described focusing on the Subba family, Vinding's comprehensive ethnography (1998) in which not only Thaksatsae Thakalis but also so-called Panchgaunle are discussed, and Fisher's critical ethnography (2001) which reflects multiple voices but almost solely from the Thaksatsae Thakalis.

ization, though frequently used in Himalayan ethnography,[50] are no more than a rough and loose summary of but one sphere of ongoing and complex processes. What should be discussed ethnographically is not the applicability of the categories but the actual mechanisms and extent of specific changes[51] as well as the relative significance of the aspects called Sanskritization or Hinduization within larger sociocultural processes.

Another interpretative strategy would be to conclude that the endeavour of village leaders to change their funeral completely was prevented in many places by the concrete resistance of essentially conservative ordinary villagers.[52] This line of argument, though certainly attractive and illuminating, is only partly applicable to this case. Certainly, villagers did not carry out Sarat in a totally different way from the now abandoned Gwon. If, however, villagers had been merely conservative, would they have omitted many details of the ritual on the one hand and started hiring Buddhist monks on the other?

This paper is based on several theoretical assumptions summarized below.[53] I hope that the discussion above is consistent with, even if it does not vindicate, these largely a priori assumptions. One can discuss rituals abstractly. For the educated young village leaders, it was evidently not very difficult to objectify their funeral, to compare it with funerals of other peoples, and to advocate reform based on the then dominant discourse of high-caste Hindus and of modernists. What is hopelessly difficult, perhaps practically impossible, is to make a plan of a new ritual concrete enough to be materialized down to the smallest details without tacitly relying on ritual habitus of their own or of outside religious specialists. And indeed the leaders failed to do this.

In any case, no one can perform a new ritual abstractly. Whenever one acts in ritual, one must recollect some antecedent, to imitate, to manipulate, or to reverse it, or repeat embodied actions semi-automatically. Thus in Sarats, in the middle of the twentieth century, villagers were forced to fill up the blanks that remained in the master plan in order to carry out their funerals. Panels C and D strongly suggest that they did so mainly by recollecting the specific details of the now abolished funeral rituals of

---

[50]Classical examples include Iijima (1963) and Jones (1976).

[51]Both Vinding (1998) and Fisher (2001) relativize the Subba-family-oriented view of the Thakali reform movement. Allen (1997) points out the "fragmented and piecemeal" manner in which Thulungs "Hinduize" themselves. Also see Höfer's very attentive multifaceted analysis of the processes of "Hinduization" among the Tamangs (1986).

[52]Boyer (1990) strongly criticizes the confusion of the repetitive nature of what he calls 'tradition' with conservativism.

[53]The last three paragraphs of this paper are strongly influenced by the discussion of a Japanese Deleuzean anthropologist, Tadashi Yanai (1995).

Gwon. Later, the memories of what they had done in previous Sarats must also have been recollected and played a part.

The process of recollection within a ritual cannot be totally anticipated beforehand. First, every reiteration of the same ritual inevitably contains some amount of creativity as no two rituals can be performed under exactly the same conditions. Nor is the range of recollection determined positively. In Changru, not only did people recollect details of the abandoned ritual while carrying out the new one. They sometimes recollected something quite foreign to Rang, hanging posters of Hindu deities on the wall, for instance. One might, on the other hand, fail to recollect some part of the ritual, as was often seen in Panel A. One could even imagine hiring Buddhist monks without being converted to Buddhism. The limit of the range of recollection, however, is defined each time only negatively, mainly through the exchange of practical utterances within the actual process of the ritual. Unless pointed out as wrong, each ritual act, or even lack of it, is temporally supposed to be legitimate. Those utterances, though sometimes deductive and in many cases based on some utterance of the same kind in the past, are not necessarily consistent with each other and are often fairly ad hoc. Just as abstract debates about a ritual can hardly determine the full details of it, concrete, contextual, and pragmatic utterances about how to carry out each part of a ritual properly hardly build up a totally coherent picture of the ritual. Actual Sarats are performed in between these two types of utterance. The former determined the framework beforehand while the latter settled each detail of it extemporaneously within each performance. And it was the accumulation of this latter sort of utterance that metamorphosed Sarat from a modern Hinduistic funeral into the present hybrid eclecticism. There is thus good reason for Sarat to be eclectic, somewhat more so than its predecessor Gwon.

REFERENCES

Allen, N.J. 1997. 'Hinduization: The Experience of the Thulung Rai', in D.N. Gellner, J. Pfaff-Czarnecka, and J. Whelpton (eds.), *Nationalism and Ethnicity in a Himalayan Kingdom*, pp. 303-24. Amsterdam: Harwood Academic Publishers.

Bennett, L. 1983. *Dangerous Wives and Sacred Sisters: Social and Symbolic Roles of High-Caste Women in Nepal*. New York: Columbia University Press.

Bourdieu, P. 1977. *Outline of a Theory of Practice,* tr. R. Nice. Cambridge: Cambridge University Press.

Boyer, P. 1990. *Tradition as Truth and Communication: A Cognitive Description of Traditional Discourse*. Cambridge: Cambridge University Press.

Dahal, D.R. 1994. 'Poverty or Plenty: A Case Study of the Byansi People of Darchula District of Far Western Nepal', in M. Allen (ed.), *Proceedings of an International Seminar on the Anthropology of Nepal: People, Problems and Processes*, pp. 36-48. Kathmandu: Mandala Book Point.

Fisher, W.F. 2001. *Fluid Boundaries: Forming and Transforming Identity in Nepal*. New York: Columbia University Press.

Fürer-Haimendorf, C. von. 1988 (1975). *Himalayan Traders: Life in Highland Nepal*. Delhi: Time Books International.

Goody, J. 1977. *The Domestication of the Savage Mind*. Cambridge: Cambridge University Press.

HMG. 2058 v.s. 'Adivasi Janajati Utthana Rashtriya Pratishthanko Vyavastha Garna Baneko Ain (An Act Made to Provide for the Establishment of National Foundation for Development of Indigenous Nationalities)', *Nepal Rajpatra (Nepal Gazette)* 51, *Atiriktamk* 67: 39-58.

Höfer, A. 1986. 'Wieso Hinduisieren Sich die Tamang? (Why do the Tamang Hinduize Themselves)', in B. Kölver (ed.), *Formen Kulturellen Wandels und Andere Beiträge zur Erforschung des Himalaya*, pp. 33-52. Sankt Augustin: VGH Wissenschaftsverlag.

Hoon, V. 1996. *Living on the Move: Bhotiyas of the Kumaon Himalaya*. Delhi: Sage Publications.

Iijima, S. 1963. 'Hinduization of a Himalayan Tribe in Nepal'. *Kroeber Anthropological Society Papers* 29: 43-52.

——. 1982. *Himalaya no Kanatakara: Nepal no Shogyo Minzoku Thakali Seikatsushi (From across the Himalayas: An Account of the Life of the Thakalis, a Merchant Community in Nepal)*. Tokyo: Nippon Hoso Shuppan Kyokai (in Japanese).

Jones, R.L. 1976. 'Sanskritization in Eastern Nepal'. *Ethnology* 15: 63-75.

Latour, B. 1987. *Science in Action: How to Follow Scientists and Engineers through Society*. Cambridge, MA: Harvard University Press.

Leder, S. 2003. *Zu einer Zeit, als Bäume und Gräser noch Sprechen Konnten ... : Sozioökonomie, Kosmologie und Mythologie der Rang-Shauka im Zentralindischen Himalaya (Once When Trees and Grasses Could still Speak ... : Socioeconomy, Cosmology, and Mythology of the Rang-Shauka in the Central Indian Himalayas)*. Frankfurt: Peter Lang.

Lewis, G. 1980. *Day of Shining Red: An Essay on Understanding Ritual*. Cambridge: Cambridge University Press.

Malkki, L.H. 1995. *Purity and Exile: Violence, Memory, and National Cosmology among Hutu Refugees in Tanzania*. Chicago and London: The University of Chicago Press.

Manzardo, A.E., D.R. Dahal, and N.K. Rai. 1976. 'The Byanshis: An Ethnographic Note on a Trading Group in Far Western Nepal'. *Contributions to Nepalese Studies* 3 (2): 83-118.

Nawa, K. 2000. 'Ethnic Categories and their Usages in Byans, Far Western Nepal'. *European Bulletin of Himalayan Research* 18: 36-57.

——. 2002. Nepal, Byans oyobi Shuhen Chiiki ni okeru Girei to Shakaihanchu ni kansuru Minzokushiteki Kenkyu (An Ethnographic Study on Rituals and Social Categories of Byans, Nepal and Adjacent Regions: Another Constellation of 'Modernity'). Tokyo: Sangensya (in Japanese).

——. n.d. a. 'Toward a Critically Eclectic Description of Ritual: Thumo and Changchimo in Byans, Far Western Nepal'. Manuscript.

——. n.d. b. 'Change and Diversity in Traditional Funerals in Byans and Adjacent Regions'. Manuscript.

Raha, M.K. and J.C. Das. 1981. 'Divergent Trends of Transformation among the Kumaon Bhotia of the Central Himalayas', in C. von Fürer-Haimendorf (ed.), *Asian Highland Societies in Anthropological Perspective*, pp. 250-65. Delhi: Sterling Publishers.

Rana Magar, B.K. 2057 v.s. 'An Ethnographic Study on the Shaukas of Byas Valley', *Janajati* 2 (1): 63-83.

Raypa, R.S. 1974. *Shauka: Simavarti Janjati (Shauka: A Borderland Tribe)*. Dharchula: Raypa Bradars (in Hindi).

Sharma, S.R. 2001. 'A Sketch of Byangsi Grammar', in Y. Nagano and R.J. LaPolla (eds.), *New Research on Zhangzhung and Related Himalayan Languages* (Senri Ethnological Reports 19), pp. 271-341. Osaka: National Museum of Ethnology.

Sherring, C.A. 1907. 'Notes on the Bhotias of Almora and British Garhwal'. *Memoirs of the Asiatic Society of Bengal* 1: 93-119.

——. 1993 (1906). *Western Tibet and the British Borderland: The Sacred Country of Hindus and Buddhists: With an Account of the Government, Religion and Customs of Its Peoples*. Delhi: Asian Educational Services.

Srivastava, R.P. 1953. '"Rang-bang" in the Changing Bhotia Life'. *The Eastern Anthropologist* 6 (3-4): 190-203.

——. 1966. 'Tribe-Caste Mobility in India and the Case of Kumaon Bhotias', in C. von Fürer-Haimendorf (ed.), *Caste and Kin in Nepal, India and Ceylon: Anthropological Studies in Hindu-Buddhist Contact Zones*, pp. 140-60. Bombay: Asia Publishing House.

Trivedi, G.M. 1991. *Descriptive Grammar of Byansi: A Bhotiya Language*. Calcutta: Anthropological Survey of India.

Ukyab, T. and S. Adhikari. 2000. *The Nationalities of Nepal*. Kathmandu: National Committee for Development of Nationalities, HMG Nepal.

Vinding, M. 1998. *The Thakali: A Himalayan Ethnography*. London: Serindia Publications.

Yanai, T. 1995. 'Soki to Hanpuku: Gendai Mapuche Shakai ni okeru Bunkateki Seisei (Reminiscence and Repetition: Cultural Genesis in Contemporary Mapuche Society)'. Unpublished Ph.D. dissertation, The University of Tokyo (in Japanese).

PART 3

FORMS OF 'SECULAR' ACTIVISM: RESISTANCE, NEGOTIATION, AND VIOLENCE

10

Bengalis Outside Bengal: The 1947 Partition of India and the Formation of a Bengali Displaced Persons' Colony in South Delhi, India

TETSUYA NAKATANI

> ... partition was a messy, long-drawn-out process. It was in no sense finally or tidily concluded in August 1947; indeed, one could argue that the process had just begun, and that it is still unfinished today.
>
> J. Chatterji, 'The Fashioning of a Frontier: The Radcliffe Line and Bengal's Border Landscape, 1947-52', in *Modern Asian Studies*

INTRODUCTION

The purpose of this paper is to consider an aspect of social dynamics in northern India by illustrating how the historical event of the Partition of India affected the social formation of post-Independence India.[1] As Chatterji (1999: 186), cited above, indicates, the Partition of India has been a long-lasting process and has had various impacts on Indian society. We can see one aspect of this among the refugees produced by Partition.

Scholarly interest in the Partition refugees has grown recently. To mention only a few, there are works on the Partition refugees' identities and historical processes (Chatterjee 1990, 1992; Tan & Kudaisya 2000),

[1] I am deeply grateful to the people of Chittaranjan Park, particularly the late Mr Jyotirndra Chakraborty, Mr B.B. Chakraborty, Dr Ananda Mukherjee, Mr Sritimay Das, Dr B.K. Bhattacharya, Mr A.K. Sen, Mr B.C. Das, Mr D.M. Sarkar, Mr Manjir Mukherjee, who helped me during my fieldwork. I wish to express my gratitude to Dr André Béteille and Dr Abhijit Dasgupta for their guidance. I would also like to thank my assistant Shantanu Deb and other friends in Chittaranjan Park.

movement and settlement processes (Nakatani 2000; Rahman & van Schendel 2003), politics and the rehabilitation movement (Chakrabarti 1990; Dasgupta 2001), experiences and memories (Chakrabarty 1996; Raj 1997; Samaddar 1997), the relation between nationalism and household worship (Ghosh 1998), gender and state (Butalia 1993; Das 1995; Menon & Bhasin 1998), and adaptation (Talukdar 1986; Waseem 1997). Literary works and narratives on Partition are well documented in Butalia (2000), Kaul (2001), Settar & Gupta (2002), and Bagchi & Dasgupta (2003).[2]

In this paper, I will focus on Bengali refugees in Delhi and illustrate how the allotment of land and the construction of a Bengali colony in South Delhi contributed to shaping a part of the subsequent urban development in the capital city. I will hereafter use 'displaced persons' instead of refugees to designate Bengali 'refugees' in Delhi, because, as we will see later, Bengalis do not regard themselves as refugees but as displaced persons and the official documents also use the term 'displaced persons'. After outlining the influx of Partition refugees to the city, I will take up the case of land allotments to Bengali displaced persons in South Delhi by the Indian government and argue that the rehabilitation of displaced persons apparently expanded the urban residential area and formed a culturally unique settlement in Delhi. The fact that the land allotment scheme was implemented long after independence meant that the Bengalis, who had previously lived scattered all over the city, came to live side by side, thus creating a centre of Bengali culture and society in the non-Bengali environment of Delhi. This has contributed to the complex multi-ethnic formation of the capital city.

THE EXPANSION OF DELHI AND THE REFUGEE INFLUX

The Partition of India in 1947 saw a mass exodus and exchange of refugees between India and Pakistan. As Pakistan consisted of two separated wings, West Pakistan and East Pakistan, an exodus of refugees occurred at both wings. According to the Census of India 1951, 4.7 million refugees came over from West Pakistan and 2.55 million refugees from East Pakistan. They were scattered in many places in India, but the major concentrations can be found in Punjab (50.5 per cent), Delhi (10.5 per cent), and Uttar Pradesh (9.5 per cent) among refugees from West Pakistan, and West Bengal (81.2 per cent), Assam (10.7 per cent), and Tripura (4.0 per cent) among refugees from East Pakistan (Government of India 1954).

---

[2] Haque (1995) reviewed studies on Partition refugees published up till 1990. Journals like *International Journal of Punjab Studies* 4 (1), 1997, and *South Asia* 18, 1995, have had special issues on Partition refugees. See also Nakatani (2003).

Delhi became one of the major destinations for refugees, particularly refugees from West Pakistan. Delhi had accepted 495,391 Partition refugees by 1951. Of half a million refugees, most came from West Pakistan regions like West Punjab (78.4 per cent), NWFP (9.0 per cent), and Sind (8.4 per cent), while the number of refugees from East Pakistan was only 3,674 (0.74 per cent of the total) (ibid.). As a result of the huge influx of refugees, there was enormous population growth in Delhi: the population rose by nearly 90 per cent between 1941 (917,939) and 1951 (1,744,072).[3]

Delhi was not prepared for this sudden and unprecedented influx. The first requirement was to provide them with immediate and temporary shelter. The camp at Kingsway was the largest in Delhi, having some 300,000 refugees. Other camps were established at Tibbia College in Karol Bagh and at Shahdara (Delhi Development Authority 1957, Chap. 1: 18). The next step was to provide the refugees with permanent rehabilitation. In addition to providing them with the houses left by departing Muslims, new townships were planned during 1948-50 by the Delhi Improvement Trust and the Central Public Works Department for the Ministry of Relief (Jain 2000: 115). Agricultural lands were acquired all around Delhi. A number of townships sprang up: Nizamuddin, Lajpat Nagar, Kalkaji, Malviya Nagar in the south, Rajendra Nagar, Patel Nagar, Moti Nagar, Ramesh Nagar, Tilak Nagar in the west, Kingsway Camp in the north (Delhi Development Authority 1957, Chap. 1: 18-19). They constitute some of the major residential and market areas of Delhi today. Business and shopping centres, schools, and other facilities were established at the same time. As a result, the urban Delhi area (agglomeration area) grew from 201.36 sq. km in 1951 to 326.55 in 1961, a 62 per cent decennial growth rate (Dupont 2000: 230).

The residential areas of refugees, or ex-refugees we should say, continued to develop. According to Datta, as the existing colonies expanded, their well-to-do inhabitants moved out to healthier and more select localities like Golf Links, Vasant Vihar, Greater Kailash, Ring Road, New Friends Colony, and Defence Colony (1986: 450), which now constitute some of the main residential areas in south Delhi. In short, the influx of the Partition refugees played an important role in the demographic and spatial expansion of Delhi after 1947.

---

[3]Though the highest demographic growth in the history of the capital was recorded in the 1941-51 period, population growth in Delhi in the post-Independence era has continued to be remarkable because of internal migration and the spatial expansion of the urban zone in all directions (see Dupont 2000). The population of Delhi (National Capital Territory) was 2,658,612 in 1961, 4,065,698 in 1971, 6,220,406 in 1981, 9,420,644 in 1991, and 13,850,507 in 2001 (Census of India figures).

ANOTHER STORY OF REFUGEE REHABILITATION IN DELHI: BENGALI DISPLACED PERSONS

The ethnic diversity of Delhi is a remarkable aspect of the city. The 'People of India' project, which was a comprehensive survey of ethnic groups in India conducted by the Anthropological Survey of India, identified 147 communities in Delhi (Ghosh & Nath 1996: xxii). Though the original population was Urdu-speaking and Hindi-speaking, Partition dramatically changed the demographic profile of Delhi. In particular, the huge influx from West Punjab has changed both demographic and socio-economic compositions of the city. They are either Hindus or Sikhs by religion, but they are both called 'Punjabis'. It is often said that Delhi is a city of Punjabis. The 'People of India' project states:

> The Punjabi refugees brought with them their business acumen and determination. They vowed to transform Delhi into a second Lahore … and to a great extent succeeded in doing so. Trade and commerce flourished. A sleeping political and administrative capital was transformed into a glittering industrial and business centre ... Here we find the blending of all the best in occidental and oriental, notwithstanding the dominating Punjabi factor.
>
> (ibid.: 3)

Though Punjabi refugees were the most influential and numerous in Delhi, this chapter will pick up another story of rehabilitation, that of the Bengalis and the history of the construction of their colony in south Delhi. Bengalis have migrated to Delhi for a long time and their presence should not be ignored in the history of Delhi. The 'People of India' project explains the importance of Bengalis in Delhi:

> The Punjabi population has increased greatly after the Partition, and has thereafter made a definite impact on the city. The Bengali-speaking population was introduced to Delhi in considerable numbers when the British shifted the capital from Calcutta to Delhi in 1912. Thereafter, they have multiplied and made their impact too. … (Ghosh & Nath 1996: 4)
>
> They first came as government employees on transfer and gradually moved on [to] other spheres and avenues of employment over the years and generations. Even five to seven decades ago, North Western India abounded with Bengali professionals … like doctors, engineers and academics. (ibid.: 86)

In Bengal they were called the *Bhadralok* class (middle-class Bengali

Hindus), who enjoyed better social positions in Bengal.[4] While they had an English education and were employed in Calcutta (West Bengal) as officers, lawyers, doctors, teachers, journalists, and so on, many of them had landed property in their native home in East Bengal. Following the transfer of the capital, Bengalis moved to Delhi on transfer and this stream of Bengali migration to Delhi continued up to Partition. Thus Bengalis in Delhi were displaced and lost their home in Bengal due to Partition. The case of Bengalis will demonstrate the longer process of the displaced person's rehabilitation and will highlight the multi-ethnic composition of Delhi.

It is unofficially claimed today that there are many Bengali settlements in and around Delhi having a total population of 500,000 (Kali Mandir Society 1998: 8). Bengalis in Delhi may be divided broadly into four categories: Bengalis who migrated from East Bengal before Partition and were displaced by Partition; Bengalis who migrated from West Bengal before Partition; Bengalis who migrated from East Bengal (East Pakistan) after Partition as displaced persons; and Bengalis who migrated after Partition as non-displaced persons. This paper will deal primarily with the first category, those Bengalis who migrated before Partition and found themselves displaced in Delhi, because they are the people who organized the association and appealed to the government for the construction of a Bengali colony. This, however, does not mean that the other categories are not included. In fact, the process of migration from East Pakistan to India continued long after Partition. Quite a few Bengalis migrated to Calcutta for education and got employed in Delhi after Partition. Their background is as displaced persons or rather refugees. The case study in this paper includes all categories.

The construction of the Bengali colony which is now called Chittaranjan Park took place over the whole period from the 1950s to the 1990s. Thus this case study equally illustrates post-Independence urban development in Delhi and the ethnic influence in it. Bengalis are conscious of their culture. In fact, they have created a 'mini Bengal' in Delhi.

---

[4] *Bhadralok* literally means the 'respectable people', the 'gentleman'. They constituted a cohort in Bengal society and played an important role in the British period. According to Munshi, *Bhadralok* can be distinguished in many ways: their position in society, education, speech, dress, style of housing, eating habits, occupations, associations, cultural values, and sense of social propriety. The most rigidly maintained feature was their abstention from manual labour. They valued landed property for the security and prestige that resulted from its possession. English education was essential to their desire for a progressive rise in social status, that is, they learnt English to seize the expanding opportunities under the British administration. Many of the *Bhadralok* were drawn from the three upper castes of Bengal Hindu society: Brahman, Kayastha, and Baidya (Munshi 1996: 33-4).

CHITTARANJAN PARK: THE CONSTRUCTION OF A BENGALI COLONY IN SOUTH DELHI

Background

Chittaranjan Park was formerly known as the 'East Pakistan Displaced Persons' Colony'.[5] There is an office of the East Pakistan Displaced Persons' Association (EPDPA) in the heart of the colony. Visitors may wonder that even half a century after Partition the organization that was named after East Pakistan and Displaced Persons is still operating. They cannot miss two big complexes situated opposite the EPDPA office: the Deshbandhu Chittarajan Memorial Society, named after a Bengali hero of the nationalist movement in colonial Bengal, which maintains a Bengali library and provides free medical services, and next to it the Bangiya Samaj, which publishes Bengali periodicals and often organizes cultural functions. If locals want Bengali cuisine, they can purchase their favourite fish and vegetables or can taste Bengali dishes at the restaurants in the market. When Bengalis wish to pray to Mother Goddess Kali, the principal goddess of Bengal, a neat and well-maintained temple complex of the Kali Mandir Society welcomes them. A number of religious and cultural programmes are organized there aimed at satisfying the religious needs of Bengalis.

The original residents of Chittaranjan Park were 'displaced persons' from East Pakistan. They do not identify themselves as refugees (*udvastu*) but as displaced persons (*vastuhara*). For them, 'refugee' means those who are uprooted and forced to leave their homes against their will due to disturbances. In other words, "refugees are those who were refused by their country".[6] They say that they were not rejected and forced to leave, because many of them were already in Delhi when Partition took place. But they are 'displaced' as they lost their home in East Pakistan.

The core group, which struggled to establish a new township for Bengalis, consisted of government employees who were transferred to Delhi. They formed an association called The Association of Central Government Employees Displaced from East Pakistan in 1954.[7] They appealed to the Indian government to provide them with rehabilitation. One of the oldest members explained:

> We were not refugees since we had served as government employees in Delhi even before Partition. But, we lost our home in

---

[5]The author conducted fieldwork in Chittaranjan Park from December 2001 to August 2002. The interviews quoted here were carried out in Bengali.

[6]Interview with Mr J. Roychoudury, a resident of Chittaranjan Park on 21 July 2002.

[7]This association was registered in 1960 under the Societies Registration Act XXI of 1860. See 'Constitution' as amended up to 2 February 1992, East Pakistan Displaced Persons' Association, Delhi.

> East Pakistan because of Partition. We have no home to go back to. What to do and where to go after our retirement? We appealed to the government to provide us with land.[8]

In addition to the fact that Bengal was divided and their home fell into a different state, East Pakistan, riots occurring in East Pakistan in 1950, particularly in Khulna and Barisal, persuaded them that they could no longer go home. Bengalis working in Delhi had wished to spend their years after retirement at home. The riots destroyed that dream (Mukhopadhyay 1979: 1).

Another aspect to the Bengalis' campaign was their observation that refugees from West Pakistan had been rehabilitated by the government:

> The government provided all conveniences and assistance to refugees from West Pakistan and established wonderful colonies like Rajendra Nagar, Patel Nagar, and Lajpat Nagar. However, the government had done nothing for displaced persons from East Pakistan (ibid.).

The present president of EPDPA made this point in the following way:

> Then Prime Minister Nehru granted rehabilitation to refugees from West Pakistan. The government established colonies for Punjabis. They got lands free or at very low cost. Why did they not do this for Bengalis from East Pakistan? We equally lost our home.[9]

The Process of Negotiation

Though the association began its organizational efforts from 1954, in the initial period it could not obtain any positive results. The members had several meetings at the residence of the then secretary, Mr Manindralal Dutta, and contacted many people. But the members were gradually disappointed. The following incident occurred at that time:

> In 1954 Mr Dutta with some other members visited the then Rehabilitation Minister Mr Meher Chand Khanna at his residence. However, Mr Khanna refused their demand and said, "There is no way to hear their words. Their demands should be rejected and we must take action against them if they demand such a thing." They were threatened by the Minister. (Mukhopadhyay 1979: 2)

According to Mr Subimal Das, one of the visitors who accompanied Mr Dutta, "We were forced out of Mr Khanna's residence" (interview 17 April 2002). As they were not officers of high rank, their voice was very weak. After this incident, Mr Dutta approached Mr S.P. Senvarma. He was a

---

[8] Interview with Mr P. Kanti Roy, one of the oldest members of EPDPA, on 24 July 2002.

[9] Interview on 15 December 2001 with the late Mr J. Chakraborty, who was president of EPDPA at the time.

Bengali originally from East Pakistan. He was joint secretary in the Ministry of Law when the association was registered in 1960 and later became Chief Election Commissioner of India. As Mr Senvarma recollects it,

> In August-September 1955 Mr Dutta invited me to the Association's annual meeting held at his residence. Some 15-16 members attended. At that time members of the association numbered only 25-30. They were all government employees. I understood their situation at the meeting ... and the incident at the minister's residence ... Then I thought the number of members should be increased. Who will listen to an association of only 25-30 members?
> (Senvarma 1973: 12)

Mr Senvarma advised the association to make an effort to increase the number of its members. Three or four years later there were around five hundred members. The more the Association sought publicity, the more its members increased. In 1956, Ms Ila Palchoudhury, a member of the Lok Sabha (Lower House), whose constituency was in West Bengal state, was welcomed as the president of the association, with Mr Senvarma as vice-president (Mukhopadhyay 1979: 3). The association continued its activities under the leadership of its secretary, Mr C.K. Mukherjee who was well known among elite circles in the Bengali community in Delhi. Their contribution, the publicity they brought to the association, and the concomitant increase in membership helped to bring their cause to fruition.

On 3 March 1960, the then Rehabilitation Minister Mr Khanna for the first time officially made an announcement concerning the rehabilitation of Bengalis in Delhi in the Rajya Sabha (Upper House):

> It is proposed to set up a colony in Kalkaji for displaced persons from East Pakistan who are already residing in Delhi and are gainfully employed in the Capital. The Central Public Works Department has been asked to prepare lay-out plans for the same.[10]

After this announcement, the membership of the association increased still further. The *Statesman* (7 March 1960) reported a meeting held in the same month in 1960:

> A meeting of the Association of Central Government servants dislodged from East Pakistan held on Saturday adopted its constitution which aimed at complete rehabilitation of its members within the Union Territory of Delhi. ... Mr S.P. Sen Varma, who presided over the meeting, stated that the Association had over 3,000 members and represented a population of nearly 20,000 displaced persons from East Pakistan ... A resolution passed by the meeting authorized the managing committee to make a representation to

[10] *Rajya Sabha Debates*, 3 March 1960, vol. XXVIII, p. 2594.

> the Rehabilitation Ministry. ... Over 1,000 members attended the meeting.

The association was renamed the East Pakistan Displaced Persons' Association (EPDPA) in 1962 to broaden the membership (Roy 1982: 25). Since displaced persons from East Pakistan were not only government employees but also included people working in the private sector, many voices came to Mr Senvarma to request him to include people other than government employees. The Rehabilitation Minister agreed with this, for political reasons. According to Mr Senvarma, the Minister was interested in their emergence as a new vote bank (Senvarma 1973: 13). In this way, the association accomplished its prime object through the pledge by the government to construct a rehabilitation colony and simultaneously became the body which represented all displaced Bengalis in Delhi.

The Allotment of Land

After the announcement by the Rehabilitation Minister in 1960, it took six years for the government to finalize the plan and schedule. During those six years, members of Lok Sabha questioned the Minister several times as to how the planning was progressing. For example, in April 1960 the Deputy Rehabilitation Minister answered that it was difficult to state at that stage when the plans would be ready.[11] In April 1963 the Rehabilitation Minister explained the main criteria for eligibility would be that the displaced person was already settled in Delhi, was gainfully employed, and did not own a house of his own and added that different sizes of plots would be developed to suit the needs of displaced persons belonging to different income groups.[12]

It was on 4 January 1966 that the government released a first Press Note to inviting applications for the allotment of plots of land. The government invited applications on two further occasions, in 1967 and 1977. According to the layout plan prepared by the Department of Rehabilitation, the total area of the colony was 218.3 acres with 2,072 plots in sizes of 320, 233, 160, and 533/450 square yards. The former three categories were for individual allottees and the last was for group housing.[13]

The first Press Note[14] defined the conditions of land allotment and eligibility for application. The land plots would be allotted on a ninety-nine-year-leasehold basis. A premium would be provisionally charged at

---

[11] *Lok Sabha Debates*, 16 April 1960, vol. XLII, p. 11949.

[12] *Lok Sabha Debates*, 18 April 1963, vol. XVII, p. 10411.

[13] Standard Note issued by the Department of Rehabilitation: Chittaranjan Park (Formerly known as E.P.D.P. Colony) near Kalkaji, New Delhi – Development and Allotment of Plots to Displaced Persons from former East Pakistan, 31 March 1980.

[14] Press Note issued on 4 January 1966, Department of Rehabilitation.

the rate of Rs.25 per square yard. Twenty per cent of the amount of the premium would be payable in advance and the balance in four equal annual instalments. The allottee had to complete construction of the house within a period of two years after possession of the plot, and so on. The eligibility for application was defined as follows:

(i) The applicant should be more than 21 years of age on the date of application.
(ii) The applicant or his wife/husband or any dependent member of his family, including unmarried daughters, does not own any house or residential plot anywhere in India.
(iii) The applicant is gainfully employed in the Union Territory of Delhi in any service/occupation or has been gainfully employed and has been continuously in residence therein from a date prior to the 31 March 1958.
(iv) The applicant is a bona fide displaced person from East Pakistan.

Then the Press Note defines 'displaced persons':

> Note-1:
>
> A 'displaced person' shall mean a person who was ordinarily resident in the territories now comprised in East Pakistan but who on account of civil disturbances or on account of the Partition of India, has migrated:
>
> (a) in the case of persons migrating from the district of Noakhali or the district of Comilla now forming part of East Pakistan, on or after 1 October 1946 and
> (b) in the case of persons migrating from any other areas in East Pakistan on or after 1 June 1947 to the territories now included in the Union of India, with the intention of taking up permanent residence within such territories.
>
> Note-2:
>
> The following persons shall also be eligible for the allotment of plots provided they had lost the use of their houses in Pakistan and have not acquired any house in any part of India:
>
> (i) Families of optee Government Servants[15] who are themselves displaced persons within the definition

---

[15]When the Partition of British India took place, the then government employees had an option, whether to serve the Indian Government or the Pakistan Government after independence. Interestingly, an ex-government employee in Chittaranjan Park first opted for the Pakistan Government expecting accelerated promotion in the new government. He later changed his option to the Indian Government. See also Rahman & van Schendel (2003).

(ii) Families with heads who had been gainfully employed in what is now India from before Partition in Government service or otherwise and are not displaced persons themselves within the definition, but whose other members migrated to India after the material dates.

To sum up, the above definition includes those who migrated from East Pakistan (East Bengal) either before or after Partition with a common condition that they had to have been gainfully employed and living in Delhi from a date prior to 31 March 1958. During interviews quite a few allottees mentioned that the condition regarding their place of origin in East Pakistan was not so difficult to fulfil. For example, those who were government employees had a description in their service book (record of the personnel section) that their original home was in East Bengal. Others had other documents such as border slips, migration certificates, or citizenship certificates that showed their place of origin. What was more difficult to establish was the condition of continuous residence in Delhi from a date prior to 31 March 1958.[16] Those in government service were liable to be transferred both inside and even outside India whenever they were so ordered. This condition limited the number of applications.

As a result, the government had to release a second Press Note on 13 August 1967 inviting more applications.[17] The Press Note stated:

> One of the conditions for the allotment of plots was that the applicant should be ... continuously in residence therein, from a date prior to the 31 March, 1958. This condition of continuous residence has adversely affected the case of some persons who went out of Delhi for short periods in the interest of public service. As some plots are still available after meeting the requirements of the applicants ... it has been decided that the condition of residence in Delhi may be relaxed.[18]

The condition was relaxed to include those who had lived in Delhi for a

[16]The reason why the date was fixed as 31 March 1958 is not clear. However, it conforms with the date of refugee rehabilitation in West Bengal. In West Bengal, those who migrated between October 1946 and March 1958 were designated as the 'old migrants'. They were the only people who were eligible for rehabilitation in West Bengal (Government of India 1976).

[17]It was not known how many plots remained available after meeting the requirements of the first allotment based on the first Press Note in January 1966. However, we can deduce the number from the statement of the Minister in charge. He mentioned in the Lok Sabha on 10 August 1967 (just three days before the second Press Note was issued on 13 August) that 1,317 persons had deposited money for the first allotment by the deadline announced by the government (Lok Sabha Debates, Written Answers, 10 August 1967). This means that some 700 plots (2,072 total plots minus 1,317 plots for the first allotment minus 55 plots for group housing) were still available for the second allotment.

[18]Press Note issued on 13 August 1967, Department of Rehabilitation.

total period of at least four years after Partition up to 31 March 1966.[19] The condition of 'continuous residence' was removed and the period of residence was shortened and counted 'in total'. In this Press Note, the rate of premium was changed and provisionally fixed at Rs.30 per square yard. Other conditions were the same as before. Applications were examined to check whether they met the conditions. Allotment letters were issued after the demarcation of the land plots and the levelling of the ground for construction.

At the same time as the second invitation for land allotment was issued, development work was implemented. Approximately 75 per cent of the planned development work had been completed by August 1967.[20] Infrastructure such as roads, drains, sewerage, sumps, overhead tanks, and pipelines for water supply, was completed, as was 40 per cent of the electrification in July 1969.[21] One year later, in July 1970, development work in the colony was, by and large, completed and about 100 houses were under construction.[22] Local people still remember the construction of the colony's first house in 1969. To celebrate the building of the first house, the EPDPA arranged a community feast on the site on 2 October 1969 (Roy 1982: 25).

In the early 1970s there were still relatively few constructed houses. The fringe areas of the colony looked like a 'jungle' and it was common to see snakes around.[23] Nonetheless, the residents began to organize community activities. For example, some residents formed a committee to organize the centenary celebration of Chittaranjan Das, after whom the colony was later named. The ceremony was first held on December 1970 and Prime Minister, Indira Gandhi attended. In 1971 the first community *puja* (Hindu festival), Sarasvati Puja, was celebrated. The first market site was established. The inaugural ceremony of a cultural organization, Bangiya Samaj, was held. In 1973 the Kali Mandir Society, which at present runs the biggest Hindu temple complex, was established, and so on (ibid.: 26-8).

As mentioned, the colony, originally known as EPDP Colony, was renamed Chittaranjan Park in 1973. There were two suggestions for a new name: 'Chittaranjan Park' and 'Purbachal' (meaning 'eastern region' or 'the locality of Easterners'). The former was proposed by those who organized the centenary celebrations of Chittaranjan Das and the latter by the EPDPA, the founder group of the colony. A referendum was held among the residents and the former suggestion was adopted. The former group tried to

---

[19] Ibid.

[20] *Lok Sabha Debates*, Written Answers, 2 August 1967, vol. VIII, p. 16307.

[21] Ibid., Written Answers, 31 July 1969, vol. XXX, p. 108.

[22] Ibid., Written Answers, 27 August 1970, vol. XLIV, p. 104.

[23] Interview with Mr Pijush Kanti Roy on 24 July 2002.

irnpress on residents "the importance of the name Chittaranjan Park not only to commemorate a man (Chittaranjan Das) but his ideology of sacrifice and service as well".[24] The members of the EPDPA proposed the name 'Purbachal' because it recalled their origins in the east and because it was already in use and accepted by many residents in the colony. They opposed the idea of Chittaranjan Park because "it is difficult to select one (among many great men) depending on the standard of their fame and patriotism".[25] This renaming of the colony was a symbolic incident and can be regarded as a milestone which transformed the colony from the transitional to the permanent, from 'a colony of displaced persons' to 'a colony of Bengalis'.[26]

Despite the fact that the colony had passed the initial period of construction and was proceeding to the stage of community formation, a plan to allot further land was announced by the government, which caused serious confusion and initiated another period of long struggle in Chittaranjan Park. The Department of Rehabilitation issued a third Press Note on 14 January 1977, ten years after the second Press Note. The conditions of eligibility were the same as the second allotment. In this Press Note, it was mentioned that the Department of Rehabilitation had a few plots for allotment to individuals and that these would be granted to displaced persons from erstwhile East Pakistan.[27] The actual number of available plots was not declared. In the end only eighty applicants received plots.

What was different from the previous two allotments was that this third allotment produced many people who could not get plots despite the fact that they were equally declared as 'eligible' as others who succeeded in getting allotments. Some of them did not accept the result and started appealing both to unlucky applicants and to the government. The leader of this movement, Mr B.C. Das, explained:

> In 1977 more than 1,600 persons applied. Among them 794 persons were declared as eligible to allotment. However, the allotment was done for only 80 plots. 714 (794 minus 80) persons remained. We were equally declared eligible. We thought it was not fair. We must have the same right to get plots. The selection of allottees

[24]B.M. Bardhan & P.C. Dhar, 'The Dream and the Reality', a souvenir titled 'Chittaranjan Bhavan Inauguration on 16 January 1993', issued by Deshbandhu Chittaranjan Memorial Society (no page number).

[25]*Purbachaler Katha*. Quarterly Publication of the EPDPA 1(2), 1972 (no page number).

[26]In this period there were already many refugee colonies for Punjabis which adopted the names of national heroes such as Lala Lajpat Rai (Lajpat Nagar), Sardar Vallabhbhai Patel (Patel Nagar), Bal Gangadhar Tilak (Tilak Nagar), and so on. By naming the colony after a Bengali hero, the people of Chittaranjan Park asserted themselves as the equal of Punjabis and simultaneously marked the locality as Bengali.

[27]Press Note issued on 14 January 1977, Department of Rehabilitation.

> was done by drawing lots. We collected the names of applicants there and made a name list. We called a meeting near Udyog Bhavan on 21 April 1978 and decided to form an association. Our twelve-year campaign began.[28]

The association was named the 'Association of Displaced Persons from East Pakistan Declared Eligible for Allotment of Plots in Delhi'.[29] This association was later officially registered. Initially they sought the cooperation of the EPDPA, but they were unable to get its support and therefore had to campaign independently for the realization of land allotments. After a long and painstaking effort, in 1984 the government decided to allot plots to them[30] and the actual implementation began around 1990, depending on the information of allottees. Their plots were not distributed in the main area of Chittaranjan Park but at its fringes.

Lastly, two group housings called DDA Flats, constructed by the Delhi Development Authority, should be mentioned. They were for low-income groups (LIG), particularly those who engaged in manual and skilled labour services such as tailors, cooks, barbers, or petty shopkeepers. They were also allotted flats as displaced persons from East Pakistan.

THE RESIDENTS OF CHITTARANJAN PARK: A SURVEY

This section will analyse some sociological aspects of the allottees in Chittaranjan Park. As Chittaranjan Park was established for displaced persons whose eligibility for land allotments was specifically defined by the government, the common characteristics of residents are supposed to be that they are displaced persons who migrated from East Pakistan and have been in Delhi for a certain period. On the other hand, there seems to be a simplistic common image of residents of Chittaranjan Park, that residents of Chittaranjan Park are well-off government employees who migrated to Delhi long before Partition and have been working there ever since.[31] This image may derive from the fact that those who initially took the initiative were government employees. We will reconsider the above image of Chittaranjan Park by looking at some basic sociological characteristics of the residents, such as the place of origin, time of arrival in Delhi, caste, academic career, and occupation. This data shows that the residents of Chittaranjan Park are in fact rather diverse.

---

[28] Interview with Mr B.C. Das, on 25 April 2002.

[29] 'Appeal', a mimeograph issued by the Association of Displaced Persons from East Pakistan Declared Eligible for Allotment of Plots in Delhi, 23 May 1978.

[30] A letter from Minister of Parliamentary Affairs, Sport and Works & Housing, 4 June 1984.

[31] This image of Chittaranjan Park residents was very often recounted to the author during his fieldwork both inside and outside Chittaranjan Park.

To gather the data I conducted a household survey in August 2002 with a sample of 122 households. Chittaranjan Park consists of twenty blocks and two DDA Flats. I selected a five per cent sample from every block and from each DDA Flat using the 2002 resident directory (*Purbachaler Katha*) issued by the EPDPA. The figures in the tables indicate the number of households.[32]

Table 10.1 shows the place of origin of each household. The first thing to note is that not all residents of Chittaranjan Park are allottees. Twelve of the 122 sample households were non-allottees. They had purchased or were renting flats in the open market. Of the 109 allottees for whom data was

Table 10.1: Place of Origin (by household)

Place of Origin	Allottee	Non-Allottee	Total
East Bengal			
Dhaka	25	0	25
Faridpur	15	3	18
Mymensingh	9	0	9
Bakarganj	8	2	10
Noakhali	8	0	8
Sylhet	7	0	7
Chittagong	6	0	6
Tippera	6	0	6
Khulna	6	0	6
Nadia	5	0	5
Jessore	2	0	2
Rajshahi	1	0	1
Other than East Bengal			
West Bengal	3	5	8
Assam	2	1	3
Bihar	1	1	2
Delhi	1	0	1
Uttar Pradesh	1	0	1
Madhya Pradesh	1	0	1
Karachi	1	0	1
Myanmar	1	0	1
Unknown	1	0	1
Total	110	12	122

Source: Author's own fieldwork.

[32] In some households, though, the first generation has already expired and the second generation takes the position of head. In such cases, too, the figure indicates the place of origin of the first generation.

available, 98 (89.9 per cent) had their origin in East Bengal.[33] The others were from West Bengal, Assam, Bihar, Delhi, and other places. Though some of them had never lived in East Pakistan, they received land because their ancestors originated in East Bengal. Some men received plots in the names of their wives.

Table 10.2 shows the year of first residence in Delhi. Of the allottees for whom the data was available, only 17 (16.3 per cent) had started living in Delhi before Partition. This figure clearly shows that the popular image of Chittaranjan Park residents is far too simplistic. Some allottees came to present Indian territory, particularly Calcutta (Kolkata), for higher education and were employed in Delhi before Partition. This stream further continued during and after Partition. The disturbances and instability in East Pakistan impelled them to migrate.

Among those who came before Partition, the experience of Mr Asok Chakraborti was typical:

> I was born in Dhaka in 1926 and migrated to Howrah, West Bengal, in 1945 because my elder brother had been working for the railways there. I completed my Bachelor's degree from Calcutta University and came to Delhi to join the Ministry of Finance in 1956.[34]

As with Mr Chakraborti, it was a widely observed trend that Hindus from East Bengal shifted to Calcutta for higher education and employment. Mr Prakash Roy similarly migrated before Partition, but his story was different. He was not displaced but his family was:

Table 10.2: Year of First Residence in Delhi (by household)

Year	Allottee	Non-Allottee	Total
Before Partition	17	0	17
In 1947-49	14	1	15
In 1950s	41	1	42
In 1960s	26	0	26
In 1970s	4	4	8
In 1980s	1	3	4
In 1990s	0	2	2
Others	1	0	1
Unknown	6	1	7
Total	110	12	122

Source: Author's own fieldwork.

[33] The 'Place of Origin' in Table 10.1 shows the district name as it was in East Pakistan.

[34] Interview with Mr Asok Chakraborti on 23 August 2002. The names given here are pseudonyms.

> I was born in 1925 in present Kustia district in East Bengal. I shifted to Birbhum district in West Bengal in 1937. I stayed with my uncle and joined Vidyasagar College. After completing my degree, I joined the Ministry of Agriculture in Delhi in May 1947. After Partition, I opted to serve in India. Muslim colleagues opted for Pakistan. In 1952 my father migrated and joined us. He was forced out of Pakistan by the attacks of Muslims. He had to surrender most of his possessions. He did not work after migration since he was very aged already.[35]

Some allottees feared violence and instability in East Pakistan and sought opportunities in India. The family of Mr Kumar Ghosh is an example of this. They first migrated inside East Bengal and later, after Partition, to India:

> We migrated from Dhaka to Dinajipur [the border district between East and West Bengal] because our mother feared oppression by Muslims. We permanently shifted to Bihar state in India in September 1947 and then shifted to Calcutta in 1948. I was only 11 years old. I graduated from Presidency College in Calcutta and joined the Ministry of Foreign Affairs in 1958. My father was a prominent lawyer in Dhaka, but he was engaged with income tax office in India. He was no longer a big lawyer in India. Loss of identity was the most difficult problem.[36]

Furthermore, allottees included those who took flight from violence and disturbance after Partition. Despite their statement that they are not refugees, some allottees were de facto refugees, as another case, that of a sixty-six-year-old man, Asutosh Chakraborti, illustrates:

> We came to Calcutta in 1950. We were forced to leave because of disturbances. The whole of East Pakistan had fallen into turmoil. As we had no relatives in Calcutta, we were like beggars. We spent a few months in a camp in West Bengal. We lived in a tent. After that I shifted to Calcutta. Though my condition was severe, I resumed my studies and graduated. I experienced hardship beyond expression. After graduation, I joined the Ministry of Information in Delhi in 1955.[37]

Table 10.3 shows caste affiliation. Taking just the allottees (i.e. excluding those who came later), out of 106 for whom the data was available, 97 (91.5 per cent) come from the higher castes (Brahman, Kayastha, and

---

[35]Interview with Mr Prakash Roy on 22 August 2002.

[36]Interview with Mr Kumar Ghosh on 28 March 2002.

[37]Interview with Mr Asutosh Chakraborti on 18 August 2002.

Table 10.3: Caste (by household)

Name of Castes	Allottee	Non-Allottee	Total
Kayastha (scribe)	43	3	46
Brahman (priest)	40	7	47
Baidya (traditional doctor)	14	0	14
Baishya (merchant)	2	0	2
Namasudra (boatman, agriculturist)	2	1	3
Buddhist	1	0	1
Goala (milkman)	1	0	1
Napit (barber)	1	0	1
Tili (oil trade)	1	0	1
Yogi (mendicant)	1	0	1
Unknown	4	1	5
Total	110	12	122

Source: Author's own fieldwork.

Baidya); these are precisely the castes that predominate among the *Bhadralok*. The following two tables (Tables 10.4 and 10.5) equally tend to show that the allottees were *Bhadralok* in that they put importance on education and occupation, in particular on service (see note 4).

The fact that Chittaranjan Park has few lower-caste residents is partly a result of the fact that services outside Bengal were mostly monopolized by the *Bhadralok* class throughout the British period and partly because after Partition the upper and middle castes migrateu from East Pakistan earlier than the lower castes. This tendency had an effect on the demographic character of Chittaranjan Park.[38] Though I did not carry out research to confirm it, it seems that there are quite a few lower castes from West Bengal around the market area working as skilled or manual labourers. In addition, it is said that there are many newcomer Bangladeshis around Chittaranjan Park and in different areas in Delhi.

Table 10.4 shows that 78 (79.6 per cent) allottees out of available 98 samples hold a Bachelor's degree and above. Most of them are highly qualified persons in comparison to average educational standards in India.

[38]In Chittaranjan Park 55.4 per cent of allottee households (56 households out of 101 for whom data is available) migrated before 1947 and 31.7 per cent of allottee households (32 households) migrated between 1947 and 1949 from East Bengal to present Indian territory. This figure indicates that many residents of Chittaranjan Park either migrated in the :tish period or shortly after Partition, though their migration to Delhi in many cases occurred later. It is said that the migrants between 1946 and 1949 were old migrants who had pre-Partition ties of occupation or kinship with West Bengal, belonged to upper and middle castes, and tended to gravitate to urban areas. Following the outbreak of communal conflict in Khulna in December 1949, migrants from East Pakistan were chiefly rural – peasant proprietors, traders, and artisans (Chatterjee 1990: 72-3).

Table 10.4: Educational Background (by household head)

Education	Allottee	Non-Allottee	Total
Ph.D.	4	3	7
Doctor of Medicine	2	0	2
Master	18	0	18
MBBS (medical)	5	0	5
Bachelor	49	4	53
Diploma	3	0	3
Class 12	5	0	5
Class 10	9	3	12
Under Class 10	3	0	3
Unknown	12	2	14
Total	110	12	122

Source: Author's own fieldwork.

Table 10.5 indicates that they are generally oriented to service rather than business. These service personnel constitute the core group in Chittaranjan Park.[39] The stress on higher education and service is found in the history of many allottees throughout, before and after Partition. Mr P.K. Majumdar was one such person:

> I was born in a village in Jessore district. My father was a Talukdar (landowner) and engaged in the jute trade. I still remember my friends and Durga Puja (religious festival for the goddess). Life was easy. We commuted by boat and steamer, seeing trees and birds. When I was eighteen years old, I moved to Calcutta in 1944 for higher education. Later, I was employed by a publisher. In 1959 I was transferred to Delhi head office. I worked as editor until my retirement.[40]

R.S. Mukherjee and S.C. Roy migrated after Partition:

> I was born in Faridpur. My native village in east Bengal was like my mother. I cannot forget it. In 1949, I came to stay with my uncle in Calcutta. I could not continue my study in East Pakistan due to disturbance. I got a border slip and registered myself. I studied art in a college for five years in Calcutta. I joined the Ministry of Education in Delhi as an artist in 1960.[41]

[39]Quite a few of these people did not move in as soon as Chittaranjan Park was developed, because Chittaranjan Park was far away from their workplace. Rather, they shifted to Chittaranjan Park after retirement.

[40]Interview with Mr P.K. Majumdar on 29 August 2002.

[41]Interview with Mr R.S. Mukherjee on 23 August 2002.

Table 10.5: Occupation (in household)

Occupation	Allottee	Non-Allottee	Total
Government services	65	1	66
Professionals*	16	4	20
Office worker in private company	15	2	17
Army	5	0	5
Business	5	2	7
Skilled labour+	3	1	4
Housewife	0	2	2
Domestic servant	1	0	1
Total	110	12	122

Source: Author's own fieldwork.
Notes:* 'Professionals' includes doctors, journalists, editors, architects, priests, engineers, professors, teachers, painters, and consultants.
+ 'Skilled labour' includes cooks, tailors, and barbers.

> I was born in Mymensingh and came to Calcutta in 1953 when I was sixteen years old. I came to India alone because there was no education, no scope in East Pakistan. I passed Bachelor and Master's in technology and Ph.D. in electronics in Calcutta University. After working in Calcutta for some time, I joined the Delhi Electric Research in 1962. I got the opportunity which I would not have got if I were in East Pakistan.[42]

This data illustrates the characteristics of the residents of Chittaranjan Park. First, allottees include not only displaced persons in their sense but also de facto refugees who directly and indirectly suffered from the disturbances in East Pakistan and sought their opportunities in India. Second, the number of those who migrated and worked in Delhi long before Partition was limited. Some allottees migrated during and after Partition. But the stream of migration continued even after Partition. Third, the purpose of migration was for higher education and employment, or flight from disturbance, or both. Fourth, allottees mainly consist of so-called *Bhadralok* middle-class people. They are high caste, educated, and service holders. Fifth, contrary to the image that they are all well off, though it may well be true that they are not poor, not all the allottees are rich. In fact, there are many categories among government employees and, as mentioned above, those who led the EPDPA movement were forced out of the Minister's residence because they were low-ranking employees. Allottees included all ranks from clerks to

[42]Interview with Mr S.C. Roy on 22 August 2002.

top-ranking IAS (Indian Administrative Service) officers and three categories of land were allotted to them depending on their respective ranking in the government. In addition, there are some people who had to give up the land they were entitled to, because they were unable to pay the advance (deposit) money to the government. Finally, today's Chittaranjan Park also includes non-allottee Bengalis. This author's survey counted twelve such persons. Six of these live in rented flats and six had purchased flats from allottees. They include Bengalis from both West and East Bengal. Though such residents are few in number, their presence shows that Chittaranjan Park is no longer exclusively a colony for allottees but also attracts other Delhi Bengalis.

FORMATION AND DEFORMATION OF A MINI BENGAL

Since the end of the 1960s Chittaranjan Park has brought together more than two thousand allottees and their family members who had lived scattered all over Delhi, thus creating a centre of Bengali settlement. Of course, Chittaranjan Park is not the only Bengali settlement in Delhi today. Durga Puja, the most famous Bengali Hindu festival, is celebrated in over 250 places in Delhi, so there are supposedly about 250 Bengali settlements of different sizes.[43] However, Chittaranjan Park is undoubtedly the biggest Bengali colony. The frequency and scale of various religious and cultural functions in other areas are not comparable to those in Chittaranjan Park. That is why non-allottees desire to live in Chittaranjan Park. Most of the non-allottees explained that they shifted to Chittaranjan Park in order to enjoy its Bengali environment.

Nowadays, nearby areas such as Govindpuri and Alakanada have become satellites of Chittaranjan Park. Bengalis come to settle in these areas because they are very close to Chittaranjan Park. They can taste the Bengali flavour and at the same time the cost of living (the price of land and house rents) is lower than in Chittaranjan Park itself. Many non-resident Bengalis who live far away regularly come to Chittaranjan Park to attend functions, to visit friends and relatives, and to purchase fish in No.1 Market.

Some organizations play an important role in maintaining and promoting Bengali culture and social welfare. There are five major sociocultural organizations in Chittaranjan Park:

---

[43] Bengali settlements for government employees are found in Timarpur, Dev Nagar, Gole Market, Lodi Road, Sarojini Nagar, Moti Bagh, Ramakrishna Puram, and Kidwai Nagar. Other important settlement areas are Pahar Ganj, Karol Bagh, Punjabi Bagh, Model Town, Tagore Garden, West Vihar, Daryaganj, and Hauz Khas. Areas such as Lakshmi Nagar, Gandhi Nagar, Pandav Nagar, Mayur Vihar on the opposite side of the Yamuna River are new. Durga Puja is celebrated in all of these localities (Kali Mandir Society 1998: 7-9).

1. Kali Mandir Society (established in 1973, running the Kali Temple and organizing religious and cultural functions);
2. Deshbandhu Chittaranjan Memorial Society (established in 1974, running a free clinic and library, teaching dance, music, drawing, karate, etc., and organizing the birth anniversary celebration of Chittaranjan Das);
3. Chittaranjan Park Bangiya Samaj (established in 1971, organizing an annual art and culture festival, issuing a newsletter; new building under construction);
4. Bipin Chandra Pal Memorial Trust (established in 1988, running an auditorium, library, clinic, organizing cultural functions, and issuing a newsletter); and
5. Purbsree Mahila Samity (established in 1973 as a women's organization, running a school for poor children, a polyclinic, and a vocational centre).

All of the above are voluntary organizations. They offer welfare services, several religious and cultural functions, and provide the residents with the chance to work as volunteers and perform community service.

Though Chittaranjan Park plays an important role as a centre of Bengali society outside Bengal, many anxieties are recognized among its residents partly due to a generation gap. How to maintain the Bengali language is one of the concerns of the older generation. As Delhi is basically a non-Bengali environment and many children and their families give higher priority to English for economic reasons, it is very difficult for a Delhi-born child to maintain Bengali. For this reason, the first ever Bengali Book Fair for Children was organized in Chittaranjan Park in May 2002. The organizer explained:

> Children of the present generation study at English-medium schools. As they read everything in English, they lose interest in their mother tongue. In West Bengal the situation is similar, but not so much as in Delhi. West Bengal has a Bengali environment. Delhi has a Hindi and English environment in place of Bengali. Bengali does not have importance here. Bengalis communicate with each other in Hindi.[44]
>
> We want to promote Bengali among children. Our intention is that we want Bengali children outside Bengal to come back to the Bengali language. Their parents are able to buy books here even if they have no relatives in Calcutta. This is a starting point. If children read, learn, and take an interest in the Bengali language, they

[44] Interview with the president of Saptarsi, organizer of the Delhi Children's Book Fair – 2002 on 1 May 2002.

> will want more on Bengali. We make efforts to do so [encourage their interest].[45]

Another concern is the problem of ageing and the overseas migration of the second generation. As the first generation becomes older and their children are no longer living with them, the pressure to sell property in Chittaranjan Park becomes strong. Quite a few of the second generation seek higher education and employment abroad. Among the 122 sample households, there are 51 persons living abroad in countries such as the USA, UK, Canada, Singapore, UAE, etc. Their children are educated abroad. In other words, the Chittaranjan Park Bengalis' migration did not stop in Delhi. It continued overseas.

There are increasing cases of inter-ethnic marriage among the younger generations. Though in many cases today marriage continues to be arranged between Bengalis, tolerance of inter-ethic marriage is to be found even among the most senior generation. P.K. Dasgupta, who is sixty-three years old, explained:

> As we have lived outside Bengal over fifty years, marriage with other caste, non-Bengalis, and foreigners are not rare any more. In the cosmopolitan atmosphere where we use to contact with Punjabis, South Indians, and foreigners, we do not mind it. If my children opt for it, I will not have any objection.[46]

This continued migration process over generations has given them a particular consciousness as Bengalis who do not stick to the 'original' Bengal. They think they are different from Bengalis in Bengal. In the process of adaptation under non-Bengali circumstances, they often reinterpret their history, rituals, and culture and create new ones. For instance, the Deshbandhu Chittarajan Memorial Society was not named because Chittaranjan Das was a nationalist hero in Bengal, but because they appreciated his philosophy of charity. Bengalis in Delhi started up an original Bengali ritual in which worship is offered to the sun in the early morning of the New Year. So their concern is not necessarily to follow the Bengali culture of Bengal or to completely recreate it outside Bengal. They are Bengalis in Delhi who have their own uniqueness as Bengalis. In addition, some people apparently separate themselves from overseas Bengalis and think of themselves in the context of internal migration. The concept of *Bahirbanga* (Inner Indian Bengali Diaspora or Bengalis residing outside of West Bengal but within the Indian territory) is becoming popular in Delhi.[47]

---

[45]Interview with the president of Saptarsi, organizer of the Delhi Children's Book Fair – 2002 on 29 April 2002.

[46]Interview with Mr P.K. Dasgupta on 27 August 2002.

[47]For example, a Delhi-based organization called *Prangshu* has organized an annual festival for Bengalis outside Bengal since 2001. See <http://www.bahirbanga.com>.

The residents of Chittaranjan Park have another concern: the increase of the non-Bengali population. According to them, the number of Punjabis is increasing in Chittaranjan Park. As the metropolitan area of Delhi has expanded, Chittaranjan Park has begun to attract new city dwellers. It is situated in the heart of south Delhi and is surrounded by newly developed exclusive residential districts like Greater Kailash I & II and the commercial and business complex, Nehru Place. According to residents, land prices have risen steeply after Nehru Place was constructed. Naturally builders and developers have started to take an interest in Chittaranjan Park. Some have contracted with allottees of Chittaranjan Park to construct multi-storeyed houses. The builders provide money and the ground floor to the original allottees (the leaseholders of the land) and sell the first and second floors to outsiders (often Punjabis). Some allottees have sold their property to builders, once they have bought out the lease from the local authority and converted their property to freehold. Some allottees told me that they had paid about Rs.20,000 per 160 square yards in order to do this.

CONCLUSION

In this paper, I have tried to illustrate how the rehabilitation of refugees has influenced urban development in the capital city of India, Delhi. The huge refugee influx from West Pakistan had a tremendous demographic impact on Delhi. Though refugees from East Pakistan were fewer in number, the rehabilitation of Bengali displaced persons in Delhi provides another story of refugee adaptation and has contributed to shaping post-Independence Delhi. As compared with Punjabi refugees whose migration was over within a few years of Partition and whose rehabilitation was completed in the early 1950s, the rehabilitation of Bengali displaced persons in Delhi took place more than twenty years after Partition. Had it been done earlier, as with the Punjabis, Chittaranjan Park might have developed as a colony exclusively for those who had worked in government service in Delhi before Partition. However, during the twenty years after Partition many Bengali Hindus from East Pakistan were forced to leave their homeland. Some of them got jobs in India and moved to Delhi. They represent a long-lasting displacement and migration process from the eastern wing of India. As a result, Chittaranjan Park consists of different persons, both displaced persons and persons who must be called refugees.

The rehabilitation of Bengalis illustrates the multi-ethnic character of Delhi. It brought together Bengalis who lived scattered in different places and resulted in the creation of a Bengali centre in Delhi. It further attracted non-allottees and newcomer Bengalis and formed an ethnic locality, called 'mini-Bengal'. The case of Chittaranjan Park clearly shows that ethnic claims affected the formation process of the capital city, in which ethnicity was instrumentally used to make appeals for land allotment. Ethnicity was mobilized in the process of community formation when historical figures like Chittaranjan Das and Bipin Chandra Pal, though they do not seem to be highlighted in West Bengal today, were used to symbolize the Bengali settlement.

Bengalis in Chittaranjan Park show a less instrumental and more expressive form of Bengali ethnic awareness, too. They consciously and unconsciously practise the Bengali way of life. For instance, worship in temples and *puja*s (religious offerings) are such cases. The Kali Mandir Society maintains three temples – to Kali, to Shiva (Shakti), and to Krishna – which cover three main religio-cosmological characters in Bengal. Any Bengali can participate in the worship of each of them as he or she wishes. The various daily offerings and weekly, monthly, and annual festivals are held in the complex. In particular, Durga Puja (the annual festival of Goddess Durga) is the most vivid expression of their Bengali traditions.

However, continuing urban development and rising land prices have added another dimension to Chittaranjan Park: outmigration by some Bengalis and the in-migration of non-Bengalis. Many Punjabis now live in Chittaranjan Park. The refugee influx affected the urban formation of Delhi and in reverse urban development has also affected the settlement of displaced persons.

Thus, we have seen two tendencies in the development of this Bengali colony. One is the construction of a mini-Bengal with different Bengali elements like historical figures, religious festivals, temples, songs, dances, dramas, lectures, libraries, food, etc. The other is the modification or deconstruction of the mini-Bengal by such factors as language erosion, overseas migration, inter-ethnic marriage, and the increase of the non-Bengali population in the locality. In this connection, the appeal of *Bahirbanga,* which seeks to chart a third direction, is unique.

When we take into account the fact that the population growth of Delhi largely depends on internal migration, we will see that Delhi is not a homeland for many residents. Though a term like *Delhiwalla* (person of Delhi) is often used in journalism, the ethnic formation of the capital city is plural and there are differences in the ways each ethnic group has adapted to life in Delhi.[48] The way in which ethnic groups are developing in India needs further and ongoing research.

---

[48]On this point, Bengalis are said to be more conscious of being Bengali than Punjabis are of being Punjabi. Aditi Mukherjee conducted a comparative study on language and attitudes between Bengalis and Punjabis in Delhi. All of her Bengali informants described themselves as Bengali and refused to accept labels such as *Delhiwalla* or even *Delhiwalla Bengali.* Punjabis are more flexible. They used a variety of labels to describe themselves (Mukherjee 1996: 71).

REFERENCES

Bagchi, J. and S. Dasgupta. 2003. *The Trauma and the Triumph: Gender and Partition in Eastern India*. Kolkata: Stree.

Butalia, U. 1993. 'Community, State and Gender: On Women's Agency during Partition'. *Economic and Political Weekly* 28 (17): WS12-24.

——. 2000. *The Other Side of Silence: Voices from the Partition of India*. London: Hurst & Company.

Chakrabarti, P.K. 1990. *The Marginal Men: The Refugees and the Left Political Syndrome in West Bengal*. Kalyani: Lumière Books.

Chakrabarty, D. 1996. 'Remembered Villages: Representation of Hindu-Bengali Memories in the Aftermath of the Partition'. *Economic and Political Weekly* 31 (32): 2143-51.

Chatterjee, N. 1990. 'The East Bengal Refugees: A Lesson in Survival', in S. Chaudhuri (ed.), *Calcutta: The Living City, Vol. 2: Present and Future*, pp. 70-7. Oxford: Oxford University Press.

——. 1992. 'Midnight's Unwanted Children: East Bengal Refugees and the Politics of Rehabilitation'. Ph.D. dissertation, Brown University.

Chatterji, J. 1999. 'The Fashioning of a Frontier: The Radcliffe Line and Bengal's Border Landscape, 1947-52'. *Modern Asian Studies* 33 (1): 185-242.

Das, V. 1995. *Critical Events: An Anthropological Perspective on Contemporary India* (Chap. 3). Delhi: Oxford University Press.

Dasgupta, A. 2001. 'The Politics of Agitation and Confession: Displaced Bengalis in West Bengal', in S. Ray (ed.), *Refugees and Human Rights: Social and Political Dynamics of Refugee Problem in Eastern and North-Eastern India*, pp. 95-129. Jaipur: Rawat Publications.

Datta, V.N. 1986. 'Panjabi Refugees and the Urban Development of Greater Delhi', in R.E. Frykenberg (ed.), *Delhi through the Ages: Essays in Urban History, Culture and Society*, pp. 442-60. Delhi: Oxford University Press.

Delhi Development Authority. 1957. *Master Plan for Delhi*, Vol. 2, Part I.

Dupont, V. 2000. 'Spatial and Demographic Growth of Delhi since 1947 and the Main Migration Flows', in V. Dupont, E. Tarlo, and D. Vidal (eds.), *Delhi: Urban Space and Human Destinies*, pp. 229-39. Delhi: Manohar Publishers.

Ghosh, G. 1998. 'God is a Refugee: Nationality, Morality and History in the 1947 Partition of India'. *Social Analysis* 42 (1): 33-62.

Ghosh, T.K. and S. Nath (eds.). 1996. *People of India Volume XX: Delhi*. Delhi: Manohar (on behalf of Anthropological Survey of India).

Government of India. 1954. *Census of India 1951: Paper No. 4, Displaced Persons*. New Delhi.

——. 1976. *Report of the Working Group on the Residual Problem of Rehabilitation in West Bengal*. New Delhi: Ministry of Supply and Rehabilitation.

Haque, C.E. 1995. 'The Dilemma of "Nationhood" and Religion: A Survey and

Critique of Studies on Population Displacement Resulting from the Partition of the Indian Subcontinent'. *Journal of Refugee Studies* 8 (2): 185-209.

Jain, A.K. 2000. *The Cities of Delhi*. Dehradun: Management Publishing.

Kali Mandir Society. 1998. *Chittaranjan Park Kalimandir Sosaiti Rajat Jayanti Barsa Smaranika (Chittaranjan Park Kalimandir Society Silver Jubilee Souvenir Brochure)*. Delhi: Chittaranjan Park (in Bengali).

Kaul, S. (ed.). 2001. *The Partitions of Memory: The Afterlife of the Division of India*. Delhi: Permanent Black.

Menon, R. and K. Bhasin. 1998. *Borders and Boundaries: Women in India's Partition*. Delhi: Kali for Women.

Mukherjee, A. 1996. *Language Maintenance and Language Shift: Punjabis and Bengalis in Delhi*. Delhi: Bahri Publications.

Mukhopadhyay, K. 1979. 'I-pi-di-pi Esosiyesan (EPDP Association)' *Purbachaler Katha (Topics of the East)*. Quarterly Publication of the EPDPA 8 (4): 1-10. Delhi: EPDPA (in Bengali).

Munshi, S. 1996. 'Social Composition of the 19th-Century Bhadralok in Calcutta'. *Bengal Past & Present* 115: 28-47.

Nakatani, T. 2000. 'Away From Home: the Movement and Settlement of Refugees from East Pakistan in West Bengal, India'. *Journal of the Japanese Association for South Asian Studies* 12: 73-109.

——. 2003. 'Refugees', in V. Das (ed.), *The Oxford India Companion to Sociology and Social Anthropology*, pp. 283-302. Delhi: Oxford University Press.

Rahman, Md.M. and W. van Schendel. 2003. 'I Am Not a Refugee: Rethinking Partition Migration'. *Modern Asian Studies* 37 (3): 551-84.

Raj, D.S. 1997. 'Partition and Diaspora: Memories and Identities of Punjabi Hindus in London'. *International Journal of Punjab Studies* 4 (1): 101-27.

Roy, P.K. 1982. 'Cittaranjan Parker "pratham" o "ghatnapanji" (The "beginning" and "chronicle" of Chittaranjan Park)'. *Purbachaler Katha (Topics of the East)*. Quarterly Publication of the EPDPA 11 (3/4): 25-32 (in Bengali).

Samaddar, R. (ed.). 1997. *Reflections on Partition in the East*. Delhi: Vikas Publishing House.

Senvarma, S.P. 1973. 'Kalkaji Kaloni (Kalkaji Colony)' *Purbachaler Katha (Topics of the East)*. Quarterly Publication of the EPDPA 2 (4): 11-16 (in Bengali).

Settar, S. and I. B. Gupta (eds.). 2002. *Pangs of Partition Volume II: The Human Dimension*. Delhi: Manohar Publishers (Indian Council of Historical Research).

Talukdar, R. 1986. 'The Styles of Adjustment of Bengali Refugees: A Sociological Inquiry 1950-1980'. Ph.D. dissertation, Jawaharlal Nehru University, New Delhi.

Tan, T.Y. and G. Kudaisya. 2000. *The Aftermath of Partition in South Asia*. London: Routledge.

Waseem, M. 1997. 'Partition, Migration and Assimilation: A Comparative Study of Pakistani Punjab'. *International Journal of Punjab Studies* 4 (1): 21-41.

11

The Bonded Agricultural Labourers' Freedom Movement in Western Nepal

TATSURO FUJIKURA

> The Kamaiya Freedom Movement emerged in the midst of the gloom and frustration pervading the ten year anniversary of democracy ... The kamaiya movement is in a sense a civil society campaign, but it is interesting to note that few kamaiyas have citizenship papers. They are struggling from the bottom up to make basic structures work for them. It seems clear that democracy, like freedom, is not simply created by government decree, but claimed through ongoing struggle.
>
> Tim Whyte, 'Afterword', in P. Lowe, *Kamaiya: Slavery and Freedom in Nepal*

INTRODUCTION

The bonded labourers' freedom movement that began on 1 May 2000 prompted the Nepali government to declare, on 17 July 2000, the emancipation of at least 16,000 bonded labourers or '*kamaiya*s' in western Nepal. This was a unique movement, which came at a unique moment in Nepali history. The year 2000 was the tenth anniversary of the restoration of multiparty democracy in Nepal. As Tim Whyte's text in the epigraph indicates, there was a popular sense of disillusionment with the democratically elected government and political leaders, including a sense that the Nepali government had become even more inefficient and corrupt than it had been under the authoritarian Panchayat regime. Many analysts regarded the Maoists' violent uprising as a result of the failure of both development *and* democracy in Nepal. The Maoists claimed their movement was aimed at replacing the current oligarchic 'democracy' with a real people's rule and building a truly progressive Nepal. By the year 2000, the Maoists had already declared four western hill districts as their 'base area'.[1]

[1] Namely, Rolpa, Rukum, Salyan, and Jajarkot districts. See Sharma (2057 V.S.).

The bonded labourers' liberation movement also emerged from rural western Nepal. The movement involved a group of people who were among the poorest and most exploited in Nepal. However, unlike the Maoists' 'People's War', it was a non-violent movement. The movement also was not led by any political party, and indeed transcended party divisions in a post-1990 Nepal where party affiliation seemed to exert decisive influences on many areas of life. There was a strong ethnic dimension to the movement, the overwhelming majority of kamaiyas being Tharus, the ethnic group indigenous to the Tarai plains. However, I shall argue that the movement also went beyond being purely an ethnic movement pursuing group rights. The movement, as we shall see, would not have emerged without its history of engagements with the transnational networks of institutions, ideas, and practices of development as well as of human rights, and the movement's demands were articulated in universalist terms. The leaders of the movement, as we shall also see, were highly critical of existing development organizations. However, they never disengaged themselves either from the institutional spaces of development or from the Nepali state. What I try to do in this paper then is to describe the politics of the kamaiya freedom movement and BASE, the organization which led the movement, as a politics of engagement which gained momentum by building heterogeneous alliances and networks and whose strength resided precisely in its hybridity, a politics that contrasts with other, more radical forms of mobilization.

I should state at the beginning, however, that this is a preliminary account of an ongoing and highly complicated social, economic, and political process; my account cannot but be partial. I believe a note on how I personally became interested in and in some ways involved in the kamaiya issue may help clarify for the readers some of the limitations and partiality of this paper. In 1994 in Chicago, I met Dilli Bahadur Chaudhari, the founder and president of the grassroots organization BASE, which I will describe in more detail later. My interest in the activities of BASE was one of the reasons why I decided to conduct my extended field research on ideologies and practices of development in western Nepal. However, at the time I began my fieldwork, in 1996, I was more interested in the conditions of life in the hills than those in the Tarai plains. Accordingly I selected Salyan district as my main fieldwork location. Salyan was the only hill district in which BASE was active, and since the district traditionally had no Tharu residents, the BASE members there consisted exclusively of non-Tharus. Although I often visited the Dang valley, south of Salyan, and had close contacts with BASE leaders and staff members, the majority of whom were Tharu, I did not make any systematic effort to explore Tharu culture and society, nor was I focused primarily on the issues of kamaiya labour during the course of my fieldwork between 1996 and 1999. It was during my return visit to Nepal from June to August of 2000 that my attention was clearly focused on the kamaiya issue. As already noted, the kamaiya freedom movement began in western Nepal at the beginning of May 2000. The movement involved not only BASE activists from western Nepal, but also intellectuals and human rights activists in Kathmandu, whom I had also known for years by then. I participated in meetings of those activists involved in the movement and participated in demonstrations in Kathmandu and in western Nepal. Subsequently, I have also made efforts to help in the rehabilitation process of the freed kamaiyas. This is why some of the passages in this paper assume the form of personal testimony. The way I approached the kamaiya issue also explains my heavy focus at this point on some of the leaders of BASE, rather than on other actors in the process, for example, other human rights and development organizations and activists who have also been involved in the kamaiya issue, political parties and politicians, and indeed kamaiyas themselves. I am currently in the process of expanding my research to include those other actors and other aspects of the process. However, I do believe that it is worthwhile, at this point, to foreground the actions of a limited set of actors, primarily the BASE leaders, focusing particularly on how they have constructed the meaning of their actions. For the purposes of this paper, when dealing with such topics as the history of the western Tarai and the characteristics of kamaiya labour, I rely largely on the works of others.

THE MEANINGS OF KAMAIYA

Kamaiya as a Human Rights Problem

The 'kamaiya system' in western Nepal, which included a form of bonded labour,[2] became a prominent issue, especially after the restoration of multiparty democracy in 1990 resulted in a dramatic increase in the activities of human rights organizations in Nepal. A Kathmandu based human rights NGO called INSEC, for example, conducted and published a research on kamaiya practices in 1992, which in their words, "shocked the nation" by showing that "slavery still existed in the form of bonded-labor

[2]A detailed account of kamaiya practices is given in the next section. When I state here that "the kamaiya system ... included a form of bonded labour", I am simply maintaining that *some* of those who were known as kamaiyas in western Nepal worked under the conditions of labour bondage as defined by international law. The most relevant international instrument here is the Supplementary Convention on the Abolition of Slavery, the Slave Trade, and Institutions and Practices Similar to Slavery (1956) to which Nepal is a signatory. Section I, Article 1 (a) of the Convention reads, in part, "Debt bondage [is] the status or condition arising from a pledge by a debtor of his personal services or of those of a person under his control as security for a debt if the value of those services as reasonably assessed is not applied towards the liquidation of the debt."

in western Nepal" (INSEC 2003). In that report, INSEC described the kamaiya system as involving "virtual buying and selling of individuals for work in agriculture and whole families may remain bonded in the system across generations" (INSEC 2003). With the help of the London-based Anti-Slavery International, INSEC continued research and advocacy work over the 1990s, making policy recommendations to the Nepali government and international organizations, including the United Nations' Economic and Social Council. The Nepali government, for its part, also began to publish reports on kamaiyas in the mid 1990s with funding from the International Labor Organization (ILO). In one such report, the Ministry of Land Reform and Management (MLRM), based on a census it conducted from January to February 1996, reported that there were 15,152 kamaiya households in the five western Tarai districts of Dang, Banke, Bardiya, Kailali, and Kanchanpur.[3] The Ministry of Land Reform and Management, in its report, claimed that the kamaiya system, which has come "under the spotlight of global and national media", not only represented a clear violation of human rights, but was also "an outcome of socio-economic and cultural conditions" that Nepal shared with many other developing countries (MLRM 1999). Thus, the kamaiya system was not just a legal problem, it was simultaneously a sign of Nepal's backwardness.

The historian, Gyan Prakash, in his study of the British colonial construction of '*kamiyas*' in northern India as bonded labourers, argued that the colonial officers made use of what he called a 'discourse of freedom' (Prakash 1990). Colonial records from the nineteenth century on, represented "history as a progression from unfreedom to freedom, as a process of restoring the loss of natural rights to liberty" (Prakash 1990: 2). Prakash argued further that:

> In post-colonial India ... the abolition of debt-bondage remains one of the issues around which the government struts and swaggers as an agent of modern progress in a land of feudal backwardness. It continues to be a question whose importance is owed, above all, to the fact that it allows modernity and tradition to appear in perpetual combat, with tradition now defined as a combination of sources of backwardness – social, economic, and cultural. (Prakash 1990: 225)

[3]In addition to the problems associated with any large-scale census, enumeration of kamaiyas is complicated by their diversity, as discussed in the next section. Besides the Ministry of Land Reform and Management, the government's Sukumbasi Samasya Samadhan Ayog (Commission for the Solution of Landless Squatter Problem) reported in 1995 that there were 17,435 kamaiya households and 25,762 individual kamaiyas in the same five districts (SSSA 1995). Backward Society Education enumerated 35,874 individual kamaiyas in 1995 (BASE 1995). Comparing different reports, Shiva Sharma and Manasa Thakurathi estimated the number of individual kamaiyas to be about 26,000 (Sharma & Thakurathi 1998: 25). For further discussions of the quantitative data on kamaiyas during the 1990s, see Sharma & Thakurathi (1998) and Chapagain (1998: Part D).

Building on Prakash's work, anthropologist Katharine Rankin, in her 1999 article, criticized the discourse surrounding the kamaiya issue in Nepal in a similar manner. In particular, Rankin argued that, with the global ascendance of a neo-liberal ideology, bonded labour in Nepal has come to serve as an example of "anachronistic negation of freedom against which the causal relationship between the market and democracy can be asserted and legitimated" (1999: 28). Rankin saw two major problems with this formulation. First, like so many other practices in the so-called Third World societies, kamaiya practices were explained as the result of a premodern and irrational organization of society – in this case, the absence of a viable labour market. This mode of explanation, Rankin argued, failed to appreciate the "diversity and historical specificity of kamaiya practices that have emerged" in Nepal's western plains (Rankin 1999: 28). The second problem that Rankin identified was that by defining emancipation through wage labour as the only real solution to kamaiya domination, the discourse of freedom masked the scope for domination inherent in 'free' labour. Thus Rankin argued that the discourse of freedom employed by human rights advocates and development policy makers was inadequate both as a representation of the reality of kamaiya practices and as a guide towards their political solution.

I agree with Rankin's observations as far as they go. However, the story I want to convey in this paper involves the moment in 2000 when kamaiyas themselves seized hold of the language of freedom in their struggle to transform their own conditions. During the kamaiya movement they represented their hopes and demands in terms of emancipation (*mukti*) and human rights (*manav adhikar*), the very vocabulary that both Prakash and Rankin find so inadequate and ultimately oppressive. Thus, we are faced with a challenge very different from that which preoccupied Prakash and Rankin. In other words, the challenge is not simply to expose the ways in which 'rights discourse' misrepresents a complex local practice. Nor is it our task to judge whether the discourse, taken by itself, represents a 'liberating' political programme. Instead, we need to start, it seems to me, with an exploration of the *pragmatics* of the language of freedom in a particular socio-historical context. I will argue that the way the kamaiya freedom movement unfolded makes clear that the transition suggested by Rankin's argument – i.e. from a locally and historically specific structure of subjugation and exploitation towards subjugation and exploitation through the 'free' market under a neo-liberal regime – is not the only possible consequence of the use of the vocabulary of human rights. In the next section, I will try to sketch what constituted kamaiya practices in western Nepal. Then I will describe the history of the grassroots organization, BASE, which led the kamaiya liberation movement, and the process of kamaiya mobilization in 2000, which led to the government's 'emancipation of the kamaiyas'.

Kamaiya Practices in Western Nepal

As I have already indicated, kamaiya practices were found in the five western Tarai districts of Dang, Banke, Bardiya, Kailali, and Kanchanpur.[4] An overwhelming majority of the kamaiyas were Tharus, an ethnic group indigenous to the Tarai.[5] There is no agreement among the locals regarding the origins of kamaiya practices. However, it is commonly pointed out that the word 'kamaiya' derives from the Tharu verb *kamaina*, which means 'to earn'. The word 'kamaiya' traditionally meant a 'hardworking man'. The feminine form of the word is 'kamalahari', a 'hardworking woman'.[6]

As already indicated, a wide variety of arrangements were called 'kamaiya' in modern-day western Tarai. Several people in the western Tarai told me that there could be as many kinds of arrangements with kamaiyas as there were landlords. However, as existing studies show, one can speak of recurring types, categories, distinctions, or characteristic arrangements within the diverse field of kamaiya practices (Sharma & Thakurathi 1998; Dhakal et al. 2000; Rankin 1999). Let me begin with the type which could most easily fall under the scope of 'bonded labour'. This type of kamaiya contract involved a person taking a loan, called *saunki*, from another farmer or a landlord and, in exchange, agreeing to work exclusively for the latter as a kamaiya (or sending his son to work as a kamaiya, as we shall see later in the case of Yagyaraj Chaudhari). The landlord in turn agreed to provide the kamaiya with a fixed amount of grain or money every year. The landlord also gave the kamaiya one set of clothes every year and guaranteed to provide shelter for those kamaiyas who were landless. Moreover, kamaiyas also had the right to demand additional credits for basic and emergency needs from their employers. These additional loans were added to the *saunki*. The term of contract was renegotiated annually on the first day of the month of Magh (January-February). At this negotiation, called *samjhauta*, the landlord asked the kamaiya whether he wanted to stay. In order to leave the landlord, kamaiya had to pay back the *saunki* or find a new employer to do so.

---

[4]Sharma and Thakurathi (1998) also include Kapilvastu, Rupandehi, and Nawalparasi as districts with kamaiya practices. However, the kamaiya mobilization I relate here, as well as most of the official and non-government programmes aimed at kamaiyas and former kamaiyas, have concentrated on the five districts listed above.

[5]Based on a field survey done in 1997, INSEC reports that the proportion of Tharus among kamaiyas was 95.9 per cent in Kanchanpur, 98.7 per cent in Kailali, 84.8 per cent in Bardiya, 77.9 per cent in Banke, and 93.8 per cent in Dang (the sample size of kamaiyas surveyed range from 353 in Banke to 604 in Bardiya: Sharma & Thakurathi 1998). When speaking of 'Tharus' in this area, we are mainly referring to Dangaura Tharus and Rana Tharus. On the construction of Tharu identity in Nepal, see Guneratne (2002).

[6]See Dhakal et al. (2000) on the ways in which the appellations 'kamaiya', 'kamalahari', and others originally referred to different roles in the division of labour in the extended Tharu household.

To turn now to a discussion of the diversity of kamaiyas, there were cases where a person worked as a kamaiya for a few years and managed to pay back the *saunki* either by himself or with help from his family members. There were also families who worked as kamaiya for the same landlord for two or three generations. There were kamaiyas who were hired as individuals by a landlord (*ek saro kamaiya*) but there were also many kept by the landlord along with their family (*bukrahi kamaiya*). Moreover, there could be two kamaiyas within the same family working for a landlord. For instance, the father and one of his sons could be working as kamaiyas for a landlord while other sons did not. There were kamaiyas with large debts, and those without any. There were landless and homeless kamaiyas who depended totally on the landlord for their shelter, and those with their own house who commuted to work. While most kamaiyas were provided fixed amounts of grain or cash each year, some received a specified share of the crop.[7]

Rankin has pointed out that kamaiyas were explicitly counted as part of the landlord's wealth and patrimony; and brothers fought over the allocation of kamaiyas when they divided up joint family property (1999: 31). Kamaiyas did not participate in village meetings called by the *bhalamansa* (or *mahatou*), the locally elected traditional leaders. They therefore had "no voice in the political, economic, and juridical matters of concern to the village as a whole", although they did participate in the village *ritual* activities suggesting that they shared with their owners "the responsibilities and benefits of residing in the domain of village divinities" (Rankin 1999: 31). As Rankin also points out, the relation between the landlord and the kamaiya was constructed in terms of patronage and dependence (Rankin 1999: 31-4). When the employer gave a set of clothes to the kamaiya, it was presented as an act of generosity. When an agreement was reached at the annual renegotiation, the landlord offered alcohol to the kamaiya and they exchanged garlands of flowers. The construction of the relation as one of patronage and dependence gave rise to a particular form of everyday power-negotiation wherein the kamaiya could demand that the landlord act as a moral and generous caretaker, and the landlord could demand that the

---

[7]There were cases where payments were based *solely* on sharecropping (usually one third to one fourth of the output going to the kamaiya) or combined with a pre-fixed amount of in-kind-or-cash payment. Thus, in a practice reported by SPACE from Bardiya, each kamaiya family was paid 8 quintals of paddy as *mashaura* (the food provided to a kamaiya family for daily consumption) plus *chaumali*. *Chaumali* was a sharecropping arrangement where, for example, if there were seven kamaiya families working for a landlord on a single tract of land, they would collectively complete all the cropping and harvesting related activities. After the harvest, the produce would be divided into four parts, three parts of which would go to the landlord, and the rest would get divided equally among the kamaiyas (Dhakal et al. 2000: 52-3).

kamaiya act as a grateful and faithful dependent.[8] In more narrowly economic terms, by keeping a kamaiya, the landlord was guaranteed a supply of labour during the peak agricultural season. From the perspective of a kamaiya, by the annual contract, he was guaranteed his minimum subsistence needs even in times when there were low demands for labour. There were indeed cases in which kamaiya arrangements appeared to be experienced as mutually beneficial. Even some of the local Tharu activists, whom I discuss below, found some cases of kamaiya-landlord relations reasonably equitable.

I referred earlier to Rankin's argument that human rights discourse embodied liberal ideology, and hence was inadequate both as a representation of the complexity of kamaiya practices and as a guide towards their political solution. As I shall argue below, the Tharu activists who led the kamaiya movement did not take 'free labour' as a necessary and sufficient solution to the problems of the kamaiyas. Yet, neither were they concerned with opposing liberal ideology and capitalist relations *as such*. In order to understand better what kamaiya practices and their 'abolition' meant for the Tharu activists – or the pragmatics of their invocations of 'human rights' and 'freedom' – in addition to the typologies of kamaiya practices discussed above, we need to locate them within the wider historical experience of Tharus in western Nepal in the twentieth century.

THE HISTORICAL TRANSFORMATION OF THE WESTERN TARAI

Until the implementation of the malaria eradication programmes in the early 1960s, Tharus were the only year-round residents of western Tarai. Although many parts of the western Tarai came under the suzerainty of different powers from at least the fourteenth century, Tharus were mostly left to themselves to conduct their local affairs (Krauskopff 1999, 2000). The last century, however, saw a progressive decline of Tharu autonomy. Under the explicit policy of the Nepali state to expand its administrative apparatus into the Tarai, high-caste Hindus of hill origin, collectively called Pahari (or 'people of the hills') by the Tharu, increasingly replaced local Tharu authorities.[9] This replacement of authorities was accompanied by

---

[8] For a classic ethnographic description of the relationship between the landlord and the 'attached labourer' under arrangements similar to the kamaiya system, see Breman (1993).

[9] As McDonaugh writes, from "the late nineteenth century on, the central government sought to undermine the position of the powerful Tharu Chaudharis, who were responsible for the administration of revenues and other duties" for the large administrative units called *praganna*. To this end, the government introduced the position of *jamindar*, and appointed Paharis to the position to be responsible for the collection of taxes at a *mauja* (one or more villages), which

Pahari encroachment of Tharu-held lands. With reference to the Dang valley, Christian McDonaugh reports (citing in part a survey done by McDougal) that:

> whereas in the 1912 revenue settlement most of the landlords were Tharus, by the late 1960s McDougal's survey found that the great majority of landlords were Pahari ([McDougal] 1968: 86-7). In Dang by this date some 80% of the Tharu were tenants and the great majority of these tenants had little or no land of their own. Around 90% of the land cultivated by Tharus belonged to Paharis.
> (McDonaugh 1997: 281)

The rate of immigration by hill people into the Tarai accelerated rapidly after the malaria eradication programme of the early 1960s.[10] Most of the Pahari migrants were able to obtain and register land in the Tarai, and many of the Tharus lost their land. Many contemporary residents of the Tarai (both Tharu and Pahari) speak of cheating and coercion involved in this process – as many Paharis used their literacy and close connections with government officers to their advantage. It is important to note that there was differentiation among the Tharus themselves: some were large landlords and others worked as tenant farmers and agricultural labourers. However, for much of its history, the Tarai was characterized by an abundance of potentially cultivable land, and tenant farmers could keep a large share of the produce. However, as McDonaugh describes in detail (1997: 281-2), the balance of power has radically shifted against the tenant farmers over the course of twentieth century.[11]

The pressure from Paharis also resulted in a dramatic increase in the emigration of Tharus from the Dang valley, which peaked in the late 1960s but continued into the 1980s. In some cases whole village communities migrated, and those sites became Pahari villages in a matter of a few years (McDonaugh 1997: 282). Those emigrating from Dang moved 'west', primarily towards Bardiya and Kailali, where, it was thought at that time, there were more unclaimed or unused patches of land and fewer Paharis than in Dang.

McDonaugh also recalls a prevalent Tharu attitude towards outsiders from his fieldwork at the end of 1970s:

> In many of the villages I visited I was struck by the quiet, even withdrawn, though dignified attitude of the Tharu … A fundamen-

---

thereby progressively replaced the much larger *praganna* as the key unit of local administration (McDonaugh 1997: 280-1). See also Krauskopff (1999, 2000).

[10] On the beliefs and debates about the Tharu genetic and/or culturally acquired resistance to malaria, see Guneratne 2002: 24.

[11] On the Tharu experiences regarding land in modern times, see also Guneratne (2002: 91-124) and works cited therein.

> tal notion … was that outsiders meant trouble. During the last few decades … [the] settlers from the hills … only brought trouble to the Tharu … Another significant factor here is the value the Tharu place on their own forms of manners and social etiquette. These were contrasted with the customary behaviour of the Pahari, who appeared to the Tharu as loud, intrusive, vociferous – and devious.
>
> (McDonaugh 1999: 225)

McDonaugh describes Tharu villages, at least up to 1980, as characterized by a tendency towards isolation from the outside world, and their identity as constructed primarily through its contrast with the Paharis. However, there were also signs of change. Thus, around the same period in Dang, Gisèle Krauskopff observed that the "younger generation" were abandoning the isolationist attitude and were beginning to identify themselves also as "Nepalis" (Krauskopff 1989: 56; cited in McDonaugh 1999: 224-5). In his detailed account of how some of the Tharu villagers began to regain control over the land (taking advantage of tenancy rights provisions and new agricultural technologies) through the 1980s, McDonaugh also notes the rapid rise in the number of Tharu children attending local schools, passing the SLC, and even going on to higher education: "Engagement with the wider world [was] also reflected in the encroachment of Nepali language along with new styles of dress" (McDonaugh 1999: 232; see also McDonaugh 1997).

Thus, it is with reference to the history of disempowerment and dispossession of the Tharus, as well as to the more recent history of Tharus' new modes of engagement with the wider world, that the contemporary significance of kamaiya practices, as well as the emergence of the grassroots organization, BASE, needs to be understood.

BACKWARD SOCIETY EDUCATION (BASE)

> My grandfather lost his land by putting a mark on a paper. So my father had to work as a kamaiya for some years. My mother was also a bonded labourer for 16 years. At school I was beaten for being a Tharu. This had an effect on my mind – I began to ask: Why do so many Tharu people become kamaiyas? Many Tharus have no education: they don't know the laws and rules of the country or the value of land. When we realized these facts we started BASE.
>
> Dilli Bahadur Chaudhari, President of BASE
> (P. Lowe, *Kamaiya: Slavery and Freedom in Nepal*. p. 81)

The origin of BASE goes back to the mid 1980s in the Dang valley. As described, there were signs of major social and cultural changes in the valley in the 1980s. One of the major events that contributed to changing the outlook of the valley was the opening of the motor road that linked the valley to Nepal's main East-West highway, which was fully opened in 1985. At the same time, USAID initiated a multi-million dollar 'integrated rural development project' in the Rapti zone, which included Dang along with three other hill districts to its north. The small town of Tulsipur, the headquarters of Rapti Zone, also became the headquarters of the USAID's Rapti project and rapidly turned into a major bazaar.[12]

Dilli Bahadur Chaudhari, the founder of BASE, was born in the late 1960s in Dumrigaun, a village lying just outside Tulsipur bazaar. As stated in the epigraph to this section, Dilli's grandfather had lost all his land to a Pahari by putting his thumbprint on a paper. Dilli's father, who engaged in electoral politics under the Panchayat system and served as a Pradhan Panch, tried all his life to have the document declared void, but was unsuccessful (cf. Ødegaard 1999: 67). After his father died, Dilli decided to start an organization with his friends. The creation of this organization for the improvement of the condition of poor Tharus was proposed and approved at the annual *khyala* (or *khel*, a traditional Tharu village meeting) at the beginning of Magh in 2042 V.S., i.e. January 1986 (BASE 2055 V.S.: 3). This action reflected, according to Dilli, his understanding of the failure of his father's efforts. Unlike his father, who tried to work through the formal political system set up by the Panchayat regime, Dilli decided to create an informal group, and had it sanctioned at the *khyala* meeting continuing outside a system of local governance installed by the state.

The organization, which began with thirty-four members, raised money in Tulsipur and the surrounding villages by forming a 'singing and dancing' troupe, as well as by working in the construction of houses. The first thing that the organization did was to run non-formal literacy classes at night for poor and mostly female Tharu workers, reflecting their views that the plight of many Tharus derived from their lack of education.[13] As I have mentioned, Tulsipur was the headquarters for the USAID's Rapti Integrated Development Project. In July 1986, Dilli and the Dumrigaun organization were approached by staff members of No-Frills, a consulting firm which was implementing USAID's Vegetable, Fruit and Cash Crop Program

[12]The Rapti Integrated Development Program "aimed to fulfill the basic needs of the poor majority, the farmers of the mid-hills" (Mainali 2003: 125). The planning document stated that the programme aimed at "improving household food production and consumption, improved income generating opportunities for poor farmers, landless labourers, occupational castes and women" (ibid.). It spent about fifty million dollars over the fifteen years (1980-95) of its operation. As Mainali points out, only a month and a half after the conclusion of the programme, the Maoist People's War was launched in the hills of the Rapti Zone (Mainali 2003, 2055 V.S.).

[13]For discussions of the notion of education as the key to personal and collective welfare and development in Nepal see, among others, Ahearn (2001) and Fujikura (2001).

(VFC). They asked Dilli to organize a 4-H club under the VFC's rural extension scheme, where Tharu farmers could learn new agricultural skills. Dilli accepted the offer and established the Dumrigaun Misrit Charpatte Yuba Club ('Dumrigaun Mixed 4-Leaves Youth Club'). Most of the members of the Dumrigaun organization hence doubled as members of the 4-H club (Cox n.d.: 13). In addition to implementing programmes for introducing a variety of new crops and livestock (including improved vegetables, corn, potatoes, rabbits, and pigs) into the Tharu villages in the valley through the youth club, No-Frills staff members also supported literacy classes with donations of pens, notebooks, and kerosene lamps. This allowed the organization's activities to expand into additional villages outside Dumrigaun.

In August 1988, Dilli attended a tribal rights conference in Thailand, with help from the director of No-Frills, who obtained funding for his trip from the Asian Adivasi Committee, a pan-Asian tribal rights organization. After the conference, Dilli spent six weeks in Bombay learning about tribal rights activism (Cox n.d.: 14-15). This was Dilli's first international exposure which also enabled him to establish connections with activists outside Nepal. In particular, he kept close contacts with activists in Maharashtra, some of whom would later play important roles in the kamaiya liberation movement in 2000. Through this trip, according to Dilli, he learnt to understand the problems of Tharus within the framework of global indigenous struggles against dispossession, exploitation, and domination.

By 1988, within three years of its establishment, the Dumrigaun organization membership had grown from 34 to 350. For the rapid expansion of the organization, Dilli credits the Tharu institution of *khyala*. As I have already mentioned, *khyala* is a traditional Tharu village council, which is attended by the male household heads of the village. The *mahatou*, or village headman, is elected at the *khyala* meeting at the beginning of the Magh month every year, ideally by unanimous consent. The *mahatou* and his house are then sanctified through ritual procedures presided over by a *guruwa* or priest. As Gisèle Krauskopff writes, the institutions of *khyala* and *mahatou* represent elements of the sociocultural tradition of the Tharu characterized by "the strong and centralized organization of villages and households" (2003: 215). The tradition emphasizes respect for the elders and the headman and encourages solidarity among the villagers (ibid.). According to Dilli, the rapid expansion of the Dumrigaun organization should be credited to the efficient indigenous institutions of *khyala* and *mahatou*.[14]

---

[14]The book published by the NGO, SPACE, dealing with a community of resettled Tharus in Bardiya, contains an oral history of the 'Kanara Movement' of 1992, which credits the efficient, large-scale movement out of the villages towards 'capturing' government forest land by the landless Tharus to the institutions of *khel* and *badghar* (or *mahatou*) (Dhakal et al. 2000: 65-6).

At the organization's general assembly in the year 2046 V.S. (1989/90), its name was changed to Shramik Mukti Sangathan (Organization for Labourers' Liberation) and an office was established in Tulsipur. The organization also applied to be officially registered as a social service organization, but the Chief District Officer of Dang refused. Instead, government officials variously accused the organization of being an organ of a political party, a Christian missionary group, a caste/ethnic organization, all of which were banned under the Panchayat regime. Around the same time, No-Frills, the group that gave the first institutional support to the Dumrigaun organization and facilitated its transnational networking, grew increasingly worried about the 'politicization' of the 4-H Club. In December of 1989, No-Frills completely withdrew its support for the Dumrigaun Club (Cox n.d.: 15). The Chief District Officer (CDO), on his part, mobilized Parashu Narayan Chaudhari, a Tharu and, at the time, the Minister of Education, to persuade Dilli to stop his activities.[15] When this did not work, the CDO had Dilli thrown in jail twice under the Public Security Act, accusing him of being a 'threat to national security' (Cox n.d.: 15).

Hence, at the time of the restoration of multiparty democracy in April 1990, the organization had no external institutional support and no official recognition as a non-governmental organization. The organization was finding it difficult to purchase kerosene for the lanterns used during night classes. Official registration was crucial for receiving financial support from development aid donors. Yet, even after the restoration of multiparty democracy, the CDO refused to register the organization as an NGO. Around this time, Dilli came to know Arjun Guneratne, then a Ph.D. candidate at the University of Chicago, working on his dissertation on the construction of Tharu identity in Nepal.[16] Guneratne put Dilli in touch with Ramanand Prasad Singh, a Tharu and Nepal's attorney general at the time. Ramanand Prasad Singh immediately called up the CDO and persuaded him, and the organization was formally registered with the district administrative office on 30 January 1991 (16 Magh 2047 V.S.) under the name Backward Society Education (BASE).

As noted earlier, by the end of the 1980s the organization was calling itself Shramik Mukti Sangathan or Organization for Labourers' Liberation. However, Dilli and other leaders of the organization felt that they would

---

[15]Parashu Narayan Chaudhari has been one of the most prominent Tharu politicians in Nepal. For his place in Tharu and national politics, see Guneratne (2002).

[16]Arjun Guneratne has told me that he was introduced to Dilli Chaudhari by Thomas Cox. Cox, in turn, had gone to Tulsipur in 1989 as a consultant to monitor and evaluate the Vegetable, Fruit and Cash Crop Project when he met Dilli Chaudhari (Cox n.d.: 1). Later, Cox, among other things, wrote the report on BASE (Cox n.d.), which I have been citing.

not be allowed to register under that name, because it sounded too much like a communist organization (which it was not), and unlike an NGO, which are supposed to be non-political. When foreigners, including anthropologists, hear the name Backward Society Education, they often cringe, because the name doesn't sound very 'politically correct'. In fact, the word 'backward' (or *pichadieko*) is used very commonly by local Nepalis. In this particular case, it was the Tharus themselves who were adopting the label of backwardness, and with it indeed the discursive framework of progress and development that designated some groups as lacking in progress, and hence in need of pedagogic intervention and transformation. Another point to note about this name is that it is English. By adopting an English name, BASE leaders were trying to be visible to an international audience. The hope was that international visibility would to some extent deter the Nepali government, or any political leaders, from persecuting BASE members.

Once registered as an NGO, BASE was indeed successful. In the fall of 1991, with the assistance of Inge Kirstine Sagild (of Norwegian Church Service, working in Dang) and Save the Children US (who wrote the grant proposal), BASE succeeded in obtaining

> a 113,000 dollar grant from the Danish Agency for International Development (DANIDA) to expand [its] literacy classes, income generating activities, health education, and other development activities. (Cox n.d.: 16)

With Danish funding, BASE was able, within three years, to expand its activities to five additional districts and to more than three hundred villages, running 700 night-classes. The five additional districts were Banke, Bardiya, Kailali, Kanchanpur, and Salyan. The last of these, Salyan, is a hill district and traditionally has no Tharu residents. In fact, even within the Tarai districts, the expanded BASE membership included a significant number of non-Tharus. This is in accordance with BASE's self-definition, not as an ethnic organization, but as an organization working for a general good, namely, for "the creation of exploitation-free society", the motto printed in many of its publications as the "vision" of BASE (e.g. BASE 2056 V.S.). BASE encouraged all those who were involved in the night classes, either as students or as volunteer teachers, to become members of BASE. A member of BASE paid an annual membership fee (1 rupee at the beginning of the 1990s) and participated in all decision-making processes, including voting to elect village, area, district, and central-level BASE committee members. Dilli and other leaders of BASE defined it as a 'membership organization' and saw it as fundamentally different from other prominent NGOs elsewhere; for example, Grameen Bank and BRAC in Bangladesh, which were organized around the activities of micro-finance.

By the spring of 2000, BASE had around 30,000 members.[17] According to the BASE constitution, general elections for its committee members should be held every five years. Up to this date (2004), the general election of BASE committee members has been held twice: during the 2052 V.S. (1995/6) general convention in Kanchanpur, and during the 2057 V.S. (2000/1) general convention, again in Kanchanpur. In both general elections, Dilli Bahadur Chaudhari was re-elected unopposed as the president.

Several long-term members of BASE have told me that there has been tension in the organization between a preference for informal negotiation and unanimous decision, on the one hand, and preference for open debates and decision by vote, on the other. Those who prefer open debate and votes in relation to one issue or another, appear to have often labelled the preference for consensus and unanimity as a sign of backwardness, or an outcome of a history of oppression. One BASE member told me: "There are people who prefer to simply obey, rather than speak up. There is still a problem of 'culture of silence' [he used the English phrase]. This is not just a problem among us Tharus. This is also a problem for the Nepali society as a whole. But in this time and age, everyone should be able to express their own opinion even if they are in the minority."

Those who have participated in BASE since its early days also told me about the attempts by different political parties to capture the organization, and the BASE responses against them. From the very beginning political parties attempted to use BASE for their own purposes and, if possible, put under their complete control. During its early years, BASE leaders guarded their organization against political takeover by prohibiting BASE officials from being active in any political party. If a political officeholder, such as a Village Development Committee chairperson, wanted to play an active role in BASE, the person was asked first to resign the position of VDC chair. A person active since the early days of BASE told me about an incident in the early 1990s wherein he took part in a general convention of the UML as a representative of his district, and was subsequently told by other BASE officials to provide 'clarification' at its general assembly. At the general meeting, he reminded other BASE members that the organization's strategies for social change included that of increasing the number of Tharus holding political positions as well as working in government agencies. He told them that the practices of asking people to resign their political positions before becoming active in BASE contradicted this strategy. He argued that politicians and political parties made important decisions for society, and Tharus should be present where those decisions were made. After this 'clarification', he told me, no further action was taken against

[17] According to BASE's annual report of 2057 V.S. Magh (2001), for example, there were 27,868 general members (BASE 2057 V.S.: 48) constituting over 800 village committees in 6 districts.

him by the organization. He also observed that in the early years after the restoration of multiparty democracy, with the fierce and sometimes violent competition among different political parties, it was natural that BASE members needed to be very vigilant against undue influences from any political party. But, he further observed, as years went by and the situation became more normalized as people grew more used to the multiparty system, most BASE members also felt that it was a good thing to have your friends in different political parties. In the latter half of the 1990s, in Salyan district, I knew BASE members who were also active in the Nepali Congress Party, the UML, the United People's Front, and the Rashtriya Prajatantra Party. Some Congress supporters did still speak about the UML trying to 'take over' BASE-Salyan. Some UML supporters similarly spoke of the possibilities of a Congress 'takeover' of BASE-Salyan. Meanwhile, some key positions of the BASE-Salyan district committee were held by Rashtriya Prajatantra Party supporters. In all the districts where the organization was active in the late 1990s, it seemed to me that BASE provided a unique forum where supporters of different political parties could come together and participate in common activities with major social and political significance.

During the 1990s, the amount of external funding and the number of donors for BASE increased; they were apparently impressed by its enormous local popularity. In addition to literacy classes, it was running programmes encouraging women's savings groups, environmental protection, skill-training for income generation, family planning, and HIV/AIDS prevention. In 1994 Dilli Chaudhari received the Reebok Human Rights Award for his efforts to improve the situation of the kamaiyas. This international recognition led to the decision by King Birendra to confer a medal of honour on him, thereby making it more difficult for government officials and other politicians to persecute him directly. As already mentioned, BASE leaders were themselves keenly aware of the importance of international (or royal) recognition. Since receiving the Human Rights Award, Dilli has often repeated in his public speeches that his friends and supporters included the former US president Jimmy Carter, a member of the Board of Advisors to the Reebok Award.

Throughout the 1990s, however, external criticism mounted that BASE was turning into just another 'regular' NGO, one that simply implemented projects dictated by international donors. BASE leaders themselves were conscious of this. They also felt that what they called the 'project approach', which involved seminars, workshops, saving-and-credit schemes, and income-generating activities, was not creating radical changes in the key areas of their concerns. Foremost among these concerns was the situation of the kamaiyas. In the next section, we will look at what BASE was doing during the 1990s regarding kamaiya issues, and how it started something very different in 2000. Before that, however, something should be said about BASE activities during its 'project-oriented' phase.

As we have seen, non-formal literacy education has been at the core of BASE activities. BASE gained many loyal members from those who studied in its literacy classes. Many of the literacy class students were non-Tharus and included a significant number from high-caste Hindu families as well. BASE thus cut across ethnic/caste divisions and gained many loyal non-Tharu members. This was possible because it defined its mission broadly as social progress through education – rather than defining it more exclusively as socio-economic advancement of the Tharus or the liberation of bonded kamaiyas.

In its adult literacy classes, BASE used textbooks published by the Ministry of Education of His Majesty's Government of Nepal. Laura Ahearn (2001) has observed that, unlike the school textbooks, the adult literacy textbooks had virtually no reference to nationalism. The adult literacy textbooks exhorted their intended audience, mainly rural women, to be hard-working, provident, self-sufficient, sanitation-conscious, non-alcohol-drinking, non-tobacco-smoking, and to practise family planning. However, unlike in the school textbooks, these exhortations were not tied to the project of nation-building. In the literacy classes run by BASE that I observed, the connection was made between the practices of learning and service to society (*samaj sewa*), but not to nationalism. This is also clear from a letter written by Parvati Adhikari (2057 V.S.), a non-Tharu graduate of the BASE literacy course, which was published in a BASE newsletter. In the letter, she wrote that literacy education enabled her to engage in *samaj sewa*. Parvati Adhikari begins her letter by saying that she always "wanted to serve the society" but due to economic problems at home, and because she had "just never heard of the idea that one should act for the betterment of society" (*samaj ko sewa garnu parne chetana ko bare thaha nahunale*), she did not know what to do. However, when she became a member of BASE, "they taught her how to spread to other people an awareness of the need to light education's lamp" (*siksha ko jyoti balna chetana ko bikas garauna siksha dinu bhayo*) (Adhikari 2057 V.S.). She also wrote that she felt BASE was like her maternal home, that its members were her own brothers and sisters, and that she was ready to accomplish any work that BASE might give her to do (ibid.).

In this connection, Dilli Chaudhari often repeated, both to BASE members and to me, that the organization had to be 'social' (in his case more often using the English word than the Nepali, *samajik*). By this he meant that BASE was a social organization engaged in social improvements and social movements. But he also meant that the organization and its members ought to be sociable, convivial, and gregarious. He wanted BASE members to be always talking with one another and with outsiders, including visiting foreigners. This insistence on being social went together with Dilli Chaudhari's view that if an individual or a group aims to work for social change, they need to have many networks and be connected with a variety of people, high and low, locally and internationally.

In describing BASE in this way I do not deny the Tharu-ness of the organization. The organization was initiated by young Tharus concerned mainly with improving the conditions of poor Tharus. The organization is still led mostly by those Tharus who initiated the organization, but now includes significant numbers of non-Tharus within its central committee as well as among its paid staff members. This situation has given rise to at least two forms of criticism of BASE which are mutually incompatible. On the one hand, BASE, and especially its top leaders, have been criticized of straying away from their 'essential' commitments, which the critics define as the advancements of Tharu causes. On the other hand, other critics have accused BASE of being 'too Tharu', disproportionately benefiting Tharus through its activities, whereas as a development organization BASE should be concerned with the welfare of all, and not just Tharus. For my part, I am trying to call attention to the ability that BASE has exhibited, to be either one or the other, or both at the same time, depending on the contexts and perspectives of its various participants. I insist on this point because the massive mobilization from 1 May 2000 would not have been possible if BASE had been an exclusively Tharu organization, and not the hybrid and inclusive one that it is.[18]

Even though BASE workers defined their activities as 'social' in nature, they were not apolitical either, even during the late 1990s. Let me illustrate this point by briefly describing scenes from BASE's general assembly held in 1999. It was held that year in Bardiya district and several thousand members from six BASE districts gathered. (BASE officially declared that there were ten thousand people.) On the morning of the first day, all members participated in a rally along the main highway, carrying placards and shouting slogans such as 'Send kamaiya children to school!', 'Saunki is void!', 'End to kamaiya system!', and 'Long live BASE!' The organizers and participants explicitly conceived of this mass rally as a *shakti pradarshan* (show of strength) by BASE. The mass rally was followed by an

[18]See Guneratne (2002: 91-124) and Krauskopff (2003) for accounts of BASE as a Tharu ethnic movement. For instance, Guneratne writes, "BASE is, in effect, an example of ethnicized politics ... ; it aims to alter the balance of power in Dang between Parbatiyas and Tharus, a profoundly political goal but one couched in the rhetoric of development" (2002: 124). It should be clear from my discussion above that I do not intend to deny Tharu ethnicity as a key dimension of BASE as a movement and an organization. However, its assumption of a form of development NGO has added novel dimensions to the organization. These new (not exclusively Tharu-focused) dimensions of the organization have also become part of the reality, not 'mere rhetoric', as many thousands of Pahari BASE members engaged in development and social service activities would testify.

open-air inaugural meeting. The main guest at that year's inaugural meeting was former Prime Minister Sher Bahadur Deuba.[19] He and other distinguished invitees, including politicians, journalists, and social activists, made speeches on the value of education, democracy, human rights, and NGOs. BASE members, including young women (both Tharu and non-Tharu) and a kamaiya, also made speeches. In front of the former Prime Minister and other distinguished guests, they criticized the government, police, and politicians for being corrupt and 'anti-people'.

At night there was a 'Let's Preserve Our Culture' programme in which groups from different districts danced, sang, and performed plays on the stage. All the groups wore elaborate dresses and staged well-rehearsed performances. Some of these groups put on traditional songs and dances. Others performed songs and dances with the underlying modern messages of the virtues of education, development, equality, and human rights. The cultural programme went on until dawn the next day. It was one of the most popular parts of the general assembly, and it seemed to me to embody the ideal pursued by the BASE leadership, for it to be a lively 'social' organization.

Even during the late 1990s, as just described, BASE was organizing lively activities imbued with potent social, cultural, and political messages. However, this situation was not satisfactory for many of the BASE leaders because none of these activities were able to bring about major changes in the main area of their concern, i.e. the situation of the kamaiyas.

KAMAIYA PROGRAMMES BEFORE 2000

As BASE leaders have often reminded themselves and others, more than half of their twelve central committee members either were themselves kamaiyas, or had a parent who was a kamaiya. They also understood the diverse situations of kamaiyas. Reflecting this recognition, in designing its programmes for kamaiyas, BASE divided them into three groups and gave top priority to the kind of kamaiyas it described as "Those who are born Kamaiya and might be second or third generation, still in debt and landless, living in a house provided by the landlord, and where all the family members work for the landlord" (BASE 1994: 15).

BASE programmes for these kamaiyas included conducting meetings with them. There was a programme for the children of the kamaiyas,

[19]Sher Bahadur Deuba of the Nepali Congress Party served as prime minister of Nepal from September 1995 to March 1997, again from July 2001 to October 2002, when he was dismissed by King Gyanendra, and again from June 2004 to February 2005, when he was put under house arrest by King Gyanendra.

helping them to attend either non-formal education classes run by BASE, or public schools, by providing financial assistance for school fees, uniforms, and stationery. BASE built a hostel for the children of kamaiyas in Dang, to separate them from the exploitative environment under the landlord. BASE also provided skill-training courses in hair-cutting, weaving, welding, and electrical wiring. It also distributed potato and onion seeds to kamaiya families free of charge (BASE 1994: 16-18).

In a 'Kamaiya Saving Programme', BASE asked kamaiya families to save a little bowl of rice each day. At the end of the month, BASE staff would collect the rice, turn it into money, and put it into a bank account. For 'regular savers', BASE provided 300 per cent matching funds at the end of the year. According to the BASE annual report for the year 1993/4, 221 kamaiya households participated in the saving programme. With the help of this programme, among the 221 households, 50 pairs of bullocks, 15 goats or sheep, 14 ducks, and 12 pigs were bought and 30 households were able to purchase land (BASE 1994: 17). However, by 1998 the kamaiya saving programme had been discontinued in favour of a 'kamaiya rehabilitation programme' involving grant assistance for "such Kamaiyas who want to leave their landlord's house but cannot due to lack of initial capital" (BASE 1998: 11).[20] The "poorest Kamaiya families" were identified by BASE committees and local kamaiya groups formed by BASE, and received up to 10,000 rupees. Of the 43 kamaiyas who received the assistance in 1999, for example, BASE reported that "8 bought land, 16 bought an oxcart, 12 bought oxen, 6 invested in a shop, and 1 bought a rickshaw" (Nørmose 2000: 69). As this list shows, the kind of life that the person was expected to lead after he stopped being a kamaiya was not confined to being a 'free labourer'. The possible paths included becoming a small merchant as well as tenant farmer or eventually an owner-cultivator. Of course, there could be a combination of any of the above.[21] I will return to this point later in my discussion of the kamaiya liberation movement.

As already indicated, BASE was not the only organization working on kamaiya issues. By the mid 1990s, there were dozens of large and small development and human rights organizations working on it as well. With millions of dollars in foreign aid flowing into Nepal for kamaiya-related projects, the kamaiya issue was becoming a virtual industry. Both govern-

---

[20]Vivek Pandit, a tribal rights activist discussed below, has been a vocal critic of savings programmes. According to him, you 'save' what is still left after spending on your basic necessities, and it may well be a good idea. But if you are speaking about those who are starving, what are they going to 'save'?

[21]Notice also that 'paying back the loan (*saunki*) to the landlord' is not included in this list. Assistance for paying back *saunki* was against the policy of BASE, because it regarded the *saunki* itself as illegal. However, Nørmose reports that out of her nineteen interviewees who had received Rs.10,000 through the rehabilitation programme, two reported that they used the money to pay back the *saunki* (2000: 69-70)

mental and non-governmental agents were producing reports on kamaiyas, running 'awareness raising' campaigns, conducting literacy, skill-training, health and family planning classes, and offering micro-credit and income-generation programmes.

Of course, some of these programmes provided some tangible benefits to kamaiyas themselves. With reference to BASE programmes, by the end of the 1990s, hundreds of kamaiya families had received assistance through the kamaiya saving or kamaiya rehabilitation support programme for obtaining some form of capital.[22] More than a thousand kamaiya children had received support for their education.[23] However, BASE leaders knew that these initiatives were far from sufficient given that there were tens of thousands of kamaiyas.

Yagyaraj Chaudhari

One of the BASE leaders who was most frustrated by this situation was Yagyaraj Chaudhari. Yagyaraj's father, Tikaram Chaudhari, was born, in Dang, into a family of landless labourers. Tikaram Chaudhari told me that, in Dang, he spent most of his time carrying loads up from the valley to the hills for his master. In the year 2007 V.S. (1950/1), Tikaram moved to Kailali in search of a better life. He eventually managed to buy a patch of land near Dhangadhi bazaar. Yagyaraj was born in 2015 V.S. (1958/9) as Tikaram's first son. When Yagyaraj was sixteen his father took a loan from a landlord because his family did not have enough to eat. In exchange for the loan Yagyaraj was sent to work for the landlord as a kamaiya. He had to leave school and work all day and night. The *saunki* was Rs.5,000, and his pay was Rs.600 a year. Under such terms Yagyaraj felt that he would never be able to pay back the loan. So he tried very hard to negotiate with the landlord, and eventually, after two years, was successful in persuading the landlord to let him work elsewhere so as to pay back what he owed. According to Yagyaraj, it was during the time he was working as a kamaiya that he began to think about how to get rid of the kamaiya system *as a whole*. Yagyaraj recalls that he thought many times that, "if only there were someone who would help me and support me, I would have raised my voice against the system" (Tharu 2057: 40).

After freeing himself from the landlord, he decided to engage in 'social work' (*samajik karya*). For him 'social work' included running for and serving as the ward chairman of Geti (the ward number 2 of Geta VDC in Kailali District), as well as serving as the chairman of the management

[22] The cumulative number of kamaiyas who received assistance through the savings or the rehabilitation programmes is unavailable since neither myself, BASE staff, nor others (e.g. Nørmose 2000: 69 n.58) could locate BASE annual reports from 1995 to 1997.

[23] Based on BASE annual reports. The remark made in the previous note also applies here.

committee of a local primary school. From these positions he along with his father helped sixty-five landless kamaiya families to obtain land from the Sukumbasi Samasya Samadhan Ayog (Commission for the Solution of Landless Problem) on the edge of a jungle in Krishnapur village. He and his father also borrowed Rs.36,000 from a merchant and lent the money to kamaiyas without interest, to help them buy bulls or pigs, or to build small houses (cf. Lowe 2002: 75). He also assisted groups of kamaiya families to move in and cultivate unregistered land in various locations (cf. Tharu 2057: 40).

In an interview for a BASE report, responding to the question why he became active in social work and kamaiya liberation, Yagyaraj replied:

> Because I had myself been fighting with the [kamaiya] problem and had been a victim of exploitation by the landlords, there was a sour feeling in my heart that it is not right (*uchit*) for a human being to be a slave to, or under oppression from, another human being. So I felt I had to raise my voice. (Tharu 2057: 40)[24]

In the early 1990s Yagyaraj heard about BASE from Inge Sagild (mentioned earlier as a Norwegian Church Service member who helped BASE obtain its first major funding from DANIDA), and decided to join the organization. He served as the treasurer of the BASE Kailali district committee for five years before he was elected to the BASE central committee. When running for a seat on the central committee in 1996 Yagyaraj argued that, rather than running educational and income-generation programmes, BASE should just start freeing the kamaiyas, one by one. After all, the Nepali constitution and civil code included articles prohibiting forced and bonded labour. Nepal was also a signatory to international conventions banning slavery and 'practices similar to slavery'.[25] Hence, according to Yagyaraj, BASE should persuade kamaiyas themselves to file petitions asking the government to guarantee their rights. At a meeting in the Land Reform Office in Kailali with various organizations working on

---

[24]The Nepali original reads: *ma pahiledekhi samasyasanga judhdai aeko ra jamindarharusanga sosit pidit bhai aekole manav bhaera manavko das tatha dabavma rahanu uchit hoina bhanne kura manmanai paglirahanthyo jasle yaspratī awaj uthaunai parcha bhani.* The word *uchit*, which I translated as 'right', above, could also be translated as 'proper' or 'suitable'.

[25]Article 20 (1) of the 1990 Constitution of Nepal states that "Traffic in human beings, slavery, serfdom or forced labor in any form is prohibited. Any contravention of this provision shall be punishable by law." Muluki Ain ('Civil Code') (part 4, section 11, sub-section 3) prohibits slavery-like practices and prescribes 3 to 10 years of imprisonment against offenders. Nepal also ratified the Slavery Convention (1926) and the Supplementary Convention on the Abolition of Slavery, the Slave Trade, and Institution and Practices Similar to Slavery (1956) in 1963. See fn. 2 for the definition of debt bondage given in the Supplementary Convention on the Abolition of Slavery, Section I, Article 1 (a). For more details on legal provisions see: Ojha (2057 V.S., 2000), Pandit (2000).

kamaiya issues, including BASE, INSEC, and other members of the Kamaiya Concern Group,[26] Yagyaraj even said:

> You are just filling your belly! You are working for kamaiyas for your salary. The kamaiya problem will not be solved in this way! ... Now we should file cases. (Lowe 2002: 76)

Yagyaraj decided to take personal action and targeted kamaiyas working for a single landlord, Shiva Raj Pant. Shiva Raj had migrated from the hills into Kailali around 1970, and once had "eighty kamaiyas in three villages" (Lowe 2002: 77). A professed Gandhian and a Nepali Congress Party leader, he had served as a minister in the year 2015 (1958/9). According to the locals, until around 1990, Shiva Raj owned about 300 *bigha*s of land (Shrestha 2057: 21). Although by 2000, his landholding had decreased to about 150 *bigha*s, and the number of kamaiyas to twenty, he was still considered the "most powerful person" and was still referred to as *Mantri* (minister) in the area (Lowe 2002: 76). Yagyaraj began to contact Shiva Raj's kamaiyas at night to persuade them to work towards their own freedom. After several meetings he convinced them to participate in a night class to be organized by BASE, and secured permission from the landlord, Shiva Raj, to let his kamaiyas "study in the evening" (Lowe 2002: 75). The night class continued for two years. In the class, Yagyaraj talked about how they could stop being kamaiyas. In the beginning the kamaiyas were sceptical of Yagyaraj's motives. However, things finally turned around and the kamaiyas began to believe in him, according to Yagyaraj, after he personally intervened in a dispute between a landlord and a young kamaiya who had eloped with a girl to another village.

After gaining their trust, Yagyaraj told the kamaiyas to demand that Shiva Raj Pant raise their wages. Earlier in the year (2000), a minimum wage law had been passed fixing it at Rs.60 a day. Each kamaiya family working for Shiva Raj Pant received 15 quintals (1.5 tons) of paddy per year. According to one calculation this was the equivalent of about Rs.13 per day.[27] Their demands for a raise were refused by Shiva Raj. Yagyaraj told them to go again after fifteen days and tell the landlord that without the

---

[26]In 1997, a number of organizations concerned with kamaiya issues formed the Kamaiya Concern Group (KCG) with INSEC playing a coordinating role. According to Robertson and Mishra (1997: 67) the group included the Kamaiya Liberation Forum, BASE, INSEC, GRINSO, Rural Reconstruction Nepal, DANIDA, Lutheran World Service, Save the Children (US), UNICEF, ActionAid Nepal, South Asia Partnership Nepal, UNDP, Social Welfare Council, and Plan International.

[27]The calculation was done by the Kamaiya Freedom Movement Working Committee and publicized on <www.freedomnepal.org> during the movement. The kamaiya families working for Shiva Raj Pant ranged in size from five to fifteen members (I cite the number from the information reprinted in Informal 2000: 48). On the Kamaiya Freedom Movement Working Committee, see fn. 29.

raise they would stop working and leave him without paying back the *saunki*. Yagyaraj also called a women's meeting and they too went to ask Shiva Raj for a raise. The landlord became very angry and relations between him and the kamaiyas and Yagyaraj became very tense. But the kamaiyas and Yagyaraj were determined not to back down (Lowe 2002: 76).

THE KAMAIYA LIBERATION MOVEMENT OF 2000

In 2000 BASE and other NGOs organized a three-day meeting and festivities leading up to May Day. The programme included song and dance competitions and speeches by kamaiyas themselves. According to Yagyaraj, Shiva Raj Pant's kamaiyas, who also took part in the programmes, felt encouraged to see so many kamaiyas like themselves and to learn that there were many people who would fight on their side. On the third day of the meeting, on 1 May, nineteen kamaiyas working under Shiva Raj Pant filed their cases with the Geta VDC office. They requested four things: (1) the enforcement of the minimum wage law; (2) cancellation of their debts; (3) rehabilitation measures; and (4) guarantees of their personal security. On 10 May a meeting was held at the VDC office with about 100 participants, including the kamaiyas, journalists, and representatives of various organizations. However, Shiva Raj Pant did not attend the meeting and the kamaiyas and their supporters decided the case needed to be taken to the District Administrative Office (BASE 2057 V.S.: 10).

BASE members wrote up statements from each of the nineteen kamaiyas and took them to the Kailali District Administrative Office in Dhangadhi.[28] However, the CDO Tana Gautam refused to register the case and insulted the kamaiyas and supporting organizations, who in turn immediately began a sit-in in front of the CDO's office on 12 May. On 14 May thousands of people (7,000-8,000 according to BASE and the Kamaiya Freedom Movement Working Committee[29] [BASE 2057 V.S.; Informal 2000]) including many kamaiyas but also a large number of non-kamaiyas, as well as non-Tharus, from Dang, Banke, Bardiya, Kailali, and Kanchanpur, gathered in Dhangadhi to protest in front of the CDO office. Although various organizations were involved in this mobilization, the overwhelming majority of the protesters were BASE members, since no other organ-

[28]Five of the statements were subsequently put on <www.freedomnepal.org> by the Kamaiya Liberation Movement Working Committee and reprinted in Informal 2000.

[29]The Kamaiya Freedom Movement Working Committee or Kamaiya Andolan Parichalan Samiti was formed during the liberation movement by the supporters of the movement with Dilli Chaudhari as the coordinator while the Kamaiya Liberation Movement Committee was also created to represent the kamaiyas themselves with Raj Dev Chaudhari, one of Shiva Raj's kamaiyas, as its chairman.

ization had a comparable mass membership or ability for mass mobilization. On 15 May the demonstrators staged a silent demonstration tying black cloth over their mouths signifying that the government was not listening to its people. On the same day, the chairman of INSEC, Sushil Pyakurel, sent letters to the Prime Minister, the general secretary of the opposition, UML, and other major political figures to take up the kamaiya issue in parliament (BASE 2057 V.S.: 10).

The sit-in continued as meetings among the supporting organizations were held daily and continuous efforts were made to attract more media attention and to involve high-level politicians. On 18 May 2000, demonstrators with lit lanterns marched in Dhangadhi bazaar in broad daylight to signify that they were looking for justice. On other days the demonstrators beat drums, pots, and pans, proclaiming that they were trying to wake up the conscience of the government officials (BASE 2057 V.S.). After twelve days of the sit-in, the landlord, Shiva Raj Pant, said he had had enough. At a meeting at the district office, he said: "I might have borrowed money from these Kamaiyas in my previous life. I grant remission of their loans. They are free to go" (Lowe 2002: 76).

The news spread rapidly and BASE encouraged other kamaiyas to file similar cases with their district administrative offices. More than a thousand kamaiyas did so. BASE also continued to organize protest rallies and sit-ins at different district headquarters in the western Tarai districts. However, the district administrative officers began declaring that they had no authority to decide the cases. In early July BASE organized a two-day meeting of kamaiyas and organizations supporting them in the western Tarai town of Nepalganj.[30] They invited Vivek Pandit, a tribal rights activist from India and the winner of the 1999 Anti-Slavery International Award, to serve as a 'facilitator' of the meeting.[31] I mentioned earlier that the cases filed by the first nineteen kamaiyas involved demands for better wages, housing, personal security, as well as cancellation of their debts. However, at this meeting in Nepalganj, Vivek Pandit and others insisted that 'freedom' was the first and foremost issue for the kamaiyas. As long as the kamaiyas were under the domination of the landlords, they could not start to build their lives as dignified human beings. After freedom, other issues could be dealt with. The goal of the movement had to be clearly defined. And the goal was freedom. Vivek, as the facilitator of the meeting, encouraged the kamaiyas to compose and sing songs about the kamaiya struggle. It was, Vivek suggested, an epic fight between good and evil, as in

[30]The following account of the Nepalganj meeting is based on an oral presentation made at Martin Chautari (Thapathali, Kathmandu) in July 2000 by Ashutosh Tiwari who participated at that meeting. Later e-mail communication with Tiwari provided additional information.

[31]Dilli Chaudhari first came to know Vivek in 1988 through his trip supported by the Asian Adivasi Committee mentioned above.

Hindi movies. There were heroes and there were villains. The heroes, of course, were the kamaiyas who deserved freedom; the villains were the landlords and the chief district officers who denied them freedom. Nepali and International NGOs were cast as friends of the heroes, facilitators of the legitimate desire of the kamaiyas to be free.

At this point, Dilli Chaudhari and other leaders of BASE felt that they needed to take the movement to the capital, Kathmandu, since the district-level administrators appeared unwilling to act. Yet BASE did not have an office in Kathmandu. So Dilli first contacted INSEC, the largest Nepali human rights organization based in Kathmandu. However, following their own programme for the liberation of kamaiyas, the leaders of INSEC told Dilli not to come to Kathmandu. They argued that comprehensive legislation for kamaiya liberation and rehabilitation, the kind that they had already drafted, needed to be passed by the parliament before the liberation process could begin (cf. Ojha 2000, 2057 v.s.). The kind of activities that BASE had helped initiate, they said, was only going to create chaos.

However, the movement had already started, and more than a thousand kamaiyas had already taken clearly antagonistic stances towards their landlords by filing petitions. So the movement could not simply be called off. Dilli Chaudhari then contacted Martin Chautari, an informal discussion forum in Kathmandu run by a group of young intellectuals. Members of this group, including Ashutosh Tiwari who worked for BASE as a volunteer in the mid 1990s, had already visited Dhangadhi during the month of June to observe the kamaiyas' movement. Dilli told the organizers of Martin Chautari that he wanted to bring in 150 kamaiyas and kamalaharis to Kathmandu within a few days, to stage a sit-in in front of the parliament building, and he wanted Martin Chautari to look after the logistics. The Martin Chautari organizers agreed. ActionAid and Save the Children US quickly came up with financial aid for logistical support. I had returned to Kathmandu in mid June 2000 and had been following the kamaiya movement through communications with Dilli Chaudhari and other activists. Since I was also a regular participant in Martin Chautari, I naturally participated in the movement's operation in Kathmandu.

The members of Martin Chautari arranged for food, lodging, and medical support for the kamaiyas. They also wrote press statements, corresponded with international human rights organizations, and held meetings of NGOs in support of the kamaiya movement. In these meetings, many organizations argued that since the kamaiya issue was complex, the movement should make many demands, including even the implementation of sweeping land-reform measures. The BASE leaders and many of the Martin Chautari members disagreed. Ashutosh Tiwari in particular kept repeating that the demand had to be simple and clear, otherwise the movement would not produce any tangible results. Since the government could not possibly deny that bonded labour was unconstitutional in Nepal as well as in violation of international human rights laws, this was the argument the movement should make.

Indeed, all the political parties, from royalists to social democrats to Marxist-Leninists to Maoists, came forward and expressed their support for the movement. Many political leaders came to Bhadrakali, across the street from the parliament, to give speeches in front of the kamaiyas. The human rights activist, Gopal Shivakoti 'Chintan', also made a speech at Bhadrakali and told the kamaiyas:

> The Nepali government is sending armed police force to western Nepal, saying that the government is trying to make the Maoists obey the Constitution. Now you came all the way from western Nepal to Kathmandu, in order to make the government itself obey the Constitution.

Journalists also came to interview the kamaiyas. The kamaiyas told them stories of suffering, or *dukha*: one kamaiya told them how having been kicked by the landlord, he had once fallen from the stairs and broken his bones; a kamalahari said the landlord once tried to rape her; a *bukrahi* related how her infant baby died because the landlord was not giving them enough food. As an example of *dukha* stories, let me relate here what Jokhini Chaudhari told the reporter, Roshan Shrestha, in an interview around the time of the movement. Jokhini Chaudhari is the wife of one of the kamaiyas who was employed by Shiva Raj Pant. By 2000, she had worked for Shiva Raj for forty-one years. When asked by the reporter to describe the saddest experience of her life (*jindagima aphulai sabaibhanda dukha lageko kura*) she told the following story. From time to time, Jokhini and others had to apply mud on Shiva Raj's house walls. Once she had her two-month-old son with her when she had to do that work. Each time she tried to take a break to breastfeed her son, she was beaten on the head and told to return to work. "My son died because he couldn't drink milk!" (Shrestha 2057: 19). Shrestha's paper also describes cases of rape of girls of kamaiya households (ibid.: 18).[32]

Legally minded supporters such as Tiwari argued that there was no need for those *dukha* stories for the purpose of the movement – rather, they had to keep repeating the clear legal arguments. In Tiwari's argument, as well as in Vivek Pandit's insistence on viewing the movement as an epic battle between good and evil, we see a radical reduction of the complexity of kamaiya practices that Katherine Rankin, as we saw earlier, reacted against. But again, we are here not primarily concerned with the accuracy of a juridical discourse as a representation of a complex local practice.

---

[32] On the abuse of kamaiyas and their family members, see also Guneratne (2002: 96-8).

Rather, we are concerned with its pragmatics. The movement participants were reducing the complexity of the issues in order, among other things, to enable the government to *act*. I am sure that very few of the movement's participants doubted the necessity of systematic land-reform measures for the effective reduction of rural poverty. However, all knew that there was not much possibility in the short run of the government devising and actually implementing an effective land-reform programme. To demand such action as the first priority was to risk creating a situation where the movement did not produce any result at all.

On the evening of the third day of the sit-in, wanting to keep up the momentum, Dilli Chaudhari and others decided that the protesters should march towards the parliament building, stop traffic, and let a few among them, including Dilli himself, be arrested. On the fourth day of the sit-in, we began to march. When the police stopped the march from reaching the parliament, Dilli and others sat down in the middle of the road. The police decided to arrest Dilli, all the kamaiyas and kamalaharis, and many of the supporters marching with them, including me.[33] In the Mahendra Police Club where we were all detained, we heard on the 5 o'clock radio news that the government, based on a cabinet meeting held earlier that day, had declared that, effective immediately, all the kamaiyas were free, and any debts they owed to the landlords were void. The government also promised to implement rehabilitation measures for the freed kamaiyas. Kamaiyas and their supporters celebrated joyfully inside the Mahendra Police Club, rubbing *abir* (red powder) on each other's faces. The general secretary of the Communist Party of Nepal (UML), Madhav Kumar Nepal, came to the Police Club and made a speech telling the kamaiyas how UML had always supported kamaiya causes and this time had forced the government to declare the emancipation by stating at the beginning of the parliamentary session that the UML would block the proceedings from going forward unless the government addressed the kamaiya issue as the first order of business. (According to my information, the UML and Congress leaders had met the night before and agreed on the scenario, i.e. UML would first

---

[33]Before the beginning of the march, Dilli Chaudhari had given a strong warning to the police officers not to injure the protesting kamaiyas and kamalaharis, or let any of them 'disappear'. Since almost all of the kamaiyas and kamalaharis were visiting Kathmandu for the first time, it was perhaps a wise decision on the part of the police to arrest *all* of them, rather than, for example, arresting a few of them and lathi-charging and dispersing the rest in different directions – in which case, a number of them might well have got lost. For my part, I was not planning on being arrested. The night before the march, someone in the meeting suggested that the presence of a foreigner with a camera might deter the policemen from using excessive force in dealing with the protesters. I had that suggestion in my mind when I approached the front line of the protest with a camera, and was immediately grabbed by a policeman and pushed into a van. I suppose they were grabbing everyone near the front line without first checking whether the person was a journalist or a foreigner.

threaten a boycott, and then the government would declare the emancipation.) Then, former Prime Minister and Nepali Congress Party leader Sher Bahadur Deuba came to the Police Club and made a speech, and we were released.

The kamaiyas and their supporters walked back to Bhadrakali, and from there embarked on a "victory rally" around Tundikhel and Ratna Park in the middle of the city. Several kamalahari whom I spoke with told me that they were extremely happy because 'we won' – echoing Vivek Pandit's exhortation earlier to regard this movement as an epic fight between good and evil.

AFTER THE EMANCIPATION

Immediately after the government's declaration, BASE organized massive rallies in western Nepal celebrating kamaiya liberation, some of which I participated in. In the Dhangadhi bazaar in Kailali, the rally by a few thousand demonstrators was headed by a Tharu dancing troupe which intermittently threw clouds of red powder into the sky. Dilli Chaudhari characterized this celebration rally, as he did other massive BASE gatherings, as *shakti pradarshan,* or a show of strength. The purpose of the rally, in addition to celebrating the victory of the kamaiyas, was to exhibit their power to the people in the bazaar including the merchants, office workers, politicians, and government officials. On the day of the rally I also accompanied Dilli to the district administrative office and police office, where he explained to the concerned officials the purpose of the kamaiya movement and that it was a peaceful one, and asked them not to randomly arrest or otherwise persecute kamaiyas or their supporters.

A newspaper cartoon a few days after the declaration depicted a man whose left leg was freed from the fetters of the 'Kamaiya System' but whose right leg was still chained to the larger fetters of poverty (Spotlight 2000). Indeed, thousands of kamaiya families left their landlords, either of their own volition or because they were forced out. They began to live in makeshift camps on public lands around the bazaars, highways, and jungles. BASE, the Lutheran World Service, and other organizations were immediately faced with the task of assisting kamaiyas with their daily food, shelter, and medical needs. The government was very slow to come up with any rehabilitation measures.

Before the start of the kamaiya liberation movement, ILO's Nepal office had been granted 3.5 million dollars by the United States Department of Labor for kamaiya-related programmes. A couple of months after the declaration of emancipation, ILO announced that it was going to implement a programme of

> direct action targeted at bonded labourers and their families to secure effective release from bondage, and sustainably reduce their poverty through training and education, livelihood improvements, and service provision. (as quoted in Chaudhari 2000)

Responding to this announcement, Dilli Chaudhari argued in his opinion article in *The Kathmandu Post* that the ILO programme represented another example of the flawed 'project mentality' in which Dilli himself and his organization had once been trapped. Dilli argued that the programme was destined to fail since it was conceived without consulting the former kamaiyas about their actual, urgent needs. Clearly, former kamaiyas needed to have housing and land issues reasonably settled before they felt like participating in a skill-training classes or a savings-and-credit group (Chaudhari 2000). Instead, the ex-kamaiya leaders and BASE demanded distribution of 10 *katthas* (1/3 hectare) of land to each kamaiya family (ibid.). Ten *katthas* of irrigated land was considered the minimum landholding for a small farming family to be food sufficient. And every kamaiya already knew how to work on the land.

After the emancipation, the government conducted a survey and declared that there were 18,245 kamaiya households in the five western Tarai districts. In conducting this survey the government divided kamaiyas into four categories:

> A: Kamaiyas who possess no house or land
> B: Kamaiyas who possess a small hut on an unregistered land
> C: Kamaiyas who possess up to 2 *katthas* of registered land and a small shelter
> D: Kamaiyas who possess more than C.
>
> (Devkota 2000: 3)

The government claimed that out of the total of 18,245 kamaiya households, there were 8,523 category A households. These households were going to be the primary beneficiaries of the government rehabilitation programmes. From the beginning of the government survey process, there were informal complaints heard that a significant number of kamaiyas were being left out (ibid.). The government's tendency towards leaving out a significant number of kamaiyas was more apparent in the actual procedure for distributing identification cards proving that the holder was really a landless former kamaiya and thus eligible to receive a land title and other rehabilitation support. The government required anyone asking for an identification card to obtain the landlord's signature certifying him as his former kamaiya. A significant number of landlords refused to sign. At the same time, there were a number of reported cases of non-kamaiyas receiving identification cards (Ban 2002; McNair 2003; Bhusal & Whyte 2001). On the whole, identification and the distribution of land became a lengthy process. Many former kamaiyas who waited in long lines at the Land Reform Office were simply told to 'come again' at the end of the day (Bhusal & Whyte 2001). By December 2000 many thousands of kamaiya families had already gone through a very heavy rainy season and were now enduring the cold weather with only a plastic sheet over their heads.

Given this condition, in January 2001, exactly six months after the emancipation, BASE helped thousands of former kamaiyas living in camps in Bardiya, Kailali, and Kanchanpur districts, to begin 'land grab' actions – they occupied unregistered land around the forests, and distributed land among themselves, 10 *kattha*s each. Some of the settlements on the captured land were burnt down by the government, including the settlement with 8,000 huts on a wide open space in Kalika in the Bardiya district which legally belonged to the government's Cotton Development Committee. However, most kamaiyas succeeded in holding on to the captured land and were able to begin cultivating. Around this time, proving the validity of Dilli Chaudhari's often repeated claim of friendship, Jimmy Carter at the request of the former sent letters with his delegates to the king and the prime minister of Nepal requesting prompt implementation of rehabilitation measures.

In their interviews in 2001 with MS Nepal,[34] many of the freed kamaiyas said that although life in the camp was hard, they felt better because they were free. They were free to get up at any time, to go and look for work if they wanted, or to meet with friends and sing and dance. Debi Lal Tharu, a kamaiya who participated in the protests in Kathmandu but was still living at the landlord's place at the time of the interview, told the interviewers:

> When kamaiya movement organizers came to talk to us about our rights the landlord was angry, so we were afraid to talk to them. We feared that we would be beaten. But I decided to talk with them anyway. I used to travel with the landlord. My job was to carry his bags, clean his clothes and be the guard. So I had been outside and seen that others had freedom. I thought it could be good for us to have it here too. We are human beings and we need human rights [*hami manis haun ra manislai manav adhikar chahincha*]. After that, I sold a small goat and went to Kathmandu to join the kamaiya movement. Now I no longer feel shy about talking face-to-face with the landlord. I had to bow many times whenever I talked to him. Now once is enough. (Lowe 2002: 43-4)

Durgi Devi Chaudhari, a freed kamalahari, told interviewers:

---

[34] A Danish NGO (Mellemfolkeligt Samvirke/Danish Association for International Cooperation) working to support freed kamaiyas in Nepal.

> The landlords say that we are lower people and they are higher. … They kept us under their feet and looked down at us. So, we didn't like to live with them, and we left. Now it is different. We are free. We don't have to work for the landlord. Now we have been made higher. Now we have courage. (Lowe 2002: 44)

Sukdaya Chaudhari, another freed kamalahari, asked:

> Shall we be led by others or lead ourselves? We should become leaders. Let us march forward for our rights. Let us go forward ourselves. Let us become leaders and teach others. Let me sing a song in Tharu … (she sings) … This song means that we were in darkness. Down there on the plain the paddy plants are dancing with the wind. Our eyes begin to open. Now my life is better. I can work however I want and go wherever I like. I have a small hut and even though it is not in good condition I manage to live comfortably, to make little improvements and be secure. The health of my children has improved and everybody respects me. Life goes on whatever the conditions may be. This is my own life and I have to be strong and make it myself. One should improve as far as possible one's own life. We have to solve our own problems. (Lowe 2002: 44)

After the declaration of an emergency by the government in November 2001, some additional kamaiya settlements were burnt down by government officials. BASE also came under increased pressure from both the Maoists and the government. The Maoists were extorting money from BASE workers, and looting and blowing up BASE offices. The Home Minister Khum Bahadur Khadka, on the other hand, accused BASE of collaborating with the Maoists and was threatening to revoke its NGO registration. Jimmy Carter again wrote a letter on behalf of BASE and, according to BASE leaders, the persecution from the government side stopped immediately after the latter received Carter's letter. However, the kamaiyas' ability to agitate for land was severely limited during the emergency, since the right to assemble, along with other fundamental rights, had been suspended.

The relationship between the CPN (Maoist) and BASE has always been contentious. It is understandable given that the former preaches violent revolution as the only way forward for Nepal, while the latter is committed to pursuing non-violent paths towards social transformation. Towards the end of the 1990s in Salyan, for example, BASE workers were regularly harassed by Maoists, and BASE meetings and training sessions were occasionally hijacked by Maoists who turned those meetings into their own propaganda sessions. However, unlike most foreign-funded NGOs working in Salyan, which were forced to close down their projects by 1998 by the Maoists, BASE remained quite active in the district beyond the close of the 1990s. Some BASE members in Salyan attributed this difference to the locally rooted nature of BASE. While the activities of most other foreign-funded NGOs were run by their staff sent in from Kathmandu, BASE activities were run by locals, so the Maoists could not just tell the BASE staff to 'leave' the district as they did other NGO personnel. Other BASE members in Salyan observed that since both BASE members and fieldworkers were from local villages (and mostly from households of medium to lower economic status) the Maoists would have risked antagonizing entire villages if they injured or killed any BASE activists.[35]

In recent years, however, Maoist attitudes towards BASE appear to have become much more antagonistic and aggressive. This is true, especially after the breakdown of the second ceasefire in August 2003 and the subsequent, dramatic escalation of military confrontation. In January 2004, the Maoists declared western Tarai as the 'Tharuwan Autonomous Region'. From the spring of 2004 the Tharuwan People's Council began to demand that NGOs and international organizations active in the region register formally with the council and pay tax to them. Around this time the Maoists also blew up the BASE office in Kailali and stepped up their propaganda campaign against BASE, accusing the organization of massive corruption. One of the reasons behind the intensified Maoist campaign against BASE at this juncture may have been that the former felt an urgent need for the consolidation of rural Tharu support for the revolutionary movement, and they saw BASE as an obstacle in this. This would be in line with a long-established Maoist tendency to expel or murder anyone who exhibits and exercises local leadership *and* does not agree with the Maoists, whether he or she belonged to Congress or Communist parties, or did not belong to any. As a result of Maoist actions, it has reportedly become very difficult to carry out many of BASE's activities in many rural areas, especially since 2003, although I have not had the opportunity to investigate systematically and measure the magnitude of Maoist control for myself.

Since early 2001 some members of international human rights organizations had made joint efforts to nominate Dilli Chaudhari and BASE for the Anti-Slavery International Award. The purpose was to raise the international profile of the kamaiya situation and BASE. The hope was that the international attention would contribute to quickening the rehabilitation processes of former kamaiyas, and to lowering the possibilities of persecu-

[35]Around 1998, in Salyan, local Maoist cadres told BASE members that BASE would be allowed to be active for another five years. At that time the local Maoists frequently said that in five years, with the progress of the revolutionary movement, there would no longer be any need for NGOs.

tion of BASE. Dilli Chaudhari and BASE were awarded the Anti-Slavery Award in December 2002 in London. During this period, BASE continued to receive assistance for programmes for freed kamaiyas from small and large donors. While many donor-assisted programmes have been helpful, especially for those kamaiyas who have already received official land titles, many BASE leaders including Yagyaraj Chaudhari have criticized the lack of international organizations that are willing to work directly on the issue of land rights.

In 2003, taking advantage of a period of ceasefire between the Maoists and the government, from 18 to 30 July, the kamaiyas organized another major campaign for land rights involving road blockades and the shutting down of district administrative offices. Through this campaign they were able to make the government reopen the identification process and distribute more land (BASE 2060). By spring 2004, according to a survey conducted by NGOs including BASE, there were 32,922 former-kamaiya families who were formally identified as such by the government. (Compare this number with 18,245, i.e. the number of kamaiya families identified by the government in its first survey after the declaration of emancipation.) According to that survey conducted by the NGOs, there were 2,789 former kamaiyas still to be identified as such by the government. The same survey reported that there were now 16,163 households classified by the government as Class A former kamaiyas. On the other hand, the number of those former kamaiyas who had actually obtained land from the government was given as 11,999. The government has given former kamaiyas between 1 and 5 *kattha*s of land each, which is far less than the 10 *kattha*s initially demanded by the kamaiya freedom movement. However, if we assume that all this land went to Class A former kamaiyas, then roughly 74 per cent of those identified as formerly landless and houseless kamaiyas have received land in their own names. Many of them have also managed to receive from the government a grant of Rs.10,000 and wood to build a house. Many of those officially settled have also received much support from international organizations. For example, the World Food Program, through German Technical Assistance (GTZ), implemented programmes for building infrastructures in freed kamaiya settlements and hired the freed kamaiyas for construction work and provided wages. Lutheran World Service and others have helped with house construction and other matters, so that one can see a number of kamaiya settlements lined with houses with cemented walls, tin roofs, and cemented and tin-roofed outhouses.

Based on the above, we can certainly observe that former kamaiyas, as a whole, have not received everything that they demanded. One of the most urgent issues remains to be the official recognition for those who are yet to be identified, so that they can also become eligible for a variety of assistance programmes. On the other hand, we cannot say that the kamaiya freedom movement has resulted in total disaster. They were not simply thrown out into the realm of the 'free market', as it were, to fend for themselves. They are struggling instead in a space where there is the presence of numerous governmental and non-governmental agencies whose mandates are to increase the welfare of disadvantaged population groups. How one manages to establish a relationship with these agencies critically affects one's fortune.

Another, more recent development we should note is the emergence of kamaiya organizations that are determined to act independently from BASE. Many of them voice strong criticism of what they have perceived as a lack of effective leadership exhibited by BASE in the post-emancipation period. They also emphasize that the movement now has to be led by and for kamaiyas themselves, and not by NGOs, such as BASE, who, they say, are deriving financial benefits in the name of kamaiyas. The effects of the diversification of kamaiya organizations and leadership remain to be seen. However, at this point, I should like to note that the demands and strategies of these new organizations are not significantly different from those adopted by kamaiya organizations working with BASE. These new organizations are also demanding provisions of land and other facilities from the government, and they have captured a government-owned (and unused) airfield in Kailali and a cotton field in Bardiya.

CONCLUSION

In conclusion, let me highlight some of the key features of this story and consider their theoretical and political implications. The success of BASE in leading the kamaiya freedom movement in 2000 ought to be attributed first of all to its strong and massive grassroots membership. The members participated in Backward Society Education, whose name, broadly construed, pointed to the need for those groups that were 'left behind' or were 'lower' to be uplifted through 'education'. I argued that the groups to be uplifted were not limited to Tharus. BASE leaders were also constantly trying to build up social networks. We saw that the BASE leadership actively sought to establish connections with international actors as well as local and national powerbrokers. This effort included involving non-Tharus (including local and national elites) in BASE activities. The nature of the associations that they built among diverse actors, however, was not simply based on utilitarian interests. The letter by Parvati Adhikari, a non-Tharu graduate from a BASE literacy class, referred to earlier, described feelings about BASE being like her maternal home, and its members her own brothers and sisters (2056 V.S.). In other words, she was saying that she had emotional attachment to the organization. She wrote that she was ready to accomplish *any* work that BASE might give her to do. She was ready to accomplish such work because of her loyalty to the organization, without the need to deliberate on the merits of each assignment from BASE.

Earlier in the chapter, we saw Katherine Rankin arguing that what she called "discourse of freedom" was intimately tied with neo-liberal ideology, and hence was not genuinely liberatory. The kamaiya freedom movement seized upon the very juridical notion of freedom that Rankin and Gyan Prakash criticized. By focusing on legal rights, the movement was able to produce a radical disruption in local operations of power, enabling, among other things, kamaiyas who had previously lived in isolation from each other to settle together and organize themselves. The main kamaiya demand of the movement after gaining freedom was not for training to turn themselves into wage labourers but for land to enable them to produce at least part of their subsistence needs by themselves. In struggling to build their new lives, they constantly engaged with the government by repeatedly visiting its offices and by means of demonstrations, road blockages, and the unauthorized occupation of public lands. Through these actions, they were challenging the government to fulfil its responsibilities as the provider of minimum welfare to its population (cf. Chatterjee 2004).

This brings us back to Tim Whyte's observation, quoted in the epigraph, that the kamaiyas were trying 'from the bottom up' to make the government work for them. Here, I should like to highlight the fact that demands of the kamaiyas are aimed at His Majesty's Government of Nepal. This point is important, given that situation, and the prevalent forms of analyses of the current political situation, in Nepal. Immediately after the declaration of emancipation, many people were speaking of the possibility that the kamaiyas thus freed would join the Maoists *en masse*. Even members of BASE had observed that *if* the government did not promptly implement rehabilitation measures *then* many of the kamaiyas might join the Maoists. The government security forces, on their part, appear to have no qualms in *presuming* kamaiya sympathies towards the Maoists. They have conducted numerous 'search operations' in freed kamaiya camps. The representatives of freed kamaiya organizations claim that there have been at least twenty well-documented cases of extrajudicial killings of freed kamaiyas by the security forces. They also testify that there have been many more cases of rape by the security personnel of women in freed kamaiya settlements.

At the time of this writing (early 2005), more than four years have passed since the declaration of emancipation. Given the government's apparent lack of commitment towards proper and complete rehabilitation, and the crimes committed by government forces against the freed kamaiyas, it is indeed somewhat surprising that the overwhelming majority of former kamaiyas have not joined the People's Liberation Army. Even those freed kamaiyas who parted with BASE, as we have seen, are still asking His Majesty's Government (HMG) to implement rehabilitation measures. Local Maoists, on their part, have been telling those still landless former kamaiyas to capture and occupy land belonging to large landlords. According to my information, kamaiyas have refused this order by the Maoists. One of the main reasons for the refusal is of course that the Maoists cannot guarantee the security of those kamaiyas who thus occupy the landlords' property. Kamaiyas who obey the order of the Maoists would become vulnerable to being killed by the government security forces. Hence the overwhelming majority of kamaiyas prefer land titles issued by the HMG. In this connection, we can also observe that Maoist actions have created obstacles against the fulfilment of kamaiya demands, as Maoists have banned government officials, including those with authority to issue land titles to former kamaiyas, from entering the rural areas that the former claim to be under their control (cf. Luintel 2061 V.S.).

I have already mentioned that one of the most recent and prominent organized actions by the freed kamaiya was the occupation of government-owned lands such as airfields. Those who occupied these lands have been demanding that the government either provide them with land titles or, if the former needs to keep those lands, provide alternative land. As to the reason why they decided to occupy government airfields and cotton fields rather than, for instance, unclaimed patches of land in the villages or near the forests, a number of freed kamaiyas told me that they were trying to 'awaken' the government. It should not be necessary to add that this is different from a revolutionary politics that aims to *replace* the current government. Those freed kamaiyas occupying the government lands are still engaged in a "politics of patience" (Appadurai 2002) and not a revolutionary politics of radical discontinuity and rapture (Onesto 2000). After more than four years since their 'emancipation', and even after the suspension of representative democracy in Nepal in October 2002, the freed kamaiyas, as Tim Whyte wrote, are engaged in democratic struggles.

REFERENCES

Adhikari, P. 2057 V.S. (2000). 'Praud Kaksha Padheki Mahila Parvati Adhikari ko Patra (Letter from Parvati Adhikari, a Woman Who Learned to Read in an Adult Education Class)', *Sanghari* 3 (12): 8.

Ahearn, L. 2001. *Invitations to Love: Literacy, Love Letters, and Social Change in Nepal*. Ann Arbor: University of Michigan Press.

Appadurai, A. 2002. 'Deep Democracy: Urban Governmentality and the Horizons of Politics', *Public Culture* 14 (1): 21-48.

Ban, J. 2002. 'Kamaiya Mukti: Pristhabhumidekhi Parinatisamma (Kamaiya Liberation: From Background to Transformation)', *Ekchin* 2: 34-9.

BASE. n.d. 'Kamaiya Sarvekshan Prativedan Vivaran, Arthik Barsa 2057/8 (Report on the Kamaiya Survey, Financial Year 2057-8)'. Unpublished document. Nepalganj: Backward Society Education (BASE) Banke office.

——. 1992. *One Year Report (October 1991 - September 1992) for Tharu Education for Transformation* (Submitted to DANIDA). Tulsipur: BASE.

——. 1993. *Second Year Report (October 1992 - September 1993) for Tharu Education for Transformation* (Submitted to DANIDA). Tulsipur: BASE.

——. 1994. *Tharu Education for Transformation: Third Year Report* (Submitted to DANIDA). Tulsipur: BASE Project Office.

——. 1995. *Kamaiya Survey Report.* Tulsipur: BASE Project Office.

——. 1998. *Annual Progress Report 1998* (Submitted to Royal Danish Embassy/ DANIDA). Tulsipur: BASE Project Office.

——. 2053 v.s. *Barsik Pragati Prativedan (Yearly Progress Report).* Chakhaura, Dang: BASE Central Office.

——. 2055 v.s. 'Bes Ke Ho?' (What is BASE?), *Sanghari* 2 (17): 2, 5.

——. 2056 v.s. *Barsik Pragati Prativedan (2056 Magh samma) [Yearly Progress Report (up to 2001)]*. Tulsipur: BASE.

——. 2057 v.s. 'Kamaiya Andolan Kailalima Kun Din Ke Bhayo? 2057 Baisakh dekhi Jestha 17 sammako Ghatna Vivaran (In the Kailali Kamaiya Movement What Happened on Which Day? Analysis of the Incidents in 2000, April-June)' *Sanghari* 3 (12): 11, 12, 10.

——. 2060 v.s. 'Mukta Kamaiya Punarsthapanaka lagi Andolan (miti 2060 Srawan dekhi 14 Gate samma): Pragati ra Samiksa (The Movement for the Rehabilitation of Freed-Kamaiyas (from July 2003): Progress and Assessment)'. Unpublished report. Dhangadhi: BASE Kailali Office.

Bhusal, S. and T. Whyte. 2001. *Freed Kamaiya Status Report, October 2001.* MS Nepal (Danish Association for International Cooperation) (cited 6 November 2001). Available from http://www.msnepal.org/reports_pubs/kamaiya_report/

Breman, J. 1993. *Beyond Patronage and Exploitation: Changing Agrarian Relations in South Gujarat.* Delhi: Oxford University Press.

Chapagain, D.P. 1998. *A Decade of Human Rights Movement in Nepal: An Assessment of the Activities of INSEC.* Kathmandu: Informal Sector Service Centre (INSEC).

Chatterjee, P. 2004. *The Politics of the Governed.* New York: Columbia University Press.

Chaudhari, D. 2000. 'Land Rights: Next Priority for ex-Kamaiyas'. *The Kathmandu Post*, 27 November, Editorial page.

Cox, T. n.d. (*c.*1994). 'Backward Society Education (BASE): The Development of a Grassroots Movement'. Tulsipur, Dang: BASE.

Devkota, B.M. 2000. 'A Status Report on the Situation of the Kamaiyas in

Kanchanpur, Kailali, and Bardiya Districts, December 2000'. Unpublished report.

Dhakal, S., J. Rai, D. Chemchong, D. Maharjan, P. Pradhan, J. Maharjan, and S. Chaudhary. 2000. *Issues and Experiences: Kamaiya System, Kanara Andolan and Tharus in Bardiya*. Kathmandu: Society for Participatory Cultural Education (SPACE).

Fujikura, T. 2001. 'Discourses of Awareness: Notes for a Criticism of Development in Nepal'. *Studies in Nepali History and Society* 6 (2): 271-313.

Guneratne, A. 2002. *Many Tongues, One People: The Making of Tharu Identity in Nepal*. Ithaca: Cornell University Press.

Informal. 2000. 'Bonded Labourers on their Road to Freedom'. *Informal* 10 (1): 46-9.

INSEC. 1996. *Human Rights Yearbook 1995*. Kathmandu: Informal Sector Service Centre (INSEC).

——. 1999. 'Maoist Activities and the Treatment of the Government', in *Human Rights Yearbook 1999*. Kathmandu: INSEC.

——. 2002. 'No. of Victims Killed by State & Maoist in Connection with "People's War"' *Informal,* June: 69-70. Kathmandu: INSEC.

——. 2003. *History*. INSEC (cited 2 February 2003). Available from http:// www.hri.ca/partners/insec/history/

Krauskopff, G. 1989. *Maîtres et Possédés: Les rites et l'ordre social chez les Tharu (Népal)*. Paris: Editions de CNRS.

——. 1999. 'Corvées (Begaari) in Dang: Ethno-Historical Notes', in H.O. Skar (ed.), *Nepal: Tharu and Tarai Neighbours*, pp. 47-62. Kathmandu: EMR.

——. 2000. 'From Jungle to Farms: A Look at Tharu History', in G. Krauskopff and P.D. Meyer (eds.), *The Kings of Nepal and the Tharu of the Tarai*, pp. 25-48. Kirtipur: Centre for Nepal and Asian Studies.

——. 2003. 'An "Indigenous Minority" in a Border Area: Tharu Ethnic Associations, NGOs, and the Nepalese State', in D.N. Gellner (ed.), *Resistance and the State: Nepalese Experiences*, pp. 199-243. Delhi: Social Science Press.

Krauskopff, G. and P.D. Meyer (eds.). 2000. *The Kings of Nepal and the Tharu of the Tarai*. Kirtipur: Centre for Nepal and Asian Studies.

Lowe, P. 2002. *Kamaiya: Slavery and Freedom in Nepal*. Kathmandu: Mandala Book Point.

Luintel, G. 2061 v.s. 'Mukta Kamaiyako Jaggama Maobadi Kheti (Maoist Cultivation on the Freed Kamaiyas' Fields)'. *Kantipur*, 22 Kattik 2061 (7 November 2004), p. 1.

McDonaugh, C. 1997. 'Losing Ground, Gaining Ground: Land and Change in a Tharu Community in Dang, West Nepal', in D.N. Gellner, J. Pfaff-Czarnecka, and J. Whelpton (eds.) *Nationalism and Ethnicity in a Hindu Kingdom: The Politics of Culture in Contemporary Nepal*. Amsterdam: Harwood.

——. 1999. 'Aspects of Social and Cultural Change in a Tharu Village Community in Dang, West Nepal, 1980-93', in H.O. Skar (ed.), pp. 223-33.

McDougal, C. 1968. *Village and Household Economy in Far-Western Nepal.* Kathmandu: Tribhuvan University.

McNair, E.E. 2003. 'Get the Bikas Flowing: Constructing Kamaiya Identity within Nepal's Circulating Systems of Discursive Relations'. BA thesis, Division of Social Studies, Bard College, Annandale-on-Hudson, New York.

Mainali, M. 2003. '"Development" vs the Maobaadis', in D. Thapa (ed.), *Understanding the Maoist Movement of Nepal*, pp. 125-7. Kathmandu: Martin Chautari.

——. 2055 v.s. 'Saghan Garibi Unmulan ra Maobad (Poverty Eradication and Maoism)'. *Haka-Haki* 2 (4): 8-14.

MLRM (Ministry of Land Reform and Management). 1999. 'Summary Report on the Socio-Economic Status of Kamaiya (Bonded Labour) in Dang, Banke, Bardiya Kailali and Kanchanpur Districts Based on Kamaiya (Bonded Labour) Census Conducted by the Department of Land Reform/HMG Nepal (DOLR) in 1995/6 (2052/3 v.s.)'. Kathmandu: HMG, MLRM, Department of Land Reform.

Nørmose, S. 2000. *BASEline Survey and Program Impact Assessment.* Tulsipur: BASE Project Office.

Ødegaard, S.E. 1999. 'BASE and the Role of NGOs in the Process of Local and Regional Change', in H.O. Skar (ed.), pp. 63-83.

Ojha, P.K. 2000. 'Need of Bonded Labor Abolition Act in Nepal'. *Informal* 10 (1): 36-42.

——. 2057 v.s. 'Bandhasram Unmulan: Paribhasha ra Kanunko Avasyakta (Uprooting Bonded Labour: Comments and the Necessity of Legislation)'. *Prachi* 8 (29): 20-2.

Onesto, L. 2000. 'Red Flag Flying on the Roof of the World: Inside the Revolution in Nepal: Interview with Comrade Prachanda'. *Revolutionary Worker,* No. 1043, 20 February.

Pandit, V. 2000. 'Kamaiya Release: Will Govt. Uphold Constitution?'. *The Kathmandu Post*, 16 July: 4.

Parajuli, R. 2057 v.s. 'Mukti Andolanka Mukhya Patra' (The Main Character of the Liberation Movement). *Kantipur*, 4 Saun: 7.

Prakash, G. 1990. *Bonded Histories: Genealogies of Labor Servitude in Colonial India.* Cambridge: Cambridge University Press.

Rankin, K.N. 1999. 'The Predicament of Labor: Kamaiya Practices and the Ideology of "Freedom"', in H.O. Skar (ed.), pp. 27-45.

Robertson, A. and S. Mishra. 1997. *Forced to Plough: Bonded Labour in Nepal's Agricultural Economy* (A Report for Informal Sector Service Centre and Anti-Slavery International). London: Anti-Slavery International.

Sharma, S. 2057 v.s. 'Char Jilla Maobadiko Hatma' (Four Districts in the Maoists' Hands) *Himal Khabarpatrika* 10 (7): 30-7.

Sharma, S. and M. Thakurathi. 1998. *A Revisit to the Kamaiya System of Nepal.* Kathmandu: INSEC.

Shrestha, R. 2057. 'Mukta ta Paiyo tara Kahan Jane?' (We Gained Freedom, but Where to Go?). *Himal Khabarpatrika* 1-15 Saun: 18-21.

Skar, H.O. (ed.) 1999. *Nepal: Tharu and Tarai Neighbours*. Kathmandu: EMR.

Spotlight. 2000. A Cartoon from *Himalayan Times*, 28 July, p. 7.

SSSA (Sukumbasi Samasya Samadhan Ayog). 1995. *Survey on Landless Bonded Labour (Kamaiya): A Report.* Kathmandu: His Majesty's Government, Department of Housing and Physical Planning.

Tharu, T. 2057 V.S. 'Yagyaraj Chaudhari Ek Samajik Karyakarta' (Yagyaraj Chaudhari, a Social Worker). *Varsik Prativedan (2056 Magh samma)* [Yearly Report (up to 2001)]. Tulsipur: BASE.

Whyte, T. 2002. 'Afterword', in P. Lowe, *Kamaiya: Slavery and Freedom in Nepal.* Kathmandu: Mandala Book Point.

12

The Sociology of Activism in Nepal: Some Preliminary Considerations

DAVID N. GELLNER AND
MRIGENDRA BAHADUR KARKI

> The ambiguous fruits of the European Enlightenment include the emergence of modern science and modern moral political philosophies and programmes ... the arguments and claims of liberalism, socialism and science have consistently found receptive audiences well beyond their North American and European heartlands.
>
> D. Held et al., *Global Transformations: Politics, Economics and Culture*

INTRODUCTION

Activism – the practice of campaigning to remake the world in line with a consciously articulated programme – is today a global phenomenon.[1] Secular activism can no doubt be traced to the Enlightenment ambition to rework the world in line with reason alone. Religious activism goes back even beyond that, to the missionary world religions, which aimed, to greater or lesser degrees, to reform or replace at least some traditional cultural practices in line with their soteriological vision. But even in the case of religious activism, it can plausibly be argued that there is a distinctively modern form of activism.

It surely cannot be doubted that the social context and impact of activism is an important topic to study and understand. In a related, though

[1] We would like to express our gratitude to the Leverhulme Foundation, UK, which has supported this research through two three-year grants. Krishna Hachhethu is also part of the project and has provided valuable comments and input to this paper. The other editors of the volume, as well as the participants in the conference at which the paper was presented, also provided valuable feedback.

differently focused work, Ashutosh Varshney (2002) has recently argued that it is precisely a rich associational life (a large number of inter-ethnic clubs and societies) that differentiates those Indian cities that manage to avoid bloody riots from those that are notoriously prone to them. The focus of Varshney's work is 'civil society' at the local urban level and the degree to which this is conducted inter-ethnically or not. He constructs a convincing argument, using both quantitative and qualitative data (and the latter from both contemporary interviews and history), that where such inter-ethnic civil society is strong, there have been far fewer riots. The focus of our project is somewhat different. In spite of the many cultural similarities with India, the history of Nepal has been distinct from India's in important ways, and the current threat to Nepal's national integrity comes from a politically inspired and rural-based political movement, rather than from urban ethnic chauvinism. We have attempted to understand the background, motivations, and personal development of diverse activists – those who build associations – of whatever sort they may be.

Activism of the modern type (i.e. excluding traditional religious reformers) may be said to have started in Nepal in the 1920s, 1930s, and 1940s, when it was severely repressed by the Rana regime. There were attempts to keep it strictly under control during the Panchayat regime (1960-90), when political parties were banned and for most of the time were forced to operate underground and/or by means of front organizations. During this period it was possible to found and run religious and cultural organizations provided they had no explicitly political content. Since 1990 and the restoration of multiparty democracy, with elections on the British ('first past the post') model, activism of all sorts has flourished. The Constitution of Nepal 1990 has guaranteed the right to form campaigning and community-based organizations; all kinds of political and quasi-political organizations have sprung up. Many of these have or seek links with international non-governmental organizations (INGOs). Activist organizations have a key role in the ongoing transformation of Nepali society. Post 1990, it is estimated that more than 30,000 community-based organizations (CBOs) and NGOs have been registered in Nepal, focusing particularly on development, awareness, advocacy, civic and human rights, the environment, children, women, peace, and so on.

Our research project was intended to attempt to understand all kinds of activism, whether in the religious, political, cultural, ethnic, or social field. In terms of regional coverage 104 activists in Kathmandu, Pokhara, and Janakpur cities were surveyed, as a pilot for a much larger survey of 800 activists, that was later completed in 2004-5. In all three cities, selected activists gave lengthy qualitative interviews as well. Kathmandu was an obvious choice of location, as many activists, and all national-level ones, are located there, at least part of the time. Pokhara as a large and heterogeneous city in the hills seemed to offer a good window on activism outside the Kathmandu Valley. Janakpur was chosen in order to have representation from the Tarai where nearly half of Nepal's population live.

There is no agreed overall definition of activists in Nepal, nor is there any overall published list, so the respondents for our sample had to be chosen by the so-called 'snowball' method; in other words, by word of mouth and recommendations from previous contacts. It will be seen, however, from Appendix Tables 12A.1, 12A.2, and 12A.6 that we have attempted to cover a spectrum of types of activist, and to cover different age groups and all political points of view. Respondents for the questionnaire were chosen from the members of major and national political parties and their front (*bhratri*, literally 'brother') organizations, from religious committees, from bodies such as the Nepal Federation of Indigenous Nationalities (NEFIN), the National Foundation for Development of Indigenous Nationalities, the Dalit NGO Federation (DNF), Dalit Commission, Women's Commission, Free Student Union, etc. It would not have been sensible, however, to have attempted to interview as many women as men, since overall there are far fewer women than men activists. Furthermore, given the current political context we did not think it wise to attempt to interview Maoist activists. Thus our coverage, though extensive, omits the extreme left of the political spectrum.

ACTIVISM DEFINED

We have defined activism above as the practice of campaigning to influence or re-make the world in line with a consciously articulated programme and we have taken activists to be members of organizations dedicated to those ends. Clearly the members of the political parties would come under this definition, as do the numerous ethnic organizations that have mushroomed in the freer environment post 1990. Cynically viewed, however, opponents of the activists in question will frequently claim that their campaigning is a mere cover for careerism, and that the person in question is no activist. In this sense, 'activist' is an appraisive term and activists will always and inevitably disagree among themselves about who 'really' deserves to be considered as such. Heaton Shrestha (2002) has described vividly the world of NGO workers and the way in which they have to foster an image as selfless social workers (*sevak*) in order to combat the notion that they are nothing more than self-interested contractors (*thekadar*), making a living out of helping the poor.[2]

[2]That the latter is the case, especially for INGO workers and organizations, is the thesis of the stinging critique of the aid business by Graham Hancock (1989).

Suffering in the cause of one's activism is one mark of its genuineness, hence the high prestige of those political activists who had spent time behind bars under the Panchayat regime in 1990, and the correspondingly low regard in which they were held after they had become ministers and enjoyed the fruits of office. That activism required courage under the Panchayat regime was clear, particularly if it was related to party, ethnic, or cultural politics, though it was relatively safe to restrict oneself to literary or religious activities (so long as no attempt was made to convert those defined as outside the religion in question). Today too, with increased violence from both the Maoists and the security forces, it is in many cases an uncertain, even dangerous, profession or vocation, as witness the brutal slaying on 15 February 2004, outside his own office in Bagh Bazaar, of Ganesh Chilwal, president of the Nepal Maoists' Victims Association.

In order to avoid endless dispute over particular cases, we include as activists all active members of political parties, ethnic, regionalist, Dalit, women's, religious, or social service organizations. At the limit there may well be organizations about which one may have doubts. We consider as activists those who devote themselves full-time, or most of their spare time, to these activities. After considerable discussion we decided to include organizations such as Rotary or Lions Clubs in the larger questionnaire survey, even though they were not included in the pilot questionnaire which is the basis of the quantitative data presented in this paper.

In order to carry out a survey we needed to have some kind of classification of types of activist organization or spheres which remained close to Nepalis' own ways of viewing things. Thus question nine of the quantitative survey discussed further below asks if the respondents have a second or third area of activism, and lists the options as follows:

- politics,
- caste/ethnicity (*jat/jati*),
- Dalit,
- Madheshi,
- language/culture,
- women,
- religion,
- human rights,
- social,
- other,
- none.

One could simplify this list by saying that there are 'essentially' four areas of activism: politics, religion, ethnicity/culture, and society. In this way of looking at the phenomena, the Nepalese categories of caste/ethnicity, Dalit,[3] Madheshi, and language/culture all fall under the

[3]The term 'Dalit' was first used by Jyotirao Phule (1827-90) for Untouchables as oppressed and dispersed by the Hindu caste system; it was taken up by Ambedkar and really popularized by the Dalit Panthers in Maharashtra in the 1970s. In Nepal, as with the word 'Janajati', it has only come into general usage after 1990. Bishwakarma (2002) lists sixty-three Dalit organizations in Nepal in 2002.

heading of 'ethnicity/culture', and women's issues, human rights, and social issues all fall under the heading of 'society'. The various subdivisions merely reflect the specificities of the Nepalese case, in which Dalits (ex-untouchables) and caste Hindu Madheshis of the Tarai are excluded minorities, but are not considered eligible for membership of the Janajati category. But if we cut the cake in that particular way, if we simplify the categories down to those four, it may help to make international comparisons, but, inevitably, the price is that it simultaneously takes us further away from the specificities, and the social realities, of the activist world in Nepal, from the emerging political culture which the activists are helping to build. The establishment by HMG Nepal of Dalit and Women's Commissions in 2001 and the National Foundation for Development of Indigenous Nationalities (NFDIN) in 2002 is a striking testament to the success of Nepali activists in defining at least these spheres as priorities for government action and resources.

However one classifies activists and their organizations, it is of course the case that many organizations combine one or more spheres of activism. Thus, ethnic organizations such as the Rai Yayokkha, Nepal Magar Sangh, Yakthung Chumlung, and the Tharu Kalyankarini Sabha concentrate on social, cultural, and ethnic issues, occasionally venturing into the religious field, as when the Nepal Magar Sangh encouraged Magars to return their religion as 'Buddhism' in the 2001 census, and the Rai and Limbu organizations encouraged the response 'Kirati dharma'. The main political parties have frequently established front organizations (principally since 1990) in order to mobilize students, youth, women, Dalits, ethnic groups or 'nationalities' (Janajati, also sometimes glossed as 'indigenous groups'), and the Maoists have done the same.

DEFINING ETHNICITY IN NEPAL

The government itself has been dragged step by step along the road to granting legitimacy to ethnic and other claims. In 1996 it accepted in full a report prepared largely by activists and set up a Janajati Pratisthan or Nationalities Commission. The report drew up a list of sixty-one Janajatis and these became the first officially recognized 'nationalities' of Nepal. In 2000 the Ministry of Local Development published a booklet with a page on each of the sixty-one (Ukyab & Adhikari 2000). Subsequently, however, the Manangis decided to merge with the Gurungs, the Shyantan, Chintang, and Thindang formed a single group called the Tingaule ('the three villages'), and the Yakkha were added as a separate group, thus making fifty-nine in all. On 10 February 2002, the list of fifty-nine, as shown in

Table 12.1, was confirmed by the Ministry of Law, Justice, and Parliamentary Affairs. Of these now officially recognized fifty-nine Janajatis, sixteen were not included as possible ethnic categories in the 2001 census, so there is no official record of their numbers. It is no coincidence that fully thirteen of these are from the mountain region, i.e. the sparsely populated high Himalayas. This region is inhabited by people speaking dialects of Tibetan (or in some cases other Tibeto-Burman languages), who share a deep commitment to forms of Tibetan Buddhism or Bon, but they have a longstanding reluctance to construct any overarching 'Tibetan' ethnic identity. Rather, as Charles Ramble (1997) has described, such groups seek either to merge with a larger group (as the Manangis have done with the Gurungs) or, more commonly, to form a small, restrictive ethnic groups on the model of the Sherpas and Thakalis. (In fact, at least four of these groups are close neighbours of the main Thakali group but are excluded by the extremely restrictive terms of the latter's self-definition.[4])

This government recognition was a great success for the Nepal Janajati Adivasi Mahasangh (Nepal Federation of Indigenous Nationalities or NEFIN in English), a campaigning umbrella body for ethnic groups, originally set up in 1990 with just seven constituent groups. It originally called itself the Nepal Federation of Nationalities (NEFEN) and only changed its name to The Nepal Federation of Indigenous Nationalities (NEFIN) at its Fifth National Conference in August 2003. This was a concession to the importance of global initiatives on behalf of indigenous people, which only really came to Nepali activists' attention after the foundation of NEFEN in 1993 with the UN's declaration of a Year (then converted to a decade) of Indigenous People.[5] NEFIN early on established the principle that each ethnic group should have one representative body as its member of NEFIN so that NEFIN can function as the federal body representing all Janajatis in Nepal. NEFIN has therefore actively encouraged the formation of new ethnic organizations where none existed.

The original proposed definition, accepted right up to the last moment, of Nepal's nationalities referred to Janajatis as "those who have their own mother languages and traditional culture but who do not fall under the traditional four-fold Varna classification of Hindu Varna System". However, in the Act establishing NFDIN, which was passed on 7 February 2002,

---

[4] See W.F. Fisher (2001) on Thakali ethnicity.

[5] For some material on NEFEN in English, see Gellner et al. (1997) and Gellner (2001). See now NEFIN's website: www.nefin.org.np.

Janajatis were defined as "a tribe or community as mentioned in the schedule having its own mother tongue and traditional rites and customs, distinct cultural identity, distinct social structure, and written or unwritten history" (NFDIN 2003: 32). In other words, explicit reference to being outside the Hindu varna system was not mentioned.

Whether the Newars should be accepted as a member of this body, and should be treated as Janajatis (and be eligible for benefits), has been a controversial question, both for many Newars and for many activists, since Newars are perceived by many Nepalis, not without reason, to be part of the Establishment. This has meant that it is hard for Newars to be accepted as leaders of the Janajati movement. Furthermore, it is highly questionable to claim that they fall outside the "Hindu Varna system" since they have an elaborate internal caste system of their own.[6] The very term 'Janajati' was unknown during the Panchayat period, and even today it is known only to the educated and only to those who follow politics. However, it is now sufficiently accepted and sufficiently used for there to be common usages; it would, we believe, be generally accepted that the primary usage of 'Janajati' is to refer to what used to be called 'hill tribes' in English or *matwali* in Nepali. Most of the time when people use the term, they do not in fact intend to include the Newars, despite the fact that Newars are included in the official schedule. We have followed this emergent usage, treating hill Janajati, Tarai Janajati, and Newar as three separate categories (see Table 12.A.1).

In 1996 and 1997, it appeared as an open question whether substantial resources would move in the direction of these first hesitant steps towards multiculturalism. In 2003, however, the embattled government of Surya Bahadur Thapa accepted the principle of reservations, on the Indian model, for Janajatis, Dalits, and women, across a wide spectrum of national life. The practicalities of institutionalizing them have yet to be worked out in many contexts. Once the principle of reservations (positive discrimination) was agreed, the problem of the wide gap in educational achievements and economic resources between different Janajatis became too pressing to ignore, and in 2004 NEFIN and NFDIN agreed a fivefold classification, also shown in Table 12.1, which would enable projects and reserved places at university and elsewhere to be targeted at the most disadvantaged groups.

---

[6] On these debates between Newar activists, see Gellner (2003); on caste among the Newars, see Toffin (1984) and Gellner & Quigley (1995). An article by Malla K. Sundar, President of the Newa De Dabu, the umbrella national body for the Newars, arguing that Newars should be considered as Janajatis because of their cultural exclusion, and urging this conclusion on other Newars essentially as a strategic policy, is available on the web in English translation (Sundar 2000).

Table 12.1: Classification of 59 Official Janajatis by NEFIN and NFDIN (2004)

Region	Classification of Indigenous Nationalities				
	Endangered	Highly Marginalized	Marginalized	Disadvantaged	Advantaged
Mountain (18)		Shiyar (Chumba) *c.* 1,000 Shingsawa (Lhomi, Karbhote) *c.* 2,000 Thudam *c.* 200	Bhote (Bhotiya) 19,261 (0.08%) Dolpo *c.* 20,000 Larke (Nupriba) *c.* 4,000 Lhopa (Mustang) *c.* 5,000 Mugali (Mugu) 10-12, 000 Topkegola (Dhokpya) 2-3,000 Walung 1,448 (0.01%)	Barhagaule (Bargaule) *c.* 2,000 Byansi (Sauka, Byasi, Rang) 2,103 (0.01%) Chairotan (Tamang Thakali, Panchgaule) *c.* 200 Marphali Thakali (Puntan, Punel) *c.* 2,000 Sherpa 154,622 (0.68%) Tangbe (Tangbedani) *c.* 400 Tingaule Thakali (Yhulkosompaimhi) *c.* 1,500	Thakali 12,973 (0.06%)
Hill (24)	Bankariya 44 Hayu 1,821 (0.01%) Kusbadiya 552 (0.00%) Kusunda 162 (0.00%) Lapcha (Lepcha, Rong) 3,660 (0.02%) Surel 149	Baramu 7,383 (0.03%) Chepang 52,237 (0.23%) Thami (Thangmi) 22,999 (0.10%)	Bhujel 117,568 (0.52%) Dura 5,169 (0.02%) Pahari 11,505 (0.05%) Free (Phri) ?? Sunuwar 95,254 (0.42%) Tamang 1,282,304 (5.64%)	Chantyal 9,814 (0.04%) Gurung (Tamu) 543,571 (2.39%) Jirel 5,316 (0.02%) Limbu (Yakthung) 359,379 (1.58%) Magar 1,622,421 (7.14%) Rai 635,151 (2.79%) Yakkha (Dewan) 17,003 (0.07%) Yolmo (Helambu) 579 (0.00%)	Newar 1,245,232 (5.48%)

Inner Tarai (7)	Raji 2,399 (0.01%) Raute 658 (0.00%)	Bote 7,969 (0.04%) Danuwar 53,229 (0.23%) Majhi (Bhumar) 72,614 (0.32%)	Darai 14,859 (0.07%) Kumal 99,389 (0.44%)		
Tarai (10)	Kisan (Kuntum) 2,876 (0.01%) Meche (Bodo) 3,763 (0.02%)	Dhanuk (Rajbanshi, Khumu) 188,150 (0.83%) Jhangad (Dhungar, Ghangar, Dhangad) 41,764 (0.18%) Santhal (Satar) 42,698 (0.19%)	Dhimal 19,537 (0.09%) Gangai 31,318 (0.14%) Rajbanshi (Koch) 97,241 (0.43%) Tajpuriya 13,250 (0.06%) Tharu 1,533,879 (6.75%)		
Total	10	12	20	15	2

Sources: Adapted from NEFIN (2004) and nefin.org.np.

Note: By mid 2006 there remained only five Janajati groups without an organization holding membership of NEFIN: Bankariya, Hayu, Kusunda, Raute, and Free. Figures and percentages (which are the percentage of the total Nepali population of 22,736,934) come courtesy of Prof. Sant Bahadur Gurung, director of NFDIN until 2006: these follow the 2001 census. Where there is no percentage this means that the group was not a category recognized by the 2001 census; thus the figures are either unknown or are based on an estimate (note that in some cases, e.g. Yolmo, the ethnic label is not widely recognized or accepted in the region, and therefore the figures are much lower than might be expected: while only 579 people returned 'Yolmo' as their ethnicity, 3,986 recorded that they spoke 'Yolmo').

HISTORICAL BACKGROUND

Conquest and Nepalization

Until 1963 and the promulgation of the new civil code the Nepali state was built upon hierarchical and highly stratified traditional Hindu notions, which included the idea that it was the king's or the state's duty to maintain that hierarchy by force. Within that order those groups that were known as 'Gorkhali', essentially the Bahuns and Chetris, were at the centre of the polity, and others belonged only thanks to association with them, association that could only come at the price of accepting lower status. When the Panchayat regime began to try and 'build the nation', it did so, inevitably, on the basis of this Bahun-Chetri culture and it suppressed all expressions of difference, except insofar as they were 'cute' folklore that evoked locality whether for Nepalis on Radio Nepal or in cultural shows put on for tourists. As far as the 'essence of the nation' went, it was the language, religion, dress, and culture of Bahuns and Chetris of the middle hills which were to form the basis of national identity. Other groups were encouraged to accept this in a process of Nepalization, a continuation of the Sanskritization and Hinduization that had already started, both among elites and in many places among many ordinary people, under the Rana regime. During the Panchayat period the state propagated, through education and state rituals, the notion of one nation (*rashtra*), one language (*bhasha*), and one (style of) dress (*bhesh*). The language was, of course, Nepali (Gorkhali, Khas Kura), and the dress was the *daura suruwal* (the hillman's long shirt with flaps attached by short ties, and distinctive trousers that are tight around the calves and baggy above the knees) plus *topi* (Nepali cap). Officials in the Panchayat regime, and still today, combine this with a Western-style tweed jacket. The king himself often added sunglasses. An official list of national symbols was also drawn up. Four (the crown, the sceptre, the royal standard, and coat of arms) identified the nation with the monarchy; two – the cow and the red blob of vermilion – were borrowed from, and emphasized the link with, Hinduism; and two – the Himalayan pheasant and the rhododendron tree – could be said to identify the nation particularly with the middle-hill region (as opposed to either the Tarai or the Mountain region).[7]

The ruling Shah dynasty and the Ranas (Thakuris), and associated

[7]The essays in Gellner et al. (1997) address many of the processes of nation-building in Nepal, both during the Panchayat regime and before. The essay by Harka Gurung appears also in Gurung (1998).

high castes – Kshatriyas (Chetris) and Brahmans (Bahuns) – have played the dominant role in Nepal's administrative unification. Consequently, these high-caste Hindus, plus certain high-caste Newars, have been able to dominate the military, legal, political, and religious sectors at the centre of the Nepali state; this means that they have also had the lion's share of the educational and other opportunities that have opened up in the last twenty years (Dahal 1998). Notwithstanding the existence of some non-Parbatiya local elites, for example Bhumihar and Jha Brahmans, Rajputs, Kayasthas in the Tarai, and of some economically elite families (Newars, Marwaris, Thakalis), the traditional model of restricted access to power has, inevitably, delayed the social advancement of the vast majority of people from other social backgrounds. Thus, for example, Panday (1989) points out that "there is an astonishing continuity in the predominance of the high caste and specific ethnic groups in state administration since the formation of the Nepali State more than two centuries and a quarter ago, which appear to have occupied 98 per cent of the top civil service posts in 1854. More than a century later, in 1969, this percentage came down only marginally, to 93 per cent." At present, of the 454 top-level civil service positions (special class and first class), 417 (92 per cent) are still occupied by the same groups. Similarly, only about 5 per cent of high civil service positions are held by women and only one of the seventy-five special class positions (NESAC 1998: 146).

The boundaries of modern Nepal were fixed, more or less as today, by the Treaty of Sagauli signed between Nepal and the British East India Company in 1816. However, in 1858, after Jang Bahadur had supported the British against the Indian rebels, he received as a reward the area known as *naya muluk* comprising Banke, Bardiya, Kailali, and Kanchanpur districts, large parts of which then became estates belonging to the Rana aristocracy. The Rana regime attempted to weld the highly diverse population under its rule – diverse in language, culture, and religion – into a single body by means of the Legal Code promulgated in 1854 (Höfer 1979). This legal code effectively gave the force of law to the hierarchical notions that structured relations between the various groups in the country.

Such legalized inequality was only dismantled with the new Legal Code of 1963. A sense of shared national identity was intended to replace the now illegal, though in practice still functioning, hierarchical social system. But traditionally excluded groups failed to prosper in the absence of economic development or the political will to indulge in social engineering. As Whelpton (1997: 49) remarks, "the reliance of the regime on the traditional aspects of Nepalese political culture meant that languages other than Nepali and values other than those of the *tagadhari* ['sacred thread - wearing', i.e. high-caste] Parbatiyas continued to be disregarded." The aim of the Panchayat constitution of 1962 was to remove political parties from politics, and to control all politics in such a way that it was based around the palace. The ideology was that only a partyless system was 'suited to the soil' of Nepal, and only by a form of indirect, bottom-up democracy could the energies of the Nepali people be 'unleashed' for development. What in fact happened was that local elites monopolized the positions that became available, and continued to govern through the continuation of older forms of the patron-client relationship, albeit with greater intra-elite competition (Ramirez 2000). By means of this competition ethnic or lower-caste families were able to use democratic procedures to win positions they might not have had otherwise; however, in its essentials, the system of social and ethnic inequalities of country, though abolished in formal terms, continued to be reproduced.

Despite this, many modernizing changes were introduced under the Panchayat regime (including a number of legal measures that are collectively known as Land Reform, 1963-4), changes which eventually would bring about the downfall of the regime itself. King Mahendra also encouraged a concerted campaign of nation-building, building schools, establishing Radio Nepal, and attempting to propagate the Nepali language throughout the kingdom. The Panchayat regime was here continuing nationalist policies that had already been initiated in the 1950s. A government educational report of 1955 advised the use of local languages only to ensure that students at the beginning of primary school could understand, thereafter advocating the exclusive use of Nepali so that "other languages will gradually disappear and greater national strength and unity will result" (cited in Whelpton 1997: 49). The banning of the use of Hindi in schools during the prime ministership of K.I. Singh in 1957 was particularly controversial in the Tarai where there were well-established schools and textbooks following the Indian system (Hoftun et al. 1999: 52). The Panchayat regime did indeed succeed in raising levels of literacy and education considerably. Literacy went from well under 10 per cent in 1961 to nearly 40 per cent in 1991, and in the same period the number of schools multiplied nearly five times (ibid.: 96, 221).

Constitutional Inclusivism and the Rise of Activism

It should have come as no surprise that once the authoritarian and controlling hand of the Panchayat regime was removed there would be an efflorescence of activism. Along with the political opening up, there has been considerable liberalization, not to say marketization, in the fields of education, health, transportation, electrification, and the media.[8] Public media are reaching throughout the country in an unprecedented way. Today, people are participating as never before in many new local political institutions, civil clubs, non-governmental and community organizations.

Nepal has had three constitutions and two government acts so far, namely, the Constitution of the Kingdom of Nepal 1958, the Constitution of Nepal 1962, and the Constitution of the Kingdom of Nepal 1990, and the Government of Nepal Act 1948, and the Interim Government of Nepal Act 1951. For the first time the ethnic, linguistic, and cultural diversity of Nepal was acknowledged constitutionally in 1990 when Nepal was defined as "a multiethnic, multilingual, democratic, independent, indivisible, sovereign, Hindu and Constitutional Monarchical Kingdom": the words 'multiethnic', 'multilingual', 'democratic', and 'Constitutional' were all new additions, when compared to the previous constitution.

VECTORS OF DIFFERENCE

Religion

One key word remained in the 1990 constitution's definition of the kingdom, to the dismay of ethnic and (non-Hindu) religious activists. That word was 'Hindu'. Although Hinduism was a key part of the legitimation of the kingdom of Nepal from the time of Prithvi Narayan Shah and before, Nepal was only actually officially labelled 'a Hindu kingdom' in Mahendra's constitution of 1962. This was, ironically, just at the time when most of the state's operation had in fact become almost wholly secular (Gaborieau 1982), and this is even more so today. Since all discrimination on the basis of caste, religion, or ethnicity, is outlawed, one commentator

[8]Private television channels now available in Kathmandu include Kantipur, Nepal 1, Image, Channel Nepal, Shangrila, Emetro, NTV Metro. According to *Kantipur* (14 January 2004), altogether fifty-six private FM stations have been registered in Nepal and of these twenty-six are in operation (not including those run by the Maoists). However, the army has urged the government to cancel the remaining thirty licences on security grounds. Kantipur, KTM Metro, Radio Sagarmatha, HBC, Image, KEC, Times are serving the Kathmandu Valley. Nepali daily newspapers include: *Kantipur*, *Himalaya Times*, *Samachar Patra*, *Annapurna Post*; in English there are *The Kathmandu Post*, *The Himalayan Times*. There are also numerous weekly and fortnightly newspapers, as well as magazines oriented to specific issues, e.g. ethnic groups, women, Dalits, or religion. Before 1990 there were essentially just the two government daily newspapers, the *Gorkhapatra* and *The Rising Nepal* in Nepali and English respectively, plus weeklies backed by different political factions. See Kharel (2000) and Onta (2002) for surveys of the media since 1990.

remarks that "it would not be far from the truth to say that Nepal is in de facto terms a secular state with the kingship as the sole Hindu institution so far as the state is concerned" (Sharma 2002: 35). This does not stop the lack of explicit commitment on the part of the state to 'secularity' or 'equidistance between religions' (*dharma-nirapekshata*) from being extremely controversial, mainly because it is taken to express the dominance of high castes (Bahuns and Chetris) over other groups. Nowadays, it is not only Janajati activists, but Maoists and political parties as well, who have taken up this issue; and in fact many liberal Hindus are not particularly attached to keeping the label 'Hindu state' either. On the other hand, whether or not the state is Hindu in its day-to-day practice, the position of the king is certainly intimately tied up with Hindu ritual (the Constitution, 27.1, specifies that the king should be a descendant of Prithvi Narayan Shah "and an adherent of Aryan culture and the Hindu religion"). Thus any attack on Nepal as a Hindu kingdom is seen by monarchists as an attack on monarchy as well.

Figures from the decennial censuses (Table 12.2) show how religion has become one of the most burning issues in Nepal. Hinduism is the majority religion in seventy out of seventy-five districts; of the rest, three, namely Rasuwa, Manang, and Mustang (with predominantly Tamang and Gurung populations), have a majority of Buddhists, and two, namely, Taplejung and Panchthar (predominantly Limbu), have a majority of Kirati religionists. The massive rise of the Kirati religion, from 1.7 to 3.6 per cent of the population, is not caused by conversion, or by high fertility on the part of Rais and Limbus, but simply by the activists' success in having 'Kirati' listed as one of the options in 2001, whereas in 1991, those who wished to have their religion recorded as Kirati had to respond 'Other' and then specify 'Kirati'. In the same way, Buddhist activists under the Panchayat regime frequently complained that the government did everything it could to increase the number of Hindus and decrease that of non-Hindus in the census (by instructing or just encouraging census takers to use 'Hindu' as a default option and not ask the question unless the respondent insisted upon it). The sudden jumps in the percentage of Buddhists, from 5.3 in 1981 to 7.8 in 1991 and 10.7 in 2001 do perhaps show that their complaints were well founded. But these jumps also show that the activists themselves have succeeded in getting across their message that it is important to make sure that their desired outcome is recorded in the census.

Perhaps the most striking case of how activists have brought about social and religious change is that of the Nepal Magar Sangh, the national body for the Magars. Its central committee published a pamphlet just before the 2001 census requesting all Magars to return their ethnicity

Table 12.2: The Religious Make up of Nepal According to the Decennial Censuses

Religion	1952/4		1961		1971		1981		1991		2001	
	Number	%	Number	%	Number	%	Number	%	Number	%	Number	%
Hinduism	7,318,392	88.9	8,254,403	87.7	10,330,009	89.4	13,445,787	89.5	15,996,953	86.5	18,330,121	80.6
Buddhism	707,104	8.6	807,991	9.3	866,411	7.5	799,081	5.3	1,439,142	7.8	2,442,520	10.7
Islam	208,899	2.5	280,597	3.0	351,186	3.0	399,197	2.7	653,218	3.5	954,023	4.2
Kirati									318,389	1.7	818,106	3.6
Christianity			458				3,891	<.1	31,280	0.2	101,976	0.5
Jainism			831		2,541		9,430	0.1	7,561	<.1	4,108	<.1
Others	684								26,416	0.1	86,095	0.4
Unstated			5,716	0.1	5,836	0.1	365,445	2.4	18,138	0.1		
Total	8,235,079	100	9,412,996	100	11,555,983	100	15,022,831	100	18,491,097	100	22,736,934	100

Source: H. Gurung (1998: 95) plus data from 2001 census.

Note: Percentages do not always add up to 100 because of rounding; the last digit of the total for 1981 has been corrected from '9' to '1'; the total for 2001 is left as reported in the 2001 census Table 18 even though it is 15 too few, and the total for 1961 has been left as reported in Gurung, even though it should read 9,349,996.

as 'Magar', their language as 'Magar', and their religion as 'Buddhist' – this despite the facts that only about 33 per cent of Magars speak Magar (Whelpton 1997: 59; Gurung 1998: 75), and there is no tradition of Buddhism among the Magars. Despite this lack of Buddhism, Magar activists, in a search for an alternative to Hinduism, have been enthusiastically taking up and propagating Buddhism over the last ten or so years, urging fellow Magars not to use Brahman priests, to boycott Dasain, and to carry out their life-cycle rituals in a Buddhist manner.[9] Of course it is activists themselves who are most likely to respond to such campaigns, and it is in this light that one should interpret the fact that 20 per cent of our sample of 104 activists reported that they were Buddhists, whereas the proportion in the population as a whole is just over 10 per cent.

It would be a mistake, however, to assume, as ethnic and Buddhist activists usually do, that there are no modernist activists among Hindus, that those who are vocal in the Hindu cause are entirely traditionalist and conservative. In fact there are Hindu organizations that set out to provide social services – free health clinics, maternity hospitals, scholarships for deprived children – in exactly the same way as the charitable arms of other religions. Jedu Nath Pokhrel, President of the World Hindu Youth Council (a 'sister organization' of the World Hindu Federation, Nepal), told us:

> In the Hindu scriptures there is nothing reactionary and nothing to do with social exclusion or Untouchability (*rudhivadi ra samajik vibhedta, chuwachut*). Nowhere is it written that there should be caste prejudice (*jatbhat*) or low castes (*tallo jat*). It is all a corruption (*vikrti*) of the people, and we have to get rid of it. There should be no Dalits; we have to get rid of prejudice (*bhedbhav*) ... We have done seminars, interactions with Dalits. We have Dalit members. We all sit together and eat together, we show this. We create the atmosphere to let Untouchables into temples. They become *sachet* (conscious) seeing us [...] and we eat together. (Interview 1 May 2003)

Language

As we have seen, the constitution recognizes that Nepal is multilingual. In fact, not only is there diversity of language, but also, in many cases, considerable variation of dialects within a short distance. The 2001 census

---

[9]For a discussion of the background to this, see Lecomte-Tilouine (2003). For quotations from and analysis of a speech by Gore Bahadur Khapangi, then President of the Nepal Magar Sangh, see Ahearn (2001).

revealed ninety-two mother tongues. Some ethnic experts claim that there are in fact between 125 and 130 languages in Nepal. Ethnic organizations such as the Kirat Rai Yayokkha, the Nepal Magar Sangh, and the Kirat Yakthung Chumlung campaigned among their own communities in order to maximize the returns for their languages in the census. The previous census of 1991 had covered a mere thirty-two national languages.[10] The censuses of 1952/54, 1961, 1971, and 1981 recorded different figures: forty-four, thirty-six, seventeen, and eighteen respectively. Needless to say, these enormous fluctuations in the numbers of languages recorded reflect indecision in the language policy of the state at the time, rather than any changes 'on the ground'. It is not surprising, then, that language is today, like religion, a significant political issue.

In the spheres of both religion and language there are important processes of 'conversion' from one to another, and at the same time both religions and languages are themselves undergoing considerable change. However, one significant difference between them, in the current Nepalese context, is that the most salient process for religion is internal change, whereas in the case of language, it is simply a shift from local languages to Nepali. Thus, despite activists carrying out programmes of linguistic revitalization, there is undoubtedly a crisis for the languages of the middle hills. Many respondents reported that the younger generation use only or predominantly Nepali, rather than the ethnic language of their parents or grandparents. This is one respect in which there is a considerable difference between the hills and the Tarai. Taraian communities are not as worried as hill ethnic groups are, and local language loss among them appears to be less. Whelpton (1997: 59) estimates that language loss among the major groups of the Nepalese hills has reached 68 per cent among the Magars, nearly 50 per cent among the Gurungs, 34 per cent among the Newars, 16 per cent among the Rais, 14.5 per cent among the Limbus, and 11 per cent among the Tamangs. Indra Bahadur Gurung, President of the Tamu Pyalu Sangh, said that his children and grandchildren hesitate to speak in their mother tongue, and he feared for the existence of the Gurung language in future. Inter-lingual marriages have also contributed to the decline of mother tongues. The Kiratis – including Rais, Limbus, Yakkha, and Sunuwar (and the Rais themselves speaking many mutually incomprehensible languages) – frequently intermarry, and

[10] Namely, Nepali, Maithili, Bhojpuri, Newari, Gurung, Tamang, Abadhi, Tharu, Magar, Limbu, Rai/Kirati, Sherpa, Thakali, Rajbansi, Satar, Danuwar, Santhal, Hindi, Urdu, Chepang, Thami, Bengali, Majhi, Dhimal, Jhangar, Marwari, Kumhale, Darai, Jirel, Byanshi, Raji, and English.

when they do, the language of the home will be Nepali. When this is combined, as it often is, with migration to towns, the children are unlikely to acquire more than a very basic knowledge of the parents' languages.

The 1990 Constitution distinguishes 'the' national language (*rashtra bhasha*) of the country, Nepali, from 'national languages' (*rashtriya bhasha*), which are defined as mother tongues spoken in the various parts of Nepal. Although Nepali is the national language, the right to primary education in one of the other national languages is guaranteed. Furthermore, the Constitution commits the government to a policy of providing support for multiculturalism in section 26, subsection 2, which reads:

> The State shall, while maintaining the cultural diversity of the country, pursue a policy of strengthening the national unity by promoting healthy and cordial relations amongst the various religions, castes, tribes, communities and linguistic groups, and by helping in the promotion of their languages, literatures, scripts, arts and cultures.

One of the ways in which the government has done this is to implement a policy of broadcasting five minutes of news on Radio Nepal in all national languages spoken by one per cent or more of the population from different regionally based offices.[11]

By the standards of the Panchayat era constitution these are radical steps. However, they fall a long way short of the hopes of many ethnic and linguistic activists, who dream of equality for all languages to match the jural individual equality that has already been achieved. At the very least they would like the right to run educational institutions in languages other than Nepali and English at the secondary level also and, even more important, for qualifications in Nepalese languages other than Nepali to be recognized as valid when applying for government service, or promotions within government service. Such concessions still seem to be some way off. In 1998, the Kathmandu city authority started to use Nepal Bhasha (Newari) as an official language alongside Nepali, and Rajbiraj municipality and Dhanusha District Development Committee both did the same with Maithili. On 19 March 1999, the Supreme Court ruled that this was unconstitutional, and they were obliged to desist.

---

[11]Radio Nepal Information Section reported (2004) that from Singha Darbar, Kathmandu, the following news programmes are broadcast: Nepal Bhasha (Newari), Hindi, Sanskrit, Bhojpuri, Tamang, Maithili, Urdu, and Sherpa; from Surkhet: Abadhi, Western Tharu, Kham Magar, and Doteli; from Pokhara: Gurung and Magar; from Dhankuta: Limbu, Bantawa (Rai), and Eastern Tharu.

Dalits

As mentioned above, since 1963 the traditional concept of touchability and untouchability has been legally proscribed. However, social practices of exclusion and inferiorization continued in many places. There was an infamous incident when Hira Lal Vishwakarma, an Assistant Minister of State during the Panchayat period, was refused entry to a tea shop in Chainpur, east Nepal, on caste grounds. No legal action was taken against the tea shop owner, but the Minister recommended that the headquarters of the district be moved to Khadbari.

The 1990 constitution (11.4) reiterated that "No person shall, on the basis of caste, be discriminated against as untouchable, be denied access to any public place, or be deprived of the use of public utilities. Any contravention of this provision shall be punishable by law." Before 1990 there were no Dalit NGOs, although a few Dalits were active in political parties. Since 1990, there has been a mushrooming of such NGOs, and the political parties have set up Dalit front organizations, though these are still fewer than those that represent other social spheres. Since 1995 there has been a confederal body, the Dalit NGO Federation, bringing together all Dalit organizations. In 2001 the government set up a National Dalit Commission, with representatives from the various political parties, a permanent body on the lines of the Women's and Janajati Commissions, to ensure that Dalit issues were addressed.

Women

The numerous unequal legal provisions, and unequal conditions of life, under which women have laboured have been amply documented by feminist researchers and activists. A landmark project, The Status of Women in Nepal, directed by Lynn Bennett and carried out through CEDA, Tribhuvan University, produced a series of eight different studies on different Nepali ethnic groups: Maithil Tamang, Newar, Parbatiya, Baragaonle, Lohorung Rai, Tharu, and Kham Magar. Each study was carried out using the same methodology and these studies clearly established that, despite considerable cultural differences in status and expectations, which did indeed make a difference to their quality of life, women and girls in all groups worked longer hours than men and boys (on average three hours longer per day) and received a smaller share of household resources (Acharya & Bennett 1981). Legally too, women still suffered during the Panchayat period from many unequal and (from a modern and feminist point of view) discriminatory provisions, which have only been addressed in 2002 with the passage of the eleventh amendment to the Law Code of 1963. This entitles women to inherit ancestral property, providing they do not marry, to have an abortion, and to seek divorce with maintenance and a share of the husband's property.[12]

Region and Dress

Different communities have various different traditional costumes. Barman Budha, an old communist leader from Thabang in Rolpa, now the Maoist 'capital', caused a stir in 1991 when he was elected an MP and turned up in Parliament in traditional Kham Magar dress (i.e. with a short piece of hempen cloth around his upper thighs, and the rest of his legs bare), and took his oath of office in the Kham language (de Sales 2003: 346). Generally, however, hill ethnic groups have not raised their voices against *daura suruwal* as the national dress of Nepal. It is rather the people of the Tarai, and particularly the Sadbhavana Party, who have campaigned at elections on the issue. Still, today, the national official dress, which is essential for formal government ceremonies, consists for men of the *daura*, *suruwal*, *kot*, and *topi*, and for women, the *sari* and *cholo* (short-sleeved blouse). No Nepali is allowed to enter the royal palace unless dressed in this way. For their own dignity and as a symbol of equal rights, Taraians want the right to enter wearing a *dhoti* and cite the slogan, first used in Janakpur in 1990 by Ram Chandra Tiwari, one of the founders of the Sadbhavana Party: *dhoti ra topiko man barabari hunu pardacha*: the *dhoti* (the traditional Tarai male dress) and the *topi* (the hillman's cap) must have equal respect.

ACTIVISM AND POLITICS UNDER THE PANCHAYAT REGIME: PERSONAL ACCOUNTS

Most of the activists in our sample grew up and had their formative experiences under the Panchayat system (only the very oldest began their activist career under the Ranas). Many of the earliest generation of activists were the sons of men who worked for the Ranas. Their fathers in many cases disagreed with the policies of their own rulers, or in some cases were humiliated or even dismissed by them.[13] In some cases they came from

[12]Previously, from 1975, women had the right to inherit only after the age of thirty-five, providing they were still unmarried, and with the proviso that if they married, the property would have to be returned. Abortion was illegal until 2002, and divorced women could only claim food from their ex-husband for a period of five years.

[13]This happened, for instance, to the father of K.P. Malla and Malla K. Sundar: he arrived one year for the annual *pajani* ceremony to find that he was not to receive a turban. He had to walk home without one, a public and humiliating form of dismissal. He refused government

wealthy landowning families, in others from more moderate backgrounds, but never from the poorest, since at that time only the better off had any education.[14]

During the Panchayat era the political parties organized underground. Many activists first became involved in literary activities and through that made contact with political activists. Depending on the generation, the first experience of politics would be through student union politics. Student politics on an organized basis began in the early 1970s and revived particularly from 1978. From that time student identities tended to be either 'leftist' or 'democrat' (i.e. a Congress supporter); in addition there were some who were supporters of the Panchayat regime, who could be classed as 'royalist'.

Education in India or the Tarai

For many, education in India was a formative experience. Educational facilities have always been much more advanced in India than in Nepal and many Nepalis have taken advantage of the open border to access them. In the case of the Dalit activists interviewed, it is striking that education in India was often a key part of their personal development, in fact the only way in which they could survive in education to the end of high school:

> When my father was young he was a *hali* (ploughman) for a Bahun. Then he went to India for more than 15 years, to Agra, Delhi, and Haryana. Later on the whole family, my elder brother and sister and me, went with him. If I hadn't gone to India, I wouldn't be here now. My mother and father were not educated, though my mother now knows [how to read]. I went to school in Agra. The schooling was in Hindi and English, up to third class. [Then I returned to school in the hills of Nepal.] At that time my elder brother was (politically) conscious (*sachet*). In the village there was a Chetri-Bahun majority. There were no Damai, but there were Magars in the hills around. [On one occasion] it was the school's *barsik diwas*, an annual function. I was a little for-

employment under the Ranas thereafter (Gellner 1996). For a similar humiliation at the hands of the Ranas of Tanka Prasad Acharya's father, and its radicalizing effect on Tanka Prasad, see J.F. Fisher (1997: 50-1).

[14] This is very clear among the Tharus. The early land activists who set up the Tharu Kalyan Samiti in 1956 were the sons of landlords. Only in a much later generation, in the 1990s, did those from much poorer backgrounds set up other mass organizations, notably Dilli Chaudhuri's BASE (see Guneratne 2002; Krauskopff 2003; and Fujikura this volume, on the different social bases of these two Tharu organizations).

> ward as a speaker, so I was one of the speakers. [When tea was served] they discriminated: the ward chairman (*adhyaksha*) forced me [to wash my cup]. I thought: There cannot be discrimination in a line of teachers. I opposed it right there. "Rather than wash it, I'll break it" [I said]. They threatened me, so I ran away. My grandfather came and took away the glass [and cleaned it]. [On normal days as well] at school the peon used to discriminate. He would have to pour water for us [rather than let us get it for ourselves]. I just didn't go for water. (30-year-old Dalit activist)[15]

> My father was working in Gonda, UP, not far from Banaras ... I had no experience of untouchability in India. When I came back to visit Nepal, there was. Once I went to a friend's house. I was stopped at the door: "Don't come in here!" (*yahan na au*). My friend was sprinkled with water and taken inside. I went to my father and asked, "Why do they do this?" He said, "Nepal's customs are like that." It was very unpleasant, very painful for me. So I joined the anti-untouchability campaign. (70-year-old Congress Dalit activist)

In a less dramatic way India's more developed education system and more conscious political environment had a significant impact on other Nepalis as well. Of those who lived in the Tarai, some were sent to boarding schools in Lucknow, Darjeeling, or Kurseong. Others went to more ordinary Indian schools and stayed in hostels or lodgings nearby. Many of those closely associated with the Congress Party received their education in India, because they were in exile. Others were drawn to the Party while studying in Banaras because they then had contact with B.P. Koirala and his followers and family. In at least one case, the activist we interviewed was drawn into leftist politics via contacts with members of the Communist Party of India while studying just over the border in Bihar.

Even for those who did not study in India, simply moving to the Tarai was often the occasion to acquire a better education than would have been available in the hills and to receive exposure to radical ideas at the same time. This was the case both for Gore Bahadur Khapangi, President of the Nepal Magar Sangh from 1992 to 2002, but an underground communist activist before 1990, and for Narayan Man Bijukche (Rohit), President of

---

[15] All the activists cited in this section are men; a fuller, less preliminary treatment would have to address this bias. For a gripping account by a woman who faced similar difficulties under the Panchayat regime, see Pokhrel & Willett (1996).

the Nepal Workers and Peasants Party. Bijukche's father had been a tax collector for the Ranas in the Tarai and stayed on there as a civil servant after 1951. Bijukche spent two years there in school, where he was impressed by the application of his teachers and by the extreme poverty of those afflicted by the floods he witnessed there.

The Influence of Progressive Ideology

For those who did not leave the country but grew up under the Panchayat regime (1960-90) it was often the visions of a communist alternative circulated in highly subsidized Chinese, Russian, and Korean imprints that were influential. There were three well-known progressive bookshops in Kathmandu: (i) the Mutual Book Centre in front of Padmodaya Campus, Putali Sadak, (ii) the one in Bhota Hiti belonging to Niranjan Govinda Vaidya, one of the founders of the Nepali Communist Party, and (iii) the Lalima Pustak Sadan in Naradevi. In addition there were the outlets of the Russians, the Russian Cultural Centre (previously in Jamal, now in Kamal Pokhari), and the Chinese, the Nepal-China Cultural Centre in New Road in front of Vishal Bazaar. There were other small progressive bookshops elsewhere, in Bhaktapur and Banepa, among other places.

The monthly magazine *Chin Sachitra* (*China Pictorial*) had a big effect on some activists. One recalled:

> It was while I was first a teacher. I used to go to get books for the children. The booksellers would sell *Chin Sachitra* for one *suka* [25 paisa] each – so cheaply! I got other books very cheaply too, e.g. Mao Tse-Tung's book. I didn't know his name before; maybe I had just heard it. The bookshop owner was a communist. He is still a UML supporter today. I was very influenced by that literature. ('PM', 51-year-old ex-left communist, Newar)

Another recalled:

> Yes, the magazine *Chin Sachitra* would come (to our village). We were struck by the similarity of the faces (to ours) and by the illustrations of development. "That was exciting, you know." We thought, "This could be the model." The people who were operating all those machines looked just like us. Aryans tended to be more in Congress, Mongoloids with the Communists. Congress was made in Banaras, Communists in China. *Chin Sachitra* was one of the key things ... Even now there are more Mongolians in the Maoists. (41-year-old Limbu ethnic activist)

It was a time when the embassies of the communist countries, just like those of the capitalist ones, sought to influence opinion. The activist cited above continued:

> When I came to study the IA, there was a lot of influence of China. I had it through study, but also from concern to help the poor. I was concerned about this from a young age. In the bazaar where I grew up there was an old lady. She had been rich but she became poor. People would say she was a witch and that one shouldn't eat from her hand. I would go and do it simply to oppose [these ideas] [lit. 'as a *vidroha*', rebellion].
>
> From the time I was studying for the SLC and afterwards this oppositional character of mine increased. It started from China's Cultural Revolution. People would discuss it in the bazaar. I heard that there were no differences of rich and poor there.
>
> Then, when I was studying for my IA, I went in to the Chinese Embassy in Naksal, next to the Jaya Nepal Cinema. I just went in, I had no special reason. I met the cultural attaché, and he dealt with me very nicely. He gave me some literature about China in Hindi and English, and also Mao's volume. I was a bit impressed. I liked Mao's 'idea'. (PM)

Another activist compared the first impact of Marxist ideas to falling in love:

> It was around '24 [1967-8] when I was studying for my IA. I met some students who were distributing the Communist Manifesto in Nepali. Later I read a lot of Mao Tse-Tung's works, and Kim Il-Sung. At first it seemed very powerful (*tagada*). But when you start to go into depth ... When you first see it, it seems most scientific. It's like the first girl you fall in love with, you don't forget it! [laughs] It was just like that. But then if you join and make an 'action plan', even if your differences of opinion are very small, they call you a traitor (*gaddar*). (56-year-old social and Limbu ethnic activist)

For an earlier generation of leftist activists, Russian or Soviet influence was much stronger than the Chinese. One explained, in response to the question, "Why weren't you attracted to the Congress Party?"

> It was like this: We'd already seen a Congress government in India. There was lots of Russian literature because India was friendly with Russia. We used to read that. The distribution system [under communism] was good: no one had to live without a

> house or without clothes, that's what we learned from this literature. At the same time one *jati* [nation or ethnic group] shouldn't dominate another, because nations had the right to self-determination. Communists also supported that. I didn't read a lot, but I did read *Vaigyanik Bhautikvad* (Scientific Materialism), *Leninka kehi Rachana* (Some Writings of Lenin), *Stalinka kehi Rachana* (Some Writings of Stalin): These were mostly in Hindi, some in English. There wasn't much Chinese influence – that only really started after 1962. The differences with Moscow began after 1961-2. From the beginning I wasn't so influenced by Mao Tse-Tung's teachings. After 1962 the world communist movement split and I was very little attracted by the Chinese line, so I never read Mao's work ... Then in 1968 there was a Youth Festival in Sofia, Bulgaria. I went as part of a delegation ... We had to make a big effort to get a passport. We spent about one week in Bulgaria. Then on our way back, I stayed several months in Moscow (I was the only one of the delegation who did so) and at that time I was dismissed (*nishkasit*) from my teaching post. It was a private college and the main person on the managing committee was of Congress inclination. So he sacked me for being a communist. It was an all-party delegation. We went as individuals. The main sponsor was the Soviet government. Pressure came from the Soviet Youth Federation to include us [the communists]. It was through the Soviet Youth Federation, through the Soviet Embassy. We flew from Kathmandu, it was all paid for. While I was in Moscow I studied communist literature. There was an institute, for philosophy. (64-year-old UML activist, Maithil)

Gorky's Mother

A novel that turns up frequently in answer to the question 'What literature influenced you in your student days?' is Maxim Gorky's *Mother*. To those who haven't read it, and perhaps even more to those who have, it may come as a surprise to learn that it had such a powerful impact. Gorky himself apparently dismissed it, saying it was "an unsuccessful thing, not only in its external appearance, because it is long, boring and carelessly written, but chiefly because it's insufficiently democratic" (cited in Freeborn 1982: 51) – a judgement that would not be assented to by the novel's many Nepali admirers. It tells the story of a mother, who, after her drunken, abusive husband dies, is gradually drawn into revolutionary activism by her son. At the outset of the book, she is illiterate and has no political understanding or consciousness, her only beliefs being a fervent Christianity and the desperate love for her son. (Except occasionally, when addressed by name, she appears in the novel as 'the mother'.) By the end she is committed to the cause of her son, lives and works with other revolutionaries, and goes happily to (what appears to be) her death for the sake of the Russian people and because her love takes in everyone except the enemies of progress. Her belief in Christianity is transformed into a faith in the necessity of fundamental, possibly violent, change and self-sacrifice to bring about a viable life for the mass of the people. The characters are simply drawn. The revolutionaries are all good and selfless; the opponents of revolution are all beastly and selfish, and frequently sadistic. The revolutionaries are devoted to the truth and the good of the poor, whatever sufferings they must go through for their sake, and there are virtually no references to serious disputes among them. This is made plausible only by the device of having the whole novel focus on the mother, her perceptions, and her gradual halting progress towards full involvement.

Towards the end of the novel, the mother's son, who is so entirely heroic as almost to be a plaster model, and his comrades are in jail. They could escape, but he refuses to do so. They are brought before a kangaroo court and he makes a set-piece speech lasting three pages in defence of revolutionary socialism:

> We are Socialists. That means we are against private property, an institution which disintegrates society, sets people against one another, creates an irreconcilable hostility of interests, resorts to falsehood in the effort to conceal or justify this hostility, and corrupts all people with lies, hypocrisy and hatred ... Our knowledge of the truth is growing all the time, and it is attracting the best people – all who are pure in spirit – even from your own circles ... socialism will take the world you have destroyed and rebuild it into one great whole, and nothing you can do will stop it! (Gorky n.d. 377-9)

At the beginning of the book, reflecting the mother's own limited understanding, there are few speeches of this sort, and no long ones. By the end they are frequent. At the very end, as she prepares to go out to spread hastily printed copies of her son's speech, she is giving them herself:

> Our children are treading the path of truth and reason, bringing love to the hearts of men, showing them a new heaven and lighting up the earth with a new fire – the unquenchable fire of the spirit. From its flames a new life is springing, born of our chil-

> dren's love for all mankind. Who can extinguish this love? ... The earth has given it birth, and life itself longs for its victory. Life itself! (ibid.: 406)

As the mother waits at a railway station she realizes she has been spotted by a police spy and that they are closing in. She opens the suitcase she has been given and scatters the pamphlets to the crowds as they arrest her. The novel ends with her being choked by a policeman.

It is the powerful symbol of a mother's love which dominates and suffuses the entire novel. It is this love which draws her into the movement and motivates her to pursue justice for all mankind. It is no doubt this universal symbol, combined with the vivid, if idealized, picture of underground revolutionaries having secret meetings and printing newspapers in hiding from brutal policemen and reactionary government officials – the overdrawn contrast of selfless fighters for progress and the future with bestial reactionaries who stand in their way – that made the novel speak so powerfully to those growing up and being educated under the Panchayat regime:

> In the second year of my IA, I was staying in the central hostel in Tahachal. There were a lot of students and I started reading Russian literature and seeing Russian films. Gorky's *Mother* was in English and Hindi. I read it in English. That was during my BA.
>
> "Why did it have such a big influence?"
>
> It was the skilful way it was written (*lekhanshaili*), it was about an ordinary worker. The subject matter was very good. Yes, lots of people were influenced by it. (PM)

> I read Gorky's *Mother* around 1960. Yes, in Hindi. Later on I read it in Nepali.
>
> "Why did it have such an impact?"
>
> It was because it is about such realistic things. It has 'feeling'. (62-year-old leftist and social activist, Newar)

> Even more than *Mother*, I was influenced by Gorky's *My Childhood*. It seemed to fit my own childhood so exactly. (56-year-old Newar ethnic activist)

> The book which influenced me most was Gorky's *Mother*. I liked the English version better; it was more straightforward (*saral*) in English than in Hindi. You could easily get it in the bazaar, or borrow it. It didn't matter whether you were Congress or Communist, everyone read it. 'The novel is a mirror of society.' Anyone's heart can be touched by that. First you are a human, then a

> communist. Anyone who has inside them what it is that makes you human will respond to Gorky, Bankimchandra, Premchand, or Devkota. (52-year-old pro-Congress lecturer, Maithil)

In the 1958 election campaign Ganesh Man Singh gave speeches against his opponent in central Kathmandu, Pushpa Lal Shrestha, the founder of the Communist Party. He attacked Pushpa Lal's praise of the Soviet Union and told people that if they really wanted to know what it was like there, they should read *Dr Zhivago*, which the Soviet government had just banned. Though the novel became popular for a short time, it does not seem to have had anything like the long-term impact of Gorky's writings.

Family Influences

In a significant number of cases, activists are born into the role. Many come from families with a history of political involvement. Some prominent leaders of ethnic movements today had fathers who held office in the Panchayat regime or were close to leaders of the Congress Party. This applies even more to political activists: many who are prominent in the Congress Party today are the sons or wives of those who were early members of the movement. This does not mean, of course, that all children of activists become activists; in many cases, however, one or more of them do.

In other cases, the family had no history of activism, and there was active opposition to the young man's choice of career or, as it was usually seen, non-career:

> My father did oppose me, he used to really tell me off (*gali garnu*). My mother also. But father became very aggressive. Father tried to hit me, but didn't succeed. My elder brother sympathized with me.
>
> "Was your father afraid?"
>
> Yes, mainly he was afraid. But the second thing was: When I got older, would I be able to earn money? Would I look after him? Would I be arrested and killed? (49-year-old UML activist, Maithil)

Understandably the same attitude was widespread among worried parents, even when they sympathized with the political opinions of their children. It was not only fear for the life of the children and for one's own future in old age. There was also the consideration that the careers of siblings would be held back because the family was associated with an opponent of the regime. That these considerations played equally, or perhaps all the more, in the case of women activists is described vividly in the autobiography of Durga Pokhrel (Pokhrel & Willett 1996), whose family cut her off for years because of her oppositional activities.

ACTIVISTS' BACKGROUNDS: THE STATISTICS

The first set of data on the pilot questionnaire respondents is presented in Table 12A.1 in Appendix below. It shows that hill Brahmans (Bahuns) make up nearly 30 per cent of our sample, whereas they are only 13 per cent of the population as a whole. It may well be that the sample simply reflects the over-representation of Bahuns in politics and the professions generally. On the other hand, our sample over-represents hill Dalits also, since they comprise 9-10 per cent of the population. Table 12A.2 shows that there is a good spread in the sample of people born throughout the country, both from north to south (by ecological zone) and from east to west. The lower representation of the mid-west and far western regions may be attributed to the lower levels of education in those regions. The high representation of the Central Development Region, especially if the Kathmandu Valley total is included, is not surprising since both Kathmandu and Janakpur are in this region. The two 'foreign-born' respondents had fathers in the Indian army.

It is notable that 73.5 per cent of the activists sampled came from rural areas and only 8.8 per cent from the Kathmandu Valley. Since 86.1 per cent of Nepalis reside in rural areas (Dahal 2003: 101) this may not seem surprising. However, when one factors in the fact that activists are almost entirely drawn from the educated (see Table 12A.3), the large number of rural activists may be significant. Undoubtedly, activism and education (formal or informal) are connected: as many as 39.4 per cent of the sample hold a Master's degree. The 2001 census recorded only 75,083 out of a total population of 23 million with a postgraduate qualification (about one-third of 1 per cent). There was only one illiterate respondent, a cadre of the Dalit wing of the RPP. Taking the graduate and postgraduate respondents together constitutes a significant majority of the sample with 63.4 per cent (whereas they are a mere 1.5 per cent or so of the population as a whole).

The data on the social status of the activists' father and grandfather (Table 12A.4), plus the answers to questions about residence (whether they had their own home, or rented while in Kathmandu), and about access to motor vehicles (Table 12A.5), suggests that the vast majority of activists are not particularly well off, and may be said to belong to the lower or middle section of the middle class. Of course, this does not apply to many leading members of the Congress and RPP who come from elite families.[16]

In selecting respondents an attempt was made to cover a broad spectrum of types of activist (Table 12A.6), to ensure that a range of age groups was represented (Table 12A.7), and that respondents were genuinely active, by selecting either central or district committee members (Table 12A.7).

In questions about major influences (Table 12A.8), many – over 30 per cent – cited family and about the same number cited the influence of a specific individual. Almost as many cited the general cultural and/or social environment. Only nine individuals claimed that books had influenced them, and most of these were leftists, thus confirming the impression that leftists are more inclined than others to be readers and to give emphasis to the written word.

CONCLUSION

As flagged by the title, this is a preliminary survey and so the material we present is likely to appear fragmentary, eclectic, and less than perfectly marshalled. In addition, any generalizations we have attempted to make have to be taken as suggestive rather than definitive. In particular, it is too early to try and draw any sophisticated conclusions from the statistical data, for example, about the rural origins of activists. Nor can we yet offer much in the way of generalizations about variations in the backgrounds of different types of activists.

Enough has been said, however, to show that under the Panchayat regime significant changes had already begun, not just in development indicators such as literacy levels, mortality rates, or measures of health but in the way in which people thought about their society and in the ways in which they wanted it to be organized. Movements of many different kinds were already under way in opposition to different aspects of the orthodoxy imposed from above. These movements – political, social, religious, ethnic, feminist, Dalit, and so on – flourished in the new, much freer atmosphere after 1990. But, in many cases, their roots go back well

---

[16]Preliminary results from the full survey of 800 activists, carried out between December 2004 and April 2005, indicate that, with more multiple responses being given than in the pilot, rather more activists had high-born grandfathers and fathers than shown in Table 12A.4 here. The figures for possession or use of a vehicle in Table 12A.5 and the full survey are very comparable (residence figures were differently compiled in the full survey: 70 per cent of activists were revealed to own their own homes).

before 1990. In so far as scholars who worked on Nepal in the Panchayat period suggested that Nepalese society was unchanging, they seriously *mis*represented it.

REFERENCES

Acharya, M. and L. Bennett. 1981. *The Rural Women of Nepal: An Aggregate Analysis and Summary of Eight Village Studies* (Status of Women Series II.9). Kathmandu: CEDA, TU.

Ahearn, L. 2001. '"We were Kings here once": Gendered Constructions of Magar Ethnicity in a Speech by Gore Bahadur Khapangi'. *Himalayan Research Bulletin* 21 (1): 7-10.

Bishwakarma, P.L. 2002. 'Dalits in Crisis'. *Dalit Empowerment Program (DEP)*, Annual Report 2002, pp. 20-3. Kathmandu: Dalit NGO Federation (DNF).

Dahal, D.R. 1998. 'The Nepalese Political Elites'. Submitted to DFID Nepal (unpublished MS).

——. 2003. 'Social Composition of the Population: Caste/Ethnicity and Religion in Nepal'. *Population Monograph of Nepal*, Vol. 1, Chapter 3. Kathmandu: Central Bureau of Statistics.

Fisher, J.F. 1997. *Living Martyrs: Individuals and Revolution in Nepal.* Delhi: Oxford University Press.

Fisher, W.F. 2001. *Fluid Boundaries: Forming and Transforming Identity in Nepal.* New York: Columbia University Press.

Freeborn, R. 1982. *The Russian Revolutionary Novel: Turgenev to Pasternak.* Cambridge: Cambridge University Press.

Gaborieau, M. 1982. 'Les rapports de classe dans l'idéologie officielle du Népal'. *Purusartha* 6: 251-90.

Gellner, D.N. 1996. 'From Literature to Linguistics to Culture: An Interview with K.P. Malla'. *European Bulletin of Himalayan Research* 11: 37-52.

——. 2001. 'From Group Rights to Individual Rights and Back: Nepalese Struggles over Culture and Equality', in J. Cowan, M. Dembour, and R. Wilson (eds.), *Culture and Rights: Anthropological Perspectives*, pp. 177-200. Cambridge: Cambridge University Press.

——. 2003. 'From Cultural Hierarchies to a Hierarchy of Multiculturalisms: The Case of the Newars of Nepal', in M. Lecomte-Tilouine and P. Dollfus (eds.), *Ethnic Revival and Religious Turmoil in the Himalayas*, pp. 73-131. Delhi: Oxford University Press.

Gellner, D.N. and D. Quigley (eds.). 1995. *Contested Hierarchies: A Collaborative Ethnography of Caste among the Newars of the Kathmandu Valley, Nepal.* Oxford: Clarendon.

Gellner, D.N., J. Pfaff-Czarnecka, and J. Whelpton (eds.). 1997. *Nationalism and*

Ethnicity in a Hindu Kingdom: The Politics of Culture in Contemporary Nepal. Amsterdam: Harwood.

Gorky, M. n.d. *Mother (A Novel in Two Parts)*, tr. M. Wettlin. Moscow: Foreign Languages Publishing House.

Guneratne, A. 2002. *Many Tongues, One People: The Making of Tharu Identity in Nepal.* Ithaca & London: Cornell University Press.

Gurung, H. 1998. *Nepal: Social Demography and Expressions.* Kathmandu: New Era.

Hachhethu, K. 2002. *Party Building in Nepal, Organization, Leadership and People: A Comparative Study of the Nepali Congress and the Communist Party of Nepal (Unified Marxist-Leninist).* Kathmandu: Mandala Book Point.

Hancock, G. 1989. *Lords of Poverty.* London: Papermac.

Heaton Shrestha, C. 2002. 'NGOs as *thekadars* or *sevaks*? Identity Crisis in Nepal's Non-Governmental Sector'. *European Bulletin of Himalayan Research* 22: 5-36.

Held, D., A. McGrew, D. Goldblatt, and J. Perraton. 1999. *Global Transformations: Politics, Economics and Culture.* Cambridge: Polity.

Höfer, A. 1979. *Caste Hierarchy and the State: A Study of the Muluki Ain of 1854.* Innsbruck: Universitätsverlag Wagner. (Reissued 2004 by Himal Books, Lalitpur, Nepal.)

Hoftun, M., W. Raeper, and J. Whelpton. 1999. *People, Politics, and Ideology: Democracy and Social Change in Nepal.* Kathmandu: Mandala.

Kharel, P. (ed.). 2000. *Media Nepal 2000.* Kathmandu: Nepal Press Institute with Danida.

Krauskopff, G. 2003. 'An "Indigenous Minority" in a Border Area: Tharu Ethnic Associations, NGOs, and the Nepali State', in D.N. Gellner (ed.), *Resistance and the State: Nepalese Experiences*, pp. 199-243. Delhi: Social Science Press.

Lecomte-Tilouine, M. 2003. 'Sur le de-Sanskritisation des Magars: ethno-histoire d'une groupe sans histoire'. *Purusartha* 23: 297-327.

NEFIN. 2004. 'Classified Schedule of Indigenous Nationalities of Nepal', document prepared by the Janajati Classification Task Force and approved by the Federal Council of Nepal Federation of Indigenous Natinonalities, 1 March 2004.

NESAC. 1998. *Nepal Human Development Report 1998.* Kathmandu: Nepal South Asia Centre.

NFDIN. 2003. *National Foundation for Development of Indigenous Nationalities (NFDIN) An Introduction.* Kathmandu: NFDIN.

Onta, P. 2002. 'Critiquing the Media Boom', in K.M. Dixit and S. Ramachandaran (eds.), *State of Nepal*, pp. 253-69. Lalitpur: Himal Books.

Panday, D.R. 1989. 'Administrative Development in a Semi-Dependency: The Experience of Nepal'. *Public Administration and Development* 9 (3) (June-August).

Pokhrel, D. and D. Willett. 1996. *Shadow over Shangrila: A Woman's Quest for Freedom*. Dulles: Brassey's.

Ramble, C. 1997. 'Tibetan Pride of Place: Or, Why Nepal's Bhotiyas are not an Ethnic Group', in Gellner et al. (eds.), *Nationalism and Ethnicity in a Hindu Kingdom*, pp. 379-413.

Ramirez, P. 2000. *De la disparition des chefs: Une anthropologie politique népalaise*. Paris: CNRS (Collection Monde Indien).

de Sales, A. 2003. 'The Kham Magar Country: Between Ethnic Claims and Maoism', in D.N. Gellner (ed.), *Resistance and the State: Nepalese Experiences*, pp. 326-57. Delhi: Social Science Press.

Sharma, S. 2002. 'The Hindu State and the State of Hinduism', in K.M. Dixit and S. Ramachandaran (eds.), *State of Nepal*, pp.22-38. Kathmandu: Himal Books.

Sundar, Malla K. 2000. 'Whether the Newars are Janajati or Not', www.newah.org/Janjati-English%20version.htm (accessed 2/9/05).

Toffin, G. 1984. *Religion et société chez les Néwars du Népal*. Paris: CNRS.

Ukyab, T. and S. Adhikari 2000. *The Nationalities of Nepal*. Kathmandu: HMG Committee for the Development of Nationalities, Ministry of Local Development.

Varshney, A. 2002. *Ethnic Conflict and Civic Life: Hindus and Muslims in India* (2nd ed.). New Haven: Yale University Press.

Whelpton, J. 1997. 'Political Identity in Nepal: State, Nation, and Community', in Gellner et al. (eds.), *Nationalism and Ethnicity in a Hindu Kingdom*, pp. 39-78.

Appendix: Tables on Activists Surveyed

(The source for all these tables is field surveys carried out by Mrigendra Karki.)

Table 12A.1: Caste/Ethnicity and Occupation

Ethnicity/Caste	No.	Per cent	Occupation	No.	Per cent
Brahman (Hill)	30	28.8	Lawyer	1	1.0
Chetri/Thakuri (Hill)	10	9.6	Technical occupation	3	2.9
Janajati (Hill)	26	25.0	Business/ Industry	13	12.5
Newar (Hill)	3	2.9	Service	5	4.8
Dalit (Hill)	17	16.3	Traditional occupation	2	1.9
Brahman (Tarai)	3	2.9	Agriculture	19	18.3
Chetri (Tarai) (Rajput/Kayastha)	1	1.0	Housewife	15	14.4
Yadav and equivalent (Tarai)	7	6.7	Student	31	29.8
Janajati (Tarai)	2	1.9	School teacher	7	6.7
Dalit (Tarai)	2	1.9			
Others (Tarai)	1	1.0	Campus teacher	8	7.7
Others	2	1.9			
Total	104	100.0	Total	104	100.0

Table 12A.2: Birthplace by Zone, Rural/Urban, and Development Region of the Country

Ecological Zone	No.	Per cent	Residence	No.	Per cent	Development Region*	No.	Per cent
Mountain	6	5.8	Rural	75	73.5	KTM Valley	9	8.8
Hill	59	56.7	Urban	27	26.5	EDR	18	17.6
Tarai	37	35.6				CDR ex. KTM	30	29.4
Foreign	2	1.9				WDR	32	31.4
						MWDR	8	7.8
						FWDR	5	4.9
Total	104	100.0	Total	102	100.0	Total	102	100.0

Note: *KTM – Kathmandu
EDR – Eastern Development Region
CDR – Central Development Region
WDR – Western Development Region
MWDR – Mid-Western Development Region
FWDR – Far-Western Development Region

Table 12A.3: Education, Religion, and Activism

Educational status	No.	Per cent	Religion	No.	Per cent
Illiterate	1	1.0	Hindu	73	70.2
Literate	11	10.6	Buddhist	20	19.2
School level	15	14.4	Muslim	2	1.9
Certificate	11	10.6	Christian	2	1.9
Diploma	25	24.0	Kirati	4	3.8
Master's	41	39.4	Others	3	2.9
Total	104	100.0	Total	104	100.0

Table 12A.4: Social Status of Grandfather and Father

Grandfather's social status	No.	Per cent	Father's social status	No.	Per cent
Elite (*thālu*)	20	19.2	Elite	2	1.9
Merchant	15	14.4	Merchant	7	6.7
Pandit	6	5.8	Pandit	3	2.9
Social activist	26	25.0	Social activist	25	24.0
Religious activist	12	11.5	Religious activist	11	10.6
Political leader	2	1.9	Political leader	22	21.2
Official/Teacher	5	4.8	Official/Teacher	15	14.4
Retired army	4	3.8	Retired army	17	16.3
Ordinary people	49	47.1	Ordinary people	31	29.8
Other	4	3.8	Other	7	6.7
Total Respondents (104)	143	137.5	Total Respondents (104)	140	134.6

Note: Percentages based on multiple responses.

Table 12A.5: Status of Residence and Possession and/or Use of Car

Living in KTM	No.	Per cent	Residence in Kathmandu	No.	Per cent	Possession of own vehicle	No.	Per cent
Permanent resident	6	5.8	Own	21	33.3	Yes	11	10.6
						No	93	89.4
50 years & above	1	1.0	Rented	39	61.9	Total	104	100.0
25-49	6	5.8	Lodge/hotel	1	1.6	Use of office vehicle	No.	Per cent
1-24	50	48.1	With relative	1	1.6	Yes	1	1.0
						Sometimes	4	3.8
Live outside KTM Valley	41	39.4	Other	1	1.6	No	99	95.2
Total	104	100.0	Total	63	100.0	Total	104	100.0

Table 12A.6: Name or Type of Main Organization to which Activist is Affiliated

Organization	No.	Per cent
NC	4	3.8
UML	2	1.9
Sadbhavana	2	1.9
Other political party	3	2.9
Student union	7	6.7
Other front organization	19	18.3
Janajati Mahasangh (NEFIN)	4	3.8
Govt. institutionalized Janajati Committee	1	1.0
Other Janajati	3	2.9
Women's Commission	2	1.9
Other women's groups	24	23.1
Dalit NGO Federation (DNF)	2	1.9
Dalit Commission	5	4.8
Other Dalit organization	10	9.6
Hindu	3	2.9
Buddhist	9	8.7
Muslim	2	1.9
Christian	2	1.9
Total	104	100.0

Table 12A.7: Level and Length of Involvement in the Organization

	No.	Per cent		No.	Per cent
Executive Central	42	40.4	Before 1951	2	1.9
Executive District	12	11.5	1951-60	2	1.9
Committee Member Central	47	45.2	1961-80	29	27.9
Committee Member District	3	2.9	1981-90	30	28.8
			After 1990	41	39.4
Total	104	100.0	Total	104	100.0

Table 12A.8: Source of Inspiration and Additional Field of Activism

Inspiration	No.	Per cent	Additional Field of Activism	No.	Per cent
Books	9	8.7	Politics	38	36.5
Event(s)	18	17.3	Ethnic	17	16.3
Individual	34	32.7	Dalit	10	9.6
Ideology	18	17.3	Madheshi	4	3.8
Family	33	31.7	Language/Culture	10	9.6
Social/cultural environment	28	26.5	Women	18	17.3
Other	17	16.3	Religious	7	6.7
Do not know	1	1.0	Human rights	39	37.5
			Social reform	39	37.5
			Other	2	1.9
			None	10	9.6
Total Respondents (104)	158	151.9	Total Respondents (104)	194	186.5

Note: Percentages based on multiple responses.

13

Challenging Goliath: People, Dams, and the Paradoxes of Transnational Critical Movements

JOANNA PFAFF-CZARNECKA

INTRODUCTION

In the Western imagination, we are assumed to know fairly well what is happening in today's world. The high standard and the easy availability of communication technologies buttress this perception. Today, we share the strong impression that global connectivity is continuously growing, enhancing our knowledge bases and increasing the density of social interactions across the globe. Moreover, more and more people seem to believe that we currently face (and contribute to) the formation of a global public sphere. In this process, the powerful image of a well-informed world community has emerged, suggesting that discourses and norms constituting a common framework of reference converge (though dissident views abound as well). Disposing of such a plethora of information and communication channels, it is easy to assume that we all dwell in a common horizon, sharing the concerns that the world society faces. This powerful picture requires some reconsideration, notwithstanding its appeal.

Human rights abuses and struggles to realize human rights are a case in point. The mass media and alternative information platforms continuously disseminate shocking information on injustice and atrocities. Simultaneously, we learn about 'gains of terrain' by movements, networks, and organizations engaged in the protection of human rights. What emerges is a picture in which various dimensions of global flows come together: the spread of information, the transnationalization and pluralization of law, as well as better and tighter means at civil society's disposal to protect and realize human rights. Despite this boost of information, connectivity, and action, several doubts remain, however, which I should like to address in this essay.

This essay seeks to highlight some hitherto little noticed difficulties faced by campaigns against human rights abuses and environmental damage at dam construction sites in South Asia. Rather than analysing the most obvious problems and obstacles that the victims and their supporters, the international human rights movements, face in their confrontation with powerful 'adversaries' such as state officials, lending agencies, and enterprises which ignore social and environmental standards, I shall concentrate instead upon some less striking, but nevertheless important problems. The existing literature and available internet sites provide accounts of successful struggles and they convey an idea of the magnitude of the social and environmental problems people at sites such as Narmada have faced. Such sources document the great significance, impact, and growth of these protest movement(s).[1] Yet they fail to acknowledge the movements' internal problems, and the assessments of their achievements are – I intend to show – too optimistic.

Thus, drawing on material from India and Nepal, I shall question the prevailing tendency in the existing literature to depict these protest movements as being well integrated and smoothly efficient. Taking this position may sound politically incorrect, but my intention is certainly not to belittle these movements or their impact. Rather, my aim is to highlight the highly complex and possibly fragmented character of those arenas where striking human rights abuses and everyday problems are contested and negotiated.[2] Against the backdrop of such ongoing struggles, it will therefore be my aim to address the limits of successful action in contexts characterized simultaneously by a striking variety of concerns and grievances, numerous and diverse stakeholders, and a multiplicity of sites of contestation. Viewed in this perspective, the accomplishments of previous struggles may appear even more conspicuous and impressive. Moreover, a proper grasp of some of the difficulties in carrying out protest movements may – I hope – contribute to strengthening them. I shall therefore consider the diverse logics of action and the internal conflicts within protest movements, the problem of an uneven distribution of resources at their disposal, as well as the problem of effectiveness due to the scattered character of sites of contestation. In this enquiry, I concur with the important observation by Johnson and Wilson (2000: 1891):

---

[1] See especially Khagram (2004), Baviskar (1995), and Sen (1999). For internet sites, see, for instance, http://www.narmada.org/sardarsarovar.html.

[2] Everyday issues such as working conditions and health can be seen as human rights problems, according to the First International Pact of Economic, Social and Cultural Rights.

> The current concern with the role of civil society in public action on development and social provisioning raises many conceptual questions. Among them is whether the concept of civil society inherently homogenizes social divisions which instead need actively to be confronted and negotiated.

At least since the Polish movement *Solidarnosc* gained global prominence and its logo captured our imaginations, the notion of 'civil society' has become a powerful image around the world. As is well known (and decried by many), this concept has been used with a great variety of connotations. Its success reflects the enhanced role of actors who neither belong to the state, nor to the economic sector, and who act outside the private domain in choosing, defining, and pursuing social goals.[3] Besides having the capacity of self-organization, civil society is expected successfully to resist the state's domination (Taylor 1990: 98) as well as other 'colonization' attempts (Habermas 1988). In debates on so-called developing societies many observers and development agencies have invested great hopes in civil society's potential not only to strengthen their societies' institutional fabrics, but also to provide badly needed correctives to either weak and/or corrupt and inefficient states (Pfaff-Czarnecka 2004).

These expectations of efficiency have been so high that Western organizations, including the World Bank, USAID, and numerous other multi- and bilateral organizations have taken to providing economic support for non-governmental organizations and to sponsoring 'new social movements' in great numbers (and this development has been reflected in a tremendous boost for NGOs in the West as well). There is a far-reaching agreement that such non-state social forms[4] tend to embody and reinforce democratic ideals through their dynamic character, their organizational potentials, as well as through their strong value stress on equality and partnership, and that they are likely to be more efficient because of their comparatively small size, specialization, and the high degree of legitimacy they enjoy.

The high ethos of partnership and equality evinced by many movements and organizations became a staple in the public understanding of what civil society is about. But it is important to see that resistance networks can be contingent and are not always stable bodies, but may rather be prone to conflict and division. In view of the immense engagement in direct action, in advocacy and the dissemination of information, I do not mean to neglect the tremendous importance of these formations. The

---

[3] Cohen & Arato (1989), Habermas (1988).

[4] In fact, so far it has proved rather difficult to produce any satisfactory definition of these non-state social formations. The synonymous use of the terms 'NGO' and 'civil society' is extremely problematic for several reasons which, for lack of space, cannot be gone into here.

question is whether failures, shortcomings, and ongoing conflicts should be silenced in social analysis. The great diversity and inequality prevailing in civil society tends to be neglected in media depictions and in current academic research. Fragmentation, power differentials, and competition have not so far received much attention.

Simultaneously, over the last ten years, three assumptions about the dynamics of civil society have significantly buttressed the legitimacy of non-governmental organizations and social movements. The first assumption is that there have been continuous 'gains in terrain' in the battles against their adversaries; the second is a firm belief in their effectiveness; third, there is the image of civil society as well integrated and consistent. The first assumption is reflected, for instance, in the well-known elegant 'spiral model' presented by Risse, Ropp, and Sikkink in 1999 that purports to explain how transnationally organized civil society works towards the realization of human rights. Risse et al. discern several stages in the cooperation between national and international civil society actors: international actors help their national partners to pressurize governments to protect human rights while operating under severe conditions, characterized by denial and backlash against their cause. In the first stage, they achieve – after prolonged battles – tactical concessions made by government. In the second stage, prescriptive status is reached (incorporating human rights into the state's legislation). In the final step, governmental behaviour consistent with international norms is achieved. Obviously, the 'spiral model' conforms to what is desirable. Risse et al. very rightly stress the onerous process leading to the realization of human rights. Nevertheless, they concentrate on cases where international pressure has ultimately proved successful, whereas in many instances, as we shall see with the example of the Narmada project(s) in India, tactical concessions can go on forever, leaving space for discretion and room for manoeuvre, to the continuing advantage of resourceful stakeholders. It is an empirical question, then, whether a movement's losses are to be seen as a temporary backlash, or, alternatively, as a durable reversal of a process they have sought to influence.

The second assumption – that civil society organizations are always effective – is reflected in Khagram's (2004) assessment of the civil society movement's decisive impact on the diminished volume of large dam constructions worldwide:

> ... I argue that the unprecedented emergence and unexpected strength of transnationally coordinated action – constituted primarily by nongovernmental organisations and social movements – has dramatically altered the dynamics surrounding big dams around the world from the local to the international levels. Critics and opponents of these projects have been strengthened by globally

> spreading norms and principles regarding human rights, indigenous peoples, and especially the environment, among others. The gradual institutionalisation of these norms and principles into the procedures and structures of states, international agencies, private sector companies, and other prominent organisations has partially been the result of the activities, and substantially contributed to the effectiveness, of these actors. (Khagram 2004: 3)

As a corrective to this view, a document prepared for the World Commission on Dams cites a number of alternative reasons why there has been a decrease in the number of large dam projects worldwide:

- Environmental and social ('safeguard') policies have become more explicit and comprehensive.
- Internal review processes have been strengthened ...
- Lending policies, especially in the power sector, seek to promote reform and encourage governments to bring in the private sector.
- Greater emphasis is being placed on sound macro-economic policies and reduction in poorly targeted subsidies ...
- Country strategies focus more on poverty alleviation and environmentally sustainable development, which has increased the emphasis on energy efficiency. (Ljung 2001: vi)

Ljung's explanation is not necessarily incompatible with an enthusiastic depiction of the role of human rights and environmental protest groups. In fact, it forcefully reflects the importance of their impact, but it attributes to them a smaller weight in assessing the overall causes of changing trends in power generation. Khagram's argument for the efficacy of the transnational protest movements may appear in a special light when we consider the serious setbacks to the movement that I discuss below.

Both Risse et al. (1999) and Khagram (2004) also illustrate the third assumption (civil society as being well integrated and consistent). Other authors, such as Manuel Castells (1996) who has worked on *spaces of flows*, and Brysk (2000) who stresses the acceleration (see the first assumption) of international connections, tend to convey a picture of transnational protest movements as well structured and connected. By contrast, Radcliffe et al. (2002) draw our attention to such movements' unruly, complex, and partly contradictory character. On the basis of a study of indigenous and political transnationalism in the Andean region, they argue against a simple 'meeting of above and below' model, as reflected in the 'spiral model'. They suggest that the issue networks they have observed operate simultaneously at diverse levels, and are full of entanglements and contradictions: "In practice, the work on Andean indigenous transnational issue networks demonstrates that the interests, agendas and practices constitutive of transnational indigenous development are radically heterogeneous" (Radcliffe et al. 2002: 14; see also Singh 1997: 13). The same observation could be made of the South Asian data I am now going to present.

CONSTRUCTING DAMS AND THEIR CONTESTATIONS IN SOUTH ASIA

During the second half of the twentieth century, in South Asia as elsewhere, very ambitious energy programmes were initiated and partly implemented. Apart from nuclear power stations, large dams were among the largest projects undertaken in order to generate electricity. At the beginning of the state-guided modernizing era, coinciding with the period when India gained its independence, everything was subordinate to the ideology of development. Its advocates embraced the idea of technical progress and economic growth, according overwhelming priority to the common good (of the nation) as opposed to the private concerns of affected population groups. Subsequently, from the 1950s onwards, numerous damming projects were initiated in India. Many remained at the planning stage, however. Significant delays were due partly to a lack of funding and partly to problems of coordination and conflicts of interest within and between governmental agencies.

It is only during the last two decades that protest movements have gained momentum in India and in Nepal, and these have slowed the pace of implementation still further. Today, India looks back at an impressive trajectory of mobilization and protest involving more and more people, organizations, and movements within India and abroad. The success of the Indian protest movement has greatly contributed to policy changes in the world at large, instigating the adoption of new approaches within the World Bank as well as within several transnational corporations operating in this field. Successful protest at one particular construction site has usually spread to other sites, providing a model for how to organize efficiently, which course of action to adopt, and which style of leadership to follow (see Khagram 2004: 33-64). Indirectly, the Indian struggles have had a positive impact in Nepal as well, as I shall discuss below. Notwithstanding the many success stories and achievements, numerous drawbacks and problems have remained, as the following two examples reveal.

Case 1: India – The Narmada Project(s)

This short account can, of course, only provide a rough summary of developments surrounding the Narmada projects, their planning and implementation, the escalating protests, and the negotiations which resulted. This is partly due to the sheer magnitude of the protest against the construction work and accompanying activities, in particular the forced displacements. Furthermore, the sheer quantity of publications that document these processes complicates the matter further since the authors often follow one of the ideological positions among the competing factions within the anti-Narmada movement. It is precisely this size and complexity that are my point of departure.

Plans to establish dams in the Narmada River Valley go back to colonial times. Subsequently "... over 3,000 dam projects, including 165 big dams, were finally approved for construction along the Narmada river's course and tributaries in 1979, constituting part of the largest river basin scheme formulated in India since Independence" (Khagram 2004: 65). Before this region became the nexus of a strong protest movement, in the initial decades, it was already the arena for interdepartmental struggles and conflicts of interests between different arms of the state apparatus, especially at the federal level. These 'internal' struggles among and within governmental agencies provide a telling picture of the meagre chances to manage projects of this scale and size.

According to Khagram (2004: 67), who has provided the most recent, concise and well-documented analysis on this issue,[5] the first proposal for the integrated development of the Narmada River Valley was made by A.N. Khosla, the Chairman of the Federal Government of India's Central Waterways, Irrigation and Navigation Commission in 1946. Despite a scarcity of trained personnel and of financial resources, an ad hoc committee was formed by the Central Ministry of Works, Mines, and Power in 1947 in order to review the preliminary estimates and to formulate priorities since the government saw the generation of power as one of the key requirements for progress, for the sake of which individual interests had to be sacrificed:

> Signalling that the displacement of people from the construction of big dams in the name of development would become a common feature in post-independence India, Prime Minister Jawaharlal Nehru told villagers while laying the foundation stone for the project [Hirakuru in Orissa] on April 12, 1948, "If you are to suffer, you should suffer in the interest of the country".[6]

In subsequent years conflicts were to escalate. The Ministry of Irrigation and Power argued for the expansion of wet rice production, an imperative that have partly collided with the task of optimizing energy generation. The

---

[5]Unless stated otherwise, the information in this subsection is based on Khagram (2004).

[6]Cited in Khagram (2004: 37) from the *Bombay Chronicle*, 12 April 1948: 5. In a similar vein, J. Nehru stated, "When I walked around the site, I thought these days, the biggest temple and mosque and gurdwara is the place where man works for the good of mankind. Which place can be greater than the Bhakra Nangal Project, where thousands of men have worked or shed their blood and sweat and laid down their lives as well? Where can be a holier place than this, which can we regard as higher?" (cited in Khagram 2004: 33).

federal states affected by the project embarked on prolonged negotiations regarding the location of important dams and over the losses of water needed for irrigation and for other dams.[7] Initially, there existed no central authority which could successfully mediate the deepening inter-state conflicts. With the splitting of the state of Bombay on 1 May 1960 into the states of Maharashtra and Gujarat, new and inexperienced bureaucracies were put in charge of planning and implementation. Subsequently, no ecological impact assessment was conducted, nor – as in the case of the Broach project (the predecessor of the Sardar Sarovar major dam project) – was any economic analysis or comprehensive financial plan undertaken. The technical designs as well as the expected outputs repeatedly shifted in the course of negotiations between the states.

At the moment when the Broach project was inaugurated in 1961, the authorities gave no consideration to its social impact. As Khagram (2004: 71) very pointedly reports,

> At that time, the first six villages (four completely, two partially) were commandeered for Kevadia Colony, the headquarters for construction of the project. The impacts on those displaced, who were mostly tribal peoples, were not examined. The people who were affected by the project were not informed in advance, nor was their participation considered necessary for successful execution of the projects. A policy of resettlement and rehabilitation was not formulated, nor was compensation awarded for the loss of lands and livelihoods. The 'outstees', as they were called, themselves were not organised, mobilised, or even aware of their rights enshrined in India's democratic constitution.

Only in 1969 did the Narmada Water Dispute Tribunal (NWDT) come into being. This can also be considered the defining moment when the diverse projects planned and under construction affecting the four Indian states of Gujarat, Madhya Pradesh, Maharashtra, and Rajasthan (Rajasthan not being considered a 'riparian' state, however) came into being as the single 'Narmada' – the largest river basin scheme the Indian state has ever sought to implement. In the course of the 1970s, this Tribunal was in charge of mediating between governmental actors, while a range of key non-state stakeholders, in particular the directly affected persons, were not involved in the NWDT's deliberations. Also, its establishment itself has instigated new conflicts (on its constitutionality as well as on its competencies and the finality of its judgements) – while still leaving many problems unresolved. In the course of the 1970s, its deliberations centred on key

[7] After four major projects (Bargi, Tawa, Punasá and Broach) were approved initially, the states of Madhya Pradesh and of the then Bombay have agreed to expand the projects to the sites of Barwah, Harinphal and Keli.

technical issues: the height of the dams, the designated areas for submersion, the priority of the individual projects, and the shares of water to be directed to the four states. It was only in the middle of the 1970s that the issue of rehabilitation measures for the displaced population appeared on the NWDT's agenda; environmental concerns continued to be left out (Dwevedi 1998). It was already realized that around 200,000 people would be evicted in the course of the construction of all the dams and channels (see narmada.org; Shihata 2000). The projects had grown significantly in scope and size. As of 31 March 2005, the construction agency gives the following striking data on the Sardar Sarovar Dam:

> A concrete gravity dam, 1210 meters (3970 feet) in length and with a maximum height of 163 meters above the deepest foundation level, is under construction across river Narmada. The dam will be the third highest concrete dam (163 meters) in India, the first two being Bhakra (226 metres) in Himachal Pradesh and Lakhwar (192 meters) in Uttar Pradesh. In terms of the volume of concrete involved for gravity dams, this dam will be ranking as the second largest in the world with an aggregate volume of 6.82 million cu.m. The first is Grand Coule Dam in USA with a total volume of 8.0 million cu.m. This dam with its spillway discharging capacity of 87,000 cumecs (30.70 lac), will be the third in the world, Gazenba (1.13 lac cumecs) in China and Tucurri (1.0 lac cumecs) in Brazil being the first two. As per the approval of Planning Commission of Government of India, the cost of SSP was estimated at Rs.64.06 billion based on the 1986-87 price level, out of which share of Gujarat was placed at Rs.49.04 billion and the share of other 3 States Madhya Pradesh, Maharashtra and Rajasthan at Rs.15.02 billion. The likely cost at 1991-92 price level works out to Rs.13,180 crores. There are two power houses for the Sardar Sarovar Project (SSP). (i) 1,200 MW River Bed Power House and (ii) 250 MW Canal Head Power House. Power benefits are shared among Madhya Pradesh, Maharashtra and Gujarat in the ratio of 57 : 27 : 16 respectively.[8]

Towards the end of the 1970s new actors entered the complex terrain of the Narmada. In 1978 the Indian authorities accepted foreign funds provided in the first place by the World Bank, the United Nations, and Japan. Almost at the same time the first domestic resistance against the Sardar Sarovar Project occurred in the state of Gujarat, but the protests were limited because of the weakness of the tribal population and their supporters. In Madhya Pradesh, a stronger protest movement formed almost simulta-

---

[8] Quoted from the homepage http://www.sardarsarovardam.org/, run by the consortium Sardar Sarovar Narmada Nigam Ltd.

neously. Its strength can be attributed, first, to the fact that with the planned height of the Sardar Sarovar Dam of 455 feet, prime agricultural lands in Nirmar district were going to be submerged, affecting especially middle-class farmers who were affluent enough to generate substantial funds for the movement. Second, members of the then oppositional party of Congress hoped to make political capital by lending their support to the movement. Subsequently, leading politicians such as Dr Shankar Dayal Sharma (former President of India) and V.C. Shukla (former Union Minister of Water Resources) were detained by the police in the course of the protest movement (Khagram 2004: 85). However, once Congress came to power, local expectations were disappointed. The elected leaders agreed to proceed with planned construction works, while stressing that they would strive to explore "the possibility of reducing the distress of the displaced persons as much as possible".[9] With the promise of compensation, resistance ended.

World Bank involvement has slowed the project implementation, in the first place due to the Bank's authorities having been compelled to conduct several studies in response to technical concerns. Also, upon its recommendation, planning groups and commissions were established in order to coordinate the project. Increasingly, the modalities of resettlement and rehabilitation (R & R) have received more and more attention. Almost from the outset, the World Bank issued several statements and sent out several missions seeking to refine its policy with regard to R & R. However, the Bank's authorities have had little impact with regard to implementation. In the same vein, the governmental Narmada Water Dispute Tribunal ruled that the affected families were to be compensated not only in cash but also in land, that they were to be supported by additional grants and financial assistance, and that full communities as units were to be relocated to the new villages. In practice, the Tribunal lacked the authority to monitor the implementation of its recommendations. People without land titles, especially those ethnic groups that relied on common property resources and on living from forest and waste land, were not included in this planning. A further drawback was that the Tribunal designed these R & R packages for farmers in Madhya Pradesh and in Maharashtra, but not for those in Gujarat.

It should come as no surprise, therefore, that Gujarat developed into a site where, from the beginning of the 1980s onwards, a strong domestic protest movement started to gain momentum. For instance, on 8 March 1984, there was "a massive march to Kevadia Colony – the construction headquarters near the Sardar Sarovar Dam site – involving all outstees

[9]Cited by Khagram (2004: 85) from the memorandum of understanding signed by the Chief Ministers of Gujarat and Madhya Pradesh on 8 August 1981.

from all the villages to be submerged in Gujarat and joined by potentially affected villagers from Maharashtra" (Khagram 2004: 89); the marchers demanded compensation. Increasingly, they were supported by domestic non-governmental organizations such as the Social Services Society or Arch Vahini, which have taken upon themselves the task of organizing the project-affected people to improve their compensation packages, to monitor their delivery, and to disseminate their findings on injustices, for example, in relation to unequal treatment in the ongoing process of R & R.

While the R & R issue has remained the most prominent concern for the growing protest movement, other issues have started to be included in their agendas as well – in this they were increasingly influenced by international debates. So, for instance, the UK-based Oxfam (besides supporting the R & R issue) began to carry out and strengthen health-related work. By the mid 1980s environmental concerns were also receiving more and more attention. The Ministry of Environment and Forests (MOEF) of Gujarat issued a confidential note to Prime Minister Rajiv Gandhi expressing concern at the environmental impact of resettlement practices. Furthermore, "[t]his criticism with respect to resettlement was connected to the increasing divergences between the MOEF on the one hand, and the federal Government of India's Ministry of Water resources and the state governments on the other, over the environmental impacts of the projects" (Khagram 2004: 97). Internationally endorsed norms of environmental protection were translated into national and state-level legislation, binding the various governments to introduce checks, balances, and standards.

The R & R issue was gaining momentum in India as well, with NGOs framing grievances in human rights terminology, and in particular adopting the language of indigenous peoples' rights. Their efforts have been supported more and more by international movements and organizations which exerted pressure on the World Bank. The World Bank, in turn, has repeatedly "urged the various Indian Governments to improve their policies on resettlement" (Khagram 2004: 89). Having received unsatisfactory answers on several occasions,[10] the Bank contracted a renowned specialist on resettlement who came up with a highly critical report, which still had little impact on actual practice. The international movement has been instrumental in pressurizing the World Bank as well as the Western governments that are involved in the dams' construction either by providing loans or by issuing guarantees to Western enterprises active on the sites.

With this strong international support, domestic protest also grew in strength. Simultaneously, the (pressurized) Wold Bank exerted pressure upon the Indian government. After November 1987, when the newly

[10] "Letters were sent to the Bank stating that 'necessary steps are being taken to formulate a rehabilitation plan' and that no Bank mission should be mounted specifically for this purpose" (Khagram 2004: 89).

appointed President of the World Bank, Barber Conable, visited India and met with numerous activists, the Government revised its course, affirming a two-hectare minimum for landed outstees:

> Two weeks later, on December 14th and 17th, three more resolutions were passed ... The first resolution granted that landed outstees, who were eligible for a minimum of two hectares of land, would be given an ex gratia payment equal to the difference between the compensation received for a submerged land-holding and the market price of buying five acres of land. ... The second and third resolutions increased the subsistence allowances and grants to be given to the outstees during the process of relocation ... The final resolution – and by far the most unexpected – completely reformed the resettlement policy by adopting the same package for all landless outstees of Gujarat, not just those cultivating unauthorised lands, that was to be given to landholding outstees. (Khagram 2004: 99)

This substantial victory of the movement was, however, soon revealed a faultline along which cracks within the movement began to emerge. For, under the new circumstances, those who objected to the dam construction as long as there was no policy for R & R and those who opposed all and any dam construction no longer stood side by side. The former, including the NGO Arch Vahini, began to cooperate with the project authorities in the implementation of policy reforms. The latter, who included the Narmada Dharanghast Samiti, claimed that, for environmental reasons a complete and comprehensive re-evaluation of the project was required. (To this they added scepticism both about the prospects for efficient implementation of resettlement policies and about the proposed economic benefits of the project.)

Subsequently, during the 1990s and thereafter, two very diverse dynamics coincided. On the one hand, the human rights regime, consisting of laws, the formal institutions for their enforcement, as well as civil society actors supporting human rights, has substantially grown in size and refined its tools. On the other hand, conflicts within the movement have intensified. The complex relationship between human rights and environmental activists is a case in point. The two movements can reinforce each other, as was the case on the occasion of the 1992 Rio UNCED Summit where the rights of indigenous peoples were brought into a direct relation with environmental concerns.[11] But they can also collide and clash – as has

[11]"Principle 22: Indigenous people and their communities and other local communities have a vital role in environmental management and development because of their knowledge and traditional practices. States should recognize and duly support their identity, culture and interests and enable their effective participation in the achievement of sustainable develop-

repeatedly been the case with national parks in many countries.[12] Again, action aiming at improving the working conditions of workers on the project sites may come into collision with both of these positions.

Activists and the immediately affected local people were able to join forces in stalling construction on the projects. To the great disappointment of the project's fundamental opponents, however, the movement has not been able to halt Narmada altogether. Nevertheless, environmental as well as human rights groups have been able to gain strong support from abroad in order not only to make the authorities acknowledge and refine legal norms, but also to work towards their realization. Increasingly, Indian activists have been joining hands with a wide array of international actors, including Oxfam, Survival International, 'The Ecologist' group, and numerous other organizations and movements in the West.

With the support of their Western allies, the domestic opposition was able to cooperate with the newly established environmental departments in pursuing environmental protection. "During the period between 1985 and 1987, what by then had become the MOEF persisted in its refusal to grant environmental clearances to either the Narmada Sagar or Sardar Sarovar Projects" (Khagram 2004: 107). At that time the World Bank was clearly on the opposing side, having already approved a $450 million loan and credit agreement for the Sardar Sarovar Project in the year 1985, and exerting pressure upon the MOEF. The rapidly growing domestic opposition that came to be guided by such charismatic leaders as Medha Patkar has subsequently accused the World Bank, among other things, of ignoring and bypassing the MOEF's concerns and decisions. On the other hand, the authorities have established two subcommittees of the Narmada Control Authority in charge of environment and welfare respectively, involving members of domestic NGOs.

In May 1988, the domestic opposition managed to gather a huge protest rally after the governments of the three riparian states withdrew some of the previously given assurances regarding resettlement. This overwhelming protest forced the Government of Gujarat (GOG) to compromise, again regaining support from the pragmatist NGOs, which deepened the rift with their more fundamentalist opponents and sometime allies. The GOG's (and other states') tactics – manoeuvring between stakeholders, making 'strategic concessions' (see Risse et al. 1999), and co-opting protesters – contributed to this rift. Nonetheless, a strong front was formed, calling

ment" (Rio Declaration on Environment and Development formulated at The United Nations Conference on Environment and Development).

[12]Khagram (2004: 97) argues that with the transnationalization of the anti-Narmada movement "there was a progressive integration of human rights, indigenous peoples, and environmental concerns". This was certainly the case among the opponents of the entire Narmada project, but within the movement diverse opinions have been voiced.

itself the 'Save-the-Narmada Movement', and it gained high visibility both in India and abroad. But state authorities were strengthening their tools as well. On 5 October 1988 the Government of India's Planning Commission granted an investment clearance of Rs.6,406 crores and the GOG imposed the Official Secrets Act, severely restricting access to information and forums for public protest (Khagram 2004: 115).

Subsequently battles and negotiations took place at diverse sites. Ever-shifting constellations of actors joined forces directly at the project's operational headquarters (Kevadia Colony), meeting at rallies and national conventions and acting abroad. Endeavours to influence the decision-making within the World Bank have proved particularly effective. American activists have successfully accessed the US Senate, Congress, and the World Bank's board of executive directors as well as its several key executives. In the same vein, in other Western countries, activists have lobbied their governments and organized concerned citizens' support. The 'gains of terrain' achieved by activists in Washington, where Congressmen and other politicians started to pressurize the World Bank, subsequently spread to other Western countries:

> The Congressional hearings and Scheurer's interventions also began to shift the perceptions of other foreign donors. Congressman Scheurer himself went a step further and raised the issue at a Washington, D.C. meeting of Global Legislators for a Balanced Environment (GLOBE), a transgovernmental coalition, and subsequently sent letters to several European and Japanese funders to take the case up in their own countries. These included the OECF of Japan which was to fund turbines manufactured by the Sumitomo and Hitachi corporations, KFW of Germany which was involved in fisheries development, CIDA of Canada which had been approached on the issue of the environmental impact assessment, and ODA of the United Kingdom, which was called upon to conduct downstream impact studies on the projects. (Khagram 2004: 119)

Eventually, the Japanese activists were successful. In 1990 the Japanese Ministry of Foreign Affairs announced the suspension of any further payments for the projects; in addition, numerous Japanese politicians signed a letter to the World Bank's president, Barber Conable, arguing for a suspension of its funding (ibid.: 120). Despite growing criticisms abroad, the Indian authorities did not alter their stance.

For the argument being advanced here the subsequent developments are of special importance. First, faced with the mounting pressure upon the World Bank, the Indian government announced on 26 March 1993 that India would forego the remaining \$170 million of the \$450 million credits and loans that had been allocated for the Sardar Sarovar Project by the World Bank. Second, no longer able to pressurize the Indian government through its external donors, activists intensified their pressure directly on the government, and in response increasingly faced repression at the project sites. Third, from 1994, the Indian Supreme Court became an important site of contest and negotiation. It considered several petitions handed in by the protest movement and in February 1997 it delivered a judgement, ordering an indefinite stay on implementation of the Sardar Sarovar Project. This judgment was celebrated by the Anti-Narmada Movement as a major victory. However,

> Gujarat authorities ... continued to build the Sardar Sarovar Project without complying with the Supreme Court's February 1997 judgment. By this time, moreover, Hindu fundamentalist groups had grown in strength and the right wing Bharatiya Janata Party (BJP) had been elected to numerous governments in India including in the State of Gujarat. ... the increasingly authoritarian nature of [the] Indian political system, along with mounting counter-mobilisation by big dam proponents, and growing attempts to privatize big dam projects began to curtail the effectiveness of big dam opponents, including the Narmada Bachao Andolan and its transnational allies. (Khagram 2004: 136)

Furthermore, in 2000, the Supreme Court made a very crucial decision which effectively reversed its 1997 ruling and supported the implementation of the damming project with little concession to the objections put forward by the Narmada Bachao Andolan (NBA). After six years of pending and deliberation, during which a stay order was issued over construction of the Sardar Sarovar Dam (Gujarat), the Court ruled in favour of the project's continuation, issuing an order that the construction works could be restarted immediately. The Supreme Court further made the point that the judiciary should have no role in deciding whether social justice was threatened through this project. Neither the objections regarding the project's environmental impact nor the shortcomings of the rehabilitation programmes were taken up.

It was a severe blow to the Indian Save the Narmada Movement that the Supreme Court questioned the legitimacy of social movements to act as public interest petitioners. Also, the Supreme Court's voicing a clear position in favour of large dam projects as beneficial to the entire nation was considered a severe affront to the movement. On the home front, therefore, the international campaigning has not proved as successful as it did in the West and especially at World Bank headquarters in Washington.

Before proceeding to the Nepalese example, I should like to identify three major sets of issues to be followed in the subsequent analysis. Of special interest are the logics of public communication. The population in the affected region and their allies carry on their battle in public social fields, and they have proved very successful in mobilizing support by successfully communicating their cause and grievances. Their public appeal has proven to be an important resource throughout the anti-Narmada struggle. Obviously, all those involved seek to communicate their truth. As a result, diverse and often conflicting definitions of the situation seek to dominate public forums. This diversity comes about as a consequence of divergent interests, drawing upon particular understandings of a given situation and mobilized in order to shape the perceptions of potential audiences. Such differences are obvious when state officials and the outstees disagree on the form and amount of compensation; they may also show that within the protest movement diverse goals are embraced. So, among the 'fundamental' opponents of the movement, the outstees will be depicted as victims of eviction and of environmental degradation; the 'pragmatists' may rather concentrate upon the amount of remuneration as well as working conditions on the constructing sites, health problems, etc.

The diversity of public depictions comes to light when Maninder Gill (1995) goes so far as to speak of the 'reign of terror' unleashed by the Narmada Bachao Andolan (NBA) on government officials as well as on those outstees who preferred to negotiate with the government in the light of a revised resettlement policy.[13] This accusation conflicts entirely with the NBA's self-promoted image as close allies of the outstees. Whereas the NBA has over and over again claimed that the indigenous people are anti-dam per se, this has been denied by other activists and scholars (see, for instance, Patel 1997 and Dhagamwar 1997). This example indicates that the victims may be depicted in differing ways, in accordance with the course of action a particular protest group is taking.

The second important set of issues is the question regarding the effectiveness of the civil society actors who face well-endowed opponents, be it state agencies, lending agencies, or transnational corporations (TNCs). The anti-globalization movements have been repeatedly depicted as David facing Goliath (Hannerz 1995; Wimmer 2001) in the literature. This discursive figure entails, of course, that the weak but resourceful protestors will win, eventually. Khagram (e.g. 2004: 137-8) is especially enthusiastic about the movement's success, pointing to its effectiveness in stalling the construction of the Sardar Sarovar, indicating how the international human rights and environmental norms have been acknowledged and incorporated into national law and highlighting the international effects of the movement. The evidence he provides substantiates these claims. However, viewed from another angle, different inferences can be drawn. For, during the

---

[13] See also Singh (1997: 13).

period when the international protest movement was growing, the state and corporate actors were gaining strength as well. Withdrawals by Japan and the World Bank, rather than being a victory for the protest movement, can be interpreted as a loss to the cause of the outstees, because thereafter the Indian authorities faced less pressure – which has allowed them to go ahead with construction. While the World Bank proved to be a learning agency and withdrew from Narmada, the homepages of those organizations active in the protest movement have recently (spring 2005) been full of vivid accounts of environmental causes under threat and human rights abuses.

The third issue regards diverse entanglements coming about in the course of project implementation. This notion was introduced by Radcliffe, Laurie, and Andolina in 2002 into the growing research on transnational solidarity movements. While observing pro-indigenous movements in the Andean region, they have reached the conclusion that in the course of transnationally organized action, dynamics at diverse levels of social organization come to coincide and to impinge upon each other. Multiple scales of interaction are involved simultaneously in negotiations, and actors and practices are not confined to a fixed location. Furthermore, "political transnationalism represents the entanglements of diverse ethnic, class and geographically dispersed institutionalized and politicized social actors around the notion of indigenous needs, and the policy and political frameworks through which to address these needs. ... we find entanglements around gender hierarchies, political affiliations, notions of professionalism, and cultural authenticity" (Radcliffe et al. 2002: 3). Such entanglements come about because development interventions, just as much as protest movements, are embodied and embedded in social practices and discourses wherever they take place. In the same vein, Gandhi draws our attention to the deeply entangled nature of negotiations in the course of the Narmada project in Gujarat:

> Resistance is a process of negotiation between actors who operate from particular positions along a spectrum of power relations. Complex, horizontal engagements of convergence and disengagement rather than static relations of dominance 'from above' and resistance 'from below' characterize the relationship between the state, adivasis and activists. (Gandhi 2003: 486)

These complexities come to light in the case of the Kali Gandaki 'A' project in Nepal as well.

Case 2: Nepal – The Kali Gandaki 'A' Project

This case needs to be seen as forming part of a larger trajectory of dam construction, the related protest, and subsequent policy reforms in Nepal, in South Asia, and worldwide. On the one hand, the design, the policies, and the modes of implementation of Kali Gandaki 'A' are to be seen in relation to the prolonged negotiations over the Arun III project in Nepal and the subsequent analyses and discussions that have occurred among experts and civil society members. The notorious Arun III was among the most prestigious and largest projects the Nepalese authorities and their international partners had ever designed for the country. Only after very severe protests by Nepali experts and activists and their Western allies, was the decision taken to give up the plan. The World Bank's decision to pull out in 1993 brought the project to an end.[14]

While human rights, and especially environmental concerns, have formed part of the protest against the Arun III, the major argument stressed the economic and managerial aspects. The opponents argued that with the magnitude of this project, the implementation would have been in foreign hands to an unacceptable degree. Furthermore, it would have created an enormous foreign debt (in addition to the already existing debt). Additionally, the problem of India's dictating the price for electricity purchase remained unresolved; given the scope of the planned electricity production, this was seen as a crucial issue. Therefore, Arun III was deemed too large for the Nepalese political economy, and unfeasible with regard to the environmental situation in the fragile Himalayan region. Projects such as Kali Gandaki 'A', tiny in comparison to other projects abroad, were thought to be more appropriate in size, and were accordingly approved.

As Kavita Rai demonstrates in her doctoral thesis, the Kali Gandaki 'A' forms part of a South Asian and possibly global pattern of negotiations over dam construction: international experiences of protest over human rights and environmental concerns have induced the authorities to revise their policies with regard to nature protection, resettlement policies, working conditions, as well as to policies regarding the dissemination of information.[15] In other words, on both sides the Kali Gandaki 'A' project has greatly benefited from the experience of previous protests and negotiations.

The 144 MW Kali Gandaki 'A' project was inaugurated in 2004 on 22 January.[16] Construction started in 1993 at a total cost of almost US $360 million which was put together by His Majesty's Government and the NEA (the Nepalese Electricity Authority), the Asian Development Bank, and

[14]That is, for the time being, for the project has not been abandoned altogether.

[15]Conducting her doctoral research under Prof. Wimmer's and my supervision, Rai has discovered that the local population failed to understand that eventually construction work would be terminated, that in general they were not able to plan any investments for the compensation they received, and that they were mostly unable to save the money they earned at the construction sites.

[16]If not specified otherwise, all information on this case is drawn from Rai 2005.

Japan's Overseas Economic Cooperation Fund.[17] The electricity generated from this project is fed to the national electricity grid. The Kali Gandaki region was found best suited for this kind of endeavour for technical, economic, and environmental reasons, as revealed in an assessment sponsored by the UNDP in 1979, as well as in an up-to-date feasibility study conducted by Norpower in 1991-2.

The Kali Gandaki area is situated in Nepal's Western Development Region, in an area comprising parts of the districts of Syangja, Palpa, Gulmi, and Parbat. The Project consists of the dam, a water reservoir, power plant, transmission lines, and a 28.5 km access road. The 5.5 km long water reservoir spreads over 65 hectares. The water is then diverted through a 6 km channel from the dam to a powerhouse. The area immediately affected consists of fertile lands, especially in Shri Krishna Gandaki VDC, the pilgrimage sites in Rudra Beni and Ridi Bazar as well as fishing and rafting sites. During construction, the NEA displaced eighteen Bote households. By 2002, there were 263 seriously project-affected families who had experienced a loss of income greater than 60 per cent, or loss of assets of more than 50 per cent. In addition, there were 1,205 project-affected families who had lost less than 50 per cent of assets. All eighteen households of the Bote ethnic group were relocated.[18] Out of the sum of US $540,000 set aside for relocations, 95 per cent was disbursed (Rai 2005: 112).

The Kali Gandaki 'A' project was among the first undertakings in Nepal for which the NEA contracted an environmental impact assessment, and it was completed in 1996. The authorities also drew up a 'Mitigation and Monitoring Plan' as well as an 'Acquisition, Compensation, and Resettlement Plan'. The results of the two plans were incorporated into the project's annual progress reports. Rai especially stresses that "for the first time in the history of hydropower project implementation, the NEA paid compensation for the acquisition of land for building an access road in addition to those in the main disturbance sites" (2005: 83). She also states that "the project-affected families received better compensation than in the past", without giving further details. Other benefits to the population consisted of a rural electrification scheme benefiting 2,671 households in 9 VDCs (Rai 2005: 85). In addition, a Micro-Credit Revolving Fund was established with US $58,895 disbursed by the Agricultural Development Bank in 1993. Tree plantation programmes were funded and a series of training courses were held in technical subjects (including tailoring) and in micro enterprise generation. Literacy classes were also made available.

---

[17]For precise data, see, e.g. http://www.adb.org/Documents/PCRs/NEP/pcr_nep_26362.pdf.

[18]This process was closely monitored by the international social and environmental panel of experts.

According to Rai, the population in the region initially welcomed the project enthusiastically and was hardly worried by its possible negative outcomes. The NEA authorities promised the villagers jobs, electricity, schools, and roads. East Consult, a Kathmandu-based consulting firm, visited and studied twelve villages to discuss impacts and concerns. The NEA also conducted public hearings. For instance, in 1994 two public meetings were attended by 1,100 affected villagers, and they were continued in the subsequent years with the help of community-based NGOs. The villagers especially welcomed the opportunity to earn money by working on construction sites, and to benefit from road and electricity access. The families who lost land were compensated in cash. Furthermore, local politicians and contractors were expected to profit in manifold ways, including new access to external personal networks in politics and administration. Support for the dam was so strong at the beginning that the villagers, along with the project authorities, denied access to the area to the Kathmandu-based human rights activists of INHURED who were trying to organize protests against the project. The latter questioned the project's viability and benefits for rural folk, its environmental impacts, and the lack of participation by local residents. The villagers, on the contrary, were afraid that the authorities would give up on the construction plans, as happened with Arun III, thus depriving them of the expected benefits.

During the ten years of Kali Gandaki 'A's implementation the key issue of the negotiations, and what little local protest occurred, was over the availability of work and the working conditions, while environmental issues were largely in the background. From the point of view of the local population, it was essential to have the bulk of the work contracted within the region and not given to migrant labourers. Furthermore, the local population's concern was that members from each local family should be employed, if they so wished, and that certain minimum standards in payment be maintained. In the course of time, the security of the working conditions came up as an increasingly important issue after several workers were killed on the construction sites. Secure working conditions are an important concern expressed in the First International Pact of Human Rights (Art. 7), but this discourse seems to have been absent in the region.

Kavita Rai suggests that in the course of the dam construction a practical process of learning was initiated. Negotiations with the authorities were initiated, regarding the selection of workers, their wages, and the security conditions. Another issue was the perception that the richer families were receiving larger compensation. The abundant availability of cash, partly reflected in high salaries (by the local standards), raised expectations, while causing opposition on the part of those lacking similar opportunities. At the same time the price of land rose rapidly. Increasingly, the villagers also began to recognize their bargaining power as workers and protesters, taking advantage of the freer political environment in the early post-1990 era. Labour unions supported them in this. At the same time villagers recognized that there were some deleterious social trends: increasing elopements, outmigration, and a growing sense of dependency on cash economy.

In the course of time, especially when construction work was nearing completion, criticisms and protests intensified significantly. More and more employees at the project sites, as well as those who had received compensation, came to realize that their earning and saving opportunities would be greatly altered once the cash flow into the region came to a close. One of the most drastic lessons was the realization that they had made poor investments with the compensation money and that conspicuous consumption, especially by young people, was a mistake. Even the better-off and better-educated villagers came to realize that having traded the productive asset of land for cash, they had failed to invest their money in a sustainable way, expecting, among other things, that opportunities to earn cash would continue to be easily available. The growing protests were then increasingly geared towards the lack of preparation of the villagers to cope with drastically changed economic conditions and the lack of inputs on the part of the project implementers to develop local markets. However, the project authorities have learnt to incorporate local leaders within wider patron-client relations, thereby diminishing the force of their protest.

We can draw three inferences from this Nepalese case. First, it brings to light, once again, the importance of the international anti-dam movement. Some achievements of the international protest movement addressing dam construction have had a direct impact in the Nepalese context, even without any strong scrutiny or protest action on the spot. Apparently, the key agents, in this case the Nepalese authorities and the entrepreneurial consortium, had incorporated previous criticisms and concerns into their policies and action plans. They anticipated the likely problems of implementation and took steps to mitigate environmental risks as well as risks of major human rights abuses. To what extent the key implementers learnt their lesson as concerned governmental or corporate agents, and to what extent the learning process was in fact reduced to strategic considerations, remains an open question, however.[19]

The second inference addresses precisely the learning effects. According to Rai, all the involved stakeholders continuously adjusted to new circumstances and they built upon the previous experiences. Most probably the Nepalese state agents, as well as the entrepreneurs, national and foreign, anticipated a high degree of publicity and close public scrutiny of their endeavours and therefore made sure to abide by standards set up elsewhere.

---

[19] In his comparative overview of dam projects in diverse political contexts, Khagram comes to the conclusion that the entrepreneurial willingness to adopt social and environmental standards coincides with high degree of democratization.

Nepal's well-developed public sphere and the excellent international networks certainly aided this process. At the same time, experiences from other countries that are less democratized and with less external dependency for funds indicate that environmental and human rights concerns tend to be less prominent among the implementers (see Khagram 2004: 139-76). In another sense the villagers have learnt many lessons, not least that construction work does not last forever and cannot be relied on as a source of employment. Another lesson learned was the necessity to consult with people in other regions in order to anticipate problems. Moreover, Rai's ethnography indicates that in Nepal the role of intermediaries (e.g. NGOs and movements) in shaping the villagers' perceptions and in the villagers' pursuit of their interests was very limited, whereas the villagers displayed great eagerness to learn from villagers living in the other regions of Nepal where dam construction had caused similar problems.

Finally, this case reveals that diverse definitions of the situation obtain, and that diverse versions of the problems and their solutions are communicated by the involved parties. The bulk of the local population saw the dam as an economic boon, at least initially, and this perception suggests that the implementers adopted successful communication strategies, whereas the issues taken up by INHURED did not address local preoccupations. Rai's account is particularly interesting because it provides insights into people's perceptions and expectations, and demonstrates the diversity of people's concerns. While selected reports from India (e.g. Baviskar 1997; Hakim 1997; Joshi 1997) focus upon the villagers' perceptions as well, the bulk of the literature concentrates upon such 'large' issues as environmental degradation and replacement, and does not pay sufficient attention to other interests expressed by the local population. Working conditions and social security issues have failed to occupy sufficient space on political agendas. Also, the villagers have not been involved in designing the modalities of resettlement themselves. It seems that such concerns have been 'covered up' by the larger issue of fundamental opposition to dams.

ON THE DIVERSITY OF 'STAKEHOLDERS' AND THEIR LOGICS OF ACTION

Both case studies taken together provide a complex picture. On the one hand, they reveal significant similarities and also commonalities. In fact, an interesting endeavour would be to follow the trajectories of negotiations around the world in order to establish precisely how experiences at one dam construction site come to impinge upon the planning, implementation, and incidence of protest at other dam construction project sites. On the other hand, the comparison has revealed significant differences. These came about not only because both cases differ in important respects (the size of the project, tackling the issue of social standards and of environmental protection by the authorities, the number of persons suffering forced displacement), but also because I have relied on authors pursuing diverse interests in their respective analyses. They adopted diverse perspectives and I have sought to reproduce them here in a multi-perspectival approach.

In this and in the following sections I shall pursue the issue of diversity and complexity even further, for constructing a dam entails a myriad of activities. To name just some of them; proving its feasibility in terms of technological and economic gains as well as future development potential, environmental and social impact assessments, creating a consortium to carry out the endeavour, attracting capital (be it from private investors, public agencies, international banks such as the World Bank and Asian Development Bank, multi- and bilateral donor agencies – often in combination), contracting firms to design and build the actual structure consisting not only of the dam, but also of channels (occasionally a discharge), access roads, devices to transport the generated energy, buildings, etc. Manifold standards need to be met and permits obtained. Overburdened with this complexity and seeking to reduce it, the responsible bodies and their representatives frequently fail to consult the persons most affected by, and involved in, the construction process, i.e. the local population – sometimes due to neglect, often for utilitarian reasons.

It is not only the case that the involved actors are diverse in their organization, function, and in their endowment of resources. They are furthermore situated at diverse sites in transnational space. They themselves are embedded in diverse societal contexts and underlie diverse types of logic. No discussion of either the Indian or the Nepalese case could possibly comprehensively convey the multiplicity of all those actors and organizations implicated in the construction even of a relatively modest dam (the Nepalese case). The discussion of the Narmada project(s) has, for instance, hardly touched upon the role of private entrepreneurs who are involved in large numbers. In fact, much of the critical literature on dam construction in India ignores the stakes involved and the role these economic actors play, and instead concentrate on the state (often seen as one actor) and on the protest/solidarity movement. But the account of the Kaḷi Gandaki 'A' project makes it clear that entrepreneurs can play a crucial role in mitigating the risk of social and environmental abuses. The concept of 'corporate citizens' that numerous transnational corporations have adopted in their self-depictions indicates an important shift in their attitude.[20] Rather than risking antagonism or face naming and shaming actions (as

[20]See, for instance, the following homepage giving names of '100 Best Corporate Citizens': http://www.business-ethics.com/100best.htm

was, for instance, the case with the firms Shell and Nike), certain corporations have therefore started to pursue strategies which are socially and environmentally sensitive. Very little is known regarding the impact of these new strategies, however. For instance, it is largely unknown how entrepreneurs and state authorities have influenced and shaped each other's actions while designing and implementing the Narmada project(s).

Both accounts have revealed, furthermore, that categories of actors are diverse in themselves. The differentiated character of the state emerges clearly from the discussion of the Narmada project(s), where competing powers (executives *vs.* judiciary), layers of authority, and areas of responsibility between the ministries have confronted each other time and again. Similar diversity was detected within the social field known today as 'civil society', as well as among the affected population, including Adivasi groups such as the Bhils, Bhilalas, and Gongs (Baviskar 1997). Not only have sections of the population come to suffer from the projects in diverse ways; the benefits have also been diverse and uneven.

Additionally, the local populations are involved in project activities in their various roles and positions. The most crucial field is certainly coping with displacement – either resisting shifting of sites, or negotiating the terms of displacement, i.e. where to go,[21] which types of compensation to accept, and which offers to reject as unsuitable or insufficient. (We know significantly more about instances of resistance, whether successful or not, than about instances of almost complete powerlessness of local populations. This situation may occur less frequently in India and Nepal, but more so in countries with a lesser degree of development of democratic institutions where projects are implemented with a still higher degree of coercion.)

During the consultations regarding the modes of resettlements, employment, and benefits, the affected populations' freedom of information, freedom of speech, and freedom to organize are at stake, and these freedoms tend to be unequally distributed. Very often, in the process of dam construction in South Asia, people have been kept unaware of the magnitude of the changes that will occur in their life, their options, and the local benefits. Whereas the authorities have neglected to provide sufficient information, in many places, local 'power-holders' have striven to establish themselves in middlemen positions, thus monopolizing communication flows and brokering discourses.

Obviously local societies are in themselves highly diversified, and are divided by class, ethnicity, caste, and gender. Some people are significantly

---

[21] From the early 1980s onwards numerous cases of very detrimental displacements (on waterlogged or arid land) have been reported in the case on Narmada project. Another problem opened up because only those populations previously living in the catchment areas were to benefit from displacement provisions, whereas families forced to leave areas where canal infrastructure was built were initially ignored.

more entrepreneurial than others when it comes to relating to external stakeholders such as contractors or civil servants. Knowledge of external rationalities, future planning, available funds and other benefits, knowledge about how to avert external interventions considered harmful, all this can be used to one's own advantage. It has repeatedly happened, however, that local elites have used privileged knowledge to the detriment of their village co-fellows (Pfaff-Czarnecka 2000). There are significant differences in the amount of resources at the disposal of the villagers and their supporters. Reports from the Narmada area indicate that within villages and between them the support for the anti-Narmada movement is fractured. Villagers and village representatives continually debate among themselves whether to accept resettlement and rehabilitation provisions or not. As Gandhi argues:

> Each adivasi's relationship to development is shaped by his or her position within the village hierarchy, and resultant relationship with state functionaries. ... A village's geographical proximity to and cultural integration with government and market actors, and its status within state boundaries is also important. ... Higher ranking village leaders with patronage relationships to bureaucrats will often manage to obtain above-average resettlement terms while others in the same village cannot. ... Given that such variegated experiences are present within villages, resettlement has produced pockets of compliance and resistance within adivasi communities in attitudes towards the Narmada project. This has found its clearest expression in adivasi communities that have distanced themselves from the (anti Narmada movement), and instead become allies of those NGOs that support the Narmada project. (Gandhi 2003: 488)

The last sentence of the above quotation draws our attention to the very diverse and competitive character of civil society action. Visions regarding the well-being of societies differ a great deal. Many organizations have been co-opted by state agencies, to work, for instance, as middlemen or even contractors at the project sites (installing handpumps or building roads). Additionally, significant power differentials and differences in the financial base obtain. Some of the movements and organizations have acquired substantial funding and do not face the immediate problem of their 'survival' in the political field. Other groups, often those working close to the villages, may be considerably worse off. It is not uncommon for various civil society actors to vie with one another for money, access to international networks, and public attention. The chances of their clients being heard and helped depend on their success in this competition.

Kavita Rai's account demonstrates that persons directly involved at construction sites – with the usual diversity in wealth, power differentials, and value orientations most common in South Asian villages – tend to expand their knowledge bases and gain enhanced access to information in the course of time. Depending upon the internal constellations of power, more or fewer villagers benefit from the available information (that is a scarce resource), uniting in actions of protest or in concerted negotiations with state authorities and with providers of working contracts. What very often looks to outside observers as action against dam projects, appears at second (and third) glance as attempts to enhance working conditions, or as action oriented towards direct benefits such as immediate access to electricity.

This insight is important for at least two reasons. First, the rationalities and strategies deployed by local actors render construction sites arenas where negotiations occur in shifting power constellations, address very diverse issues, and underlie diverse logics. While, for instance, the villagers may strive for such material benefits as long-term employment, the authorities will be careful not to make conflicts escalate. Second, it is also worth noting that the villagers' goals may not go hand in hand with environmental concerns, as the Narmada case has amply revealed. Public representations of legal battles geared to broader international audiences tend to address big issues, while in their everyday life members of local societies are frequently engaged in more specialized negotiations. Therefore, a wide space for contestations opens up in the transnational realm where dam constructions are negotiated.

PLURALIZATION AND FRAGMENTATION IN THE TRANSNATIONAL MOVEMENT AGAINST DAMS

The global spread of the movement that critically scrutinizes dam constructions is truly impressive, but ambivalence surrounds it as well. Among its impressive features – besides the numerous success stories that have been mentioned above – are (a) the high degree of visibility of the movement, provided by excellent internet sites and well-publicized actions; (b) the establishment of the World Commission of Dams, which has become the key platform for the dissemination of information and for deliberations; and (c) the very wide and differentiated web of those sites where action is carried out. The example of the Narmada project(s) has forcefully demonstrated how multiple and diverse are the forums where negotiations take place. Protest and deliberations have been occurring directly at the construction sites, at governmental headquarters in the riparian states, in New Delhi, inside and outside (street demonstrations) the US Congress, inside and outside the World Bank, and within governmental and departmental organizations and commissions in Japan and in numerous Western countries – to name just some of the major arenas. Especially in the local sites of the Narmada project, *satyagraha* actions have been carried out repeatedly by Adivasi populations in the villages that would eventually be submerged (Gandhi 2003); officials were refused entry (*gaon bandhi*) and the roads blocked (*rasta roko*). Such actions geared at specified locales, and seeking to avert immediate atrocities, have been accompanied by large-scale international NGO movements and pressure politics at various spots of the globe (especially in the above-mentioned Western cities), deploying environmentalist and anti-globalization rhetoric and protesting against gigantic projects while advocating smaller-scale and more decentralized solutions.

Therefore, multiple scales of interaction have been involved, often simultaneously. At some sites specialized persons and specialized practices prevail, while in many others there is no fixed localization within which actors or practices are found (see also Radcliffe et al. 2002). The transnational support movement for the Narmada protestors has created spatial continuities (concerted action) as much as discontinuities ('lifting' concerns out of their immediate contexts), and it has created what Radcliffe et al. (2002: 2) call "relational spaces" in a double sense. On the one hand, Narmada-related actions carried out at such remote sites as the World Bank headquarters and the Japanese Ministry of Foreign Affairs have impinged upon each other as well as upon Indian decision making. On the other hand, the concerns of the Narmada movement have spread to Nepal where the planning and implementation of the Kali Gandaki 'A' project were modified according to social and environmental standards drawn up elsewhere. Therefore, there have been manifold supra-local consequences of the anti-Narmada movement.

It is their world-spanning character and the multiplicity and diversity of negotiation sites that provide the transnational protest movements with the necessary strength and flexible infrastructure. By seeking to capitalize upon it, the popular (self) depictions of such movements disseminated by civil society actors actively seek to highlight the powerful, dispersed, differentiated, and supple character of this social field. This is what renders their actions successful. But there are limitations stemming from precisely this complex set-up. The World Bank's adoption of stronger standards on social and environmental issues and reforming its organization can certainly be seen as a success for transnational protest movements. However, the shift in orientation within the World Bank and within several Western governmental agencies has failed to provide guarantees that social and environmental abuses would stop at the Narmada construction sites. When the Indian government decided to do without further World Bank loans, the Western allies lost much of their capacity to exert external pressure.

According to Singh:

> The discontinuation of World Bank funding did not diminish the Gujarat's [*sic*] government's resolve to complete the project. If anything, the government's commitment to the speedy completion of the project was strengthened, in the absence of the World Bank's restraining influence. (Singh 1997: 12)

Hence, a 'gain in terrain' at one site of contestation does not necessarily translate into effects at other related sites. Also, while Nepal directly benefited from the learning process within the World Bank with the abandonment of Arun III, little impact of such refined policies can be so far observed in other parts of the world.[22] More authoritarian governments seek nowadays to forgo World Bank funds and opt for other financial sources, in order to endure less pressure.

In fact, the notion of 'concerted action', which I have just used above, does not do justice to the contestations carried out at diverse sites. The term 'concerted' may mean 'collaborative', 'joint', or 'mutual' – that is, terms embracing the key civic values 'solidarity' and 'partnership'. I was trying to show, however, that crucial differences in their perceptions and goals obtain not only between such diverse stakeholders as state officials, entrepreneurs, and outstees. Among the affected population and between the diverse advocacy groups substantial differences in grievances and priorities exist which have repeatedly been turned into rifts and bones of contention. We cannot therefore ignore the clashes of interests within the entire protest movement. Given the diverse nature of contemporary societies, it should not come as a surprise that individual persons and groups embrace divergent truths and act accordingly.

But the transnational audiences, for whom public discourses are geared, have hardly had the chance to grasp these complexities. For one of the major logics of the public sphere is to have messages to disseminate which are rather simple and which relate well to general concerns. It is easier to attract attention through such general notions as 'environmental deterioration' or 'human rights abuses' rather than the arguably smaller, but for those affected very important, concerns such as work conditions and social security. Issues that are strong enough to reach public forums become enlarged, as if transformed by a magnifying glass, whereas smaller concerns that have lacked public attraction at a given moment are silenced and fade away.

Thus one problem lies in the nature of the political communication that civil society actors engage in. There is 'popular noise' in the global system (borrowing the title of a conference held at the Institute for World Society

---

[22] For instance, huge damming projects with enormous numbers of displacements are currently going on in China on the Yangtse River.

Studies, at the University of Bielefeld, organized by Urs Staeheli et al.) in the sense that attractive public images and discourses spread around through global mass media very fast, affecting the imaginations of those belonging to 'global audiences' (a substantial portion of humanity still does not participate in it, of course). In recent years, many narratives and discursive figures have developed and spread around the globe. Cases of dispute and patterns of legitimacy (legal language, legal representation) have been constructed according to prevailing modes in discursive fields. Human rights campaigns have been socially constructed in such a way as to attract the maximum of attention and support. Those persons reporting abuses cater – consciously or unconsciously – to public images of what a legitimate grievance is, and what a victim should look like.

Moreover, *grievances have been matched to recognized human rights abuses*. John Meyer[23] even goes so far as to talk of a coercive force of public opinion over individuals, forcing them into uniform patterns of expression, and socializing them according to recognized norms and depictions. Additionally, the capricious character of mass communication brings about a selection of particular cases acquiring more visibility than others. While 'global audiences' may like to imagine that they have perfect access to information, many local victims lack access to transnational networks and to the public sphere. Jai Sen's (1999) excellent account of the conflicts accompanying the Narmada project draws a very sharp picture of the ways in which the dynamics of local resistance have been shaped by the agendas of global civil society. We should also not overlook practices of 'window-dressing' when foreign donors make it a point to have civil society's and Adivasis' voices heard. Such invocations tend to be of a rather sweeping character. Capturing public attention becomes therefore a very important communicative strategy, and public forums turn for this reason into embattled sites of contestation.[24]

Arenas where rights are negotiated are equally contested, but these are structured by different mechanisms. With the proliferation of negotiation sites, and with the multiplicity of goals, grievances, and perspectives, it

---

[23] In a lecture given at the conference 'World State' organized by the Institute for World Society Studies at the Centre for Interdisciplinary Studies, University of Bielefeld.

[24] Here we can note yet another paradox. During the Narmada Bachao Andolan campaigns, national NGOs sought the support of international partners who – with the help of the US Congress – exerted pressure on the World Bank and on their own government! In Randeria's formulation:

> As social movements and NGOs in the South link up with powerful northern and especially North American NGOs to use US Congressional hearings as a forum to put pressure on multilateral development banks in general, and the World Bank in particular, in order to change their policies and reform their structures, they not only reinforce existing asymmetries in power between the North and the South but also lend greater legitimacy to these institutions. (Randeria 2003: 315-16)

does not come as a surprise that diverse legal orders come into conflict with each other. Of course, diverse orientations are already inherent in any given legal system. A single legal system may need to incorporate and to combine diverse legal norms (for instance, environmental protection and minority rights). Opponents put forward conflicting arguments, and the courts may reach different judgments in the course of time (as was the case with the Indian Supreme Court's verdict on the Narmada projects during the 1990s). But in such complex undertakings as damming projects, diverse laws come to confront each other and disputes are carried out at diverse sites of contestations (see World Commission 2000).

Most of the involved stakeholders vary in their definition of the situation. Views diverge over the facts (e.g. the gravity of the environmental impact), over methods (e.g. labour intensive or technology intensive implementation), over goals (e.g. the common good created by the enhanced availability of energy *vs.* local losses), over values (e.g. progress *vs.* protection of livelihood and environment), as well as regarding the role to be played by the affected citizens.

Given the variety of stakeholders – members of local societies, civil servants and politicians, bilateral and multilateral donor agencies, funding institutions as well as entrepreneurs – divergent constructions of social situations, cases, and rights obtain. Not only do values such as 'progress', 'the common good', 'efficiency', or 'equity' collide, but so does the stress put upon the priority of rights by individual persons and organizations. For instance, human rights standards do not necessarily go hand in hand with environmental standards. Furthermore, substantial conflicts erupt around the notion of property when parties to a dispute attempt to justify their claims to ownership by appeal to different rights.

The expansion of the human rights regime and the growing acceptance of human rights (even when grievances are not necessarily expressed in this terminology) worldwide have significantly contributed to the enhancement of people's chances of fighting against the abuses they face. More and more legal and non-legal tools are at the disposal of people who were defenceless until recently. From what we know about the means deployed in recent cases, it is safe to infer that the transnationalization of law and the pluralization of means have opened up multiple channels of participation through which protest can be voiced. It seems, furthermore, that a multiplicity of forums makes it possible to find flexible solutions that fit the given circumstances. Such opportunities make it possible, among other things, to find decentralized solutions through immediate interaction such as the alternative dispute resolution as widely recommended by the World Commission on Dams.

On the other hand, we simply do not know to what extent this multiplicity opens up an avenue for the stronger stakeholders to diversify their means as well. The more various the interpretations of a situation and the more legal systems and forums available to the people, the greater insecurity and uncertainty are likely to be. All actors learn about the opening up of opportunities coming with the proliferation of laws and forums in which to negotiate. We know little about the chances of realizing rights and enforcing courts' rulings, as for instance, when accused firms, governments, or persons take resort to tactical concessions (see Risse et al. 1999) of which a full range exists today.

Given their diverse rationalities and interests, most stakeholders have their reasons for invoking particular laws or for approaching particular courts.[25] However, with such strong and manifold stakeholders involved in the implementation of dam projects as transnational corporations, public and private investors, as well as professional groups such as engineers, it cannot be ignored that with the multiplication of contestation sites their tools of enforcement tend to be strengthened. For while loss-suffering populations and their civil society allies find new room for manoeuvre in the pluralizing world of law and mitigation, new options open up for the other stakeholders as well.

CONCLUSION

The aim of this paper was to ask a few questions which have not yet received due attention in the ongoing debates on the realization of human rights and environmental protection. I have tried to suggest that the world audience may be too optimistic regarding current potentials to realize human rights. Individual persons, (non-governmental) organizations, move-

---

[25]Guenther Teubner and Andreas Fischer-Lescano (2004) inquire into changes in global legal pluralism concentrating on the ongoing fragmentation of global law. Two dimensions of this fragmentation are discerned: fragmentation along the lines of cognitive expectation (economy, science, technology), and fragmentation due to the substantial privatization of law. They decry the weak normative compatibility as well as the breaking down of law hierarchies. In the context of dam construction both dimensions are important:

> Standard contracts within the *lex mercatoria* reflecting the economic rationality of global markets collide with World Health Organisation norms that derive from fundamental principles of the health system. The *lex constructionis*, the worldwide professional code of construction engineers, collides with international environmental law. The World Trade Organisation Appellate Panel is confronted with colliding human rights regimes and environmental protection regimes. Indeed, the tempestuous character of rationality conflicts is such that they have even fragmented the very centre of global law, where courts and arbitration tribunals are located. ... Globally dispersed courts, tribunals, arbitration panels and alternative dispute resolution bodies are so closely coupled, both in terms of organisation and self-perception, with their own specialised regimes in the legal periphery [i.e. outside international and state courts] that they necessarily contribute to global fragmentation. (Teubner & Fischer-Lescano 2004: 3)

ments, and networks – all those persons, networks, organizations and movements currently understood as 'civil society' – have played an immensely important role all over the world by enhancing connectivity and by continuously alerting the public to human rights abuses.

There is an ambivalence inherent in this formation, however, as I have attempted to demonstrate, lying in a variety of issues. One problem is the widespread perception that civil society will eventually manage all existing problems. Civil society actors themselves need to convey the impression of their efficiency in order to attract new supporters and to strengthen their legitimacy. Therefore, several convictions are nourished that may be illusory: regarding the easy access to information (on abuses), regarding the capacity to outwit powerful and scheming adversaries, and regarding the efficacy of means such as exerting pressure through lobbying and through 'naming and shaming'. While the discussions of dam construction in India and Nepal have indicated the organizational strength of civil society actors, it has also revealed some of their weaknesses and failures. The actual scope of this transnational protest movement's strength still remains unknown.

Moreover, the human rights regime – that is, the totality of legal and extra-legal norms, instruments of litigation and instruments at their disposal in order to achieve rule-consistent behaviour – is significantly more fragmented and more prone to contradictions and challenge than is usually acknowledged. Corresponding to such fractures, particular deficiencies in realizing human rights have come to light, such as mutual contestations of each other's truth, which are, however, well hidden from the public eye. I wonder, however, whether the substantial increase in litigation, civic action, and 'gains in terrain' we have witnessed over the last twenty years have not drawn our attention away from the fact that there persist very substantial gaps in our knowledge of persisting human rights abuses.

The underlying idea leading me to this question comes with the realization that our knowledge of human rights abuses is very selective. Uncountable examples of previously undiscovered crimes against human beings (such as the instances of torture in Iraq's prisons) provide a good example of how long the public is kept unaware of such occurrences – and the very fact that such atrocities are made public is no proof that all atrocities come to light. The substantial selectivity about what becomes 'hot news' and which human rights abuses fail to attract public attention is a further cause for doubts on this score.

How fragmented or, conversely, how integrated – and if so, by what means – the human rights regime is at present, remains an empirical question. In order to answer it, we need more collaborative exchange and more pooling of our information. Let us agree that we still know little in this very important field.

REFERENCES

Baviskar, A. 1995. *In the Belly of the River: Tribal Conflicts over Development in the Narmada Valley*. Delhi: Oxford University Press.

——. 1997. 'Displacement and the Bhilala Tribals of the Narmada Valley', in J. Drèze, M. Samson, and S. Singh (eds.), *The Dam and Nation: Displacement and Resettlement in the Narmada Valley*, pp. 103-35. New York: Oxford University Press.

von Benda-Beckmann, K. 2000. 'Transnationalisation of Legal Pluralism'. Unpublished conference manuscript.

Brysk, A. 2000. *Democratising Civil Society in Latin America*. Journal of Democracy 11 (3): 151-65.

Castells, M. 1996. *The Rise of the Network Society*. Oxford: Blackwell.

Cohen, J. and A. Arato 1989. 'Politics and the Reconstruction of the Concept of Civil Society', in A. Honneth et al. (eds.), *Zwischenbetrachtungen im Prozess der Aufklärung*, pp. 482-502. Frankfurt: Suhrkamp.

Dhagamwar, V. 1997. 'The NGO Movements in the Narmada Valley: Some Reflections', in J. Drèze, M. Samson, and S. Singh (eds.), pp. 93-102.

Drèze, J., M. Samson, and S. Singh (eds.). 1997. *The Dam and Nation: Displacement and Resettlement in the Narmada Valley*. New York: Oxford University Press.

Dwevedi, R. 1998. 'Resisting Dams and "Development": Contemporary Significance of the Campaign against the Narmada Projects in India'. *European Journal of Development Research* 10: 135-83.

Ferguson, J. 1999. *Expectations of Modernity: Myths and Meanings of Urban Life on the Zambian Copperbelt*. Berkeley: University of California Press.

Gandhi, A. 2003. 'Developing Compliance and Resistance: The State, Transnational Social Movements and Tribal Peoples Contesting India's Narmada Project'. *Global Networks* 3 (4): 481-95.

Gill, M. 1995. 'Resettlement and Rehabilitation in Maharashtra for the Sardar Sarovar Project', in W.F. Fisher (ed.), *Working towards Sustainable Development: The Damming of the Narmada River in Western India*. New York: M.E. Sharpe.

Gupta, A. 1995. 'Blurred Boundaries: The Discourse of Corruption, the Culture of Politics and the Imagined State'. *American Ethnologist* 22: 375-402.

——. 1998. *Postcolonial Development: Agriculture in the Making of Modern India*. Durham: Duke University Press.

Gupta, A. and J. Ferguson (eds.). 1997. *Anthropological Locations: Boundaries and Grounds of a Field Science*. Berkeley: University of California Press.

Gyawali, D. and A. Dixit. 2000. 'Mahakali Impasse: A Futile Paradigm's Bequested Travails', in D. Kumar (ed.), *Domestic Conflict and Crisis of Governability*, pp. 236-304. Kathmandu: CNAS.

Habermas, J. 1988 (1981). *Theorie des Kommunikativen Handelns*, I & II. Frankfurt: Suhrkamp.

Hakim, R.P. 1997. 'Resettlement and Rehabilitation in the Context of "Vasava" Culture', in J. Drèze, M. Samson, and S. Singh (eds.), pp. 136-67.

Hannerz, U. 1995. '"Kultur" in Einer Vernetzten Welt: Zur Revision Eines Ethnologischen Begriffs', in W. Kaschuba (ed.), *Kulturen – Identitäten – Diskurse.* Perspektiven Europäischer Ethnologie, pp.64-8. Berlin: Akademieverlag.

Jayal, N.G. 2001. *Democracy and the State.* Delhi: Oxford University Press.

Johnson, H. and G. Wilson. 2000. 'Biting the Bullet: Civil Society, Social Learning and the Transformation of Local Governance'. *World Development* 28 (11): 1891-1906.

Joshi, V. 1997. 'Rehabilitation in the Narmada Valley: Human Rights and National Policy Issues', in J. Drèze, M. Samson and S. Singh (eds.), pp. 168-83.

Khagram, S. 2004. *Dams and Development: Transnational Struggles for Water and Power*. Delhi: Oxford University Press.

Ljung, P. 2001. *Trends in the Financing of Water and Energy Resources Projects.* World Commission on Dams (http://www.dams.org), downloaded April 2005.

Mosse, D. 2005. *Cultivating Development: An Ethnography of Aid Policy and Practice.* London: Pluto Press.

Patel, A. 1997. 'Resettlement Politics and Tribal Interests', in J. Drèze, M. Samson, and S. Singh (eds.), pp. 66-92.

Pawar, S.N., R.B. Patil, and S.A. Salunkhe (eds.). 1996. *Environmental Movements in India.* Jaipur and Delhi: Rawat Publications.

Pfaff-Czarnecka, J. 2000. 'Complex Communities in Nepal-Himalaya, or: Solidarity as a Way of Life and as a Global Category', in R.P. Thapa and J. Baaden (eds.), *Nepal – Myths & Realities*, pp. 457-77. Delhi: Book Faith India.

——. 2004. 'High Expectations, Deep Disappointment: Politics, State and Society in Nepal after 1990', in Michael Hutt (ed.), *People's War in a Hindu Kingdom: Maoism in Nepal,* pp. 166-91. London: Hurst.

Radcliffe, S., N. Laurie, and R. Andolina. 2002. 'Indigenous People and Political Transnationalism: Globalisation from below Meets Globalisation from above'. (Downloaded from the homepage http://www.transcomm.ox.ac.uk/ in October 2003.)

Rai, K. 2005. *Dam Development: The Dynamics of Social Inequality in a Hydropower Project in Nepal.* Göttingen: Cuvillier Verlag.

Raina, V., A. Chowdhury, and S. Chowdhury (eds.). 1997. *The Dispossessed: Victims of Development in Asia.* Hong Kong: Arena.

Randeria, S. 2003. 'Glocalization of Law: Environmental Justice, World Bank, NGOs and the Cunning State in India'. *Current Sociology* 51 (3/4): 305-28.

Risse, T., S.C. Ropp, and K. Sikkink (eds.). 1999. *The Power of Human Rights.* Cambridge: Cambridge University Press.

Sen, J. 1999. 'A World to Win: But Whose World Is It, Anyway?', in J.W. Foster and A. Anand (eds.), *Whose World Is It Anyway? Civil Society, the United*

Nations and the Multilateral Future, pp. 337-90. Ottawa: United Nations Association in Canada.

Shihata, I. 2000. *The World Bank Inspection Panel in Practice*. Washington DC: Oxford University Press.

Singh, S. 1997. 'Introduction', in J. Drèze, M. Samson, and S. Singh (eds.), pp. 1-25.

Subba, B. 2002. 'Water, Nepal and India', in K.M. Dixit and S. Ramachandaran (eds.), *State of Nepal,* pp. 119-36. Patan Dhoka: Himal Books.

Taylor, C. 1990. 'Modes of Civil Society'. *Public Culture* 3 (1): 95-118.

Teubner, G. and A. Fischer-Lescano. 2004. 'Regime-Collision: How the Emergence of Private Governance Regimes Changes Global Legal Pluralism'. Unpublished conference manuscript.

Wimmer, A. 2001. 'Globalisations *avant la lettre*: A Comparative View on Isomorphization and Heteromorphization in an Interconnecting World'. *Comparative Studies in Society and History* 43 (3): 435-66.

World Commission. 2000. 'Participation, Negotiation and Conflict Management in Large Dam Projects' (World Commission on Dams' Review Document V.5), see http://www.dams.org/

14

Maoists, People, and the State as Seen from Rolpa and Rukum

KIYOKO OGURA

INTRODUCTION

Since the Communist Party of Nepal (Maoist) launched its People's War in February 1996, two districts in Rapti Zone, Rolpa and Rukum, have remained continuously at the centre of their activities.[1] On 13 February 1996, the first day when the Maoists launched the People's War, they attacked the police posts in Holeri, Rolpa, and in Radijula, Rukum, and seized some rifles and explosives.[2] Even before the Maoists started their insurgency, they had launched two political campaigns in those districts in 1995 called the *Si-Ja Abhiyan* (campaign) and the *Miteri Abhiyan.* The person in-charge was Comrade Badal or Ram Bahadur Thapa, a politburo member of the CPN (Maoist) and a member of its negotiating team during the second ceasefire of 2003. The *Si-Ja Abhiyan* was named after the two mountains, Sisne in Rukum and Jaljala in Rolpa. Both campaigns were aimed at strengthening the party organization in those areas through exchanges between the cadres of each district. The exchanges included the performance of revolutionary songs and dances and the construction of schools and roads.[3]

At the beginning of their insurgency, and in the course of establishing their base area, the Maoists' activities were centralized in these two districts. In total, 146 persons were killed by the Maoists and the state during the first two years of the insurgency. Of these, 106 persons were killed in

---

[1]I would like to thank David Gellner for his help in editing this paper.

[2]On the same day they also attacked a police post in Sindhuli and a government office of the Small Scale Farmers' Development programme in Gorkha, where they burnt some documents.

[3]According to the explanation of Santos Budha Magar, a member of the United Revolutionary People's Council.

Rolpa and Rukum.[4] The Maoists adopted the strategy of attacking police stations in the villages, a strategy that was successful since almost all the police posts except that in the district headquarters had been evacuated by the middle of 2002. In the absence of any state authority, the Maoists were easily able to establish their rule over the people.

Between 26 February and 15 March 2003, I travelled around Rukum and Rolpa, the heartland of the Maoists' base area. The main destination of this trip was Thabang located in north-east Rolpa and known as the 'capital' of the Maoists. The main purpose of my trip was to discover, if I could, the root causes of why the Maoists insurgency had begun in this area. In addition to this trip, I conducted interviews with the relevant people from these two districts in the Kathmandu Valley and in Libang, the seat of Rolpa district headquarters, in June 2002. In this way I was able to find many 'seeds' of the insurgency in this area.[5] The historical backgrounds of Rolpa and Rukum are different. In Rukum there is a strong Thakuri influence. According to Whelpton (1991: 7), Thakuris as a caste "included the ruling dynasty of Gorkha and of the other hill principalities and who proclaimed themselves the descendants of Rajput refugees fleeing Muslim invaders on the plains." This Thakuri influence is clearly visible in the 'three Shah politicians' of the Panchayat era, Dhruba Bikram Shah, Lokendra Bahadur Shah, and Gopalji Jung Shah, who are discussed in a later section. By contrast, in Rolpa, Thakuri influence is much less strong. Despite this difference, the structure of confrontation between the people and the state can be seen as developing in both districts in various ways from the time of the Panchayat regime onwards. In this chapter, mainly based on testimonies of the persons I interviewed, I will try to show how the 'seeds' of revolt gradually developed and grew in these two districts.

KHOLAGAUN, WESTERN RUKUM: MAOIST RULE

Anti-State Feeling Created by the Police

After a twenty-two hour bus trip from Kathmandu, we arrived in Sitalpati in Salyan district. Three Maoists, one of them a journalist from the Maoist mouthpiece, the *Janadesh* weekly paper, had accompanied me from Kathmandu.[6] Although one month had already passed since the declaration

---

[4]According to the data of INSEC (Informal Sector Service Centre). INSEC's data lists 8057 victims who were killed either by the state or by the Maoists in connection with the People's War from 13 February 1996 to 28 October 2003. Rukum had the highest toll, namely, 808, of Nepal's 75 districts, and Rolpa had the second highest toll, 750.

[5]For two other valuable attempts to find the causes of the Maoist insurgency, see de Sales (2003) and Gersony (2003); cf. Maharjan (2000) and Thapa (2003).

[6]I was able to establish contact with the Maoists in Kathmandu after the declaration of the ceasefire.

of the ceasefire by both sides in the night of 29 January 2003, the three Maoists asked me not to talk to them during the trip. However, after arriving in Sitalpati, they told me that we could talk openly from there onwards as we had entered their *adhar ilaka*, that is, their base area. Maoists attacked Sitalpati Police Post near this bazaar in February 2002, killing thirty-five policemen, almost half of all the police force stationed there.[7] After that incident, police no longer stayed in this bazaar. Taking another bus, we headed north and arrived at the last stop in Tharmare VDC, Salyan. The only police post was withdrawn from this village in July 2001 following the Holeri incident.[8] We spent two nights there waiting to be contacted by some local Maoists from Rukum. I came to know at this point that we would be taken to western Rukum to attend the mass gathering at which the newly elected Rukum District People's Government would be declared.

We were given a small ceremonial send-off by the Maoist people's government of Tharmare,[9] in which, in front of a small 'mass meeting' we were presented with garlands and red *tika*s (later I received the same treatment in Rukumkot and Thabang). We left for Rukum on foot. We walked all day and passed several examples of infrastructure built by what they call the *naya satta* (new power),[10] that is, the local Maoist people's governments. From Balchaur VDC, Salyan, to Kholagaun VDC, Rukum, a footpath about 20 km long had just been completed along the Jarikhola River by the local people under the direction of two village people's governments. We crossed some wooden bridges built by the *naya satta*. It was already after seven in the evening when we arrived in Kholagaun VDC, where, inside a large tent set up near the river, a closed meeting of the Samyukta Jilla Jana Parishad Rukum (United District People's Council Rukum), that is, the district-level people's government of Rukum, was going on under dim lighting generated by their own power plant.

---

[7]According to a central committee member of the Maoist women's organization who participated in this action, around 500 Maoists were involved in this attack and six of them were killed. I met this woman Maoist in Tharmare. Her husband was killed by the police in Rukum in 1998 and their only child, a five-year-old only daughter, has been brought up in a Maoist school.

[8]In this incident Maoists attacked the police post in Holeri situated in southern Rolpa and abducted seventy policemen. Prime Minister Girija Prasad Koirala asked the king to deploy the Royal Nepalese Army to rescue the abducted policemen but the army was not deployed. This was one of the factors which led to Koirala's resignation immediately afterwards.

[9]According to the chairman of the people's government of Tharmare, it was formed around July 2000. This chairman was the third one. At the time when I travelled there, people's governments had been set up in forty-three of Salyan's forty-seven VDCs.

[10]Maoists call the state power, including the government and the king, *purano satta* (old power). During the second peace talks held between the government and the Maoists, the latter claimed that talks should be held between two *satta*s, each of which had its own army, that is, the king with his Royal Nepalese Army and the Maoists with their People's Liberation Army.

In Kholagaun white radish flowers were in full bloom. The villagers, whose biggest population groups are Chetri and Magar, derive a small income from selling radish seeds. Kholagaun is also famous in this area for the quality of its vegetable production. This village was ruled by the king of Jajarkot until it was captured by the forces of the Nepali Congress Party during the 1950s movement against the Ranas. Even after that and up until around 1980, *karindas*, clerks of the landlords, used to come to collect tax from the villagers. Anti-establishment feelings, awakened by the Nepali Congress, did not surface during the Panchayat regime as there was no party organization in the village before the pro-democratic movement was launched in 1990. The political change of 1990 brought some parties to the village, including the Nepali Congress and the Samyukta Jan Morcha Nepal (SJM, or United People's Front Nepal), a parent party of the CPN (Maoist).[11] It was then that political confrontation started, leading to a murder case. Ganesh Shah, an ex-*karinda* and an ex-Pradhan Panch (village headman) of Kholagaun, was murdered by the supporters of the Samyukta Jan Morcha in the month of Bhadra (August-September), 1994. Com. Manjil, a Maoist in Kholagaun, explained the reason why Ganesh Shah was killed:

> During the Panchayat regime Ganesh Shah became the Pradhan Panch by benefiting from his relationship with a *mukhiya* (village leader) and he forced the villagers to work for him, for example, by having them carry stones when he built his house. After 1990 he joined the Nepali Congress and moved the police station to his house for his own security. He tried to avoid his political enemies from the village by using the police force. That is why he was killed as a part of the class struggle.[12]

On the evening of my second day in Kholagaun, family members of twenty victims killed by the state assembled in one place. All twenty victims, including three non-Maoists and one sympathizer, were killed after the Kilo Sierra Two police operation launched in May 1998 to control the insurgency.[13] Some of the victims' families clearly stated that they had joined

[11]The SJM was a political front for the underground party, the CPN (Unity Centre). In May 1994, the CPN (Unity Centre) split into two groups, one led by Nirmal Lama and the other by Prachanda (Pushpa Kamal Dahal) due to differences between them over launching a People's War. The faction of the SJM led by Baburam Bhattarai joined Prachanda's group and they formed the CPN (Maoist) in March 1995 to launch the People's War.

[12]Another Nepali Congress member, Hari Bhakta Oli, who was an ex-District Development Committee chairman of Rukum, was murdered by the Maoists on 15 January 1999. Manjil said that he was killed because he made false accusations against people and had them sent to jail.

[13]The government has never admitted the existence of this operation. According to Sarun Batha Magar, chairman of the District People's Government of Rukum, during this operation

the Maoists because their family members were killed by the state. The case of a sixty-four-year-old woman was typical. Both her sons were killed by the police, together with three other villagers, at one place while they were 'playing' *Bhailo* during the Tihar festival of October 1998.[14] Her twenty-five-year-old elder son had just returned from India where he had worked as a labourer for a year. This woman joined the party nine months after her sons' deaths and became a member of the women's front. She said to us firmly, "Though I have no sons any more, the party comrades are cultivating our fields and helping to build a house. Now the party is my son and my sons are the party."

A nineteen-year-old girl, who had lost her husband during the Maoists' attack on Jumla in November 2002,[15] showed her strong hatred towards the state when she said, "I am always thinking about how to take revenge on the enemy." When I asked who her enemy was, she replied: "Everybody who belongs to the state power." She also joined the Maoist women's front after her husband's death. Sorrow was hardly visible in the faces of victims' families. An eighteen-year-old boy, who had lost his elder brother during the attack on the police post in Ghartigaun of Rolpa in February 2000,[16] said, "I didn't feel sad at all even when I heard the news of my brother's death. I knew that during the revolution it could happen at any time." His brother was one of the activists who had been arrested on the charge of murdering Ganesh Shah. His motivation for joining the Maoists was a strong antipathy towards Hinduism. They are from a Dalit (Untouchable) caste and the younger brother became a member of Dalit Mukti Morcha (Dalit Liberation Front) after his brother's death.

A fifty-eight-year-old woman had a more particular story. Her husband, who was a member of the Maoists' peasant front, was killed by policemen in the village in 1999. After one month her eldest daughter, a member of the women's front, was killed by the police in the village as well and her second eldest daughter died during the Mangalsen attack in Accham district in February 2002.[17] She herself had been tortured by the police several

---

around fifty to sixty people were killed by the police in Rukum alone. He said most of the victims were not Maoists but members of the general public. After this operation the number of people killed by the security forces increased rapidly.

[14] *Bhailo* is the custom of going from house to house singing and dancing in order to collect money.

[15] In this attack the Maoists killed forty-two persons including a CDO and three members of the general public.

[16] This was the first major attack on a police post by the Maoists. Of the thirty-nine stationed there, fifteen policemen, including an inspector, were killed.

[17] This was the Maoists' biggest military action until the attack on Beni, the district headquarters of Myagdi, on 20 March 2004 (on which see Ogura 2004). They carried out simultaneous attacks on the army barracks, the district police office and the CDO office in Mangalsen, as well as at the airport of Sanfebagar in Accham district, killing more than 140 people

times. Now all the remaining family members apart from herself – that is, her two sons and her fourteen-year-old youngest daughter – are active Maoists. Feelings of hatred towards the state could be seen even among the general public here, such as a woman with whom I shared a bed for two nights while staying in Kholagaun. She said to me in the dark after getting into the bed:

> When there was a police post in this village, we could not even light a lamp during the night as it might cause the police to raid us on suspicion that Maoists were hiding there. I used to sleep with a sickle by my bedside as I had to sleep alone in this room. It is definitely the brutality of the police that caused anti-state feelings among the villagers in this village.

People's Government

The mass meeting was held in Chaurjahari, the next village over from Kholagaun, on 3 March 2003, in the grounds of the high school. It started in the afternoon and was attended by thousands of people from the neighbouring villages. All twenty-five members of the newly elected Samyukta Jilla Jana Parishad Rukum (United District People's Council of Rukum)[18] were introduced to the public there. The election had been held on 1 March in a closed session of the council in Kholagaun. This council is the third one after the first district-level people's government was formed in Rukum in December 2000. According to its chairman, Sarun Batha Magar, the usual working term of the council as fixed by the party is two years but since that time they have been holding elections every year because they are in a war situation and some members may be transferred to another area after several months. In Rukum, in all VDCs except Khalanga the seat of the district headquarters, the Maoists have formed their own people's governments. Representatives of thirty-seven village people's governments,[19] who had been elected through voting in their own village three months before, attended this third council meeting. They elected twenty-five district council members including a chairman, a vice-chairman, and the representatives from twelve areas and from various fronts, those of peasants, students, women, Dalits, intellectuals, cultural

---

including the CDO. In the army barracks, fifty-five, including a captain, were killed and only four escaped alive.

[18]Of twenty-five members, only three were women. Twelve were Magars and the others were two Dalits, five Chetris, and six Bahuns.

[19]The CPN (Maoist) took seven VDCs of Rukum and six VDCs of Rolpa to form a separate Bishes Jilla (Special District) in April 2002 (the names of the VDCs are given below). Thus these VDCs were not represented at this meeting.

groups, industrialists (most of whom are shopkeepers), Magars,[20] and the People's Liberation Army. Sarun Batha Magar, a thirty-eight-year-old ex-high school teacher,[21] was unanimously elected as chairman for the second time.

According to Sarun Batha Magar, the Maoists started to form local *jana samiti* (people's committees) in villages in Rukum where they were well organized one year after launching the People's War. In the beginning the party nominated the members of the committees but by August 1999 elections for village-level people's governments were instituted. The first election was held in the adjoining VDCs of Rugha and Khara and then they held elections in various other villages. In December 2000 chairmen and vice-chairmen of all the village people's governments in Rukum assembled and the first district-level people's government was formed. In fact, this was the first Maoist district-level people's government anywhere in Nepal.

The main guest at the mass meeting was Santos Budha Magar,[22] a member of the United Revolutionary People's Council Nepal,[23] that is, the Maoists' central people's government, and the president of the Magarat Rashtriya Mukti Morcha (Magarat National Liberal Front). This forty-two-year-old leader from Thabang is also a former teacher. After giving *tika* to all the council members, he gave a two-hour-long address to the mass gathering. The main subject of his speech was the peace talks with the government that were to begin shortly afterwards. In his speech he used the same logic as other Maoist leaders to analyse the situation as it was then:

> There are two *satta* (powers) in this country. The *naya satta* (new power, the Maoists) that has *jana sena* (people's army) and the *purano satta* (old power; the government) that has *shahi sena* (royal army). At present, these two *sattas*' strength is in equilibrium. That is why we have to come to a table of talks between these two powers. ... We came to the table of talks again to find a way to stop the war. If a cat was surrounded without being given a way out, it would bite a man. ... We have already postponed our demand for a republic and we have been making it clear that we

[20]In both Rukum and Rolpa districts the Magars form the largest ethnic group.

[21]He taught English at the high school in Banfikot VDC until January of 1999. He became a communist while studying at college. He said the necessity of revolution was his motivation for joining the communists.

[22]He was the first chairman of Rolpa District People's Government, which was formed in March and declared in May 2001. He is also a central committee member of the CPN (Maoist).

[23]The Maoists declared the formation of this thirty-seven-member central government on the same night that they resumed military action by attacking the army barracks and the district police office in Ghorahi, Dang, on 23 November 2001. Dr Baburam Bhattarai became the chairman of this Council. The Council was actually formed three months before it was announced, at the general convention held in Kureli VDC, Rolpa.

> are ready to accept the multiparty-system. So the government also has to make a concession. Holding elections for a constituent assembly is our last demand.[24]

The issue of the *jana sena* (people's army) or the People's Liberation Army[25] also seemed to be very important for the party leadership. After the mass meeting, an almost three-hour-long play entitled 'The family of the royal army and the family of the people's army' was staged by their cultural group, 'Sisne Cultural Family', until three o'clock in the morning. Santos Budha told me later that they tried to convey the message through this comic play that foreign intervention was increasing in Nepal and that it might well come about that the Royal Nepalese Army and the People's Liberation Army would have to fight together to defeat a foreign power. His logic may sound unrealistic but it reflects the party's vague policy on the future of the People's Liberation Army. The question of the future of the People's Liberation Army is definitely one of the biggest issues that will face both sides if there is ever another ceasefire. When I asked Sarun Batha Magar about this issue, he answered:

> At present the supreme commander of Royal Army is the King but no army should be controlled by an individual, rather it should be controlled by an institution. So we will demand that a national army should be formed under the control of the Parliament and both our People's Army and the Royal Army should be included in it. But that does not mean that both the armies will be mixed, it means that two armies will work under the same policy and the same command. We will not give up our weapons until our aim is accomplished.

It seemed that the Maoist government had just started to function like a state as they had recently, for the first time passed an annual budget of

[24]The Maoists' main demand is to hold an election for a constituent assembly which will make a new constitution. In an interview in March 2003, Krishna Bahadur Mahara, who was a member of the Maoists' negotiating team, told me that they had not yet given up their ultimate aim of establishing a republic but they wanted the people to decide what kind of political system was needed in Nepal through a constituent assembly.

[25]Some time before I went to Rukum and Rolpa, the first division of the People's Liberation Army had just been formed in west Nepal. There were three brigades at that time. During the ceasefire the PLA definitely expanded in size. At the beginning of 2004 the Maoists had two divisions, seven brigades, and nineteen battalions. Prachanda clarified in his statement, issued on 1 September 2004 after their week-long central committee meeting held in Rolpa in August, that they had formed another division in central Nepal in order to have three divisions, nine brigades, and twenty-nine battalions. Some Maoists I met in Rolpa in September 2004 said that the newly formed Central Division, whose commander is Pasang, covers an area from Rolpa and Rukum in the west to the Kathmandu Valley in the east. Prachanda also disclosed in his statement that they had decided to develop 100,000 personnel of their *jana-militia* into company level forces under the district and regional headquarters.

Rs.2,300,000 for Rukum district at the council meeting.[26] The newly elected chairman, Sarun Batha Magar, told me that the revenue was collected mainly through taxes. They had made regulations that the villagers would have to pay 2 per cent of the land price at the time of buying land and that businessmen 5 per cent of their income. He said that the 'business tax' is more flexible as they collect tax from shopkeepers on the basis of self-statements. The council would spend this budget mainly on building infrastructure, such as irrigation canals and roads. The chairman said that they also have a plan to build five small-scale hydroelectric power plants to add to the existing two in the district. They opened two primary schools run by the people's government in Duli VDC in 2002. In addition, they had a plan to open three more schools within a year, where they will give children practical education in subjects such as agriculture and handicrafts.[27]

When I asked Sarun Batha Magar about the main job of the people's government, he answered:

> There are some works we have to do such as development and construction of infrastructure and social service, but the most important work is to make the people aware about politics. Our first priority is politics and only then, development and other work. We believe that politics have to lead everything else. We are trying to teach the people, by means of political campaigns, to carry out development work for themselves.

People's governments also have a judicial role. They give judgments on various cases from simple fighting between villagers to murder. According to Magar, the most frequent cases with which they have to deal are to do with landownership, because most of the people are peasants. He said, "We get the people involved in the investigation of cases and we make criminals do social work, such as constructing toilets and building roads as a punishment." The Maoists have established a prison for criminals in Kholagaun in a captured house that belonged to Nirmal Shah whose relative Ganesh Shah was murdered by the supporters of the Samyukta Jan Morcha, as mentioned above. Seventeen criminals, some of them just suspects, were in the prison when we visited. Maoists in the village said that of the seventeen criminals, four were suspects in murder cases. In this asylum criminals had to work in the fields all day and received political education every day as well.

---

[26]According to an article published in *Janadesh* (24 March 2003), the district-level people's governments of the Bishes Jilla, Rolpa, Dang, and Salyan also passed budgets for the first time of, respectively, Rs.7,000,000, Rs.5,200,000, Rs.3,500,000, and Rs.2,300,000. Interestingly, the newly established Bishes Jilla had the biggest budget.

[27]When I travelled around western Rolpa in September 2004, I came to know that the Maoists had opened thirty-six *Janabadi* (communist) schools in Rolpa and Rukum districts, where they teach a new curriculum including the ideology of communism.

RUKUMKOT, EASTERN RUKUM: CONFLICTS WITH THAKURIS

Rukumkot, a Thakuri Village

It was in the early morning of 5 March when I left Chaurjahari for the east. At this point I came to know that I was going to my main destination, Thabang in north Rolpa, by way of Rukumkot. It would take two days on foot to reach Rukumkot, situated in eastern Rukum. A newly elected member of Rukum District People's Government accompanied me as a guide. Despite the fact that we were in the heart of the Maoists' base area, to my surprise we saw very few armed Maoists en route, except some on leave. One of them, a battalion member and a Thakuri by caste, was going out of the district to have his weak eyesight checked after visiting his parents in Rukum. He had participated in eight or nine attacks including some major ones, such as those on Sitalpati Police Post in Salyan, Satbariya Armed Police Post in Dang, and the battle of Lisne peak following the major attack on the security forces' camp in Gam, Rolpa. Interestingly, he also took part in the attack on Salleri, the headquarters of Solukhumbu district in November 2001, in which the Maoists killed twenty-seven policemen, five soldiers of the Royal Nepalese Army, and a CDO (Chief District Officer). The next day the government declared a nationwide Emergency and deployed the Royal Nepalese Army. He told me that sixty-five members of no. 2 platoon from Rapti Zone had gone to eastern Nepal and stayed there for three months in order to command some attacks. He also said that there were no local Maoists in the team that carried out the attack on Salleri.

After two days' walk along the Sanobheri River we arrived in Rukumkot, the main settlement of Shobha VDC. This beautiful village is located on a small plateau. It was the season of peach blossom. The villagers here are blessed with fertile soil. But the fertile soil must have attracted the former rulers as well. Thakuris from Jumla settled in this village about 640 years ago and ruled over this area until the time of Prithvi Narayan's son, Bahadur Shah. Their descendants still live here and one of them, Kumar Mohan Bahadur Shahi, married princess Shobha, the younger sister of King Gyanendra. The name of this village, previously called Bahunthana, was changed to Shobha after she visited it to perform her husband's family's religious rites.

During the Kilo Sierra Two operation in 1998, more than a thousand policemen were stationed in Rukumkot to carry out operations in eastern Rukum. However, after the Maoists attacked the police station on the top of the hill in April 2001, killing thirty-two policemen,[28] there are no police in

[28]This police post was built on top of a hill, being moved out of the village for their security. According to a Maoist who participated in this attack, there were around 500 Maoists, of

this village.[29] There is a compound with government offices in the centre of Rukumkot, but after the withdrawal of the police post, most of the offices, including the Nepal Bank, the Agricultural Development Bank, and Agriculture Service Centre, were closed. When I visited, Maoists were using the buildings as their people's government offices. There were still sixteen government officers working in the village, including the staff of a health post, officers of the Forest Ministry, and a member of the technical staff for a drinking water project. The chairman of the village people's government told me that the Maoists don't stop government works that are essential for the daily life of the villagers.

The majority of the population of this village comes from the Thakuri and Chetri castes. Many Magars also live in the higher part of the village. This village of Rukumkot is the easternmost extension of settlement by Thakuris and Bahuns in the district. From here, eastwards, there are very few households of Chetri or Bahuns. Although some Dalits and other groups, plus a small number of Gurungs and Newars[30] live there, eastern Rukum is still the Magars' land. The CPN (Maoist) formed the Bishes Jilla (Special District), as noted above, by combining seven VDCs in eastern Rukum and six VDCs in northern Rolpa in order to establish a Magar autonomous region in April 2002. It can also be said that this region of the Bishes Jilla is in fact the real heartland of the Maoists.[31]

Political Competition Between the Three Shahs During the Panchayat Period

Under the Panchayat regime, a major confrontation between the public of eastern Rukum and the state occurred in 1973, relating to the transfer of the district headquarters from Rukumkot to Musikot.[32] But before discussing

---

whom 200 were members of the PLA. There were 217 policemen in the police post. During the attack eight Maoists were killed. He said the police surrendered within thirty-five minutes of the start of the attack.

[29] Later, during the Emergency, the security forces came to Rukumkot three times, twice in August and once in October 2002. When they came in August, they destroyed some houses including those of the village people's government chairman. Later, Maoists forced the families of policemen and soldiers of the Royal Nepalese Army in the village to repair those houses.

[30] Some Shrestha 'Newars' live in Gunam of Mahat VDC. Though they have the family name Shrestha, they speak the Kham language and marry Magars.

[31] The central committee meeting of the CPN (Maoist) held in August 2004 in Rolpa decided to dissolve this Bishes Jilla and formally to declare the establishment of their base area consisting of three districts, Rolpa, Rukum, and Salyan. A Rolpa district committee member, whom I met in Ghartigaun, Rolpa, in September 2004, told me that they had dissolved the Bishes Jilla because it was attracting too much attention from the government.

[32] Actually, the district headquarters was transferred to Khalanga from Bahunthana but local people usually use the names 'Musikot' and 'Rukumkot'. 'Kot' means the place where the kings used to live.

this incident, it is necessary to give some historical and political background on Rukum, as, in my opinion, there is a close relationship between this history and the root cause of why this area became the stronghold of the Maoists. The following explanation was given to me by Lokendra Bahadur Shah, a resident of Rukumkot and a descendant of Thakuri families there. Although there are some differences from the history of Rukum as given in Rajyaram Subedi's book (2054 V.S.), *Karnali Pradeshko Madhyakalin Itihas (The Medieval History of Karnali Region)*, I quote Shah's account as he gave it to me.

There used to be three Thakuri families who ruled over their own territories in Rukum. According to Lokendra Bahadur Shah, the oldest one was the *raja* (king) of Rukumkot. They came from Jumla to Rukumkot accompanied by some Bahuns (Gautam), some Chetris (Budhathoki), and some Damais around 640 years ago.[33] One of the Chetris killed a *Bhote raja*, the ruler of that area, by means of a plot.[34] From then on the Thakuri *raja* started to reign over the area. The first king divided his land among his sons. The eldest son became the king of Jajarkot, the second the king of Rukumkot, and the fourth the king of Salyan.[35] The third son went to Galkot in Baglung at the request of the people there. Around the time of Bahadur Shah, the younger son of Prithvi Narayan Shah, the last king of Rukumkot, Raj Shahi, was killed by members of his own family in the course of a power struggle. The people of Rukum asked Bahadur Shah to send his forces to control the situation but the group who killed the king ran away and Rukumkot joined the united Nepal. Since that time there has been no king in Rukumkot. The last king, Raj Shahi, had two sons the younger of whom had five sons. Of these, the eldest son, Indra Bahadur Shahi, joined the Royal Nepalese Army and married Shanta Devi Shree, a daughter of the Ranas. Their great-grandson is Kumar Mohan Bahadur Shahi who married Princess Shobha, King Gyanendra's younger sister. The Rana government gave some villages near Rukumkot as *birta*[36] to Shanta

[33]According to Subedi (2054 V.S.: 353), the third son of Malaibamma, the king of Jumla, came to Rukum to rule over the area around AD 1400. The seventh king of Rukum, Jaya Bhadra, was expelled from his state by his people after he raped two Magar girls. After that, the Shahi Thakuris of Jumla came to Rukumkot as rulers.

[34]According to Lokendra Bahadur Shah, a Budhathoki Chetri killed this *Bhote raja* after pledging friendship. The story is that one day the Budhathoki invited the *Bhote raja* and requested him to sit down on a carpet under which he had dug a deep hole. The *Bhote raja* fell into the hole and the Budhathoki killed him by covering him up with stones and soil. He said that the ancestors of this Chetri (Budhathoki) family in Rukumkot even now do *puja* to a stone on the spot where the *Bhote raja* was killed on the *Navami* day of the Dasain festival.

[35]According to Subedi (2054 V.S.: 104), King Malaibamma of Jumla divided his territory among his four sons and a son-in-law. He gave Salyan to his first son, Jajarkot to his second son, Rukum to his third son, Dailekh to his youngest son, and Jumla to his son-in-law.

[36]According to Regmi (1978: 39), "*Birtas* were given to individuals in appreciation of their services to the state, as ritual gifts, or as a mark of patronage."

Devi Shree. Although her family lived in Kathmandu, Indra Bahadur's brother, as a *karinda*, used to collect taxes from the people who lived on their *birta* land, and sent them to Kathmandu. Lokendra Bahadur Shah, one of the 'three Shah politicians' since the Panchayat regime in Rukum, is a grandson of this Indra Bahadur's brother.

Another Thakuri *raja* in Musikot came from Jumla much later than the kings of Rukumkot, when Bahadur Shah's force attacked their land for the second time.[37] The area of the present eight VDCs[38] of southern Rukum including the present district headquarters of Khalanga[39] were given to them as *birta*. Gopalji Jung Shah, the youngest of the "three Shahs", is the sixth generation of this Musikot *raja*. Kumar Khadga Bikram Shah, who married princess Sharada, the elder sister of King Gyanendra, is his relative.[40] There used to be another Thakuri *raja* in Banfikot, who at one time had separated from the Jajarkot king. Dhruba Bikram Shah,[41] the most senior of the 'three Shahs' is a descendant of this Banfikot *raja*.[42] Incidentally, Dhruba Bikram's mother is an elder sister of Gopalji Jung's father; in other words, Gopalji and Dhruba are cousins.

During the Panchayat regime these three descendants of the Thakuri *rajas* became members of the Rashtriya Panchayat, the then Parliament, one after another.[43] Since there was only one seat for the Rashtriya Panchayat from Rukum district, there was naturally intense competition between them. The transfer of the district headquarters happened in April 1973 when Dhruba Bikram Shah was a Rashtriya Panchayat member. The district headquarters was moved from Rukumkot to Musikot according to

---

[37]According to Subedi (2054 V.S.: 355), the fifth king of Rukum, Jayatabam, divided his territory among his seven sons. The first son got Rukum (Rukumkot), the second son Musikot, the third son Banfikot, the fourth son Gotam, the fifth son Athbis, the sixth son Jahari, and the youngest son Khagena. The Nepal Army took over Musikot at the time of its fifth king. After that, Musikot was given to some Brahman as *birtas*. After Jumla was attacked by Bahadur Shah's army, the family of the last Jumla king escaped to Musikot and settled there. Gopalji Jung Shah is a descendant of this family.

[38] They are Khalanga, Chibang, Arma, Shimli, Bhalakcha, Chaukabang, Sangkh, and Shalapakha.

[39]Now the headquarters of Rukum is called 'Jumlikhalanga', named after their original place 'Jumla'.

[40]The grandfathers of Gopalji Jung Shah and Kumar Khadga Bikram Shah were brothers. Kumar Khadga Bikram and princess Sharada were among the ten royal family members who died in the palace massacre on 1 June 2001.

[41]He passed away in 2003. His son, General Bibek Shah, is a former military secretary to the king.

[42]According to Subedi (2054 V.S.: 361), the fifth king of Rukum, Jayatabom distributed Banfikot to his third son Jagadibam. After Banfikot was absorbed into a united Nepal, the families of Thakuris from Jumla came there and began to live in the palace.

[43]First Dhruba Bikram Shah became a member of the Rashtriya Panchayat, then Lokendra Bahadur Shah, then Gopalji Jung Shah, and finally Dhruba Bikram once again.

the decision of the Zonal Commissioner. Immediately after that, thousands of people from Rukumkot and the eastern part of Rukum got together and marched to Musikot, holding local weapons in their hands, in order to get back the headquarters from the people of Musikot. The next day this huge mass of people arrived near the present airport in Musikot, where the CDO declared a curfew. The crowd started throwing stones and the administration forces opened fire, killing a youth from Rukumkot and injuring many others. A couple of months later, the administration issued warrants for the arrest of around two hundred people from eastern Rukum in relation to this incident, and twenty-three persons were arrested. Two of them were detained in Ghorahi jail for a year.[44]

The people from eastern Rukum still claim that the transfer of the district headquarters was a conspiracy by Dhruba Bikram Shah and Gopalji Jung Shah.[45] Lokendra Bahadur Shah of Rukumkot, who was a vice-chairman of Rukum District Panchayat at that time said:

> King Birendra was expected to visit Rukumkot from Surkhet in January 1973 and the people of Rukumkot were preparing to welcome the King to our village. I was chairman of the welcome committee. But what happened was that the King went to Musikot instead of coming to Rukumkot and after returning to Surkhet he declared that the district headquarters of Rukum would be moved to Musikot. This happened as a result of lobbying by Dhruba Bikram Shah, Kumar Khadga Bikram Shah, Home Minister Sundar Prasad Shah, and Home Secretary Khadga Bahadur Singh. After I became a Rashtriya Panchayat member in 1974, when I met the King I tried to convince him to transfer it back to Rukumkot again but it never happened.
>
> Due to this incident, anti-state sentiment increased among the people in eastern Rukum as they thought it was sheer injustice. Furthermore, all the development works were centralized in western Rukum because the powerful politicians who had strong connections with the state were there. Chaurjahari airport and the dam in Banfikot were built while Dhruba Bikram was in power and Musikot airport was built after Gopalji Jung became a Parliament member. By contrast, most of the development projects in eastern Rukum, including irrigation plans in Rukumkot, Pipal, and Pokhara VDCs, were cancelled after 1990. This made it easy for

---

[44] One of the two who were detained in Ghorahi jail for a year told me that most of the twenty-three people who were arrested were non-political.

[45] At the time of this incident, Dhruba Bikram Shah was a Rashtriya Panchayat member and Gopalji Jung Shah was chairman of Khalanga Village Panchayat. Musikot was in Khalanga Village Panchayat.

> the Maoists to convince the people to join them in eastern Rukum. If the district headquarters had remained in Rukumkot, fewer people in this area would have joined the Maoists.

Tara Prasad Gharti Magar, a former chairman of Rukum District Panchayat, also claimed that after the district headquarters moved to Musikot, it had become much easier for anti-Panchayat groups to campaign. He said, "In addition to that, there were very few Nepali Congress activists in that area. Only some communist organizations existed. Naturally, it [conflict] assumed an aspect of communists fighting against the state."

Keshar Man Roka Magar from Jang VDC in eastern Rukum, who is a former Nepali Congress Member of Parliament,[46] gave an account with a slightly different nuance. He said:

> The leaders of Rukumkot were so crazy to get the headquarters returned to Rukumkot that they directed the villagers in eastern Rukum to send one member from every household to march on Musikot. We were told that any family which had not sent a member in the march had to pay Rs.500 as a penalty. That is why we were obliged to send family members to Musikot. During the Panchayat regime the people in Rukum were divided into two groups, the one in western district led by Dhruba Bikram Shah and Gopalji Jung Shah, and the other in the eastern district led by Lokendra Bahadur Shah. The western group won out all the time because their leaders had more power. That is why conditions of development in the eastern district fell behind.

The power triangle between the three Shahs in Rukum changed after the Rashtriya Panchayat election of 1981. Until then the two cousins, Dhruba Bikram and Gopalji Jung, were in the same faction and Lokendra Bahadur of Rukumkot was alone. But the situation changed after all three Shahs stood for the 1981 election and Gopalji Jung won. After this election Lokendra Bahadur and Dhruba Bikram approached each other and the former supported the latter during the Rashtriya Panchayat election of 1986. As a result, Dhruba Bikram won and Lokendra Bahadur became the chairman of Rukum District Panchayat the following year. After the multiparty system was restored in April 1990, Dhruba Bikram and Lokendra Bahadur joined the Rashtriya Prajatantra Party (National Democratic Party) and Gopalji Jung joined the Nepali Congress.[47] Gopalji Jung

[46] He was elected from the number 1 constituency of Rukum in 1999 and became Assistant Minister in the Ministry of Local Development in 2001.

[47] He had joined the Nepali Congress students' wing, the 'Nepal Student Union', in 1970 while he was studying in Tri Chandra College in Kathmandu. After the change of 1990, he rejoined the NC. After the division of the Nepali Congress in 2002, he joined the Nepali Congress (Democrat) led by Sher Bahadur Deuba.

won from the number two constituency of Rukum in 1991 and 1994. He joined the cabinet of Sher Bahadur Deuba as Assistant Minister of Industry and was promoted to State Minister in 1995.

Anti-Thakuri Sentiment among the Magar Community

In Rukum anti-Thakuri sentiment developed into anti-state sentiment particularly among the Magars who have the biggest population in this district. Tara Prasad Gharti Magar, who belongs to the Magar community, said:

> The transfer of the district headquarters from Rukumkot to Musikot was done on the initiative of Thakuris. They tried to rule over the people and split our community. Although we live near Musikot, we took a neutral position because we didn't want to follow the Thakuris. ... The land in this area used to belong to us Magars but outsiders, the Thakuris, took it.

Some characteristic sentiments of Magars towards Thakuris are revealed in the following incident that occurred in Jipsing, Magma VDC, situated in western Rukum. Some fifteen or sixteen families of Shahi, descendants of the Thakuri *raja*s, live in Jipsing. Magars of this village used to have to collect honey from the nests of jungle bees high up on the cliffs and present it to the Thakuris every year. But about one year before the political changes of 1990, a dispute arose between the Magars and the Thakuris, and the Magars stopped collecting honey for the Thakuris. After the dispute, the villagers made a new rule that the Magars would collect honey only for themselves and the Thakuris and Chetris could do so for themselves alternately every two years. A thirty-four-year-old teacher from Jipsing who told me this story, added:

> The Thakuris used to dominate the Magars in the village. Senior people like my grandfather used to say, "Thakuris are relatives of *Ishwar* (God), so don't think that they did wrong things. If you did so, it would be a sin." But we youths wanted to seek equality with them, so we stopped collecting honey for Thakuris. We even asked them to pay cash for the honey we had presented to them up till then.

Personal anger towards Gopalji Jung Shah was also seen on the part of some political figures. One of them said, "Since the time of the Panchayat regime, the majority of the Magar community in Rukum was against Gopalji Jung Shah. We, the supporters of the CPN (Masal), gave votes for Lokendra Bahadur Shah during the election of 1981 only because he stood against Gopalji Jung Shah." I heard similar sentiments from the Magars of eastern Rukum. They said, "After 1990 we joined the Rashtriya Prajatantra Party because Gopalji Jung joined the Nepali Congress. If he had joined the

CPN (UML), we might have joined the Maoists." A former Pradhan Panch of a village from eastern Rukum said:

> Since the 1986 election we refused to vote for Gopalji Jung and supported Dhruba Bikram's faction. Because of this, after 1990, the administration accused hundreds of Magars in our area in various court cases. The then ruling party Nepali Congress and the administration tried to hinder the opposition from carrying out political activities. Many people who were accused were forced to leave the village to avoid detention. Many of them became Maoists later.

It seems that a series of confrontations between Magars and Thakuris developed into conflicts between the Magars and the state.

In Takasera, there is another aspect to opposition to the state. Many Magars were converted to Christianity after David Watters, an American linguist from the Summer Institute of Linguistics, started living there around 1970 to carry out research on the Kham language. After the state was informed about his religious activities, the local administration intervened and detained more than a hundred people between 1981 and 1986. Although not many Christians joined the Maoists, two, Sukho Kham and Gopal Budha, were accused of involvement in the Maoist insurgency and were killed by the state in Takasera. After their murder, the Maoists convinced the father of Gopal Budha to become chairman of the people's government in Takasera and he accepted. The father was also killed by the security forces in 2001.

THABANG, NORTHERN ROLPA: A HISTORY OF RESISTANCE AGAINST THE STATE

Thabang as the Capital of the Maoists

Thabang is situated 15 km south-east of Rukumkot. I finally left Rukumkot for Thabang, the main destination of my trip, early in the morning of 8 March 2003. A local guide accompanied me. We walked up along the rapidly flowing river towards the south for a couple of hours and then ascended for an hour to reach the centre of Mahat VDC on top of the hill. The CPN (Maoist) included this Magar village in their Bishes Jilla. The ruins of the police post faced an open space in the village. The Maoists attacked this police post in September 1999, killing seven policemen and one activist of the Nepali Congress. After the attack they abducted the person in charge of the police post, DSP Thule Rai, and released him three months later. The villagers still have clear memories of another incident that happened in September 2002. There was a battle between the Maoists and the security forces in the jungle near the village during the night. The next day some Maoists returned to the village and were taking a meal. Just then, the security forces arrived, surrounded the village, and started to fire. They even entered houses and fired on the villagers. Eleven people, all Magars, were killed. Only two of them were Maoists. The others were all innocent villagers including two small children, two women, and two deaf mutes.

It was about three hours' walk from Mahat to the centre of Thabang. At the entry point of Thabang VDC, which is the border of Rolpa and Rukum districts, a Maoist sentry examined us. We had to walk for one hour more to reach the main village, called Thulogaun (big village). As we approached Thulogaun we could see red communist flags on tall poles attached to houses here and there. It was around five in the afternoon when we arrived. The scenes I saw immediately after passing through the entrance gate that the Maoists had constructed astonished me. They were quite different from what I had seen in the other villages I had passed through. The first scene that caught my eye was of some ten or twelve young men weaving *doko*s (baskets) from bamboo just in front of the gate, and then I saw other young men playing volleyball in a spacious courtyard. Nearby, some girls were busy cooking beef curry and *atho* in huge pots.[48] There were scenes of collective life everywhere. We were taken to what the Maoists called *hamro sahakari hotel* (our cooperative dining room), where many people were going in and out after drinking tea or eating dried meat. An old Magar woman in traditional dress, around sixty years old and speaking in the Kham language, was working there. To my surprise, she returned a *lal salam* (the red salute), the Maoists' greeting, to everybody who entered the dining room. The dining room seemed to be a meeting place for Maoists staying in Thabang temporarily. Because of the obvious and vigorous activities going on there, Thabang just looked like the capital of the Maoists. Later I came to know that Thabang was in fact the capital of the Bishes Jilla.

A couple of days after I arrived in Thabang, I learnt that a company of the People's Liberation Army, the Maoist military front, was quartered there. They had their headquarters in a big house,[49] where a Maoist doctor and his assistant were checking the sick. They also ran a pharmacy nearby.

---

[48]*Atho* is the main meal of this area. It is made by pouring maize flour into boiling water and mixing it for a while; in other parts of Nepal it is known as *dhindo*. Thabang is also famous for its potato production but rice cannot be grown as it is located at about 7,000 feet above sea level. Barley, wheat, and maize are the main crops of the village.

[49]This house was destroyed by the security forces when they stayed in Thabang in February 2004. They destroyed the health post there as well. The security forces carried out the operation after they came to know that a huge mass meeting had been held in Thabang to declare the formation of Magarat Autonomous Region in January 2004.

The Maoists were staying in the houses captured by them. There were many vacant houses whose owners had left the village. Most of them were against the Maoists and had left to live in Libang, the district headquarters of Rolpa, or in towns like Nepalganj or Ghorahi in the Tarai. Many youths had even gone abroad to get jobs. It was clear that people could not live in Thabang without being Maoists and without helping the Maoists. In the centre of the main village the ruins of fifteen houses destroyed by the security forces were clearly visible. During the Emergency the security forces stayed in Thabang for forty-five days, from the end of March until May 2002.[50] They burnt down these houses on the second day after their arrival.

According to Bar Prasad Gharti Magar, chairman of the Thabang village people's government, the first village-level people's government in the base area was formed in Thabang in the month of Bhadra (August-September), 1997. He said that they had started to organize *jana satta* (people's power) in this village immediately after the change of 1990. The majority of villagers voted for the Samyukta Jan Morcha (United People's Front) in the first general election after the restoration of democracy in 1991,[51] but thereafter all voting in elections was boycotted in Thabang. Bar Prasad Gharti was elected as the second chairman without opposition when the new village people's government was formed in September 2002. They formed a fifty-two-member *jana samiti* (people's committee) consisting of a chairman, a vice-chairman, and five representatives from each of the ten wards. The Gaun Samyukta Jana Samiti (Village United People's Committee) consisting of *jana samiti* members plus representatives from five fronts – students, women, Dalits, intellectuals-businessmen, and the *jana sena* (people's army) – holds general meetings and is the main decision-making body.

Bar Prasad Gharti said that the main job of the village people's government is to manage power within the village. According to him, they have set up seven departments for that purpose. They are the Departments of Investigation, Culture, Social, Education, Health, Security, and Development & Construction. They have already carried out some development works such as constructing new paths connecting Thabang to the neighbouring villages, Uwa and Mirul. One person from each household has to

[50]The security forces withdrew from Thabang after the Maoists attacked the army camp in Gam VDC on 7 May 2002. Gam is situated in north-east Rolpa. In this, one of the biggest attacks by the Maoists, nearly seventy soldiers and policemen were killed and the Maoists also suffered heavy casualties.

[51]Their candidate was Krishna Bahadur Mahara, politburo member and spokesperson of the CPN (Maoist). Although Barman Budha was from this village, the party gave him the ticket for constituency number 1 in Rolpa so that he could compete with Bala Ram Gharti Magar, a politician of the Rashtriya Prajatantra Party. Barman won, getting two thousand more votes than Bala Ram, who came second.

participate in these construction works. He said they had a plan to build a hydroelectricity plant in Thabang within two years.

The CPN (Maoist) formed the Bishes Jilla (Special District) in April 2002, and its first people's government was formally declared in a mass meeting that was held in Thabang on 25 February 2003. Thirteen VDCs – Chunbang, Mahat, Kankri, Kol, Takasera, Hukam, and Maikot from eastern Rukum district and Thabang, Uwa, Mirul, Jelbang, Rangkot, and Kureli from north Rolpa district – were included in this model district. While I was in Thabang, the round-table meeting of the Bishes Jilla representatives had just started in the building of the Thabang people's government.[52] Some eighty intellectuals from the area, most of them schoolteachers, attended the meeting. All the speakers, including the vice-chairman of the Bishes Jilla and a district party in-charge, seemed to be trying to convince the participants that their three demands – that is, (1) a national-level round-table meeting attended by the King, Maoists, and all the political parties, (2) an all-party government, and (3) elections for a constituent assembly – were essential.

Man Prasad Shrestha,[53] vice-chairman of the Bishes Jilla, explained to me the purpose of creating this new district:

> More than 95 per cent of the population in the Bishes Jilla is Magar. The point of forming the Bishes Jilla is to establish an autonomous region of Magars in this area. We have the right to have our own culture, religion, and government. The administration in this area will be run by Magars. We will also teach our own Kham language in schools.

Bar Prasad Gharti, the chairman of Thabang people's government, added:

> The party is going to carry out new programmes here as a model district. The main aim of the Bishes Jilla is to politicize all the people in the area by teaching them the ideology of Maoism. We are going to give the people ideological education regarding the political issues, including why we started the People's War. In fact, we have already started informal classes about communism in the schools in Thabang.

---

[52] After the ceasefire was declared at the end of January 2003, the Maoists' strategy was to hold 'round-table meetings' attended by local intellectuals and other party activists at the district level in order to convince community leaders to support their demands.

[53] Man Prasad Shrestha is originally from a village very close to Thabang, Gunam in Mahat VDC. His wife, Dhan Maya, was killed by the police in Kankri VDC in March 1996. According to a report by INSEC (Informal Sector Service Centre), a police squad fired indiscriminately in front of her shop, killing the thirty-five-year-old Dhan Maya, a fifty-year-old farmer, and the sixty-seven-year-old Chandra Bahadur Shrestha who was a district leader of the Rashtriya Prajatantra Party and a former vice-chairman of Rukum District Panchayat.

The Bishes Jilla is in fact the original place for Athara Panthis (the followers of the Eighteen Magar states, explained in the next section) where the most original culture of the Magars remains. The common language there is Kham. Some new developments concerning the Bishes Jilla appeared in Maoist news reports at the beginning of 2004. The CPN (Maoist) declared the formation of the Magarat Autonomous Region People's Government at a mass meeting attended by – they claimed – 75,000 people on 9 January 2004 in Thabang, the capital of Bishes Jilla. The meeting of 130 representatives was held on 7 and 8 January, and they elected twenty-seven members to form the government. Santos Budha Magar, a senior communist from Thabang and a member of United People's Revolutionary Council Nepal, was elected as president. According to *Maoist Information Bulletin-8,* distributed by the Maoists via e-mail on 20 January 2004, they formed this government "as per the party's known policy of granting autonomous rule along with right of self-determination to the oppressed nationalities and regions". They added "A campaign is now underway to form autonomous people's governments in the [other] liberated areas."[54] According to Santos Budha, the Magarat Autonomous Region includes the following fourteen districts: Rolpa, Rukum, Pyuthan, Salyan, Dang (only the northern part), Baglung, Gulmi, Arghakhanchi, Myagdi, Syangja, Palpa, Nawalparasi (only the mountain side), Tanahun (only half), and the Bishes Jilla.[55]

Thabang, Village of Resistance

Thabang used to be known as 'the communist village' even during the Panchayat period. I tried to find out how this Magar village turned into a communist stronghold. For an explanation we have to go back about half a century. The following is a history based on the testimony of three Thabangis: Barman Budha Magar,[56] the seventy-four-year-old former member of parliament of the Samyukta Jan Morcha and the person mainly responsible for making Thabang a communist village, Kaman Jhankri,[57] one of the oldest communists in Thabang, and Santos Budha Magar.

---

[54] After the declaration of the Magarat Autonomous Region People's Government, the Maoists, one by one, formed eight autonomous regions. Of these, five are ethnically based and three are regionally based. The former are the autonomous regions of Tharuwan (Tharu), Tamuwan (Gurung), Kirat (Rai and Limbu), Tamang, and Newa (Newar), and the latter three are based in Bheri-Karnali, Seti-Mahakali, and Madhesh.

[55] He revealed this when I met him for the second time in September 2004. He also told me that they had formed a Jana Pratinidhi Sabha (People's Representative Assembly) which had 130 members of whom 95 were elected, 15 were nominated by the party, and 20 were from the People's Liberation Army.

[56] As mentioned above, he became famous for swearing allegiance in Parliament in traditional Magar dress. He lives in the Kathmandu Valley at present.

[57] He is around seventy years old. He became a member of the CPN in 1969 and formed a three-member 'cell committee'. He was Pradhan Panch of Thabang from 1987 to 1990. He said he had been elected without opposition as most of the villagers in Thabang at that time had already become communists.

Thabang was a part of a grant of *birta* land that was presented to Shanta Devi Shree after her marriage to Indra Bahadur Shahi, a grandson of the last Rukumkot king.[58] The *birta*-owner used to appoint a *mukhiya*, a community leader of the village, who would collect tax from the villagers and hand it over to his *karinda*, a clerk of the *birta*-owner. Barman Budha remembers that in his time it was Upendra Bahadur Shah, father of Lokendra Bahadur Shah, one of the three Shah politicians in Rukum, mentioned earlier. The villagers had to pay tax to the *birta*-owner until the *birta* system was finally abolished in 1959. The *mukhiya* had to collect Rs.349 from the whole village annually and to pay it in silver coins. Barman Budha remembers that a new *mukhiya* was appointed every several years and disputes relating to the *mukhiya*'s work occurred frequently between the villagers in Thabang. The *karinda* sometimes intervened to settle such quarrels.

Krishna Jhankri was appointed the *mukhiya* around 1952. This 'Krishna Mukhiya' introduced a new village rule prohibiting the villagers, on sanitary grounds, from keeping pigs. As most of the villagers did not follow the rule, he started punishing them. Confrontations began between Krishna Mukhiya's group and Barman Budha's group in 1954. The confrontations turned violent in 1955. At first Barman's group attacked Krishna's group and Barman was detained by the police for three days. Then, in June 1955, seven people including Barman Budha were detained in custody in Pyuthan for a month on the trumped-up charge of being communists despite the fact that they knew nothing about communism.[59] After their release they returned to Thabang but Krishna Mukhiya's group expelled the seven and their families from the village. They were compelled to stay outside the village for six months.

In the spring of 1956, Mohan Bikram Singh, a famous communist leader, stopped in Thabang with three comrades, including Khagulal Gurung. They had just been released from jail in Salyan and were returning to their homes in Pyuthan by way of Rukum and Rolpa. Barman said they were the first political persons who had ever visited Thabang. Mohan Bikram and the other communists stayed in Thabang for several days and while there they succeeded in convincing Barman's and Krishna Mukhiya's groups, to stop fighting each other and to form a peasant organization together. At that time, since the activities of the communist party were banned, they set up a peasant organization to act as a front for the party. Barman explained why they agreed to form a peasant organization: "De-

[58]Barman Budha told me that he had learnt this when he went to see Thabang's land ownership documents, in connection with a land dispute case between Thabang and Uwa.

[59]It has been claimed that Mohan Bikram Singh and Barman Budha met while they were in jail in Pyuthan but both of them denied this. In fact, Barman and Mohan Bikram had never met each other before Mohan Bikram's visit to Thabang.

spite the fact that we didn't know anything about politics, we had been charged with being communists. That is why we were curious to know what communism was." In just this same way, non-Maoists today have joined the Maoists after their families and relatives have been killed on the mere suspicion of being Maoists.

Barman Budha became the secretary of this six-member peasant organization. After Krishna Mukhiya died of tuberculosis, Barman became *mukhiya* in 1958. During the first general election in 1959, all the voters of Thabang voted for Khagulal Gurung who ran as the candidate of the Communist Party of Nepal in the Pyuthan constituency.[60] Although Mohan Bikram never visited Thabang again, Khagulal came frequently after his visit of 1956. After this election, the eyes of the administration started to fix on Thabang. But communism started to take root in a more organized way after the first primary school was established in Thabang in 1959 on the initiative of Barman Budha. At first Barman employed an ex-Indian Gurkha soldier who lived in Thabang to teach in the school. Later, in 1965, he invited Khiman Singh Gurung, a communist of Pyuthan belonging to Mohan Bikram Singh's group, as teacher. According to Khiman Singh,[61] who was born in 1930, he taught in Thabang for two years. He held *ratri pathshala* (night school) once a week for a year, where he taught communist ideology to both young and old through the medium of communist songs. In 1968 another communist, Deepak K.C., came from Pyuthan to take up the position of school principal and worked for the party in Thabang.[62]

In the early 1970s, another conflict began between ex-Pradhan Panch Ram Kumar Budha's group and Barman Budha's group. Ram Kumar, who had a close relationship with the administration, tried to turn the people of Thabang into Panchayat supporters and started to report on the political activities of Barman's group to the administration in Libang. Because of Ram Kumar's reports, Kaman Jhankri and others were accused of being communists and were arrested under the Public Security Act in 1973. Conflict between the two groups intensified and culminated in a gun battle around 1975. Kaman was also detained in Libang jail for a month in 1978. However, the majority of the people in Thabang had already become supporters of communism by the 1970s and Ram Kumar's attempts

---

[60] In this election the Nepali Congress candidate, Anirudra Sharma, won. At that time Thabang was in Pyuthan district. The boundaries were redrawn and it was included in Rolpa district in 1963.

[61] I met him in Pyuthan in October 2004. He does not have any relationship with the Maoists now.

[62] According to Santos Budha Magar, Deepak K.C. is now the chief of the social and welfare department of the Magarat Autonomous Region People's Government. For a time he was chairman of the Maoists' Pyuthan District People's Government.

eventually fizzled out. Later some of his supporters gave up and others left Thabang to live elsewhere.

At the time of the national referendum in 1980, to decide whether to continue the Panchayat system or to introduce the multiparty system, all the votes in Thabang were cast for the multiparty system. Barman Budha was Pradhan Panch of Thabang, a position which he won three times. He was arrested without any charge under the Security Act and detained for twenty-seven months in jails in Libang and Ghorahi. He was in jail when all the voters of Thabang boycotted the general election of 1981. Thabang was the only village in Rolpa where not a single vote was cast in this election. It is certain that the administration was displeased by this. Santos Budha Magar, who was in high school at that time, remembers the villagers saying that if Barman had been out of jail, they would have followed his lead. But as he was not, they followed the CPN's (Fourth Convention) decision to boycott this election.

There is a widely believed story about Barman Budha Magar that he burnt the photographs of the king and queen which hung on the wall of the Village Panchayat office while he was Pradhan Panch. In fact, this is not true. The true story of what happened in 1981 is as follows. While Barman Budha was in jail, Barman Roka, who was a supporter of the Panchayat system and then Upa-Pradhan Panch (vice-chairman of the Village Panchayat) in Thabang, was beaten by a villager during a gathering of villagers in the Village Panchayat office. During the melée the photographs of the king and the queen on the table were accidentally knocked to the ground. Barman Roka reported this incident, and claimed that the royal couple's photographs had been deliberately burnt by Barman Budha and other villagers. Despite the fact that he was in jail at the time of the incident, Barman was accused of the anti-state crime of burning the royal couple's photos.

After the boycott of the general election, a major police operation was launched in Thabang in October 1981.[63] The police force set up camp in the grounds of the high school and stayed there for nearly a month. During the operation the police arrested eight persons including Kaman Jhankri who was detained in Tulsipur jail in Dang district for the next two and a half years. Many Thabangis can still remember this *2038 sal ko Kartik operation*. Santos Budha Magar, who was in class ten at the high school and a representative of the student wing of the party at that time, said:

> The police surrounded the village in the early morning of 5 Kartik. They detained students, teachers, and even a post officer. We were able to escape from the village and we stayed outside for a while.

[63]When this operation was launched, Bala Ram Gharti Magar, one of the Rashtriya Panchayat members from Rolpa, was Defence Minister.

> After this operation, anti-state sentiment among the people in Thabang grew stronger and we formed armed teams to drive back our enemies using *khukuri*s, sticks, and even guns. Even before that the administration had already targeted the villagers of Thabang and many people had been accused of various charges including murder.

After the Kartik operation, a police area post was established in Thabang. Before that a post office and a health post had been the only signs of government presence in Thabang. The police post continued to be stationed there until it was withdrawn from the village in 1998 due to the insecurity caused by the Maoist insurgency.

While Barman Budha was Pradhan Panch of Thabang, there was another incident which demonstrates the anti-establishment spirit of the Thabangis. It happened before the general election of 1981. Rolpa District Panchayat decided to construct roads all over the district through *shramadan* (voluntary labour contributions) from the villagers. The district administration assigned the Thabang people to make a road from the border of Dang district to Libang. After discussions among themselves, the people of Thabang decided to refuse to participate in this work because it would be too far from their village.[64] It would take four days to walk to the border of Dang from Thabang. In addition to the distance, the people were suffering from food scarcity that year. Santos Budha explained why they decided to reject the demand:

> We thought the administration was pocketing public money budgeted for construction works – so why should we work voluntarily? We felt it was an injustice. So we decided that we would go to do the work on condition that the administration would either give some budget to our school or they would pay us for the labour work or they would change the place to near by our village. Barman Budha conveyed this decision to the administration in Libang but they didn't listen to us, so we refused to go to do the work.

Conflicts between the Villagers of Thabang

I had already met some villagers from Thabang the previous year in June 2002. I met them at a small house built in front of the district police office in Libang, the seat of the district headquarters of Rolpa. The thirty-six-year-old Kalam Roka Magar, his father,[65] his two wives, and his six

---

[64]According to Bam Kumari Budha Magar, the villagers of Kotgaun also refused to participate in road construction. But in this case the reason was more personal: they simply wished to oppose the current Pradhan Panch of their village.

[65]His father is Barman Roka who was vice-chairman of Thabang Village Panchayat in 1981 and accused Barman Budha of burning the photographs of the king and queen.

children were living there. Kalam Roka became vice-president of Thabang VDC in the local election of 1997.[66] As he was the only candidate who stood in that election and there was no voting in Thabang, he was automatically elected.[67] He said that the Nepali Congress party nominated him as a candidate against his will. Since then he has been living in Libang with his family because the Maoists and their supporters in Thabang would not let them live there.[68] Some youths I met along with Kalam Roka said. "If you stay in Thabang for five days, you are compelled to be a Maoist. Otherwise, you cannot live there." They claimed that the situation has been like that in Thabang since around 1997, one year after the People's War started. These youths were preparing to go to seek work in the Persian Gulf. They said they had to pay Rs.15,000 to the Maoists when going abroad.

Kalam Roka returned to Thabang with the security forces and some government officers at the end of March 2002.[69] When they arrived in Thabang, almost all the villagers had already run away from the village and only some old people had stayed behind. After the Maoists attacked the camp of the security force in Gam VDC, situated in north-eastern Rolpa, killing nearly seventy security personnel there, the security forces in Thabang withdrew to Libang. After returning from Thabang, Kalam Roka received a letter from the Maoists in the name of "your enemy *Thabangi janata* (people of Thabang)". It was a death threat to him saying that if he returned to Thabang, they would kill him. The letter was full of highly emotive expressions of hatred towards him. Within a couple of years after the Maoists started the People's War, four villagers were killed by the Maoists in Thabang. Kalam Roka claimed that all of them had been murdered to settle personal scores, and not for political reasons.

In Thabang more than 90 per cent of the inhabitants are Magars. Some Dalits (Kami and Damai),[70] and a few Gurung families live in the village, but there are no Bahun or Chetri-Thakuri households. The appearance of

---

[66] In this local election, polling was not conducted in six VDCs in Rolpa.

[67] Dil Bahadur Budha Magar was also elected as VDC president of Thabang in the same way. He also lives in Libang.

[68] According to the CDO of Rolpa, interviewed in June 2002, around 420 refugees who could not live in their own villages due to threats from the Maoists were living in Libang.

[69] According to Kalam Roka, he, as VDC vice-president, and fourteen government officers went to Thabang with the security forces. The government officers collected tax and bank loans from villagers during their stay. On the second day after the security forces arrived, they burnt fifteen houses in the centre of the village.

[70] According to Barman Budha, around thirty households of Damai lived in the area around the main village and about eighty households of Kami above it before he left Thabang in 1996. He said that Dalits in Thabang did not own their own land before but after he became *mukhiya*, on his initiative, in around 1968, they were given land. Barman said that untouchability was barely enforced against Dalits in Thabang in his generation and there were even some cases of inter-caste marriage between Magars and Dalits.

the main village of Thabang is different from other villages. Although there is no shortage of space to build, the houses are all closely clustered together. Barman Budha Magar explained it as follows:

> In the old days Thabang was frequently attacked by forces from the direction of Rukum. They thought it would be easy to defend themselves if they lived close together. Also, most households in Thabang have their fields high up at a distance of two or three hours' walk away. We have to go there very early in the morning and come back every evening after dark. It is like the life of bees. So people here want to live clustered close together.

Barman Budha said that conflicts between the villagers were also very common. Now seventy-four years old, he remembers that he used to join in fights with sticks already when he was still a small boy of three or four years of age. Barman Budha, a symbol of resistance in Thabang, has never returned to his own village after the Maoists started the insurgency in 1996.[71] He is now living a kind of sheltered life near the capital and is keeping his distance from politics. He does not directly support the Maoists' stand but commented about the People's War as follows:

> Leaders who had read books written by Mao and Lenin taught us that the people in this country were not equal. The majority of positions in government offices have been occupied by people from the higher *jati*s (castes). The situation in which higher *jati*s dominate lower *jati*s has not yet changed. Now Magars are trying to get back their rights through the People's War.

THE SEEDS OF COMMUNISM IN RUKUM AND ROLPA

The Mohan Bikram Factor

Pyuthan district in Rapti Zone is known to have produced many communist leaders, including Mohan Bikram Singh, general secretary of the CPN (Unity Centre-Masal),[72] and Kiran, or Mohan Baidya,[73] one of the leading

[71] When the security forces came to Thabang in March 2002, they destroyed one of his houses. His other house, which had been occupied by the Maoists, was destroyed by them in February 2004.

[72] This party was formed by combining the CPN (Masal) and the CPN (Unity Centre) in 2002.

[73] According to a TV interview with Hom Prasad Shrestha, an ex-Bheri Karnali Brigade Commander of the PLA, who surrendered to the government, Kiran was the party-in-charge of eastern Nepal. However, he was arrested by the Indian police in Siliguri in India in March 2004. Kiran is one of the most senior leaders of the Maoists. He was the first general secretary of the CPN (Mashal) but was demoted for being responsible for the *sectar kanda* in 1989, and Prachanda or Pushpa Kamal Dahal became general secretary. Deepak Mahato, a former

members of the CPN (Maoist). Most of the Maoist leaders, including party president Prachanda, were influenced, to a greater or lesser degree, by Mohan Bikram Singh.[74] They were in the same party until the faction led by Mohan Baidya split from Mohan Bikram's party, the CPN (Masal), to form the CPN (Mashal) in 1985. Baburam Bhattarai remained in Mohan Bikram's party until 1991. Mohan Bikram was born, the son of the *mukhiya* of Okharkot VDC in Pyuthan, in the middle of the 1930s. According to Mohan Bikram's own testimony, he first joined the Nepali Congress. However, after being arrested and detained in jail for two years due to his involvement in the student movement in Kathmandu, he joined the Communist Party of Nepal. He returned to Pyuthan in February of 1954 and started a peasant movement. He organized a *jana shiksha shivir* (people's training camp) in Bijayanagar of Pyuthan where around 150 people lived collectively and learnt about communism for three months. The following year he was arrested again and was put in jail for two years. He was elected a central committee member in the second Congress of the CPN in 1957 and was arrested again in 1961, to be detained in various jails for the next nine and a half years. Khiman Singh Gurung, who is one of the oldest comrades of Mohan Bikram, said that the participants of the 'people's training camp' had joined the party and become the followers of Mohan Bikram.[75]

Though Mohan Bikram Singh was behind bars for many years, his cadres were actively spreading communism in Pyuthan and its neighbouring areas, including Rolpa and Rukum. As mentioned above, Khiman Singh Gurung and Deepak K.C. went to work in Thabang as schoolteachers and preached communism among the villagers. According to Santos Budha Magar, Kiran frequently came to Thabang as the chief of the party in Rolpa

---

student leader of the CPN (Mashal), told the weekly paper *Jana Astha* (7 Phalgun, 2059) that Prachanda was able to become the leader of the CPN (Mashal) owing to this *sectar kanda*. He also said that the *sectar kanda* was actually the beginning of the Maoists' People's War. The CPN (Mashal) adopted the policy of boycotting the election of 1986 and decided to attack police boxes in Kathmandu. According to Deepak Mahato, they attacked nine police boxes injuring some policemen. After this incident many activists of the CPN (Mashal) were arrested by the authorities and as a result its party organization became weak. The party later reached the conclusion that this policy was wrong and Kiran, who was then the general secretary, and all the politburo members were demoted for adopting it. This incident was called the *sectar kanda*.

[74] Ever since the start of the People's War, Mohan Bikram Singh has been opposed to it. In an interview with him in April 2002 in Kathmandu, where he still lives a 'half-underground' life, he told me, "I am not against the People's War as such but the time has not yet come. Because they started it at an inappropriate time, other parties like the King and India are benefiting from it."

[75] Khiman Singh himself could not participate in the camp because he was a teacher in a public school. He became a communist after he began to teach in the school established by Mohan Bikram and his comrades in Narikot, a village close to Mohan Bikram's birthplace, Okarkot.

district around 1980. Badal or Ram Bahadur Thapa, one of the politburo members, also worked in this area from 1986 as the chief of the party for Rapti Zone and played an important role in establishing the party's organization.[76] Badal, who is one of the most popular Maoist leaders, is a Magar but does not speak the Magar language as he grew up in Chitwan district where his father, an ex-Indian Army soldier, and family had settled.[77]

Communists of Rukum

Aside from these activities inspired by Mohan Bikram Singh, there was another movement in Rukum even before the people of Thabang had become communists. According to Tara Prasad Gharti Magar, a former chairman of Rukum District Panchayat, Kami Budha Magar was the first communist in Rukum. He was an ex-Indian Army soldier and one of the activists who had rebelled with K.I. Singh in Bhairahawa against the Delhi agreement in 1951. After K.I. Singh escaped to China, Kami Budha returned to Rukum and formed an alternative government. Two members of this government are still alive in Bhalakcha VDC in Rukum. To avoid arrest by the administrator in Salyan, Kami Budha went to Humla in northwestern Nepal, where he and his group captured the government office and stayed for some time. But he was arrested and taken to Jumla where he was killed by the police in 1955.

In Rukum as well, Mohan Bikram's group was active during the Panchayat regime. One of the main places where they carried out their organizational activities was in schools. In 1966, when Tara Prasad Gharti Magar was in the ninth class of high school in Musikot, he came under the influence of a teacher from Dang and became a communist.[78] This teacher belonged to Mohan Bikram's group. On their own initiative, Tara Prasad and three colleagues formed the first 'cell committee' of communists in Rukum in the month of Mangsir (November-December), 1966. They were class ten student Dhruba Jung Malla, teacher Dilli Bahadur Malla, and peasant Iskanda Sharma, whose son 'Prabhakar' or Janardan Sharma is today a politburo member of the CPN (Maoist). Soon after the formation of this committee in Khalanga, the same kind of cell committees were formed in Bhalakcha and then in Chaukabang. According to Tara Prasad, in Rolpa district as well, in the same year four cells were formed in Thabang, Libang, Gajul, and Rugha (Rugha was included in Rukum district in 1978). They

---

[76]Mohan Bikram Singh also mentioned a woman activist called 'Jaljala' (her real name was Bidhya Dhakal) who worked to establish the party organization during her stay in Thabang in 1977. She died in an accident in New Delhi in 1981.

[77]Badal studied engineering in the former Soviet Union. He was widely claimed to be the 'military chief' of the Maoists but the party vigorously denied it through its *Maoist Information Bulletin* - 1 (10 January 2002).

[78]At present Tara Prasad does not belong to any party.

formed a Rolpa District Committee with representatives of these four cell committees, but it did not function well as they could not communicate with each other because of the distance between them.

In December 1972, the four cell committees of Khalanga, Bhalakcha, Chaukabang, and Rugha (all these villages are situated in southern Rukum at present) united and formed the first district-level committee of communists in this area, which they named the Rukum-Rolpa District Committee (at that time Rugha was still in Rolpa). Thabang, Gajul, and Libang's committees were not included because they were too far away. Tara Prasad became secretary of this seven-member committee. Most members of this committee were Magars and teachers by profession. Tara Prasad was also a teacher in the Bhalakcha secondary school. He was again elected as the committee chairman. This committee functioned until the Rukum District Committee was formed in 1974.

According to Tara Prasad, they formed all of those committees independently, not under the direction of the party, that is, the Communist Party of Nepal. They were not satisfied with the main party line, represented by Pushpa Lal Shrestha. He said:

> From the beginning, our committee took the policy of introducing a republican system through armed struggle. All the time we believed in armed struggle, though we never went into action.[79] We had contact with the party but we didn't follow them. We were the followers of Mohan Bikram Singh. We used to think that whatever Mohan Bikram said was true. While he was in jail, we kept contact with his cadres. After Mohan Bikram formed the CPN (Fourth Convention) in 1974, we joined that party.

The Role of Teachers in the Expansion of Communism

Tara Prasad Gharti Magar acknowledges that communism spread through schools in Rukum. He said that most of the headmasters of the four high schools in Rukum were communists. Tara Prasad himself was headmaster of the secondary school in Bhalakcha and made his school a base for carrying out his political work from 1973 to 1976. He said that Masta Bahadur Shrestha,[80] the headmaster of the high school in Rukumkot, and Dilli Raj Sharma,[81] headmaster of the high school in Chaurjahari, were the

---

[79]Tara Prasad said they went to Gorakhpur in India to see Pushpa Lal Shrestha and to buy weapons. However, they weren't able to buy any.

[80]He is from Gunam in Mahat VDC of Rukum.

[81]He was from Dang district and also the headmaster of Rukumkot high school. A former parliament member, Keshar Man Roka Magar who studied in the high school in Rukumkot, said Dilli Raj Sharma had taught the ideologies of communism to Masta Bahadur Shrestha when the latter was a student of a high school in Rukumkot.

main persons who worked for the spread of communism. They used the elected Panchayat bodies also. Tara Prasad was elected as chairman of the Rukum District Panchayat with the support of the CPN (Fourth Convention) in 1982. During his tenure of five years, he exercised his right to appoint schoolteachers and government officers to advance the party's work in the villages. He said, "We sent a lot of communist activists as teachers and village Panchayat secretaries in order to establish our organization in the villages." As a result, some areas in Rukum became strongholds of communism during the Panchayat era. Tara Prasad remarked:

> Even in the time of the Panchayat system, government officers from the district headquarters Khalanga were afraid to come to the south crossing the Sanka River, because in villages like Bhalakcha, Chaukabang, and Rugha, villagers used to punish corrupt officers.

The activities of the communists intensified still further after the Nepal Rashtriya Shikshak Sangathan (Nepal National Teachers Union) was formed following the referendum of 1980. Krishna Bahadur Mahara, who is today a spokesman and politburo member of the CPN (Maoist), was then a teacher in the secondary school in Libang.[82] He led the union's committee for Rolpa and Masta Bahadur Shrestha led the committee for Rukum. Both of them were active members of the CPN (Masal), the mother party of today's CPN (Maoist). Tara Prasad said that after the formation of this organization most of the teachers in the area came to follow the activists of the CPN (Masal), and later the CPN (Mashal) after Mohan Baidya's faction split from the CPN (Masal) in 1985, when they launched movements against the administration to raise their salaries and pensions, etc. An ex-member of this organization in Libang, Krishna Bahadur Gharti Magar, said:

> Up to 1990 almost 80 per cent of all the teachers in Rolpa were members of this organization. Furthermore, among the members nearly 80 per cent became supporters of the Samyukta Jan Morcha (United People's Front or SJM).

The SJM was formed in January 1991 by the merger of various communist parties including the faction of the CPN (Masal) led by Baburam Bhattarai. The SJM functioned as the political front for the CPN (Unity Centre),

---

[82]Many of the people I met in Rolpa mentioned Mahara's major role in recruiting Rolpa students to communism. They said that he used to use the honorific *tapain* even to his students (his juniors). Several people reported that when one of his students from a poor family was injured, Krishna Bahadur Mahara collected money for his treatment and took him to hospital himself. A teacher I met in Libang in October 2004 said that most of the young Maoist leaders from Rolpa, who are now in their twenties or early thirties come from villages close to Libang, such as Jangkot, Kotgaun, and Korchabang. It was the students of precisely these villages who went to the high school where Krishna Bahadur used to teach.

which had been formed in November 1990 from some leftist parties including the CPN (Mashal) led by Prachanda, who is today the president of the CPN (Maoist). The CPN (Maoist) was formed from a faction of the CPN (Unity Centre) led by Prachanda and a faction of the Samyukta Jan Morcha led by Baburam Bhattarai in 1995.

Tara Prasad claimed that activities of this Nepal Rashtriya Shikshak Sangathan actually laid the foundations for the Maoists in Rolpa and Rukum. This can clearly be seen in the backgrounds of the Maoist leaders from Rolpa. Almost all the leaders from Rolpa are ex-members of Nepal Rashtriya Shikshak Sangathan, including politburo member Krishna Bahadur Mahara, central committee member Jakku Prasad Subedi, who was formerly the elected chairman of Rolpa District Development Committee, Santos Budha Magar, who is a member of the United Revolutionary People's Council Nepal, and Dependra Pun, who was known as the party in-charge of Rolpa district. Pasang or Nanda Kisor Pun, the famous division commander of the People's Liberation Army, was also a primary schoolteacher in Rangsi VDC, Rolpa, and a member of the Sangathan.[83]

Santos Budha Magar said that, after the restoration of multiparty democracy in 1990, he was given the responsibility of working for the cultural front of his party, the Samyukta Jan Morcha Nepal. After he was transferred to the high school in Thabang, he formed a cultural group consisting of teachers and students to stage songs and dances. The same kind of cultural teams were formed in high schools in Rangsi, Nuwagaun, and Libang-Gajul (one team from two high schools). According to Santos Budha:

> These four cultural teams were formed to spread our party's politics in Rolpa after 1990 and we used these teams for campaigning in the general election of 1991 as well. Besides the cultural campaign, we started a 'punishment campaign' against corrupt persons. We made them return money they took and even gave them some physical punishments like forcing them to do *uth bas* [repeated standing up and sitting down, a common Maoist punishment even now]. We spread our party politics among the people in Rolpa through these campaigns.

Confrontations between the Nepali Congress and the Samyukta Jan Morcha

When I visited Libang, the Rolpa district headquarters, in June 2002, I heard many detailed accounts of harassment by members of the Samyukta

[83]Pasang was the Western Division commander of the PLA but became the Central Division commander after the reorganization of September 2004. He is a member of the Maoists' seventeen-member politburo.

Jan Morcha.[84] The harassment began soon after the restoration of multi-party democracy in 1990. One of the Rolpa district committee members of the CPN (UML) said:

> While party activities were banned under the Panchayat regime, we didn't even know what communism was, but after 1990 some villagers joined political parties like the Nepali Congress (NC), the CPN (UML), the Rashtriya Prajatantra Party (RPP),[85] and the Samyukta Jan Morcha (SJM). In fact, many people joined the RPP in my village in the beginning. But because members of the SJM were very aggressive and gave punishment to ex-Panchas by beating them or hanging a *jutta-ko mala* (a garland of shoes) around their neck, many people were obliged to leave the party. As a result, supporters of the SJM became more active in the village. They started forcing us to attend their party gatherings.

A former member of Rolpa District Development Committee from Mirul VDC said that he had no other option but to join the NC to protect himself because supporters of the SJM harassed anyone who refused to join their party. A teacher from Korchabang VDC, a member of Nepal Shikshak Sangh (Nepal Teachers' Association), had a garland of shoes hung around his neck after the election of 1991 because he had voted for the NC.[86] Sometimes the harassment took the extreme form of murder. According to data collected by Krishna Bahadur Gharti Magar in Libang, nine persons were killed by the supporters of the Samyukta Jan Morcha between October 1991 and the launching of the People's War in February 1996.[87]

A major confrontation between the supporters of the Samyukta Jan Morcha and those of the Nepali Congress and the Rashtriya Prajatantra Party took place in Gam VDC, situated in north-east Rolpa, during a local festival in September 1994. On the day of a religious gathering, the supporters of the NC and RPP beat up those of the SJM including a VDC

---

[84] I interviewed twenty-two refugees living in Libang in June 2002. Of these, sixteen were either NC members or NC supporters. Of the sixteen, only one had been an NC member since before 1990; all the others joined the NC only after 1990. Two were VDC presidents and four were vice-presidents. The security forces set up a barbed-wire security fence around the entire bazaar of Libang after a VDC representative from Bhabang was shot dead by Maoists in the bazaar in April 2000.

[85] This party was formed by the Panchayat supporters after 1990.

[86] He had been living in Libang since receiving a death threat from the Maoists in May 1998. Another person who received a death threat in his village was Dol Bahadur Budha, who was then an NC area secretary; he was murdered by the Maoists in December 1998. After 1990, the Nepal Rashtriya Shikshak Sangathan divided into separate party-aligned organizations. Supporters of the Nepali Congress formed the Nepal Shikshak Sangh.

[87] According to the data of INSEC (Informal Sector Service Centre), in total 228 persons were killed by the Maoists in Rolpa between the start of the insurgency in February 1996 and 28 October 2003. This is the largest total out of all of Nepal's seventy-five districts.

representative.[88] Exactly a year later, on the day of the same festival in 1995, several hundred supporters of the SJM gathered in Gam and attacked the supporters of the NC and the RPP. Soon after this incident the government started 'Operation Romeo', in November 1995, to control the activities of the SJM in Rolpa, arresting many people during a two-month operation.[89] According to the villagers I met in Libang, this operation mainly targeted north and east Rolpa where most of the inhabitants are Magars speaking the Kham language.

Conflicts became particularly intense during elections. One example is the conflict in Iribang VDC during the first local elections under the multiparty system in 1992. On the day that candidates had to register their names, supporters of the SJM assembled at the registration venue with arms and refused to allow the candidates of other political parties to register. As a result, the SJM won all the eleven seats in the VDC including those of the president, the vice-president, and nine ward representatives. In VDCs such as Gajul, Mirul, Jelbang, and Phagam as well, the SJM won all the seats.[90] In the general election held in 1991, the SJM won in both constituencies of Rolpa. Barman Budha Magar from Thabang won in constituency number one and Krishna Bahadur Mahara from Libang won in constituency number two. In this election the CPN (UML) cooperated with the SJM by withdrawing its candidates in both Rolpa and Rukum. In the local elections of 1992 the SJM occupied most of the seats on the District Development Committee including the chairman and vice-chairman, both of whom were members of the Nepal Rashtriya Shikshak Sangathan. Jakku Prasad Subedi, an ex-teacher from Gajul VDC and currently a central committee member of the CPN (Maoist), became the first DDC chairman. Krishna Bahadur Gharti Magar, a resident of Libang and an NC member said:

> Through the victories of both the general election in 1991 and the local election in 1992, the Samyukta Jan Morcha actually captured Rolpa. I think the confidence built in Rolpa affected the Maoist leadership and caused them to decide that they could launch the People's War at the national level.

---

[88] In Gam VDC, except for two ward representatives who won from the RPP and the NC, the SJM won all the seats including those of president and vice-president in the local elections of 1992.

[89] Though the government claimed that nobody was killed during this operation, some villagers from Gam whom I met in Libang said that seven persons (six supporters of the SJM and one supporter of the CPN (UML)) were killed by the police in Gam VDC during Operation Romeo. They said the police harassed not only SJM supporters but also other opposition parties' supporters, i.e. those of the CPN (UML) and the RPP, during the operation.

[90] According to the testimony of people from those villages. They said there were no nominations from other parties in Gajul and Jelbang.

Nepali Congress supporters resisted the harassment of the SJM supporters by making both real and fake charges against them. This caused the confrontation between the two groups to intensify still further, and some people blamed the Nepali Congress and its supporters for their abuse of state power. Former member of the Rashtriya Panchayat, Bam Kumari Budha Magar, said:

> The Nepali Congress supporters in Rolpa were just like duplicates of the Panchas (supporters of the Panchayat system). They got personal benefits from the authorities by using their connections with the people in power. It was exactly how Panchayat supporters used to behave during the Panchayat regime.

In Rukum the SJM won in constituency number two in the general election of 1991; as in Rolpa, it had the cooperation of the CPN (UML). The other seat was won by the Nepali Congress candidate, Gopalji Jung Shah, the youngest of the three Shah politicians in Rukum during the Panchayat regime (discussed above). During the election campaign of 1991, he was also harassed by the supporters of the SJM, who hung a garland of shoes around his neck and smeared black powder on his face in Rugha VDC, one of the communist strongholds from Panchayat days. The fifty-five-year-old Gopalji Jung Shah said:

> Actually, the supporters of the Samyukta Jan Morcha had already started their People's War in an undeclared way in this area back in 1991. After they boycotted the general election of 1994, they began the insurgency openly.

The villagers in Kholagaun claimed that Ganesh Shah, who had been murdered by the supporters of the SJM in 1994, was a close associate of Gopalji Jung Shah and had joined the NC after 1990. Gopalji Jung said that two other NC supporters in Rukum, Lal Bahadur K.C. and Garbir Batha, were killed by the SJM before the Maoists started the insurgency. However, a former communist in Rukum claimed that both of them were killed for personal, not political reasons. He said, "In fact, most of the cases of conflict between supporters of the NC and the SJM happened due to personal causes. However, the NC side claimed to be victims of the Samyukta Jan Morcha in order to get support from the state power." According to him, after 1990, the administration filed various charges against more than 1,300 people in Rukum, most of them supporters of the Samyukta Jan Morcha, under a public crime act. He said, "Most of the accused were Magars and Dalits. Many of them left their villages to escape detention and joined the Maoists."

MAGARS, COMMUNISM, AND THE STATE

It is no accident that the Maoists' People's War started in Rolpa and Rukum. Although the geographical factor, that is, closeness to Pyuthan where the charismatic radical communist leader Mohan Bikram Singh and his group were based, is one of the important factors, it is also a fact that there was an adequate foundation in that the local community was ready to accept communist ideas and activities. It seems that strong anti-state sentiments had been cultivated in Rolpa and Rukum for a very long time. That is particularly clear in Rukum where some Thakuri families from outside ruled the area. Even after they lost their royal or *birta*-owning status, they continued to dominate the people as politicians or local elites under the Panchayat regime. As a result, the antipathy to the Thakuris and their followers grew stronger, in particular among the Magars who consider themselves to be the former occupants of this area since long before Thakuris came to live there. Many Magars from this area I talked with expressed their strong antipathy to Thakuris quite openly. The former communist leader in Rukum claimed:

> We have felt that we Magars and other castes are second-class citizens of the country and Thakuris who have affiliations with the royal family and the state are the first-class citizens. The state created these classes. Because of this historical background, the Magars in this area can easily become supporters of a republican system. In fact, most of the educated persons from the Magar community in Rukum have become communists.

In contrast to Rukum, there have never been powerful Thakuri kings in Rolpa. Though there were Thakuri kings in Gajul and Khungri, they were never ambitious about ruling over the people. In the case of Thabang, the villagers showed their resistance directly towards the administration. Thabang incurred the anger of the state and attempts to suppress the people's opposition began. It required a strong internal cohesion within the community for the people in Thabang to be able to resist the state. Unity means avoiding internal opposition. They slowly drove out anyone who did not support them and this made village unity even stronger.

During my trip to Rukum and Rolpa, I had the impression that the nature of traditional Magar society may have a deep relationship with the fact that this area became a heartland of the Maoists. It is clear if one sees the contribution of the Magars from this area to the leadership of the Maoist military front. Two of the three commanders who lead divisions, that is, the biggest units of the People's Liberation Army, are Magars from Rolpa district. Pasang or Nanda Kisor Pun, who is the commander of the Central Division of the PLA, is from Rangsi VDC, and Ananta or Barsaman Pun, the commander of the Eastern Division, is from Jankot VDC. It would not be too much to say that the Magars of Rolpa and Rukum are the main source of leaders for the Maoist insurgency. Although I have not yet been able to collect enough information about the historical and cultural background of Magars in those districts as I could not conduct a long-term field survey, I will try to describe some similarities between the Magar community in this area and the Maoists. The following information is based on a series of interviews with Bam Kumari Budha Magar, who is a former Rashtriya Panchayat member from Rolpa and is now working for the conservation of the Magar language and culture in this area.[91]

Before the Thakuris and other castes migrated to Rukum and Rolpa, this area used to be a part of the Athara Panthis, that is, of the Athara Magarat (Eighteen Magar states). Before the *baise-chaubise rajyas* (the 22 and the 24 kingdoms) ruled by Thakuris were established in western Nepal, these eighteen small Magar states ruled over the hill region from the west of Gulmi district to Bheri-Karnali Zone. According to Bam Kumari Budha Magar, the last king of the Athara Magarat, Dare Jaitam ruled in Jankot, situated in central Rolpa, around four or five hundred years ago. For some unknown reason, after Dare Jaitam was killed by a landslide, no king replaced him.[92]

In Bam Kumari's phrase, there was a kind of "natural communism" in the society of the Athara Magarat. She claims that a sense of equality is a basic cultural feature of the society descended from the Athara Magarat:

> In the Athara Magarat, the king and the people were on equal terms both in terms of physical work and in social activities. The kings were rulers and the people were as well. Kings also had to carry loads and cultivate their own fields.

According to a myth, the people's main source of livelihood in the Athara Magarat was hunting. Besides hunting animals, they cultivated small fields at the edge of the forest in order to plant barn millet and buckwheat. Later they started pasturing animals. They worked in groups and took decisions collectively. Bam Kumari continued:

> All the members of the community had to participate in commu-

---

[91]She was nominated as a Rashtriya Panchayat member in 1981 when she was a teacher at Bal Kalyan Secondary School in Libang. This is the same school where Maoist leader Krishna Bahadur Mahara used to teach. She was born in Korchabang, Rolpa, in 1951 and lives in Kathmandu at present. She does not belong to any political party now. She is one of the Magar leaders who believe that Magars in the Athara Magarat have been oppressed by outsiders, that is, Thakuris and Bahuns, and the state.

[92]According to Subedi (2054 V.S.: 354), Jayatabam, the fifth king of Rukum, was called 'Dare Jaitam' as well. Subedi writes that the first king of Gajul in Rolpa, Tutha Singh, married a daughter of Dare Jaitam.

> nity work voluntarily. Anyone who didn't follow a rule decided on by the community was punished. Community involvement was considered as an important factor of the society. The Maoist way of requiring people to be involved in development works such as building roads and bridges in their base areas is similar to the tradition of the Athara Magarat.

According to Bam Kumari, who worked as a recorder or secretary of the *kachahari* (an assembly of villagers) from her teenage years, there used to be a democratic culture of group decision making in the Athara Magarat:

> The king used to rule only for one generation. If a king died, a new king was elected by an assembly of representatives of the community. For a long time, the *kachahari* functioned as a decision-making body of the community. In some villages in Rolpa it functioned right up to the time when the Maoists started the insurgency.

Santos Budha Magar, the president of Magarat Autonomous Region People's Government who comes from Thabang, also stressed the communist-like nature of Magar society:

> We Magars were indigenous people who used to be hunters. Group work was our common working style and a capacity for strong unity has been characteristic of the Magar community. The way we think is: "We live together and die together." The concept of joint ownership among the members of the community is also deep-rooted in Magar society. We share even small pieces of food. When there was not enough food, everybody starved. All these characteristics of Magar society are actually common to the feelings of communists. That is why Magars can easily accept the ideology of the communists.

Khiman Singh Gurung, who lived in Thabang as a schoolteacher for two years, expressed his impressions of the community there as follows:

> I was very surprised to hear women calling men by name there, which was very uncommon in my own village in Pyuthan. Women and men were more equal in Thabang than in any other village. I was also astonished to see Dalits coming freely into the houses of Magars. They didn't enter the kitchen but they did enter other rooms. The custom of untouchability still remained to some extent in Thabang but it was much less strict than in other villages. They also had the custom of working jointly in the fields. I could see the culture of communists in the society there. Due to the nature of the community, communist ideas could easily influence the villagers of Thabang.

Bam Kumari claimed that it was the influence of outsiders, i.e. of the Thakuris, that changed the traditionally democratic society of the Magars. She said:

> They brought seasonal farming and feudalism into the society of the Athara Magarat. They also introduced the hereditary system for *mukhiya*s (village leaders) and *beth* (forced service) system so that other villagers had to serve *mukhiya*s. This created classes within the community.

It can be clearly seen in the language how the influence of the Thakuris and their followers has changed the Magars' culture. In Rolpa and Rukum, Magars in the villages with a purely Magar population still speak their original Kham language, but those from the villages inhabited by Thakuris and other castes speak only Nepali. Magars in the Athara Magarat were originally shamanists and customarily ate beef, which is prohibited by Hinduism. Bam Kumari Budha said:

> Chetris and Bahuns speak contemptuously of Magars as *danra khane, bhanra laune manche,* that is, people who eat beef and wear canvas made of hemp.

A teacher from Magma VDC in Rukum also taught me the same phrase. In his village, Magars stopped speaking the Kham language long ago. He said:

> Magars in my village used to say that they called Thakuris from Jumla to live there during the *baise-chaubise rajya* period for their own security. It can be said that in the course of adjusting their lives because of the existence of a threat from outside, Magars eliminated their own history for the sake of their own security.

Both Bam Kumari and a teacher from Magma VDC pointed out that the state's indifference towards the local people's welfare contributed to the present situation. According to them, Magars in this area have lost their sources of income, one by one, because of state policies. Magars there used to plant hemp for multiple purposes and its product, marijuana, was a good source of income for them until the government banned it during the Panchayat era. Then they started to sell *yarchagumba,* that is, insects whose scientific name is *Cordyceps sinensis,* which are used for herbal medicines and have a good market in China and other Asian countries. However, the government policy of charging a high tax on it made it difficult for the local Magars to sell. Another source of income was sheep pasturing. Many Magars used to live by herding flocks of hundreds of sheep. But this also became difficult to continue due to the lack of big pastures after the government introduced the policy of 'community forests'. A teacher from Magma VDC said, "Now there is no other way to survive than selling sheep to go to work abroad."

Bam Kumari mentioned the role of Magars in the Maoists' People's War in a document entitled 'Questions of the Athara Magarat area for the talks between the government and the Maoists', which she handed over to Badal, who is from the Magar community and was a member of the Maoist talks team in 2003. (She no doubt hoped that the question of Magar autonomy and the survival of the Kham language and culture would be addressed in the talks.) She wrote:

> Although the glorious and very original tradition of the Magars has been, to some extent, damaged by the state's suppression, it is still in the state that we are proud of. We think that Magar language and Magar culture of Athara Magarat areas have given strength to the present Maoists' People's War.

CONCLUSION

There are definitely plenty of causes that have made Rolpa and Rukum the most affected areas of the Maoist insurgency. Comparing all the different cases of conflict that have occurred in this area, one of the main causes seems to be the antipathy towards the state that started to develop a long time ago. The Maoists utilized this sentiment by planting among the people the idea that their biggest enemy is the state and the political system. I noticed that there were two words frequently used by the Maoist supporters I met in the base area. They were *ghrina* (hatred) and *dushman* (enemy). A nineteen-year-old girl, already quoted earlier, who had lost her Maoist husband in the attack on Jumla, said that she really hated the state power (*rajya-satta mathi dherai ghrina cha*). Strong emotion showed in her face as she spoke. A Magar woman in Thabang, whose innocent younger sister had been killed by the police in December 1996, frequently used the word *dushman* to refer to 'the state', including the police, the Royal Nepalese Army, and the government, in her conversation. These two feelings indicate the main motivation, for them as for many others, to join the Maoists.

REFERENCES

Gersony, R. 2003. 'Sowing the Wind ... : History and Dynamics of the Maoist Revolt in Nepal's Rapti Hills'. Report to Mercy Corps International.

Maharjan, P.N. 2000. 'The Maoist Insurgency and Crisis of Governability in Nepal', in D. Kumar (ed.), *Domestic Conflict and Crisis of Governability in Nepal.* Kathmandu: CNAS, TU.

Maoist Information Bulletin – 1 (Occasional Bulletin of the Communist Party of

Nepal (Maoist) (10 January 2002). http://www.cpnmaoist.org/cpnm/documents/bulletin_1.htm

Maoist Information Bulletin – 8 (Occasional Bulletin of the Communist Party of Nepal (Maoist) (8 January 2004). http://www.cpnmaoist.org/cpnm/documents/english/information_bulletin8. htm

Ogura, K. 2004. 'Realities and Images of Nepal's Maoists after the Attack on Beni'. *European Bulletin of Himalayan Research* 27: 67-125.

Regmi, M.C. 1978. *Thatched Huts & Stucco Palaces: Peasants and Landlords in 19th-century Nepal*. Delhi: Vikas Publishing House.

de Sales, A. 2003. 'The Kham Magar Country: Between Ethnic Claims and Maoism', in D.N. Gellner (ed.), *Resistance and the State: Nepalese Experiences*, pp. 326-57. Delhi: Social Science Press. (Also published in 2000 in *European Bulletin of Himalayan Research* 19: 41-71, 2003, in D. Thapa (ed.), *Understanding the Maoist Movement of Nepal* [Kathmandu: Martin Chautari], and in French in 2003 in *Purusartha* 22: 271-301.)

Subedi, R. 2054 v.s. *Karnali Pradeshko Madhyakalin Itihas (The Medieval History of Karnali Region)*. Kathmandu: Sajha Prakashan.

Thapa, D. with B. Sijapati. 2003. *A Kingdom under Siege: Nepal's Maoist Insurgency, 1996-2003*. Kathmandu: The Printhouse.

Whelpton, J. 1991. *Kings, Soldiers and Priests: Nepalese Politics and the Rise of Jang Bahadur Rana 1830-1857*. Delhi: Manohar.

AFTERWORD

15

A Note on the 'Substantialization' of Caste and Its 'Hegemony'

JONATHAN PARRY

Political and Social Transformations, says the title. But *what* is transformed? From what and since when? Given the remarkable range of social phenomena that the essays contained in this volume cover, I shall have to be selective. Though I will make brief reference to other contributions, this endnote will focus on some of the issues arising from those in Part 1, where it is pre-eminently caste that is in question. This is in line with a long tradition of scholarship on the Indian subcontinent that has seen this institution as 'hegemonic', as a 'totalizing' framework which has in significant measure and over long stretches of time determined the life chances of much of the population and decisively shaped other aspects of social life. Its significance, however, has often been questioned, though from different directions. In a broad-brush way, we might identify three.

Colonial administrators, as Béteille (1996) reminds us, had been wont to insist that India would never shake off the shackles of caste; the nationalists to insist that it would. Wishful thinking aside, on the eve of Independence educated Indians had the evidence of their eyes. In a whole library of writings, those same administrators had depicted the system as founded on ritual rules derived from religious values. But if all the minutiae that regulated commensality and distance pollution were really at its heart, then the urban intelligentsia could in good faith conclude that it was on the way out. What they did not see was that "the future of caste lay not with religion but with politics" (ibid.: 159). So when M.N. Srinivas made that case in his 1957 Presidential Address to the Indian Science Congress on 'Caste in modern India' (Srinivas 1962), he was received with scepticism and accused of exaggeration in a *Times of India* editorial. When Srinivas took up his chair at the Delhi School of Economics in 1959, he was surprised to discover

> that caste was not even mentioned in discussions among Westernised intellectuals, especially economists such as those who inhabited the DSE. On the rare occasions it was mentioned, it was only to point out that caste was giving way to class. Discussing caste and its manifestations was somehow regarded as characteristic of reactionaries ... (1995: 48)

But though they assumed that it was now in rapid retreat, few in such circles would have doubted its ancient roots or significance.

Around three decades later, and on the other side of the world, doubts were raised on both scores by a new generation of South Asia specialists. The 'traditional' caste system was in reality a relatively recent invention, and the past 150 years had seen its crystallization and consolidation rather than its decline. In Dirks' formulation (1987: 8), "colonialism created much of what is now accepted as Indian 'tradition', including an autonomous caste structure with the Brahman clearly at its head ...". Though it was not invented out of nothing, caste 'as we know it today' is a creation of colonialism, and "it was under the British that 'caste' became a single term capable of expressing, organizing, and above all 'systematizing' India's diverse forms of social identity, community, and organization" (Dirks 2001: 5). How never colonized Nepal, with a highly elaborated caste hierarchy at its political and geographical core, fits into this picture is never quite clear.[1] Though Bayly (1999) shifts some of the blame from the British – 'caste society' had begun to emerge by the beginning of the eighteenth century and even in 'the distant past' there had been "recognizably castelike ideologies and practices" (ibid.: 25) – she too stresses the relatively recent origins of 'the system' and the role that colonialism played in consolidating it. Even in independent India, it appears to have grown in strength – an appearance created by focusing on its political, and occluding its economic and religious, dimension.

'Primordially' encompassing, but now of declining significance; unformed and inchoate in the unexpectedly recent past, but progressively sharply delineated and coercive – between these two extremes recent South Asian scholarship has found a third way. Caste is, and never was, the kind of hegemonic 'totalizing' institution that it is often cracked up to be, and the notion of hierarchy is in reality no more than a self-serving 'Orientalist' fiction.[2] "I, too, was lured in earlier research by the siren of caste," admits Inden (1990: 82), who now rejects "the idea that makes caste rather than

---

[1] Compare Quigley (1993: 125) who endorses Dirks' view that Brahmanical pre-eminence was a product of the British *raj*, but not his claim that the same can be said of 'the caste system'. Hocart had it right. "Caste is fundamentally about kingship and ritual ..." (ibid.: 121). The British created neither, and Nepal "belies the claim of a growing number of scholars that caste emerged out of the colonial experience in India" (Quigley 1994).

[2] A position which in places Dirks also seems to adopt, thus blurring the boundary between the last two tendencies.

kingship or a polity the constitutive institution of Indian civilization ..." Along convergent lines, Appadurai (1986: 745) suspects that Dumont's *Homo Hierarchicus* (1970) will prove to have been "the last major work to make caste the central problematic of Indian society", and describes it as the "swan song" for a now outmoded way of looking at India. 'Putting hierarchy in its place', the title of a second Appadurai piece (1992), is a precondition for the development of a more convincing (or politically correct?) sociology of India. Once more it is reactionaries who dwell on it.

The timing is intriguing. In the opening paragraphs of his paper for this volume, Surinder Jodhka provides – from the perspective of a non-diaspora son-of-the-soil social scientist – a rather different picture of the direction in which the central preoccupations of the field had been moving. Previously taken up, he tells us, with issues of development and economic change, the 1980s and 1990s saw a "paradigm shift" which brought caste – amongst other issues about identity – back to the centre of the stage. Its return should not surprise us. When, in August 1990, the V.P. Singh government decided in principle to implement the recommendations of the Mandal Commission with regard to reservations in central government employment for the 'Other Backward Classes', there had been riots and demonstrations in many parts of north India during which numbers of young upper-caste men had immolated themselves. Just when they decided in Chicago that caste mattered much less than 'orientalist' sociology supposed, college students from the Hindi belt were dousing themselves with kerosene in protest at caste reservations. True, they did not claim to be defending caste privilege. Both supporters and opponents of Mandal said they were against caste (Béteille 1991); but of its significance in Indian public life neither were in any doubt. Nor presumably are those affected by recent 'caste wars', which in Bihar alone had by 1995 killed more people than the six years of conflict in Kashmir (Bayly 1999: 345).

There is, as all this suggests, no solid consensus on what caste was in past centuries, nor on how 'hegemonic' it has ever been. That complicates the task of identifying the directions in which it has changed. It is complicated further by the obvious facts that the weight of caste bears unevenly on people located at different points in the *class* hierarchy; and that – to cite Jodhka again – caste was not exactly the same thing in the Punjab as in Tanjore or the Kathmandu Valley. On the outermost Himalayan fringes of 'northern South Asia', it was nothing more than keeping some distance from Untouchables.

Despite these difficulties, the task is not hopeless if we confine ourselves to broad trends over the past one hundred years or so. Though nobody seriously supposes that caste ever regulated all aspects of social life, there is little doubt that at the end of the nineteenth century it deeply affected many. Most would accept that Bouglé (1971 [1908]) had accurately characterized the morphology of the system in terms of a *hierarchy* of castes; a division of labour between them and the *interdependence* that results from it, and their mutual 'repulsion' or *separation*.

If Bouglé is taken as a baseline, there is considerable agreement on the way that things have moved. While the hierarchical ordering and interdependence of castes have been greatly eroded, the stress on their separation remains. The consequences for social cohesion are potentially grave and the political implications potentially sinister. Such developments were already identified by Ghurye (1950), whose insights were extended and elaborated by his former student, Srinivas (1966). According to Srinivas, the complementarity between castes was being replaced by competition; as the vertical ties between them disintegrate, new forms of horizontal solidarity uniting formerly differentiated grades within the caste have developed. The ritual considerations that had in the past governed interactions between castes have lost much of their hold, and – especially in the political field – a new spirit of antagonistic rivalry has grown up. Thus a trend towards the fusion of structurally adjacent units has gone along with an increased sense of difference from other like blocs.

Dumont's theory of caste has been so comprehensively (and in my view unjustifiably [Parry 1998]) slated that it is now usually passed over in silence. That part of it, however, that builds on the writings just alluded to and that has to do with the so-called 'substantialization' of caste, continues to be invoked with some regularity. To me that is curious. It has become, I believe, an increasingly questionable characterization of contemporary trends. His discussion (1970: Chap. 11) sets out from the "very unsatisfactory" state of the literature on "social change" in India, the extent of which has been greatly exaggerated. There has, as yet, been no change to "the living nucleus of society" (Dumont 1970: 219) – to its fundamental values. What we have is a

> ... transition from a fluid, structural universe in which the emphasis is on interdependence and in which there is no privileged level, no firm units, to a universe of impenetrable blocks, self-sufficient, essentially identical and in competition with one another, a universe in which caste appears as a collective individual (in the sense we have given this word), as a substance (ibid.: 222).

This transition is, however, confined to the politico-economic domain which "is encompassed in an overall religious setting. ... Everything happens as if the system tolerated change only in one of its secondary spheres" (ibid.: 228).

This last point first. Dumont cites Ghurye's discussion with approval and credits him with having first identified the substantialization of caste. Central to Ghurye's account, however, was an attenuation of the preoccupation with impurity, a relaxation of the rules of commensality, and a general muting of the values of hierarchy. If, as *Homo Hierarchicus* supposes, purity and hierarchy are at "the living nucleus of society", it is not easy to see – as Ishii (this volume) implies – how Dumont can consistently claim that change is confined to a "secondary sphere". Indeed, Béteille has repeatedly emphasized that though the morphology of caste may in many respects remain, the legal, moral, and religious values that underpin it have changed profoundly (e.g. Béteille 1991). Whatever he thinks or says privately, no significant public figure today is prepared to defend caste openly; and values so shame-faced that they cannot be spoken must surely lose moral force. Major modern Hindu religious leaders are more likely to attack caste than defend it (Béteille 1996). In short, it is possible to argue that the termites have gnawed at least as effectively at the ideological props of the system as at its morphological 'superstructure'. As the chapters by Jodhka and Tanabe in this volume remind us, however, the religious ideology has never been unitary and has for centuries contained anti-hierarchical strands. Even if the rate of their progress accelerated greatly over the course of the twentieth century, we cannot therefore assume that the termites only arrived with the British.

In an early development of it, Barnett (1977) gives Dumont's thesis a rather literal ('ethnosociological') spin. 'Substantialization' involves important changes in South Asian thinking about bodily substance; and these in turn reflect the breakdown of old interdependencies with the move to town, and the political and economic advantages of mobilizing on a wider scale. In the past, Kontaikkatti Vellalars (KVs for short) had thought of themselves as sharing a certain quality of 'blood purity', but this could be modified by actions and styles of life. On the basis of these, KVs also saw themselves as differentiated into a series of localized, endogamous, and ranked bilateral kindreds (*vakaiyaras*). Under modern conditions, the endogamous boundaries between them have been renegotiated, the reformers establishing the principle that all KVs – regardless of *vakaiyara* – are substantially the same. Variations in lifestyle and differences in behaviour – in 'codes of conduct' – were now irrelevant to one's fixed, innate, and immutable identity as a member of the KV caste with KV 'blood' – 'blood' that is qualitatively different from that of other castes. Instead of interdependent units in a hierarchical holistic order, castes become something like ethnic groups, each potentially separate and independent of the others. But since blood and behaviour (biogenetic substance and code of conduct) are conceptually de-coupled, it now becomes possible to conceive of people of a different caste but with a similar lifestyle as the same kind of people as oneself, and new identity choices become available. Though the importance of changes in notions about bodily substance to this development is debatable, the trend itself is real and important. In modern milieu, individuals have a significantly wider range of possible identities to choose from, and these may have as much, or more, salience than caste. Caste as a hegemonic framework loses some of its grip.

Reflecting on the way things have changed in Ramkheri between his first fieldwork there in 1954-6 and his latest visit in 1992, Mayer reports that caste membership has remained as unambiguous as ever and that inter-caste marriage is still not regarded as even "a theoretical possibility" (1996: 57). Overt reference to hierarchical ranking is today, however, avoided. At village feasts, most now eat together in a single unbroken line with people belonging to castes with whom they would never have inter-dined in the past – even if the import of this change is muted by serving only *pakka* food which has always been acceptable within wider limits than (boiled) *kaccha* food, and even if in private contexts inter-dining may still be avoided. Castes are no longer referred to as *jatis* ('breeds' or 'species') because of the hierarchical connotations of this term, and the more neutral *samaj* (community) is used instead. But while the ranking of castes is now downplayed, what is increasingly emphasized is their *difference*, expressed as a matter of different dietary habits (*khan-pin*) and different styles of life (*rahan-sahan*). It is these that provide the overt ideological justification for the continued separation of castes and the absolute injunction to endogamy.

These trends, Fuller (1996: 12-13) argues, are however accompanied

> ... by the increasing differentiation of status, power and wealth developing *within* each caste – a development which is itself contributing to the decline of clear-cut caste ranking and hence, paradoxically, to an increasing normative emphasis on difference *between* castes. Substantialisation is, in effect, a self-contradictory process, because as it develops castes actually become more heterogeneous.

This puts in question the generality of Ishii's earlier claim that "intracaste cohesion seems to be increasing", and Gellner's comment on it that what is involved is the emergence of "competing internally egalitarian blocs" (quoted by Ishii, this volume). It is, as I would see it, Fuller's differentiation, rather than Ishii and Gellner's cohesion and equality, which is the dominant trend. I am, however, unclear how the 'paradox' Fuller identifies is logically entailed; why the decline in clear-cut caste ranking resulting from differentiation within castes should necessarily lead to a greater emphasis on their difference. While Mayer's analysis would suggest that these changes were indeed concomitant, from Barnett's account it would seem that more or less the opposite may happen. Instead of differences of lifestyle between castes becoming the ideological bedrock for their separation, differentiation within the caste has become the basis for a new sense of identity with people of other castes whose lifestyle is similar to one's own. It is in other words just as plausible to suppose that intra-caste differentiation makes it increasingly difficult to sustain a strong sense of inter-caste difference. It is not only hierarchy and interdependence that have been significantly undermined; in many parts of South Asia, it is now, I believe, the sense of separation that is being progressively eroded – as much in Mayer's own ethnography, if not in his analysis of it, suggests.

One problem, then, with Dumont's notion of substance is that it "conveys a sense of homogeneity" (Béteille 1996: 172). This seldom exists, and in my experience it is as common for people to invoke the notion of *rahan-sahan* to explain, not why it is important to marry within the caste, but why one should limit the choice to caste members of equivalent wealth and occupational status. *Rahan-sahan* also marks *intra*-caste difference. As this suggests, it is not always easy in the abstract to specify the level of segmentation at which the substantialized unit exists. In the political context it may be one thing, in the matter of marriage another. Given that such a segmentary logic persists, and given that segmentation is a *relational* matter, the extent to which it can be justly said that we have witnessed the passage from structure to substance seems questionable.

Nor is it to me clear what it means to say that castes have become 'collective individuals', a phrase which Fuller (1996) and Ishii (this volume) reproduce from Dumont as if it were transparent. Dumont's own gloss that he intends 'individual' "in the sense we have given this word" is not entirely helpful in that he identifies more than one. I take it, however, that the meaning he has in mind is the one that valorizes the individual – in the manner of Durkheim's essay on 'Individualism and the intellectuals' (1975 [1898]) – as a quasi-sacred being and the ultimate repository of value. "Each particular man in a sense incarnates the whole of mankind. ... What is still called 'society' is the means, the life of each man is the end" (Dumont 1970: 9). But whether castes are now thought of as 'individuals' in this sense is doubtful. As substantialized units that compete for political and economic advantage, they may claim to be acting legitimately, but it is uncertain that others believe them or would unequivocally endorse the view that the life of each caste 'is the end'. They are more likely to condemn them as 'casteist'. Dumont quotes Tocqueville approvingly to the effect that individualism is a modern value.

> Our fathers were only acquainted with egotism. Egotism is a passionate and exaggerated love of self, which leads a man to connect everything with his own person, and to prefer himself to everything in the world. (Tocqueville, cited in Dumont 1970: 17)

When castes act today as substantialized blocs in the political arena, they are more likely to be seen as 'collective egotists' than as 'collective individuals'.

Ishii's conclusion in this volume that substantialization in the Newar village he studied is a partial and patchy process is almost certainly true more generally. But especially important is his finding that the dominant trend amongst the higher and middle castes is their "partial merger" rather than their separation. This closely parallels what I have myself reported for the ex-villages-cum-labour colonies that fringe the Chhattisgarh steel town of Bhilai (Parry 1999). Disregarding the divide between local sons-of-the-soil and immigrant outsiders, the deepest social cleavage in these *bastis* is between the Untouchable Satnamis and the so-called 'Hindu' castes of the old village hierarchy (nearly all of the others). In the past, only people of one's own caste were generally invited to wedding feasts. Today, guests from all 'Hindu' castes in the neighbourhood are likely to be called, and all sit together in a single unbroken line to eat food that invariably includes boiled rice. The new liberalism cannot therefore be explained – as for Ramkheri Mayer suggests that it might be – by the casuistic acquiescence of the higher castes in the more egalitarian spirit of the age, but only on the condition that the food now served is of a type acceptable from inferiors. But if today the 'Hindu' castes publicly inter-dine in a manner that proclaims their equality, it is still almost unthinkable that a Satnami would join them. This structural realignment has significant parallels in the matter of marriage. Primary unions are – barring elopement – arranged by the parents and are invariably caste endogamous. Rates of marital breakdown are however high, and both partners generally contract secondary unions of their own choice. Increasingly they do so with people of castes different to their own. Such unions are generally (if grudgingly) tolerated unless they cross the Hindu-Satnami divide, and the children of them accepted as members of the caste of their father (Parry 2001). The broad trend, then, has been for the boundaries between the Hindu castes to become more permeable and to lose much of their former salience, while that between Hindus and Satnamis has remained – with some qualification – largely intact and has therefore been thrown into sharper relief. A decline in the spirit of hierarchy has been accompanied by a *declining* preoccupation with separation and difference.

This lends some support – as also does Jodhka's chapter in this volume – to Bayly's (1999: 340) assessment that:

> ... the paramount manifestation of caste in Indian life today is not so much the phenomenon of "substantialization" ... but the distinction between those who can proclaim clean caste origin and those whom higher caste people can stigmatise as *avarna*, i.e. innately unclean and polluted.

It might, however, be argued that this phenomenon is itself a logical development of substantialization, which ultimately results in a two-bloc system that opposes 'clean' to 'Untouchable' castes. Indeed Fuller (1996: 25) has suggested that a notionally unitary Hindu communal identity might be seen as the apotheosis of substantialization, a proposition with which the chapter by Lobo and Das published here seems consistent. The picture that emerges from it is one of increasing social and residential segregation between Gujarati Hindus and Muslims; and perhaps their most chilling finding is that amongst Hindus "shades of grey and ambivalence ... only rarely and in small measure" mitigate the blanket negative stereotyping of Muslims. One of two contradictory conclusions seems possible. When all 'clean' castes proclaim a common identity in opposition to 'Untouchables', or all Hindus in opposition to Muslims, this is merely an extension of the segmentary logic of the 'traditional' system. Not much has changed. Alternatively, when all 'clean' castes or all Hindus begin to think of themselves as a single undifferentiated substantialized bloc, things have changed so much from the system as Bouglé characterized it that we are entitled to conclude that it has now been fundamentally transformed. Not only have hierarchy and interdependence been reduced to a vestigial form, but little is left of separation when the only people from whom one is separated are 'Untouchables', or Muslims.

An ideological muting of difference within such very broad categories is undoubtedly present, but it should not be overstated. Bahujan Samaj Party propaganda does not eliminate the sense of separation between Sweepers and Leatherworkers, any more than communal antagonism and *Sangh Parivar* rhetoric in practice create a unified Hindu identity that disregards divisions of caste. A fascinating insight, I note parenthetically, into one of the constraints that confronts organizations like the Rashtriya Swayamsevak Sangh in their efforts to persuade marginalized populations to become 'proper' homogenized Hindus by performing 'proper' homogenized Hindu rituals is provided by Nawa's paper in this volume. Not that *Hindutva* missionization is relevant to the context he describes. It is rather that Byansis' efforts to identify themselves as 'Hindus' by adopting what they conceive to be orthodox Hindu mortuary rites have over time been subverted by the complexity of ritual itself. In any lengthy and elaborate new ritual, and unless there are authoritative specialists to guide one, the question that at some point inevitably arises is: "what on earth is it that we are supposed to do next?" And when one is stuck for an answer, the obvious solution is to fall back on elements that seem to fit from the old and now discarded ritual form. As a result of this process, performances of the by now not so new Byans' funeral have become increasingly hybridized and variable. Hindu ritual, to say nothing of the Hindus who perform it, may thus prove more recalcitrant to homogenization than the reformers suppose. In any event, all the evidence – including that contained in Part 1 of this collection – suggests something significantly less radical than a trend towards the creation of a unified 'clean' caste, or Hindu, identity that successfully suppresses internal differences.

In part at least, Tanabe's ethnography is – as he notes – consistent with a conventional substantialization account, though his intention is to go beyond it. The ideological world that his village informants inhabit is one still based on the separation of discrete caste units, and – to some degree – on an interdependence between them which results from a division of labour in the ritual sphere. What they reject, however, is the hierarchy and coercion from which this organic conception of society has hitherto been inseparable. What provides them with the ideological resources to do so are the egalitarian values that have long been part of the indigenous repertoire. Though in the past these values remained subordinate and marginalized, today they have moved into the mainstream of village thinking. That such egalitarian strands are available to be picked up by subalterns when circumstances seem to demand has long been recognized (e.g. Holmström 1971; Parry 1974) – and indeed they are sometimes picked up by people who could not by any stretch be described as subalterns (e.g. Singer 1968). What is more surprising is the source to which Tanabe traces them – the ritual of sacrifice, and more precisely the first of its phases which 'corresponds to the process of death and destruction'. 'Surprising' because the more usual associations of sacrifice – as in the *Purusa-sukta*, the alleged prototype for all future sacrifices – are with the creation of a *hierarchical* social order. However that might be, the evidence that egalitarian values are significantly present in the first phase of the rite is hard to assess from Tanabe's compressed account of it. One might, moreover, wonder why people would choose to found their vision of a brave new world of equality on a ritual phase that culminates in death and destruction – especially when these are immediately followed by another that shows that rebirth and reconstruction are "achieved through the principles of 'hierarchy' and 'centrality'".

If Tanabe's evidence would suggest that the separation of castes is not seriously questioned, Jodhka's seems more ambivalent. In many practical respects, the social distance between Dalit *Mazhabi* Sikhs and upper caste *Sardars* has clearly closed. They are no longer residentially segregated; with the exception of cremation grounds, Dalit rights of access to public facilities and spaces are no longer disputed, and Dalit women are now often employed as domestic servants in upper-caste houses. Paradoxically, however, it seems likely that these gains have been partly achieved through a strategy of separation, by achieving some autonomy and escaping from old patronage-based relations of dependence. As the chapters by Ishii, Hachhethu, and Tanabe also demonstrate, the decline of hierarchical interdependence between castes is not just the mechanical effect of inexorable market forces, but is also a product of active and conscious assertions of dignity that have involved the repudiation of demeaning caste obligations and of roles that imply dependence. It is not only in the economic sphere, however, that liberation is sought. Rather than risk humiliation in upper-caste spaces, Dalits have set up their own Gurdwaras and community centres. But in the

Punjab, Jodhka argues, they were oppressed less by the ideology of pollution than by their position of dependence in the agrarian political economy. It is on this that their emancipatory efforts have focused, and their success has depended on the availability of alternative sources of employment.

Though caste is not at the centre of Abhijit Dasgupta's contribution, the political developments he traces for a village in northern Bengal have a significant bearing on its changing trajectories. In the 1978 panchayat elections that he witnessed during his first fieldwork, party support was to a large extent divided along caste lines. By the time of the 2003 elections, however, this congruence had broken down. Castes no longer voted as blocs; and in the political arena at least the separation between them as substantialized units had declined. But that is Bengal, and it would be wise to remember Ishii's caution about the patchy quality of these processes.

In this volume, however, it is Hachhethu's enormously engaging semi-autobiographical piece that speaks most directly to Ishii's point about the "partial merging" of castes. This is perhaps not surprising in that he too writes of a Newar community in the Kathmandu Valley – of the ancient city of Bhaktapur and, especially evocatively, of the neighbourhood in which he grew up. In terms of general prosperity, educational attainments, consumption patterns, dress and other markers of difference, there has, since his childhood in the 1960s and early 1970s, been a remarkable closing of the gap between the upper-caste Brahmans, Chatharis and Shresthas and the middle-ranking Jyapus. As a result of the diversification of the economy, the Jyapus have prospered; and their former economic dependence on the upper castes – and with it the deference they had previously accorded them – has markedly diminished. Commensal restrictions have been greatly relaxed and amongst the educated there are now an increasing number of love marriages. But if all this seems to support Ishii's proposition, there are countervailing currents. Despite the accelerating differentiation amongst them, in the political sphere Jyapus have emerged as a bloc which supports the NWPP, a Bhaktapur-based communist party. As a result of its influence, however, the opposition between them and their erstwhile masters and patrons (who vote Nepali Congress) is now couched in the language of class. That notwithstanding, political competition has led to a revival of a sense of caste separateness. Caste, however, "is no longer at the core of city life. A new form of associational life which transcends traditional caste values and custom is thriving ...".

Hachhethu is not alone in reporting an increasing incidence of inter-caste marriages, especially in urban contexts. In this volume, Nakatani, for example, comments on the growing number of inter-ethnic unions amongst Delhi Bengalis, a large proportion of which are presumably also inter-caste. It is of course true that the extent to which such marriages are subversive of caste depends on circumstances – on whether the couple are ostracized; on whether their children are condemned to some caste-less limbo or are readily assimilated to the caste of one of their parents (most usually the father); on the degree to which contact is maintained, and kinship is recognized, between these children and their 'cousin-brothers' and 'sisters' who are of a different caste to themselves. But whatever the answer to these questions, the escalating frequency of such unions is highly significant. Of Bouglé's three defining characteristics of caste, in the modern world it is supposedly only their separation that persists with real stubbornness; and the most significant manifestation of this is the supposedly inviolable injunction against inter-caste marriage. In the last resort, as received wisdom has it, the reproduction of caste relies on the rule of endogamy. It is therefore astonishing that what Béteille (1996: 164) describes as "the only satisfactory full-length study" of inter-caste marriage (by Kannan) was published in 1963!

In summary, then, I have tried to suggest that Dumont was in error to argue that change has not touched the fundamental values on which the 'traditional' system was founded. Nor is the conventional view that separation and an ideological stress on difference has now become the bedrock of the system an entirely convincing account of current trends. Keeping Ishii's caution in mind that we are dealing with a very uneven process, a more plausible picture is his "partial merging" of castes and a decline in their sense of separateness. *Pace* Fuller, I would argue that under modern conditions, in which there is a greater range of alternative identities to choose from, increasing differentiation within the caste is in the long term likely to prove incompatible with a strong conviction in the differences between castes. Of particular importance here is the – admittedly still insufficient – evidence for a growing incidence of inter-caste marriage and of weakened sanctions against it.[3] Even where Dalit groups – as in Jodhka's account – self-consciously pursue a strategy of separation, it is not to proclaim their difference, but on the contrary in protest at not being treated as *the same*.

True, this picture is partly contradicted by developments in the political sphere where – as in Hachhethu's ethnography – castes often emerge as substantialized blocs in competition with each other. In the case Dasgupta describes, however, this trend has been sharply reversed and on a macro-level it is difficult to know which of these two trajectories will prevail in the future. Whichever, it would be wise to remember that politics is not the whole of social life, and that most of the time most people regard it as a dirty business with which they want little to do. If sociology in the past suffered some tunnel vision that produced an excessive preoccupation with the ritual

[3] And we are not only dealing with marriages that are between partners of proximate caste status or are 'with the grain' – that is, in the hypergamous *anuloma* direction for which there is some *shastric* sanction.

and religious aspects of caste, today there is perhaps some danger of over-privileging the political aspects and of ignoring what has been happening to caste in other domains of social life.

What has been happening, as I see it, is that the 'space' that caste occupies, and the degree of 'hegemony' it exercises over the lives of large sections of the population, has contracted. As Barnett's discussion brought out, other identity choices have become more readily available and in many contexts these have greater significance than caste. In this volume, take Nakatani's account of Delhi's Chittaranjan Park. What matters is to be a member of the Bengali *bhadralok.* Whether one is a Brahman or a Kayastha counts in most circumstances for much less, and it is Punjabis of any caste – rather than Bengalis of lower caste – that residents dread as neighbours. And there are of course many other urban contexts in which regional ethnicity, or religious community, are in daily life more salient identities than caste. So often also are identities based on occupation and education, and on the distinctions in tastes and lifestyles that are associated with them. Hachhethu's conclusion can be generalized: new forms of associational life that transcend caste have become increasingly significant.[4]

It can therefore justly be said that one of the major strengths of this volume is that many of its papers focus on voluntary associations and civil society organizations of a sort that are becoming increasingly significant for an understanding of South Asian society. It would, however, take me too far from the central concerns of this note to comment on these contributions in detail, and I shall restrict myself to some extremely perfunctory observations on their political aspects.

Mio's account (Chap. 8) of the voluntary associations of young middle class Udaipur men who have introduced, and now organize, four new Hindu festivals in the town, brings out clearly the complexity of their relationship to the Hindu nationalist movement. The four associations he discusses span the whole spectrum from one that is under the direct control of the Bajrang Dal and is in effect a recruitment vehicle for it, to one that determinedly keeps all political parties at arms' length. In none do considerations of caste appear to be significant. For villages in the Kathmandu Valley, Ishii draws attention to the mushrooming of multi-caste youth clubs and Maharjan (Chap. 7) to the growth of multi-ethnic and multi-caste Vihar (Theravada) Buddhist associations. Crucial to both has been the relationship between local society and the state – the Nepalese constitutional reforms of 1990 that guaranteed freedom of association, and disillusioned opposition to the Rana regime during the early days of Vihar Buddhism. In the Bengal village that

[4]To claim that they have grown in significance is not, of course, to say that they did not exist in the past – though many, like the *akharas* (gymnasia) that have long been popular in many north Indian towns and in which Brahmans and Yadavs might exercise together, would have excluded Untouchables.

Dasgupta studied, by contrast, the actions of the state have led to a recent decline of civil society organizations – in particular of those that have had a long-standing role in championing the cause of sharecroppers and landless labourers in the area. In the interests of perpetuating its power, the ruling party has ensured that the panchayats have become the real locus of political and economic influence in the north Bengal countryside, with the result that the leverage that these organizations are able to exert has greatly decreased. The poorer sections of rural society find their former champions much enfeebled at a time when the commitment of the state government and the ruling party to its pro-poor development agenda has also significantly weakened. By its actions, then, and in highly complex ways, the state enormously influences the strength, vitality and growth of associational life, and that in turn affects the way that such organizations intersect with – and may provide some counterweight to – caste and other forms of 'primordial' identity.

In Nepal, it is often these other forms that are of greater significance. I refer in particular to the ethnic groups or 'nationalities' that have now been officially scheduled as *Janajati*s with a view to implementing a system of reservations, as Gellner and Karki (Chap. 12) explain, on the Indian model. They have even been 'ranked' into five different grades according to their degree of 'backwardness'. It is hard to suppress the suspicion that the outcome is likely to be the development of a vested interest in backwardness, a hardening of these identities and of the boundaries between groups, and their transmutation into entities that more closely resemble substantialized castes.

As the chapters by Dasgupta and Hachhethu remind us, caste and class struggles are often intertwined as there is commonly a significant congruence between these two dimensions of inequality. That may also apply to the relationship between these other ethnicities and class, as Fujikura's fascinating paper (Chap. 11) illustrates. But though the majority of those involved in the bonded labour (*kamaiya*) liberation movement he describes were Tharus, Fujikura is concerned to stress that ethnicity was of secondary significance, and that this was a pre-eminently class-based movement – at least in the eyes of its leadership and notwithstanding the fact that Tharus had been reduced wholesale to servitude by land-grabbing Pahari outsiders. What is especially striking about the situation he describes is the lack of any great sympathy amongst *kamaiya*s for the Maoist movement, and their continuing hopes in the Nepalese state, which they dream might actually deliver on promised rehabilitation measures and grant them title to a parcel of land. Ethnic antagonism would appear to be more muted, and faith in the state firmer, than one might in the circumstances expect.

The contrast with the picture that emerges from Ogura's final chapter in this volume is in some ways unexpected. In its staunchest heartland, the backbone of the Maoist movement are the Magars, and Ogura suggests that there is possibly some kind of elective affinity between the *relatively* egalitarian and communal nature of their 'traditional' social order and Maoist ideology.[5] That particular ethnic groups might be more predisposed to throw in their lot with the Maoists than others is not at all surprising; and nor is the sense of deep antipathy for the Nepalese state that Ogura conveys so forcefully. What I do find surprising in her account, however, is how muted the rhetoric of class conflict seems to have become in a movement that has generally represented itself in that idiom. The leadership of the bonded labourers' struggle was concerned to play down ethnicity, and to define its objectives in class terms; and its membership has remained surprisingly sanguine about the state. In their iconic stronghold, by contrast, the Maoists appear to be surprisingly reticent about class and to base their appeal on a strong sense of ethnic identity and separateness, and on an unmitigated hatred for the state. Though many Indians complain that the effectiveness of their state is seriously subverted by competition between substantialized caste blocs, the dangers of ethnic competition destroying the Nepalese polity may perhaps prove significantly greater.

---

[5] I underscore 'relatively' because the equality actually seems to have been somewhat limited. Though 'Untouchables' could enter Magar houses, they were still excluded from the kitchens.

REFERENCES

Appadurai, A. 1986. 'Is Homo Hierarchicus?'. *American Ethnologist* 13: 745-61.

——. 1992. 'Putting Hierarchy in Its Place', in G. Marcus (ed.), *Rereading Cultural Anthropology*, pp. 34-47. Durham: Duke University Press.

Barnett, S. 1977. 'Identity Choice and Cultural Ideology in Contemporary South India', in K. David (ed.), *The New Wind: Changing Identities in South Asia*, pp. 393-414. The Hague: Mouton.

Bayly, S. 1999. *Caste, Society and Politics in India from the Eighteenth Century to the Present (The New Cambridge History of India IV. 3)*. Cambridge: Cambridge University Press.

Béteille, A. 1991. 'The Reproduction of Inequality'. *Contributions to Indian Sociology* 25 (1): 3-28.

——. 1996. 'Caste in Contemporary India', in C. J. Fuller (ed.), *Caste Today*, pp. 150-79. Delhi: Oxford University Press.

Bouglé, C. 1971 (1908). *Essays on the Caste System*, tr. D. Pocock. Cambridge: Cambridge University Press.

Dirks, N. 1987. *The Hollow Crown: Ethnohistory of an Indian Kingdom*. Cambridge: Cambridge University Press.

——. 2001. *Castes of Mind: Colonialism and the Making of Modern India*. Princeton: Princeton University Press.

Dumont, L. 1970. *Homo Hierarchicus: The Caste System and Its Implications*. London: Weidenfeld and Nicolson.

Durkheim, E. 1975 (1898). 'Individualism and the Intellectuals', in W.S.F. Pickering (ed.), *Durkheim on Religion*. London: Routledge and Kegan Paul.

Fuller, C.J. 1996. 'Introduction: Caste Today', in C.J. Fuller (ed.), *Caste Today*, pp. 1-31. Delhi: Oxford University Press.

Ghurye, G.S. 1950. *Caste and Class in India*. Bombay: Popular Book Depot.

Holmström, M. 1971. 'Religious Change in an Industrial City of South India'. *Journal of the Royal Asiatic Society* 1: 28-40.

Inden, R. 1990. *Imagining India*. Oxford: Blackwell Publishers.

Kannan, C.T. 1963. *Intercaste and Inter-Community Marriage in India*. Bombay: Allied Publishers.

Mayer, A. 1996. 'Caste in an Indian Village: Change and Continuity 1954-1992', in C.J. Fuller (ed.), *Caste Today*, pp. 32-63. Delhi: Oxford University Press.

Parry, J.P. 1974. 'Egalitarian Values in a Hierarchical Society'. *South Asian Review* 7 (2): 95-121.

——. 1998. 'Mauss, Dumont and the Distinction between Status and Power', in W. James and N.J. Allen (eds.), *Marcel Mauss: A Centenary Tribute*, pp. 151-72. Oxford: Berghahn Books.

——. 1999. 'Two Cheers for Reservation: The Satnamis and the Steel Plant', in

R. Guha and J. Parry (eds.), *Institutions and Inequalities: Essays in Honour of André Béteille*, pp. 128-69. Delhi: Oxford University Press.

——. 2001. 'Ankalu's Errant Wife: Sex, Marriage and Industry in Contemporary Chhattisgarh'. *Modern Asian Studies* 35 (4): 783-820.

Quigley, D. 1993. *The Interpretation of Caste*. Oxford: Clarendon Press.

——. 1994. 'Is a Theory of Caste still Possible?', in M. Searle-Chatterjee and U. Sharma (eds.), *Contextualising Caste: Post-Dumontian Approaches*, pp. 25-48. Oxford: Blackwell Publishers. (Revised version published 2002 in *Social Evolution and History* 1 (1): 140-70.)

Singer, M. 1968. 'The Radha-Krishna "bhajanas" of Madras City', in M. Singer (ed.), *Krishna: Myths, Rites and Attitudes*, pp. 90-138. Chicago: Chicago University Press.

Srinivas, M.N. 1962. *Caste in Modern India and Other Essays*. Bombay: Asia Publishing House.

——. 1966. *Social Change in Modern India*. Bombay: Allied Publishers.

——. 1995. 'Sociology in Delhi', in D. Kumar and D. Mookherjee (eds.), *D. School: Reflections on the Delhi School of Economics*, pp. 31-52. Delhi: Oxford University Press.

Abbreviations

(Np) Nepali
[Diacritical marks are omitted for editorial reasons.]

BASE: Backward Society Education. An NGO in south-western Nepal for "the creation of exploitation-free society"
BDP: Bhaktapur Development Project. A German-aided project run for twelve years from 1974 to 1986 working primarily on the renovation of historical monuments.
BJP: Bharatiya Janata Party
BM: Bhaktapur Municipality
BSP: Bahujan Samaj Party
CBS: Central Bureau of Statistics (Nepal)
CDO: Chief District Officer (Nepal)
CEDA: Center for Economic Development and Administration, Tribhuvan University, Nepal
CIDA: Canadian International Development Agency
CPN: the Communist Party of Nepal
CPN (UML): the Communist Party of Nepal (Unified Marxist-Leninist). The largest left party in Nepal
CPI (M): the Communist Party of India (Marxist)
DDA: Delhi Development Authority
DNF: the Dalit NGO Federation (Nepal)
DSE: Delhi School of Economics
DSP: Deputy Superintendent of Police (Nepal)
EPDPA: the East Pakistan Displaced Persons' Association
FB: Forward Block
FGD: focus group discussion
GLOBE: Global Legislators for a Balanced Environment
GOG: Government of Gujarat
GWB: Government of West Bengal
HMG: His Majesty's Government of Nepal
IAS: Indian Administrative Service

INHURED: International Institute for Human Rights, Environment and Development
INSEC: Informal Sector Service Centre. A Kathmandu-based human rights NGO
KFW: Kreditanstalt für Wiederaufbau (Reconstruction Bank of Germany)
KPP: Kamtapuri People's Party
KV: Kontaikkatti Vellalars
LFG: the Left Front Government
LIG: low-income groups
MLRM: the Ministry of Land Reform and Management
MOEF: Ministry of Environment and Forests
MP: Madhya Pradesh
NBA: the Narmada Bachao Andolan (the movement to save Narmada)
NC: Nepali Congress, a liberal democratic and centrist party in Nepal.
NEA: the Nepalese Electricity Authority
NEFEN: the Nepal Federation of Nationalities or Nepal Janajati Mahasangh (Np). A campaigning umbrella body for ethnic groups in Nepal, originally set up in 1990.
NEFIN: the Nepal Federation of Indigenous Nationalities or Nepal Adivasi Janajati Mahasangh (Np). Changed its name from NEFEN in 2003.
NESAC: Nepal South Asia Centre
NFDIN: the National Foundation for the Development of Indigenous Nationalities, founded in 2002 (Nepal)
NPC: National Planning Commission
NWDT: the Narmada Water Dispute Tribunal
NWFP: North-West Frontier Province (India)
NWPP: Nepal Workers and Peasants Party. A leftist party in Nepal.
OB: Operation Barga
OBC: Other Backward Classes
OECF: Japanese Overseas Economic Cooperation Fund
R & R: resettlement and rehabilitation
RPP: Rashtriya Prajatantra Party. A conservative party in post-1990 Nepal
RSS: Rashtriya Swayamsevak Sangh
SC: Scheduled Caste
SJM: Samyukta Jan Morcha Nepal (United People's Front Nepal). A leftist party in Nepal.
SLC: School Leaving Certificate, taken after finishing the tenth grade, usually around the age of 16 (Nepal)
SSC: Secondary School Certificate (India)
ST: Scheduled Tribe
TMC: the Trinamul Congress (Bengal)
UML: *see* CPN (UML)
UNCED: United Nations Conference on Environment and Development

UNDP: United Nations Development Programme
USAID: US Agency for International Development
VDC: Village Development Committee, the new name for Village Panchayats after 1990 (Nepal)
VHP: Vishva Hindu Parishad
Vihar: a place where there is a statue of the Buddha in a hall where people can be accommodated for worship and meditation, Buddhist monastery
WBPA: The West Bengal Panchayat Act
WBPKS: The West Bengal Provincial Krishak Sabha

Glossary

(B) Bengali
(By) Byansi
(H) Hindi
(Np) Nepali
(Nw) Newari (Nepal Bhasa)
(U) Urdu
[Diacritical marks are omitted for editorial reasons.]

adhiar: sharecropper in north Bengal (B)
ahimsa: non-violence
anagarika: a celibate status between monastic and lay invented by Dharmapala, a Sri Lankan Buddhist reformist. [lit. 'homeless one']
anchal panchayat: block council introduced by the 1973 WBPA (B)
astashil: Eight Precepts (Buddhism)
baha, *bahi*: the temple-monastery complexes of traditional Vajrayana Buddhism (Nw)
Bahirbanga: inner Indian Bengali diaspora, Bengalis residing outside of West Bengal but within the Indian territory (B)
banja: a vendor (Nw)
ban syayegu: to offer animal sacrifices (Nw)
Bhadralok: middle-class Bengali Hindus [lit. 'respectable people', 'gentlemen'] (B)
bhajan: devotional hymns (Np, Nw, H)
bhakti: devotionalism
bhante: term of address for a Theravada monk, used colloquially in Nw as a term of reference
bhojan: (communal) meal, formal term for meal
bidi: Indian-style leaf cigarettes (H, Np)
birta: the land given to individuals in appreciation of their services to the state, as ritual gifts, or as a mark of patronage (Np)
chibhadyah: a small *stupa* (Nw) = *chaitya* (Sanskrit, Np)
Dalit: 'the depressed', former 'untouchable' castes

dapha: a set of Newar musical instruments, a prayer recitation group with such a set (Nw)
daura suruwal: the Nepali hillman's long shirt and distinctive trousers (Np)
de-bhway: a village feast (Nw)
Gau Vikas Samiti: (Np) = VDC
gram panchayat: village council introduced by the 1973 WBPA
granthi: a Sikh reader and custodian
guruma: a nun; wife of a religious leader (Nw)
guthi: organizations with a hereditary membership whose main purpose is to carry out ritual matters; land donated to such organizations or temples (Nw, Np)
gwon: the 'traditional' funeral in Byans (By)
Hindutva: 'Hinduness' (emphasized by Hindu nationalists in contemporary India)
jana samiti: people's committees (Np)
jharphuk: exorcism by blowing, brushing, and tantric incantations (H, Np)
jotedar: big landowner (B)
joter rajniti: the politics of alliance (B)
kamaiya: bonded labourers (Np)
karinda: a clerk of a landlord (Np)
kattha: =1/20 *bigha*. 1/30 hectare in mid-west Nepal Tarai (Np)
khet: paddy fields (Np)
khyala: a traditional Tharu village council (Tharu)
langar: a place where free meal is seved, free community kitchen; the food served in Gurdwara (Punjabi)
madrassa: Islamic School
mandal: a committee (H)
maulavi: a Muslim spiritual teacher (U)
mohalla: ward, neighbourhood
mukhiya: traditional village leader (Np)
naya satta: 'new power', the Maoists in the Maoist usage (Np)
panchayat: 1. 'Traditional' local or caste councils supposed to exist widely in South Asia. 2. Elected local councils to serve as institutions of local self-government in India after independence. 3. Local (village, district) and national councils in the 1962-90 'partyless democracy' period in Nepal.
panchayati raj: local government (India)
panchashil: Five Precepts (Buddhism)
para: hamlets or residential units (B)
paritran: 'protection' verses in Theravada Buddhism (Np, Nw)
pariyatti: elementary instruction in Buddhism (Pali)
pathi: about 4.5 litres (Np)
phuru: puffed rice (By)

Pradhan Panch: the head of the panchayat (Nepal)
purano satta: 'old power', the Nepali government in Maoist usage (Np)
rahan-sahan: styles of life (Np)
Rashtra: nation
ropani: 1 *ropani* of land = 0.0509 hectare (Np)
Sadbhavana Party: a Tarai-based party in Nepal
samuha: a Buddhist institution, lit. a group
sarpanch: the head of a local or *gram panchayat* (India)
sarat: the new funeral in Byans (By)
saunki: loan (Tharu)
se yamo: a long oral recitation with a peculiar tune to send the soul of the dead in traditional funerals in Byans, carried out by two male specialists called *se yakcha* (By)
shramadan: voluntary labour
sramanera: a monastic novice (Buddhism)
taluka: a subdivision of a *zilla* or district (U)
thum: custom (By)
thumo: to worship or to celebrate by tossing up offerings (By)
tika: red paste dot placed in the centre of one's forehead as a blessing (Np, H)
tol: locality (Np)
topi: Nepali cap
upasaka: lay Buddhist (male)
upasika: lay Buddhist (female)
ustad: a master (U)
vaidya: traditional medical practitioner, Ayurvedic physician (Np, H)
ya: an animal into which the soul of the deceased enters in traditional funerals in Byans (By)
yatra: tour, pilgrimage, procession
yimo: a typical gesture turning round one's hand inward horizontally (By)
zilla parishad: district council introduced by the 1973 WBPA

Personal Name Index

Subject Index